WHAT *IS* THE PERFECT NAME FOR YOUR BABY?

. . . a common name that's easy to remember?

. . . a name so unique your baby will be the only one with the name?

. . . a name that honors a relative or friend?

. . . a name with religious significance?

. . . an important sounding name?

. . . a cute name?

. . . a popular name?

Or a name that sounds just right to you . . .
and will sound right to your child?

THE GREATEST BABY NAME BOOK EVER
will help you make the choice

Other Avon Books by
Carol McD. Wallace

20,001 NAMES FOR BABY

THE GREATEST
BABY NAME BOOK EVER

CAROL McD. WALLACE

AVON BOOKS  NEW YORK

AVON BOOKS, INC.
1350 Avenue of the Americas
New York, New York 10019

Copyright © 1992, 1998 by Carol McD. Wallace
Published by arrangement with the author
Visit our website at www.AvonBooks.com
Library of Congress Catalog Card Number: 97-94317
ISBN: 0-380-78982-5

First Avon Books Printing: March 1998

AVON TRADEMARK REG. U.S. PAT. OFF. AND IN OTHER COUNTRIES, MARCA
REGISTRADA, HECHO EN U.S.A.

Printed in the U.S.A.

WCD 10 9 8 7 6 5 4 3 2

Contents

Abbreviations

Af	African	*Lat*	Latin
Arab	Arabian	*masc*	masculine
Celt	Celtic	*ME*	Middle English
comb form	combining form	*Nig*	Nigerian
Czech	Czechoslovakian	*NAm Ind*	North American Indian
Dan	Danish	*Nor*	Norwegian
dim	diminutive	*OE*	Old English
Egypt	Egyptian	*OF*	Old French
Eng	English	*OG*	Old German
fem	feminine	*ONorse*	Old Norse
Fr	French	*OWelsh*	Old Welsh
Gael	Gaelic	*Per*	Persian
Ger	German	*Pol*	Polish
Gk	Greek	*Port*	Portuguese
Haw	Hawaiian	*Rus*	Russian
Heb	Hebrew	*Scand*	Scandinavian
Hung	Hungarian	*Scot*	Scottish
Ir	Irish	*Sp*	Spanish
It	Italian	*Teut*	Teutonic
Jap	Japanese	*var*	variant
		Viet	Vietnamese

Introduction

My elder son got a hamster for his tenth birthday. Before we left the store, he insisted that somebody tell him the gender of his new pet, which was quite a production because only one member of the staff knew how to figure this out, and she was selling somebody a whole tank full of goldfish. I couldn't fathom why this was so important to Will, since we have no intention of breeding hamsters, but he looked at me as if I were completely dense and said, "Mom, how can I name it unless I know if it's a boy or a girl?"

Actually, *I* was being dense. Of course he had to name it—*her*, actually. This was how the hamster became not just one of a bunch of squirmy furry handfuls in a cage, but his own pet: Bonnie. (Named after his assistant teacher, who claimed to be honored.) Bonnie, who has her own little rodent personality. The one and only Bonnie-the-hamster.

Names are hugely important. Every culture in the world acknowledges this with ceremonies and traditions. In China you grow through names as your circumstances change: your "milk" name changes to your "book" name when you enter school, for instance. Some African cultures give long genealogical names, while others give names invoking certain deities. Catholic children traditionally take an additional saint's name when they are confirmed. Some Muslims believe that angels pray in houses where men named Muhammad or Ahmad live, making these names hugely popular wherever Islam predominates.

AMERICAN NAMES

Here in America, we have our own traditions. The most important one is the tradition of inventing yourself. This is the country, after all, that people come to in order to be something they couldn't be at home. American names have often reflected that freedom. Our names are full of aspiration and potential. Some cultures give names that reflect history, but Americans tend to look forward rather than back. Maybe in the old country (Greece or Italy, for instance), baby boys are named after their paternal grandfathers, but this is the U.S., and this child will be known as—Clint. You can go anywhere with a name like Clint.

Assimilation names have been the rule for a long time. This may be a melting pot, but the predominant culture is Anglo, and for generations, fitting in has meant giving or choosing an English-style name: Isaac instead of Yitzhak, Joan instead of Siobhan. Times are changing, though. Yes, the names at the tops of all the charts are basically English. But the names in the next tier down may not be. For girls the Gaelic Caitlin, Scandinavian Kristen, and French Danielle are hugely popular. Not because of any huge Gaelic or Scandinavian swell in immigration, but because at this moment, parents like the way these names sound.

There are two reasons for the exotic nature of many popular names. One, of course, *is* immigration, which is changing the face of parts of America that used to be homogeneous. Attitudes toward it are changing, too: newcomers to the U.S. increasingly take pride in their background and reflect that pride when they name their children. Americans who have been here for a generation or two are also turning to their roots to find inspiration for their children's names. An Italian-American Mark may name his son Marco, for instance.

A related factor is the phenomenal pace of communications nowadays. Long ago, for most folks, the pool of names was very small. You could name a child for yourself, for your parents, for somebody you knew, maybe for some Biblical character. Those would be all the names you had ever heard. It would never occur to a farmer in 18th-century Massachusetts, for instance, to name a child Marco. At the turn of the century, fifty percent of American children were given one of the top ten names for their gender. I was born in 1955 and given a very fashionable name, Carol. Throughout my life I have generally been one of three or four Carols in any gathering of a few dozen people. But this kind of intense use doesn't happen as much anymore, except perhaps in tightly knit communities.

Nowadays, the top ten names account for only twenty-five percent of children. Another researcher puts it this way: in 1990, a little more than three percent of American boys were named Michael, which was then the number one name for boys. That's one in every thirty-three boys. Looking at the class lists of my sons' school, I see a few names (Dylan, Alexandra) repeated more regularly than others, but they are the exception. Startling variety is the rule.

Fashions in names also spread much more quickly now than they used to. Tyler is the top name on some 1995 popularity lists: ten years ago, it wasn't even in the top fifteen. As people across the country are linked by computers, as they watch TV or read magazines, notions about names spread like wildfire. Oprah Winfrey's website on America Online featured a baby name bulletin board where parents posted their suggestions. So a mom in Santa Monica can suggest that Cameo is a nifty name for a baby girl, and within days, babies in Kansas, Florida, and Ohio are introduced to their grandparents as Cameo.

WHAT DO PARENTS WANT?

Long ago, the meaning of a name was important: the Puritans named their daughters after "virtues" like Silence and Temperance. In some cultures this is still true, but in the U.S., meaning is secondary. How else can you account for the popularity of Brendan, which seems to mean "stinking hair"? General cultural associations are more important. Names like Ethel or Seymour that remind parents of elderly relatives, for instance, are barely seen. (The name Hilary seemed to be surging toward popularity until the election of President Clinton, then dropped out of sight. Apparently few parents are willing to have it thought that they are naming a child after Hillary Clinton.)

But the majority of today's popular names haven't been used often enough to carry any real associative baggage. Parents are choosing them primarily for the sound. The hugely popular name Caitlin, for instance, is one of a cluster of related names that are also frequently used: Kaylin, Kathlyn, Kayleigh, Hayleigh, Hallie, Kelly, Katie. For boys, the fashion is less clearly defined, but names that begin with ''J'' and names that end in ''-in'' are stylish. What's more, parents are very ready to simply make names up. Does anybody have a grandmother named Brianna?

Of course, parents are much more conservative when it comes to boys' names. The top names for boys tend to be more familiar and certain neutral classics—like David, Michael, and Andrew—have been steadily used for years. For girls, parents are more likely to use a noun (Diamond, Rosemary), adapt spelling (Brittney), or borrow a formerly male name (Madison, Tyler, Mackenzie). I think we're all aiming for more or less the same thing: a name that is unusual without being downright weird.

There are exceptions, of course. Many parents still choose to delight a living relative or honor someone's memory by naming a child for someone else. Chances are when you meet a kindergartner with a frankly unfashionable name like Norma, that's how the choice was made. There are also parents who revel in flouting convention, and they may pick retro-cool names like Buster. But most of the time, most of us would like a name that is somewhat familiar, but still individual.

SO HOW DO YOU CHOOSE?

There are a lot of possibilities out there: there are tens of thousands in this book alone. But eliminating most of them is going to be easier than you think. When my younger sister was pregnant we sat down with this book, and after sifting through it, came up with exactly three possibilities—Simon, Mark, and Peter. She named her son Cooper. (Go figure.) There are baby name books with elaborate work sheets, but I favor a low-tech approach. You'll be able to eliminate the huge majority of candidates on the following grounds:

Leaves you cold. If a name doesn't speak to you or your partner, forget it. There are plenty of other options.

Unpleasant associations. Your old love interest, an uncle with bad breath, a character in a book you once read . . . these things are strong, and you should pay attention to them.

No nickname. I would have liked to have named a son after my father-in-law, but his name is Thornton. He was called "Thornt" for much of his youth. I didn't consider that helpful, and "Thorny" was out of the question. Parents are much more inclined to use complete names than they used to be: Robert is rarely trimmed down to Bob, for instance. But two syllables is the maximum number most people, especially schoolchildren, are likely to use.

Too trendy. If you have a feeling that a name is getting too fashionable, you are probably right. As the possessor of a once-popular name, I can sincerely urge you to look elsewhere.

Too odd. We were going to name our younger son Hugh. The hospital orderly, as he wheeled the infant and me out of the recovery room, asked me, "What's the baby's name?" I proudly answered "Hugh," and he said, "What?" I instantly realized that this was not an exchange I wanted to repeat thousands of times.

Too pretentious. Is it a name that a child can use? Think twice before naming a baby after your favorite poet or mountain peak. The famous "playground test" should weed out the duds here. If you call the name across a crowded playground, do you feel foolish? Or do heads whip around to stare at you? ("Who would name a child Everest?")

Hard to pronounce. Apparently Demi Moore has to correct everyone who tries to pronounce her name with the accent on the first syllable ("It's De*Mee*"). That seems like a lot of trouble. Why not just select something self-explanatory?

Hard to spell. Many parents, eager to individualize names, tinker with them phonetically. Some research suggests that unusually spelled names suggest negative qualities to many people. The more remarkable the spelling, the more difficulty it is likely to cause.

Sounds wrong with last name. Long or unusual last names seem to require simple first names, while plain last names can support more elaborate first names. If a child's last name is going to be hyphenated, take that into account. Your child could end up with a real mouthful.

The initials spell out something silly. Natasha Elizabeth Riley-Dodd will not thank you.

Once you've gotten down to a short list, mull things over. This is the point when you play with different endings, different spellings (Catherine or Katharine?), and combinations of first and middle names. It's not necessary to give a middle name, of course, but it can be a good way to use an unmanageable family name, and it can also give children more options as they get older. English actress Melissa Bell named her first son Diesel Thomas William, reasoning that if he got tired of Diesel (*if!*) he could move on to one of his more conservative middle names.

If you don't mind hearing the unvarnished truth you can try out possible names on your friends and family, but be prepared for people to say, "I've never met an Arthur I liked" or "You can't possibly call her Tootsie!" So if you are intent on using a very unusual name, you might prefer to keep your ideas secret until you have the baby. It's a little hard for even the most opinionated onlooker to look at an infant and say, "Why in the world did you name her Demetria?" It's also a good idea to take this book or your short list to the hospital. Sometimes name and baby just don't match up, and it's necessary to rethink.

The beauty of the process is that you really can't go wrong. Even if you feel you're compromising on a name, within days it will have lost all its other associations. It becomes, quite simply, the name of your baby. So of course it will turn out to be the perfect name.

If It's A
BOY...

Aaron Heb. "Exalted, on high." In the Old Testament, Aaron was the brother of Moses. The name was unusual until the 17th century, when so many Old Testament names first came into prominence. It has been fashionable, especially in the U.S., since the 1970s, and is very steadily used without being particularly trendy. U.S. Vice President Aaron Burr; baseball star Hank Aaron; composer Aaron Copeland.

Aaran, Aaren, Aaronas, Aarron, Aeron, Aharon, Arand, Arend, Ari, Arin, Arnie, Arny, Aron, Aronne, Arran, Arron, Arun, Erin, Haroun, Ron, Ronnie, Ronny

Abbas Heb. "Father"; Arab. "Stern." One of Muhammad's uncles was named Abbas. This is one of those cases where Judaism and Islam demonstrate their common roots. Israeli statesman Abba Eban.

Ab, Abba, Abbe, Abbey, Abbie, Abo

Abbey Dim. Abbot, Abelard, Abner. Political activist Abbie Hoffman.

Abbie, Abby

Abbott Heb. "Father." An abbot is the head of a monastic community, so the original bearers of this name (as a surname) may have worked for an abbot. Its use as a first name occurred mostly in the 19th century. In the 1940s and early 1950s Bud Abbott served as straight man to short, chubby comedian Lou Costello. Baseball player Jim Abbott.

Ab, Abad, Abba, Abbe, Abbey, Abbie, Abbot, Abby, Abe, Abot, Abott

Abda Arab. "Servant."

Abdi Heb. "My servant." Old Testament name.

Abdul Arab. "Servant of." Often used in combination with another name, as in "Abdullah," or "Servant of Allah." Basketball star Kareem Abdul-Jabar.

Ab, Abdal, Abdall, Abdalla, Abdallah, Abdel, Abdell, Ab-

della, Abdellah, Abdoul, Abdoull, Abdoulla, Abdoullah, Abdull, Abdullah, Del

Abdullah Arab. "Servant of Allah." One of the most common names in the Islamic world, and the name of Muhammad's father. A royal name in Saudi Arabia.

Abdalla, Abdallah, Abdella, Abedellah, Abdulla

Abe Dim. **Abraham.** Heb. "Father of many."

Abey, Abie

Abednego Aramaic "Servant of Nego." One of the three Biblical unfortunates thrown in the fiery furnace by King Nebuchadnezzar, and rescued by an angel. Another form of the name is **Azuriah.**

Abejundio Sp. "Like a bee."

Abejundo

Abel Heb. "Breath." Abel was the younger son of Adam and Eve, who was slain by his older brother, Cain. Abel has survived with steady use ever since the 6th century, and surprisingly enough, Cain also occurs from time to time.

Abe, Abell, Abey, Abie, Able

Abelard OG. "Highborn and steadfast." Made famous by the 12th-century French philosopher Pierre Abelard, who fell in love with and seduced his student Heloise. Her uncle and guardian had him emasculated, even though he married Heloise. She became a nun, he became a monk.

Ab, Abbey, Abby, Abe, Abel

Abiah Heb. "My father is the Lord." Another Old Testament name, used for women as well as men in the Bible. Unusual in real life.

Abia, Abija, Abijah

Abida Heb. "God knows."

Abidan

Abiel Heb. "My father is God." Old Testament name that the Puritans used in the U.S., but rare since.

Abiell, Abyel, Abyell, Ahbiel

Abimelech Heb. "My father is king." Occurred occasionally in the 19th century.

Abir Heb. "Strong."

Abeer, Abeeri, Abiri

Abisha Heb. "Gift of God."

Abidja, Abidjah, Abijah, Abishai

Abner Heb. "My father is light." Old Testament name that came to some prominence in the late 16th century. Use fell off in the 20th century, and the name is now mostly associated with Al Capp's comic strip *Li'l Abner*. Some potential for revival, though, as the name has a masculine, uncompromising air that should be appealing to today's parents. Inventor of baseball Abner Doubleday.

Ab, Abbey, Abbie, Abby, Abna, Abnar, Abnor, Avner, Eb, Ebbie, Ebby, Ebner

Abraham Heb. "Father of many." First of the Hebrew patriarchs. In the Bible, Abraham has a son named Isaac when he is 100 and his wife Sarah is 90. The name was popular while Abraham Lincoln was president (and even more so after his assassination), but it has faded from use since 1900. To both Christians and Jews, the important point about Abraham is his great age, so his name may seem unfitting for an infant.

Abarran, Abe, Abey, Abie, Abrahamo, Abrahan, Abram, Abrami, Abramo, Abran, Avram, Avrom, Bram, Ibrahim

Abram Heb. "He who is high is father." Var. **Abraham**.

Abe, Abey, Abie, Abramo, Avram, Avrom, Bram

Absalom Heb. "Father is peace." The handsome son of King David who connived to steal his father's throne. He died in battle, caught by his hair in an oak tree and executed by one of his father's soldiers. King David then lamented, "Would God I had died for thee, O Absalom, my son, my son!" Also in the title of a tragic novel *Absalom, Absalom* by William Faulkner. Little used today, perhaps because of its traditional associations with terrible grief.

Absalon, Abshalom, Absolom, Absolon, Avshalom, Avsholom

Abundio Sp. from Lat. "Abundant."

Abbondio, Abondio, Aboundio, Abundo

Acacio Sp. from Gk. "Free of malice." **Acacia**, the feminine version, refers to a blossoming tree that symbolized, to Christians, the resurrection of Christ.

Accacio

Ace Lat. "Unity." Connotations of superiority come from the fact that the ace is the playing card with highest face value. The term "flying ace" goes back to World War I (when planes were both novel and hazardous). Turns up occasionally for children of cool intellectual parents, but most likely as a nickname.

Acer, Acey, Acie

Achav Heb. "Uncle." Old Testament name.

Achiav

Achidan Heb. "My brother judged." Old Testament name.

Abidan, Amidan, Avidan

Achilles Gk. Place name; also hero of the *Iliad*, as the greatest of the Greek heroes fighting the Trojans. He was all but invulnerable, having been dipped in the River Styx by his mother. She held him, however, by the heel, which was thus his one weak point: hence "Achilles' heel."

Achill, Achille, Achillea, Achilleus, Achillios, Achillius, Akil, Akilles, Akillios, Akillius, Aquil, Aquiles, Aquilles, Quilo

Achim Heb. "God will judge."

Acim, Ahim

Achiram Heb. "My brother is well born."

Achishar Heb. "My brother sings." Old Testament name.

Amishar, Avishar

Ackerley OE. Place name: "Oak meadow." Surname transferred to first name.

Accerly, Acklea, Ackleigh, Ackley, Acklie, Ackerlea, Ackerleigh, Ackerly

Acton OE. Place name: "Oak tree settlement." Another surname transferred to a first name, also the pseudonym used by Charlotte Brontë's sister Anne, who wrote as "Acton Bell." (The three sisters purposely chose masculine-sounding pseudonyms.)

Adael Heb. "The Lord witnesses."

Adayel

Adair Scot. Gael. Place name: "Oak tree ford." Recently becoming more popular.

Adaire, Adare, Adayre

Adalard OG. "Noble and courageous."

Adelard, Adellard

Adalfieri It. from Ger. "Noble oath."

Adelfieri, Edelfieri

Adalgiso Sp. from Ger. "Noble lance."

Adelgiso, Edelgiso

Adalric OG. "Highborn ruler." The Old German particle

"-ric" is found in more common names lik and Richard.

Adalrich, Adalrick, Adelric, Adelrich, Adelrick

Adam Heb. "Son of the red earth." In the Bible, God created Adam—the first man—out of the "red earth" and breathed life into him. Steadily used from the Middle Ages until the 1700s, and again beginning in the 1970s. An appropriate name for the first boy in a family that has produced many girls. Congressman Adam Clayton Powell, Jr.; rock star Adam Ant.

Ad, Adamo, Adams, Adan, Adao, Addam, Addams, Addem, Addie, Addis, Addison, Addy, Ade, Adem, Adhamh, Adnet, Adnon, Adnot

Adamson OE. "Son of Adam."

Adamsson, Addamson

Adar Heb. "Noble."

Addison OE. "Son of Adam." Transferred surname. The English poet and essayist Joseph Addison was popular and influential through the 18th century. Addison is now turning up more and more as a girl's name.

Ad, Addeson, Addie, Addy, Adison, Adisson

Addy Teut. "Awe-inspiring; highborn." Also short for Adam, etc.

Addie, Ade, Adi, Ado

Adel OG. "Noble, highborn." More familiar as a particle of other names.

Adal, Edel

Adelar OG. "Noble eagle." Var. **Abelard.**

Adal, Adalar, Adalard, Adelard

Adelphe Fr. from Gk. "Brother."

Adelfo, Adelfus, Adelpho, Adelphus

Aden Place name (for a region of South Yemen, formerly a British colony, and an important seaport) or a variation on **Aidan.**

Aiden

Adham Arab. "Black."

Adil Arab. "Righteous, fair." Currently popular in the Arabic world.

Adeel

Adlai Heb. "My ornament." Used in the Old Testament, and very rare, though brought to public notice by statesman Adlai Stevenson.

Ad, Addie, Addy, Adley

Adler OG. "Eagle." More common as a surname, especially in the U.S.

Ad, Addler, Adlar

Admon Heb. "Red." From the same root that gives us Adam.

Adnah Heb. "Ornamented."

Adin

Adnan Arab. Meaning unclear: possibly "To settle." Arms magnate Adnan Khashoggi.

Adney OE. Place name: "The noble's island."

Adolph OG. "Noble wolf." The Latinized form Adolphus arrived in Britain in the mid–19th century, having been a German and Swedish royal name and also a saint's name. Almost unheard-of since the rise of Adolf Hitler and World War II. Filmmaker Adolph Zukor; French actor Adolphe Menjou; fashion designer Adolfo; beer magnate Adolph Coors.

Ad, Addolf, Addolph, Adolf, Adolfo, Adolfus, Adollf, Adolphe, Adolpho, Adolphus, Dolf, Dolph, Dolphus

Adonia Heb. "God is my lord." Old Testament name: one of King David's sons.

Adon, Adonias, Adonijah, Adoniya

Adonis Gk. In Greek myth, Adonis was a young man so beautiful that Aphrodite, goddess of love, became enamored of him. The name has come to epitomize male beauty, which would make it very hard to live with.

Addonis, Adohnes, Adones

Adrian Lat. "From Adria," a north Italian city. First popular in the 1950s in Britain, and used also as a woman's name, though it seems to be holding steady as a choice for male children. Hollywood costume designer Adrian; 12th-century pope Adrian IV (the only English pope in history).

Ade, Adiran, Adrain, Adrean, Adreean, Adreyan, Adreeyan, Adriano, Adrien, Adrin, Adrino, Adryan, Aydrean, Aydreean, Aydrian, Aydrien, Hadrian, Hadriano, Hadrien, Haydrian, Haydrien

Aegeus Gk. "Kid, young goat." The name actually refers to a shield made of goatskin that was the sign of Zeus, and also occurs as Egidio and Giles. In Greek myth, King

Aegeus was the father of Theseus, who slew the Cretan monster the Minotaur. When Aegeus mistakenly thought Theseus had been killed on his venture, he threw himself into the sea near Athens, which is now known as the Aegean.

Aigeos, Aigeus

Aeneas Gk. "He who is praised." The Trojan hero of Virgil's *Aeneid*. Legend has it that he founded the Italian colony that was the origin of Rome. Football player Aeneas Williams.

Aennea, Aineas, Aineias, Aineis, Ainnas, Eneas, Enné, Enneas, Enneis, Enneiss

Aeolus Gk. "Variable, changeable." In Greek myth Aeolus was the god of the winds. In the 19th century a brand of church organs was manufactured under the "Aeolian-Skinner" brand name, referring to the fact that a constant, even flow of air was necessary to produce sound from an organ.

Aeolos, Aiolos, Aiolus

Aeson Gk. Unknown meaning. In Greek myth, the father of Jason. Since the name Jason has been so fashionable, this name may hold considerable appeal for some.

Afif Arab. "Chaste."

Afton OE. Place name. A surname that has come into use as a first name.

Affton

Agamemnon Gk. "Working slowly." Name of one of the great heroes of Greek myth: a mighty warrior who commanded the Greeks at the siege of Troy. His proficiency in battle did not exempt him from the typical tragedy of Greek legend: his daughter Iphigenia was sacrificed before the Trojan War, and when he came home from the war his wife Clytemnestra killed him.

Agamemno, Agamenon

Agapito Sp. from Gk. "Loving-kindness, charity." The root is the Greek word *agape*, and there was a Pope (later Saint) Agapetus in the 6th century.

Agapeto, Agapetus, Agapios

Agathias Gk. "Good." This can be considered the masculine version of **Agatha**.

Agathios, Agathius, Agathos

Agnolo It. "Angel." More common in the U.S. in the Spanish form, Angelo.

Ahab Heb. "Father's brother." Pleasant way to honor an uncle, though literary types may be reminded of the mad sea captain in Herman Melville's novel *Moby Dick*.

Ahearn Celt. "Horse-lord."

Ahearne, Aherin, Ahern, Aherne, Hearn, Hearne, Herin, Hern

Ahmed Arab. "Greatly praised." Name often used for the prophet Muhammad, and favored by Muslims in the U.S. The name is in fact commonly used throughout the Islamic world.

Achmad, Achmed, Ahmaad, Ahmad, Ahmod, Amahd, Amed

Ahsan Arab. "Compassion."

Ehsan, Ihsan

— **Aidan** Gael. "Fire." Saint Aidan was a 7th-century Irish monk. The name is also used for women. Actor Aidan Quinn.

Aden, Aidano, Aiden, Aydan, Ayden, Edan, Eden, Eidan, Eiden

Aiken OE. "Made of oak." English writer Conrad Aiken.

Aicken, Aikin, Ayken, Aykin

Aimé Fr. "Much loved." More common as Aimée, a girl's name, or even as Esmé, a variant once well used in Scotland.

Aimery Teut. "Hardworking ruler."

Aimerey, Aimeric, Amerey, Aymeric, Aymery, Imre

Aimon Fr. from Teut. "House." Also possibly phonetic variant of the Irish **Eamon**, in turn a version of **Edmund**.

Aimond, Aymon, Haimon, Heman

Ainsley Scot. Gael. Place name: "His very own meadow." A last name converted to a first name, used by both sexes.

Ainsley, Ainsleigh, Ainslie, Ansley, Aynslee, Aynsley, Aynslie

Ainsworth OE. Place name: "Ann's estate."

Answorth

Ajax Gk. "Alas." Name from Greek mythology: a hero of the Trojan war. He was King of Salamis, and a huge, daring warrior, but he went mad and killed himself when his prowess as a fighter was cast into doubt. To Americans, may recall a kitchen cleanser.

Aias

Akbar Arab. ''Great.''

Akeem Var. **Hakeem** (Arab. ''Judging thoughtfully''). Although it is very exotic, this name ranks above such all-American classics as Howard and Nelson in usage. Its use is probably inspired by basketball player Hakeem Olajuwon, who was known as Akeem when he first came to the U.S.

Ahkeem, Akhim, Akim, Hakeem, Hakim

Akim Rus. Dim. **Joachim**, Heb. ''God will judge.''

Akmal Arab. ''Perfect.''

Aqmal

Alaire Fr. from Lat. ''Joyful.'' Var. **Hilary**. The root is the same as that for ''Hilarious,'' though the meaning has shifted a bit. Alaire, unfortunately, sounds like the name of a car.

Alair, Allair, Helier, Hilaire, Hilary, Larie, Lary

Alamar Sp. from Arab. ''Gilded, covered with gold.'' Baseball player Roberto Alomar.

Alomar

Alan Ir. Gael. Possible meanings are ''Rock'' or ''Comely.'' Widely used in the Middle Ages, then again from the 19th century to the late 20th, with a boom around the 1950s influenced by the popularity of actor Alan Ladd. Now waning, like most fifties names. South African author Alan Paton; lyricist Alan Jay Lerner; playwright Alan Bennett; astronaut Alan Shepard; actor Alan Alda; poet Allen Ginsberg.

Ailean, Ailin, Al, Alain, Alair, Aland, Alann, Alano, Alanson, Alen, Alin, Allan, Allayne, Allen, Alley, Alleyn, Alleyne, Allie, Allin, Allon, Allyn, Alon, Alun

Alard OG. ''Noble and steadfast.''

Adlar, Adlard, Al, Allard

Alaric OG. ''Ruler of all'' or ''Highborn ruler.'' Alaric I was the 5th-century king of the Visigoths who sacked Rome.

Al, Alarick, Alarico, Aleric, Alerick, Allaric, Allarick, Alleric, Allerick, Alric, Alrick, Ullrich, Ulrich, Ulrick

Alastair Gael. Var. **Alexander**, (Gk. ''Man's defender'').

Generally a Scottish name, though it appears occasionally throughout the English-speaking world. Most of the variants are different phonetic spellings of the name. TV commentator Alistair Cooke; actor Alistair Sim.

Al, Alasdair, Alasteir, Alaster, Alastor, Alaisdair, Alaistair, Alaister, Aleister, Alester, Alistair, Alistar, Alister, Allaistar, Allaster, Allastir, Allistair, Allister, Allistir, Allysdair, Allysdare, Allystair, Allyster, Alysdair, Alysdare, Alystair, Alyster

Alban Lat. "From Alba," a city on a "white" hill, the oldest city in the ancient kingdom of Latium. The first Christian martyr on British soil was Saint Alban, after whom a cathedral town (which is also a pilgrimage destination) is named. Not to be confused with Albin, which has a different root.

Al, Albain, Albany, Albie, Albin, Albinet, Albion, Albis, Alby, Albys, Alvan, Alvin, Alvy, Auban, Auben, Aubin

Albern OG. "Noble courage."

Albert OE. "Highborn, brilliant." Most widely used during the lifetime of Queen Victoria's German prince consort, Albert. Their many children and grandchildren carried the name to most of the royal families in Europe, but their eldest son's first move as king was to drop it. Out of style since the 1920s; in fact it has a seriously quaint air. Scientist Albert Einstein; Prince Albert of Monaco; actor Albert Finney; philosopher Albert Camus; artist Albrecht Dürer; baseball player Albert Belle.

Adalbert, Adalbrecht, Adelbert, Adelbrecht, Ailbert, Al, Alberto, Albie, Albrecht, Albrekt, Alvert, Alvertos, Aubert, Bert, Bertie, Berty, Dalbert, Delbert, Elbert, Elbrecht, Ulbricht

Albin Lat. "White, pale-skinned." From the root that gives us the word "albino." Common in Roman and medieval times, but not in the modern era.

Al, Alben, Albinson, Alpin, Aubin

Albion Celt. "Mountain." Used in England until the 1930s; "Albion" is a poetic name for Britain.

Alcander Gk. "Strong."

Alcinder, Alcindor, Alkander, Alkender

Alcott OE. Place name: "The old cottage."

Alcot, Allcot, Allcott, Alkott

Alden OE. "Old friend." Surname transferred to first name, but unusual.

Al, Aldin, Aldwin, Aldwyn, Aldwynn, Elden, Eldin, Eldwin, Eldwyn, Eldwynn

Aldo OG. "Old." An Italian name that is occasionally used in the U.S. A Renaissance printer named Aldus Manutius designed the first italic typeface.

Aldus, Alldo

Aldous OG. "Old." Medieval name that was brought back in the 19th century to slight popularity. Proof, if proof were needed, that meaning is usually a secondary consideration when names are chosen. Made most famous by writer Aldous Huxley.

Al, Aldis, Aldivin, Aldo, Aldon, Aldus, Alldo, Eldin, Eldis, Eldon, Eldous

Aldred OE. "Old counsel."

Alldred, Eldred, Eldrid, Elldred

Aldrich OE. "Old leader." A name that has some prominence in America as a family related to the Rockefellers.

Al, Aldric, Aldridge, Aldrige, Aldritch, Alldrich, Alldridge, Allric, Alrick, Audric, Eldrich, Eldridge, Eldritch, Elldrich, Rich, Richie, Richy, Ritch, Ritchey, Ritchie, Ritchy

Aldwin OE. "Old friend." See Alden.

Aldwinn, Aldwinne, Aldwyn, Aldwynne, Alswynn, Elden, Eldin, Eldwin, Eldwyn, Eldwynn

Alem Arab. "Wise man."

Alerio

Aleron Lat. "Winged one."

Aileron

Alex Dim. Alexander. Baseball player Alex Ochoa.

Alec, Aleco, Aleck, Alecko, Aleko, Alick, Alik, Elex

Alexander Gk. "Man's defender." Given great prominence by Alexander the Great and steadily used worldwide, as the numerous variants show. It was a royal name in Scotland, where it is still highly popular, and it is widely used in the U.S. without having attained trendy status. Offshoots like Alec or even Zander are starting to show up as given names. English poet Alexander Pope; U.S. statesman Alexander Hamilton; actors Sir Alec Guinness, Alec Baldwin; U.S. Secretary of State Alexander

Haig; Soviet writer and dissident Aleksandr Solzhenitsyn; writer Alexandre Dumas.

Al, Alasdair, Alastair, Alaster, Alcander, Alcinder, Alcindor, Alec, Aleco, Alejandro, Alejo, Alek, Aleksander, Aleksandr, Alessandre, Alessandri, Alessandro, Alex, Alexandre, Alexandro, Alexandros, Alexei, Alexi, Alexio, Alexis, Alic, Alicio, Alick, Alik, Alisander, Alissander, Alissandre, Alistair, Alister, Alistir, Alix, Allistair, Allister, Allistir, Alsandair, Alsandare, Iskander, Sacha, Sander, Sandero, Sandor, Sandro, Sandros, Sandie, Sandy, Sascha, Sasha, Saunder, Saunders, Sikander, Xander, Zander, Zandro, Zandros

Alexis Gk. "Helper." Usually thought of as a diminutive of **Alexander**, though it has a different etymological root. More commonly a girl's name.

Alejo, Aleksei, Aleksi, Aleksio, Aleksios, Aleksius, Alexei, Alexey, Alexi, Alexios, Alexius, Alexy

Alfonso Sp. Var. **Alphonse** (OG. "Ready for battle.") A royal name in Spain, but little used in the U.S. in this form or as Alphonse.

Alfons, Alfonsin, Alfonsino, Alfonz, Alonso, Alonzo, Alphons, Alphonsus, Alphonzus, Alphonz, Foncho, Fonz, Fonzie, Fonzo

Alford OE. Place name: "The old river-ford."

Aldford, Allford

Alfred OE. "Counsel from the elves." After wide medieval use, the name fell out of sight until a 19th-century revival; Queen Victoria even named her second son Alfred. Out of fashion since the 1920s, and to parents who remember *Mad Magazine*'s gap-toothed Alfred E. Neuman, a highly unlikely choice. English King Alfred the Great; poet Alfred Tennyson; movie director Alfred Hitchcock.

Ahlfred, Ailfred, Ailfrid, Ailfryd, Al, Alf, Alfeo, Alfey, Alfie, Alfre, Alfredas, Alfrey, Alfredo, Alfredos, Alfy, Avery, Elfred, Fred, Freddie, Freddy, Fredo

Alger OE. "Spear from the elves." Possibly a diminutive of **Algernon**. Medieval name revived with the 19th-century hunger for a picturesque past, but never common. State Department official Alger Hiss.

Al, Algar, Allgar, Allger, Elgar, Elger, Ellgar, Ellger

Algernon OF. "Wearing a mustache." A first name in several hugely powerful English aristocratic families, and given wider use in the latter half of the 19th century in Britain. Oscar Wilde used it for a brainless fop in *The Importance of Being Earnest*. All but unknown now. English poet Algernon Swinburne.

Al, Alger, Algernone, Algey, Algie, Algy, Aljernon, Allgernon

Algis OG. "Spear."

Ali Arab. "The high, exalted one." One of the ninety-nine attributes of Allah proposed by Muhammad as excellent names for boy children.

Aly

Alison OE. "Son of the highborn." More common as a girl's name, in spite of the "-son" ending.

Alisson, Allcen, Allison, Allisoun, Allson, Allyson

Allard OE. "Highborn and courageous." Politician Allard Lowenstein.

Adelard, Adelhard, Alhard, Alhart, Allart

Almanzo Family name of uncertain meaning. Famous from the *Little House* books: Almanzo Wilder tells Laura that a distant English ancestor's life had been saved during the Crusades by an Arab named El Manzoor. "They changed it after a while in England, but I guess there's no way to improve it much." Which just goes to show that 150 years ago parents also made fanciful choices for names.

Almarine OG. "Work ruler." Has nothing to do with the sea.

Almarin, Almarino

Alon Heb. "Oak tree." The feminine form, Alona, is more common.

Allon

Alonzo Var. **Alphonse**. OG. "Ready for battle." This form is marginally more popular than Alfonso, perhaps because of the fame of basketball star Alonzo Mourning.

Alanso, Alanzo, Allonso, Allonzo, Allohnso, Allohnzo, Alohnso, Alohnzo, Alonso, Lonnie, Lonny

Aloysius OG. "Famous fighter." Latinized version of Luigi or Louis, also related to Clovis and Ludwig. The 16th-century Italian Saint Aloysius is patron saint of students.

Ahlois, Aloess, Alois, Aloisius, Aloisio, Aloys, Lewis, Louis, Ludwick, Ludwig, Lutwick

Alpha Gk. First letter of the Greek alphabet, corresponding to ''A.'' More likely to be used for a girl, because of the ''-a'' ending. Still, in the Biblical Book of Revelation, Jesus says, ''I am Alpha and Omega, the beginning and the end.''

Alfa

Alpheus Heb. ''He who follows after.'' Biblical, used in the 19th century, now very unusual.

Alfaeus, Alfeos, Alfeus, Alpheaus, Alphoeus

Alphonse OG. ''Ready for battle.'' Alfonso is a royal name in Spain, thus very popular; this form is less used in the U.S., though even Alonzo, the most popular variant, is unusual. French writer Alphonse Daudet.

Affonso, Al, Alfie, Alfo, Alfons, Alfonso, Alfonsus, Alfonzo, Alfonzus, Alford, Alfy, Alonso, Alonzo, Alphonso, Alphonsus, Alphonzo, Alphonzus, Fons, Fonsie, Fonz, Fonzie, Phauns, Phons, Phonz

Alpin Gael. ''Fair one.''

Alpine, Macalpin, McAlpin, McAlpine

Alston OE. Place name: ''Noble one's settlement.''

Alsdon, Alsten, Alstin, Allston, Allstonn

Alta Lat. ''Elevated.'' As in Alta, Utah, thousands of feet above sea level.

Alto, Altus

Altair Gk. from Arab. ''Bird.'' Also the name of the brightest star in the constellation Aquila. It is about ten times as bright as the sun.

Alltair, Altaer, Altayr

Alter Yiddish. ''Old, old man.'' The Yiddish equivalent of Aldous.

Altman OG. ''Old man.'' Last name occasionally used as a first name. Film director Robert Altman; department store magnate Bernard Altman.

Alterman, Altermann, Altmann, Eltman, Elterman, Eltermann

Alton OE. Place name: ''Old town.'' Activist Alton Maddox.

Aldon, Allton, Alten

Alucio Sp. from Lat. "Bright, shining." The significant root here is *lux*, or "light," as in "lucid."

Allucio, Alucido, Aluxio, Aluzio

Aluf Heb. "Leader, one in charge."

Alouf, Aluph

Alured Lat. Var. **Alfred**.

Ailured

Alva Heb. Possibly "brilliance"; also related to Latin **Albin**. Old Testament name rarely used for men or women, in spite of Thomas Alva Edison's fame.

Alba, Alvah

Alvar OE. "Army of elves." Very rare. Architect Alvar Aalto.

Albaro, Alvaro, Alvarso, Alverio

Alvin OE. Several possible sources: the second element, "vin," means "Friend," but Al could indicate "Elf," "Noble," or "Old." Radio characters Alvin and the Chipmunks have given the name an irresistibly comical cast, however. Choreographer Alvin Ailey.

Ailwyn, Al, Aloin, Aluin, Aluino, Alva, Alvan, Alven, Alvie, Alvy, Alvyn, Alwin, Alwyn, Alwynn, Aylwin, Elvin, Elwin, Elwyn, Elwynn

Alvis Origin unclear. Possibly from an Old Norse legend involving the dwarf Alviss; possibly a modern blend. First appeared in the mid–20th century, but never widespread.

Alviss, Alwis, Alwyss

Amadeo Sp. from Lat. "Loved by God." The Latin version is Amadeus, given great prominence by the 1984 film about Mozart.

Amadee, Amadei, Amadeus, Amadi, Amadieu, Amadis, Amado, Amando, Amati, Amato, Amatus, Amyas, Amyot

Amadour Fr. from Lat. "Lovable." A Saint Amadour, purportedly founder of a French shrine (Rocamadour), has been venerated by the Catholic church, but recent research indicates he probably never lived.

Amador, Amadore

Amahl Heb. "Labor, hard work." Familiar to Americans as the young hero of Gian Carlo Menotti's often-performed opera *Amahl and the Night Visitors*.

Amal, Amali, Amel

Amalio Sp. from OG. "Industrious." The masculine equivalent of Amelia.
Amelio

Amarillo Sp. "Yellow." Place name: a city in Texas. Rather a mouthful for a baby, but it has a certain rakish flair.

Amasa Heb. "Bearing a burden." Occasionally used in the 19th century, but little-known today.

Amaury Var. **Maurice** (Lat. "Dark-skinned, Moorish.")
Amory

Ambrose Gk. "Ever-living." Saint Ambrose was the 4th-century bishop of Milan who baptized Saint Augustine. The name is more widely found on the Continent than in English-speaking countries. Writer Ambrose Bierce; Civil War General Ambrose E. Burnside.
Ambie, Ambroeus, Ambrogio, Ambroise, Ambros, Ambrosi, Ambrosio, Ambrosios, Ambrosius, Amby, Brose

Amerigo It. Var. **Emery**, OG. "Home ruler." It's fitting that the United States, founded on the principle of home rule, should have taken its nickname "America" from Italian explorer Amerigo Vespucci.
America, Americo, Americus, Amerika, Ameriko, Amerikus

Ames Origin unclear, but may be related to the Latin word for love, *amor*.
Aimes, Aymes

Amiel Heb. "God of my people."
Amyel

Amin Arab. "Honest, trustworthy."
Ameen, Amein

Amir Arab. "Ruler, commander." This is the term for a high-ranking and powerful official in many different capacities in the Muslim world.
Ameer, Amiran, Emeer, Emir

Amitai Heb. "Truth."
Amitay

Amjad Arab. "Full of glory."

Ammar Arab. "Long-lived."

Ammon Heb. "Teacher, builder." Biblical name: one of the sons of David, and place name: a country northeast of the Dead Sea. The Ammonites and the Israelites were frequently at war. The town of Amman in Jordan is situated in what was Ammon.

Amon, Amnon

Amory OG. "Home ruler." Var. **Emery**. Writer Cleveland Amory.

Aimory, Amery, Amorey

Amos Heb. "Borne, carried." A prophet of the Old Testament. The name has been little used in this century, perhaps because of lingering negative connotations from the highly politically incorrect radio show *Amos 'n Andy* that flourished in the 1940s and 1950s. Novelist Amos Oz.

Amoss

Amram Heb. "Mighty nation." Biblical name: the father of Moses.

Amyas Lat. "Loved one." Possibly an anglicized version of Amadeus, though sometimes considered a masculine variant of **Amy**. Unusual.

Amias, Amyes, Amyess

Anael Biblical: the name of an archangel.

Anastasius Gk. "Resurrection." Much more common in the feminine version, **Anastasia**.

Anastas, Anastase, Anastagio, Anastasio, Anastatius, Anastice, Anastius, Anasto, Anstas, Anstasios, Anstasius, Anstice, Stasio, Stasius

Anatole Gk. "From the east." Anatolia is a region of Turkey, which, of course, is east of Greece. French novelist Anatole France.

Anatol, Anatolio, Anatoly, Antal, Antol, Antole, Antolle, Antoly

Anchor The object as name. Most likely to be a transferred last name, possibly originating as some kind of occupational name.

Ancher, Anker

Anders Scand. Var. **Andrew**. Painter Anders Zorn.

Ander, Anderson, Andersson

André Fr. Var. **Andrew**. Traditionally, parents have chosen English-style names for boys in the U.S., but this preference seems to be changing; names with a foreign flair are inching into acceptability, if not into trendiness. Pianist André Watts; actor André Gregory; composer/conductor André Previn; tennis player Andre Agassi; football player Andre Rison.

Andrae, Andras, Andrei, Andrej, Andrey, Andres, Andris, Ohndrae, Ohndre, Ondre, Ondrei, Ohnrey, Ondrey

Andrew Gk. "Masculine." In the Bible, Andrew was the first of the twelve apostles. Legend has it that after his crucifixion on an X-shaped cross, his bones were transported to Scotland, where he is patron saint. The "Saint Andrew's Cross," representing Scotland, appears on the flag of the United Kingdom. Andrew is one of the top ten names for boys in the U.S., and a classic example of American parents' conservatism when it comes to choosing masculine names. U.S. Presidents Andrew Jackson, Andrew Johnson; industrialist Andrew Carnegie; Prince Andrew, Duke of York; actors Andy Devine, Andy Griffith, Andy Garcia; artists Andrew Wyeth, Andy Warhol; baseball player Andruw Jones.

Aindrea, Aindreas, Anders, Andie, Andonis, Andor, André, Andrea, Andreas, Andrei, Andrej, Andres, Andresj, Andrewes, Andrews, Andrezj, Andrey, Andrius, Andro, Andros, Andru, Andruw, Andy, Dandie, Dandy, Drew, Dru, Drud, Drugi, Ohndrae, Ohndré, Ondré, Ondrei, Ohnrey, Ondrey

Androcles Gk. "Glorious man." According to a Latin myth, Androcles was a mild-mannered slave who once removed a thorn from the paw of a lion. When Androcles, a Christian, was later tossed into an arena to face the traditional band of ravenous lions, he encountered the lion who owed him a favor, and who set him free. G.B. Shaw later used this tale as the basis for a play about Christian faith.

Androclus

Aneurin Welsh. "Honor." Mostly limited to Wales. British politician Aneurin Bevan.

Aneirin, Nye

Anfernee Modern name, made famous by basketball star Anfernee Hardaway, who is generally known as "Penny." His name may be a phonetic variant of Anthony.

Anferney, Anfernie

Angel Gk. "Messenger." Angelo is most often used now,

even in English-speaking countries, as Angel is usually considered a girl's name (although in Thomas Hardy's 1891 novel *Tess of the D'Urbervilles*, a major character is named Angel Clare). Both forms are popular in Spanish-speaking countries. Jockey Angel Cordero.

Ange, Angell, Angelmo, Angelo, Angie, Angy, Anjel, Anjelo, Anyoli, Ohngel, Ohnjel, Onjel, Onjello, Onnjel, Onnjelo

Angus Scot. Gael. "Sole or only choice." In Celtic myth Angus Og is a god of such attractive traits as humor and wisdom. The name has been more widely used in Scotland, and in the U.S. tends to be reminiscent of breeds of cattle such as the Black Angus.

Anngus, Ennis, Gus, Guss

Anicho Ger. "Ancestor, predecessor."

Aniketos Gk. "Unconquered, invincible." The name has survived in a small way in Catholic countries because of a 2nd-century martyred pope who was later canonized.

Aniceto, Anicetus, Anisio

Annan Celt. "From the brook."

Anscom OE. Place name: "Valley of the awesome one." "Combe" is an Old English term for a deep, narrow valley.

Anscomb, Anscombe, Anscoombe

Ansel OF. "Follower of a nobleman" or variant of **Anselm**. Use is very likely to refer to photographer Ansel Adams, who portrayed the American wilderness so eloquently.

Ancell, Ansell

Anselm OG. "God-helmet." Saint Anselm was Archbishop of Canterbury in the 12th century, and one of the formative influences on medieval Christian thought. The name survives best as Selma, a variant of the feminine form. Painter Anselm Kiefer.

Anse, Ansel, Anselme, Anselmi, Anselmo, Anshelm, Anso, Elmo, Selmo

Ansley OE. Place name: "The awesome one's meadow."

Ainslea, Ainslee, Ainsleigh, Ainsley, Ainslie, Ainsly, Annslea, Annsleigh, Annsley, Anslea, Ansleigh, Anslie, Ansly

Anson Unclear origin and meaning, perhaps OG. Possibly

on of Ann," though "Son of the divine" seems more likely. Baseball great Cap Anson.

Annson, Ansson, Hanson

Anstice Var. Anastasius.

Anstiss

Antaeus Greek myth name. He was the son of the earth and the sea, a wrestler who was invincible while his feet touched the ground. Hercules vanquished him by lifting him in the air. *Antaeus* is the name of a literary magazine.

Antaios, Anteo, Anteus

Antenor Sp. from Gk. "Combatant, antagonist." A Trojan in the *Iliad*. The name survives in Spanish-speaking countries. South American silver magnate Antenor Patiño.

Anthony Lat. Clan name of the Romans, possibly meaning "beyond price, invaluable." The 3rd-century hermit Saint Anthony, who, according to legend, lived alone in the wilderness for over eighty of his hundred-some years, is patron saint of the poor. In England the name is usually spelled—and pronounced—without the "h." This form is well used in the U.S., and so, to a lesser extent, are variants **Antonio** and **Antoine**. Actors Anthony Quinn, Anthony Hopkins, Anthony Perkins, Tony Curtis, Antonio Banderas; photographer Antony Armstrong-Jones, Earl of Snowdon; composer Anton Bruckner; playwright Anton Chekhov; basketball player Anthony Mason.

Anntoin, Antin, Antoine, Anton, Antone, Antonello, Antoney, Antoni, Antonin, Antonino, Antonio, Antonius, Antons, Antony, Antuwan, Antwahn, Antwohn, Antwon, Antwuan, Toney, Toni, Tony

Antioch Place name: city in what is now Turkey that was a center of Christianity from around 300 A.D. until the 18th century.

Antiochus

Antoine Fr. Var. Anthony. Popular in the U.S. in recent years. Football player Antone Davis.

Antione, Antjuan, Antuan, Antuwain, Antuwaine, Antuwayne, Antuwon, Antwahn, Antwain, Antwaine, Antwan, Antwaun, Antwohn, Antwoin, Antwoine, Antwon, Antwone

Antonio Sp. Var. Anthony. This form is even more popular than Antoine, no doubt owing to the number of Spanish-speaking immigrants to the U.S. Saint Anthony of Padua is a very important saint in the Catholic church, venerated on June 13.

Antolin, Antonito, Anton, Tony

Anwar Arab. "Shafts of light." Made famous by Egyptian President Anwar Sadat.

Anwell Welsh-Celt. "Loved one."

Anwel, Anwil, Anwill, Anwyl, Anwyll

Apollo Gk. "Manly." In classical myth, Apollo is the god who drives the sun across the sky in a carriage, and also rules over healing and prophecy, speaking through the famous oracle at Delphi.

Apollon, Apollos, Apolo

Apolonio Sp. from Gk. "Follower of Apollo." The feminine form, **Apollonia**, is somewhat more familiar.

Apollonios, Apollonius

Apostolos Gk. "Apostle, disciple."

Aquila Lat. "Eagle." Despite the feminine "-a" ending, used in the 19th century as a revival of an ancient Roman name.

Acquila, Acquilino, Acquilla, Akila, Akilino, Akilla, Aquilina, Aquilino, Aquilla

Aquilo Roman myth name: the personification of the North Wind. Interesting choice for a winter baby.

Aquilino, Aquillo

Aram Assyrian. "Heights." This was an ancient place name, referring to Syria. The language spoken there in pre-Christian times was called Aramaic.

Arram

Arcadio Sp. from Gk. Ancient place name: Arkadios was a region of Greece; the name has come down to us as Arcadia, which is a kind of pastoral paradise. As Arkady, well used in Russia.

Alcadio, Alcado, Alcedio, Arcadios, Arcadius, Arkadi, Arkadios, Arkadius, Arkady

Arcelio Sp. from Lat. "Altar of heaven."

Arcelius, Aricelio, Aricelius

Archard Anglo-Ger. "Holy, powerful."

Archerd

Archelaus Gk. "Ruler of the people." Not uncommon in the ancient world; Herod the Great had a son of that name who is mentioned in the Bible. Rare today.

Archelaios, Arkelaos, Arkelaus

Archer OF. "Bowman." Originally surname indicating occupation (like Miller, Smith, or Baker), mildly popular in the 19th century. Philanthropist Archer Huntington.

Archibald OG. "Noteworthy and valorous." Brought to Britain with the Norman Conquest, and popular largely in Scotland, where it was in the top twenty until the 1930s. Virtually invisible in the U.S. Poet Archibald MacLeish.

Arch, Archaimbaud, Archambault, Archer, Archibaldo, Archibold, Archie, Archimbald, Archimbaldo, Archy, Arquibaldo, Arquimbaldo

Archimedes Gk. "To contemplate first." The name of a brilliant Greek mathematician in the 2nd century B.C.

Arkimedes, Arquimedes

Arden Lat. "Burning with enthusiasm." The Forest of Arden in Shakespeare's *As You Like It* is a magically beautiful place.

Ard, Arda, Ardie, Ardin, Ardon, Ardy, Arrden

Ardley OE. Place name: "Home-lover's meadow."

Ardly, Ardsley, Ardsly

Ardmore Lat. Eng. "More zealous."

Ardmorr

Argento Lat. Eng. "Silvery." The country of Argentina is named for the silver its early Spanish settlers hoped to find there, but did not.

Argentino, Argentio

Argus Gk. "Vigilant guardian." In Greek myth, a creature with 100 eyes, who was later changed into a peacock with eyes on his tail feathers.

Argos

Argyle Scot. Place name. Also given to the indigenous knitting pattern of interlocking diamonds that occasionally surfaces in American fashion.

Argyll

Ari Heb. "Lion." This name is a particle of the more familiar Ariel.

Arie, Arik, Arri, Ary, Arye

Aric OG. "Ruler." Also an element of many other names, like Alaric and Frederick. Aric actually contains the elements of Richard in reversed order.

Arick, Arric, Arrict, Arrick, Eric, Erick, Erric, Errick, Erik, Ric, Rickie, Ricky

Ariel Heb. "Lion of God." In Shakespeare's *The Tempest*, Ariel is a sprite who can disappear at will. The name has the connotation of something otherworldly, and though Shakespeare's Ariel is male, the name is used mostly for girls. Israeli statesman Ariel Sharon.

Aeriell, Airel, Airyel, Airyell, Arel, Arie, Ariell, Arik, Aryel, Aryell

Ares Gk. Myth name: Ares was the god of war, and one of the lovers of Aphrodite, the goddess of beauty. In Roman myth he was known as Mars.

Aries Lat. "A ram." The name of the astrological sign for those born from March 21 to April 19.

Ares, Arese, Ariese

Arion Gk. myth name: Arion was a poet from about 700 B.C. He is sometimes erroneously identified with Orion, who was the mighty hunter and gave his name to a constellation.

Aryon

Aris Dim. **Aristeo**. A modern shortening.

Arris

Aristeo Sp. from Gk. "The best." The root is also the root of the word "aristocrat," which appears in the following names as well.

Aris, Aristio, Aristo, Aristos

Aristides Gk. "Best." Aristides was a famous Athenian general and statesman during the Golden Age of Athens.

Aristeides

Aristotle Gk. "Superior." Indelibly associated with the Greek philosopher Aristotle, though given prominence in recent years by the fame of Jacqueline Kennedy's second husband, shipping magnate Aristotle Onassis.

Ari, Arie, Aristotelis, Aristotellis, Arri, Ary

Arledge OE. Place name: "Lake with the hares." TV magnate Roone Arledge.

Arlidge, Arlledge, Arrledge

Arlen Ir. Gael. "Pledge, oath."

Arlan, Arlenn, Arles, Arlin, Arlyn, Arllen, Arrlen

Arliss Old name of confused origin. Possibly goes back to a Hebrew word meaning "Pledge."

Arley OE. Place name: "Hare-meadow."
   Arlea, Arleigh, Arlie, Arly
Arlo Sp. "Barberry tree." Enjoyed a spurt of popularity in the early 1970s, possibly attendant on the fame of singer Arlo Guthrie. With the current interest in artifacts of the '70s, combined with new interest in "-o" endings for boys' names, Arlo may see a spurt of use.
   Arlow, Arlowe, Arrlo
Armand Fr. Var. **Herman**, OG. "Army man." The most commonly used form in the U.S. is Armando, which is unusual but not as scarce as Herman itself. Actor Armand Assante.
   Almando, Arman, Armande, Armando, Armani, Armin, Armon, Armond, Armonde, Armondo, Ormond, Ormonde, Ormondo
Armani Though the root of this name is probably Herman, in the late 20th century it most likely refers to the Italian fashion designer Giorgio Armani. Football player Armani Toomer.
   Amani, Armahni, Armoni
Armin Lat. Var. **Herman**, OG. "Army man." Actor Armin Mueller-Stahl.
   Arman, Armen, Arminio, Arminius
Armon Heb. "Chestnut."
   Armoni
Armstrong OE. "Strong arm."
Arnaud Fr. Var. **Arnold**.
   Arnald, Arnaldo, Arnauld, Arnault
Arne OG. "Eagle." Var. **Arnold**.
   Arney, Arni, Arnie
Arnett OF/Eng. "Little eagle." Broadcaster Peter Arnett.
   Arnat, Arnet, Arnot, Arnott, Ornet, Ornette
Arno OG. "Eagle-wolf."
   Arnoe, Arnou, Arnoux, Arnow, Arnowe
Arnold OG. "Strength of an eagle." Brought to Britain with the Norman invasion, faded out after the 13th century, and briefly revived in the late 19th century. Unusual today, perhaps because it has vaguely dorky connotations. English novelist Arnold Bennett; golfer Arnold Palmer; actor Arnold Schwarzenegger.

Arnaldo, Arnaud, Arnauld, Arnault, Arndt, Arne, Arney, Arni, Arnie, Arnoldo, Arnot, Arny

Arran Scot. Place name. The Isle of Arran is off the Atlantic coast. There is also a group of Aran islands on the west coast of Ireland. Tradition has it that the elaborate style of sweater known as ''Aran'' developed in these islands, so that when the corpse of a drowned fisherman washed up on shore, his family could identify him by his unique handmade garment. Also possibly a phonetic variant of Aaron, even though the sources are unrelated.

Arren, Arrin, Arron

Arrigo It. Var. **Henry** (OGer. ''Estate ruler''). **Enrico** is the other variation.

Arrio Sp. ''Belligerent.''

Ario, Arryo, Aryo

Arsenio Gk. ''Masculine.'' Saint Arsenius was one of the Desert Fathers of Christianity, who lived in the 4th century A.D. His most famous saying was, ''I have often been sorry for having spoken, but never for having held my tongue.'' Ironically, his most famous modern namesake is the comedian Arsenio Hall.

Arcenio, Arcinio, Arsanio, Arseenio, Arseinio, Arsemio, Arsen, Arsene, Arsenios, Arsenius, Arseno, Arsenyo, Arsinio, Arsino

Artemus Gk. Probably ''Follower of the goddess Artemis.'' New Testament name occasionally used in the 19th century. Apollonius and Dennis (Dionysus) are the analogous ''follower of'' names: it's remarkable that they have survived so long after worship of the Greek pantheon died out. Author Artemas Ward.

Art, Artemas, Artemis, Artie, Artimas, Artimis, Artimus, Arty

Arthur Celt. Possibly ''Bear'' or ''Rock.'' Linked with King Arthur, the legendary British hero of the Round Table, and often used in the Middle Ages, but unfashionable until the early 19th century, when Arthur Wellesley, the Duke of Wellington, vanquished Napoleon. The Victorian enthusiasm for the romance of the past probably promoted its use, and the name's popularity only began to wane in the 1920s. It is still familiar, but not common. Columnist Art Buchwald; actor Art Carney; tennis star Arthur Ashe;

writer Arthur C. Clarke; playwright Arthur Miller.

Arrt, Art, Artair, Arte, Arther, Arthor, Arthuro, Artie, Artor, Artro, Artur, Arturo, Artus, Arty, Arthur

Arundel OE. Place name: "Eagle valley."

Arondel, Arondell, Arundale, Arundell

Arvad Heb. "Exile, voyager."

Arpad, Arv, Arvid, Arvie

Arvin OG. "People's friend."

Arv, Arvid, Arvie, Arvy, Arwin, Arwyn

Ary Var. **Ari**. Heb. "Lion."

Arye, Aryeh

Asa Heb. "Doctor." Another Old Testament name made popular by the Puritans in the 17th century. Now unusual.

Ase

Asad Arab. "Luckier."

Assad

Asael Heb. "God has made." Old Testament name rarely used in the 19th century in the U.S.

Asaya, Asayel, Asahel, Asiel

Asaph Heb. "Gathered up." Old Testament name, again, scarcely used.

Asaf, Asiph

Ascanius Latin myth: son of Aeneas. His other name, Iulus, was the theoretical root of the name of the clan to which Julius Caesar belonged.

Ascot OE. Place name: "Eastern cottage." More specifically, the name of England's famous racetrack near Windsor Castle, and also a style of tying a cravat.

Ascott, Escot, Escott

Asgard ONorse. "Gods' courtyard." The eternal dwelling place of the Scandinavian gods. It was allegedly in the center of the universe, accessible only by a rainbow bridge.

Ash Tree name: the ash tree was common both in England and Scandinavia.

Ashe, Asshe

Ashbel Heb. "Fire of Bel." Bel was a deity in the pre-Christian pantheon.

Ashby OE. Place name: "Ash tree farm."

Ash, Ashbie, Ashbey, Ashburn, Ashton

Asher Heb. "Felicitous." Old Testament name brought into English use by the Puritans.
  Ash, Asser

Ashford OE. Place name: "Ford near ash trees." Musician Nick Ashford.
  Ash, Ashenford

Ashley OE. Place name: "Ash tree meadow." Originally a surname that migrated to first-name status, possibly helped along by Ashley Wilkes in Margaret Mitchell's *Gone With the Wind*. Though originally used for boys, it is now so hugely popular for girls that an infant named Ashley will be presumed to be feminine.
  Ash, Ashely, Asheley, Ashelie, Ashlan, Ashleigh, Ashlen, Ashli, Ashlie, Ashlin, Ashling, Ashlinn, Ashly, Ashlyn, Ashlynn

Ashraf Arab. "More honorable."

Ashton OE. Place name: "Ash tree settlement." More popular in the 19th century than now, though this is the kind of name Anglophile parents of the 21st century may make more popular. Choreographer Sir Frederick Ashton; museum executive Ashton Hawkins.
  Assheton, Ashtun

Ashur Semitic. "Warlike one." A name used by various Assyrian kings, who lived up to its meaning.
  Asher

Asim Arab. "Guardian."
  Aseem

Aslan Literary name: invented by the author C.S. Lewis for the magical lion in *The Lion, the Witch and the Wardrobe* and the following books in the Chronicles of Narnia.

Aston OE. Place name: "Eastern town." Famous for an English sports car, the Aston Martin.

Astraeus Gk. myth name: Astraeus was one of the Titans, the gigantic race that walked the earth before mankind. He was the father of the winds.
  Astraios

Aswin OE. "Spear-friend."
  Aswinn, Aswyn, Aswynn

Athanasius Gk. "Endless life."
  Atanasio, Atanasios, Atanasius, Athan, Athanasios

Athens Gk. Place name: the capital of Greece. Athens is

considered the cradle of democracy, and many cities in the United States bear its name.

Athenios

Atherton OE. Place name: "Town by the spring." The town of Atherton in Northern California is more likely to be named after early settlers called Atherton.

Athelstan OE. "Highborn rock." Used by Anglo-Saxon royalty and revived slightly by Sir Walter Scott's use of it in *Ivanhoe*. Now extremely rare.

Athol Scot. Place name, meaning unclear. The Duke of Atholl, in Scotland, is the only British citizen entitled to maintain his own private army.

Atholl

Athos Literary name: one of the three musketeers from Alexandre Dumas's famous novel of that name.

Atif Arab. "Compassionate."

Ateef, Atiph

Atlas Gk. "To carry." Atlas was a mythical Titan who bore the weight of the world on his shoulders, so the name bears connotations of great strength.

Attlas

Atley OE. Place name: "The meadow." Indicates an ancestor who, once upon a time, lived in a house near (or "at") a meadow. The same pattern is true for the following names, all based on features of a long-ago English landscape. English politician Clement Attlee.

Atlea, Atlee, Atleigh, Attlee, Attleigh, Attley

Atticus Lat. "Of Athens." The name of a famous Roman man of letters who lived in last years (109–32 B.C.) of the Roman empire. He is sometimes considered the first "publisher" because he had slaves copy important contemporary works like the letters of Cicero. In America the name resounds from association with Atticus Finch, the heroic lawyer of Harper Lee's *To Kill a Mockingbird*.

Attila OG. "Little father." Generally remembered because of Attila the Hun, the Germanic king whose cruel invasions of the Balkans and Gaul helped hasten the end of the Roman Empire. One of his nicknames was "the scourge of God."

Atila, Atilano, Atilo, Attilia, Attilio

Atwater OE. Place name: "The water."

Attwater

Atwell OE. Place name: "The well."

Atwood OE. Place name: "The wood."
  Atwoode

Atworth OE. Place name: "The farmstead."

Auberon OG. "Highborn and bearlike." Also possibly a form of Aubrey. Better-known, though no more common for it, as Oberon, King of the Fairies in Shakespeare's *A Midsummer Night's Dream*. English writer Auberon Waugh.
  Auberron, Oberon, Oberron, Oeberon

Aubrey OF. "Elf ruler." Originally a man's name that arrived in England with the Norman Conquest. Now used by girls as well, thus no doubt dooming its use as a boy's name. The 19th-century artist Aubrey Beardsley; biographer John Aubrey.
  Alberic, Alberick, Alberik, Aube, Auberon, Aubry, Averey, Averie, Avery, Oberon

Audley OE. Place name of uncertain meaning.

Audric OG. "Noble ruler." Var. **Aldrich**.

August Lat. "Worthy of respect." The feminine version, **Augusta**, and the longer Latin version, **Augustus**, are more widely (though still infrequently) used in English-speaking countries. Sculptor Auguste Rodin; painter Auguste Renoir.
  Agostino, Agosto, Aguistin, Agustin, Agustino, Augie, Auguste, Augustin, Augustine, Augustino, Augusto, Augustus, Augie, Augy, Austen, Austin, Gus, Guss

Augustine Lat. Dim. **August**. The 5th-century bishop Saint Augustine is famous for the frank *Confessions*, in which he says, "Oh God, make me chaste—but not yet."
  Aguistin, Agustin, Augie, Augustin, Augy, Austen, Austin, Austyn

Augustus Lat. "Worthy of respect." Given historical glamor by Roman emperors and German princely families, who brought it to Britain in the 18th century, when it became very fashionable. Now little used. Sculptor Augustus Saint-Gaudens; painter Augustus John; beer magnate Augustus Busch.
  Augie, Augustin, Augy, Austen, Austin, Austyn, Gus, Guss

Aurelius Lat. "Golden."
  Aurelio, Aurelo, Oriel
Austin Oral form of Augustine, contracted by everyday speech. Now most often a family name transferred to a first name. Steadily used without being fashionable.
  Austen, Austyn, Ostyn, Ostynn
Autry Var. **Audrey** (OE. "Noble strength"). Actor Gene Autry.
  Autrey
Avenall OF. Place name: "Oat pasture."
  Aveneil, Aveneill, Avenel, Avenell, Avenil, Avenill
Averett Var. **Everett** (OE. "Boar hardness").
  Averet, Averit, Averitt, Averret
Averill Most likely derivation is OE. "Boar-warrior," though may also be related to French **Avril**, "April." Industrialist and statesman Averell Harriman.
  Ave, Averel, Averell, Averil, Averyl, Averyll, Avrel, Avrell, Avrill, Avryll, Haverell, Haverill
Avery OE. "Elf-ruler." Currently quite scarce, but a real candidate for popularity. Var. **Alfred, Aubrey**. Philanthropist Avery Fisher.
  Averey
Aviel Heb. "God is my father."
  Avyel
Avram Heb. Var. **Abraham**.
  Aviram
Avishai Heb. "Gift of my father."
Avital Heb. "Father of dew." Also used as a girl's name in Israel. In a dry climate like that of the Middle East, dew has great significance.
  Amital
Avner Heb. form of Abner ("My father is light").
  Abner
Axel OG. "Father of peace" and Scan. Var. **Absalom**. Rock star Axl Rose.
  Aksel, Ax, Axe, Axell, Axil, Axill, Axl
Aylmer OE. "Highborn and renowned." The homonym Elmer is the more common form of this very old English name.
  Aillmer, Ailmer, Allmer, Ayllmer, Elmer, Eylmer

Aylward OE. "Awesome guardian" or "Highborn guardian."

Ayman Arab. "Lucky, blessed."

Azim Arab. "Protector, defender."
Asim, Aseem, Azeem

Aziz Arab. "Strong, mighty." Another one of Allah's ninety-nine attributes, and thus a familiar name in the Muslim world.

Azrael Biblical name: the archangel who is charged with care of those born under the sign of Scorpio (Oct. 23 to Nov. 21). He appears in both Muslim and Jewish stories.

Azriel Heb. "God is my help."
Azreel, Azryel

Azuriah Heb. "Aided by Jehovah." Although twenty-eight different biblical characters are known by this name, it is all but obsolete today. Actor Hank Azaria.
Azaria, Azariah, Azria, Azriah, Azuria

MR. SMITH AND MR. LI

Over one-third of the immense population of China shares five last names: Wang, Chen, Liu, Zhang, and Li. Nearly half of the people in South Korea share three names: Lee, Kim, and Park. In Scandinavia so many citizens share names ending in "-sen" or "-son" that the government encourages them to choose new last names to minimize confusion.

In the United States, things are very different. A 1984 collation of various government records turned up 1.7 million last names. About 25,000 of them were unique: in other words, 25,000 people in America were the only people with that last name. But one cliché turns out to be accurate: the most common last name is still Smith (followed by Johnson, Williams, Brown, and Jones).

Babson OE. "Son of Barbara." Unusual in that it is based on a mother's name rather than a father's name.

Babsen, Babsson

Bachelor Middle French "Unmarried man." Usually a family name.

Bachellor, Batcheler, Batcheller, Batchelor, Batchellor

Bacchus Mythology name: Bacchus is the Greek god of wine, equivalent to Dionysus. He is also the god of poets, perhaps a more encouraging notion for parents.

Bailey OF. "Bailiff." Occupational name: in the Middle Ages a bailiff was a minor officer of the law. When it appears, this is usually a transferred last name, but if its occasional use for girls takes off, parents of boys will hesitate to use it.

Bail, Bailee, Bailie, Baillee, Baillie, Baily, Baley, Baylee, Bayley, Bayly

Bainbridge Ir. Gael. "Pale bridge." Also a place name: an island in Washington state, across Puget Sound from Seattle.

Bain, Banebridge, Baynbridge, Bayne, Baynebridge

Baird Gael. "One who sings ballads." The more familiar form in English, of course, is Bard. This is an occupational name.

Bar, Bard, Barde, Barr, Bayerd, Bayrd

Baker OE. Occupational name transferred to surname and, in the 19th century, to a first name. Politician James Baker.

Balbo Lat. "Mutterer."

Bailby, Balbi, Balbino, Ballbo

Baldemar OG. "Bold and renowned." Like many of the more exotic names, use of this one has been prolonged by the fact that it is a saint's name. Saint Baldomar was a blacksmith who became a monk and is the patron saint

40

of blacksmiths, a profession much less common than it used to be.

Baldomar, Baldomero, Baumar, Baumer

Balder OE. "Courageous army." In Norse myth the god Balder is called "the good," and reigns over summer, light, and innocence. Of course, in Norway, "bald" may not mean "hairless."

Baldor, Baldur, Baudier

Baldric OG. "Brave ruler." "Bald," obviously, is the particle meaning "brave" in these Old German names. "Ric," as in Frederick and Richard, is the particle that means "ruler."

Balderic, Balderik, Baldrick, Baudric

Baldwin OG. "Brave friend." Unusual in English-speaking countries, though Baudoin is a royal name in Belgium. Author James Baldwin.

Bald, Baldewin, Baldovino, Balduin, Balduino, Baldwinn, Baldwyn, Baldwynn, Balldwin, Baudoin

Balfour Gael. "Grazing land." Also the name of a town in northern Scotland. In Robert Louis Stevenson's *Kidnapped*, David Balfour is the young, idealistic hero. The Balfour Declaration of 1917 was a declaration of British support for limited Jewish settlement in Palestine. It was named for its author, British Foreign Secretary Arthur James Balfour, and Balfour was occasionally used as a first name in Israel afterward.

Balfer, Balfor, Balfore, Ballfour

Ballard OG. "Brave and strong."

Balthasar Gk. "God save the king." Along with Caspar and Melchior, one of the three kings who brought gifts to the baby Jesus, though they are not named in the Bible. Actor Balthazar Getty.

Baldassare, Baltasar, Baltazar, Balthasaar, Balthazaar, Balthazar, Balto, Belshazzar

Bancroft OE. Place name: "Field of beans." Many of the most common Anglo-Saxon place names that have become first names refer to simple, homely agricultural landmarks. Hubert Howe Bancroft was a prominent historian in the western United States whose collection forms the nucleus of the Bancroft Library of the University of California.

Ban, Bancrofft, Banfield, Bank, Binky

Banner OF. "Flag." This is probably an occupational name referring to someone whose job was to carry a flag or banner.
Bannerman

Banning Ir. Gael. "Small fair one" or "Son of the fair one."

Bannock Scot. Gael. "Unleavened oat bread." The name may indicate an ancestor who was a baker.
Bannoch

Baptiste Fr. from Gk. "Baptizer." Reference to John the Baptist, who baptized Jesus in the River Jordan. The Spanish form, Bautista, may be slightly more common in the U.S.
Baptist, Battista, Battiste, Bautista

Barak Heb. "Lightning." Name of an Old Testament warrior. Has a rather pugnacious sound, too.

Barber OF. "Beard." Originally an occupational name; the French word for beard is *barbe*, and long ago, men who wished to have their facial hair cut or trimmed would have it done professionally, as not everyone possessed a razor.
Barbar, Barbour

Barclay OE. Place name: "Where birches grow." This is the form most favored in Scotland; Berkeley is more common elsewhere. Barclays is the name of one of the biggest banks in Britain. Basketball player Charles Barkley.
Bar, Barcley, Barklay, Barkley, Barklie, Barrclay, Berk, Berkeley, Berkie, Berkley, Berklie, Berky

Bard Ir. Var. Baird.
Bar, Barde, Bardo, Barr

Barden OE. Place name: "Barley valley."
Bardon, Borden, Bordon

Bardolf OE. "Ax-wolf." A drunken fool named Bardolph figures in four of Shakespeare's plays.
Bardolph, Bardou, Bardoul, Bardulf, Bardulph

Bardrick Teut. "Ax-ruler." Just as many of the Anglo-Saxon names relate to farming, numerous Teutonic names relate to fighting.
Bardric, Bardrich

Barend OG. "Hard bear."

Barker OE. Possibly "Shepherd," though the name may also relate to birch trees, as in Barclay. Used more often in the 19th century. In the U.S. a barker is also someone who delivers a glib sales talk to attract customer

Birk

Barksdale OE. "Birch valley."

Barlow OE. Place name: "The bare hillside." Joel Barlow was an early American statesman.

Barlowe, Barrlow

Barnabas Heb. "Son of comfort." In the New Testament, Barnabas is a companion of Paul's and uncle of the gospeler Mark. Barnaby is used more often now in Britain. One of Charles Dickens's lesser-known novels is entitled *Barnaby Rudge*. The name is used from time to time among literary parents.

Barna, Barnaba, Barnabé, Barnabee, Barnabey, Barnabie, Barnabus, Barnaby, Barnebas, Barnebus, Barney, Barni, Barnie, Barny, Bernabé, Burnaby

Barnes OE. Place name: "Near the barns." The name's slightly rakish aura probably goes back to Jake Barnes, hero of Hemingway's novel *The Sun Also Rises*.

Barnett OE. Place name: "From the land that was burned." Or possibly a contraction of the English aristocratic title "Baronet." Duke, Earl, and Baron are used as first names from time to time.

Barnet, Barney, Barnie, Baronet, Baronett, Barrie, Barron, Barry

Barney Var. **Barnabas**. This contraction was used more often until a large purple dinosaur hijacked it. Now his fame is so widespread that it will be ages before Barney could possibly be a child again.

Barny

Barnum OE. Possibly a contraction of "Baron's home." In the U.S., inseparable from Phineas T. Barnum, founder of Barnum & Bailey's circus and one of America's great showmen.

Barnham

Baron OE. The title of nobility used as a first name. In England, a baron is the lowest rank of hereditary peerage that entitles the holder to serve in the House of Lords. Of course, none of these nobility names are actually used in countries where there is still an official aristocracy.

Baronicio, Barren, Barron

Barrett OG. "Bear-strength." Used as a first name mostly in the 19th century, possibly because of the fame of English poet Elizabeth Barrett Browning.

Baret, Barrat, Barratt, Barret, Barrey, Barrie, Barry

Barrington Eng. Place name now fairly common as a first name in Britain. Perhaps a bit of a mouthful for the more democratic U.S.

Barry Gael. "Sharp, pointed." Also a place name turned into a first name used by both sexes. Possibly influenced by the fame of Sir James Barrie, author of *Peter Pan*, since it cropped up as a first name during the height of his renown. Barry (with the "-y") was quite popular in the 1950s. Senator Barry M. Goldwater; singer Barry Manilow; baseball player Barry Bonds.

Barree, Barrey, Bari, Barrie, Baris

Bart Dim. Bartholomew. Football player Bart Starr.

Barrt

Bartholomew Heb. "Farmer's son." One of the twelve apostles. The name was common in the Middle Ages but was not revived in the 19th century, as so many medieval names were. Extremely unusual today: three syllables seems to be the maximum length parents are willing to shout across a playground.

Bart, Bartel, Barth, Barthélémy, Bartho, Barthold, Bartholoma, Bartholomäus, Bartholomé, Barthlomeo, Barthol, Barthold, Bartholomeus, Bartlet, Bartlett, Bartolomé, Bartolomeo, Bartolommeo, Bartomé, Bartow, Bartt, Bat, Bertel

Bartlet Dim. Bartholomew. Literary types for generations have relied on *Familiar Quotations* compiled by John Bartlett, first published in 1855.

Bartlett, Bartlitt

Barton OE. Place name: "Barley settlement," or possibly "Bart's town."

Bart, Barten, Barrton

Bartram OE. "Bright raven." See **Bertram**.

Barthram

Baruch Heb. "Blessed." Many languages have a form of this name: in English, Benedict; in Italian, Benedetto; in French, Benoît; in Spanish, Benito. American philanthropist Bernard Baruch.

Baruchi, Boruch

Basil Gk. "Royal, kingly." Brought to England by the Crusaders, having been common in the eastern Mediterranean. Unusual in the U.S., but more often used in Britain. Also the name of a common herb. As is obvious from the range of variants, the name has been widely used throughout Europe, though in the U.S. it seems a bit affected, probably because the only Basil most Americans know of is the British actor Basil Rathbone, who played Sherlock Holmes in fourteen films in the 1940s.

Basile, Basilic, Basilides, Basileios, Basilie, Basilio, Basilius, Bazeel, Bazeelius, Bazil, Bazyli, Vasilios, Vasilis, Vasilius, Vasilus, Vassilij, Vassily, Wassily

Bassett OE. "Little person." Descriptive surname transferred to first name. Also the name of a very short-legged hunting dog, the basset hound, possibly called that because its torso is so low (*bas* in French) to the ground.

Basset

Bastian Dim. Sebastian (Lat. "From Sebastia").

Bastien

Battista It. "Baptizer." For John the Baptist. This name survives best in countries with a strong Roman Catholic tradition. Often children are given the two-part name "Gian Battista" or "Jean-Baptiste."

Baptist, Baptiste, Bautista

Baxter OE. Occupational name: "Baker."

Bax, Baxley

Baxley ME. "Baker's meadow."

Baxlea, Baxlee, Baxlie, Baxly

Bay Geographic name (to describe an indentation of land in a coastline) or plant name. The term "bay" is used for several different kinds of trees, including the bay laurel, whose leaves are used as an herb and were also twined into wreaths by the Greeks, to crown victors. The name is equally unusual—and equally appropriate—for boys or girls, and is usually a family name.

Bayard OE. "Russet-haired." A famous French knight of the 15th century, the Seigneur de Bayard, was known as "the irreproachable and fearless." In French medieval romance, Bayard (or Baiardo, or Bajardo) is a magical horse given to the hero Rinaldo. The horse was a bright bay color. In the U.S., three generations of Bayards were senators from Delaware in the eighteenth and nineteenth centuries.

Baiardo, Bajardo, Bay

Bayless OF. "One who leases a bay." Perhaps refers to a fishing ancestor.

Bayless

Bayou Geography name: a slow-moving river or swamp. Used most generally in the southern United States.

Beacher OE. Place name: "Near the beech trees." Generally a last name. The 19th-century preacher Henry Ward Beecher.

Beach, Beachy, Beech, Beecher, Beechy

Beacon OE. "Signal light." Usually a bright light on a hilltop.

Beagan Ir. Gael. "Small one."

Beagen, Beagin, Beegan, Beegin

Beal OF. "Handsome." Var. **Beau**.

Beale, Beall, Bealle, Beals

Beaman OE. Occupational name: "Beekeeper." Athlete Bob Beamon.

Beamann, Beamen, Beeman, Beamon, Beemon

Beamer OE. "Trumpet player."

Beemer

Beasley OE. "Meadow of peas."

Beals, Beaslie, Beasly, Peaseley, Peasly

Beattie (masc. **Beatrice**) Ir. Gael. from Lat. "Bringer of gladness."

Beatie, Beatty, Beaty

Beau Fr. "Handsome." Dim. **Beauregard**. Used somewhat in the U.S. in the last thirty years. Nowadays the name is likely to be heard as the less formal "Bo." English dandy Beau Brummel; actor Beau Bridges; sports star Bo Jackson.

Beal, Beale, Bo, Boe

Beauchamp OF. Place name: "The beautiful field." Pronounced by the English as Beecham.

Beecham

Beaufort OF. Place name: "The beautiful fort."

Beaumont OF. Place name: "The beautiful mountain." More common in the 19th century than it is today. English playwright Francis Beaumont.

Beauregard Fr. "Beautiful gaze." In Patrick Dennis's novel *Auntie Mame*, Mame marries Beauregard Jackson Burnside, a caricature of Southern courtesy. Dennis took his name from the names of three prominent Confederate generals, Pierre Beauregard (who fired on Fort Sumter), Thomas Jackson (known as "Stonewall"), and Ambrose Burnside (better known for his whiskers, now called "sideburns"). Could also be taken to mean, in modern parlance, "easy on the eye." A lot for a boy to live up to.

Beau, Bo

Becher Heb. "Young man, firstborn."

Beck OE. Place name: "Small stream." The term is still in use in rural Scotland.

Becker

Bede OE. "Prayer." Saint Bede was an influential 7th-century English church historian. He is also supposed to be the first documented writer of English (as opposed to Latin) prose, though his English works have been lost.

Beda

Bedell OF. "Messenger." A somewhat unusual last name.

Bedall

Beebe OE. "Bee farmer."

Belden OE/OF. Place name: "Pretty valley."

Beldene, Beldon, Bellden, Belldene, Belldon

Belindo (masc. **Belinda**.) Probably intended to mean something like "Handsome," though Belinda may go back to an Old German word meaning "Dragon."

Bellindo

Belisario Sp. from Gk. "Swordsman."

Belisarios, Belisarius

Bell Dim. **Bellamy**. May also be an occupational name, for a bell ringer.

Bellamy OF. "Handsome friend." Many Americans know this as a last name from the popular TV series *Upstairs, Downstairs*.

Belamy, Bell, Bellamey, Bellamie, Bellemy

Bellarmine It. "Beautifully armed."

Belmont OF. "Beautiful mountain." A frequently found place name in America.

Bellmont

Belton ME. Place name: "Beautiful town." Or possibly "town of the bells."
Bellton

Beltran Sp. Var. **Bertram** (OG. "Bright raven") or **Bertrand** (OG. "Bright shield").
Bertran

Belvedere It. "Beautiful to see." This is the name of a gallery in the Vatican that contains some of the greatest classical Greek statues, among them the *Apollo Belvedere*, which took its name from the gallery.
Bellveder, Bellvedere, Bellvidere, Belveder, Belvider, Belvidere

Bemus Gk. "Foundation."
Beamus, Bemis

Ben Heb. "Son." Also dim. **Benedict, Benjamin, Benson**, etc. Now given as an independent name. Many Hebrew names combine Ben with another name, so that Ben-Baruch, for example, means "Son of the blessed." Playwright Ben Jonson; actors Ben Gazzara, Ben Stiller, Ben Vereen; football player Ben Coates.
Benn, Benny

Benedict Lat. "Blessed." Saint Benedict, founder of a monastic order, brought the name to prominence. Bennett is the more common form, especially in the U.S., where every schoolchild learns the tale of Revolutionary War traitor Benedict Arnold. Italian dictator Benito Mussolini.
Ben, Bendick, Bendict, Benedetto, Benedick, Benedicto, Benedictos, Benedictus, Benedikt, Benedikte, Bengt, Benito, Bennedict, Bennedikt, Bennet, Bennett, Bennie, Bennito, Bennt, Benoît, Bent, Venedictos

Benigno Lat. "Kind, well-born." From the root that gives us "benign."

Benjamin Heb. "Son of the right hand." In the Old Testament, the younger son of Jacob and Rachel. Brought into use by the Puritan fondness for Old Testament names, and persistent until the end of the 19th century. As the many variants show, it has been widely used all over Europe. After several decades of disuse, came back to great popularity by the 1970s, and is now quite standard. Diplomat and inventor Benjamin Franklin; U.S. President Benjamin Harrison; jazz musician Benny Goodman; pediatrician and oracle Benjamin Spock; British Prime Minister Benjamin Disraeli.

Ben, Benejamen, Beniamino, Benjaman, Benjamen, Benjamino, Benjamon, Benjee, Benjey, Benji, Benjie, Benjiman, Benjimen, Benjy, Benn, Bennie, Benno, Benny, Benyamin, Benyamino, Binyamin, Binyamino, Venyamin, Yamin, Yamino, Yemin

Bennett Fr. Var. **Benedict**. Choreographer Michael Bennett; humorist Bennett Cerf; author William Bennett; aviation pioneer Floyd Bennett.

Benet, Benett, Bennet, Benoit

Benoni Heb. "Son of my sorrow." In the Old Testament, Rachel, mother of Benjamin, knew she was dying after his birth and called him Benoni, but Jacob, his father, changed the name to Benjamin.

Benson OE. "Son of Ben." Originally a surname, transferred to a first name in the 19th century.

Bensen, Benssen, Bensson

Bentley OE. "Meadow with coarse grass." Place name become surname become first name, more common for boys but used occasionally for girls. Irresistibly linked in most minds with the luxurious English car.

Ben, Bentlea, Bentlee, Bentley, Bentlie, Bently, Lee

Benton OE. Place name. As in Bentley, refers to a kind of "bent" or coarse grass. Artist Thomas Hart Benton; film director Robert Benton.

Benvenuto It. "Welcome." In Italy, often refers to the joy at the birth of a long-awaited child. Goldsmith Benvenuto Cellini.

Bienvenido

Beresford OE. Place name: "Ford where barley grows." Used as a first name principally at the turn of the century. Film director Bruce Beresford.

Berg Ger. "Mountain." Often found as a suffix in German surnames like Kleinberg ("Small mountain"), Goldberg ("Gold mountain"), or Hochberg ("High mountain").

Berger, Bergh, Burg, Burgh

Bergen Scand. "Lives on the hill." Bergen is a major port city in Norway.

Bergin, Birgin

Berger Fr. Occupational name: "Shepherd."

  Bergeron

Berilo Sp. from Gk. "Pale green gemstone." Masculine version of **Beryl**. The beryl was considered a token of good luck.
Berillo

Berkeley OE. Place name: "Where birches grow." In the U.S., probably most famous as the San Francisco suburb that is home to a branch of the University of California.
Bar, Barcley, Barklay, Barkley, Barklie, Barrclay, Berk, Berkie, Berklee, Berkley, Berky, Birkeley, Birkley

Berlin Ger. "Borderline." The capital city of the united Germany that used to have a border in its very heart.
Berlyn

Bern OG. "Bear." Also possible nickname for Bernard.
Berne, Bernie, Berny, Bjorn

Bernal OG. "Strength of a bear." Occasionally used in English-speaking countries, but more common on the Continent.
Bernald, Bernhald, Bernhold, Bernold

Bernard OG. "Bear/courageous." Brought to England with the Norman Conquest. Two famous medieval saints bore the name; one was a founder of a monastic order. The other, for whom the shaggy brown and white dogs are named, is patron saint of mountain climbers. A fairly common name until the 18th century and revived a bit around 1920, but now unusual. Playwright George Bernard Shaw; statesman Bernard M. Baruch; film director Bernardo Bertolucci.
Barnard, Barnardo, Barney, Barnhard, Barnhardo, Barnie, Barny, Bear, Bearnard, Bern, Bernardo, Bernarr, Bernd, Berndt, Bernhard, Bernhardo, Bernie, Bernis, Bernt, Burnard

Berry Botanical name used for both boys and girls, though the boy's name is more likely a derivative of Bernard or a transferred surname. Pop music impresario Berry Gordy.

Bert OE. "Shining brightly." Dim. **Albert, Egbert, Robert**, etc. Used more often as a nickname. Its popularity among show-business types of a certain age (Miss America emcee Bert Parks; actors Burt Lancaster and Burt Reynolds) suggests a jaunty, masculine connotation.
Bertie, Berty, Burt, Burty, Butch

Berthold OG. "Bright strength." Unusual in English-speaking countries, but not unheard of. Playwright Bertolt Brecht.

Bert, Bertell, Bertil, Berthoud, Bertol, Bertoll, Bertold, Bertolde, Berton

Berton OE. Place name: "Bright settlement."

Bert, Bertie, Burt, Burton

Bertram OG. "Bright raven." Norman name revived in the Victorian era. Rare since the 1930s. Architect Bertram Goodhue.

Bart, Bartram, Beltran, Beltrano, Berton, Bertran, Bertrand, Bertrando, Bertranno

Bertrand OG. "Bright shield." Also possibly a variation on **Bertram**. Philosopher Bertrand Russell.

Berwyn OE. "Bear friend" or "Bright friend."

Berwin, Berwynn, Berwynne

Bethel Heb. "House of God." Another Biblical place name: the spot where Abraham built an altar. Unusual as a first name.

Betuel

Bevan Welsh. "Son of Evan." Mostly 20th-century use, though there may be some spillover from the popularity of soundalike Devon. British politician Aneurin Bevan.

Beavan, Beaven, Bev, Beven, Bevin, Bevon, Bevvan, Bevvin, Bevvon, Bivian

Beverly OE. "Of the beaver-stream." Originally an English place name transferred to a surname, then a first name for both sexes. Probably still most famous as a place name, referring to Beverly Hills. The English spelling is usually Beverley. In the U.S., this is more likely to be considered a girl's name.

Beverlea, Beverleigh, Beverley, Beverlie

Bevis OF. Place name: Beauvais is a town in France famous for the manufacture of tapestries. Other possible derivations are Welsh, "Son of Evan," and something related to the French word for "bull," *beuve*. This anglicized version is very unusual.

Beauvais, Beavess, Beavis, Beviss

Biagio It. "Stutterer." Related to Blaise.

Biaggio

Bickford OE. Place name: "Ax-man's ford."

Bienvenido Sp. "Welcome."
Benvenuto

Biff American slang: "To hit." The root of this expression is mysterious, and it is very unlikely to be used today.

Bill Dim. **William**. Used occasionally as an independent name. Before mid–19th century, Will was the more common nickname. Nowadays the many boys named William (one of the top twenty names in the U.S.) are much more likely to have their names shortened to a form with a "W." Actors Bill Cosby, Bill Bixby; designer Bill Blass; singer Billy Joel; comedian/actor Billy Crystal.
Billie, Billy, Byll

Bing OG. Place name: "The hollow shaped like a pot." Another source claims that modern use of the name is inspired by singer Bing Crosby, who was given the nickname after a comic-strip character. His given name was actually Harry.

Bingo Origin unknown. The name of a very popular game. Usually used as a nickname.

Birch OE. Place name: "Where birch trees grow." Not uncommon in the 19th century. Senator Birch Bayh.
Birk, Burch

Birchall OE. Place name: "Birch hall."
Birchell, Burchall, Burchell

Birkett ME. Place name: "Birch coastland."
Birket, Birkit, Birkitt, Burket, Burkett, Burkitt

Birkey ME. Place name: "Island of birch trees."
Birkee, Birkie, Birky

Birley OE. Place name: "Meadow with the cow byre." Not related to the homonym Burleigh.
Birlie, Birly

Birney OE. Place name: "Island with the brook."
Birnie, Birny, Burney, Burnie

Birtle OE. Place name: "Hill of birds."
Bertle

Bishop OE. "Bishop." Probably originally meant "One serving the bishop," or "Bishop's man."
Bishopp

Bjorn Scand. Var. **Bernard**. The fame of tennis player

Bjorn Borg is probably responsible for the use of this name in English-speaking countries.

Bjarn, Bjarne, Bjorne

Black OE. "Dark-skinned."

Blackburn OE. Place name: "Black brook." Used as a first name mostly in the 19th century. In Scotland, "burn" is still the term for a little brook.

Blackburne, Blagburn

Blackstone OE. Place name: "Black stone."

Blackwell OE. Place name: "Black well."

Blagden OE. Place name: "Dark valley."

Blaine Ir. Gael. "Slender." Surname used since the 1930s as a first name, mostly for boys but occasionally for girls.

Blane, Blayne

Blair Scot. Gael. Place name: "Plain" or "Flat area." Surname now used as first name, again more common for boys. Like many similarly transferred names, Blair was used for girls in greater numbers starting in the early 1980s. British politician Tony Blair.

Blaire, Blayr, Blayre

Blaise Lat./Fr. "One who stutters." Used for both sexes, though more common for men. The alternate spelling of Blaze probably refers to fire instead. French philosopher Blaise Pascal.

Biagio, Blaize, Blas, Blase, Blasio, Blasios, Blasius, Blayse, Blayze, Blaze

Blake OE. Paradoxically, could mean either "Pale-skinned" or "Dark." Surname used as a first name for either sex, most often in the U.S. Director Blake Edwards; *Dynasty* character Blake Carrington.

Blakely OE. Place name: "Dark meadow" or "Pale meadow." See **Blake**.

Blakelee, Blakeleigh, Blakeley, Blakelie

Blakeney OE. Place name: "Dark island" or "White island."

Blakenie, Blakeny

Blanco Sp. "Fair, white."

Bianco

Blanford OE. Place name: "Gray man's ford."

Blandford

Blanton Lat/Fr. "Mild, bland."

Blandon

Blaze Lat. "One who stutters." Anglicized form of Blaise, though for a child of the 21st century the name spelled this way is more likely to invoke flames.
Biaggio, Biagio, Blaise, Blaize, Blase, Blasien, Blasius, Blayse, Blayze

Bligh OE. "Bliss." This name is related to Bliss and Blythe, but because of the fame of English sea captain William Bligh, whose crew on HMS *Bounty* mutinied in 1789, it has taken on connotations of severity, even tyranny. Apparently Bligh did not learn much from the first mutiny, for men under his command staged rebellions twice more, in 1794 and in 1808.
Bly

Bliss OE. "Intense happiness."

Blondell OE. "Little fair-haired one."
Blondel

Blythe OE. "Happy, carefree." Made famous by the opening lines of Shelley's poem "To a Skylark" ("Hail to thee, blithe spirit!") and Noel Coward's play *Blithe Spirit*.
Bligh, Blithe

Bo Dim. **Robert, Beauregard**. Rare as a given name, more likely to be a nickname. Swaggering macho connotations (possibly because of the rhyme with "Yo!"?) seem to limit use for babies. Football coach Bo Schembechler; sports star Bo Jackson.
Beau, Boe

Boaz Heb. "Swiftness." Used for several Old Testament characters (including the second husband of Ruth), and revived with the Puritan passion for Old Testament names. Now very rare. Socialite Boaz Mazor.
Boas, Boase

Bob Dim. **Robert**. OE. "Bright fame." Used independently from time to time. The usual habit for naming, however, is to give the full form of a name, even if the parents never intend to use anything but the nickname. And while Bobby was as common as Susie and Linda for children of the 1950s and '60s, that's all the more reason for today's little Roberts to be called Robbie or Rob instead of the pedestrian Bob. Comedian Bob Hope; singer Bob Dylan; chess master Bobby Fischer; activist minister Bob Castle.

Bobbee, Bobbey, Bobbie, Bobby

Boden OF. "One who brings news."

Bodin, Bowden, Bowdoin

Bogart OF. "Bow strength." In current use probably always refers to actor Humphrey Bogart.

Bogey, Bogie, Bogy

Bolívar Sp. from Polish. "Mighty, warlike." Use most likely reflects the fame of revolutionary Simón Bolívar, who in the early 19th century helped liberate much of northern South America from Spanish rule.

Bolevar, Bollivar

Bolton English surname of uncertain meaning, though the "-ton" particle probably refers to a town. Singer Michael Bolton.

Bollton, Bolten, Boltin

Bonamy Fr. "Good friend."

Bonami

Bonar OF. "Gentle, mannerly." From the French *debonnaire*. The famous line from the Sermon on the Mount, "Blessed are the meek," translates into French as *"Heureux sont les debonnaires."* In English, "debonair" now means something closer to "nonchalant" or "urbane," as personified by Fred Astaire. British politician Bonar Law.

Bonnar, Bonner

Bonaventure Lat. "Blessed undertaking." The Italian Saint Bonaventure was a 13th-century cardinal who, in spite of his great learning, was modest and practical. He was known as "The Seraphic Teacher."

Bonaventura, Buenaventura

Bond OE. Occupational name: "Man of the soil." Or as many baby boomers will remember, "Bond. James Bond."

Boniface Lat. "Fortunate, of good fate." Also commonly, though erroneously, taken to mean "Doing good." Name of a number of early popes.

Boni, Bonifacio, Bonifacius

Booker Uncertain origin; may allude to "the Book," i.e., the Bible. Another possibility is an Anglo-Saxon derivation from the word for "Beech tree." American reformer Booker T. Washington.

Boone OF. "Good." The French adjective is *bon* or *bonne*.

Backwoods connotations courtesy of 19th-century explorer Daniel Boone.

Booth OG. Place name: "Dwelling place." Surname whose 19th-century use as a first name was probably a tribute to Salvation Army founder William Booth. In the U.S., made famous also by Lincoln's assassin John Wilkes Booth, though his precedent would hardly have promoted use. Author Booth Tarkington.
Boot, Boote, Boothe, Both

Borden OE. Place name: "Vale of the boar."
Bordin

Boris Slavic. "Warrior." Russian playwright Aleksandr Pushkin and composer Modest Mussorgsky both based works on the career of the bloodthirsty 16th-century czar Boris Godunov, who became cartoon character "Boris Badenov" in *The Rocky and Bullwinkle Show*. Consequent faint comic connotations linger. Horror-movie actor Boris Karloff; author Boris Pasternak; tennis star Boris Becker.
Boriss, Borris, Borys

Bosley ME. Place name: "Meadow near the woods." The French root in this and the following names is *bois*, or "woods."
Boslea, Boslee, Bosleigh, Bosly

Boston ME. Place name. The English town for which the capital of Massachusetts is named was originally called "Saint Botolph's town," according to some. Others suggest the simpler derivation "Town by the woods." Usage in the U.S. is very likely to refer to the historic city on the Atlantic that is home to so many institutions of higher learning.

Boswell ME. Place name: "Well near the woods." James Boswell was an 18th-century man of letters and the biographer of his contemporary, the lexicographer Samuel Johnson.

Bosworth ME. Place name: "Fenced farm near the woods."

Botolph OE. "Messenger wolf." An obscure 7th-century English saint who was very popular in the Middle Ages. He founded a monastery in England, which is thought to

have been in the Lincolnshire town of Boston (Botolph's town).
Botolf, Botolff, Botulf, Botulph

Bourbon Place name: county in Kentucky where the liquor is made. Originally the last name of the royal family of France; still the name of the royal family of Spain. Bourbon Street in New Orleans is still a famous tourist attraction for jazz fans.
Borbon

Bourne OE. Place name: "The stream." A little stream is still called a *burn* in Scotland. Or possibly OF. "Boundary, milestone." Scottish poet Robert Burns.
Born, Borne, Bourn, Burn, Burne, Byrn

Bouvier Lat./Fr. "Ox." Made famous, of course, by Jacqueline Bouvier Kennedy, so the associations may be feminine rather than masculine.

Bowen Welsh. "Son of the young one."
Bowin

Bowie Scot. Gael. "Blond." Col. James Bowie, scout and originator of the knife that bears his name. Former baseball commissioner Bowie Kuhn.
Bow, Bowen

Boyce OF. Place name: "Woods."
Boice, Boise

Boyd Scot. Gael. "Blond." Possibly also a place name, for the Scottish Isle of Bute. Actor Boyd Gaines.
Boid

Boyne Ir. Gael. "White cow." Also an historic place name in Ireland: at the 1690 Battle of the Boyne, the Protestant King William III defeated the Catholic King James II, who fled to France, thus permitting the firm establishment of the Protestant monarchy.
Boine, Boyn

Boynton Eng./Gael. "Town near the Boyne."

Bracken Plant name: a large, coarse fern. Lovers of English literature are familiar with the word, if not with the plant itself.

Brad OE. "Broad." Also diminutive for Bradley and other "Brad-" names. Quite scarce as a given name. Actor Brad Pitt.
Bradd

Bradburn OE. Place name: "Wide stream."

Braden OE. Place name: "Wide valley."
  Bradan, Bradin, Bradon, Braiden, Braidin, Brayden, Braydon

Bradford OE. Place name: "Wide river-crossing." Name of the first governor of the Plymouth colony, William Bradford, and a fairly common place name both in England and in the U.S.
  Braddford, Bradfurd

Bradley OE. Place name: "Wide meadow." Used since the mid–19th century, more in the U.S. than in other English-speaking countries. It's hard to know why Bradley alone among this group of names became firmly entrenched as a first name: possibly the familiarity of the "-ley" ending contributed to this. The fame of actor Brad Pitt may inspire parents to use Bradley even more often, though it is quite steadily used already. Senator Bill Bradley.
  Brad, Bradd, Bradlea, Bradleigh, Bradlie, Bradly, Bradney, Lee

Bradshaw OE. Place name: "Broad forest."

Brady OE. Place name: "Wide island." This name is in the air again, possibly as a result of the recent "Brady Bunch" movies. It has all the qualifications for a trendy name for either sex: the right combination of novelty and familiarity with an Anglo-Saxon aura. Baseball player Brady Anderson.
  Bradey, Bradie, Braedy, Braidie, Braidy, Braydie

Brainard OE. "Courageous raven."
  Brainerd, Braynard

Bram Ir. Gael. "Raven." It is curious that so many names refer to the raven, a bird that historically has stood for death and destruction. Bram, of course, can also be a shortened version of Abraham. *Dracula* author Bram Stoker.
  Bramm, Bran, Brann

Bramwell OE. Place name: "Well where the broom grows" or "Raven well." Author Bramwell Bronte.
  Brammell, Bramwel, Bramwyll, Branwell, Branwill, Branwyll

Branch Lat. "Paw, extension." This word probably became a place name by referring to a branch in a river or a path. Branch Rickey was the general manager of Brooklyn Dodgers, who hired Jackie Robinson.

Brand OE. "Firebrand." Also, diminutive of **Brandon**. In this country the name may have faint manly connotations of life on the rugged range.

Brander, Brandt, Brant, Brantley, Brantlie

— **Brandon** OE. Place name: "Broom-covered hill." Also a variant of Brendan, which does not quite share its popularity: Brandon was the tenth most popular boy's name in New York City in 1994, and ranked number four in the state of Florida in 1995. Families new to the U.S. sometimes look for a jump in assimilation by choosing an Anglo-Saxon name like this one. TV executive Brandon Tartikoff.

Brand, Branden, Brandin, Brandyn, Brannon, Branton

Branley OE. Place name: "Raven meadow."

Branlea, Branlee, Branlie, Branly

Brannon Ir. Gael. Elaboration of the particle ("bran" or "bram") that means "Raven." Though unusual, this name is close enough in sound to the popular Brendan and Brandon so that it may be taken up by parents looking for an uncommon yet pronounceable Gaelic name.

Brannan, Brahnen, Brannin

Brant OE. "Proud." Brant County and Brantford in southern Ontario are named for Joseph Brant, the Mohawk chieftain who led the Iroquois tribes into Canada after the American Revolution. Media executive Peter Brant.

Brandt, Brannt, Brantt

Branton Gael./Eng. "Raven settlement." May also be a variant of **Brandon**.

Brannton, Branten, Brantin

Braulio Sp. from Ger. "Glowing." Saint Braulio was a bishop in 7th-century Spain. Jockey Braulio Baeza.

Bravilio, Bravlio

Bravo It. "Excellent, courageous." This is the exclamation that accompanies a brilliant performance, traditionally in an opera house. It is also the word that means "B" in the radio operators' alphabet: Alpha, Bravo, Charlie....A jaunty name for the 21st century.

Brahvo, Bravvo

Brawley OE. Place name: "Meadow at the slope of the hill."

Brauleigh, Braulie, Brauly, Brawlea, Brawleigh, Brawlie, Brawly

Braxton OE. "Brock's settlement." Brock is an informal word for badger.

Bray ME. "Cry out." For instance, donkeys bray. It's still a good name.

Brae

Brazier ME. Occupational name: "works with brass."

Braiser, Braser, Brasier, Braizer, Brazer

Brazil Place name: largest country in South America. The name may come from the red dye-woods found in the country.

Brasil

Breck OE. Place name: "Gap," as in a gap in a stone wall. Breck also refers to a stretch of sandy, rolling land. A romantic character in Robert Louis Stevenson's *Kidnapped* is named Alan Breck, but the average American parent may remember instead a brand of shampoo.

Breckinridge OE. Place name: "Ridge with bracken."

Brackenridge

Breed Unclear origin. May be an occupational name having to do with the breeding of animals, or may refer to Saint Brigid, also known as Bride, the Irish abbess.

Breedlove

Brendan Ir. Gael. "Smelly hair." Very few names actually mean anything as negative as this. The Irish Saint Brendan, known as "The Voyager," is supposed to have sailed as far as the Canary Islands. This name has usually been popular among families of Irish descent. Playwright Brendan Behan.

Brendano, Brendin, Brendon, Brendyn, Brennan, Brennen, Brennon

Brennan Ir. Gael. "Teardrop." Not as common as Brendan or Brandon, but still occurs from time to time.

Brenan, Brennen, Brennin, Brennon, Brenyn

Brent OE. Place name: "Mount, hilltop." Use as a first name dates back only sixty years or so, and has been particularly strong in Canada. Sportscaster Brent Musburger.

Brennt, Brentan, Brenten, Brentin, Brenton, Brentt, Brentyn

Brenton Possibly OE. Place name: "Brent's town." It is also possible that families arrive at this name by combining the popular Brandon with Brent, to end up with something a little different.

Brenten, Brentin, Brentton, Brenttyn

Brett Celt. "Man from Britain." Publicized by American writer Bret Harte. Quite popular in Australia and steadily used in the U.S. Baseball players Brett Butler, Brett Saberhagen.

Bret, Brette, Bretton, Brit, Briton, Britt, Britte

Bretton Fr. "From Brittany." The northwest corner of France is called Brittany, and, like Cornwall across the English Channel, was home to a heavily Celtic civilization. French painter Jules Breton.

Breton

Brevard Lat. "Short, brief."

Brewster OE. Occupational name: "Brewer." Transferred to a surname, thence to a first name.

Brewer, Bruce

Brian Ir. Gael. Ancient name of obscure meaning, though many sources translate it as "strength." Ireland's most famous King, Brian Boru, liberated the country from the Danes in 1014, and the name has been much favored in Ireland. A spell of popularity lasted from the 1920s to the 1970s, and though Brian is no longer trendy, it is still one of the top thirty names for boys in the U.S. Actor Brian Dennehy; film director Brian De Palma.

Briano, Briant, Brien, Brion, Bryan, Bryant, Bryen, Bryent, Bryon

Brice Var. **Bryce.** The "i" spelling was more common in the 19th century.

Bricio, Brizio

Brickell OG. "Little bridge."

Brickel

Bridgely OE. Place name: "Bridge meadow."

Bridgley

Bridger OE. "Lives near the bridge." James Bridger was one of the 19th-century frontiersmen who explored the West. He was probably the first European-American to

see the Great Salt Lake, and he built Fort Bridger, on the Oregon Trail.
Bridge

Briggs OE. "Bridges." Brigg was a term, probably influenced by German, that lingered in Scotland.

Brigham OE. Place name: "Little village near the bridge." Most uses of the name probably honor Mormon leader Brigham Young.
Brigg, Briggham, Briggs

Brinley OE. Place name: "Burnt meadow." Used mostly in England and Wales.
Brindley, Brindly, Brinlee, Brinleigh, Brinly, Brinsley, Brynly

Bristol Place name: an ancient and important city in England, with one of the most important ports on the west coast. Many cities in the U.S. were named after it.
Bristow

Britannicus Roman prince, son of Claudius, who was named for his father's conquests in Britain around 50 A.D. He should have become emperor of Rome but was pushed aside in favor of his younger half-brother Nero, and eventually poisoned. If parents use this name, it may be for its resemblance to the fashionable Brittany.

Britton OE. "From Britain."
Bretton, Briton

Brock OE. "Badger." Unusual transferred surname with mostly American use. It is used about as often as Noah, Stuart, and Bruce, all of which seem much more familiar.
Broc, Brocke, Brok

Brockholst OE./ONorse: "Badger's den." A family name in Old New York.

Brockley OE. Place name: "Meadow of the badger." May remind hearers of the unpopular leafy green vegetable.
Brocklea, Brocklee, Brocklie, Brockly

Brockton OE. Place name: "Badger settlement."
Brockten, Brocktin, Brocton

Broderick ONorse. "Brother." Traveled from Ireland to Scotland as a surname. Actor Broderick Crawford.
Brod, Broddy, Broder, Broderic, Brodric, Brodrick, Ric, Rick, Rickey, Rickie, Ricky

Brody Ir. Gael. "Ditch." This name has a lot of potential.

It is short, easy to say, sounds "boyish," and is extremely unusual without being in any way peculiar.

Brodee, Brodey, Brodie, Broedy

Brogan Ir. Gael. "Sturdy shoe." The root for our word "brogue," which has also come to mean the Gaelic accent.

Broggan

Bromley OE. Place name: "Meadow where broom grows." Broom is a shrub related to heather.

Bromlea, Bromlee, Bromleigh, Broomlie

Bromwell OE. Place name: "Well where broom grows."

Bromwyl

Bronco Mexican Sp. "Rough, unbroken horse." As anyone who has ever seen a cowboy movie knows, a bronco is the horse that bucks off his rider.

Bronko

Bronson OE. "Brown one's son." Actors Charles Bronson and Bronson Pinchot.

Bron, Bronnson, Bronsen, Bronsin, Bronsonn, Bronsson

Brook OE. Place name: "Near the stream or brook." Wide fame of actress Brooke Shields will probably go far to terminate use of this name for boys. Director Brooks Atkinson.

Brooke, Brookes, Brookie, Brooks

Broughton OE. Place name: "Settlement near the fortress."

Brown ME. "Russet-complected." This is such a firmly entrenched last name that it would be hard to use it as a first name. Football player Dave Brown.

Bruce OF. "From the brushwood thicket." Norman place name brought to fame by the Scottish king Robert Bruce, who won Scotland's independence from England in 1327. Naturally popular as a first name in Scotland, and among Americans who cherish Scottish ancestry. Singer Bruce Springsteen; actor Bruce Willis.

Brucey, Brucie

Bruno OG. "Brown-skinned." Saint Bruno was the 11th-century founder of the Carthusian order of monks. Orchestral conductor Bruno Walter; actor Bruno Kirby.

Bruin, Bruino

Brunswick OG. "Bruno's village." The German word is

"Braunschweig." It was an independent state in pre-unification Germany.

Brutus Lat. "Meaningless, unintelligent." Shakespeare scholars know Brutus as the traitor who schemed to assassinate Julius Caesar.
Bruto

Bryan Var. **Brian**. Actor Bryan Brown; singer Bryan Ferry.
Bryen

Bryant Var. **Brian**. TV commentator Bryant Gumbel.

Bryce Unclear origin; may refer to followers of a 5th-century French bishop, Saint Brice. Bryce Canyon, in Utah, is one of the great natural splendors of the West.
Brice

Bryson OE. "Son of Brice."
Brysen, Brysin

Bubba Ger. "Boy." More commonly a nickname, usually for someone rather large.

Buck OE. "Buck deer." "Buck" was also a 19th-century term for a dandy, or a young man who cut a fine figure. It may have been used first as a nickname. Probably not related to the slang word for "dollar." Actor Buck Henry; baseball player Bucky Dent.
Buckey, Buckie, Bucky

Buckley OE. Place name: "Meadow of the deer." Author William F. Buckley.

Buckminster OE. Place name: "Monastery where deer dwell." Made famous by architect Buckminster Fuller.

Bud Modern slang, short for "buddy." Some sources think this is a child's pronunciation of "brother." Rarely given as a first name, but fairly common as a nickname in the middle years of the 20th century. Actor Buddy Ebsen; comedians Bud Abbott, Buddy Hackett.
Budd, Buddey, Buddie, Buddy

Buell OG. Place name: "Hill."
Buel, Bueller, Buhl, Buhler

Bunyan English name of unclear meaning, though it may be related to the French *bon*, or "Good." In America, it bears connotations of the mythic lumberjack Paul Bunyan and his blue ox Babe.

Burchard OE. "Castle strong."
Bucardo, Burckhardt, Burgard, Burgaud, Burkhart

Burford OE. Place name: "Ford near the castle."
  Bufford, Buford
Burbank OE. Place name: "Riverbank where burrs grow."
  Luther Burbank was a famous turn-of-the-century plant
  breeder who introduced many useful strains of fruits and
  vegetables in the U.S.
Burdett ME. "Bird."
  Burdette
Burgess OE. "Citizen." Related to the French word bour-
  geois, which has come to mean something like "middle
  class." Generally a transferred last name. Actor Burgess
  Meredith; poet Gelett Burgess.
  Burges, Burgiss, Burr
Burke OF. "From the fortified settlement."
  Berk, Berke, Birk, Bourke, Burk
Burl OE. "Knotty wood." Some highly prized 18th-century
  furniture is made with a "burled" walnut veneer. Singer
  Burl Ives.
  Burle
Burleigh OE. Place name: "Meadow with knotty-trunk
  trees."
  Burley, Burlie, Byrleigh, Byrley
Burnaby ONorse. "Fighter's estate."
Burne OE. Place name: "The brook." Related to Bourne.
  **Beirne, Bourn, Bourne, Burn, Burnis, Byrn, Byrne,
  Byrnes**
Burnell OF. "Small brown one." Football player Mark
  Brunell.
  Brunel, Brunell, Burnel
Burnet OE. Transferred surname of unclear origin, mostly
  used in the 19th century. It may have something to do
  with a brook ("burn"), or with brown ("brunet") col-
  oring.
  Bernet, Bernett, Burnett
Burney OE. Place name: "Island of the brook."
  Beirney, Beirnie, Burnie
Burr OE. "Bristle." In the U.S., made famous by Jeffer-
  son's Vice President Aaron Burr, who is probably best
  known for having killed his political enemy Alexander
  Hamilton in a duel in 1801. Actor Raymond Burr.
Burroughs OE. Place name: "In the borough or burrow."

The holes in the ground that animals live in and the administrative division (similar to county) come from the same word, *burgh*, which means dwelling place or town. Burgess is another derivative. Author William Burroughs.
Burrows

Burt Var. **Bert**, dim. **Albert, Bertram**, etc.

Burton OE. Place name: "Fortified enclosure." Like many of the older place names, used as a first name in the 19th century. The exploits of African explorer and writer Sir Richard Burton may have influenced its use. In the 20th century, of course, the Richard Burton most people know is the one who was married to Elizabeth Taylor. Actor Burt Lancaster.
Bert, Burt, Burtt

Busby Scot./ONorse. Place name: "Village in the thicket." A busby is also a tall military hat made of fur, such as those worn by the British soldiers who guard Buckingham Palace. Choreographer Busby Berkeley.
Busbee, Busbey, Busbie, Bussby

Buster Nickname of unknown origin, made famous by silent film star Buster Keaton. A hugely popular comic strip character of the 1930s was called Buster Brown. His pageboy haircut, sailor hat, and round collar were all dubbed "Buster Brown" after him. The name continued into the early 1960s as a brand of shoe with an advertising jingle that ended, ". . . with the boy and the dog and the foot inside." Swimmer/actor Buster Crabbe.

Butcher OE. Occupational name: "Butcher." Nickname Butch is sometimes used to address a stranger in a slightly derogatory way: "Listen, Butch . . ." The popular movie "Butch Cassidy and the Sundance Kid" did little to popularize the name.
Butch

Butler OE. Occupational name: "Bottle bearer." Originally the household servant in charge of wines and liquors. Nicholas Murray Butler was an influential turn-of-the-century president of Columbia University.
Buttler

Byford OE. Place name: "By the ford."

Byram OE. Place name. Var. **Byron**.

Byrd OE. "Birdlike."
   Bird, Byrdie
Byron OE. Place name: "Barn for cows." The term "byre" is still used. Use as a first name probably in tribute to the poet Lord Byron, since it dates from the 1850s. Though a first-rate poet, he was also famous for his wildness and debauchery: he was characterized by one acquaintance as "mad, bad, and dangerous to know."
   Beyren, Beyron, Biren, Biron, Buiron, Byram, Byran, Byren, Byrom

---

NAMING TRIVIA

Puritan William Brewster sailed for America on the *Mayflower* in 1620. With him were his two sons, who had the classic Puritan names of Love and Wrestling.

Wall Street Journal editor Vermont Royster was born in 1914, and named for his grandfather. Grandfather Royster had this unusual name because his father named all of his children for states in the Union.

American painter Charles Willson Peale had eleven children, all named after famous painters. Three of them—Raphaelle, Titian, and Rembrandt—actually lived out their father's obvious desires and became painters themselves.

The first child born in an English colony in North America was Virginia Dare. Born in 1587 in Roanoke, Virginia, she was named after Elizabeth I, England's Virgin Queen.

The nun known to the world as Mother Teresa was born in Albania and christened Agnes Gonsha Bojaxhiu.

The Marx Brothers changed their names as they developed their comic act. Harpo was originally known as Arthur, Chico as Leonard, and Groucho as Julius Henry. It's enough to make you wonder if the seven dwarves didn't have different names before they met up with Walt Disney.

Distinguished author Toni Morrison's original name was Chloe Anthony Wofford.

Boxing champion George Foreman has four sons, all of whom are named George.

Zane has recently become mildly trendy among urban intellectual types, as a boy's name redolent of the Wild West. Zane Grey was the author of the immensely popular *Riders of the Purple Sage* and dozens of other Western novels. He himself, though, was born in Zanesville, Ohio, with the jokey name of Pearl Grey. It's no wonder he turned tough guy after that.

Samuel Clemens, better known to posterity as Mark Twain, had a brother named Orion. He himself took a while to settle on Mark Twain as his pseudonym: other names he tried included Sergeant Fathom and W. Apaminondas Adrastus Blab.

The name Jennifer may be considered the first truly trendy name. In 1960 it was only around seventy-first on the list of most popular names; by 1970, it was number one.

Names that are extremely trendy are also likely to go out of fashion: Betty, a top-five name in 1930, is now almost never used. Other outdated names from the '30s are Dorothy, Doris, and Shirley.

The best-used boys' names over the last forty years are James, John, Joseph, Richard, Robert, Thomas, and William. Boys' names that have become fashionable and then faded away are Donald, Ronald, Gary, and Mark.

On some baby name lists, Tristan is used almost as often as Jason. Other surprises in the middle ranks are Connor, Caleb, Logan, and Dakota.

The new category of geography names seems to be taking hold for girls: Savannah occurs quite often, with Sierra some distance behind.

When flower names were first used, in the nineteenth century, it was home-grown English flowers that became popular, like Violet and Rose. The only popular flower name now is the exotic Jasmine, which may have been boosted to that point by the Walt Disney version of *Aladdin*.

Football player Deion Sanders, widely acknowledged to be a brilliant athlete, has never been one to hide his light under a bushel. His estimation of himself is clear in the names chosen for his two eldest children: Deion, Jr., and Deiondra.

Some people just can't resist a pun: there are folks in U. S. phone books with the names Frank N. Stein, Minnie Vann, and M. T. Head.

Looking for inspiration? Turn to Detroit—or to Japan. Children have recently been given the following car names: Transam, Tercel, Corvette, Neon, Ferrari, and Porsche.

Caballero Sp. "Horseman." In the U.S., this comes quite close to a cowboy.

Cable OF. "Rope." Cable is generally a very thick rope, though the word is also used to describe chains (as in an anchor cable) and the insulated wires that transmit electric messages. The first permanent telegraphic cable across the Atlantic was laid in 1866.

Cabell

Cabot Fr. Probably "to sail." The name of a 15th-century English explorer who probably made a landfall in Canada in 1497. Also, more recently, the name of a prominent Boston mercantile and shipping family.

Cabbot

Cadby OE. "Fighting man's settlement." A short, neutral, masculine-sounding name.

Cadbee, Cadbey, Cadbie

Caddis OE. "Worsted fabric." Also a kind of fly that trout like to eat, making this a potential choice for a fisherman's son.

Caddice, Caddiss

Caddock Welsh. "Eagerness for war."

Cadock, Cadog

Cade OE. "Round" or "Lump."

Caide, Caden, Kade, Kaden, Kayde

Cadell Welsh. "Battle." Political consultant Patrick Caddell.

Caddell, Cadel

Cadman Anglo-Welsh. "Battle man."

Cadmus Gk. "From the east." In Greek myth, Cadmus is the founder of the city of Thebes who ultimately turned into a serpent. He is also credited with the invention of writing in letters.

Cadmar, Cadmo, Cadmos, Cadmuss, Kadmos, Kadmus

Caduceus Gk. In Greek myth, the caduceus was the insignia of Hermes (called Mercury by the Romans): a winged staff with two serpents twining up it. Because Hermes was the patron of doctors, it has become the symbol for medicine.

Caesar Lat. Clan name of obscure meaning, possibly "Hairy, hirsute." The term "caesarean" for a surgical delivery of a baby came about because the famous Roman emperor Julius Caesar was born that way. It has become a generic term for emperor, translated into German (*kaiser*) and Russian (*czar*). Actor César Romero.

Caezar, Casar, César, Cesare, Cesaro, Kaiser, Seasar, Sezar

Cain Heb. "Spear." Adam and Eve's elder son, who slew his brother Abel. Surprisingly enough, used with some frequency, at least in the 19th century. Homonym Kane has a different source. Actor Michael Caine.

Caine, Kain, Kaine

Caird Scot. Gael. Occupational name: "Traveling met-alsmith." Another term would be "tinker," or "worker with tin."
Caerd, Cairde, Kaird, Kairde

Cairn Scot. Gael. Place name: "Mound of rocks." Cairns were built as long ago as the Stone Age as memorials, grave markers, and landmarks. Many of these ancient cairns can still be seen in the British Isles.
Cairne, Cairns, Kairn, Kairne, Kairns

Cairo Place name: the capital city of Egypt. The name comes from an Arabic word meaning "Victorious."

Caius Lat. "Rejoice." Var. **Gaius.** A 16th century English physician endowed a college at Cambridge University which is called "Gonville and Caius." In the inscrutable British fashion, the name is pronounced "Keys."
Cai, Caio, Kay, Kaye, Keye, Keyes, Keys

Cajetan (It. "From Gaeta.") Var. **Gaetan.**
Cajetano, Kajetan, Kajetano

Cal Dim. Calhoun, Calvin, etc. Baseball star Cal Ripken, Jr.

Calder OE. "Stream." Little rivulets are such important features in the English landscape that regional terms for them abound, and several (Brook, Burn) have traced the typical path from geographical feature to place name to surname to given name. Sculptor Alexander Calder.

Caldwell OE. Place name: "Cold well."

Cale Var. **Caleb.** Another possible source is Irish Gaelic, "Thin, slender." Race driver Cale Yarborough.
Cael, Caile, Cayle, Kale

Caleb Heb. Either "Dog" or "Courageous." An Old Testament name brought to America with the Puritans, where it was fairly common until around 1920. It has shot up out of obscurity recently, moving close to the top fifty boys' names in America. Author Caleb Carr.
Cal, Cale, Cayleb, Kaleb, Kayleb, Kaylob

Caley Ir. Gael. "Lean, slight." Very similar to the trendy Kayla/Caitlyn group of girls' names, so that an infant named Caley would probably be taken for a girl.
Cailey, Caily, Kayley

Calhoun Ir. Gael. Place name: "The narrow woods." John Calhoun was a 19th-century American statesman, Vice

President under Andrew Jackson, whose writings and ideas on states' rights contributed heavily to the Southern states' formation of the Confederacy.
Callhoun, Colhoun, Colquhoun

Callis Lat. "Chalice, goblet."
Callice, Callys, Callyx

Calogero It. "Fair old age." Name of a saint, a Sicilian hermit.
Calogeros, Kalogeros, Kalogerus

Calumet Fr. from Lat. "Straw, little reed." This was the term that the French in Canada used for the Indian peace pipe, a highly ornamental pipe smoked on ceremonial occasions. One of the great horse-racing stables of the 20th century was Calumet Farms.
Callumet

Calvert OE. Occupational name: "Calf-herder." English surname. In the U.S., borne by George Calvert, founder of Maryland. The Calvert dynasty, George, Cecilius, and Charles, ruled the colony of Maryland from 1632 until 1689, though only Charles actually lived in the New World. Their proprietorship of Maryland ended when, as Catholics, they were ousted by the newly Protestant regime in England.
Calbert

Calvin Lat. "Hairless." Roman clan name turned surname. Transferred to first name as a tribute to 16th-century Swiss religious reformer John Calvin, whose thinking deeply influenced the Presbyterian, Methodist, and Huguenot branches of Protestantism. U.S. use has probably been influenced by President Calvin Coolidge, though today the name probably conjures up fashion designer Calvin Klein first and foremost. Composer Calvin Hampton; Italian author Italo Calvino.
Cal, Calvino, Kalvin, Vinnie

Camden Scot. Gael. Place name: "The twisting valley."
Camdin, Camdon

Cameron Scot. Gael. "Crooked nose." Clan name derived from the facial feature. In Scotland, the Camerons were a powerful clan. Little used as a first name until the middle of this century, but now very well established. The exposure given it by (female) actress Cameron Diaz may persuade parents that it is a girl's name.

Cam, Camaeron, Camedon, Camron, Camry, Kameron, Kamrey

Camillo Masc. **Camilla** (Lat. meaning unclear). Most sources trace the name to the young girls who assisted at pagan religious ceremonies. Saint Camillus de Lellis was a 16th-century Italian founder of hospitals, and is patron saint of nurses and the sick.

Camillus, Camilo, Comillo

Campbell Scot. Gael. "Crooked mouth." Name of a very famous Scottish clan, again referring to a distinguishing feature. The hereditary heads of the Campbell clan, the Dukes of Argyll, at one time controlled vast acres of the Scottish highlands and commanded the loyalty of thousands of men. In the U.S. the primary association is probably with soup. Use as a first name dates back only to the 1930s. Actor Campbell Scott.

Campbel

Campion ME. "Champion." The name of a small wild-flower and of an English Catholic martyr (Edmund Campion). A fictional detective, Albert Campion, features in the popular murder mysteries of Margery Allingham.

Campian

Canby ME. Place name: "Settlement near the reeds." Another term for reeds is "canes." Film critic Vincent Canby.

Canbey, Canbie

Candelario Sp. "Candles." Refers to the Catholic feast of Candlemas, February 2. The feast marks the day the Holy Family took the baby Jesus to be presented at the temple. It was customary to bless all the candles for the succeeding year on the day of this feast.

Candelareo, Candelaro, Candelerio, Candelero

Candido Lat. "White, pure." Voltaire's famous novel *Candide* makes fun of the theory that "All is for the best in the best of all possible worlds." The term "candid" has come to mean "frank, without guile."

Candide, Candidio

Canfield ME. Place name: "Field of reeds." Dick Canfield was a famous gambler and casino operator in the late 19th century, and the Canfield form of solitaire was named for him.

Canning Fr. Occupational name: "Official of the church." Var. **Cannon**. Has nothing to do with preserving food in glass jars, which is what canning means to most of us.
Cannan

Cannon Fr. Occupational name: "Official of the church." Not, as might be expected by the spelling, related to fire-arms.
Canon, Kanon

Canute Scand. "Knot." Brought to Britain by the 11th-century King Canute of Norway and Denmark, who became King of England in 1016. Very rare, except in those of Scandinavian descent. Football coach Knute Rockne.
Cnut, Knut, Knute

Canyon Sp. "Footpath." Geography name: canyons, deep ravines, are notable features of the Western American landscape. Basketball player Rick Barry named a son Canyon.

Capp Fr. Occupational name: "Chaplain." Easily confused with the small hat attached to the head of many American boys. Still a brisk, breezy name.
Cap, Capps

Carden OE. Occupational name: "Wool carder." The production of woolen cloth, from sheep to bolt of fabric, requires many steps, and many of these steps have given last names (Shepherd, Shearer, Weaver) to the English language. Carding is the part of the process when the wool is combed to remove impurities.
Card, Cardin, Cardon

Carew Lat. "Chariot." Baseball player Rod Carew.
Carewe, Crew, Crewe

Carey Welsh. Place name: "Near the castle." Distinct from Cary, which has another source. By the 1950s, this form was usually a girl's name, often a nickname for Caroline. Actor Jim Carrey.
Carrey

Carl Var. **Charles** (OG. "Man.") Use in America was fairly steady from 1850 to 1950 (probably as a result of intensive German and Scandinavian immigration), but it dropped off in the 1960s. It is still steadily used but is

nothing like fashionable. Poet Carl Sandburg; journalist Carl Bernstein; astronomer/author Carl Sagan; psychologist Carl Jung.
Carel, Karel, Karl

Carleton OE. Place name: "Farmer's settlement." Only used as a first name since around 1880. In the U.S., usually spelled without the "e."
Carl, Carlton, Charlton

Carley ME. Place name: "Farmer's meadow."
Carleigh

Carlin Ir. Gael. "Little champion." Comedian George Carlin.
Carling, Carly

Carlisle OE. Place name: "The fortified tower." Also the name of a very old city in northwest England. Historian Thomas Carlyle.
Carley, Carlile, Carly, Carlyle

Carlos Sp. Var. **Charles** (OG. "Man"). This form of Charles is increasingly popular in the U.S. Film directors Carlos Saura, Carlo Ponti.
Carlo, Carrlos

Carlow Irish place name: a major town and a county in inland Ireland.
Carlowe

Carlsen Scand. "Carl's son."
Carlssen, Carlson, Carlsson, Karlsen, Karlssen, Karlson, Karlsson

Carmelo It. from Heb. "Garden." Biblical place name: Mount Carmel is in Israel and is often referred to in ancient writings as a kind of paradise. Scarcely used in the U.S. Fashion designer Carmelo Pomodoro.
Carmel, Carmeli, Carmello, Karmel, Karmelo, Karmello

Carmichael Scot. Gael. "Follower of Michael." Possibly referring to partisans of Saint Michael.

Carmine Lat. "Song." Though carmine also means "Purplish red" (from an Aramaic word meaning "Crimson"), the Latin source is more likely, since the name is almost exclusively used by families of Italian descent.
Carman, Carmen, Carmin, Carmino, Karman, Karmen

Carney Ir. Gael. "The winner."
Carny, Kearney

Carollan Ir. Gael. "Little champion." In the U.S., likely to be confused with a variant of Caroline.
Carlin, Carling, Carolan

Carpenter Lat. "Carriage maker." Another occupational name turned last name, rarely occurring as a first name.
Charpentier

Carr Scand. "From the swampy place."
Karr, Ker, Kerr

Carrington ME. Meaning unclear: most likely a place name, given the "-ton" ending.
Carington, Caryngton

Carroll OG. "Man." An anglicized version of Charles, occurring from time to time as a family name, though it is too much like Carol (which was very popular in the '60s) to be an appealing boys' name for most parents. Author Lewis Carroll; signer of the Declaration of Independence Charles Carroll; actor Carroll O'Connor.
Carolus, Carrol, Caroll, Cary, Caryl, Caryll

Carson OE. "Son of the marsh-dwellers." Nineteenth-century frontiersman Kit Carson was a scout and guide in the exploration of the West as well as an important factor in the Mexican War. Carson City, Nevada was named for him, and to this day an aura of rakishness and daring clings to the name.

Carswell OE. Place name: "Well where the watercress grows."
Caswell

Carter OE. Occupational name: "One who drives carts." Former President Jimmy Carter; football player Ki-Jana Carter.
Cartier

Carvell OF. "Swampy dwelling." Political strategist James Carville.
Carvel, Carvil, Carville

Carver OE. Occupational name: "One who carves wood."

Cary OE. Place name: "Pretty brook." Distinct from Carey. Use in the 19th century as a first name was quite rare, but when actor Archibald Leach renamed himself Cary Grant, numerous families suddenly found the name Cary appealing.

Case Fr. "Box."

— **Casey** Ir. Gael. "Vigilant." Possibly also a short form of Casimir. Made famous by the song about the engineer of the Cannonball Express train, Casey Jones. Since Casey is moving into the top fifty or so names for girls in the U.S., it is probably more generally thought of as a girl's name now. Baseball personality Casey Stengel; radio disc jockey Casey Kasem.
Cacey, Cayce, Caycey, Kasey

Cash Dim. Cassius (Lat. "Vain"). Also a slang word for money, of course. Singer Johnny Cash.
Casshe

Casimir Slavic. "Bringing peace." Associated with Poland for her famous 11th-century king, who brought peace to the nation.
Casimeer, Casimire, Casimiro, Casmir, Kasimiro, Kazimierz, Kazimir

Casper Origin unclear, though many sources suggest Per. "He who guards the treasure." Originally Jasper, Germanicized to Caspar. French is Gaspard. Traditionally one of the Three Kings (perhaps the one carrying the gold) was named Caspar. Americans who grew up in the 1960s and their movie-going children will also be reminded of Casper the Friendly Ghost. Defense Secretary Casper Weinberger.
Caspar, Cass, Gaspar, Gaspard, Gasparo, Gasper, Jasper, Kaspar

Caspian Place name: the Caspian Sea is the largest inland body of water in the world, lying between Russia and Asia: its southern coast is in Iran. Author C. S. Lewis named a principal character Caspian in one of his *Chronicles of Narnia*.

Cassander Sp. from Gk. "Brother of heroes." A king of Macedonia, contemporary of Alexander the Great, who married Alexander's half-sister and later murdered his widow.
Casander, Casandro, Cassandero

Cassian Lat. Clan name: "Fair, just."
Casiano, Cassio

Cassidy Ir. Gael. "Ingenious, clever." On the verge of being taken over as a girl's name, a process that can only

be hastened by the fact that TV celebrity Kathie Lee Gifford named her daughter Cassidy.
Cassady, Cassedy, Cassidey

Cassiel The archangel who watches over Capricorns.

Cassius Lat. ''Vain.'' Historically, Cassius was a Roman politician who was behind the plot to murder Julius Caesar. In Shakespeare's play, Caesar says, ''Yon Cassius has a lean and hungry look; He thinks too much: such men are dangerous.'' Boxer Cassius Clay (now Muhammad Ali).
Cash, Cass, Cassio

Castor Gk. ''Beaver.'' In classical myth, along with Pollux, one of the heavenly twins immortalized in the constellation Gemini. They were considered the patron gods of seafarers, appearing to them in Saint Elmo's fire.
Caster, Castorio, Kastor

Catlin Ir. var. Catherine (Gk. ''Pure''). An unusual last name. George Catlin was an American traveler and artist of the mid–19th century who is particularly famous for his penetrating portraits of Native Americans.
Cattlin, Katlin, Kattlin

Cato Lat. ''All-knowing.'' Cato was a particularly high-minded Roman statesman of the time of Julius Caesar. The ''o'' ending is mildly fashionable for boys' names.
Cayto, Kaeto, Kato

Catullus Lat. Meaning obscure. One of the greatest Roman poets. A name for a family with scholarly tendencies.
Catullo

Cavan Ir. Gael. ''Handsome.''
Kavan

Cavanagh Ir. Gael. ''Follower of Kevin.'' Principally an Irish last name.
Cavanaugh, Kavanagh, Kavanaugh

Cecil Lat. ''Blind one,'' from a Roman clan name. Used in Roman times, then resurfaced in the Victorian era, possibly given a boost by the fame of industrialist (and founder of Rhodesia) Cecil Rhodes. Little used in this century. Film director Cecil B. De Mille; photographer Cecil Beaton; baseball player Cecil Fielder.
Cecil, Cecilio, Cecilius, Celio

Cedric OE. ''War leader.'' Used in two 19th-century literary landmarks (*Ivanhoe* and *Little Lord Fauntleroy*), which probably increased its popularity in Britain. Actor Sir Cedric Hardwicke.

Caddaric, Ced, Cedrick, Cedro, Rick, Sedric, Sedrick, Sedrik

Celesto Lat. "Heavenly." The masculine version is scarce except in Catholic countries, where the memories of Popes Celestine I and V (both saints) keep the name alive.

Célestine, Celestino, Celindo, Selestine, Selestino, Silestino

Celso It. from Lat. "High, lofty." As in "Gloria in excelsis. . . ." The same particle is also found in various words for sky, like *ciel* (French) and *coelum* (Latin).

Celsius, Celsus

Cephas Heb. "Rock." New Testament name; what Jesus called his apostle Simon. Peter is the Latin translation by which he is more commonly known. Cephas was in steady (if infrequent) use until the 20th century.

Chad Origin cloudy; possibly OE. "Fierce." Saint Chad was a 7th-century English bishop. The name enjoyed a burst of popularity beginning in the late 1960s, reaching the top 50 names for American boys, but its popularity has declined since the mid-eighties. Actors Chad Everett, Chad Lowe.

Chadd, Chaddie

Chadwick OE. Place name: "The fighter's settlement." Has been used commercially as a generic WASP name.

Chadwyck

Chai Heb. "Living, vital."

Hai

Chaim Heb. "Life." Male version of **Eve**. Hyman is more common in English-speaking countries. Author Chaim Potok.

Chayim, Chayyim, Haim, Hayvim, Hayyim, Hy, Hyman, Hymen, Hymie, Manny

Chairo Sp. A diminutive and variant of **Jerome** (Gk. "Sacred name"), via **Hieronimo**.

Chiro, Hairo, Hiro

Chalkley OE. Place name: "Chalk meadow."

Chalklea, Chalklie

Chalmers OF. Scottish occupational name meaning "Ser-

vant of the chambers.'' French ties with Scotland (in league against their mutual enemy England) were very strong until the unification of Scotland with England in the early 17th century.
Chalmer, Chambers

Chamberlain ME. Occupational name: "Chief officer of the household." A chamberlain was an administrative post in a large royal or noble household. Actor Richard Chamberlain.
Chambellan, Chamberlin, Chambers

Champion ME. "Warrior." The word has come to mean the supreme winner in a competition, of course. Choreographer Gower Champion.
Campion, Champ, Champeon

Chanan Heb. "He was compassionate."
Hanan

Chance ME. "Good fortune." Also var. **Chauncey**. Used more often than one might expect.
Chanse, Chantz, Chanze

Chancellor ME. Occupational name: "Chief secretary, record keeper." Rather unwieldy as a first name, and it does not provide any obvious nicknames. Broadcaster John Chancellor.
Chance, Chancelor, Chansellor, Chaunce

Chand Sanskrit. "Moon, light."
Chandak, Chandan

— **Chandler** OF. Occupational name: "Candle merchant."

Chaney Fr. "Oak tree." Actor Lon Chaney.
Chainey, Chany, Cheney

Chang Chinese. "Smooth, free, unhindered."

Chaniel Heb. "Grace of God."
Chanyel, Haniel, Hanniel, Hanyel

Channing OF. Occupational name: "Official of the church." Related to Cannon. Another possibility is OF. "Canal."
Canning, Cannon, Canon

Chanoch Heb. "Dedicated." The English version is Enoch.
Channoch, Chanok, Hanoch, Hannoch, Hanok

Chantrey From OF. "Singing." A chantry, in the Middle Ages, was an endowment of funds to support the singing

(chanting) of masses for an individual's soul. This may
be an occupational name.
Chantry

Chaparral Sp. "Dwarf oak." Chaparral is the term used
to describe various kinds of low-growing ground covers
such as the mesquite found in the southwestern U.S. The
name thus has associations with the wide-open spaces.
Chaparall

Chaplin ME. Occupational name: "Secretary." A chaplain
was usually a minor ecclesiastical position, and has come
to mean something like the spiritual guide of a secular
organization, like a hospital chaplain. Actor Charlie Chaplin.
Chaplain, Chaplinn, Chappelin

Chapman OE. "Peddler." Chapmen usually sold chap-
books, pamphlets intended for a wide audience, even in
the days of low literacy rates.
Chap, Chappy, Manny

Chappel OE. Occupational name: "One who works at the
chapel."
Capel, Capell, Capello, Cappel, Chappell, Chaps

− **Charles** OG. "Man." The English term "churl," meaning
"serf," comes from the same root. Has been a staple ever
since the era of the Emperor Charlemagne, and a royal
name in many European countries, including England,
where the next king will probably be Charles III. In America, it was one of the top five names for the first three-
quarters of this century, but has since been displaced by
such exotics as Ryan, Zachary, and Tyler. Naturalist
Charles Darwin; French president Charles de Gaulle; author Charles Dickens; actor Charlie Chaplin; basketball
player Charles Barkley.
**Carel, Carl, Carlo, Carlos, Carrol, Carroll, Cary, Caryl,
Chad, Charley, Charlie, Charlot, Charls, Charlton,
Charly, Chas, Chay, Chaz, Chazz, Chick, Chip, Chuck, Karel, Karl, Karol, Karolek, Karolik, Karoly**

Charlton OE. Place name: "Charles's dwelling." Also
possibly a variation on Carlton. Used as a given name for
the last hundred years. Actor Charlton Heston.
Carleton, Carlton, Charleston, Charleton

Chase OF. "Hunter." Quite steadily used, possibly influenced by a character on TV's *Falcon Crest*. Painter William Merritt Chase.

Chace, Chayce, Chayse

Chauncey ME. Contraction of Chancellor. Broadcaster Chauncey Howell.

Chance, Chancey, Chaunsey, Chaunsy, Chawncey

Chaviv Heb. "Loved one." Closely resembles an Arabic name with the same meaning, Habib.

Habib, Haviv

Chaz Dim. **Charles** (OG. "Man"). This off-hand nickname is used from time to time on its own. Actor Chazz Palmintieri.

Chas, Chazz

Chesley OE./Lat. "Meadow of the camp."

Cheslea, Cheslee, Chesleigh, Cheslie, Chesly

Chesney OE. Place name referring to a camp.

Cheney, Cheny, Chesnie, Chesny

Chester Lat. "Soldier's camp." Place name from Roman Britain, gradually evolved into a first name most common in the U.S. Virtually unused now, however. President Chester Arthur; newscaster Chet Huntley.

Cheston, Chet

Cherokee Native American Indian tribe. The Cherokee originally lived in the southeastern U.S., especially the mountainous areas of Tennesee, Georgia, Alabama, and the Carolinas. The tribe was deported en masse to territory west of the Mississippi in 1838, undergoing enormous hardships. The Cherokee were farmers, and one of the first tribes to produce a written language.

Cherut Heb. "Liberty."

Cheroot, Heroot, Herut

Chetwin OE. Place name: "Little house on the twisted path."

Chetwen, Chetwyn, Chetwynn

Chevalier Fr. "Knight." Comedian Chevy Chase.

Chevy

Chevron Fr. A V-shaped heraldic insignia, often used to indicate rank in the armed services.

Cheyenne Native American tribe indigenous to Minnesota, the Dakotas, and Montana. The Cheyenne were some of the fiercest opponents of European settlement in the West. The capital city of Wyoming is Cheyenne.

Chayan, Chayann, Shayan, Shayanne, Sheyenne

Chick Dim. **Charles** (OG. "Man"). Musician Chick Corea.

Chic, Chik

Chico Sp. Dim. **Francis** (Lat. "Frenchman") via **Francisco**.

Chilton OE. Place name: "Farm near the well."

Chelton, Chill

Chino Sp. "Chinese." Also a California place name: an agricultural area east of Los Angeles. "Chinos" is also a term for khaki-colored trousers.

Chip Nickname commonly used among WASP families, especially if the string of chosen surnames seems unwieldy for a small child. Also occurs as a nickname for Charles. Baseball player Chipper Jones.

Chipper

Choni Heb. "Gracious."

Honi

Chris Dim. **Christian, Christopher**. Actors Chris Cooper, Chris O'Donnell, Chris Sarandon.

Chriss, Kris

— **Christian** Gk. "Anointed, Christian." A girl's name that (contrary to the usual movement) became a male name, possibly after the huge success of John Bunyan's *Pilgrim's Progress* (1684), whose hero is called Christian. In Britain and Australia, especially popular in the 1970s. Now steadily used in the U.S. French fashion designers Christian Dior, Christian Lacroix; Dr. Christiaan Barnard; actor Christian Slater; basketball player Christian Laettner.

Chrestien, Chrétien, Chris, Christer, Christiano, Christie, Christo, Christy, Cristian, Cristiano, Cristino, Cristy, Kit, Kris, Krister, Kristian, Kristo, Krystian, Krystiano

Christmas Name of the holiday, used occasionally through the 19th century for December 25 babies, but now usually replaced by the French, and somewhat subtler, form, Noel.

Christopher Gk. "Carrier of Christ." The much-loved story of Saint Christopher is that he lived alone by a river, carrying travelers across the ford on his back. A child whom he was carrying became almost too heavy to bear, and proved afterward to be the Christ child. Actually the tale has little basis in fact, and probably springs from the literal translation of the name, which originally meant carrying Christ in one's heart. Nevertheless, Christopher is still venerated as patron saint of travelers and drivers. In the modern era the name was little used until a revival in the 1940s, possibly influenced by the popularity of A.A. Milne's *Winnie the Pooh*, whose human hero is called Christopher Robin. Hugely popular right through the 1980s and 1990s, the name is still among the top five boys' names nationwide. Explorer Christopher Columbus; actors Christopher Plummer, Christopher Reeve; architect Christopher Wren.

Chris, Christie, Christof, Christoffer, Christoforo, Christoforus, Christoph, Christophe, Christophoros, Christos, Cris, Cristóbal, Cristoforo, Cristovano, Kester, Kit, Kitt, Kris, Kriss, Kristo, Kristofel, Kristofer, Kristoffer, Kristofor, Kristoforos, Kristos, Krzysztof, Stoffel, Tobal, Topher

Chuck Dim. **Charles** (OG. "Man"). Scarce as a given name, and not even that common as a nickname these days. Cartoon director Chuck Jones; musician Chuck Mangione; Colonel Chuck Yaeger.

Churchill OE. Place name: "Hill of the church." Use as a first name is probably homage to English statesman Sir Winston Churchill.

Churchil

Cicero Lat. "Chickpea." Most famous for the Roman orator and statesman who lived in the 1st century B.C. Like Cato, probably came to the U.S. as a slave name.

Cid Sp. from Arab. "Lord." El Cid was a heroic Spanish knight of the 11th century whose story is told (and embroidered) in numerous medieval epics. Easily confused with the nickname for Sidney.

Cyd

Cimarron Place name: a city in western Kansas and a river that runs 650 miles across the Great Plains from New Mexico to Oklahoma. It was made famous by an Edna Ferber novel that was the basis for movies made in 1933 and 1961.

Cimeron, Simarron, Simeron

Cincinnatus Legendary consul of ancient (5th century B.C.) Rome, a statesman who, according to legend, preferred farming but performed his civic duty by leading the state.

Cipriano Sp. from Gk. "From Cyprus." Saint Cyprian was a third-century bishop of Carthage.

Ciprien, Cyprian, Cyprien, Siprian, Siprien, Sipryan

Ciriaco It. from Gk. "Lord."

Ciro Sp. var. **Cyrus** (Per. "Sun" or "Throne").

Cirrus Lat. "Lock of hair." The name of a wispy, filmy cloud formation.

Claiborne Fr./Ger. Place name: "Boundary with clover" or OE. "Boundary of clay." U.S. Senator Claiborne Pell.

Claiborn, Claibourn, Claibourne, Clayborn, Clayborne, Claybourn, Claybourne

Clair Masc. **Claire** (Lat. "Bright"). Very scarce as a masculine name.

Claire, Clare, Claro

Clancy Ir. Gael. "Red-haired fighter's child." An almost stereotypically Irish name.

Clancey, Claney

Clare Dim. **Clarence**. Very unusual for boys. In Thomas Hardy's tragic novel *Tess of the D'Urbervilles*, Tess falls in love with, and is abandoned by, a man named Angel Clare.

Clair, Claire, Clarey, Clayre

Clarence Lat. "Bright." An alternate source is the title Duke of Clarence, created for a 14th-century royal prince who married a girl from the Clare family. The bearers of the title have been ill-fated: the third, for example, was said to have drowned in a barrel of wine. In the late 19th century, prompted by the Victorian interest in the picturesque and medieval, Clarence was immensely popular, but gradually acquired the connotations of effete aristocracy and has been neglected recently. Lawyer Clarence Darrow.

Clair, Claran, Clarance, Clare, Clarens, Claron, Clarons, Claronz, Clarrance, Clarrence, Klarance, Klarenz

Clark OF. Occupational name: "Cleric, scholar." Surname transferred to first name, heavily influenced by the fame

of actor Clark Gable. Also made famous by "mild-mannered" Clark Kent, alter ego of Superman in the popular comic strip. It does not, somehow, seem to be very suitable for a child, which may account for its neglect.
Clarke, Clerc, Clerk

Claude Lat. "Lame." Name of a Roman clan that produced the emperor immortalized in Robert Graves's novel (and subsequent TV dramatization) *I, Claudius*. Claude was used in the 19th century, but not in great numbers. Painter Claude Monet; composer Claude Debussy; Congressman Claude Pepper; actor Claude Rains.
Claud, Claudan, Claudell, Claudianus, Claudicio, Claudien, Claudino, Claudio, Claudius, Claudon, Clodito, Clodo, Clodomiro, Klaudio

Claus Dim. **Nicholas** (Gk. "People of victory"). Actor Klaus Kinski.
Claes, Clause, Klaus

Claxton OE. Place name: "Clark's town."

Clay OE. Occupational or place name involving clay. Clay that occurs naturally in the earth was a tremendous natural resource in earlier times. Most famous modern bearer was probably Cassius Clay, later Mohammad Ali, the boxing champion; he, in turn, had originally been named for a 19th-century abolitionist. American statesman Henry Clay.
Claye, Klay

Clayborne OE. Place name: "Brook near a clay-bed" or "Border near a clay-bed."
Claiborn, Claiborne, Clay, Claybourne, Clayburn, Klaiborn, Klaibourne

Clayland OE. Place name: "Land of clay."

Clayton OE. Place name: "Settlement near the clay-bed." Given as a first name since the early 19th century.
Klayton

Cleander Combined name: possibly "Leander" (Gk. "Lion-man") and Cleanth.

Cleanth Gk. Derivation unknown; possibly derived from the name of a Stoic Greek philosopher, Cleanthes. The name was used occasionally in both French and English dramas of the 17th and 18th centuries. Critic Cleanth Brooks.

Cleandro, Cleante, Cleanthes, Cleanto, Cleneth, Clianth, Clianthes, Kleanth, Kleanthes

Cleary Ir. Gael. "Learned one."

Cleavant OE. Place name: "Cliff." Related to Cleveland. Actors Cleavant Derricks, Cleavon Little.

Cleavon, Cleevant, Cleeve, Cleevont

Clement Lat. "Mild, giving mercy." A name borne by fourteen popes as well as the author (Clement Clark Moore) of "A Visit From St. Nicholas." Nevertheless, little used in English-speaking countries. Artist Francesco Clemente; baseball player Roberto Clemente.

Clem, Clemencio, Clemens, Clemente, Clementino, Clementius, Clemmie, Clemmons, Clemmy, Klemens, Klement, Klementos, Kliment

Cleon Gk. "Renowned."

Kleon

Cleophas Gk. "Vision of glory." New Testament name: husband of one of the Marys who stood at the foot of the Cross.

Cleo, Cleofas, Cleofaso, Cleophus

Cletus Gk. "Called forth, invoked."

Anacletus, Cletis, Cletos, Kletos, Kletus

Cleveland OE. Place name: "Hilly area." During the fame of U.S. President Grover Cleveland, several towns were named after him, and the surname became a first name, though only in the U.S. Writer Cleveland Amory.

Cleavon, Cleaveland, Cleavland, Cleon, Cleve, Clevon

Cliff OE. "Steep slope." Or Dim. **Clifford, Clifton**. Actor Cliff Robertson; singer Cliff Richard.

Cliffe, Clyff, Clyffe

Clifford OE. Place name: "Ford near the cliff." Surname transferred to first name, most popular in the late 19th century. Older siblings of a new baby may be familiar with Clifford the Big Red Dog, the hero of many children's books. Playwright Clifford Odets.

Cliff, Clyff, Clyfford

Clifton OE. Place name: "Town near the cliff." Another transferred surname, more common in the U.S. than in Britain.

Cliff, Cliffeton, Clift, Clyffeton, Clyfton, Clyffton

Clinton OE. Place name: "Settlement near the headland."

An illustrious 18th-century governor of New York, De Witt Clinton, left his name on many New York City locations. Cannot be used now without reference to President Bill Clinton. Actor Clint Eastwood; singer Clint Black.
Clint, Clintt, Klint

Clive OE. Place name: "Cliff." Given some publicity by a famous English soldier, Robert Clive, for his exploits in India. Thackeray used it as a first name in an 1855 novel, but its real popularity in England didn't come for another hundred years. Never widely used in the U.S. Critic Clive Barnes.
Cleve, Clyve

Clovis OG. "Renowned fighter." Early form of the name that would eventually become Ludwig or Louis. King Clovis I was the first Christian king of the Franks, and later kings' use of the name Louis probably harks back to the dynasty he founded in the 5th century. The name is rare, however, in the 20th century. Fashion designer Clovis Ruffin.
Clodoveo, Clovisito, Clovio, Clovito

Cloy Derivation unclear: may come from OF. "Nail" as an occupational name having to do with the nails in horseshoes.
Cloyce, Cloyd

Cluny Ir. Gael. "From the meadow."

Clyde Scot. place name: the River Clyde penetrates western Scotland as far as Glasgow. This name is very scarce today, though it was somewhat familiar a hundred years ago.
Clydell

Coakley OE. Place name: "Charcoal meadow." Before coke was a drug or a soft drink, it was the flammable residue from burning coal, and a valuable source of fuel.
Coakly, Cokeley, Cokelie, Cokely

Cobb OE. The word has had many meanings, but the most likely source for the name is probably "cottage." Baseball player Ty Cobb.
Cobbett

Cobden OE. Place name: "Valley with the cottage."
Cobdenn

Cobham OE. Place name: "Village with the cottage." Cob is also an ancient term for a male swan, the head of a herring, and the seed-head of clover, any of which could actually be the source for this name.
Cobbham

Coburn Derivation unclear: "burn" most likely refers to a small stream. One theory holds that Coburn is a variant of Cockburn, making it a place name: "Stream of the rooster." Actor James Coburn.
Coburne, Cockburn, Cockburne

Coby Possibly dim. **Coburn:** possibly an invented name. Resemblance to the trendy Cody favors the latter notion. Basketball player Kobe Bryant; soccer player Cobi Jones.
Cobey, Cobi, Cobie, Kobe, Kobey, Kobie, Koby

Cockrell OF. "Young rooster."
Cockerell, Cockrill

Cody OE. "Pillow." Some sources suggest "son of Odo." Use as a first name was probably influenced by the fame of Buffalo Bill Cody, frontier scout and entrepreneur, who took his "Wild West Show" around the U.S. and Europe at the turn of the century. Current extensive use is probably influenced in part by the fact that Cody is a celebrity child's name; Frank and Kathie Lee Gifford named their son Cody.
Codey, Codie, Kody

Coffin ME. "Basket, container." The word is related to "coffer." Most likely this was an occupational name, referring to a coffin maker. An unlikely choice, unless this is a family name.
Coffen

Colbert OE. "Renowned mariner."
Cole, Colt, Colvert, Culbert

Colburn OE. Place name: "Cold brook" or "Coal brook."
Colbourn, Colbourne, Collbourn, Collburn

Colby OE. Place name: "The dark farmstead." Shooting up the popularity charts, probably coasting on the appeal of similar-sounding Cody.
Colbee, Colbey, Colbie, Collby

Colden OE. Place name: "Dark valley."
Collden, Coldin, Colldin

Cole Dim. **Nicholas** (Gk. "People of victory") and names

...ning with Cole, such as Coleman. Monosyllabic names are out of favor now but Cole has a special appeal—is that because it sounds "cool?" Or because it sounds like trendy Kyle? Composer Cole Porter; outlaw Cole Younger.

Coleman OE. "Follower of Nicholas." Also contraction of the Latin word for "dove"; probably influenced by the Irish Saint Columba.
Colman

Coleridge OE. Place name: possibly "Cole's ridge" or "Dark ridge." English majors will remember English poet Samuel Taylor Coleridge, author of *The Rime of the Ancient Mariner* and the famously unfinished *Kubla Khan*, written under the influence of opium.
Colerige, Colridge, Colrige

Colgate OE. Place name: "Dark gate." Associated in the U.S. with a soap-manufacturing company, and of course a college. It was originally called Hamilton Literary and Theological Seminary, but was renamed Colgate University in 1890 for its benefactor, William Colgate, of the soap fortune.
Colegate

Colin Gael. "Young creature." Also Dim. **Nicholas** (Gk. "People of victory"). Well-known in the Middle Ages, and popular in Britain in the middle of this century, but didn't spread in any numbers to the U.S. until quite recently. It now hovers at the bottom of the top 100 names. U.S. General Colin Powell.
Colan, Cole, Collin, Colyn

Colley OE. "Dark-haired." Use as a first name is rare. Philanthropist Collis Huntington.
Collie, Collis

Collier OE. Occupation name: "Coal miner."
Colier, Colis, Collayer, Collis, Collyer

Collins Ir. Gael. "Holly." Author Wilkie Collins.

Colt OE. Occupational name. Perhaps a long-ago owner of a colt, or breeder or trainer of colts, was first given this name as a surname. In America it is reminiscent of the Colt revolving-breech pistol, or revolver, the brainchild of 19th-century inventor Samuel Colt.

Colter OE. Occupational name: "Colt-herd."

Colton OE. Place name: "Dark settlement" or possibly "Colt-settlement" or "Cole's settlement." This rather neutral name is used with surprising frequency.
Coleton, Colilton, Colston

Colum Lat. "Dove." Short for Columba or Columban. Saint Columba was a 6th-century Irish missionary who founded a monastery on the Scottish island of Iona. His contemporary, Saint Columban, also Irish, was a missionary in France, Switzerland, and Italy. Actor Colm Wilkinson.
Calum, Callum, Collumbano, Colm, Colombain, Columbano, Columbanus, Columcille

Columbus Variant of the Latin word meaning "dove." Christopher Columbus, of course, was the Italian explorer who discovered America. The name is used from time to time by parents with a taste for the exotic.
Colombe, Colombo

Colville OF. Place name of Norman origin and obscure meaning
Colvile, Colvill

Colwyn Welsh. Place name, for a river in Wales.
Colwin, Colwynn

Comanche Name of a Native American tribe. Indigenous to the Great Plains, they were expert horsemen who opposed European annexation of the West.

Como Lat. "Province." Place name: a province and lake in Northern Italy. Como is exceptionally beautiful.

Comstock OE. Unclear meaning. The Comstock Lode of silver in Nevada, discovered by scout and trapper Henry Comstock, was the richest silver mine in America in the 19th century.

Comus Greek myth name: Comus was the Greek god of mirth and hilarity. He is usually represented in art as a young man with a torch and a goblet.

Concord ME. "Peace." A Puritan virtue name and also a place name: the capital city of New Hampshire and the small town northwest of Boston linked with the American Revolution and later home to a bevy of 19th-century literary figures.

Conan Ir. Gael. "High, lifted up." Taken to Ireland some time after the Norman Conquest, but almost unknown un-

til the fame of Sherlock Holmes's creator, Sir Arthur Conan Doyle. A more modern example is the movie character Conan the Barbarian, whose creators were probably unaware of the name's previous use or origin. Talk show host Conan O'Brien.
Con, Conant, Conn, Connie

Conlan Ir. Gael. "Hero."
Conlen, Conley, Conlin, Conlon, Connlyn

Connor Ir. Gael. "High longing" or possibly "Lover of wolves." A name whose appeal has extended well beyond the Irish community. Irish author Conor Cruise O'Brien.
Conor

Conrad OG. "Courageous advice." Despite occasional increases in its numbers, a name that has never been widely popular in English-speaking countries. In the Middle Ages, several German kings bore this name, however. Anthropologist Konrad Lorenz; hotelier Conrad Hilton; author Joseph Conrad.
Con, Connie, Conrade, Conrado, Corrado, Cort, Curt, Konrad, Kort, Kurt

Conroy Ir. Gael. "Wise man."

Constantine Lat. "Steadfast." The form Constant was popular among the Puritans (as a virtue name) and was revived in the 19th century to occasional modern use. Constantine, the Latin form, was the name of the first Roman emperor and eleven Byzantine emperors, as well as a royal name in Greece. The Russian czars, in a bid to legitimize Russia as the new home of Orthodoxy, also used the name. Steady 19th-century use has now dwindled to neglect.
Constans, Constant, Constantin, Constantino, Constantius, Constanz, Costa, Konstantin, Konstantio, Konstanz

Consuel Sp. "Consolation."
Consuelo

Conway Welsh. "Holy river" or Ir. Gael. "Hound of the plain." Rare. Musician Conway Twitty.
Conwy

Coney ME. "Rabbit."

Cook Lat. "Cook." Occupational name, one of the fifty most common surnames in England, but an unusual first name in the 20th century.
Cooke, Cookie

Cooper OE. Occupational name: "Barrel maker." Novelist James Fenimore Cooper; actor Gary Cooper.

Coop

Cope ME. "Cape." This is probably an occupational name referring to the long cape worn by a bishop of the Catholic or Anglican church.

Corbin Lat. "Dark as a raven." Most common in the 19th century. Actor Corbin Bernsen.

Corbet, Corbett, Corbie, Corbit, Corbitt, Corby, Corbyn, Cory, Korbyn

Corcoran Ir. Gael. "Ruddy." A 19th-century financier, William Corcoran, founded a significant art gallery in Washington, D.C.

Cochran, Cork, Korcoran

Cordell OF. Occupational name: "Rope maker." Used with some regularity among African-American families. Football player Kordell Stewart.

Cord, Cordas, Cordelle, Kordell, Kordelle

Corey Ir. Gael. Place name: "The hollow." Transferred to a surname and used as a first name for either sex. Also diminutive for "Cor-" names. It is currently much more popular for boys, perhaps because golfer Corey Pavin keeps it in the limelight as a masculine name. Actor Corey Feldman.

Correy, Corrie, Corry, Cory, Currie, Curry

Corin Lat. "Spear." The name, which refers both to a male saint and to an early Roman god of war, is more commonly given to boys. As a girl's name, it may even be a variant of Corinne. Actor Corin Redgrave.

Coren, Corrin, Cyran, Koren, Korin, Korrin

Cormick Gael. "Chariot driver."

Cormac, Cormack, Cormic

Cork Ir. Gael. Place name: "Swamp, marsh." A seaport, city, and county in Ireland.

Corliss OE. "Benevolent, cheery."

Corless, Corley

Cornelius Lat. "Like a horn." Comes from a famous Latin clan name, and was often used under the Roman Empire. Turns up from time to time, usually as a family name. Railroad millionaire Cornelius Vanderbilt.

Con, Connie, Cornall, Corneille, Cornelious, Cornell, Cornelus, Corney, Cornilius, Kornelious, Kornelis, Kornelius, Neal, Neel, Neil, Neely

Cornell Fr. Var. **Cornelius**. Cornell University, in Ithaca, N.Y., was founded by 19th-century telegraph pioneer Ezra Cornell. He was for a while the largest stockholder in Western Union.

Cornall, Cornel, Corney

Cornwallis OE. "Man from Cornwall." Surname transferred to a first name in the 19th century. In the Revolutionary War, famous English general George Cornwallis lost the battle of Yorktown to Washington and Lafayette, but was later more successful putting down other colonial rebellions in India and Ireland.

Corridon Ir. Gael. "Spear." An unusual Irish last name.

Cort OG. "Brave." Actor Bud Cort.

Corty, Court, Kort

Cortez Sp. last name: may mean "Court-dweller." May also refer to explorer Hernán Cortés, who conquered Mexico for Spain in the 16th century.

Cortes, Kortes, Kortez

Corwin OE. "Heart's friend or companion."

Corwan, Corwinn, Corwyn, Corwynn

Corydon Gk. "Battle-ready."

Coridon, Coryden, Coryell

Cosgrove Ir. Gael. "Victorious champion."

Cosgrave

Cosmo Gk. "Orderliness, organization." Saint Cosmas, a martyr, was patron saint of the Italian city of Milan, and the name was further spread there by the fame of Cosimo de' Medici, Grand Duke of Tuscany. His friend the Duke of Gordon took the name to Britain in the 17th century, but it was never widely used and is now the name of an American soccer team.

Cosimo, Cosmé, Kosmo

Costas Gr. Var. **Constantine** (Lat. "Steadfast"). Sportscaster Bob Costas.

Costa, Kostas, Kostis

Coster OE. "Peddler." The full word was "costermonger," which meant "seller of costards." Costards were a kind of cooking apple.

Cotton Plant name. May originally have been an occupational name from England, though the cotton plant, requiring a warm climate, was never a big source of industry in Britain. In the U.S., use may refer to the great Massachusetts clergyman Cotton Mather, whose writings contributed to the Salem witch trials. He was named for his grandfather, early American clergyman John Cotton. Actor Joseph Cotten.
Cotten

Coty Fr. Possibly "small hillside." More likely, however, to be a respelling of the popular Cody.

Coulson Surname derived from Nicholas (Gk. "People of victory"), mostly 19th-century use. Minister Charles Colson.
Colson

Council Lat. "Group of people."
Counsel

Courtland OE. Place name: "Land of the court."
Cortland, Cortlandt, Court, Courtlandt

Courtney OE. "Court-dweller." Surname transferred to first name; usually feminine in U.S., though still given to boys. Immensely popular for girls in the late eighties, which will probably limit its use as a boy's name in the future. Actor Tom Courtenay, actor Courtney Vance.
Cortney, Courtenay, Courtnay, Curt

Covert ME. Place name: "Shelter." Refers to a small area of woods that gives shelter to game.
Couvert

Covell OE. Place name: "Slope with the cave."

Covey ME. "Brood of birds." Author Stephen Covey.
Covvey

Covington OE. Place name: "Settlement near the cave."

Cowan Ir. Gael. Place name: "Hollow in the hill."
Coe

Cowrie Shell name: cowrie shells have long been used as currency in eastern Africa, and have a significant place in African American culture.
Courey, Cowrey, Cowry

Coy Unclear meaning: possibly "woods" or "quiet place."
Coye

Coyle Ir. Gael. "Follows the battle."

Cox ME. Occupational name: "Coxswain." A coxswain used to be in charge of the rowboats aboard large ships.
Coxe, Coxey

Craddock Welsh. "Love." Anglicization of a Welsh name, more common as a surname.
Caradoc, Caradog, Cradock

Craig Gael. "Rock." (Think "crag.") Surname that has become very popular since its introduction as a first name only fifty years ago. Though not exactly fashionable now, Craig is still steadily used. Baseball player Graig Nettles.
Graig, Craigie, Craik, Kraig

Cramer OG. "Peddler." A "cram" was a peddler's pack, and our term "to cram together" comes from that word.
Cram, Kram, Kramer

Crandall OE. Place name: "Valley of cranes." A dell is another term for a small valley, familiar to most of us from the song "The Farmer in the Dell." Yes, that's what that meant.
Crandal, Crandell

Crane OE. "Crane." This fairly common last name was probably an occupational name referring to the simple hoisting machine that resembles the long-legged bird. Cranes have been in use since early times.
Crain, Craine, Crayn, Crayne

Cranford OE. Place name: "Ford with the crane." This name probably refers to the water-dwelling birds.
Cranfurd

Cranley OE. Place name: "Meadow with the cranes."
Cranlee, Cranleigh, Cranly

Cranston OE. Place name: "Settlement of cranes." U.S. Senator Alan Cranston.

Craven OE. Last name, formerly place name, of unclear meaning. As an adjective, however, the usual definition is "cowardly." Mostly 19th-century use.

Crawford OE. Place name: "Ford of the crows." Particularly well used in Scotland, as both a surname and a given name.
Crawfurd

Cree Native Canadian tribe: the Cree originated in areas from Quebec to Alberta. Some of the guides for the famous Northwest explorations of North America came from Cree tribes, as they were great warriors and travelers.

Creed From Lat. *Credo*, "I believe." A creed is a statement of belief, usually religious.

Creek Place name: "Small river." Such an important feature of any rural landscape that there are many local terms for it: brook, burn, etc.

Creik

Creighton OE. Place name: "Rocky spot."

Crayton, Crichton

Cresswell OE. Place name: "Well where watercress grows."

Carswell, Creswell, Creswill

Crisanto Sp. from Gk. "Gold flower." Usually refers to a chrysanthemum. Possibly because of the name (which sounds like "holy Christ") as many as eight minor saints of this name have been venerated, but they are no longer acknowledged by the Catholic church.

Cresento, Crisento, Crizant, Crizanto

Crispin Lat. "Curly-haired." Saint Crispin, supposedly a 3rd-century martyr (though there is some doubt about his legend), is patron of shoemakers, and Henry V fought the battle of Agincourt on his feast day, October 25. The name was somewhat popular in Britain in the 17th and 18th centuries, and was revived in the 1960s, but has not spread to the U.S. in significant numbers. Actor Crispin Glover.

Crépin, Crispian, Crispino, Crispo, Crispus, Crisspin

Crockett ME. "Crook." Probably an occupational name, and the crook referred to is a shepherd's crook. Author Crockett Johnson; frontiersman David Crockett.

Crock, Crocket, Croquet, Croquett, Krock

Crofton OE. "Settlement of the cottages."

Croft, Crofft, Croffton

Cromwell OE. Place name: "Winding stream." Limited use as a first name, probably out of admiration for 17th-century English reformer Oliver Cromwell. Actor James Cromwell.

Cronus Greek myth name: the youngest Titan (predecessors of the Greek gods) and father of Zeus, Hades, Poseidon, and Demeter. He ruled over earth until he was

overthrown by the Olympian gods, his children.
Cronan, Kronos

Crook OE. Occupational name: "Crook." As with Crockett, the name probably indicates a shepherd ancestor.
Crooke, Crookes, Crooks

Crosby Scand. Place name: "At the cross." Singer Bing Crosby.
Crosbey, Crosbie

Crosley OE. Place name: "Meadow of the cross."
Croslea, Crosleigh, Crosly, Crosslee, Crossley, Crosslie

Crowell OE. Place name: "Well at the cross." The "cross" might refer to a spot where two roads cross.

Crowther OE. Occupational name: "Fiddler."
Crothers

Cruz Sp. "Cross."

Cuba Place name: the largest island in the West Indies, since 1959 a Communist country under the control of Fidel Castro. Actor Cuba Gooding, Jr.

Cullen Ir. Gael. "Handsome." Poet William Cullen Bryant.
Cullan, Cullin, Cullinan

Culley Ir. Gael. Place name: "The woods."
Cully

Culver OE. "Dove." Related to Colum and Columba, the Latin forms.
Colver, Cully

Cunningham Ir. Gael. "Village of the milk pail." Football player Randall Cunningham.
Conyngham, Cunninghame

Curley OE. "Strong man." Related to Charles, via Anglo-Saxon *ceorl*, or "churl."

Curragh Ir. Gael. "Moor." Also a place name: a plain in Kildare in Ireland where the army trained, also the site of a famous racecourse.

Curran Ir. Gael. "Hero."
Currey, Currie, Curry

Currier ME. Occupational name: "Groom, one who curries a horse." Currying in this case means brushing. This may also be a corruption of "courier," or messenger.
Currie, Curry

Curt Dim. **Courtney, Curtis, Conrad**. Most common in

the U.S., but not often a given name. Musician Kurt Cobain; actor Kurt Russell.

Kurt

Curtis OF. "Polite, courteous." Surname used as first name, notably in the U.S. since the 1950s. Used quite steadily. General Curtis Le May; golfer Curtis Strange.

Curcio, Curt, Curtell, Curtice, Curtiss, Kurtis

Custodio Sp. "Guardian." Refers to the guardian angels of mankind.

Cuthbert OE. "Famous, brilliant." Saint Cuthbert was a much-loved 7th-century English bishop. He was most famous in northern England and Scotland, and his name was most common there, though it fell out of favor after the 1930s. Never popular in America.

Cutler OE. Occupational name: "Knife maker."

Cyprian Gk. "From Cyprus." Steadily used in Britain until the 17th century, but never transferred to the U.S.

Ciprian, Cipriano, Ciprien, Cyprien

Cyrano Gk. "From Cyrene." Use is bound to recall Edmond Rostand's popular play *Cyrano de Bergerac* (1897), based on the life of the 17th-century author and swashbuckler of that name.

Cyril Gk. "The lord." Popularity confined to Britain, from the turn of the century to the 1930s. Actor Cyril Ritchard.

Ciril, Cirilio, Cyrill, Cyrille, Cirillo, Cyrillus, Cirilo, Kiril, Kyril

Cyrus Per. "Sun" or "Throne." Famous Persian emperor who appears in the Old Testament; he allowed exiled Jews to rebuild Jerusalem. Puritan use brought it to the U.S., where it was somewhat popular, but faded in modern times. Inventor Cyrus McCormick; former Secretary of State Cyrus Vance.

Ciro, Cy

Dabney OF. Place name: "From Aubigny." This is an old Virginia name, given with pride to establish a connection with a 1649 immigrant to the New World named Cornelius d'Aubigny. It is used for both boys and girls. Actor Dabney Coleman.

Dabnee, Dabnie, Dabny

Dacey Ir. Gael. "From the South" or Lat. "From Dacia," an area that is now Romania. The form Dacian enjoyed a burst of popularity in the 1970s along with other "-ian" names like Damian and Dorian.

Dace, Dacian, Dacius, Dacy, Daicey, Daicy

Dack Origin unclear. The name may be considered a variant of Dag (ONorse, "Day"), but it would be unknown without the fame of actor Dack Rambo.

Daedalus Gk. "Craftsman." In Greek myth, Daedalus was the designer of King Minos's labyrinth. So as not to lose the services of this master craftsman, Minos had him imprisoned in the labyrinth. To escape, Daedalus made wings from wax and feathers for himself and his son Icarus. Icarus, however, disregarding his father's instructions, flew too close to the sun. The wax in his wings melted and he fell into the sea and died.

Daidalos, Dedalus

Dag Scand. "Daylight." In Norse mythology the god Dag is the son of light. Diplomat and author Dag Hammarskjöld.

Dagget, Daggett, Dagny

Dagan Heb. "Grain, the earth."

Dagon

Dagobert OG. "Bright day, shining day." Most familiar, probably, in the Spanish form Dagoberto. Many of these old German names (like Adalgiso and Braulio) survive in Spanish form. This may date back to the days when Spain and the German princedoms formed part of the Holy Ro-

man Empire, although many of these names are al[...]
names of obscure saints, long venerated in the Spanish
church. This name may be the source for the racial slur
"dago." It is almost certainly the source for the cartoon
character Dogbert.

Dagbert, Dagoberto

Dagon Aramaic: meaning unknown. Old Testament name:
Dagon was a god of the Canaanites.

Dagwood OE. Place name: "Shining forest." Virtually
preempted by a character from the popular comic strip
Blondie. Dagwood was the harassed husband of a dizzy
blonde and the name is still occasionally found on menus
as the name of a sandwich.

Dahy Ir. Gael. "Quick-footed."

Dahey

Dai Welsh. "To shine." Also a nickname for David.

Dailey Ir. Gael. "Assembly." Daly is another common
form of this name.

Daley, Daly, Daily

Dainard OE. "Bold Dane."

**Danehard, Danehardt, Daneard, Daneardt, Dainehard,
Dainhard, Daynard**

Daivat Hindi. "Power, strength."

Dakota American place name: the word may be Sioux for
"allies," though another source suggests "forever smiling." Despite its "-a" ending, this name is used (perhaps
because of the percussive consonants or the ruggedness it
evokes) for both boys and girls. Used with some regularity. Furniture designer Dakota Jackson.

**Daccota, Dakoda, Dakodah, Dakoeta, Dakotah, Dekota,
Dekohta, Dekowta**

Dalbert OE. "Bright-shining one."

Del, Delbert

Dale OE. Place name: "Valley." Originally a surname
meaning "one who lives in the valley." The term "dale"
is still used in parts of England. Most famous as a first
name in the 1930s. The fame of Roy Rogers' consort Dale
Evans may have made this a girl's name. Success guru
Dale Carnegie.

Daile, Daley, Dallan, Dalle, Dallin, Dayle

Dallas Scot. Gael. Place name: a village in northeastern
Scotland, used as a first name since the 19th century and

apparently unrelated to Dallas, Texas, which was named for a U.S. vice president. Few modern Americans, however, will fail to make the connection between the name and the city.

Dal, Dalles, Dallis, Delles

Dallin OE. Place name: "From the valley." Related to Dale.

Dallan, Dallen, Dallon

Dalton OE. Place name: "The settlement in the valley." Novelist Dalton Trumbo.

Daleton, Dalton, Dalten

Daly Ir. Gael. "Assembly." Common Irish surname, used since the 1940s as a first name. Decathlon champion Daley Thompson.

Daley, Dawley

Dalziel Scot. Gael. Place name: "The small field."

Damario Sp./Gk. "Calf." This is more familiar (though still scarce) as a girl's name, **Damaris**.

Damarios, Damarius, Damaro, Damero

Damaskenos Gk. "From Damascus." Damascus is an ancient city in what is now Syria.

Damascus, Damaskinos

Damek Slavic. Var. **Adam** (Heb. "Son of the red earth)."

Adamec, Adamek, Adamik, Adamok, Adham, Damick, Damicke

Damian Gk. Meaning not clear: possibly "To tame," although the Greek root is also close to the word for "spirit." The name was revived in various forms (Damon, Damien) in the 1950s, having been neglected since the Middle Ages. Still quite steadily used. Author Damon Runyon; ballet dancer Damien Woetzel.

Daemon, Daimen, Daimon, Daman, Damen, Dameon, Damian, Damiano, Damianos, Damianus, Damien, Damion, Damon, Damyan, Damyen, Damyon, Dayman, Daymian, Daymon, Demyan

Dan Dim. **Daniel** (Heb. "God is my judge"). Used from time to time on its own. Actors Dan Ackroyd, Dan Blocker.

Dana OE. "From Denmark." Also possibly a place name referring to an English river. Surname first used as a boy's name in the 19th century, but now almost exclusively a girl's name, and a specifically American one. In 1840 Boston writer Richard Henry Dana, Jr. published the maritime classic *Two Years Before the Mast*, about his voyage in a sailing ship around Cape Horn to California. Artist Charles Dana Gibson; actor Dana Carvey.

Dane, Danie

Danar Invented name, taken from *Star Trek*. The character Danar is a magnificent human specimen.

Danaus Gk. myth name: a king whose fifty daughters married the fifty sons of his brother Aegiptos.

Denaus, Dinaus

Dane OE. "Dane." In the days when England was subject to regular invasions from Scandinavia, a Dane may have been an enemy. This form of the name is now more popular than Dana for boys. Actor Dane Clark.

Dain, Daine, Dayne

Daniel Heb. "God is my judge." In the famous Old Testament story, Daniel is thrown into a den of lions because he insists on praying to his God while a captive in Babylon; he was, of course, rescued by the same God. The name has been used with moderate frequency until a spurt of popularity in the late 1950s, which endured until today; Daniel is still quite common without being trendy. Today's parents may have fond memories of the TV-inspired "Daniel Boone" coonskin hats they wore in the 1960s. Novelist Daniel Defoe; entertainers Danny Thomas, Danny Kaye; Senator Daniel Patrick Moynihan; actors Daniel Day-Lewis, Danny De Vito, Danny Aiello.

Dan, Danal, Dane, Daneal, Danek, Dani, Danial, Daniele, Danil, Danilo, Danko, Dannel, Dannie, Danny, Danyal, Danyel, Deiniol

Dante Lat. "Lasting, enduring." Actually a nickname, since Italian poet Dante Alighieri's full name was Durante, and modern use of the name almost always refers to him. English artist Dante Gabriel Rossetti.

Dantae, Dantay, Dontae, Dontay, Donté

Danton Fr. May mean "from Anton," a place name, or may refer to an ancestor named Anthony. *Dantan* means "long ago" in poetic French. The famous Danton this name calls to mind, though, is Georges Danton, one of the key figures in the French revolution.

Danube Geography name: the second largest river in Eu

rope, it wanders through Germany, Austria, Hungary, and finally empties into the Black Sea.
Donau

Daphnis Greek myth name. Daphnis (not to be confused with the female Daphne) appears in two tales as a love-struck shepherd. The more widely known story is the pastoral romance of Daphnis and Chloë.

Daquan Invented name. Parents who invent names for boys generally stop at two syllables, though girls' names often run on to three. The "qu-" sound, which occurs so rarely in English, is a popular element of invented names in the African-American community.
Daquanne, Dequan, Dequanne, Dekwan, Dekwohn, Dekwohnne

Dar Heb. "Pearl."

Darby OE. Place name: "Park with deer." Derived from Derby, a surname used as a first name. Darby is occasionally used for girls.
Darbey, Darbie, Derby

Darcy Ir. Gael. "Dark." Also Norman place name, "from Arcy." It was possibly this connotation of Norman aristocracy that Jane Austen sought when she named the haughty hero of *Pride and Prejudice* "Mr. Darcy." In Britain, more likely to be a boy's name, but in the U.S., more likely to be feminine.
D'Arcy, Darcey, Darsey, Darsy

Dardanos Greek mythology name: the founder of Troy and the surrounding country, Dardania. He was a son of Zeus.
Dard, Dardanio, Dardanios, Dardanus

Darian Invented name. Adrian, Darius, Marion, Darren: this name includes a number of familiar elements combined in a new way. This process is increasingly popular with today's parents. See **Darrien**.
Darien, Darion, Darrian, Darrien, Darrion

Darius Gk. "Rich, kingly." Darius the Great was a renowned emperor of Persia in the 5th century B.C., who permitted the Jews to rebuild the temple in Jerusalem. The name is especially popular with African American parents. Composer Darius Milhaud.
Darias, Dariess, Dario, Darious, Darrius, Derrius, Derry

Darnell OE. Place name: "The hidden spot."
Darnall, Darnel

Darnley ME. Place name: "Grassy meadow." Darnel is a specific kind of grass. This name resonates with history beyond the mere place it commemorates, however: Henry Stewart, Lord Darnley, was the second husband of Mary, Queen of Scots, and father of James VI of Scotland and I of England.

Darold Invented name: Harold with a "D."
Darrold

Darrah Ir. Gael. "Dark oak." This was originally an Irish last name.
Darach, Darragh

Darrel Transferred surname, possibly originated as a French place name, like Darcy. There are many forms, of which Darryl is the favorite by a nose. In fact, that spelling, and the popularity of the name in the 1950s, may stem from the fame of film producer Darryl Zanuck. Baseball star Darryl Strawberry; musician Daryl Hall.
Darral, Darrell, Darrill, Darrol, Darroll, Darry, Darryl, Darryll, Daryl, Derrel, Derrell, Derril, Derrill, Deryl, Deryll

Darren Ir. Gael. "Great." Originally a surname, first used as a given name in this century. Its popularity was probably influenced by the TV series *Bewitched*, in which the rather hapless leading man was named Darren. Though hardly fashionable, it is still very steadily used.
Daren, Darin, Daron, Darran, Darrin, Darring, Darron, Darryn, Derrin, Derron

Darrien Modern combined name: possibly an elaborated form of Darren or a retooling of Dorian. It is possible, but unlikely, that this name is a reference to the eastern part of Panama known as Darien, which later gave its name to one of New York City's poshest suburbs. John Keats's famous sonnet "On First Looking Into Chapman's Homer" ends by comparing the poet's wonder to that of Cortés, glimpsing the Pacific Ocean for the first time "Silent, upon a peak in Darien."
Darian, Darion, Darrian, Darrion, Darryan, Darryen

Darrow OE. "Spear." Use may be a tribute to the great labor lawyer Clarence Darrow.
Darro

Darshan Sanskrit. "Vision."

E. Place name: the river Dart is a small river in southern England. Dartmouth is a town at the mouth of the river. A dart, of course, is also a small arrow.

D'Artagnan OF. "From Artagnan." D'Artagnan is one of the central characters in the famous Alexandre Dumas novel *The Three Musketeers*.

Darton OE. Place name: "Settlement of the deer."

Darwin OE. "Dear friend." Naturalist Charles Darwin.
Darwon, Darwyn, Derwin, Derwynn

Dathan Heb. Meaning unclear: possibly "spring" or "fountain." In the Old Testament, Dathan rebelled against Moses.

Davenport OF. Unknown origin. The word is occasionally used as a term for a large sofa. It is a place name and a last name in the U.S.

Davian Modern combined name: David plus Ian, or David plus Dorian.
Daivian, Daivyan, Davien, Davion, Davyan, Davyen, Davyon

David Heb. "Dear one." In the Old Testament, the young David used his slingshot to kill the mighty giant Goliath, and went on to become King of Israel and author of the Psalms. He has been a favorite subject of artists, notably sculptors of the Italian Renaissance like Michelangelo and Donatello. Saint David is the patron saint of Wales, so the name is popular there, and in Scotland, where David was a royal name. In the U.S. the name is used by Jewish and Christian families alike, and has been in the top ten boys' names for the last forty years. Explorer David Livingstone; actor David Niven; baseball star Dave Winfield; TV host David Letterman; musician David Bowie.
Daffy, Daffyd, Dafydd, Dai, Dave, Daven, Davey, Davi, Davie, Davidde, Davide, Davidson, Davie, Davies, Davin, Davis, Davon, Davy, Davyd, Davydd

Davis OE. "David's son." Contraction of surname that cropped up in the Middle Ages. Confederate President Jefferson Davis; actor Brad Davis.
Dave, Davidson, Davies, Davison, Daviss, Davy

Dawson OE. "David's son." Another form of the medieval surname.
Daw, Dawe, Dawes

Day OE. "Day." Familiar as a last name but scarce as a first name. Author Clarence Day.

Daye

Dayanand Hindi. "He who loves compassion."

Daymond Modern name: Raymond with a "D." Resemblance to Damon makes it sound familiar.

Daimond

Dayton OE. Place name: possibly "Day's settlement" or "David's settlement." Also a city in Ohio.

Daytan, Dayten

Deacon Gk. "Messenger." A deacon is a Christian clergyman, usually lower in the hierarchy than the minister or pastor. Football player Deacon Jones.

Deakin, Deecon, Deekon, Diakonos

Dean OE. Place name: "Valley," or occupational name: "Church official." Surname used as a first name, mostly since the 1950s. Actor Dean Martin; U.S. Secretaries of State Dean Acheson, Dean Rusk.

Deane, Deen, Dene, Deyn, Dino

DeAndré Modern name: André with the prefix "De-." Names for boys are, as a rule, more conservative than names for girls. Even African-American parents, who show great invention in choosing their children's names, tend to be less adventurous, but DeAndré is common enough to be on some popularity lists.

D'André, DeAndrae, DeAndray, Diandray, Diondrae, Diondray

DeAngelo Modern name: Angelo with the prefix "De-." The least common of these "De-" names.

D'Angelo, DiAngelo

Dearborn OE. Place name: "Brook of the deer."

Dearbourn, Dearburne, Deerborn

Debonair Fr. "Urbane, nonchalant." Perhaps a Norman family name: it could have meant "of good lineage." To moderns, debonair is the word you use to describe Fred Astaire.

Debonnair, Debonnaire

Decatur Last name of unclear origin. There is a process called "decating" in the manufacture of cloth. "Deca-" is the Greek word particle meaning "ten," but it might also mean "pure," as Catherine does. The name is probably used in tribute to Stephen Decatur, an early 19th-century naval hero. There are several U.S. towns named for him.

Deccan Place name: an area in central India.

Decimus Lat. "Tenth," as in tenth child. In the 1990s, opportunities for use seem negligible.
Decio

Declan Ir. Unknown meaning: name of a saint, popular in Ireland. The singer Elvis Costello was born Declan Patrick McManus.

Dedrick Var. **Theodoric** (OG. "The people's ruler"). Also the source for the better-known Derek. Football player Dedric Ward.
Dedric, Diederick, Dietrich

Dee Scot. Place name: a significant river that runs into the North Sea at Aberdeen.

Deems OE. "Judge's child."

Deepak Sanskrit. "Little lamp." Author Deepak Chopra.
Dipak

DeForest ME. Place name: "Living near the forest."
Defforest

DeJuan Modern name: Juan with the "De-" prefix.
DaJuan, DaJuwan, DeJuwan, DeWuan, DeWonn

Dekel Heb. "Palm tree."

Delaney Ir. Gael. Meaning unclear: possibly "Offspring of the challenger." May also have something to do with "swarthy," or be a place name referring to the Slaney river.
Delaine, Delainey, Delainy, Delane, Delany

Delano OF. Surname of unclear origin: possibly "nighttime" (*de la nuit*) or "nut tree" (*de la noix*). It would be merely one of those odd family names if it had not been made famous by U.S. President Franklin Delano Roosevelt.

Delbert OE. "Day-bright." Also possibly a variant of **Albert** (**Adelbert**), OE. "Highborn, brilliant." The title of a very popular comic strip is the variation **Dilbert**.
Bert, Bertie, Dalbert, Dilbert

Delius Gk. "From Delos." Delos is a tiny Greek island that was sacred to the ancient Greeks, who believed that Apollo and Artemis had been born there.
Deli, Delios, Delos

Dell OE. Place name: "Small valley." As in the old song "The Farmer in the Dell." May also be a diminutive of names like Delbert or Odell.

Delling ONorse. "Scintillating."

Delmore OF. "Of the sea." The more familiar form, at least as a place name, is the Spanish Delmar. Use is American only. Poet Delmore Schwartz.

Delmar, Delmer, Delmor

Delphin Gk. "Dolphin." This is a French form of a name with a complex origin. It alludes to the Greek town of Delphi, home of a famous oracle. The Greeks believed that Delphi was the earth's womb; the dolphin's shape resembles that of a pregnant woman. A 4th-century French bishop, later a saint, was named Delphin. The feminine form, **Delphine**, has survived much better than this form.

Delfin, Delfino, Delfinos, Delfinus, Delphino, Delphinos, Delphinus, Delvin

Delroy Fr. "The king." More common forms are Elroy and Leroy.

Delroi

Delwin OE. "Proud friend" or "Bright friend."

Dalwin, Dalwyn, Delavan, Delevan, Dellwin, Delwyn, Delwynn

DeMarcus Modern name: Marcus with the prefix "De-." Marcus also tends to shade into Marquez, which comes from an entirely different root.

Damarcus, DaMarkiss, DeMarco, Demarkess, DeMarko, Demarkus, DeMarquess, DeMarquez, DeMarquiss

Demas Biblical name: a companion who forsook Paul. This may be the source for Deems, another obscure name.

Dimas

Demetrius Gk. "Follower of Demeter." It has been little used in English-speaking countries, though its Greek and Russian forms are well known in those countries. Lately, however, the urge toward exoticism in the U.S. (or perhaps high levels of immigration) has brought it to more frequent use. On one list, Demetrius ranks above old standbys like Albert, Glenn, and Arthur. Composer Dimitri Shostakovich.

Dametrius, Demetri, Demetrice, Demetris, Demitrios,

Dhimitrios, Dimetre, Dimitri, Dimitrios, Dimitrious, Dimitry, Dmitri, Dmitrios, Dmitry

Demos Gk. "The people." Also possibly homage to Greece's most famous orator, Demosthenes. This is the word that forms the root of "democracy." Rare, even in Greece.

Demas

Dempsey Ir. Gael. "Proud." Boxer Jack Dempsey.

Dempsy

Dempster OE. "One who judges." Gossip columnist Nigel Dempster.

Denali Geography name: Mount McKinley, over 20,000 feet high and America's highest mountain, rises out of Denali National Park in Alaska. Denali means "the big one" in the language of the Athabaskan Indians.

Denby Scand. Place name: "The Danes' village." Film critic David Denby.

Danby, Denbey, Denney, Dennie, Denny

Denham OE. Place name: "Village in a valley."

Denholm Scot. Place name. In the public eye currently because of the English actor Denholm Elliott.

Denley OE. Place name: "Meadow near the valley."

Denlie, Denly

Denman OE. Surname derived from place name: "Man who lives in the valley."

Denmark Geography: name of one of the Scandinavian countries. Also a possibly combined name, marrying Dennis and Mark.

Dennis Gk. "Follower of Dionysius." Dionysos was the classical Greek god of wine, but the name also appears in the New Testament. Saint Denis is the patron saint of France. The name has had alternating centuries of favor and disfavor (16th out, 17th in), reaching the height of its 20th-century popularity around 1920. Actors Dennis Quaid, Dennis Christopher, Dennis Hopper; sailor Dennis Conner.

Den, Denies, Denis, Dennes, Dennet, Denney, Dennie, Dennison, Denny, Dennys, Denys, Deon, Dion, Dionisio, Dionysius, Dionysus, Diot

Dennison OE. "Son of Dennis."

Den, Denison, Dennyson, Tennyson

Denton OE. Place name: "Settlement in the valley."
Denny, Dent, Denten, Dentin

Denver OE. Place name: "Green valley." The Colorado capital was named after the 19th-century governor of the Kansas Territory, James W. Denver. The late singer John Denver.

Denzel Cornish place name, used as a first name almost exclusively in Britain. Actor Denzel Washington.
Denzell, Denziel, Denzil, Denzill, Denzyl

Deodar Sanskrit. "Divine wood." The name of an exceptionally tall species of cedar, native to India, that is also grown in California and England, where it is sometimes known as the "god tree."

Deon Var. **Dion**. See below.

Derby OE. Place name: "Park with deer." Variant spelling of Darby. The English, in their confusing way, pronounce this word "Darby." This is also the name of a hat with a hard round crown, and America's most famous horse race, the Kentucky Derby. The race got its name from the English Derby, which was instituted by the Earl of Derby in 1780.
Derbey, Derbie

Derek OG. "The people's ruler." Most common of the many anglicized forms of Theodoric, popular starting around 1890, peaking in the 1930s, but still in the top fifty names for boys. Basketball player Derrick Coleman.
Darrick, Darriq, Dereck, Deric, Derick, Derik, Deriq, Derk, Derreck, Derrek, Derrick, Derrik, Derryck, Derryk, Deryk, Deryke, Dirk, Dirke, Dyrk

Derland OE. "Land with deer."
Durland

Dermot Ir. Gael. "Without envy."
Dermott, Diarmid, Diarmuid

DeRon Modern name: Ron with the "De-" prefix. Depending on where the accent lies, this could be a variation of Darren.
Daron, DeRronn

Derry Ir. Gael. Place name: City in Northern Ireland formerly known as Londonderry. Also short form of Derek, Dermot, etc. Photographer Derry Moore.
Derrie

Derward OE. "Deer keeper."
Durward

Derwent OE. Place name: there are three rivers called "Derwent" in England, possibly from the ancient word *dwr*, meaning "water."

Derwin OE. "Dear friend."
Darwin, Darwyn, Derwyn, Derwynn, Durwin

Deshan Hindi. "Of the nation."
Deshad, Deshal

DeShawn Modern name: Shawn with the "De-" prefix.
Dashaun, Dashawn, Desean, DeShaun, D'Shawn

Desiderio It. "Desired." Several names come from this Latin root; the girl's name Desirée is analogous. Saint Desiderius was a 7th-century bishop and martyr in France. The name Didier, which is quite common in France, evolved from this root. Comedian Desi Arnaz.
Deri, Derito, Desi, Desideratus, Desiderios, Desiderius, Diderot, Didier, Dizier

Desmond Ir. Gael. "From South Munster." Munster was an ancient kingdom in Ireland. Used in England since 1900, and briefly popular around 1920, but unusual now. South African cleric and activist Bishop Desmond Tutu.
Des, Desmund, Dezmond

Detleff Germanic name of uncertain meaning and origin.
Detlef, Detlev

Deval Hindi. "Divine." The Sanskrit root *deva* means "god."
Deven

Deverell OE. Place name: "Bank of the river."

Devereux OF. Meaning unclear. Probably a place name having to do with water *(eau)*, or somehow related to the Old English Everard ("Board hardness").
Deveraux

Devin Ir. Gael. "Bard, poet," or possibly "Young deer." May also come from the French *divin*, meaning "divine." The name, spelled either this way or with an "o" instead of an "i," is also popular for girls, but is still used more often for boys.
Dev, Devinn, Devon, Devyn, Devynn

Devine Ir. Gael. "Ox" or OF. "Divine."

Devlin Ir. Gael. "Fierce courage."
Delvin, Devland, Devlen, Devlon, Devlyn

Devon English and American place name; Devon is a county in southwestern England, and several towns in the United States have been named after it. There is no clear-cut "feminine" or "masculine" spelling for this name, but the *o* spelling is somewhat more common for girls.
Deven, Devin, Devonn, Devyn

Dewey Welsh. Var. **David** (Heb. "Dear one"). Bookish parents may remember the Dewey Decimal System, invented by Melvil Dewey in 1876 and the organizing principle for the majority of American libraries until the Libary of Congress got in on the act and changed all the numbers.
Dewi, Dewie

DeWitt Flemish. "Blond." Early American statesman De Witt Clinton.
Dewitt, Dwight, Witt

Dexter Lat. "Right-handed" or OE. "Woman dyer." Modern use, more common in Britain. Football player Dexter Carter.
Dex

Diamond OE. "Bright guardian." Also, for girls, a jewel name. Actor Lou Diamond Phillips.

Diarmid Ir. Gael. "Free man." The anglicized version is Dermot.
Diarmaid, Diarmait, Diarmi

Dice ME. "Dice." The small numbered cubes used in games. Comedian Andrew Dice Clay.
Dyce

Dick Dim. **Richard** (OG. "Dominant ruler"); also **Frederick** (OG. "Peaceful ruler"). Figure skater Dick Button.

Dickinson OE. "Dick's son."

Didier Fr. "Much-desired." From **Desideratus**. Male form of **Desirée** currently popular in France.

Diego Sp. Var. **James** (Heb. "He who supplants"). The Mexican peasant to whom the Virgin of Guadalupe appeared was named Juan Diego. Painter Diego Rivera.
Dago

Dieter OG. "Army of the people."

Dietrich Ger. Form of **Theodoric** (OG. "People's ruler"). See **Derek**.
Dedrick, Derek, Deke, Diederick, Dirk

Digby ONorse. "Town by the ditch." Like many English surnames adapted from place names, became a first name in the late 19th century without ever becoming very widespread.

Diggory English name of uncertain meaning, though it may be a place name, referring to a dyke.
Diggery, Diggorey, Digory

Dillon Ir. Gael. "Loyal." Often confused with its popular homonym, the Welsh Dylan. Actor Matt Dillon.
Dillan, Dilon, Dyllon, Dylon

Dinesh Sanskrit. "Lord of the day" or "Sun." Writer Dinesh D'Souza.

Dingo Australian. The wild dogs of Australia, similar to foxes.

Dino Usually a diminutive of **Dean** or any number of names that end in "-dino," like **Bernardino**. Movie producer Dino DeLaurentiis.

Dinsmore Ir. Gael. Place name: "The hill fortress."
Dinnsmore

Diogenes Greek philosopher, a cynic and ascetic who believed that the simple life was the good life: taking this principle seriously, he is said to have lived in a tub.

Dion Probably short for Dionysius, but often used without reference to the longer name. Singer Dion (of Dion and the Belmonts); football player Deion Sanders.
Deion, Deon, Deonn, Deonys, Deyon

Dionysius Myth. name: Dionysius was the Greek god of wine (known to Romans as Bacchus). The name survived into the Christian era, possibly because of the man named Dionysius who was converted by Saint Paul, and is traditionally considered the first bishop of Athens. Dennis is an offshoot of this name.
Dion, Dionio, Dionisio, Dioniso, Dionysios, Dionysos, Dionysus

Dirk Var. **Derek** (OG. "The people's ruler"). "Dirk" is also the Scottish term for a small, very sharp knife. Flemish painter Dierick Bouts.
Dierck, Dieric, Dierick, Dirck

Dixon OE. "Son of Dick." Scottish surname transferred to first name. Author Dixon Wecter.
Dickson, Dix

Doane OE. Place name: "Low, rolling hills."
  Doan
Dobbs Possibly OE. Occupational name having to do with painting ("daubing"). May also be related to Robert.
Dodge OE. Name of unclear meaning; may be related to Roger. Dodge was a prominent name in American history even before the Dodge family began manufacturing cars.
  Dod, Dodds, Dodgson
Doherty Ir. Gael. "Harmful." Surname common in Ireland, transferred occasionally to first-name status.
  Docherty, Dougherty, Douherty
Dolan Ir. Gael. "Black-haired."
Dolph Dim. **Adolph** (OG. "Noble wolf"). Actor Dolf Lundgren.
  Dolf, Dollfus, Dollfuss, Dollphus, Dolphus
Dominic Lat. "Lord." A name popular among Catholic families possibly because of the fame of Saint Dominic, founder of an important monastic order. Use has spread since the 1950s. Still more common in Britain than the U.S. Clever for a child born on Sunday, "the Lord's day." The French version, Dominique, is often a girl's name in the U.S. Opera star Placido Domingo; basketball player Dominique Wilkins.
  Demenico, Demingo, Dom, Domenic, Domenico, Domenique, Domingo, Domini, Dominick, Dominie, Dominik, Dominique, Domino, Dominy, Nick
Domino Lat. "Lord, master." May refer to the rectangular game pieces marked with dots: in theory they are called dominoes because the loser of each game called out "Domino" to the winner.
Donahue Ir. Gael. "Dark fighter." TV host Phil Donahue.
  Donahoe, Donohoe, Donohue
Donald Scot. Gael. "World mighty." Common in Scotland for centuries, and popular elsewhere for some fifty years, peaking in 1925 but less popular since the 1950s, perhaps because Disney preempted the name by giving it to a cartoon duck. Nevertheless, it is still more common than either George or Peter. Actor Donald Sutherland; real estate tycoon Donald Trump; singer Donny Osmond.
  Donal, Donaldo, Donall, Donalt, Donaugh, Donel, Donelson, Donnel, Donnell, Donnie, Donny

Donato Lat. "Given."
Donatien, Donatus
Donnelly Ir. Gael. "Brown-haired fighter."
Donnell
Donovan Ir. Gael. "Dark." Surname become first name or, in the case of the pop singer who recorded "Mellow Yellow" in the late 1960s, only name.
Donavon, Donevin, Donevon, Donoven, Donovon
Dontavius Modern name: Probably a combination of the quite popular Donté, and Octavius.
Dantavius, Dawntavius, Dewontavius, Dontavious
Donté It. "Lasting." This is a respelling of Dante: this form is popular among African-American families.
Dantae, Dantay, Dohntae, Dontae, Dontay, Dontey
Dooley Ir. Gael. "Dark hero." In the early 20th century author Finley Peter Dunne wrote more than 700 hugely popular newspaper essays that saw the world through the eyes of Martin Dooley, a fictitious Irish bartender on Chicago's West Side.
Dor Heb. "Generation."
Doram, Doriel, Dorli
Doran Ir. Gael. "Fist" or "Stranger, exile."
Dore, Dorian, Doron, Dorran, Dorren
Dorian Gk. Place name: "From Doris," an area in Greece. Introduced by Oscar Wilde in *The Picture of Dorian Gray*; the hero of the tale is a beautiful young man who succumbs to a life of vice. Notwithstanding this discouraging precedent, the name has had some popularity in the U.S.
Dore, Dorien, Dorrian, Dorrien, Dorryen
Doron Heb. "Gift."
Doran, Doroni
Dorsey Probably from the French d'Orsay, meaning "From Orsay." Band leader Tommy Dorsey.
Dorsee, Dorsie
Dotson Probably a respelling of Dodson (and thus a variation on "Roger's son"). Author Dotson Rader.
Dotsen, Dottson
Dougal Celt. "Dark stranger." Most common in Scotland.
Doyle, Dougall, Dugal, Dugald, Dugall

Douglas Scot. Gael. Place name: "Black water." The name of a hugely powerful Scots clan. Though it was originally a girl's name, by the 19th century Douglas was used for boys. Its period of great popularity, which peaked in the 1950s, seems to have been inspired by the actors Douglas Fairbanks, father and son. Fairly steadily used, though not fashionable. Author Douglas Adams; General Douglas MacArthur.
Douglass, Dugaid

Dov Heb. "Bear."

Dow Ir. Gael. "Dark-haired."
Dowan, Dowe, Dowson

Doyle Ir. Gael. "Black stranger." Var. **Dougal**. Authors Paddy Doyle, Arthur Conan Doyle.

Drake ME. This is an unusually specific name, for it derives from the word *draca*, which was the medieval term for "dragon." Originally Drake designated the man who kept the inn with the dragon trademark, or the "Sign of the Dragon." It followed the usual route of becoming a surname, and thence a first name. English explorer Sir Francis Drake.

Draper OE. Occupational name: a draper was a man who sold cloth.

Drew Welsh. "Wise." Dim. **Andrew** (Gk. "Masculine"). Used as an independent name since the 1960s. Football player Drew Bledsoe.
Dru, Druw

Driscoll Meaning and derivation unclear: possibly Celtic "sorrowful."
Driscol

Drummond Celt. Meaning unclear. Use as a first name is concentrated in Scotland.

Drury OF. "Loved one." Drury Lane is a famous street in London's theater district, and also the home of the Muffin Man in a well-known children's song.
Drew, Drewry, Dru

Dryden OE. Place name: "Dry valley." Poet John Dryden.

Duane Ir. Gael. "Swarthy." Used primarily since the 1940s, predominantly in the U.S. Dwayne is the most popular spelling.
Dewain, Dewayne, Duwain, Duwaine, Duwayne, Dwain, Dwaine, Dwayne

Dudley OE. Place name: "People's field." Aristocratic family name in England, used as a first name since the 19th century. The absurd Canadian mountie Dudley Do-right was a staple character in the 1960s *Rocky and Bullwinkle Show*. Actor Dudley Moore.

Duff Gael. "Swarthy." There are many English surnames turned first names that derive from the Gaelic *dubh*, which means dark. They may describe places (i.e., Douglas), or personal characteristics, as in this case.
Duffey, Duffie, Duffy

Dugan Ir. Gael. "Swarthy."
Doogan, Dougan, Douggan, Duggan

Duke Lat. "Leader." Last name transferred to first name, or possibly an abbreviation of the highly unusual Marmaduke. Current use is probably inspired either by John Wayne (who was nicknamed "Duke"), or the great jazz musician Duke Ellington.

Dumont Fr. Place name: "Of the mountain."

Dunbar Gael. "Castle headland."

Duncan Scot. Gael. "Brown fighter." A royal name in early Scotland: There was a King Duncan in 11th-century Scotland whose cousin Macbeth murdered him. Shakespeare later picked up the tale in his tragedy *Macbeth*. The name disappeared until a spell of 19th-century use in Scotland and a flurry of mostly English popularity in the 1950s and 1960s. Never a big hit in the U.S. Cabinetmaker Duncan Phyfe.
Dunc, Dunn

Dundee Gael. "Fort on the Tay." The Tay is a river in Scotland, and Dundee is a city there.

Dunham Gael. "Brown man."

Dunley OE. Place name: "Meadow with the hill."
Dunlea, Dunleigh, Dunlie, Dunly, Dunnlea, Dunnleigh, Dunnley

Dunlop Scot. Gael. Place name: "Muddy hill."

Dunmore Scot. Gael. Place name: "Big fortress on the hill."

Dunn Gael. "Brown." Writers Dominick and John Gregory Dunne.
Dunne

Dunstan OE. Place name: "Brown hill with stones." Name of an English saint who was Archbishop of Canterbury in the 10th century. Rarely used, even in Britain.
Dunsten, Dunstin, Dunston

Dunton OE. Place name: "Hill settlement."

Durant Lat. "Enduring." Much more common as a last name. Dante is an abbreviated version. The 19th-century historians Will and Ariel Durant; American painter Asher Durand; entertainer Jimmy Durante.
Dante, Durand, Durante

Durward OE. Occupational name: "Warder at the gate." Derward

Durwin OE. "Dear friend."
Derwin, Derwyn, Durwyn

Duryea Unclear derivation: possibly related to Latin "Lasting." Since this is most often an Irish last name, a Gaelic origin seems more likely.

Dustin OG. "Brave warrior," or OE. Place name: "Dusty area." Use of the name is almost certainly influenced by the fame of actor Dustin Hoffman, and it's quite substantial.
Dustan, Dusten, Duston, Dusty, Dustyn

Duvall Fr. Place name: "Of the valley." Actor Robert Duvall.
Duval

Dwayne Ir. Gael. "Swarthy." Many English names are based on the Gaelic particle *dubh*, which means "Dark."
Duane, Duwain, Duwayne, Dwain, Dwaine

Dwight Flemish. "White or blond." Var. **DeWitt**. Some sources claim Dwight is a contraction of a surname derived from Dionysius. Given fame in the U.S. by two Yale University presidents, and by President Dwight D. Eisenhower. Its moderate use as a first name was probably inspired by him, and had trailed off by the 1970s. Baseball player Dwight Gooden.

Dwyer Ir. Gael. "Dark wise one." This was originally an Irish last name, occasionally transferred to a first name.
Dwire

Dyer OE. Occupational name: "Dyer." Curiously enough, Dexter refers to a female dyer.

Dylan Welsh. "Son of the sea." Welsh legend tells of a sea-god named Dylan, but modern use of the name, which has spread well beyond Wales, is probably homage to poet Dylan Thomas. The best-known example of this tribute is singer Bob Dylan, whose last name was originally Zimmerman. Some of the variant spellings given below are more closely related to homonym Dillon.
Dillan, Dillon, Dyllan, Dylon, Dylonn

Dyson OE. Last name that is probably a contraction of Dennison. Transferred to first-name use in the 19th century.

Eagle Bird name. The eagle is America's national bird, of course. Since certain Native American tribes have traditionally named children after birds and animals, this name has an aura of the open spaces of the west.

Eamon Ir. Var. **Edmund** (OE. "Wealthy protector"). Irish President Eamon de Valera may have been the inspiration behind the spurt of popularity between the 1950s and the 1970s. The name is rare in America.
Amon, Aimon, Aymon, Eamonn

Earl OE. "Nobleman, leader." The most popular of the English titles of nobility to be used as a first name, though Baron and Duke also occur. In the democratic U.S. it is probably a transferred surname rather than an allusion to the hereditary aristocracy. Author Erle Stanley Gardner; actor Errol Flynn; basketball star Earl ("the Pearl") Monroe; musician Earl Scruggs; Chief Justice of the U.S. Supreme Court Earl Warren.
Earle, Earlie, Early, Erl, Erle, Errol, Erroll, Erryl, Rollo

Earland OE. Place name: "Earl's land." Earl is the oldest title in the aristocracy, which probably explains the number of words that incorporate the title. The Erland spelling, for linguists, comes from Old Norse and means "Foreigner."
Erland

Earlham OE. Place name: "Earl's village."

Earlston OE. Place name: "Earl's settlement."
Earlton

Early ME. "Early, soon" or OE. "Earl's meadow." Confederate General Jubal Early.
Earley, Earlie, Erlie, Erly

Earvin Var. **Irvin** (OE. "Sea friend"). Made famous by basketball star Earvin "Magic" Johnson.

Eastman OE. "Man from the East." Painter Eastman Johnson; photography pioneeer George Eastman.

Eaton OE. Place name: "Settlement on the river."
Eatton, Eton, Eyton

Eban Heb. "Stone, rock." Israeli statesman Abba Eban.
Eben

Ebenezer Heb. "Rock of help." In the Old Testament, Samuel created a memorial to his victory over the Philistines and called the stone Ebenezer. The name came to America with the Puritans, and was, improbably enough, at one point almost as popular a name as John. It was fading by the 19th century, and Ebenezer Scrooge in Charles Dickens's *A Christmas Carol* probably hastened its disappearance.
Eb, Ebbaneza, Eben, Ebeneezer, Ebeneser, Ebenezar, Eveneser, Evenezer

Eberhard OG. "Courage of a boar." Var. **Everett**. Pencil magnate Eberhard Faber.
Eberardo, Eberhardt, Eberdt, Ebert, Everard, Everhardt, Evrard, Evreux

Eberlein OG. "Small boar."
Eberle, Eberley

Ebisu In Japan, the god of hard work and also of good luck.

Eckhard OG. "Brave edge, brave point." Refers to the point of a sword.
Eckard, Eckardt, Eckhardt, Ekkehard, Ekkehardt

Edbert OE. "Wealthy and bright."

Edel OG. "Noble." Unusual as a name in itself, but the first syllable of many combined forms such as Adalric and Adelaide. Biographer Leon Edel.
Adel, Adlin, Edelin, Edlin

Eden Heb. "Pleasure, delight." It is a short step from the Hebrew meaning of the word to its general association with Paradise. The name is used for girls as well as boys. English statesman Sir Anthony Eden.
Eaden, Eadin, Edin, Ednan, Edyn

Edgar OE. "Wealthy spearman." A royal name in Anglo-Saxon England which, like Edmund, endured through the Norman invasion and the resulting influx of Norman names. In Shakespeare's *King Lear*, Lear's son is called Edgar. Revived, like many Anglo-Saxon names, at the turn of the century, but the revival was short-lived. Poet Edgar Allan Poe; puppeteer Edgar Bergen; artist Edgar Dégas; author Edgar Rice Burroughs.

Eadgar, Eadger, Ed, Eddie, Edgard, Edgardo, Ned, Neddy, Ted, Teddie

Edison OE. "Son of Edward." Inventor Thomas Edison.

Eddison, Eddy, Edson

Edmar OE. "Wealthy sea."

Edmund OE. "Wealthy protector." A popular, and sainted, king of the East Angles in the 9th century gave the name enough popularity to survive the Norman Conquest. Astronomer Edmund Halley; poet Edmund Spenser; explorer Sir Edmund Hillary; Governor Edmund "Pat" Brown; Senator Edmund Muskie.

Eadmund, Eamon, Eamonn, Ed, Eddie, Edmon, Edmond, Edmonde, Edmondo, Ned, Neddie, Ted, Teddy

Edom Heb. "Red."

Edric OE. "Wealthy ruler." Anglo-Saxon name that was pushed out of fashion by the Normans in the 11th century but revived briefly at the end of the 19th.

Ederic, Ederick, Edrich, Edrick

Edsel OE. Place name: "Wealthy man's house." Linked in most minds to automotive pioneer Edsel Ford, and the ill-fated car named after him. The name is still used in the Ford family.

Edward OE. "Wealthy defender." A name with long-lasting popularity throughout the English-speaking world. Used by kings of England (including the saint Edward the Confessor) since before the Norman Conquest, and still a staple in the royal family. Though less of an obvious choice since the 1930s, it is still popular. As a nickname for Edward, Eddie has been replaced by Ted, Teddy, or Ned. Photographer Edward Steichen; ballet dancer Edward Villella; U.S. senator Edward Kennedy; poet Edward Lear; artist Édouard Manet; Edward, Duke of Windsor.

Eadward, Ed, Eddie, Eddy, Edik, Édouard, Eduard, Eduardo, Edvard, Edvardas, Ewart, Lalo, Ned, Neddie, Ted, Teddie

Edwin OE. "Wealthy friend." Anglo-Saxon name revived at the end of the 19th century, and used with some frequency since then. Astronaut Edwin "Buzz" Aldrin; Attorney General Edwin Meese III.

Eadwinn, Ed, Eddy, Edlin, Eduino, Edwyn, Ned, Neddy, Ted

Efigenio Variant of **Eugene** (Gk. "Noble").

Ephigenio, Ephigenios, Ephigenius, Efigenios, Efigenius

Efisio It. from Lat. "Ephesian, from Ephesus." Ephesus was one of the early Christian communities; Saint Paul addressed two of his letters to the Ephesians.

Efrat Heb. "Honored."

Ephrat

Efrem Var. **Ephraim** (Heb. "Fertile, productive"). Actor Efrem Zimbalist, Jr.

Efi, Efraim, Efrayim, Efren, Efrim

Efron Heb. "Lark."

Efroni, Ephron

Egan Gael. "Burning." Irish use predominates.

Eagan, Eagen, Egann, Egon

Egbert OE. "Brilliant sword." Another 19th-century Anglo-Saxon revival, now little heard.

Egerton OE. Place name: possibly "Edgar's settlement." Occurs as a surname in the English aristocracy. Transferred to first-name use mostly in Britain.

Edgerton

Egidio It. "Kid, young goat." The anglicized version is Giles.

Egil Scand. "Edge, point." As in the point of a weapon.

Eigil

Eginhard Ger. "Sword power."

Eginard, Eginhardt, Einhard, Einhardt, Enno

Egmont Fr./Ger. "Fearsome protection."

Egmond

Egon German name, having to do with the point of a sword. Prince Egon von Furstenburg.

Egor Rus. "Farmer." Currently popular in Russia, but very exotic in English-speaking countries.
Igor, Ygor

Ehud Heb. "Love."

Eilam Heb. "Forever, eternal." In the Old Testament, the name of one of Noah's grandsons.
Elam

Eilert Scand. "Hard point."

Eilif ONorse. "Immortal."

Eilon Heb. "Oak tree." This name is used in many different spellings, for girls and for boys.
Eilan, Elan, Elon, Ilan, Ilon

Einar ONorse. "Battle leader." Refers to the heroes of Valhalla, in the Old Norse legends.
Ejnar, Inar

Einion Welsh. "Anvil."

Eion Ir. Var. **John** (Heb. "The Lord is gracious"), by way of **Ian**.
Ean, Ion

Eilad Heb. "God is for ever."

Eladio Sp. from Gk. "Greek."

Elbert Var. **Albert** (OE. "Highborn/shining"). The long form is Ethelbert, but it is virtually obsolete.

Elbridge OE. Place name: "Old bridge."
Ellbridge

Elchanan Heb. "God is gracious." Old Testament name. Many of these names beginning with "El-" (Hebrew for "God") have survived because they are mentioned in the Bible. They were adopted by the American Puritans, and often survived into the 19th century without seeming the least bit exotic to a Biblically literate population.
Elchana, Elhanan, Elhannan, Elkanah

Elden Var. **Alden** (OE. "Old friend"). Also possibly "valley of the elves." Surname changed to first name.
Eldin, Eldon, Eldwin, Eldwyn, Elton

Elder OE. Place name: "Elder trees." Also, in U.S., may denote a forebear who had high standing in one of the Protestant churches that are governed by councils of elders.
Eldor

Eldon OE. Place name: "Sacred hill." Used since the 19th century.

Eldorado Sp. "The golden man." Mythical South American country, avidly sought by Europeans like Pizarro, Coronado, and Francis Drake. The name has also been used steadily as a place name.

Eldred OE. "Old counsel." Anglo-Saxon name lost in the onslaught of Norman names, and brought back in the 19th-century craze for the picturesque remnants of the past.
Aldred, Eldrid

Eldridge Ger. "Sage ruler." Eldrick, a variation, is the given name of golfer Tiger Woods. Civil rights activist Eldridge Cleaver.
Eldredge, Eldrege, Eldrich, Eldrick, Eldrige

Eleazer Var. **Lazarus** (Heb. "The Lord will help"). The 19th-century fondness for obscure biblical names (Eleazer among them) tends to confirm the stereotype of the repressed religious Victorians. If nothing else, they must have read their Bibles carefully to come up with these names.
Elazar, Eleasar, Eleazaro, Eli, Elie, Eliezer, Ely

Eleodoro Sp. from Gk. "Gift from the sun."
Heliodoro, Heliodoros

Elford OE. Place name: "Old ford."
Ellford

Elger OE. "Spear from the elves." Variation of **Alger**, which is marginally more widely known.
Elgar, Ellgar, Ellger

Eli Heb. "On high." In the Old Testament, Eli was Israel's high priest. This was a very holy name to the Hebrews. The Puritans used it freely, and it persisted through the 19th century but faded after the 1930s. American inventor Eli Whitney; author Elie Wiesel; actor Eli Wallach.
Elie, Eloi, Eloy, Ely

Eliachim Heb. "The Lord will establish."
Eliakim

Eliam Heb. "God is my nation."
Elami

Elian Sp. from Lat. Based on a clan name, Aelia.

Elias Gk. Var. **Elijah**. Most common in the 17th century.

Spread widely by Greek translations of the Bible, and by the King James version, in which Elijah is referred to as Elias.

Elice, Ellice, Ellis, Elyas

Elihu Heb. "God, the Lord." Like Eleazer, occasionally used in the 19th century.

Elijah Heb. "The Lord is my God." A great prophet in the Old Testament. Felix Mendelssohn, reputedly Queen Victoria's favorite composer, wrote an oratorio about him in 1846. The name was most popular in the early 19th century. Film director Elia Kazan; actor Elijah Wood.

Eli, Elia, Elias, Elie, Elihu, Eliot, Eliyahu, Eljah, Elliot, Ellis, Ely, Elyot, Elyott

Elimelech Heb. "My God is kind." Old Testament name.

Eliron Heb. "My God is song."

Eliran

Eloi Fr. from Lat. "Elect, selected." Saint Eligius, or Eloi, was a 6th-century metalworker and engraver of coins who later founded a monastery and a convent. He is patron of blacksmiths, watchmakers, and other metalworkers.

Eligio, Eligius, Eloy

Eliphalet Heb. "God delivers me." In the Old Testament, this is the name of one of David's sons. It was occasionally used in 19th-century America.

Elifalet, Elifelet, Eliphelet

Elisha Heb. "The Lord is my salvation." The successor to Elijah, as recounted in the Old Testament. Puritan name in the 17th century, a bit more widespread in the 19th, and all but obsolete now.

Eli, Elisee, Eliseo, Elisher, Eliso, Lisha

Eliyahu Heb. "The Lord is my God." This is the Hebrew form of Elijah.

Elkanah Heb. "God has made." A man's name in the Old Testament, but occasionally used for girls as well. A variant spelling of **Elchanah**.

Elkana

Ellard OG. "Noble and valorous."

Allard, Allerd

Ellery OE. Place name: "Island with elder trees." Some sources propose a relationship to Hilary. The famous fictional detective Ellery Queen is probably the best-known user of the name.

Ellary, Ellerey

Ellesmere ME. "Elllis's pond." Mere is a term related to "marine" that came to mean a pond, or even a swamp.

Ellington OE. Place name. Possibly "Ellis's town." Used in 21st century America, however, the name almost has to refer to the great jazz musician Duke Ellington.

Elliott Anglicization of Elijah or Eli. Surname first used as a given name in modern Scotland, quite popular in the U.S. Though the various spellings don't alter the pronunciation one whit, this is the most common form. Poet T. S. Eliot; actor Elliott Gould; Attorney General Elliot Richardson.

Eliot, Eliott, Elliot, Elyot, Elyott

Ellis Anglicization of Elias. Surname transferred to first name. Ellis Bell was the pseudonym used by Emily Brontë; when they first began publishing, each of the Brontë sisters chose a name that could be considered masculine. Anne was Acton Bell, and Charlotte was Currer Bell.

Elliss, Ellyce

Ellison OE. "Son of Ellis." Author Ralph Ellison.

Elison, Elisson, Ellson, Ellyson, Elson

Ellsworth OE. Place name: "Nobleman's estate" or possibly "Ellis's estate." Painter Ellsworth Kelly.

Ellswerth, Elsworth

Ellwood OE. Place name: "Nobleman's wood" or "Ellis's wood."

Elwood

Elman OE. "Noble man." A contraction of Edelman.

Elmer OE. "Highborn and renowned." Anglo-Saxon name that has been much more popular in the U.S. than in Britain, especially in the late 19th century. Sinclair Lewis's well-known novel *Elmer Gantry*, published in 1927, was about a compelling charlatan of a minister. It was shocking, successful, and discouraging to parents who were considering Elmer as a name for their babies. Cartoon character Elmer Fudd.

Aylmar, Aylmer, Aymer, Ellmer, Elmir

Elmo Lat. from Gk. "Amiable" or It. "Godly helmet."

Var. **Anselm**. Saint Elmo is the common name for Saint Erasmus, a 4th-century bishop and martyr who is patron saint of sailors. Saint Elmo's fire (also the name of a popular movie in the early 1980s) refers to the electrical discharges occasionally sighted at the top of a ship's mast. Parents who already have children may know Elmo as a furry red toddler-monster featured on *Sesame Street*. Giving a child this name could be quite confusing right through the preschool years.

Elmore OE. Place name: "Moor with elm trees." Author Elmore Leonard.

Elof Swed. "Only heir."
Elov, Eluf

Elois Var. **Louis** (OG. "Renowned in battle"). Nowhere near as familiar as the feminine version, Eloise, though the more elaborate Aloysius is another variant.
Alois, Aloysius

Elon Heb. "Oak tree." See **Eilon**.

Elpidos Gk. "Hoping."
Elpido

Elrad OE. "Noble counsel."
Ellrad, Ellrod, Elrod

Elroy Var. **Leroy** (Fr. "King").
Elroi, Elroye

Elsdon OE. Place name: "Hill of the nobleman."
Elsden, Elisdon

Elston OE. Place name: "Settlement of the nobleman."
Ellston

Elton OE. Place name: "Old Settlement" or "Ella's town." Musician Elton John.
Alton, Eldon, Ellton

Elvin OE. "Elf friend" or "Highborn friend." Var. **Alvin**.
Elven, Elwin, Elwinn, Elwyn, Elwynne

Elvio Sp. from Lat. "Blond, fair."

Elvis Scand. "All-wise." Variants are rare, since use, as in the case of singer Elvis Costello (né Declan Patrick McManus), is almost always influenced by the fame of Elvis Presley. The prominent Elvises in their late '20s and early '30s attest to this name's popularity during the singer's heyday. Figure skater Elvis Stojko; football player Elvis Grbac.
Alvis, Alvys, Elvio, Elviss, Elvo, Elvys

Elwell OE. Place name: "Old well."
  Elwill
Elwin Var. Elvin.
  Elvin, Elvis, Elvyn, Elwin, Win, Wynn
Elwyn Welsh. "Fair brow." Easily confused with Elwin, but more likely to be found in Wales, where it has a different meaning altogether.
  Elwin, Elwynn
Elwood OE. Place name: "Old wood."
  Ellwood, Woody
Ely OE. Place name (a river in South Wales and a cathedral and town in Cambridgeshire) turned surname. Or, more likely, a variant of **Eli**.
— **Emerson** OG. "Emery's son." First-name use may be tribute to Ralph Waldo Emerson, the transcendentalist philosopher and "sage of Concord."
Emery OG. "Home ruler." Saw 19th-century use as a first name, predominantly American rather than British. Architect Emery Roth.
  Amerigo, Amery, Amory, Emerey, Emeri, Emerich, Emmerich, Emmery, Emmory, Emory
Emil Lat. "Eager to please." The French form, Émile, took root slightly earlier in English-speaking countries. Used only since the mid–19th century, without any great period of popularity. French author Émile Zola; actor Emilio Estevez.
  Aimil, Aymil, Emelen, Émile, Emilian, Emiliano, Emilianus, Emilio, Emilion, Emilyan, Emlen, Emlin, Emlyn, Emlynn
Emir Arab. "Prince, ruler."
  Amir, Ameer, Emeer
Emlyn Welsh place name given some prominence by playwright and actor Emlyn Williams.
Emmanuel Heb. "God is among us." Used in both the Old and the New Testaments, and as another name for Jesus. Slight use in the 17th century grew gradually right through the 19th century, then tailed off. In the U.S. Manuel is fairly common among Catholics of Hispanic descent, who also use Jesus quite freely. Fashion designer Emanuel Ungaro; pianist Emmanuel Ax.

Eman, Emanual, Emanuel, Emanuele, Emmanual, Emmonual, Emmonuel, Emonual, Emonuel, Imanuel, Immanuel, Immanuele, Manny, Manual, Manuel, Manuelo

Emmett Various derivations are possible, including OG. "Energetic, powerful," OE. "An ant," or even a last name relating to Emma. Given by Irish and Irish-American families to celebrate early 19th century Irish patriot Robert Emmet, who tried to overthrow English rule in Ireland with French help. Famous clown Emmett Kelly; football player Emmitt Smith.
Emmet, Emmit, Emmitt, Emmot, Emmott

Emmons English last name, possibly related to the Irish Eamon.

Emrys Welsh from Gk. "Immortal." The Welsh version of Ambrose.

Endicott OE. Place name: possibly "Cottage on the end." A name to reckon with in Massachusetts, where Endicotts have been prominent since 1628. Massachusetts governor Endicott Peabody.
Endecott

Endymion In Greek myth, a youth renowned for his beauty.
Endimion

Eneas Var. Aeneas (Gk. "He who is praised").
Enneas, Ennes, Ennis

Engelbert OG. "Angel-bright." Entertainer Engelbert Humperdinck (whose original name, less memorable if more euphonious, was Arnold Dorsey).
Bert, Berty, Ingelbert, Inglebert

Ennis Var. Angus (Ir. Gael. "Sole or only choice").

Enoch Heb. "Vowed, dedicated." Old Testament name for the father of Methuselah. Briefly popular from the 1860s to 1880s, inspired by Tennyson's famous and sentimental poem "Enoch Arden." Now scarce.
Enock

Enos Heb. "Man." Old Testament name for one of Adam and Eve's great-grandsons. Mildly revived, not by the Puritans, but in the 19th century. Obscure in this century.

Enrico It. Var. Henry (OG. "Estate ruler"). Use by English-speaking families probably reflects the fame of operatic tenor Enrico Caruso.
Erico, Errico

Ensign Lat. "Badge." Possibly used in reference to the naval rank: an ensign is the most junior naval commissioned officer.

Enzo It. Var. **Henry** (OG. "Estate ruler").
  Enzio

Epaminondas Gk. Meaning unknown. Epaminondas was a 4th-century B.C. military genius who invented fighting in organized units, known as "phalanxes."

Ephah Heb. "Darkness." Old Testament name.

Ephraim Heb. "Fertile, productive." Old Testament name used mostly in the 18th and 19th centuries. This spelling was most common in the U.S.
  Efraim, Efrain, Efrayim, Efrem, Efren, Efrim, Efrym, Ephraem, Ephream, Ephrem, Ephrim, Ephrym

Epicurus Gk. Meaning unknown. A philosopher of great influence, who proposed that philosophy's purpose should be to make life happy. He wrote extensively on the nature of pleasure, and believed that intellectual and aesthetic pleasure, and the joys of friendship, were more important than the joys of the flesh. The word "epicure," which has its root in his name, means someone who enjoys the pleasures of the flesh, which is a misunderstanding of the philosopher's teachings.

Epifanio Sp. from Gk. "Bringing light." In English, the term is "epiphany," and in the Catholic calendar, it is the season that follows Christmas.
  Epefano, Epefanio, Epephanio, Epifan, Epifano, Epiphany

Epimetheus Gk. "Afterthought." In Greek myth, the husband of Pandora (who opened the famous box, loosing trouble on the world) and brother of Prometheus, who brought fire to mankind.

Erasmus Gk. "Loved, desired." The 16th-century Dutch humanist philosopher Geert Geerts wrote as Desiderius Erasmus. (Desiderius is the Latin form of Erasmus.) He may have been thinking of Saint Erasmus, who is more popularly known as Saint Elmo. Use of the name was greatest in the latter half of the 19th century, and probably refers to the philosopher rather than the saint.
  Erasme, Erasmo, Ras

Erastus Gk. "Beloved." In the New Testament, Erastus was a missionary sent out by St. Paul.
Eraste, Rastus

Ercole It. "Splendid gift." This is the Italian version of Hercules.
Ercolo

Erhard OG. "Strong resolve."
Erhardt, Erhart

Eric Scand. "All-ruler." In spite of the renown of Viking explorer Eric the Red (who colonized Iceland around A.D. 985) and his son Leif Ericsson, who reputedly discovered North America half a millennium before Columbus, Eric was little used until the turn of the 19th century. It caught on, however, becoming fashionable in Britain in the 1920s, in the U.S. some 50 years later. It is very solidly used today. Author Erich Segal; musician Eric Clapton; skater Eric Heiden.
Aeric, Aerick, Aerric, Aerrick, Aerricko, Arreck, Arric, Arrick, Erek, Erich, Erick, Erik, Eriq, Errick, Eryk, Rick, Rikky

Erie American place name: one of the Great Lakes, the famous canal from Albany to Buffalo, and a tribe of Native Americans who lived in western New York state and Ohio. The Erie Canal, completed in 1825, linked America's inland waterways with the Atlantic via the Hudson River.

Erin Ir. Gael. Name for Ireland. Mostly used by girls, and not in Ireland itself.

Erland OE. "Noble's land" or ONorse "Foreigner, stranger." Actor Erland Josephson.
Arlan, Erlend

Erling OE. "Noble's son."

Ermin Var. **Herman** (OG. "Army man").
Erman, Ermano, Erminio, Ermino

Ernest OE. "Sincere." Its great popularity at the turn of the 20th century was only confirmed by Oscar Wilde's play *The Importance of Being Earnest*. Fell out of use after the 1930s. It could be argued that that was the era when being earnest began to lose its desirability. Author Ernest Hemingway; actor Ernest Borgnine; entertainer Ernie Kovacs.
Earnest, Ernesto, Ernestus, Ernie, Erno, Ernst

Eros Greek mythology name: Eros was the god of love. Since in our era Eros generally refers to sexual love, this seems a tricky name to give a baby.

Errol Origin unclear, though most sources consider it a variation of Earl. It may also derive from a Scottish place name; there have been Scottish Earls of Erroll for more than 600 years. The most famous modern Errol was dashing movie actor Errol Flynn.

Erroll, Erryl, Erryle, Eryle, Rollo

Erskine Scot. Gael. Place name: "High cliff." Transference from last name to first occurred only in this century. Novelist Erskine Caldwell.

Erv, Erve, Ervine, Ervyn, Erwin, Erwyn, Erwynn, Irvin

Ervin Scot. Gael. Place name, or "Beautiful." Var. **Irving** (OE "Sea friend"). General Erwin Rommel.

Erving Var. **Irving** (OE. "Sea friend"). Basketball player Julius Erving.

Ervine

Esau Heb. "Hairy." In the Old Testament the story is told of how Esau came out of the womb covered with hair, while his twin brother, Jacob, was hairless. The name was used somewhat in the 19th century.

Esbjorn ONorse "Godly bear." Well used in Scandinavia.

Asbjorn, Esbern

Escott OE. Place name: "Hut near the stream."

Escot

Eskel ONorse "Divine cauldron." The name refers to a cauldron used for sacrifice to the gods.

Askel, Askell, Eskil

Esias Gk. from Heb. "God is salvation." This name is a variant of the much more common **Isaiah**.

Esaias, Esiason, Esiasson

Esmé Fr. "Esteemed." Related to the more modern French form, *aimé*, which is the root of Amy. Originally a male name brought to Scotland by a French cousin of James VI. Now used mostly for girls, though scarce.

Esmay, Esmeling, Ismay, Ismé

Esmond OE. "Protected by grace." Survived the Norman Conquest as a last name, but was not rediscovered as a first name until the late 19th century, and was never widely used.

Essex OE. Place name: "Eastern." A county in southeastern England that gave its name to many towns in America. In Anglo-Saxon England, there was a kingdom of Essex.

Esteban Sp. Var. **Stephen** (Gk. "Crowned").

Estes Place name of uncertain meaning, though some sources relate it to the Latin *aestus* or tide, suggesting that it means something like "by the estuary." It may also be realted to "east." Estes Park, Colorado, a popular resort high in the Rockies, was named for its first settler.

Eston OE. Place name: "Eastern town."

Ethan Heb. "Firmness, steadfastness." An Old Testament name given fame in the U.S. by Revolutionary War leader Ethan Allen, who captured Fort Ticonderoga with only eighty-three men. Fairly well used now and may receive a boost from the glamor of actor Ethan Hawke and Ethan Hunt, hero of the film *Mission: Impossible*.
Aitan, Eitan, Etan, Ethen

Étienne Fr. Var. **Stephen** (Gk. "Crowned").

Ethelbert OE. "Highborn, shining." The original form of Albert. A 6th-century king of Kent whom Saint Augustine converted to Christianity. The name was revived in the 19th century but is now extremely scarce.

Ethelred OE. "Noble counsel." The name of a king of the West Saxons, and of a king of the English, around the year 1000. The latter was known as "Ethelred the Unready" in later years because he was such an incompetent ruler.
Aethelred

Ethelwulf OE. "Noble wolf." A king of the West Saxons in the 9th century.
Aethelwolf, Aethelwulf, Ethelwolf

Ethelwin OE. "Noble friend." Anglo-Saxon name that followed the same cycle of 19th-century revival and 20th-century disuse.
Ethelwyn, Ethelwynne

Ettore It. "Loyal." The Italian version of Hector. Designer Ettore Sottsass.

Euan Ir. Gael. "Little swift one." Possibly also a variant of **Evan** and thus, in a roundabout way, yet another version of John.

Ewan, Ewen

Euclid Gk. Mathematician, generally considered the inventor of geometry.

Euclides

Eudocio Gk. "Well thought of."

Eugene Gk. "Wellborn." In use since the early Christian era, and chosen by four popes. After centuries of disuse, it was dusted off in the 19th century and became very popular in the U.S. No longer in the first rank, but still occurs. Senator Eugene McCarthy; playwrights Eugene O'Neill, Eugène Ionesco; artist Eugène Delacroix.

Efigenio, Efigenios, Efigenius, Ephigenio, Ephigenios, Ifigenio, Ifigenios, Iphigenio, Iphigenius, Eugen, Eugenio, Eugenius, Evgeny, Gene

Eulogio Gk. "Reasoning well."

Euodias Gk. "Good fortune." New Testament name; it occurs in Paul's Letter to the Philippians.

Euphemios Gk. "Well spoken." Masculine version of Euphemia, which was popular in the 19th century.

Eufemio, Eufemios, Eufemius, Euphemio, Euphemius

Euphrates Turkish. "Great river." Name of the river, 1,700 miles long, that flows through Asia Minor. The valley between the Tigris and the Euphrates is often known as "the cradle of civilization."

Eufrates

Euripides Gk. Meaning unknown. Greek playwright of the 5th century B.C., author of many of the classic Greek tragedies such as *Medea* and *The Trojan Women*.

Eusebius Gk. "Devout." Name of a number of saints, the best-known of whom was a 4th-century Italian bishop.

Esabio, Esavio, Esavius, Esebio, Eusabio, Eusaio, Eusebio, Eusebios, Eusavio, Eusevio, Eusevios

Eustace Gk. "Fertile." Brought to Britain with the Normans, but never hugely popular there. Most common in the late 19th century, little used in the U.S. The last names Stacey and Stacy come from Eustace. (As girls' names, they are diminutives of **Anastasia**.)

Eustache, Eustachios, Eustachius, Eustachy, Eustaquio, Eustashe, Eustasius, Eustatius, Eustazio, Eustis, Eustiss

Evan Welsh. Var. **John** (Heb. "The lord is gracious.")
Most common in Wales, but well-known in all English-
speaking countries ever since the mid–19th century. Quite
well used among today's parents.
Euan, Euen, Evans, Even, Evin, Evyn, Ewan, Ewen, Owen

Evander Gk. "Good man." The root "andr-" also appears
in the much more common Andrew. A figure in Roman
mythology. Fighter Evander Holyfield.

Evangel Gk. "Good news." Masculine version of the more
common Evangline.
**Evangelin, Evangelino, Evangelo, Vangelios, Vangelis,
Vangelo**

Evelyn Surname transferred to first name, and more common for girls than boys. Author Evelyn Waugh's first wife
was also called Evelyn; their friends referred to them as
"He-Evelyn" and "She-Evelyn."
Evelin

Everard OE. "Boar hardness." Norman name more com-
mon as a surname, but revived in the 19th century.
German form is Eberhard. Now rare.
Eberhard, Everardo, Evered, Everhart, Evrard, Evraud

Everest OE. Probably related to Everett. The highest mountain in the world, Mount Everest in the Himalayas, was
named for a 19th-century surveyor of India, Sir George
Everest. Fashion designer Timothy Everest.

Everett OE. "Boar hardness." Surname deriving from Ev-
erard, used as a first name in the 19th century. Senator
Everett Dirksen.
**Averett, Averitt, Eberhard, Eberhardt, Everard, Evered,
Everet, Everitt, Evrard, Eward, Ewart**

Everild OE. "Boar battle."
Evald, Evaldo, Everald, Everhild, Everildo

Everley OE. Place name: "Boar meadow." Singing group
the Everly Brothers.
Everlie, Everly

Everton OE. Place name: "Boar settlement." Used as a
first name only in this century.

Evo Var. **Yves** via **Ivo** (OG. "Yew wood.")

Ewald OE. "Law-powerful."
Evald, Evaldo, Euell, Ewell

Ewan Scot. Gael. Unclear origin: perhaps "Young man"

or a variant of **Eugene**. Use confined to Scotland until the mid–20th century, but now spreading.

Euan, Euen, Ewen

Ewert OE. Occupational name: "Shepherd." Literally, "Ewe-herder."

Evart, Evarts, Evert, Ewart

Ewing OE. "Law-friend." Unusual, though some families may have been inspired to use it in the 1980s by the Ewing family on the popular TV series *Dallas*. Basketball player Patrick Ewing.

Ewin, Ewynn

Eyolf Norwegian "Lucky wolf."

Eyulf

Ezekiel Heb. "Strength of God." An important Old Testament prophet. Since the end of the 19th century, very scarce.

Esequiel, Ezechiel, Eziechiele, Eziequel, Zeke

Ezer Heb. "Help, aid."

Eizer, Ezar, Ezri

Ezio It. from Lat. Possibly a clan name, possibly related to the Greek word meaning "Eagle." Singer Ezio Pinza.

Ezra Heb. "Helper." Old Testament prophet. The Puritans brought the name to America, where it was most used in the 19th century. Poet Ezra Pound.

Azariah, Azur, Esdras, Esra, Ezer, Ezri

Fabian Lat. Clan name, possibly meaning "One who grows beans." Name of a 3rd-century saint/pope, and latterly of a 1960s pop star. Not much used in the intervening 1700 years. Art director Fabien Baron.

Fabe, Fabek, Faber, Fabert, Fabianno, Fabiano, Fabianus, Fabien, Fabio, Fabion, Faebian, Faebien, Fabius, Fabiyus, Fabyan, Fabyen, Faybian, Faybien, Faybion, Faybionn

Fabrice Fr. from Lat. "Works with the hands."

Fabriano, Fabricius, Fabritius, Fabrizio, Fabrizius

Fabron Fr. "Young blacksmith."

Fabre, Fabroni

Factor OE. Occupational name: "Businessman." A factor was the agent or steward of a large estate. The term is still sometimes used in Scotland. Cosmetics magnate Max Factor.

Fadi Arab. "Savior."

Fagan Ir. Gael. "Little ardent one." The wily con artist Fagin in Dickens's *Oliver Twist* has probably put an indelible stamp on this name, particularly given the fame of the musical and movie versions.
Fegan, Feggan, Fagin

Fahd Arab. "Panther, leopard." This is a popular name in Arabic countries, perhaps because it is the name of Saudi Arabia's king. It bears connotations of courage and fierceness.
Fahad

Fairbairn Scot. "Fair-haired child."

Fairbanks OE. "Bank along the pathway." Also the name of a significant town in Alaska. Actor Douglas Fairbanks.

Fairchild OE. "Fair-haired child."

Fairfax OE. "Blond."

Faisal Arab. "Resolute." King Faysal of Saudi Arabia.
Faysal, Feisal

Falkner OE. Occupational name: "Falcon trainer." Author William Faulkner.
Falconer, Falconner, Faulconer, Faulconner, Faulkner, Fowler

Fallows OE. Place name: "The fallow field." Fallow means "not planted." Before the discovery of crop rotation, farmers used to let fields lie fallow to gather moisture or to kill weeds. Author James Fallows.
Fallow

Fane OE. "Happy, joyous."
Fain, Faine

Faolan Ir. Gael. "Little wolf."
Felan, Phelan

Faraj Arab. "To cure."
Farag

Faramond OE. "Traveler's protection."
Faramund, Farrimond, Farrimund, Pharamond, Pharamund

Fargo Origin unknown. William George Fargo was one of the original founders of Wells Fargo, a shipping company in the West, that dominated banking in the gold rush camps for a time. Fargo later became president of the American Express Company. Fargo, North Dakota, was named for him.

Farley OE. Place name: "Meadow of the sheep" or "Meadow of the bulls." Surname transferred occasionally to first name. Actor Farley Granger; author Walter Farley.
Fairlay, Fairlee, Fairleigh, Fairlie, Farlay, Farlee, Farleigh, Farlie, Farly, Farrleigh, Farrley, Lee, Leigh

Farmer OE. Occupational name: "Farmer." A fairly common last name.

Farnell OE. Place name: "The fern hill." Originally a surname.
Farnall, Fernald, Furnald

Farnham OE. Place name: "Meadow with ferns." Common surname with a little spurt of late–19th-century use as a first name.
Farnam, Farnum, Fernham

Farnley OE. Place name: "Field with ferns."
Farnlea, Farnlee, Farnleigh, Farnly, Fernleigh, Fernley

Farold OE. "Mighty voyager."

Farouk Arab. "Discerning truth from falsehood." The last king of Egypt, deposed in 1952, was King Faruq.
Faruq, Faruqh

Farquhar Scot. Gael. "Very dear one." First-name use is occasional, and mostly Scottish.
Farquharson, Farquar, Farquarson

Farr OE. "Voyager." As in, someone who goes *far* away.

Farrar ME. "Blacksmith." The French term, which obviously contributes to this name, is *ferrier*, for someone who works with iron (*fer*). Blacksmiths are sometimes called "farriers."
Farrer, Farrier, Farrior, Ferrar, Ferrars, Ferrer, Ferrier

Farrell Ir. Gael. "Hero, man of courage."
Farrel, Farrill, Farryll, Ferrel, Ferrell, Ferrill, Ferryl

Faunus Latin "Animal." In Roman myth, the god of nature. He was attended by little fauns, half man and half goat.
Fawnus

Faust Lat. "Fortunate, enjoying good luck." Very rare as a first name, no doubt owing to the literary connotations, for the legendary Faust sells his soul to the devil. His story was retold by Marlowe, Goethe, Wagner, and Thomas Mann, among others.
Faustino, Fausto, Faustus

Favian Lat. "Man of wisdom."

Faxon OE. "Hair." This is the kind of neutral two-syllable name that is very popular among parents just now.

Fay Ir. Gael. "Raven." Extremely rare as a boy's name, though somewhat popular for girls.
Faye, Fayette

Fedor Ger. Var. **Theodore** (Gk. "Gift from God"). Author Fyodor Dostoyevsky.
Faydor, Feodor, Fyodor

Feivel Yiddish form of **Phoebus** (Gk. "Brilliant one").
Feiwel

Felim Ir. Gael. "Ever good."
Feidhlim, Phelim

Felipe Sp. Var. **Philip** (Gk. "Lover of horses"). The current Crown Prince of Spain is named Felipe.
Filip, Filippo, Fillip, Flip, Lippo, Pip, Pippo

Felix Lat. "Happy, fortunate." Not common in America, possibly because of a strong association with Felix the Cat and, more recently, *The Odd Couple's* Felix Unger. American physicist Felix Bloch.
Fee, Felic, Felice, Felicio, Felike, Feliks, Felizio, Felyx

Felton OE. Place name: "Settlement on the field."
Felten, Feltin

Fenris Scandinavian myth name: Fenris was a giant wolf who had the power to threaten the gods.

Fenton OE. Place name: "Settlement on the marsh." First used as a given name in the 19th century, but never widespread.

Fenwick OE. "Village on the marsh."

Ferdinand OG. "Bold voyager." A name that has always been more popular in Southern Europe than in the English-speaking countries. Explorers Ferdinand Magellan, Hernán Cortés; former Philippines president Ferdinand Marcos.
Ferd, Ferdie, Ferdinando, Ferdo, Ferdynand, Fernand, Fernandas, Fernando, Hernán, Hernando, Nando

Ferenc Hung. "Free man." This is a variant of **Francis**. Playwright Ferenc Molnar.

Fergall Ir. Gael. "Brave, manly."
Fearghall, Forgael

Fergus Ir. Gael. "Highest choice." Mostly Scottish use.
Fearghas, Fearghus, Feargus, Fergie, Ferguson, Fergusson

Fermin Sp. "Strong." The famous running of the bulls in Pamplona, Spain, takes place in honor of a bishop and saint named Fermin.
Firmin

Fernley OE. Place name: "Fern meadow." Used since the late 19th century as a first name for children of both sexes, though primarily in Britain.
Farnlea, Farnlee, Farnleigh, Farnley, Fernlea, Fernlee, Fernleigh

Ferrand OF. "Gray-haired."
Farand, Farrand, Farrant, Ferrant

Ferris Ir. Gael. Possibly derived from Fergus, or else, via Pierce, an Irish variant of **Peter**. Brought to attention in the 1980s by the movie *Ferris Bueller's Day Off*.
Farris, Farrish, Ferriss

Festus Lat. "Joyous, festive."

Fiacre Saint's name of unknown meaning: Fiacre was an Irish saint who built a hospice in France. He is patron of gardeners, and hemorrhoid sufferers pray to him for relief.

Fico Derivation disputed: possibly an Italian contraction of Federico.

Fidel Lat. "Faithful." The Puritans named boys Faithful, but Fidel is the modern form. However, since Fidel Castro's rise in Cuba, it is unlikely to be used by today's parents.
Fadelio, Fedele, Fidele, Fedelio, Fidal, Fidalio, Fidelio, Fidelis, Fidelix, Fidelo, Fido

Fielding OE. Place name: "The field." Author Henry Fielding.
Feilding, Field, Fielder

Filbert OE. "Very brilliant." Saint Philibert was a 7th-century monk who gave his name to a nut, since his feast day falls at the time when the nuts are ripe. In the U.S., filberts are more usually known as hazelnuts. The name is uncommon in any of its forms.
Bert, Filberte, Filberto, Philbert, Philibert, Phillbert

Filmore OE. "Very famous." Historically best-known under the presidency of Millard Fillmore (1850–1853), but nostalgic rock fans may also remember the famous rock and roll venues in San Francisco and New York.
Fillmore, Filmer, Fylmer

Finbarr Ir. Gael. "Fair-haired." One of the more prominent of the many abbotts and bishops who kept the Catholic Church alive in Ireland during the 7th and 8th centuries. One tale about Saint Finbarr is that he crossed the Irish Sea on horseback.
Barr, Barra, Finbar, Finnbar, Finnbarr, Fionn, Fionnbharr

Finian Ir. Gael. "Fair." Perhaps familiar from the 1968 film *Finian's Rainbow* (Fred Astaire's last musical), but little used as a first name.
Finan, Finnian, Fionan, Fionn, Phinean, Phinian

Finlay Ir. Gael. "Fair-haired courageous one." Most often used in Scotland, where it is a common last name. Author Finley Peter Dunne.
Findlay, Findley, Finlea, Finlee, Finley, Finn, Finnlea, Finnley, Lee, Leigh

Finn Ir. Gael. "Fair" or OG. "From Finland." Many of the names above and below have *fionh* as a root.
Fin, Fionn, Fingal, Fingall

Fintan Ir. Gael. "Little fair one." Saint Fintan was another Irish abbot, whose monastery subsisted at a remarkable level of austerity. Fintan himself lived solely on bread and water.

Finnegan Ir. Gael. "Fair." Common Irish surname. Given some prominence by James Joyce's last novel, *Finnegan's Wake*.
Finegan

Fiorello It. "Little flower." Would be almost unknown in the U.S. without the fame of New York mayor Fiorello La Guardia.

Fisher OE. Occupational name: "Fisherman." Actor Fisher Stevens.
Fish, Fischer, Fisscher, Visscher

Fisk ME. "Fish." Probably an occupational name, indicating an ancestor who was a fishmonger.
Fiske

Fitch ME. Animal name: a fitch is a mammal related to the ferret or ermine. Use as a name probably goes back to an ancestor who hunted or kept fitches, rather than relating to the late–19th-century fashion for nature names.

Fitz OF. "Son of . . ." Usually short for one of the "Fitz-" names below. Derives from the Norman *filz* or "son."

Fitzgerald OF./OG. "Son of the spear-ruler." In the U.S., famous as the middle name of John F. Kennedy, and the last name of his grandfather, who was known as "Honey Fitz."

Fitzhugh OF./OG. "Son of intelligence." American painter Fitzhugh Lane.

Fitzpatrick OF./Lat. "Son of the nobleman."

Fitzroy OF. "Son of the king."

Flaminio Sp. "Roman priest."
Flamino

Flann Ir. Gael. "Ruddy, red-haired."
Flainn, Flannan, Flannery

Flavian Lat. "Yellow hair." Originally a Latin clan name, and common enough in the Roman Empire, but never revived in an English-speaking country.
Flavel, Flavelle, Flaviano, Flavien, Flavio, Flavius, Flawiusz

Fleetwood OE. Place name: "Woods with the stream." Very likely to refer to the band Fleetwood Mac.

Fleming OE. "Man from Flanders." Flanders is now Belgium. Author (and James Bond creator) Ian Fleming.
Flemming, Flemmyng, Flemyng

Fletcher ME. Occupational name: "Arrow-maker."
Flecher, Fletch

Flint OE. Place name: "Stream." Denotes an ancestor who lived near a stream. In the U.S., "flint" is a kind of stone. Publisher Larry Flynt.
Flynt

Florent OF. "In flower." The feminine version, Florence, is far more popular. Impresario Florenz Ziegfeld.
Fiorentino, Florentin, Florentino, Florentz, Florenz, Florinio, Florino, Floris, Florus

Florian Lat. "Blooming." Most common in Middle European countries.
Florien, Florrian, Floryan

Floyd Welsh. "Gray-haired." Anglicization of Lloyd. Boxing star Floyd Patterson.

Flynn Ir. Gael. "Son of the ruddy man."
Flin, Flinn, Flyn

Folke Scand. "People's guardian."
Folker, Volker, Vollker

Forbes Scot. Gael. "Field." Used mostly in Scotland. Magazine founder Malcolm Forbes.

Ford OE. Place name. "River crossing." Most Americans will automatically associate the name with the car. Author Ford Madox Ford; automotive pioneer Henry Ford.
Forden, Fordon

Forest OF. Occupational name, "Woodsman," or place name, "Woods." Most common in the U.S., spelled "Forrest," as in Winston Groom's novel and the popular film *Forrest Gump*. Novelist E. M. Forster; actor/director Forrest Whittaker.
Forester, Forrest, Forrester, Forster, Foster

Fortney Lat. "Strong one." May gain usage from its familiarity, since it rhymes with the popular Courtney. On the other hand, the pull of Courtney may make Fortney a girl's name.
Fortenay, Forteney, Forteny, Fortny, Fourtney

Fortune OF. "Lucky."
Fortunato, Fortunatus, Fortune, Fortunio, Fortuny

Foster OE. Occupational name: "Woodsman." Var. **Forest**.

Fouad Arab. "Heart."
Fuad

Fowler OE. Occupational name: "Bird trapper."

Fox OE. "Fox." This is probably different from the numerous German names based on "Wolf," which refer to the fierce nature of the beast in a mythic way. This name probably refers either to a fox-catcher or to the location of a fox's den. Journalist Fox Butterfield; English statesman Charles James Fox.
Foxe, Foxen

Franchot Fr. Var. **Francis**. Actor Franchot Tone.

Francis Lat. "Frenchman" or "Free man." France was originally the Kingdom of the Franks. Saint Francis of Assisi gave the name its first fame; though he was named

John, he had been nicknamed Francis because h[...]
had him taught French as a boy. The name traveled to
England via France, and was popular in the 17th and 19th
centuries. Frank is more often used now probably owing
to the rise of the feminine version and homonym Frances.
Philosopher Sir Francis Bacon; composer Franz Josef
Haydn; King François I of France; playwright Ferenc
Molnar; French president François Mittérrand; film
director Francis Ford Coppola; "Star Spangled Banner"
author Francis Scott Key; football players Fran Tarkenton,
Franco Harris.

Chico, Ferenc, Feri, Fran, Franco, Francesco, Franche, Franchesco, Franchesko, Franchot, Francisco, Franciscus, Franciskus, François, Franio, Frank, Frankie, Franko, Frann, Frannie, Frans, Fransisco, Frants, Frantz, Franz, Franzel, Franzen, Franzin, Frasco, Frascuelo, Frasquito, Paco, Pacorro, Panchito, Pancho, Paquito

Frank Dim. **Francis** or **Franklin**. Used as an independent
name since the 17th century, and very popular at the turn
of the 20th century right through the 1930s. Now less
used, though it is still more popular than such old standbys as Henry, Frederick, or Roger. The durable popularity
of its most famous bearer, Frank Sinatra, may do something to keep it in the public consciousness. Astronaut
Frank Borman; actors Frank Langella, Franco Nero; architect Frank Lloyd Wright; musician Frank Zappa.

Franc, Franco, Franck, Francke, Frankie

Franklin ME. "Free landholder." Surname transferred to
first name, popular in the U.S., especially in the 1930s
and 1940s as homage to President Franklin Delano Roosevelt. President Franklin Pierce apparently made less of
an impression, as his term (1853–1857) did not inspire a
surge of infant Franklins.

**Francklin, Francklyn, Frank, Franklinn, Franklyn, Frank-
lynn**

Frazer Derivation unclear, possibly OE. "Curly hair" or
an old French place name. [Relationship to the French
fraise (charcoal) is debated.] Used mostly in Scottish families, though a popular TV sitcom of the late nineties may
have changed that.

Fraser, Frasier, Frazier

Frayne ME. "Foreign."
Fraine, Frayn, Frean, Freen, Freyne
Frederick OG. "Peaceful ruler." Taken by the Hanoverian
  kings to Britain, where it began a steady ascent to great
  popularity that only faded in the 1930s. No longer fashionable, but sufficiently common so that it doesn't sound
  outlandish. Actor Fred MacMurray; dancer Fred Astaire;
  cartoon character Fred Flintstone; children's TV personality Fred Rogers; composer Frédéric Chopin; abolitionist
  Frederick Douglass; philosopher Friedrich Nietzsche.
**Eric, Erich, Erick, Erico, Erik, Eryk, Federico, Federigo,
  Fred, Fredd, Freddie, Fredek, Frédéric, Frederich, Fred-
  erico, Frederigo, Frederik, Fredi, Fredric, Fredrick, Fred-
  rik, Frido, Friedel, Friedrich, Friedrick, Fridrich, Fridrick,
  Fritz, Fritzchen, Fritzi, Fritzl, Fryderyk, Ric, Rich, Rick,
  Ricky, Rik, Rikki**
Freeborn OE. Use of the descriptive term. May date back
  to slave days, or to the era of widespread serfdom, when
  to be born free was worthy of commemoration.
Freed OE. "Free" or Ger. "Peace."
Fried
Freedom Use of the word as a given name is more common
  than one might think.
Freeman OE. See **Freeborn**.
**Free, Freedman, Freeland, Freemon, Friedman, Fried-
  mann**
Fremont OG. "Protector of freedom." Explorer John Fré-
  mont.
French ME. "From France." Transferred last name.
Frewin OE. "Free friend."
Frewen
Frey Scand. "Lord, exalted one." In Norse myth, Frey is
  the fertility god, and also the handsomest of all the deities.
Frick OE. "Brave man." Industrialist and philanthropist
  Henry Clay Frick.
Fridolf OE. "Peaceful wolf."
Freydolf, Freydulf, Friedolf, Fridulf
Friedhelm OG. "Peace helmet."
Friedelm
Fritz Ger. Dim. **Frederick**. Film director Fritz Lang.
Frits

Frode ONorse. "Wise."

Frost OE. "Freezing." Poet Robert Frost.

Fry ME. "Seedling, offspring." As in "small-fry."
  Frye, Fryer

Fulbright OG. "Very bright." See **Filbert**. The name has become famous through the Fulbright Scholar program, which sends (very bright) American graduate students to study abroad.
  Fulbert, Philbert, Philibert, Philbert

Fulgentius Lat. "Brilliant, shining." Veneration of a North African bishop and saint of the 5th century keeps this elaborate name alive.
  Fulgencio

Fulke OE. "Folk, people." A very old name in England, still used in families that trace their lineage back hundreds of years. A bit odd, however, in the rather newer United States.
  Fulk, Fawke, Fowke

Fuller OE. Occupational name: "One who shrinks cloth." The woolen fabric that was such a staple of the medieval English economy needed to be treated by fullers before it was made into clothes. The surname was most often used as a first name in the 19th century.

Fulton OE. Place name: "Settlement of the fowl" or "People's estate." Surname used as first name: in the U.S., possibly a compliment to Robert Fulton, inventor of the steamboat. Catholic bishop Fulton J. Sheen.

Fursey Ir. Gael. Meaning unknown: the name of one of the many 7th-century Irish missionary saints who tried to convert the Angles to Christianity.

Fyfe Scot. Gael. Place name: Fifeshire is an area of Scotland. American cabinetmaker Duncan Phyfe.
  Fife, Fyffe, Phyfe

Furman Ger. "Ferryman."
  Fuhrman, Fuhrmann, Furmann

Fyodor Rus. from Gk. "Divine gift." Var. **Theodore**. Author Fyodor Dostoyevsky.
  Fedor, Feodor, Fyodr

IT'S A PUPPY, IT'S A KITTEN, IT'S A BABY!

Every now and then parents go a little too far in choosing inventive names for their children, and it seems that the name they've picked would really be more suited to a pet. Could this be some cosmic confusion? Some of the hottest names for pets right now have been borrowed from the human world: Max is the top choice for dogs, with Jake, Molly, and Sam right up there. Cats are being named Max, too, with Samantha and Callie also popular. Cat people will not be surprised, though, to know that the number one name for felines is still, yes, Kitty.

Gabbo ME. "Scoff, joke."

Gable OF. Dim. **Gabriel**. When used, is probably influenced by the fame of actor Clark Gable, who was often known by just his last name.

Gabriel Heb. "Hero of God." Gabriel is an archangel who appears in Christian, Jewish, and Muslim texts. The name was uncommon in English-speaking countries, except for a spell of use in the 18th and 19th centuries, but is now used quite steadily in the U.S., perhaps because of the universality of Gabriel's story. Musician Peter Gabriel; author Gabriel García Marquez; football player Roman Gabriel.

Gab, Gabbi, Gabbie, Gabby, Gabe, Gabi, Gabie, Gabriele,

Gabrielli, Gabriello, Gabrielo, Gaby, Gavriel, Gavril, Gavrilo

Gad Heb. "Fortune, luck." In the old Testament, one of Jacob's twelve sons, and founder of one of the twelve tribes of Israel.

Gadi

Gadiel Arab. "God is my fortune."

Gaddiel

Gadish Heb. "Shock of corn." Appropriate for boys born near Shavuot, the Jewish harvest festival that usually falls in October.

Gael Eng. "Speaker of Gaelic." Refers to one of the Celtic peoples of Scotland or Ireland. As a name, would be confused with Gail, which is traditionally female.

Gale

Gaetan It. Place name: Gaeta is a region in Southern Italy; the Gulf of Gaeta is just north of Naples.

Cajetan, Cajetano, Gaetano, Gaeton, Kajetan, Kajetano

Gage OF. "Oath." The British General Thomas Gage was the Governor of the Massachusetts Bay Colony at the outbreak of the Revolutionary War.

Gaige

Gahan Possibly a Scottish variant of **John**. Cartoonist Gahan Wilson.

Gehan

Gaillard ME. "Brave, cheerful, spirited." Also the name of a 16th-century dance.

Gaillhard, Gaillardet, Galliard

Gaines English last name of uncertain derivation. It may have something to do with today's meaning of "gain," "to get."

Gains, Gayne, Gaynes

Gair Ir. Gael. "Small one."

Gaer, Geir

Gaius Lat. "Rejoice." This is probably the root of our word "gay," which used to mean "jolly." A Gaius appears in the New Testament, and another one was a Roman jurist of the 2nd century. Caius is a variation that occurs from time to time in England.

Cai, Caio, Kay, Kaye, Keye, Keyes, Keys

Gal Heb. "Wave, roller, swell."

Galbraith Ir. Gael. "Foreign Briton." In Ireland, the name would have been used most commonly to describe a Scot. Economist John Kenneth Galbraith.
Galbrait, Galbreath, Gallbraith, Gallbreath

Gale Ir. Gael. "Foreigner"; OE. "Cheerful, happy." Much more common now as a girl's name, when it is usually a diminutive of Abigail. Football player Gale Sayers.
Gael, Gaell, Gaelle, Gail, Gaill, Gaille, Gaile, Gayle

Galen Gk. "Healer" or "Tranquil." A 2nd-century Greek physician named Galen was for centuries the only authority on the emergent practice of medicine. The name is seeing a flicker of trendy use among intellectuals.
Gaelan, Gaillen, Gaillen, Galeno, Galin, Gaylen, Gaylin, Gaylinn, Gaylon, Jalen, Jalin, Jalon, Jaylen, Jaylon

Galil Heb. "Hilly." This is the word that gives the name to Galilee, a hilly area in Israel.

Galileo It. "From Galilee." The name of the great 16th- and 17th-century Italian astronomer who built the first astronomical telescope and confirmed Copernicus's theory that the planets revolve around the sun.

Gall Derivation unknown. May possibly refer to Gaelic, since Saint Gall was one of the many 7th-century Irish monks who brought Christianity back to the continent of Europe after the Dark Ages.

Gallagher Ir. Gael. "Foreign helper." Actor Peter Gallagher.

Gallatin American place name: a county and river in Montana. They were probably named for Albert Gallatin, a Swiss-born American statesman of the early 19th century, but to outdoors people, the name Gallatin bears connotations of the unspoiled West.

Galloway Old Gael. "Foreign Gael." Another name for a Scot. The Irish population includes a strong Scottish strain.
Gallway, Galway

Galo Sp. from Lat. "From Gaul." Gaul was the Roman name for France.
Gallo

Galt OE. Place name: "Steep wooded land." May also be

derived from the Old German word particle that gives us Walter ("People of power").

Galton OE. "Owner of a rented land."
Galt, Galten, Gallton

Galvin Ir. Gael. "Sparrow" or "Brilliantly white."
Gallven, Gallvin, Galvan, Galven, Galvon

Galway Irish place name: a city in Western Ireland. Critic Galway Kinnell; flutist James Galway.

Gamal Arab. "Camel."
Gamali, Gamul, Gemal, Gemali, Gemul, Jamal, Jammal, Jemaal, Jemal

Gamaliel Heb. "Recompense of God." An obscure biblical name probably brought to the U.S. by the Puritans. Little used since the 19th century. President Warren Gamaliel Harding.
Gamliel, Gmali

Gamble ONorse. "Old." A household name in this country as part of the former soap-manufacturing company Procter & Gamble.
Gamblen, Gambling, Gamel, Gammel, Gamlin

Ganesh Sanskrit. "Lord of the throngs." Ganesh is the Hindu god of wisdom, usually portrayed as a squat little man with an elephant's head.

Gannet OG. "Goose." A fish-eating web-footed sea bird related to the booby. Gannets are found in northern climates and live on cliffs and rocks.
Gannett

Gannon Ir. Gael. "Fair-skinned."

Gardner ME. Occupational name: "Gardener." In the eastern U.S., reminiscent of two distinguished families, known as the "blind" Gardners (the name has no *i*) or the "sighted" Gardiners. The former are famous for the Isabella Stewart Gardner Museum in Boston; the latter for Gardiner's Island on Long Island Sound.
Gardell, Gardener, Gardenner, Gardie, Gardiner, Gardnar, Gardnard

Gareth Welsh. "Gentle." The name of one of King Arthur's knights. Used in Britain since the 1930s, but rare elsewhere.
Garith, Garreth, Garret, Garyth

Garfield OE. "Spear field." Use as a first name probably

honored President James Garfield, though indignation at
his untimely death outweighed admiration for his skills,
since his term lasted only a few months before he was
assassinated in 1881. More recently the statesman has
been upstaged by a fat orange cartoon cat who has made
the name his own.

Garland OE. Place name: "Land of the spear" or OF.
"Wreath." Musician Garland Jeffreys.

Garlan, Garlen, Garlend, Garlin, Garlind, Garllan

Garman OE. "Spearman."

Garmann, Garmen, Garmin, Garmon, Garrman

Garner ME. "To gather grain." Possibly a place name or
occupational name originally, denoting an ancestor who
lived near a granary, or who helped harvest grain. Actor
James Garner.

Garnar, Garnier

Garnett OE. "Spear" or OF. "Red like a pomegranate."
Although the girl's name is more likely to be a jewel
name in the tradition of Pearl or Ruby, for boys, Garnet
is usually a transferred last name. In England, boys may
have been named for a famous Victorian soldier, Sir Garnet Wolseley.

Garnet

Garnock Old Welsh. Place name: "River of alder trees."

Garrard OE. "Spear-hard" or "Spear-brave." Related to
Gerard via the German form, Gerhard.

Gerhard, Gerhardt, Gerard

Garrett Var. **Gerard** dating from the Middle Ages.
Equally, it may be a variation of **Gareth/Garth**.

**Gareth, Garrard, Garret, Garreth, Garretson, Garrith,
Garritt, Garrot, Garrott, Garyth, Gerrit, Gerritt, Gerrity,
Jared, Jarod, Jarret, Jarrett, Jarrot, Jarrott**

Garrick OE. "Spear-rule." Eighteenth century English actor David Garrick did much to revive the fame of Shakespeare, and he is commemorated with street and building
names in the theater district of London. Newscaster Garrick Utley.

Garek, Garreck, Garrik, Garryck, Garryk

Garrison ME. "Protection, stronghold." Author Garrison
Keillor.

Garrisson

Garroway OE. "Spear-fighter."
 Garraway

Garson OE. "Gar's son." Gar in this case may be a diminutive of **Garrett, Gareth, Garland**, etc., or even a shortening of Garrison.

Garth Scand. Occupational name: "Keeper of the garden." Used as a first name in this century, but never widely. Illustrator Garth Williams.

Garton OE. Place name: "Triangle-shaped settlement."
 Gorton

Garvey Ir. Gael. "Rough peace."
 Garrvey, Garrvie, Garvie, Garvy

Garvin OE. "Spear-friend."
 Garvan, Garven, Garvyn, Garwen, Garwin, Garwyn, Garwynn

Garwood OE. Place name: "Wood with fir trees."
 Garrwood, Woody

Gary OE. "Spear." Popularized by film idol Gary Cooper, whose name was originally Frank. Very fashionable from the 1950s to the 1970s, and still steadily used. Cartoonists Garry Trudeau, Gary Larson.
 Gari, Garey, Garrie, Garry

Gaspar Var. **Caspar**. Possibly Persian. "He who guards the treasure."
 Caspar, Casper, Gaspard, Gasparo, Gasper, Jaspar, Jasper, Kaspar, Kasper

Gaston Fr. "Man from Gascony." Gascony is a region in the south of France whose inhabitants are reputed to be hot-tempered. Since the unlucky and boorish suitor in Disney's cartoon film of *Beauty and the Beast* is named Gaston, the name has taken on new connotations of foolishness.
 Gascon

Gates OE. Place name: "Near the gates." An infrequently transferred last name.

Gaurav Hindi. "Pride."

Gauthier Teut. "Strong ruler." The anglicized version of this name is Walter. Fashion designer Jean-Paul Gaultier.
 Galtero, Gaultier, Gautier, Gualterio, Gualtiero

Gavin Welsh. "White falcon" or "Little falcon." As Gawain, this was the name of one of King Arthur's knights.

The Scottish form, Gavin, has spread from Scotland to broad acceptance in Britain, especially in the last thirty years. Still rare in the U.S. Actor Gavin MacLeod.

Gavan, Gaven, Gavyn, Gavynn, Gawain, Gawaine, Gawayn, Gawayne, Gawen, Gwaine, Gwayn

Gaylord OF. "Lively, high-spirited." This is the most familiar version of Gaillard. Author Gayelord Hauser.

Gaillard, Gailard, Galliard, Gay, Gayelord, Gayler, Gaylor

Gaynor Ir. Gael. "Son of the fair-skinned one." From a different root than the feminine version; for male children, this is strictly a transferred last name, and unusual at that.

Gaine, Gainer, Gainor, Gay, Gayner, Gaynnor

Geary ME. "Variable."

Gearey, Gery

Gedaliah Heb. "God is great."

Gedalia, Gedaliahu, Gedalio, Gedalya

Geddes Scottish last name of disputed meaning. It may be related to "goad," a pointed rod used to drive livestock.

Gaddis, Geddis

Gefen Heb. "Vine."

Gafni, Gefania, Gefaniah, Gefanya, Gefanyah, Gefanyahu, Geffen, Gephania, Gephaniah

Gemini Lat. "Twins." Name of the astrological sign of the Twins, who govern the period from May 21 to June 20.

Gemelli, Geminiano

Gene Dim. Eugene (Gk. "Well-born"). Used as an independent name since the late 19th century, especially in America. Actors Gene Kelly, Gene Wilder, Gene Hackman.

Genio, Geno, Jeno

Genesis Gk. "Origin, beginning." Genesis is the first book in the Old Testament, and relates the story of the creation of the world.

Gennesis, Ginesis, Jenesis, Jennesis

Gennaro It. "Of Janus." Janus was an ancient Roman god with two faces, one which looked to the old year, one to the new year. He gave his name to the month of January. A Saint Januarius was martyred in the 4th century A.D. According to one source, a vial said to contain his blood, which is preserved in the cathedral at Naples, actually

turns to liquid eighteen times year. There is n[
explanation for this.

Gennarius, Gennaros, Januario, Januarius

Gentian Flower name: the gentian was named after an ancient king of Illyria (now Yugoslavia's coast). Gentians
are brilliant blue, with fringed petals. Though flower
names are usually feminine, the "-ian" ending is still
masculine (Dorian, Julian).

Genshian, Jenshian, Jentian

Gentile Lat. "Foreigner, heathen." The term "gentile" is
often used to characterize someone as non-Jewish. Italian
painter Gentile da Fabriano.

Gentilo

Geoffrey Var. Jeffrey. OG. Unclear, something to do with
"peace." Norman name popular through the Middle Ages
in Britain, and revived in the mid–19th century after a
350-year rest. The peak of its popularity was the 1970s
in the U.S., and it is no longer a favorite, though the
"Jeff-" spelling occurs quite often. Performer Geoffrey
Holder; medieval poet Geoffrey Chaucer; fashion designer
Geoffrey Beene.

**Geoff, Geoffery, Geoffroy, Geoffry, Geofrey, Jefery, Jeff,
Jefferey, Jefferies, Jeffery, Jeffree, Jeffrey, Jeffry, Jef-
frie, Jeffries, Jefry, Jeoffroi, Jephers, Jepherson, Je-
phrey, Jephry**

— **George** Gk. "Farmer." The popularity of the dragon-
killing Saint George (patron of Boy Scouts, soldiers, and
England) is undimmed by the fact that little proof of his
existence can be found. George was a royal name in England, and admiration for George Washington in the U.S.
gave the name a parallel popularity in the renegade colonies from the 18th century until the middle of the 20th.
Now less common but still a steady presence. Rock star
George Michael; fashion designer Giorgio Armani; comedians George Burns, George Carlin; baseball legend
George "Babe" Ruth; U.S. President George Bush.

**Egor, Georas, Geordie, Georg, Georges, Georgi, Georgie,
Georgios, Georgius, Georgiy, Georgy, Gheorghe, Giorgi,
Giorgio, Giorgios, Giorgius, Goran, Gyorgy, Gyuri, Igor,
Jerzy, Jiri, Jorgan, Jorge, Jorgen, Jurgen, Jurek, Jurik,
Yorick, Yorik, Yurik, Ygor**

Geraint Lat. "Old." From the same root as "geriatric." A Sir Geraint figures in certain Arthurian legends; the name is sparingly used in Britain.

Gerant, Jerant, Jeraint

Gerald OG. "Spear ruler." Old name revived in the 19th century. Most popular in the middle of this century, but now less common. U.S. President Gerald Ford; TV journalist Geraldo Rivera.

Garald, Garold, Gary, Gearalt, Geralde, Geraldo, Gérard, Geraud, Gerek, Gerhard, Gerik, Gerold, Gerolld, Gerolt, Gerollt, Gerrald, Gerrard, Gerri, Gerrild, Gerrold, Gerry, Geryld, Giraldo, Giraud, Girauld, Girault, Jerald, Jerold, Jerri, Jerrold, Jerry

Gerard OE. "Spear brave." Closely related to Gerald, and its use follows a similar pattern, though it is still increasing. Particularly popular in Ireland. Poet Gerard Manley Hopkins; actor Gérard Depardieu.

Garrard, Garrat, Garratt, Garrett, Gearard, Gerardo, Geraud, Gerhard, Gerhardt, Gerhart, Gerrard, Gerri, Gerry, Girard, Girault, Giraud, Gherardo, Jarard, Jared, Jerard, Jerardo, Jerarrd, Jerrott

Geremia It. Var. Jeremiah (Heb. "The Lord exalts").

Gerlach Scand. "Spear sport."

Gerlaich

Germain Fr. "From Germany." There were several early saints called "Germanus" for their national origin, the most famous of whom gave his name to a church in Paris, Saint Germain-des-Près. Singer Jermaine Jackson; football player Joe Germaine.

Germaine, German, Germane, Germanicus, Germano, Germanus, Germayn, Germayne, Germin, Jermain, Jermaine, Jermane, Jermayn, Jermayne

Geronimo It. Var. **Jerome** (Gk. "Sacred name"). Famous as the name of an Apache Indian chief and also as the cry with which American parachutists in World War II would leap from airplanes. Nobody knows why.

Heronimo, Herinomos, Hieronimo, Hieronymus, Jeronimo, Jeronimus

Gerontius Lat. "Old man."

Gershom Heb. "Exile." Old Testament name, appearing, appropriately enough, in Exodus. The Puritans adopted it and brought it to the U.S., where it is rare, but like many Hebrew names, kept alive by Orthodox Jewish families.

Gersham, Gershon, Gershoom, Gerson

Gervase OG. Meaning unclear; possibly "With honor." Because of the popularity of a Saint Gervase, the name has been steadily used by English Catholics, but is otherwise unusual.

Garvey, Gervais, Gervaise, Gervasio, Gervasius, Gervaso, Gervayse, Gerwazy, Jarvey, Jarvis, Jervis

Gethin Welsh "Dark-skinned."

Gethen, Gethyn

Gevariah Heb. "Strength of Jehovah."

Gevaria, Gevarya, Gevaryah, Gevarayahu

Ghalib Arab. "Victorious."

Ghassan Arab. "Youth, prime of life."

Giacomo It. Var. **Jacob** (Heb. "He who supplants"). The name of one of musician Sting's sons.

Gian Italian-style respelling of **John** (Heb. "The Lord is gracious") possibly via the nickname Gianni. Shows up occasionally in combination, as in Gian-Carlo and Gianfranco.

Gianney, Gianni, Gianny

Gibor Heb. "Strong one."

Gibbor

Gibson OE. "Son of Gilbert." Actor Mel Gibson.

Gibb, Gibbes, Gibby, Gibbons, Gibbs, Gillson, Gilson

Gideon Heb. "Feller of trees" or "Mighty warrior." A biblical judge and hero who, with an army of only 300 men, liberated the Israelites from the Midianites. The latter-day Gideons are the group responsible for placing Bibles in hotel bedrooms. Oddly enough, Gideon did not benefit from the 1980s craze for Old Testament names that dusted off names like Joshua and Jeremy.

Gideone, Gidi, Gidon, Hedeon

Gifford OE. Either "Brave giver" or "Puffy-faced." It is astonishing how rarely the derivations of names mean anything negative; this exception to that rule is used as a first name from time to time. Sports figure Frank Gifford; U.S. conservation pioneer Gifford Pinchot.

Giffard, Gifferd, Gyfford

Gilad Arab. "Hump of a camel." Heb. "Monument, site

of testimony.'' Gilead is a Biblical place name, referring to the fertile region east of the Jordan.

Giladi, Gilead

Gilam Heb. ''Joy of a people.''

Gilbert OG. ''Shining pledge.'' Norman name much used in the Middle Ages, but use tapered away to mostly local favor in Scotland and Northern England. Very unusual in the U.S. Author Gilbert Chesterton.

Bert, Bertie, Burt, Gib, Gibb, Gil, Gilberto, Gilburt, Gill, Giselbert, Giselberto, Giselbertus, Guilbert

Gilby ONorse. ''Estate of the hostage'' or Ir. Gael. ''Blond boy.''

Gilbey, Gillbey, Gillbie, Gillby

Gilchrist Ir. Gael. ''Christ's servant.''

Gillchrist

Giles Gk. ''Kid, young goat.'' The link with a shield or shield-bearer (sometimes the translation given for Giles) probably comes from the kidskin that ancient shields were made of. In modern times the name, a particular favorite in Scotland, was popular in Britain in the 1970s.

Égide, Egidio, Egidius, Gide, Gil, Gilles, Gillis, Gilliss, Gyles, Jiles, Jyles

Gill Ir. Gael. ''Servant.'' Also a diminutive of the many Irish names that begin with ''Gil-.''

Ghillie, Gilley

Gillanders Scot. Gael. ''Servant of Saint Andrew.'' Scottish Gaelic, though not identical with the Irish language, does share the particle ''Gill-,'' meaning servant, and it shows up in several names. In the Highlands in Victorian times, ''ghillie'' was a term for a kind of outdoor servant.

Gillean Ir. Gael. ''Servant of Saint John.'' Related to Gilchrist, Gillespie, Gilmore, etc., which all use the ''Gill'' particle, meaning ''servant.''

Gilean, Gilian, Gillan, Gillen, Gilleon, Gillian, Gillion, Gillon

Gillespie Ir. Gael. ''Son of the bishop's servant.''

Gillaspie, Gillis

Gillett OF. ''Young Gilbert.'' Poet Gelett Burgess.

Gelett, Gelette, Gillette

Gillies Scot. Gael. ''Servant of Jesus.''

Ghilles, Ghillies, Gilies, Gillis, Gilliss

Gilmer OE. "Renowned hostage."

Gilman Possibly Ir. Gael. "Manservant" or OE. "Gilbert's man."
　Gillman

Gilmore Ir. Gael. "Servant of the Virgin Mary."
　Gillmore, Gillmour, Gilmour

Gilon Heb. "Joy."
　Gil, Gili

Gilroy Ir. Gael. "Servant of the redhead."
　Gilderoy, Gildray, Gildroy, Gillroy, Gillray, Gilray

Gilson OE. "Son of Gilbert."
　Gillson

Gino It. Dim. **Ambrogino** (Gk. "Ever-living") or **Luigino** (OG. "Renowned warrior") or possibly **Eugene** (Gk. "Well-born").
　Geno, Jeno, Jino

Giovanni It. Var. **John** (Heb. "The Lord is gracious"). In an indication of just how polyglot America is becoming, Giovanni is used about as often as Stuart, Morgan, or Francis. The spellings of today's versions may part company with the Italian version, though. Artist Giovanni Bellini; author Giovanni Boccaccio.
　Geovanney, Geovanni, Gian, Gianni, Giannino, Giovan, Giovanno, Giovel, Giovell, Jovan, Jovanney, Jovanni, Jovanno

Girvin Ir. Gael. "Small rough one."
　Girvan, Girven, Girvon

Giulio It. Var. **Julius** (Lat. "Youthful").
　Giuliano

Giuseppe It. Var. **Joseph** (Heb. "The Lord increases"). Composer Giuseppe Verdi.

Giustino It. Var. **Justin** (Lat. "Just, fair").
　Giustinian, Giustiniano, Giusto

Gjorn Scand. "God of peace."
　Gjurd

Glade OE. "Shining." Place name, referring to a clearing in the woods.
　Glades

Gladstone OE. Place name: "Kite-shaped stone." Used in the 19th century in tribute to the great British Prime Minister William Ewart Gladstone.

Gladwin OE. "Lighthearted friend."
Gladwinn, Gladwyn, Gladwynne

Glanville OF. Place name: "Settlement of oak trees."

Glen Ir. Gael. Place name: "Glen." A glen is a narrow valley between hills. As a surname, Glen would indicate an ancestor who lived in such a valley. Singer Glen Campbell; band leader Glenn Miller; pianist Glenn Gould.
Gleann, Glenn, Glennard, Glennie, Glennon, Glenny, Glin, Glinn, Glyn, Glynn

Glenavon OE. Place name: "Valley near the Avon." The Avon is a river in England.
Glenavin, Glennavin, Glennavon

Glendon Scot. Gael. Place name: "Settlement in the glen."
Glenden, Glendin, Glenton

Glendower Welsh. "Valley of water."
Glin, Glyn, Glynn, Glyndwer, Glyndwr

Glenville Gael. Place name that has been used occasionally as a first name. Along with Glendon, it has probably gained legitimacy from the popularity of Glen as a given name.
Glanvill, Glanville, Glenvill

Glover OE. Occupational name: "Maker of gloves." Actor John Glover; tap dancer Savion Glover.

Gobind Sanskrit. "The cow finder." A prominent 17th-century guru of the Sikhs was named Guru Gobind Singh, and Govind is one of the names of Krishna, the principal Hindu deity.
Gobinda, Govind, Govinda

Goddard OG. "God-hard." Film director Jean-Luc Godard.
Godard, Godart, Goddart, Godhart, Godhardt, Gothart, Gotthard, Gotthardt, Gotthart

Godfrey OG. "God-peace." Popular medieval name that faded very gradually to its near-disuse today. The fact that it was the name of a valet in the 1936 comic film *My Man Godfrey* might indicate that there was something indefinably buffoonish about the name by that date.
Giotto, Godefroi, Godfry, Godofredo, Goffredo, Gottfrid, Gottfried

Godric OE. "God-ruler."
Goderick, Godrick, Goodrick

Godwin OE. "Friend of God" or "Good friend." Anglo-Saxon name that, though it did outlast the Norman Conquest in England, did not benefit from the 19th-century revival that resuscitated many ancient names, so it is almost unknown in the U.S.

Godden, Godding, Godewyn, Godin, Godwinn, Godwyn, Goodwin, Goodwyn, Goodwynn, Goodwynne

Golding OE. "Little golden one." *Lord of the Flies* author William Golding.

Golden, Goldman

Goldsmith OE. Occupational name: "Gold worker." Financier Sir James Goldsmith.

Goldschmidt, Goldshmidt

Goldwin OE. "Golden friend." Film pioneer Samuel Goldwyn.

Goldewin, Goldewyn, Goldwinn, Goldwyn, Goldwynn

Goliath Heb. "Exile." Though babies are frequently named for David, the Old Testament bard, very few are given the name of the giant he killed with his slingshot. Even Cain, the first assassin, has inspired more parents. Nevertheless, the name is used from time to time.

Golliath, Golyath

Gomer OE. "Famous battle" or "Good fight." Also an Old Testament name. Grown-up fans of the goofy marine depicted by Jim Nabors in the 1960s TV series "Gomer Pyle" may have trouble taking the name seriously.

Gonzalo Sp. "Wolf." Tennis star Pancho Gonzales.

Consalvo, Goncalve, Gonsalve, Gonzales

Goodman OE. "Good man." This term used to be used as a title, like Mister. Actor John Goodman.

Goodmann, Guttman, Guttmann

Goodwin OE. "Good friend."

Goodwinn, Goodwyn, Goodwynn

Goodyear OE. "Good year." In the U.S. this name is associated with the Goodyear blimp or with tires, but even car buffs may be surprised to learn that Charles Goodyear, the inventor of vulcanized rubber, patented his process in 1844 and died in debt. What's more, the first practical use of his product was for shoes.

Gordon OE. Meaning unclear, possibly a place name meaning "Hill near meadows" or "Triangular hill." Histori-

cally associated with Scotland, but principal use has been 20th century. Balladeer Gordon Lightfoot; photographer Gordon Parks; hockey player Gordie Howe.
Gordan, Gorden, Gordie

Gore OE. "Spear" or "Wedge-shaped object." "Gore" is also an old term for a small, triangular-shaped piece of land, so this may be considered a place name, denoting an ancestor who lived on or near such a piece of land. Author Gore Vidal.
Goring

Goren Heb. "Barn floor, granary." Refers to the grain harvest.
Gorin, Gorren, Gorrin

Gorham OE. Place name: "Village near the wedge-shaped piece of land." Or possibly "Spear village." Gorham is the name of a silver company based in Rhode Island.

Gorman Ir. Gael. "Small blue-eyed one."

Gorrell OE. Place name: "Thicket in the marsh."

Gorton OE. Place name: "Settlement near the wedge-shaped piece of land." Also possibly a respelling of Gordon.
Gorten

Gould OE. "Gold." Actor Elliott Gould.

Gouverneur Fr. "Governor." A name that showed up occasionally in Early American families.
Governor

Gower Old Welsh. "Pure."

Grady Ir. Gael. "Renowned." A transferred Irish last name.
Gradea, Gradee, Gradey, Graidey, Graidy

Graham OE. "Gray homestead." Mostly Scottish name that was popular in Britain in the 1950s, without ever being much used in America. Author Graham Greene; inventor Alexander Graham Bell.
Graeham, Graeme, Grahame

Granger Middle French. "Farmer." Grange organizations used to dot the agricultural portions of the U.S., offering services to farm communities.
Grainger, Grange

Grant Fr. "Tall, big." Another Scottish name, but one that has been more popular in the U.S. as a first name, probably inspired by President Ulysses S. Grant. With a very

few exceptions, monosyllabic names are not fashi
now, but Grant is used somewhat steadily. Painter Grant
Wood; actor Hugh Grant.

Grantham, Grantley

Grantland OE. Place name: "The large fields," or possibly
"Granta's fields."

Grantleigh, Grantley, Grantly

Granville OF. Place name: "Big town." Though never frequent, use of the name has diminished since the 1960s,
possibly because its slightly aristocratic sound has seemed
too undemocratic for the age of equality.

Granvil, Granvile, Granvill, Grenville

Graves OE. Place name. Commemorates an area near a
community burying ground. Fairly common as a last name
in Britain. Poet Robert Graves.

Gray OE. "Gray-haired." Poet Thomas Gray.

Graye, Grey

Graydon OE. Possibly "Son of the gray-haired one" or a
place name: "Gray settlement."

Grayton

Grayson OE. "Son of the gray-haired man."

Graydon, Greydon, Greyson

Graziano It. "Beloved, dear."

Gracian, Graciano

Greeley OE. Place name: "Gray meadow" or perhaps
"Green meadow." American use of the name (which is
far from widespread) may reflect admiration for 19th-
century journalist and politician Horace Greeley.

Greelea, Greeleigh, Greely

Greenwood OE. Place name: "Green wood."

— **Gregory** Gk. "Watchful, vigilant." A staple name in the
Middle Ages, used by sixteen popes and ten saints. Modern popularity dates from the 1940s, which means it is
probably linked to actor Gregory Peck's rise to stardom.
Like most names that were very fashionable in the 1950s,
it is now a bit out of style. Cyclist Greg LeMond; musician Gregg Allman; actor Gregory Hines.

**Graig, Greer, Greg, Greger, Gregg, Greggory, Grégoire,
Gregoor, Gregor, Gregori, Gregorio, Gregorius, Gregos,
Grigor, Grigori, Grigorios, Grygor, Grzegorz**

Gresham OE. Place name: "Village surrounded by pasture."

Greville OF. Place name used occasionally in Britain.
Grevill

Gridley OE. Place name: "Level meadow."
Gridlie, Gridly

Griffin Lat. "Hooked nose." The name of a mythical beast, usually half eagle (hence the hooked nose), half lion. Use as a name may be connected to the frequent heraldic use of the animal. Actor Griffin Dunne.
Griff, Griffen, Griffon, Gryffen, Gryffin, Gryphon

Griffith Welsh. "Strong chief." Used most often as a first name in the 16th through the 18th centuries. This is the kind of slightly nostalgic name that seems ripe for revival, except that it's hard to say in a hurry.

Grimaldo Ger./Sp. "Powerful protector." Grimaldi, a related name, is the last name of the royal family of Monaco.
Grimaldi

Grimshaw OE. Place name: "Dark woods."

Grimsley OE. Place name: "Dark meadow."
Grimslea, Grimsleigh, Grimslie, Grimsly

Griswold OF./Ger. Place name: "Gray woods."
Griswald

Grosvenor OF. "Great hunter." Grosvenor is the last name of one of the richest families in Britain. Their stake in London real estate is commemorated in names like Grosvenor Square.
Grosveneur

Grover OE. Place name: "Grove of trees." American use was probably inspired by President Grover Cleveland, but has faded since the mid–20th century. Parents of *Sesame Street* viewers are more likely to be reminded of the self-proclaimed "cute, furry, lovable little monster" Grover.

Guerrant Fr. "Fighting, at war."

Guido It. Var. **Guy.**

Guildford OE. Place name: "Ford with yellow flowers."
Gilford, Guilford

Guillaume Fr. Var. **William** (OG. "Will-helmet"). Poet Guillaume Apollinaire.
Guglielmo, Guilherme, Guillermo, Gwillym, Gwilym

Gulshan Hindi. "Garden."

Gulzar Arab. "In bloom, flourishing."

Gunther Scand. "Warrior." Author Günter Grass.
Guenter, Guenther, Gun, Gunn, Gunnar, Gunner, Gunners, Guntar, Gunter, Guntero, Gunthar, Guntur

Gur Heb. "Cub, young lion."
Guri, Guriel, Gurion, Guryon

Gus Dim. Augustus (Lat. "Worthy of respect").
Guss, Gustav

Gustave Scand. "Staff of the gods." A royal name in Sweden; used elsewhere in Europe in the 17th century, and in England in the 19th century. American use (which is uncommon) tends to harken back to Scandinavian ancestry. Composer Gustav Mahler; writer Gustave Flaubert.
Gus, Guss, Gustaf, Gustaff, Gustaof, Gustav, Gustavo, Gustavus, Gustovo, Gustus, Gusztav

Guthrie Ir. Gael. Place name: "Windy spot." Folk singer Woody Guthrie.
Guthree, Guthrey, Guthry

Guy Unclear origin, though some sources make a case for French "Guide" or Old German "Warrior." Made infamous in 1605 by Guy Fawkes, scapegoat of a plot to blow up the Houses of Parliament; in Britain, November 5 is still Guy Fawkes Day, when a dummy was traditionally burned in effigy. The English shunned the name for 200 years, but it became acceptable again by the mid–19th century, and use was increasing by the 1950s. To Americans, it is still a very English-sounding name.
Guido

Gwalchmai Welsh. "Battle hawk."

Gwynn OWelsh. "Fair."
Guinn, Gwin, Gwyn, Gwynedd

Gyandev Sanskrit. "God of wisdom."
Gyan

Habakkuk Heb. "Embrace." One of the minor prophets in the Old Testament. One of the more outlandish-sounding prophet names to anglophone ears, and it has never been widely used.
Habacuc, Habbakuk

Habib Arab. "Loved one."
Habeeb

Hackett OF./Ger. Occupational name: "Little hewer" (of wood).
Hacket, Hackit, Hackitt

Hackman OF./Ger. Occupational name: "Hewer, hacker" (of wood). Actor Gene Hackman.

Hadar Heb. "Splendor, ornament" or "Respect."
Hadaram, Hadur, Heder

Hadden OE. Place name: "Hill of heather."
Haddan, Haddon, Haddin, Haden, Hadon

Hadi Arab. "Rightly guide."

Hadley OE. Place name: "Heather meadow." Interior designer Albert Hadley.
Hadlea, Hadlee, Hadleigh, Hadly, Leigh

Hadrian Var. **Adrian** (Lat. "From Adria"). Adria was a north Italian city. A Roman Emperor Hadrian was responsible for the building of a vast wall across northern Britain, parts of which still stand.
Adrian, Adriano, Adrien, Hadrien

Hadriel Heb. "Splendor of Jehovah."

Hadwin OE. "Friend in war."
Hadwinn, Hadwyn, Hadwynne, Hedwin, Hedwinn

Hafiz Arab. "One who guards."
Hafeez, Hapheez, Haphiz

Hagen Ir. Gael. "Youthful one." Also a Germanic version of Hakon (see following).
Hagan, Haggan

Hagley OE. Place name: "Enclosed meadow."
Haglea, Haglee, Hagleigh, Hagly

Haig OE. Place name: "Enclosed with hedges." Douglas Haig was a prominent English soldier in World War I.

Haidar Arab. "Lion."

Haider, Haydar, Hyder

Haim Heb. "Life." Variant spelling of **Chaim**.

Hayim, Hayyim

Hakeem Arab. "Wise, all-knowing." One of the ninety-nine attributes of Allah, which the prophet Muhammad considered good choices for names. Basketball player Hakeem Olajuwon.

Hakim

Hakon Scand. "Of the highest race" or "Chosen son." A royal name in Norway, but little used in English-speaking countries.

Haaken, Haakin, Haakon, Hacon, Hagan, Hagen, Hakan, Hako

Hal Dim. Most commonly of **Henry** (OE. "Home ruler"). In Shakespeare's plays about Henry IV, his son (to become Henry V) is affectionately known as "Prince Hal." Actors Hal Holbrook, Hal Linden.

Halbert OE. "Shining hero."

Halburt

Haldan Scand. "Half-Danish." The name takes on a certain significance when you consider that in ancient Britain, the Danes were fierce and frequent invaders.

Haldane, Halden, Halfdan, Halfdane, Halvdan

Haldor ONorse. "Thor's stone."

Halldor, Halle

Hale OE. Either place name: "From the hall," or "Healthy hero." Revolutionary War hero Nathan Hale was hanged by the British as a spy. His famous last words on the scaffold were "I regret that I have but one life to lose for my country."

Hal, Hayle

Haley OE. Place name: "Hay meadow" or Ir. Gael. "Ingenious, clever." The widespread use of Hayley as a girl's name probably spells the end of its use as a boy's name. Football player Charles Haley.

Hailey, Haily, Haleigh, Halley, Hallie, Hayleigh, Hayley

Halford OE. Place name: "Valley ford" or "Hal's ford."

Hallford

Hali Gk. "The sea."

Hall OE. Occupational name: "Worker at the hall." In this case, the hall would signify a large house or manor. Musician Darryl Hall.

Hallam OE. Place name: "The valley."
  Hallem

Hallberg ONorse. "Rock mountain."
  Halberg, Halburg, Hallburg

Halle ONorse. "Rock." Considering the Scandinavian influence in the formation of English, it's probably impossible to sort out derivations of various "Hall-" names.

Halley OE. Either place name: "Meadow near the hall" or "Holy." This is a different name from the homonym Haley, but will probably also be discarded as a boy's name as the retro-charming Hallie becomes more popular for girls. Astronomer Edmund Halley.

Halliwell OE. Place name: "Holy well."
  Hallewell, Hallowell, Hellewell, Helliwell

Hallward OE. Occupational name: "Guardian of the hall." Like many of these Anglo-Saxon names, it is unusual as a first name.
  Halward, Halwerd, Hawarden

Halsey OE. Place name: "Hal's island."
  Hallsey, Hallsy, Halsy

Halstead OE. Place name: "The manor grounds."
  Hallstead, Hallsted, Halsted

Halton OE. Place name: "Estate on the hill."
  Halten, Hallton, Halton

Halvard ONorse. "Guardian of the rock."
  Hallvard, Hallverd, Hallvor, Halvar, Halver, Halverd, Halvor

Ham Heb. "Heat." Old Testament name, one of the sons of Noah. Little used; the names of Noah's other two sons, Shem and Japheth, are even more rare.

Hamal Arab. "Lamb."
  Amahl, Amal, Hamahl

Hamar ONorse. "Hammer."

Hamid Arab. "Thankful, praising."
  Hameed

Hamilton OE. Place name of several possible meanings such as "Home-lover's estate" or "Hill with grass." It was the surname of several aristocratic British families and made the transition to a first name in the early 19th century. U.S. statesman Alexander Hamilton; figure skater Scott Hamilton.

Hamel, Hamelton, Hamil, Hamill

Hamill OE. "Scarred." May refer to the facial characteristic of a distant ancestor. Actor Mark Hamill; newspaper editor and writer Pete Hamill.

Hamel, Hamell, Hammill

Hamish Scot. Var. **James** (Heb. "He who supplants"). Almost unknown outside of Scotland.

Hamlet OG./Fr. "Village, home." This name, like Hamlin, derives from a German root that means "home." Hamlet was a common first name until the beginning of the 19th century, but now its use would inevitably recall Shakespeare's tortured Danish prince so frequently seen on screen and stage. This would not necessarily have been the case in the 17th and 18th centuries, when Shakespeare's work was not so widely performed. Author Dashiell Hammett.

Hammet, Hammett, Hammond, Hamnet, Hamnett

Hamlin OG. "Little home-lover." Actor Harry Hamlin; Abraham Lincoln's Vice President, Hannibal Hamlin.

Hamblin, Hamelin, Hamlen, Hamlyn

Hammer OG. "Hammer maker; carpenter." An ancient occupational name.

Hammar, Hammur

Hammond OG. "Home protector."

Hampden OE. Place name: "Home in the valley." Related to **Hampton**, below.

Hampton OE. Place name: "Home settlement." A name with enormous resonance in the South. Hampton Beach, Virginia, is the oldest English settlement in continuous existence in the U.S., and Hampton Roads is the channel to one of the greatest natural harbors on the eastern seaboard. South Carolina planter Wade Hampton was an important soldier in the Revolutionary War and his grandson Wade Hampton was an important Confederate general and later Governor of South Carolina. Musician Lionel Hampton.

Hampten

Hancock OE. Meaning obscure, probably related to poultry

in some way. Bostonian patriot John Hancock was the first man to sign the Declaration of Independence. His name lingers on in a huge insurance conglomerate and an ultra-modern glass building in downtown Boston.
Handcock

Hanford OE. Place name: "High ford."

Hani Arab. "Full of joy."

Hanif Arab. "Devout devotee of Islam." Filmmaker Hanif Kureishi.

Hank Dim. **Henry** (OE. "Estate ruler"). Usually a nickname rather than a given name. Baseball star Hank Aaron.

Hanley OE. Place name: "High meadow."
Handlea, Handleigh, Handley, Hanlea, Hanlee, Hanleigh, Hanly, Henlea, Henlee, Henleigh, Henley

Hannibal Punic. "Grace of Baal." The name of a great general of Carthage, a kingdom in North Africa. He was a great enemy of the Roman Empire and masterminded one of the military feats of all time when he crossed the Alps with a baggage train of elephants to invade Italy.

Hanoch Heb. "Vowed, dedicated." A variant of **Enoch**.

Hans Scand. Var. **John** (Heb. "The Lord is gracious"). Most familiar from the diminutive, **Hansel**, in the fairy tale "Hansel and Gretel." Writer Hans Christian Andersen.
Hannes, Hanns, Hansel, Hanss, Hanzel

Hanson Scand. "Son of Hans."
Hansen, Hanssen, Hansson

Hansraj Sanskrit. "Swan king."

Harbin OF./Ger. "Little bright warrior."
Harben

Harcourt OF. "Fortified farm."
Harcort

Harden OE. Place name: "Valley of the hares."
Hardin, Hardon

Harding OE. "Son of the courageous one." This name is closely related to Hardy. U.S. President Warren G. Harding.
Hardinge

Hardwick OE. "Courageous one's settlement."
Harwyck

Hardwin OE. "Courageous friend."
Hardwen, Hardwinn, Hardwyn, Hardwynn

Hardy OG. "Bold, brave." Writer Thomas Hardy; designer Hardy Amies.
Hardey

Harel Heb. "God's mount."
Harrel, Harrell

Harford OE. Place name: "Ford of the hares." Like many place names turned surnames, this was used as a first name in the 19th century.
Harfurd, Harrford, Harrfurd

Hargrove OE. Place name: "Grove of the hares." In modern times it seems curious that ancient names took such close note of the whereabouts of rabbits, but they might have constituted a significant portion of the average person's diet in those days.
Hargrave, Hargreaves

Harkin Ir. Gael. "Dark red."
Harkan, Harken

Harlan OE. Place name: "Army land."
Harland, Harlen, Harlenn, Harlin, Harlyn, Harlynn

Harley OE. Place name: "The long field." Familiar to most people as half of the name of a great motorcycle, the Harley-Davidson.
Arlea, Arleigh, Arley, Harlea, Harlee, Harleigh, Harlley, Harly

Harlow OE. Place name: "Army hill." Musician Arlo Guthrie.
Arlo, Harlow, Harlo, Harloe

Harmon Var. Herman (OG. "Army man"). Actor Mark Harmon.
Harman, Harmann, Harmonn

Harmony Lat. "Concord, joining." New Age name.
Harmonio

Harold Scand. "Army ruler." An Anglo-Saxon name revived to great popularity in the mid–19th century. It was greatly in vogue until the turn of the century, but is now rare. British Prime Minister Harold Macmillan; playwright Harold Pinter.
Araldo, Aralt, Aroldo, Arry, Garald, Garold, Hal, Harald, Haralds, Haroldas, Haroldo, Harry, Herold, Herrold, Herrick, Herryck

Harper OE. "Harp player."
Harpur

Harrell Heb. "God's mount."

Harrington OE. Place name: possibly "Herring town" or "Harry's town."

Harrison OE. "Son of Harry." Harrison is the more popular version of this name, but neither it nor Harris has been used much as a first name in the latter part of this century. Actor Harrison Ford.
Harris, Harriss, Harrisson

Harry Dim. **Henry** (OE. "Home ruler"). Since about 1920, Harry has been used as an independent name about as frequently as Henry. In the U.S. this may have something to do with admiration for President Harry S Truman. Actor Harry Belafonte; U.S. Supreme Court Justice Harry A. Blackmun; magician Harry Houdini.

Harshad Hindi. "Bringer of joy."

Hart OE. "Stag." Poet Hart Crane; actor Hart Bochner.

Hartford OE. Place name: "Stag ford."

Hartley OE. Place name: "Stag meadow."
Hartlea, Hartlee, Hartleigh, Hartly

Hartman OG. "Hard, strong man."
Hartmann

Hartwell OE. Place name: "Well of the stags."
Harwell, Harwill

Hartwig Ger. "Courageous in battle."

Harun Arab. "On high, exalted."
Haroon, Haroun

Harvey OF. "Burning for battle" or "Strong and ardent." Norman name revived in the 19th century, but now uncommon. Many people may recall the Jimmy Stewart movie *Harvey*, in which he was upstaged by a giant invisible rabbit. Playwright Harvey Fierstein.
Harvee, Harvie, Herve, Hervey

Harwood OE. Place name: "Wood of the hares."
Harewood

Hashim Arab. "Crusher of evil."
Hasheem, Hisham

Haskel Heb. "Intellect." Cinematographer Haskell Wexler.
Haskell

Haslett OE. Place name: "Headland with the hazel trees." Literary critic William Hazlitt.
Haslit, Haslitt, Hazel, Hazlett, Hazlitt

Hassan Arab. "Handsome." A very popular name i
Arabic world, and one of the more familiar Muslim names
even in America.
Hasan

Hastings OE. "Son of the austere man."
Hastey, Hastie, Hasting, Hasty

Havelock Scand. "Sea competition." Author Havelock Ellis.

Haven OE. Place name: "Sanctuary, safe harbor."
Hagan, Hagen, Havin, Hogan

Haward ONorse. "High guardian." Possibly related to
Howard, which it resembles to the ear.
Hawarden

Hawes OE. Place name: "Hedged area." May also refer to
the fruit from hawthorne trees, known as "haws." They
are small and resemble berries.
Haws

Hawk OE. "Falcon, bird of prey." Use of this name
may be related to the perennial popularity of Alan Alda's
character Hawkeye, on the long-running TV serial
"M*A*S*H."

Hawkins OE. "Little hawk."
Hawkyns

Hawley OE. Place name: "Hedged meadow."
Hawleigh, Hawly

Hawthorne OE. Place name: "Where hawthorn trees
grow." Use in the U.S. may reflect admiration for the
novelist Nathaniel Hawthorne.
Hawthorn

Hayden OE. Place name: "Hedged valley." Most commonly used in Wales. Football player Pat Haden.
Haden, Haydn, Haydon

Hayes OE. Place name: "Hedged area." U.S. President
Rutherford B. Hayes; baseball player Charlie Hayes.
Hays

Hayward OE. Occupational name: "Keeper or guardian of
the hedged enclosure."

Haywood OE. Place name: "Hedged forest." Writer Heywood Broun.
Heywood, Woody

Hazaiah Heb. "God decides."

Hazard OF. "Chance, luck."
  Hazzard
Hazen Var. **Hayes**.
  Hazin
Hazleton OE. Place name: "Settlement near hazel trees."
Hazlewood OE. Place name: "Wood of hazel trees."
Heath ME. Place name: "Heath." In Britain a "heath" is a large, open space that's not under cultivation. Football player Heath Shuler.
Heathcliff ME. Place name indicating a cliff near a heath. Most parents today would automatically associate it with the passionate hero of Emily Brontë's *Wuthering Heights*.
Heber Heb. "Togetherness." An Old Testament name used by the Puritans but rare in this century.
  Hebor
Hector Gk. "Holds fast." One of the great heroes of the Trojan War, though today the verb "to hector" means to bully or browbeat. Designer Ettore Sottsass.
  Ector, Ettore
Heddwyn Welsh. "Fair peace."
  Hedwin, Hedwyn, Hedwynn
Hedley OE. Place name: "Heathered meadow." Used in Britain in the late 19th century, but rare in the U.S.
  Headleigh, Headley, Headly, Hedly
Hedeon Rus. Var. **Gideon** (Heb. "Feller of trees").
Heimdall ONorse mythology name. One of the sons of Odin, the principal Norse god, he was one of the founders of the human race. The name means "White god."
  Heiman, Heimann
Heinrich Ger. Var. **Henry**.
  Heine, Heini, Heinie
Heinz Ger. Var. **Hans** (Heb. "The Lord is gracious").
  Hines
Heladio Sp. "Born in Greece."
  Eladio, Elado, Helado
Helgi ONorse. "Productive, successful, happy." Well used in Scandinavia. Ballet dancer Helgi Thomassen.
  Helge, Helje, Helji
Heller Ger. "Bright, brilliant."

Helmut Ger. "Brave protector." Photographer Helmut Newton.
   Hellmut, Hellmuth
Henderson OE. "Son of Henry."
   Hendrie, Hendries, Hendron, Henryson
Hendrick OG. "Estate ruler." Variant form of **Henry**.
   Hendrik
Henley OE. Place name: "High meadow." Variant of **Hanley**, but made famous by the English town that hosts an annual worldwide rowing regatta and has given its name to a style of shirt.
   Henlee, Henlie
Henry OG. "Estate ruler." Norman name that took root in Britain and became a royal name used by eight kings and, most recently, for the younger son of the Prince of Wales. This exposure may give new popularity to a name that was extremely common until the first quarter of this century and is now used less than unusual names like Marcus, Adrian, and Randall. Explorer Henry Hudson; actor Henry Fonda; author Henry James; poet Henry Wadsworth Longfellow; artists Henri Matisse, Henri de Toulouse-Lautrec, Henri Rousseau; playwright Henrik Ibsen.
   Arrigo, Enrico, Enrikos, Enrique, Enzio, Hal, Hank, Harry, Heike, Heindrick, Heindrik, Heiner, Heinrich, Heinrick, Heinrik, Heinz, Hendrick, Hendrik, Henerik, Henning, Henri, Henrik, Henrique, Henryk, Heriot, Herriot, Hinrich
Herbert OG. "Bright army" or "Bright warrior." Norman name that faded in the Middle Ages, to be revived enthusiastically in the 19th century. Now unusual. U.S. President Herbert Hoover.
   Bert, Bertie, Erberto, Harbert, Hebert, Herb, Herbie, Heribert, Heriberto
Hercules Gk. Meaning not quite clear: Possibly "Glorious gift" or "Glory of Hera." The legendary Greek hero who exhibited incredible strength. In modern times his physical strength might have been rivaled by the intellectual power of his namesake, Agatha Christie's fictional detective Hercule Poirot.
   Ercole, Ercolo, Ercule, Herakles, Hercule, Herculie
Heribert Ger. "Renowned army."

Herman OG. "Army man." Another 19th-century revival of a Norman name, this one especially a U.S. favorite. Uncommon since the turn of the century. Authors Herman Hesse, Herman Melville.

Armand, Armando, Armin, Ermanno, Ermano, Ermin, Harman, Harmon, Hermann, Hermie, Herminio, Hermon

Hermes Gk. Myth name: the messenger god, with wings on his heels. The corresponding Roman god is Mercury. Choreographer Hermes Pan.

Ermes, Hermilo, Hermite, Hermus

Hernando Sp. Var. **Ferdinand** (OG. "Bold voyager").

Herndon OE. Place name: "Heron valley."

Herne OE. "Heron." Probably used to indicate a place where herons were to be found.

Hearne, Hern

Hernley OE. "Heron meadow."

Hernlea, Hernlee, Hernlie, Hernly

Herrick OG. "War ruler." The 17th-century poet Robert Herrick.

Herrik, Herryck

Hershel Heb. "Deer." As Herzl, this name is often used to commemorate Theodor Herzl, an early Zionist. Football player Herschel Walker; actor Herschel Bernardi.

Hersch, Herschel, Herschell, Hersh, Hertzel, Herzel, Herzl, Heschel, Heshel, Hirsch, Hirschel, Hirschl

Hesed Heb. "Kindness."

Hesperos Gk. "Evening or evening star." The Greeks referred to Italy as Hesperia, since the sun set and the evening star rose there.

Hesperios, Hespero, Hesperus

Hewett OF. Dim. **Hugh** (Ger. "Small intelligent one").

Hewet, Hewie, Hewitt, Hewlett, Hewlitt

Hewney Ir. Gael. "Green."

Owney

Hewson OE. "Hugh's son."

Heywood OE. Place name: "Hedged forest." Variant of Haywood.

Hezekiah Heb. "God gives strength." Old Testament name little used since the 19th century.

Hezeki

Hideo Jap. "Excellent man." Baseball player Hideo Nomo.

Hieremias Gk. Var. **Jeremiah** (Heb. "Jehovah lifts up").

Hieronymos Gk. Var. **Jerome** (Heb. "Sacred name"). Painter Hieronymus Bosch.

Hierome, Hieronim, Hieronimos, Hieronymus

Hilary Gk. "Cheerful, happy." The name comes from the same root as the word "hilarious." Although it was used for boys (including a pope and a saint) until the 17th century, it was revived at the turn of the 20th century as a girl's name, and after years with a Hillary as First Lady, it will be hard to reclaim this name for male babies.

Helario, Hilaire, Hilar, Hilarid, Hilarie, Hilario, Hilarion, Hilarius, Hillary, Hillery, Hilliary, Hilorio, Ilario, Illario

Hildebrand OG. "Battle sword."

Hildebrandt, Hillebrand

Hill OE. Place name. Indicates a remote ancestor who lived on or near a hill.

Hillard OG. "Hard warrior."

Hilliard, Hillier, Hillyer

Hillel Heb. "Greatly praised." Sometimes used in honor of the celebrated 1st-century Jewish scholar Rabbi Hillel.

Hilliard OG. "Battle guard" or OE. Place name: "Yard on a hill."

Hiller, Hillierd, Hillyard, Hillyer, Hillyerd

Hilton OE. Place name: "Hill settlement." Hotelier Conrad Hilton.

Hylton

Himesh Hindi. "Snow king."

Hippolyte Gk. Meaning not entirely clear, but alludes to horses. The Hippolytus in Greek legend, son of Theseus, was dragged to death by his bolting chariot horses. Extremely rare.

Hippolit, Hippolitos, Hippolytus, Ippolito

Hiram Heb. Meaning not clear, possibly "Most noble." Old Testament name little used in the 20th century, though fairly popular in the 19th.

Hi, Hirom, Hy, Hyrum

Hiroshi Jap. "Generous."

Hitchcock OE. Meaning unclear. Film director Alfred Hitchcock.

Hjalmar ONorse. "Army helmet." Another warlike name from England's northern neighbors.

Hjalamar, Hjallmar, Hjalmer

Hobart A particularly American (though unusual) variant of **Hubert** (OG. "Bright or shining intellect").
Hobard, Hobert, Hobey, Hobie, Hoebart

Hockley OE. Place name: "High meadow."
Hocklea, Hocklee, Hocklie, Hockly

Hockney OE. Place name: "High island." Artist David Hockney.
Hockny

Hobbes OE. Variant of **Robert** (OE. "Bright fame"). Seventeenth-century English philosopher Thomas Hobbes wrote that life without government was "solitary, poor, nasty, brutish, and short." The popular cartoon character (a stuffed tiger) created by Bill Watterson was named after the philosopher.
Hob, Hobbs

Hobson OE. "Son of Robert."
Hobbson

Hodgson OE. "Son of Roger."
Hodge, Hodges

Hoffman Ger. "Courtier." *Hof* means court or castle in German.
Hofman, Hofmann, Hoffmann

Hogan Ir. Gael. "Youth."

Holbrook OE. Place name: "Stream near the hollow." Actor Hal Holbrook.
Brook, Holbrooke

Holcomb OE. "Deep valley." "Combe" is a term, sometimes used in England, for a deep, narrow valley.
Holcombe, Holcoomb

Holden OE. Place name: "Hollow valley." The hero of J.D. Salinger's coming-of-age novel *The Catcher in the Rye* is named Holden Caulfield.

Holiday OE. "Holy day."
Holliday

Hollis OE. Place name: "Near the holly bushes" or "Holly-tree grove." Used as a girl's name with some frequency as well.
Holliss, Hollister

Holmes ME. Place name: "Islands in the river." Arthur Conan Doyle's fictional detective Sherlock Holmes.

Holt OE. Place name: "Woods, forest."

Homer Gk. "Security, pledge." The name of the classical poet, author of the *Iliad* and the *Odyssey*. More popular in the U.S. than elsewhere, especially in the 19th century, but scarcely used today. Artist Winslow Homer.
Homere, Homero, Homeros, Homerus, Omero

Honesto Sp. "Honest man."

Honoré Lat. "Honored one." Familiar because of a fashionable neighborhood and a shopping street in Paris called the Faubourg Saint-Honoré.
Honoratus, Honorius

Hooker OE. Possibly an occupational name referring to a shepherd's hook or crook. Joseph Hooker was a prominent Union general in the Civil War.

Hooper OE. Occupational name: "Maker of hoops," the metal circles that bound barrels.

Hopkins Welsh. "Robert's son." Hob was a long-ago nickname for Robert.
Hopkin, Hopkinson, Hopkyns, Hopper, Hoppner

Horace Lat. Clan name, possibly meaning "Timekeeper." Late 19th-century use may have been inspired in part by the famous Roman poet Horace. British Admiral Horatio Nelson; journalist Horace Greeley; basketball player Horace Grant.
Horacio, Horatio, Horatius, Horaz, Oratio, Orazio

Horsley OE. Place name: "Horse meadow."
Horslea, Horsleigh, Horslie, Horsly

Horst OG. "A thicket." Photographer Horst P. Horst.
Hurst

Horton OE. Place name: "Gray settlement." Dr. Seuss character Horton of *Horton Hears a Who*.
Horten, Orton

Hosea Heb. "Salvation." Name of an Old Testament prophet, but less popular, even in the 19th century, than other prophets' names like Joel or Amos. Unless the "-a" is pronounced clearly, Hosea is likely to be taken for José.
Hoshea, Hoseia, Hosheia

Houghton OE. Place name: "Settlement on the headland."
Hough

Houston OE. Place name: "Settlement on the hill" or

"Hugh's town." Sam Houston was the first president of the republic of Texas, before Texas entered the United States.

Hewson, Huston, Hutcheson, Hutchinson

Hovannes Central European var. **John** (Heb. "The Lord is gracious") via **Johannes**.

Howard OE. Meaning unclear, possibly occupational name indicating a watchman of some kind. Millionaire Howard Hughes; sportscaster Howard Cosell.

Howie, Ward

Howe OG. "Lofty one" or ME. Place name: "Hill." Elias Howe patented the first sewing machine in 1845.

How

Howell Welsh. "Eminent, remarkable." The anglicized version of Hywel, a name mostly used in Wales. Authors William Dean Howells, Howell Raines.

Howel, Howells

Howland OE. Place name: "Land with hills."

Howlan, Howlen

Hoyt ONorse. "Spirit, soul."

Hoyce

Hubbard Var. Hubert.

Hubert OG. "Bright or shining intellect." An old European name that was popular around the turn of the century, but is now rare. U.S. Vice President Hubert Humphrey.

Bert, Hobard, Hobart, Hubbard, Hube, Huberto, Hubie, Humberto, Uberto, Ulberto

Hudson OE. "Hugh's son." Explorer Henry Hudson was the first European to visit the Hudson River, which he found while searching for a northwest passage to India. On a later voyage he sailed into Hudson Bay in Canada.

Hugh OG. "Mind, intellect." Popular medieval name, steadily used (though at a diminishing rate) in the modern era. Its widespread use in the Middles Ages resulted in spin-off names like Hudson, Hewson, and Houston. Film director Hugh Hudson; *Playboy* founder Hugh Hefner; U.S. Supreme Court Justice Hugo Black; actor Hugh Grant.

Hew, Hewe, Huey, Hughes, Hughie, Hugo, Hugues, Huw, Ugo

Hulbert OG. "Bright grace."

Bert, Hulbard, Hulburd, Hulburt

Humbert OG. "Renowned Hun." Made famous narrator of Vladimir Nabokov's *Lolita*, Humbert Humbert. Italian author Umberto Eco.

Umberto

Hume Scottish Var. **Holmes** (ME. "Islands in the river.") Scottish philosopher David Hume.

Hulme

Humphrey OG. Meaning unclear, but alludes to peace. In the Middle Ages, the form Humfrey was used in England, but Humphrey was the usual form from 1700 on. Never immensely popular, especially since the 1960s. Actor Humphrey Bogart.

Humfrey, Humfrid, Humfried, Humfry, Humph, Humphery, Humphry, Hunfredo, Onfré, Onfroi, Onofredo, Onofrio

Hunt OE. The word as a name, perhaps originally a shortening of Hunter or Huntington.

Hunter OE. Occupational name: "Hunter." A name that was obscure until the early 1990s, then shot into middling popularity. Seems to be subsiding back into disuse. Journalist Hunter Thompson.

Hunt

Huntington OE. Place name: "Hunter's settlement." Railroad magnate and philanthropist Henry Huntington.

Hunt, Huntingdon

Huntley OE. Place name: "Meadow of the hunter."

Huntlea, Huntlee, Huntleigh, Huntly

Huon Var. **John** (Heb. "The Lord is gracious"), probably via **Juan**.

Hurlbert OE. "Shining army."

Hulbert, Hurlburt, Hurlbutt

Hurley Ir. Gael. "Sea tide."

Hurlee, Hurleigh, Hurly

Hurst ME. Place name: "Thicket of trees." Sometimes occurs as a place name in combination with the tree name, as in Elmhurst or Pinehurst.

Hearst, Hirst, Horst

Hussein Arab. "Small handsome one." The name of the King of Jordan.

Husain, Husayn, Husein

Hutton OE. Place name: "Settlement on the bluff." Actor Timothy Hutton.

Hutten

Huxford OE. Place name: "Hugh's ford."

Huxley OE. Place name: "Hugh's meadow." Author Aldous Huxley.

Huxlea, Huxlee, Huxleigh, Huxly

Hyacinthe Fr. "Hyacinth." Owing to the English-speaking tradition of flower names for girls, unlikely to be used as a boy's name, despite its origin as a male name. French painter Hyacinthe Rigaud.

Hyacinthos, Hyacinthus, Hyakinthos

Hyatt OE. Place name: "Lofty gate."

Hayatt, Hiatt

Hyde OE. Place name referring to a "hide," a measure of land current in the early Middle Ages. It amounted to about 120 acres.

Hyman Anglicized variant of **Chaim** (Heb. "Life").

Hayim, Hayyim, Hymie, Mannie

Iago Sp. Var. **James** (Heb. "He who supplants"). The Spanish name for Saint James, Santiago, was given to a number of geographical features (rivers, lakes, mountains) in South America, as well as the capital city of Chile. Still, most English-speaking parents will remember the treacherous villain of Shakespeare's *Othello* and pass this name by.

Jago, Yago

Ian Scot. Var. **John** (Heb. "God is gracious"). One of the few Scottish names that has achieved really broad popularity since the beginning of this century, though John still outranks it on the charts. Ian's popularity stems from the current longing for the name that is just a little bit out of the ordinary. James Bond's creator Ian Fleming; actor Ian McKellen.

Ean, Eann, Eion, Eon, Iain, Ion

Ib Dan. "Baal's pledge." Baal was an ancient god of the Semites. Dancer Ib Andersen.

Ibrahim Arab. Var. **Abraham** (Heb. "Father of many"). This form of the name is more common in Moslem countries.

Icarus Mythology name: Icarus was the son of Daedalus, the designer of the Labyrinth in Knossos who was held prisoner by King Minos. Daedalus made wings out of wax and feathers to facilitate his and Icarus's escape, but Icarus flew too close to the sun. The wax melted, and he fell into the sea.
Ikaros, Ikarus

Ichabod Heb. "The glory is gone." An Old Testament name brought to the U.S. by the Pilgrims and given fame by Washington Irving, who named a character Ichabod Crane in *The Legend of Sleepy Hollow*.
Ikabod, Ikavod

Idan Heb. "Era, time."

Ido Heb. "Evaporate" or Arab. "To be mighty." This is one case where a word means radically different things in Hebrew and Arabic. Frequently there is similarity between names in the two languages.
Iddo

Idris Welsh. "Eager lord." Mostly used in Wales around the turn of the century.

Ignatius Meaning unclear, though some sources suggest Latin "Ardent, burning" (from the same root as "ignite"). The most famous Ignatius is Saint Ignatius of Loyola, founder of the Society of Jesus, popularly known as the Jesuits. The name is rare in English-speaking countries.
Iggie, Ignac, Ignace, Ignacio, Ignacius, Ignatious, Ignatz, Ignaz, Ignazio, Inacio, Inigo

Igor Rus. Var. **Ingvar** (Scand. "Ing's soldier"). Composer Igor Stravinsky.
Inge, Ingemar, Ingmar

Ihab Arab. "Gift."

Ilan Heb. "Tree." This name is used in many forms, and is particularly popular in the feminine version, **Ilana**.
Eilon, Elam, Elan, Ilon

Ilario It. Var. **Hilary** (Gk. "Cheerful, merry").

Ilias Gk. Var. **Elijah** (Heb. "The Lord is my God").
Ilie

Ilya Rus. Var. **Elijah** (Heb. "The Lord is my God"). Nostalgic TV fans will remember the glamorous Russian Illya Kuryakin from the series *The Man from U.N.C.L.E.*
Ilia, Illya

Imad Arab. "Support, mainstay."

Immanuel Var. **Emmanuel** (Heb. "God is among us").
Imanoel, Imannuel, Imanuel

Imre Hung. Possibly a variant of **Emeric** (OG. "Home ruler"). Little used outside Hungary. Another source for the same name is Heb. "My words."
Imray, Imri, Imrie

Ince Hung. "Innocent."

Indio Modern name. Possibly a masculine version of **India**, perhaps a reference to Native Americans.
Indeeo, Indeio, Indyo

Ingemar Scand. "Ing's son." Ing, in Norse mythology, was a powerful god of fertility and peace. His name is an element in several modern names. Film director Ingmar Bergman.
Ingamar, Ingemur, Ingmar

Inglebert Var. **Englebert** (OE. "Angel-bright").
Ingbert, Ingelbert

Ingo Dan. "Meadow" or Scand. "Lord."

Ingram OE. "Raven of Anglia." A first name until the 17th century, now more commonly a surname that is occasionally transferred.
Ingraham, Ingrahame, Ingrams, Ingrim, Yngraham, Yngraham

Ingvar Scand. "Ing's soldier."
Ingevar

Inigo OE. Var. **Ignatius**. In modern times, likely to be homage to the great English architect Inigo Jones.

Inman OE. Occupational name: "Innkeeper."
Innman

Innis Scot. Gael. Place name: "Island."
Ennis, Innes, Inness, Inniss

Innocenzio It. "Innocent." Thirteen popes have chosen to be called "Innocent."
Innocent, Innocenty, Inocencio

Inver Gael. "Estuary." Most commonly combined with the names of rivers, as in Inverness, which means "Estuary of the Ness."

Ioanis Rus. Var. **John** (Heb. "The Lord is gracious").

Ioakim Rus. Var. **Joachim** (Heb. "God will judge").
  Ioachim, Ioachime

Ion Pronounced with a long "I," this is a Greek mythology name, referring to a son of Apollo who became the ancestor of the Ionians. (The western Greek islands, including Corfu, are still known as the Ionian islands.) If the name is pronounced with an initial long "E" sound, however, it is clearly a respelling of Ian.
  Eion

Iosef Rus. Var. **Joseph** (Heb. "Jehovah increases").
  Iosif, Iosip

Ira Heb. "Watchful." Old Testament name revived in the 19th century, but never very popular. Lyricist Ira Gershwin.

Irenio Sp. from Gk. "Peace." The masculine form of Irene.
  Irenaeus, Ireneus

Irving OE. "Sea friend." Also a Scottish place name. Used as a first name since the middle of the last century. Composer Irving Berlin; author Irving Stone.
  Earvin, Erv, Ervin, Irv, Irvin, Irvine

Irwin OE. "Boar friend." Revived from roughly 1860 to 1940s, but little used since. Author Irwin Shaw; clown Bill Irwin.
  Erwin, Erwinn, Erwyn, Irwinn, Irwyn

Isaac Heb. "Laughter." In the Old Testament, Abraham's son, born when his father was 100 years old. God tested Abraham's faith by ordering him to sacrifice Isaac, and when Abraham was willing to do so, God sent an angel to stop him. The scene has often been portrayed in western art, but moderns may wonder about the effect of this scene on Isaac. The Puritans used the name enthusiastically, and it remained popular through the 18th century, fading very gradually. Less fashionable in the last fifty years. Scientist Isaac Newton; angler Izaak Walton; authors Isaac Bashevis Singer, Isaac Asimov.
  Ike, Ikey, Ikie, Isaak, Isac, Isacco, Isak, Issac, Itzak, Izaak, Izak, Izik, Izsak, Yitzhak, Zack, Zak

Isaiah Heb. "The Lord helps me" or "Salvation of God." Like so many Old Testament names, popular with the Puritans in the 17th century, brought to America, and revived by the Victorians. Now rare. Basketball player Isiah Thomas.

Isa, Isaia, Isaias, Isia, Isiah, Issiah, Izaiah, Iziah

Isam Arab. "Protection, security."

Isandro Sp. from Gk. "Man's liberator." Related to Alexander.

Isander, Isandero, Ysander, Ysandro

Ishaan Hindi. "The sun."

Isham OE. Place name: "Home of the iron one."

Ishmael Heb. "The Lord will hear." Old Testament name immortalized in the first line of Herman Melville's *Moby Dick*: "Call me Ishmael." The name has been used in literature to indicate an outcast, since Ishmael, son of Abraham by his servant Hagar, was cast out of Abraham's household when Isaac (the legitimate son) was born. The Arab peoples were descended from Ishmael's twelve sons. The Arabic version of this name is Ismail.

Ismael, Ismail, Ysmael, Ysmail

Isidore Gk. "Gift of Isis." Isis was the principal goddess of ancient Egypt, and Isidore was a popular name among the ancient Greeks. There are several saints named Isidore, but the name is probably most famous in its feminine form, Isadora.

Dore, Dorian, Dory, Isador, Isadore, Isidor, Isidoro, Isidorus, Isidro, Issy, Izidor, Izydor, Izzy, Ysidro

Iskander Arab. Var. **Alexander** (Gk. "Man's defender").

Ismail Arab. A variant of **Ishmael**, who built the temple of Kaaba at Mecca. Film director Ismail Merchant; football playing brothers Raghib and Qadry Ismail.

Ishmael, Ismaal, Ismael, Ismal, Ismayl, Izmail, Ysmal, Ysmail

Ismat Arab. "Protecting." Related to Isam.

Israel Heb. Meaning unclear, though some sources suggest "Wrestling with the Lord," for this was the name given Jacob in the Old Testament after his three-day bout with his Lord. Came to be synonymous with the Jewish people, and was consequently used as the name for the new Jewish state founded in 1948. Author Israel Shenker.

Yisrael

Issachar Heb. "His reward will come." Old Testament name: one of the twelve sons of Jacob who founded the

Twelve Tribes of Israel.

Isachar, Yisachar, Yissachar

Istvan Hung. Var. **Stephen** (Gk. "Crowned"). Film director Istvan Szabo.

Itai Heb. "The Lord is at my side."

Ittai, Itiel

Italo It. "From Italy." Novelist Italo Calvino.

Itamar Heb. "Palm island."

Ithamar, Ittamar

Ivan Rus. Var. **John** (Heb. "God is gracious"). Used in English-speaking countries for the last hundred-odd years. Tennis star Ivan Lendl.

Ifan, Iwan

Ivo OG. "Yew wood." Since yew wood was used for bows, the name may have been an occupational one meaning "archer." The most famous form is probably Ives from the old nursery rhyme "As I was going to St. Ives/I met a man with seven wives . . ." Uncommon nevertheless.

Ivair, Ivar, Iven, Iver, Ives, Ivon, Yves, Yvo

Ivor ONorse, meaning unclear. Possibly related to Ivo or to Ingvar. Used now and then in Britain, scarce in the U.S. Songwriter Ivor Novello.

Ifor, Ivar, Iver, Yvor

Iyar Heb. "Light."

Iyyar

THE LETTER "J"

Names starting with "J" have been stylish for boys for the last twenty-five years. The trend began when Jason appeared on the charts in 1970, joining perennials John, James, Joseph, and Jeffrey. By 1980, Jason was extremely fashionable. Joshua and Justin, apparently riding on its coattails, were on some top ten lists. By 1990 Jason had skidded, Joshua was hot, and Jonathan and Jacob were starting to climb.

Jabbar Arab. "Consoler."
   Jabar
Jabez Heb. "Borne in pain." Old Testament name that lasted fairly well until around 1930.
   Jabes, Jabesh
Jabir Arab. "Consolation."
Jace Dim. **Jason** (Heb. "The Lord is my salvation"). Far from common, but nevertheless well established for a name that didn't even exist twenty years ago.
   Jacey, Jacian, Jaice, Jayce
Jacinto Sp. from Gk. **Hyacinth** (Flower name). There was a 3rd-century Saint Hyacinth, and the name has been used for both sexes. In Greek legend, Apollo loved a beautiful youth of the name; the hyacinth flower sprang up from his blood when he died.
   Giacintho, Giacinto, Jacindo
Jack Familiar form of **John** (Heb. "The Lord is gracious") or less often, **Jacob** (Heb. "He who supplants"). Was used as an independent name from the 1850s to the 1920s, then subsided. Currently experiencing quite a little renaissance, possibly because of its slightly rugged downhome aura. Christie Brinkley, for instance, named her son Jack. Actors Jackie Gleason, Jack Nicholson; comedian Jack Benny; exercise guru Jack LaLanne.
   Jackie, Jackman, Jacko, Jacky, Jacq, Jacqin, Jak, Jaq
Jackson OE. "Son of Jack." May indicate an ancestor's admiration for U.S. President Andrew Jackson, or in Southern families, Civil War General Stonewall Jackson. Possibly driven by Jack's popularity (or the current fashion for "J" names), Jackson is quite well used. Artist Jackson Pollock; singer Jackson Browne.
   Jack, Jackie, Jacksen, Jacky, Jakson, Jaxen, Jaxson
Jacob Heb. "He who supplants." In the Old Testament, Jacob, Esau's brother, impersonates his brother at his

blind father Isaac's deathbed by covering his hands with a goatskin ("for Esau was a hairy man"), securing the blessing meant for the elder son. His ten sons and two grandsons were the founders of the twelve tribes of Israel, the name Jacob himself received after wrestling with an angel. Very steadily used now, though boys named Jacob seem to be called "Jake" in large numbers. Senator Jacob Javits.

Cob, Cobb, Cobby, Giacamo, Giacobo, Giacomo, Giacopo, Hamish, Iacopo, Iacovo, Iago, Iakob, Iakobos, Iakov, Jaco, Jacobo, Jacobi, Jacoby, Jack, Jackie, Jacko, Jacky, Jacques, Jacquet, Jago, Jaime, Jake, Jakie, Jakob, Jakov, Jakub, James, Jamesie, Jamey, Jamie, Jamsey, Jay, Jayme, Jim, Jimmie, Seamus, Shamus, Yakov

Jacques Fr. Var. **James** via **Jacob**. Familiar from the well-known song "Frère Jacques." Undersea explorer Jacques Cousteau.

Jacot, Jacque, Jaq, Jaques

Jade Sp. Jewel name, for the semiprecious green stone. Jewel names are commonly used for girls, but the brisk monosyllable of this name (and the fact that it has not been widely used) makes it an appealing choice for a boy.

Jaide, Jayde

Jael Heb. "Mountain goat." Also used for girls, although rare in either case.

Yael

Jafar Arab. "Stream." It will be quite some time before Jafar loses its villainous connotations, courtesy of Disney's *Aladdin*.

Jaffar

Jagger OE. Occupational name. Possibly "One who cuts," as in jagged edges of cloth; also possibly "A peddler." Modern parents who choose this name will no doubt be thinking of musician Mick Jagger instead, making this name incredibly cool instead of merely obscure.

Jago Variant of **Jacob** or **James**, similar to **Iago**.

Jahan Sanskrit. "The world." Shah Jahan, the 16th-century emperor of India, built the Taj Mahal.

Jehan

Jaime Sp. Var. **James**. Quite well used in the polyglot U.S.

Jaimey, Jaimie, Jayme, Jaymie

Jaimini Sanskrit. "Victory."

Jair Heb. "He enlightens." Jairus, in the New Testament, is the man whose daughter Jesus raised from the dead.

Jake Dim. Jacob. Used independently since the 1960s, and quite steadily chosen by today's parents.

Jaladhi Hindi. "Ocean."
Jaladi, Jeladhi, Jeladi

Jalal Arab. "Greatness, superiority, renown."
Jallal, Jalil, Jaliyl, Jela, Jellal

Jalen Modern name, probably Galen (Gk. "Healer" or "Tranquil") with a "J." Since there is no standard spelling for many of these modern names, phonetic spellings abound, each one more imaginative than the last.
Jaelan, Jaelin, Jaelon, Jailin, Jaillen, Jaillin, Jailon, Jalan, Jalin, Jalon, Jayelan, Jayelen, Jaylan Jaylen, Jaylon, Jaylonn

Jamal Arab. "Handsome." Very popular in the U.S. among black or Muslim families. TV star Malcolm-Jamal Warner.
Jamaal, Jamahl, Jamall, Jamaul, Jameel, Jamel, Jamell, Jamil, Jamill, Jammal, Jemaal, Jemahl, Jemal, Jemall, Jimal, Jimahl, Jomal, Jomahl, Jomall

Jamar Modern name, a variant of Jamal.
Jamarr, Jemar, Jemarr, Jimar, Jimarr

James English variant of Jacob. In the New Testament there are two apostles known as James, though the Old Testament version of the name is always Jacob. The apostles are known a bit unfairly as James the Greater and James the Less. The name was popularized by the Stuart kings James I and II, and has been a stable favorite ever since. Like John, this is a tremendously popular old standby. Writer James Joyce; actors James Mason and Jimmy Stewart; entertainer Jimmy Durante; five U.S. presidents: James Buchanan, James Garfield, James Madison, James Polk, Jimmy Carter.
Diego, Giacomo, Giamo, Hamish, Iago, Jacques, Jago, Jaime, Jaimes, Jaimey, Jaimie, Jameson, Jamesie, Jamesy, Jamey, Jamie, Jamison, Jaymes, Jaymie, Jaymz, Jim, Jimmie, Jimmy, Seamus, Seumas, Seumus, Shamus

Jameson OE. "Son of James."
Jaimison, Jamieson, Jamison

Jamie Dim. **James**. Traditionally mostly Scottish, but currently quite steadily used as an independent name. However, since it is very popular as a girl's name, this phenomenon may fade.

Jaime, Jaimie, Jamee, Jamey, Jayme

Jan Dutch. Var. **John** (Heb. "The Lord is gracious"). Painters Jan Van Eyck, Jan Vermeer.

Hans, Janek, Janos

Janesh Hindi. "Leader of the people."

Janson Scand. "Jan's son." Used as a first name only in this century.

Jansen, Janssen, Jansson, Jantzen, Janzen, Jenson, Jensen

Janus Lat. "Gateway." Janus was the Roman guardian of doors as well as of beginnings and endings. He had two faces, one of which looked forward and the other backward, and gave his name to the first month of the year, January.

Gennadi, Gennaro, Janan, Janiusz, Januarius, Janusz, Jenaro, Jenarius, Jennaro

Japheth Heb. "He expands." Along with Ham and Shem, one of Noah's sons. Little used, except by the Puritans.

Jareb Heb. "He will struggle."

Jardine Fr. "Garden." The name of a significant financial concern based in Hong Kong.

Jared Heb. "He descends." Related to Jordan. Old Testament name used by the Puritans, and suddenly, inexplicably popular in the 1960s. Very widely used now as well.

Jarad, Jarid, Jarod, Jarrad, Jarrard, Jarred, Jarrid, Jarrod, Jerad, Jerod, Jerrad, Jerred, Jerrod

Jarek Slavic. Dim. of the many Slavic names that begin with "Jaro-," a word particle that means "spring."

Jarlath Ir. Gael. Ancient name of unclear origin.

Jarleath, Jarlaith

Jarman OG. "German." Film director Derek Jarman.

Jarmann, Jerman

Jaromir Slav. "Famous spring."

Jaron Modern name. Possibly Darren with the fashionable initial "J." Invented names are chosen for their sound and for their novelty; their source doesn't really matter at all.

Jaran, Jaren, Jarin, Jarran, Jarren, Jarrin, Jarron

Jaroslav Slavic. "Beauty of spring." A popular name in the Czech Republic. Historian Jaroslav Pelikan.
Jarek, Jaroslaw

Jarrell Var. **Gerald** (OG. "Spear ruler"). Poet Randall Jarrell.
Jarrall

Jarrett Var. **Garrett** (OE. "Spear-brave").
Jarett, Jarret, Jarrot, Jarrott, Jerrett, Jerrot, Jerrott

Jarvis Var. **Gervase** (OG. Meaning unclear: possibly "with honor"). This version is used more often than the somewhat effete-seeming source. Musician Jarvis Cocker.
Jarvey, Jary, Jervey, Jervis

Jascha Slavic Var. **James** (Heb. "He who supplants"). Violinist Jascha Heifetz.
Jasha

Jason Heb. "The Lord is salvation." The name is actually a variation of **Joshua**, formed by biblical translators. Jason was a legendary Greek hero who, after many adventures, recovered the Golden Fleece from an enemy kingdom. The name was phenomenally popular in the 1970s after centuries of sporadic use, and is still very well used, as its variety of phonetic variations attests. Now on the wane. Actor Jason Robards.
Jace, Jacen, Jaisen, Jaison, Jase, Jasen, Jasin, Jasun, Jay, Jayce, Jaysen, Jayson

Jasper Eng. Var. **Caspar** (Possibly Persian. "He who guards the treasure"). Jasper is also a strikingly colorful variety of quartz. Painter Jasper Johns.
Gaspar, Gasper, Jaspar, Jesper

Javier Sp. Var. **Xavier**. Meaning obscure, but refers to Saint Francis Xavier.
Havier, Haviero, Javi, Javiero

Jay Lat. "Jaybird." A medieval name that has survived especially in the U.S., where it is given to boys and girls alike. Its use may be inspired by the first Chief Justice of the U.S. Supreme Court, John Jay. Financier Jay Gould; comedian Jay Leno; author Jay McInerney; actor Jaye Davidson.
Jae, Jaye, Jeh

Jazz Improvisational modern music. The origin of the word is unknown, and it is only occasionally adopted as a proper name.

Jean Fr. Var. **John** (Heb. "The Lord is gracious"). In France it is frequently combined with other names, as in Jean-Claude, Jean-Paul, Jean-Philippe. Author and artist Jean Cocteau; playwright Jean Molière; author Jean-Paul Sartre; actor Jean-Claude Van Damme.

Jeb Nickname of dashing Confederate General James Ewell Brown Stuart. He was a wily commander of the cavalry, and died during the Civil War. The name is occasionally carried on in a Southern family.

Jed Dim. **Jedidiah**. Lent a certain rustic aura by Jed Clampitt, a character on the popular 1960s TV show *The Beverly Hillbillies*.
Jedd, Jedediah

Jedidiah Heb. "Beloved of the Lord." Old Testament name that was used by the Puritans in the 17th century.
Jedd, Jedediah

Jeff Dim. **Jefferson, Jeffrey**. Used as an independent name in this century. Actors Jeff Daniels, Jeff Goldblum.

Jefferson OE. "Son of Jeffrey." Surname used as a first name. A sterling example of this use is President of the Confederacy Jefferson Davis, who was born in 1808, during the presidency of Thomas Jefferson.
Jeff, Jeffers, Jeffersson, Jeffey, Jeffie

Jeffrey OG. Meaning unclear, but refers to "peace." Norman name popular through the Middle Ages in Britain and revived in the mid–19th century after a 350-year rest. The peak of its popularity was the 1970s in the U.S., with this form preferred to Geoffrey. Still steadily used, however.
Geoff, Geoffrey, Geoffroi, Geoffroy, Geoffry, Geofrey, Geofry, Godfrey, Godfry, Gottfried, Jefery, Jeff, Jefferey, Jefferies, Jeffery, Jeffree, Jeffries, Jeffry, Jeffy, Jefry, Jeoffroi, Joffre, Joffrey

Jehoiakim Heb. "God will judge." A longer version of Joachim.
Akim, Jehoioachim, Jehoiakin, Joachim, Joakim, Joaquin, Josquin, Yachim, Yakim

Jehu Heb. "He is God."

Jellimiah Var. Jeremiah.

Jem Dim. James or Jeremiah. Rare as nickname or independent name.

Jenkin Flemish. "Little John." A name as popular and well used as John has naturally produced numerous last names as well, some of which find their way back to first-name status.

Jenkins, Jenkyn, Jenkyns, Jennings

Jens Scand. Var. John.

Jensen, Jenson, Jensson

Jeremiah Heb. "The Lord exalts." Old Testament prophet who lived in Jerusalem when it fell to the Babylonians. The Book of Jeremiah is so relentlessly gloomy in outlook that "jeremiad" has become the term for a lengthy denunciatory complaint. The Puritans used Jeremiah somewhat, but Jeremy has eclipsed it in modern times.

Dermot, Dermott, Diarmid, Geremia, Jem, Jemmie, Jereme, Jeremia, Jeremias, Jeremija, Jeremiya, Jeremy, Jermyn, Jerry, Yeremia, Yeremiya, Yeremiyah

Jeremy Modern form of Jeremiah. One source suggests that the modern penchant for Jeremy was sparked by a 1960s TV series called *Here Come the Brides*. This may be true, since the Jeremy on the show had brothers named Jason and Joshua, names that were simultaneously fashionable. The vogue for Jeremy and Jason is fading, though Joshua is one of the top five names in the U.S. Actor Jeremy Irons.

Jem, Jemmie, Jemmy, Jeramee, Jeramey, Jeramie, Jere, Jereme, Jeremie, Jeromy, Jerry

Jericho Biblical place name: one of the oldest cities in Palestine, and the first one that Joshua conquered when he brought the Israelites back into the promised land. An old spiritual relates how "Joshua fit the battle of Jericho . . . and the walls came tumbling down." Though not historically a proper name, Jericho has the familiar "Jer-" particle and the trendy -o ending that may bring it to popularity.

Jerico, Jericko, Jerrico, Jherico

Jerick Modern name: Derek (OG. "The people's ruler") with a "J." Six of the top twenty boy's names on one 1990 survey began with "J," and many parents like to update names by substituting the fashionable "J" for a different initial consonant.

Jerack, Jereck, Jerek, Jerrick, Jerrik, Jerriq

Jermaine Var. **Jarman** (OG. "German"). Made famous by Michael Jackson's older brother Jermaine.

Germain, Germaine, Jermane, Jermin, Jermyn

Jeroboam Old Testament name: a king of the Israelites who permitted the worship of idols. Because he was a big man, a very large bottle of champagne is known as a jeroboam.

Jerome Gk. "Sacred name." The 5th-century Saint Jerome was responsible for a Latin translation of the Bible. He is often portrayed with a lion, from the legend that he removed a thorn from the lion's pad and the beast rewarded him with lifelong fidelity. The name has been best used in the 16th and 19th centuries. Songwriter Jerome Kern; choreographer Jerome Robbins.

Gerome, Geronimo, Gerrie, Gerry, Hierome, Hieronim, Hieronimo, Hieronimos, Hieronimus, Hieronymos, Hieronymus, Jairo, Jairome, Jeroen, Jeromo, Jeronimo, Jerrome, Jerron, Jerrone, Jerry

Jerrell Modern name: probably a variant of **Gerald**, perhaps influenced by Darrell.

Gerall, Gerrall, Jerall, Jerel, Jeril, Jeroll, Jerrill, Jerroll, Jerryll

Jerry Dim. **Jeremy, Gerald**, etc. Scarce as a given name. Jockey Jerry Bailey.

Gerrey, Gerry, Jerre, Jerrey, Jerrie

Jerzy Pol. Var. **George** ("Farmer"). Writer Jerzy Kozinski.

Jesimiel Heb. "The Lord establishes."

Jessimiel

Jessamine English var. **Jesse**. Very unusual, and likely these days to be confused with the fashionable girl's name Jasmine. Author Jessamyn West.

Jessamyn

Jesse Heb. "The Lord exists." The biblical father of King David. In America the formidable athlete Jesse Owens (whose success at the 1936 Olympics chagrined the Nazis) has given the name great resonance for black families; the fame of politician Jesse Jackson may continue to do so. Outlaw Jesse James.

Jess, Jessie, Yishai

Jesus Heb. "The Lord is salvation." Used mostly by families of Latin American origin, but Joshua, from the same Hebrew derivation, is tremendously popular.
Jesous

Jethro Heb. "Preeminence." Old Testament name that occurred from time to time until the late 19th century. A flicker of modern use may have been inspired by the rock group Jethro Tull.
Jeth, Jethroe

Jett Mineral name: jet is a shiny black substance used for making jewelry. Jette is a girl's name in Scandinavia. In the U.S. this name is more likely to conjure up aircraft.
Jette

Jevon Modern name. Possibly Devon with a "J," though the accent is sometimes placed on the last syllable.
Jeavan, Jeaven, Jeavin, Jevan, Jeven, Jevin, Jevvan, Jevven, Jevvin, Jevvyn

Jim Dim. **James** (Heb. "He who supplants."). Used occasionally as an independent name.
Jimi, Jimmee, Jimmey, Jimmie, Jimmy, Jimson

Jivan Hindi. "Life."

Joab Heb. "Praise Jehovah."

Joachim Heb. "God will judge." Composer Josquin Des Pres.
Akim, Ioakim, Jachim, Jakim, Joacheim, Joaquim, Joaquin, Josquin, Yachim, Yakim

Joash Heb. "Given by the Lord."

Job Heb. "The afflicted." In the Old Testament, the Book of Job recounts the trials of an innocent man who was sorely tried by his God but remained faithful: hence "the patience of Job." Revived by the Puritans and used fairly steadily since the 17th century.
Joab, Jobe

Jock Familiar var. **Jacob** or **John** (Heb. "The Lord is gracious"). A slang term for a Scotsman, probably because the local accent turns Jack into Jock. Not actually used in Scotland, and in the U.S. avoided because it is a slightly derogatory term for an athlete. Sportsman Jock Whitney.
Jocko

Jody Familiar var. **Joseph** (Heb. "Jehovah increases"). In Marjorie Kinnan Rawlings's Pulitzer Prize–winning novel

The Yearling, the young hero is called Jody, but the name is more likely to be used for a girl.

Jodey, Jodi, Jodie

Joe Dim. **Joseph**. Sometimes given as an independent name. Baseball player Joe DiMaggio; boxer Joe Louis.

Joel Heb. "Jehovah is the Lord." Along with Amos, the most common of the Old Testament prophets' names, though Hosea also occurs. For some reason the parents of the late 20th century who have scoured the Old Testament for names have had a strong predilection for those beginning with "J." Actors Joel McCrea, Joel Grey.

Yoel

Joffrey Var. **Jeffrey** (OG., meaning unclear).

Jophrey

Johar Hindi. "Jewel."

John Heb. "The Lord is gracious." Given a sound foundation by two crucial saints, John the Baptist and John the Evangelist. (There are another thirty-odd significant saints named John.) The name has been used by twenty-five popes, an English king, and endless numbers of parents all over the world. In the English-speaking countries it was the most popular boys' name for over 400 years, losing ground only in the 1950s. Now some of its variants, like Ian and Sean, are gaining. Almost every country that was predominantly Christian has a version of the name, some of which—Hans, Giovanni, and Evan, for instance—barely resemble this English form. Actors John Gielgud, John Barrymore, John Wayne, Johnny Depp; four U.S. presidents: John F. Kennedy, John Tyler, John Adams, John Quincy Adams; poet John Donne; Beatle John Lennon; composer Johannes Bach; TV star John Tesh; football player John Elway.

Anno, Ean, Eian, Eion, Euan, Evan, Ewan, Ewen, Gian, Giannes, Gianni, Giannis, Giannos, Giovanni, Hannes, Hanno, Hans, Hanschen, Hansel, Hansl, Iain, Ian, Ioannes, Ioannis, Ivan, Ivann, Iwan, Jack, Jackie, Jacky, Jan, Jancsi, Janek, Janko, Janne, Janos, Jean, Jeanno, Jeannot, Jehan, Jenkin, Jenkins, Jens, Jian, Jianni, Joannes, Joao, Jock, Jocko, Johan, Johanan, Johann, Johannes, Johon, Johnie, Johnnie, Johnny, Jon, Jona, Jonnie, Jovan, Jovanney, Jovanni, Jovonni, Juan, Juanito, Ju-

wan, Sean, Seann, Shane, Shaughn, Shaun, Shawn, Vanek, Vanko, Vanya, Yanni, Yanno, Zane

Johnson OE. "Son of John." Mostly 19th-century use. Playwright Ben Jonson; track star Michael Johnson.

Jonson, Johnston

Jolyon Var. **Julian** (Lat. "Young"). Jolyon Forsyte is a major character in John Galsworthy's series of novels *The Forsyte Saga.*

Jonas Gk. Var. **Jonah** (Heb. "Dove"). Jonah is the biblical hero who was swallowed alive by a whale, in whose belly he lived for three days. He had been thrown overboard by sailors from the ship he was traveling on in order to calm a stormy sea; by extension, the term "Jonah" means someone who brings bad luck. The name, nevertheless, has been used with some frequency, though never immense popularity. Medical pioneer Jonas Salk.

Jonah, Jonaso

Jonathan Heb. "Gift of Jehovah." Related to Nathan, rather than to John, though the alternate Johnathan spelling clouds this issue. In the Old Testament, the great friend of King David. Used in the 17th century, then neglected from the 18th century until the 1940s. Some of its current extensive use probably comes about because it resembles John. Today's parents seem a bit reluctant to give a child a name of just one syllable, so Jonathan may be used instead. English author Jonathan Swift; actors Jon Voight, Jonathan Taylor Thomas.

Johnathan, Johnathon, Jon, Jonathon

Jones Surname derived from John. Particularly popular in Wales.

Jordan Heb. "Descend." Named after the River Jordan. First used in the Middle Ages by Crusaders returning from the Holy Land. Revived slightly in the 19th century. Unusual in that it is quite popular for both boys and girls. Male use has the edge at the moment. Possibly the fame of basketball star Michael Jordan, and Nike's extensive line of Air Jordan athletic shoes, maintains the perception that this is a masculine name.

Giordano, Jared, Jarred, Jarod, Jarrod, Jarrot, Jarrott, Jerad, Jerred, Jerrod, Jerrot, Jerrott, Jordaan, Jordao, Jordon, Jori, Jory, Jourdain, Jourdan, Jud, Judd

Jorge Sp. Var. **George** (Lat. "Farmer").

Jorgen Dan. Var. **George** (Lat. "Farmer").

  Jeorg, Jerzy, Jorg, Jori, Joris, Jurgen, Juri

Jory Dim. **Jordan**.

  Jorey, Jorie

José Sp. Var. **Joseph**. The most popular of the Latino names in the U.S. Baseball player José Canseco; opera singer José Carreras.

  Joseito, Pepe, Pepito

Joseph Heb. "Jehovah increases." Name that occurs for principal figures in both the Old and the New Testaments of the Bible. It has been less widely used than John and has fewer international variants, probably because of the relative prominence of these figures. The Old Testament Joseph, though significant, was not a saint. For hundreds of years, Catholic parents named their children exclusively after saints, and the two Biblical Johns (as well as dozens of Saint Johns) were far more important than the New Testament Saint Joseph, whose role in Jesus' life is small. Actor Josef Sommer; writers Joseph Conrad, Joseph Wambaugh; revolutionary Che Guevara; painter Joseph W.M.A. Turner.

  Che, Giuseppe, Giuseppino, Iosep, Iosef, Iosif, Iosip, Jessop, Jessup, Jo, Jodi, Jodie, Jody, Joey, Joop, Joos, José, Josef, Joseito, Josep, Josip, Josif, Josephe, Josephus, Joss, Josue, Joszef, Jozef, Osip, Pepe, Pepito, Peppi, Pino, Pipo, Sepp, Seppi, Yousef, Yusif, Yussuf, Yusuf, Yusup, Yuszef

Joshua Heb. "The Lord is salvation." An Old Testament hero, Moses' successor. Passed over by the Puritans, revived somewhat in the 18th century, and currently immensely fashionable in the U.S. It may be cherished by parents precisely beccause it has no history, and therefore no connotations, positive or negative. Painter Joshua Reynolds; director Joshua Logan.

  Josh, Joshuah, Josua, Josué, Joushua, Jozua, Yehoshua

Josiah Heb. "The Lord supports." An Old Testament king of Judah. Most common in the 18th century, now rather rare. Why is Joshua one of the top five names in the U.S. while Josiah, so apparently similar, is rare? Ask a parent

with a son named Josh. Porcelain entrepreneur Josiah Wedgwood.
Josia, Josias

Joss English name that may be a variant of **Joseph** or a surviving morsel of Jocelyn, which was a masculine name until early in this century. Actor Joss Ackland.
Joslin, Josslin

Jotham Heb. "The Lord is upright." Old Testament name.

Jove Mythology name: the Roman name for the sky god whom the Greeks knew as Zeus. He was also called Jupiter.

Joyner OE. Occupational name: "Carpenter."
Joiner

Juan Sp. Var. **John** (Heb. "The Lord is gracious"). Basketball player Juwan Howard; baseball player Juan Gonzales; King Juan Carlos of Spain.
Juwan

Jubal Heb. Meaning uncertain, though it may come from the Hebrew term for a ram's horn, like the word "jubilee." Jubal is said to have invented musical instruments. Confederate general Jubal Early.

Judah Heb. "Praise." In the Old Testament, Judah is the ancestor of one of the Twelve Tribes of Israel. Jude is the more common form.
Jud, Judas, Judd, Jude

Judd Var. **Jordan** (Heb. "Descending"), used as a last name and transferred to first name use. Given exposure by two actors, Judd Hirsh and Judd Nelson.
Jud

Jude Lat. Var. **Judah**. Very unusual, probably because of the traitorous apostle Judas Iscariot. There was, however, another apostle named Jude who now enjoys some popularity as the patron saint of lost causes. The literary-minded will associate this name with Thomas Hardy's novel *Jude the Obscure*.
Jud, Judah, Judas, Judd, Judsen, Judson

Jules Fr. Var. **Julius**. Author Jules Verne; playwright Jules Feiffer.

Julian Lat. Var. **Julius**. First took hold in the 18th century, and became fashionable in the 1950s through 1970s. Steadily used today. Musician Julian Lennon.
Jolyon, Julyan, Julianus, Julien

Julius Lat. Clan name: "Youthful." Common in Christian Rome and revived in the 19th century. This form and the Spanish form, Julio, are used about the same amount. Singers Julio Iglesias, Julius La Rosa; basketball player Julius Erving.

Giulio, Jolyon, Jule, Jules, Julio

July Dim. **Julius**. Or possibly the month name. If it's pronounced like the month, it is less likely to be taken for the girl's name Julie.

Julee, Juley, Juli

Juniper Plant name: evergreen shrub with berries from which gin (known as *genever* in Dutch) is traditionally distilled.

Junius Lat. "Young." Rare. Financier Junius Spencer Morgan; football coach June Jones; author Junot Diaz.

June, Juneau, Junio, Junot

Jupiter Roman mythology name: the sky god, supreme Roman deity, corresponding to the Greek god Zeus. Lightning bolts were thought to be messages from Jupiter to mortals on earth.

Juppiter

Jurgen Scand. Var. **George** (Lat. "Farmer"). Actor Jürgen Prochnow.

Jorgen

Juri Slavic. Var. **George** (Lat. "Farmer").

Jaris, Yuri

Justin Lat. "Fair, righteous." Another name well used by Roman Christians, but unusual elsewhere until very recently. It is now extremely fashionable, right up there with Joshua, James, and John. Actor Justin Henry.

Giustino, Giusto, Joos, Joost, Just, Juste, Justen, Justinas, Justinian, Justinius, Justino, Justinus, Justis, Justo, Justus, Justyn

Juvenal Lat. "Young." The name of a Roman satiric poet of the 1st century A.D.

Kaden Modern name, probably formed in response to the popularity of Kayla, Kaitlin, etc., for girls. The "-en" ending is perceived as masculine (Damien, Julien) in the way that "-ie" endings are considered feminine. Though meanings are almost irrelevant when it comes to a name like this, parents could extract an Old German reference to a swamp or an Old English word meaning "round" from *kaden*.

Caden, Caidan, Caiden, Caidin, Caidon, Caydan, Cayden, Caydin, Caydon, Kadan, Kadin, Kadon, Kaidan, Kaiden, Kaidin, Kaidon, Kaydan, Kayden, Kaydin, Kaydon

Kadir Arab. "Capable, competent." As Al-Qadir, this is one of the ninety-nine attributes of Allah.

Kadeer, Qadeer, Qadir

Kadmiel Heb. "Who stands before God." Old Testament name.

Kahn Heb. from Ger. "Priest."

Kai Possibly variant spelling of **Kay**; some sources suggest South African, "Beautiful."

Keh

Kaiser Var. **Caesar** (Lat. Possibly "Hairy"). The connotations, of course, are of imperial rule, as in Germany's Kaiser Wilhelm.

Kaleb Heb. "Dog." Anglicized as Caleb. Old Testament name.

Caleb

Kalil Arab. "Friend." Writer Kahlil Gibran.

Kahil, Kahleel, Kahlil, Kaleel, Khaleel, Khalil

Kalogeros Gk. "Lovely old age." A concept to be wished for, but an unwieldy name for a small child.

Kamal Arab. "Perfection, perfect."

Kameel, Kamil

Kane Welsh. "Beautiful" or Ir. Gael. "Warrior's son." Surname transferred occasionally to first name in this century.

Cahan, Cahane, Cain, Kahan, Kahane, Kain, Kaine, Kayne, Keane

Kaniel Heb. "The Lord supports me."

Kari ONorse. "Puff of wind" or "Curly hair." Mythology name, but also long used as an attribute name for someone with curls.

Kareem Arab. "Highborn, generous." This is the name of the current Aga Khan. Basketball star Kareem Abdul-Jabbar.

Karam, Karim

Karl OG. "Man." Var. **Charles**. The Germanic form of the name; as Carl, it was fairly well used in the U.S. from 1850 to 1950. "K" spellings are not as readily adopted for boys' names as they are for girls'. Fashion designers Karl Lagerfeld, Karl Kani; economist Karl Marx; basketball player Karl Malone.

Carl, Kale, Karel, Karlan, Karlens, Karli, Karrel, Karol, Karoly

Karmel Heb. "Garden." Biblical place name: Mount Carmel is in Israel, and is often referred to in ancient writings as a kind of paradise. This name is most often seen as Carmelo in the U.S.

Carmel, Carmeli, Carmelo, Karmeli, Karmelli, Karmelo, Karmello, Karmi

Karr Var. **Carr** (Scand. "From the swampy place").

Kasi Sanskrit "Shining." Also possibly a respelling of Casey, which used to be primarily a boy's name.

Kasee, Kasey, Kasie

Kaspar Var. **Caspar** (Possibly Per. "He who guards the treasure"). Originally Jasper. Traditionally one of the Three Kings (perhaps the one carrying the gold) was named Caspar.

Kasper

Katzir Heb. "Harvesting."

Katzeer

Kauai Hawaiian place name: the "Garden Island," considered by some to be the most beautiful in the Hawaiian archipelago.

Kawai

Kaufman Ger. "Merchant."

Kauffmann, Kaufmann

Kavan Ir. Gael. "Handsome."
Cavan, Kayvan, Kayven

Kavanagh Ir. Gael. "Follower of Kevin." Principally an Irish surname.
Cavanagh, Cavanaugh, Kavanaugh

Kay Old Welsh. "Rejoicing." Ancient name borne, in legend, by one of the knights of the Round Table. Now all but obliterated as a male name by the women's name Kay, which is a diminutive of **Katherine**.
Kai, Keh

Kazimierz Var. **Casimir** (Slavic. "Bringing peace"). Associated with Poland for her famous 11th-century king who brought peace to the nation.
Kaz, Kazimir, Kazmer

Keane OE. "Sharp." As in a "keen wit" or with a "keen eye." Actor Edmund Kean.
Kean, Keen, Keene

Kearney Var. **Carney** (Ir. Gael. "The winner").
Karney, Karny, Kearny

Keaton English place name, meaning unknown. Used as a first name in the U.S. in recent years. May be influenced by actor Michael Keaton.

Keats English last name: meaning unknown. John Keats was one of the great English romantic poets, who, despite his death at the age of 26, left a large body of unmatched verse.

Kedar Arab. "Powerful."
Kadar, Keder

Keefe Ir. Gael. "Handsome; lovable, loved."
Keeffe

Keegan Ir. Gael. "Small and ardent."
Keagan, Keagen, Keegen, Keeghan, Kegan

Keelan Ir. Gael. "Small and slim."
Kealan, Keallan, Keallin, Keilan, Keillan, Kelan

Keeley Ir. Gael. "Handsome." Also possibly a variant of Kelly (Ir. Gael. "Eager for battle").
Kealey, Kealy, Keelie, Keely

Keenan Ir. Gael. "Small and ancient." Two actors, Keenan Ivory Wayans and Keenan Wynn, have brought this name to the attention of the public, and it is the most common of these Irish names (with the exception of Keith and Kevin).
Keen, Keenen, Kienan, Kienen

Kefir Heb. "Young lion."

Keir Gael. "Dark-skinned, swarthy." Actor Keir Dullea.

Keith Scot. Gael. "Forest." Originally a place name, adopted as a first name for non-Scots in the 19th century. Peaked in the 1960s in the U.S., but still fairly steadily used. Baseball player Keith Hernandez; Rolling Stone Keith Richard; actor Keith Carradine.

Kelby ONorse. Place name: "The farm near the spring."
Kelbey, Kelbie, Kellby

Kell ONorse. Place name: "Spring."

Kellagh Ir. Gael. "Battle, strife, warfare."
Kellach

Kellen May be related to Kell, or to an Old German word that means "swamp."
Kellan, Kellin

Keller Possibly Ir. Gael. "Dear friend" or OG. "Cellar-keeper," which probably referred to someone whose cellar was stored with ales or wines.

⚊Kelly Ir. Gael. "Warrior." Originally a common Irish last name, and very popular as a girl's first name from the 1950s. Use for boy babies has diminished accordingly. TV producer David Kelley.
Kelley, Kellie

Kelsey OE. Place name, incorporating a word particle that means "Island." Until ten years ago this was a boy's name, but by 1995, it was one of the top twenty girls' names in the U.S., often with the more "feminine" spelling of Kelsie or Kelcie.
Kelsie, Kelsy

Kelton OE. Place name: "Town of the keels." Probably originally referred to a town where ships were built.
Keldon, Kelltin, Kellton, Kelten, Keltin, Keltonn

Kelvin Meaning and origin unclear: possibly OE. "Keel friend" (keel, in this case, standing in for ship) or a place name alluding to a river. Brief spurt of use in the 1920s was mostly British, but there has been a recent resurgence in America. Football player Kelvin Bryant.
Kelvan, Kelven, Kellven, Kelvon, Kelvyn, Kelwin, Kelwinn, Kelwyn

Kelvis Modern name: Elvis with the popular "K-" initial consonant.

Kellvis, Kelviss, Kelvys

Kemp ME. "Fighter, champion." Basketball player Shawn Kemp.

Kempton ME. Place name: "From the warrior's settlement."

Kemuel Heb. "Helper of God." Considered as Samuel with a consonant shift, the name has potential for popularity, though most of currently the hot "K-" names seem to be based on Gaelic sources.

Ken Dim. Kenneth and other "Ken-" names. Used independently, but parents who played with Barbie dolls in the 1960s may be hard put to name a baby after Barbie's boyfriend Ken. Baseball player Ken Griffey, Jr., singer Kenny Rogers.

Kenney, Kennie, Kenny

Kendall OE. Place name: "The valley of the Kent," a river in western England. Some sources also suggest "the bright river valley." In either case, a transferred surname used as a first name since the 19th century. There is a real vogue for "Ke-" names and Kendall, Kelvin, Kendrick, Keaton, Keegan, and the like are surprisingly well used.

Kendal, Kendel, Kendell, Kendill, Kendle, Kendyl, Kendyll, Kenny

Kendrick OE. "Royal ruler." Revived as a first name in the 19th century, and benefitting from the fashion for "Ke-" names. It is the sound, rather than the meaning, that makes these names popular.

Kendricks, Kendrik, Kendryck, Kenric, Kenrick, Kenricks, Kenrik

Kenelm OE. "Brave helmet." The name of a 9th-century king of Mercia (one of the kingdoms that predated a united England) who was later canonized.

Kenhelm, Kennelm

Kenley OE. Place name: "The king's meadow."

Kenlea, Kenlee, Kenleigh, Kenlie, Kenly

Kenn Welsh. "Bright water." Also a variant of **Kenneth**.

Kennard OE. "Brave and strong."

Kennaird

Kennedy Ir. Gael. Some sources suggest "Helmet-head,"

while "Ugly-head" is also offered, which would make this one of the rare names to refer to negative characteristics or habits possessed by ancestors. Use of Kennedy as a first name may be inspired by President John F. Kennedy. In that case "ugly-head" seems inaccurate.
Canaday, Canady, Kennedey

Kenneth Ir. Gael. "Handsome" or "Sprung from fire." Originally a favorite Scottish name that spread starting in the late 19th century. Very popular in the U.S. in the 1950s and 1960s, and one of the most widely used of the "Ke-" names. Art historian Kenneth Clark; actor-director Kenneth Branagh.
Ken, Kennet, Kennett, Kennith, Kenny

Kent OE. Place name: a county in England. Familiar as a surname, and used in the U.S. as a first name. In the 1930s and 1940s monosyllabic names (Clark, Burt, Kirk) seemed to project a manly aura and enjoyed a consequent burst of popularity. Football player Kent Graham; artist Rockwell Kent.
Kennt, Kentt

Kenton OE. Place name: "The royal settlement." In use as a first name since the 1950s.
Kentan, Kentin, Kenton

Kenward OE. "Brave or royal guardian."

Kenway OE. "Brave or royal fighter."

Kenyatta Used in recognition of Jomo Kenyatta, first president of Kenya as an independent country.

Kenyon Ir. Gael. "Blond."

Keon Modern name, possibly related to the girl's name **Kiana**, or an adaptation of the popular Deon.
Keion, Keioni, Keyawn, Keyon, Kion, Kiohn, Kionn

Kepler Ger. "Hatter, cap maker." Astronomer Johannes Kepler.
Kappler, Keppel, Keppeler, Keppler

Kerem Heb. "Vineyard."

Kermit Ir. Gael. "Without envy." A variant of **Dermot**, made famous (and virtually unusable) by the popular green Muppet, Kermit the Frog.

Kern Ir. Gael. "Small swarthy one." Kern was also a term, used especially in Scotland or Ireland, for a lightly armed footsoldier.
Curran, Kearn, Kearne, Kearns

Kernaghan Ir. Gael. "Victorious."
Carnahan, Kernohan

Kerr Scand. Place name: "The swampy place." Used basically in Scotland as a first name.
Carr, Karr

Kerry Irish place name: Kerry is a county in southwestern Ireland. Also, according to some sources, "dark-haired." Used more often for girls. Football player Kerry Collins; basketball player Kerry Kittles.
Kearie, Keary, Kerrey, Kerrie

Kerwin Possibly OE. "Swamp friend" or Ir. Gael. "Little dark one."
Kervin, Kervyn, Kerwinn, Kirwan, Kirwen

Keshet Heb. "Rainbow."

Kester Gaelic. Dim. **Christopher** (Gk. "Bearing Christ").

Kettil Swedish. "Cauldron." Huge kettles for sacrifices played a part in the old Scandinavian religion.
Keld, Kjeld, Ketil, Ketti

— **Kevin** Ir. Gael. "Handsome" (a meaning that certainly applies to two famous Kevins, actors Kline and Costner). Originally an Irish name that spread to wider use in the 20th century. Most popular in the 1960s, but still fairly standard.
Kevan, Keven, Kevon, Kevyn

Keyes OE. Probably an occupational name having to do with possession of keys. In the Middle Ages, locks would have been quite novel, and the man in charge of their keys would bear quite a responsibility. Francis Scott Key, author of "The Star-Spangled Banner."
Key, Keys

Keyshawn Modern name combining two popular elements, Shawn and the voguish "Ke-" particle. Football player Keyshawn Johnson has given this name exposure.

Khadim Arab. "Servant." Used in the U.S. as Kadeem.
Kadeem, Kadeen, Kahdeem, Khadeem

Khalid Arab. "Never-ending."

Khalil Arab. "Friend." See **Kalil**.

Kibo African place name: the highest summit in Africa, atop Mount Kilimanjaro. The peak is at 19,710 feet.

Kieran Ir. Gael. "Dark, swarthy." Becoming popular in Ireland, and showing some signs of spreading further afield. Actor Kieran Culkin.

Ciaran, Keiran, Keiron, Kernan, Kieren, Kiernan, Kieron, Kierren, Kierrin, Kierron

Kidd ME. "Kid, young goat." Probably an occupational name, possibly indicating an ancestor who kept goats. Pirate Captain William Kidd.

Kidder

Kiefer Ger. "Barrel maker." Actor Kiefer Sutherland; painter Anselm Kiefer.

Keefer, Kieffer, Kiefner, Kieffner, Kiefert, Kuefer, Kueffner

Killian Ir. Gael. "Small and fierce." From the same root as Kelly.

Kilean, Kilian, Killean

Kim Dim. "Kim-" names like **Kimball** and **Kimberly**. Also the title of a famous Kipling novel, but the days when children were named for Kipling characters is long since past, and Kim is almost always a girl's name now.

Kimball OE. "Bold war-leader."

Kimbal, Kimbel, Kimbell, Kimble

Kimberly OE. Place name: the "-ly" suffix indicates a meadow. The *Facts on File Dictionary of First Names* traces the masculine use of the name to the Boer War, when many English soldiers were fighting in the South African town of Kimberley. It has been virtually taken over by girls, however, and was a great favorite in the 1960s.

Kim, Kimbo, Kimberleigh, Kimberley

Kincaid Celt. "Battle leader."

King OE. "King." A last name since the Middle Ages. Modern use may be homage to Martin Luther King.

Kingman OE. "King's man." U.S. Ambassador Kingman Brewster.

Kingsley OE. Place name: "King's meadow." Surname transferred to first name, particularly in Britain. Novelist Kingsley Amis; actor Ben Kingsley.

Kingslea, Kingslie, Kingsly, Kinsey, Kinslea, Kinslee, Kinsley, Kinslie, Kinsly

Kingston OE. Place name: "King's settlement."

Kingswell OE. Place name: "King's well."

Kinnard Ir. Gael. Place name: "The tall hill."
   Kinnaird

Kinnell Ir. Gael. Place name: "Top of the cliff."

Kipling Origin unclear. Possibly related to Kip, below: may even mean "small pointed hill." Usage is likely to reflect admiration for the great English poet and storyteller Rudyard Kipling, who gave the world *Kim*, *The Jungle Book*, and the *Just So Stories*.
   Kippling

Kipp OE. Place name: "Pointed hill."
   Kip, Kyp

Kiran Sanskrit. "A ray of light."

Kirby OE. Place name: "Church village." Mostly 19th-century use. Baseball player Kirby Puckett.
   Kerbie, Kerbey, Kirbey, Kirbie, Kirkby

Kiril Gk. "The Lord." As Cyril, used in Britain around the turn of the century.
   Cyril, Cyrill, Kirill, Kirillos, Kyril, Kyrill

Kirk ONorse. "Church." Some 19th-century use in Britain, but it was really brought into circulation by actor Kirk Douglas. Unusual today, but not unheard-of.
   Kerk, Kirke

Kirkland OE. Place name: "Church land." In the era when last names were being formed in England, everyone was Catholic and the church played a central role in everyday life.
   Kirtland

Kirkley OE. Place name: "Church meadow." Like the following names, this became a last name after being a place name, and is only occasionally used as a first name.
   Kirklea, Kirklee, Kirklie, Kirkly

Kirkwell OE. Place name: "Church spring."

Kirkwood OE. Place name: "Church forest." Author James Kirkwood.

Kit Dim. **Christopher** (Gk. "Bearer of Christ"). A nickname for Christopher long before Chris was thought of. Christopher Columbus named the Caribbean island of Saint Kitts for himself and Saint Christopher, the patron saint of travelers.
   Kitt

Klaus Var. **Claus** (Dim. **Nicholas**; Gk. "Victorious people"). Even spelled with the more anglicized "C," unusual in English-speaking countries. Actor Klaus Maria Brandauer.
Klaas, Klaes

Klein Ger. "Small." German last names are not transferred to first names as often as their English counterparts.
Kleiner, Kleinert, Kline

Klemens Var. **Clement** (Lat. "Mild, giving mercy").
Klemenis, Klement, Kliment

Knightley OE. Place name: "Knight's meadow."
Knight, Knightlea, Knightlee, Knightlie, Knightly, Knights

Knoll OE. Place name: "Little hill." Conspiracy theorists will remember the "grassy knoll" at the scene of John F. Kennedy's assassination. The word is scarcely used otherwise.
Knolles, Knollys, Knowles

Knox OE. Place name. May be a variant of **Knoll**. Religious reformern John Knox founded the Scottish Presbyterian church in the mid–16th century.

Knud Dan. "Kind."

Knut Scand. "Knot." Brought to Britain by the 11th century King Canute of Norway and Denmark, who became the King of England in 1016. Very rare, except in those of Scandinavian descent. Football coach Knute Rockne; author Knut Hamsun.
Canute, Cnut, Knute

Kobi Hung. Variant **Jacob** (Heb. "Supplanter"). A couple of young athletes (basketball player Kobe Bryant, soccer player Cobi Jones) have brought this unusual name to the notice of the public. Did their parents know they were choosing a Hungarian nickname for Jacob? Probably not: the name has other sources as well, just as it has numerous spellings. Kobe Bryant was named for a special Japanese brand of beef.
Cobe, Cobey, Cobi, Cobie, Coby, Kobe, Kobey, Kobie, Koby

Kodiak Place name: island group at the western end of the Strait of Alaska. Settled in the 18th century by Russians.

Kody Var. **Cody** (OE. "Pillow"). The "C" spelling for this popular name is standard, but today's parents seek departure from the standard, so this spelling may become more common.

Kodey, Kodi, Kodie

Kofi Ghanaian. "Born on Friday." Some African names that are pronounceable to English-speakers are becoming more visible in America.

Kojo Ghanaian. "Born on Monday."

Konrad Var. **Conrad** (OG. "Courageous advice"). Despite occasional increases in numbers, a name that has never been widely popular in English-speaking countries. Anthropologist Konrad Lorenz.

Kord, Kort, Kunz

Konstantin Var. **Constantine** (Lat. "Steadfast"). The form Constant was popular among the Puritans (as a virtue name) and was revived in the 19th century to occasional modern use. Constantine, the Latin form, was the name of the first Christian Roman emperor, and a royal name in Greece.

Konstant, Konstantio, Konstanty, Konstanz, Kostas

Kornel Var. **Cornelius** (Lat. "Like a horn"). Comes from a Latin clan name, and as Cornelius, was often used under the Roman Empire. Painter Kees Van Dongen.

Kees, Kornelisz, Kornelius, Kornell

Koren Heb. "Gleaming."

Koresh Heb. "Cultivator, digger, farmer."

Choresh

Kramer Var. **Cramer** (OG. "Peddler"). People may think of the character from the popular TV show "Seinfeld."

Krispin Var. **Crispin** (Lat. "Curly-haired"). Saint Crispin, supposedly a 3rd-century martyr, is patron of shoemakers. The name was somewhat popular in Britain in the 17th and 18th centuries, and was revived in the 1960s, but has not spread to the U.S. in any significant numbers.

Kristian Var. **Christian** (Gk. "Anointed, Christian"). A girl's name that (contrary to the usual movement) became a male name, possibly after the huge success of John Bunyan's *Pilgrim's Progress* (1684), whose hero is called Christian.

Krist

Kristofer Var. **Christopher** (Gk. "Carrier of Christ"). The much-loved story of Saint Christopher is that he lived alone by a river, carrying travelers across the ford on his back. A child whom he was carrying became almost too heavy to bear, and proved afterward to be the Christ child. Actually, the tale has little basis in fact, and probably springs from the literal translation of the name, which originally alluded to carrying Christ in one's heart. Actor Kris Kristofferson.

Kristoffer, Kristofor, Kristopher, Kristophor, Krzysztof

Kumar Sanskrit. "Male child."

Kurt Ger. Var. **Conrad** (OG. "Courageous advice"). Actor Kurt Russell; author Kurt Vonnegut; U.N. Secretary General Kurt Waldheim.

Kwame Ghanaian. "Born on Saturday." The most widely used of these names from the Akan people of Ghana.

Kwasi Ghanaian. "Born on Sunday." Former Congressman Kweisi Mfune.

Kweisi, Kwesi

Kyle Scot. Place name: "Narrow spit of land." Well-traveled parents may have crossed the Kyle of Lochalsh to reach the Isle of Skye. Kyle is one of the two dozen most popular names in the U.S. for boys, and a "feminine" version of the name, Kylie, is almost as hot for girls. This seems to be the result of the craze for "K-" names rather than the significance of the name itself. Actor Kyle MacLachlan.

Kyler Dutch "Bowman, archer." As Schuyler/Skylar becomes ever hotter, Kyler is likely to follow, unless the girls get to it first.

Cuyler, Kylor

Kynaston OE. Place name: "Royal peace settlement."

Kyrone Modern name: Tyrone (Ir. Gael. "Land of Owen") with a "K."

Keirohn, Keiron, Keirone, Keirown, Kirone, Kyron

Laban Heb. "White." Old Testament name revived by the Puritans. Has appeared sporadically since.
Lavan
Lachlan Scot. Gael. Either "Belligerent" or "From the fjord-land," which would refer to Norway, thus indicating a Viking ancestor. The name is unusual, even in Scotland.

Lachman Ger. Place name: "Man from the lake."
Lachmann

Lacrosse Fr. "The cross." Lacrosse is a game played with a long racquet with a netted pocket: its name comes from the French term for a crozier, or bishop's crook. This is also the place name for a city and county in Wisconsin that was originally a fur trading post.

Lacy OF. Place name of obscure meaning, used as a boy's name in the 19th century and more commonly for girls today, probably owing to the double whammy of the "feminine" "-y" ending and the connotations of one fabric that even the dressiest guys don't wear.
Lacey, Lacie

Ladd ME. "Manservant or young man." Most likely to be a transferred surname. Actor Alan Ladd.
Lad, Laddey, Laddie, Laddy

Ladislas Slavonic. "Glorious rule." Related to Vladislav. The variants like **Laszlo** are more common. This was a royal name in medieval Hungary.
Lacko, Ladislaus, Laslo, Laszlo, Lazlo

Lafayette French name of uncertain meaning, though it may refer to faith (*foi*). First used in this country in homage to the French general the Marquis de Lafayette, whose participation in the American Revolution included both military action and solicitation of French help for the cause. During a return trip to the U.S. (1824-25), Lafayette was welcomed as a hero.

Laird Scot. "Lord of the land."

Lake Geography name: a small, contained body of water.

Names of this sort have become fashionable in the late 1990s as parents search for ever more unusual choices.
Laike, Laiken, Laikin, Laken, Lakon

Lakshman Hindi. "Auspicious, foreseeing good fortune."

Lalo Lat. "To sing a lullaby." Musician Lalo Schiffrin.
Lale, Lallo

Lamar OG. "Land famous." Plutocrat Lamar Hunt.
Lamarr, Lemar, Lemarr

Lambert OG. "Land-brilliant." Medieval and Renaissance use was encouraged by veneration for the Belgian martyr Saint Lambert, but in the more secular times since, nothing has occurred to save it from neglect.
Bert, Lambart, Lamberto, Lambirt, Landbert

Lamont Scand. "Man of law." Mostly U.S. use around the 1940s. Bicycle racer Greg LeMond.
Lammond, Lamond, Lemond

Lance Var. **Lancelot**. Mildly popular on its own in the middle of this century. Parents may have erroneously thought it referred to the medieval jousting weapon. It is fairly widely used, misunderstood or not.
Lantz, Lanz, Launce

Lancaster OE. Place name: a city and county that probably took its name from the river Lune, in western England. It was the center of much industry in the 19th century, and several cities in the U.S. also bear this name.
Lancashire, Lancester, Lanchester, Lankester

Lancelot OF. "Servant." Most famous, of course, for the knight of the Round Table who seduced King Arthur's wife, Guinevere. Used as a first name in the romantic 19th century, rare since the middle of this century.
Launcelot

Lander ME. Occupational name: possibly "Laundry-man" or "Landowner." More probably the latter, since the laundering trade, in medieval Britain, was unlikely to provide much of a career. Another, possibly more credible derivation is German, "Picket fence," which would make this a place name. Lander, Wyoming, was named after explorer and Civil War general Frederick W. Lander.
Land, Landers, Landis, Landiss, Landor, Landry

Landon OE. Place name: "Grassy plain."
Land, Landan, Landen, Landin

Lane ME. Place name. "A small roadway or path." More common for boys than for girls, though still unusual for both. This is the kind of name that is likely to be a mother's maiden name transferred to a first name.
Laine, Layne

Lang ONorse. "Tall one."
Lange

Langdon OE. Place name: "Long hill."
Landon, Langden

Langford OE. Place name: "Long ford." Many English place names are just compounds of familiar elements that still exist in our spoken language.

Langhorne OE. "Long horn." May refer to ancient possession of a cow with this distinguishing characteristic. This is an old Virginia name, borne by the illustrious Nancy Langhorne Astor, the first woman ever to serve as a member of Britain's House of Commons.
Langhorn

Langley OE. Place name: "Long meadow." As fans of adventure novels and films know, Langley, Virginia is home to the Central Intelligence Agency.
Langlea, Langlee, Langleigh, Langly

Langston OE. Place name: "Long town" or "Tall man's town." The "Lang-" element could have two meanings in this instance. Author Langston Hughes.
Langsden, Langsdon, Langton

Langward OE. Descriptive/occupational name: "Tall guardian."

Langworth OE. Place name: "Long paddock."

Lanier OF. Occupational name: "Woolworker."

Lanny Dim. **Roland** (OF. "Famous land"). More common as a nickname.

Lansing Possibly related to Lancelot. Also a place name: the capital of Michigan was named for an early American statesman named John Lansing.

Laramie Place name: a city in southern Wyoming, named for 19th-century fur trapper Jacques Laramie. The original spelling of his name is not entirely certain; it may have been Lorimier or LaRamee.

Larch Nature name: a kind of deciduous evergreen. The eastern larch is also known as a tamarack; the western larch is grown commercially as a lumber tree. The word "larch" comes from its Latin name, *larix*.

Laredo Place name: a city in southern Texas, on the Rio Grande. It was founded by Spaniards in 1755. The plaintive folk song "As I Walked Through the Streets of Laredo" may be familiar to some parents.

Largo Sp. "Tall, long." As in Key Largo, Florida. In musical terms, *largo* indicates a very slow tempo.

Lark ME. Nature name, used since the 1950s, mostly in the U.S. and predominantly for girls. Larks are usually thought of as playful, lighthearted songbirds.

Larkin Ir. Gael. "Rough, fierce." Poet Philip Larkin.

Larrimore OF. "Armorer."
   Larimore, Larmer, Larmor, Lorimer

Larron Modern name: possibly Darron with an "L," or a variant of Lawrence.
   Laren, Larin, Laron, Larran, Larren, Larrin

Larry Dim. **Lawrence**. Given as an independent name in this century, and with some regularity today. In fact this form is used more often than Lawrence, in spite of modern parents' reluctance to use nicknames. Basketball player Larry Bird.

Lars Scand. Var. **Lawrence**. Artist Carl Larsson.
   Larsen, Larson, Larsson

Laszlo Hung. "Famous ruler." A variant of the more unwieldy **Ladislas**.
   Laslo, Lazlo

Latham Scand. Place name: "The barn." Football player Lamar Lathom.
   Lathom

Lathrop OE. Place name: "Farmstead with barns."

Latif Arab. "Gentle, kind."
   Lateef, Lateeph, Latiph

Latimer ME. Occupational name: "Interpreter." Possibly one who could translate into Latin.
   Lattemore, Lattimore, Latymer

Laud Lat. "Praise." Archbishop of Canterbury William Laud.

Laughlin Ir. Gael. "Dweller at the fjord-land." This was the Irish term for invaders from Scandinavia.
   Loughlin

Lauriston OE. Place name: "Lawrence's settlement."

LaVerne This is actually the name of a classical goddess—of minor criminals, no less. The name has been used widely as a girl's name, but does sometimes occur for boys. It sounds enough like the romance languages' word for green (*vert*, *verde*) to have acquired misplaced con-notations of green trees or springtime.

Lavern, Levern, Leverne, Luvern, Luverne

Lawford OE. Place name: "The hill-ford." Actor Peter Lawford.

Lawler Ir. Gael. "Mutterer."

Lawlor, Loller, Lollar

Lawrence Lat. "From Laurentium." Laurentium was a city south of Rome known for its numerous laurel trees. Though the place no longer exists, the name endures, at first given staying power by the popularity of Saint Lawrence (who was martyred by being grilled alive). Brought to Britain with the Norman Conquest, and after an eventual 19th-century decline, was soundly revived in the U.S. in this century. Popularity began to tail off after the 1970s. Actor Laurence Olivier; band leader Lawrence Welk; actor Laurence Fishburne; football player Lawrence Taylor; author Laurens Van Der Post; opera singer Lauritz Melchior.

Larance, Laranz, Larenz, Larrance, Larrence, Larrens, Larrey, Larry, Lars, Laurance, Lauren, Laurence, Laurens, Laurent, Laurentios, Laurentius, Laurenz, Laurie, Laurits, Lauritz, Lavrans, Lavrens, Lawrance, Lawrey, Lawrie, Lawry, Lenci, Lon, Lonny, Lorant, Loren, Lorenc, Lorencz, Lorens, Lorentz, Lorenz, Lorenzen, Lorenzo, Lorin, Loritz, Lorrence, Lorrenz, Lorry, Lowrance

Lawson OE. "Son of Lawrence." Used as a first name mostly since 1850. Author Robert Lawson.

Lawton OE. Place name: "Hill-town." Actor Charles Laughton.

Laughton, Loughton

Lawyer Modern occupational name. Perhaps the mother who first used this name hope that her son would become an attorney. Football player Lawyer Milloy.

Lazarus Heb. "The Lord will help." Biblical name: Lazarus was the man whom Jesus raised from the dead. Little used, perhaps since in the Middle Ages it became a synonym for "leper."

Eleazer, Lazar, Lazare, Lazarillo, Lazaro, Lazear, Lazer, Lazzaro

Leander Gk. "Lion-man." The mythical Greek Leander swam across the Hellespont to visit his beloved, Hero. This was a saint's name as well, but has never been very widely used.

Ander, Leandre, Leandro, Leandros, Leanther, Lee, Leiandros, Leo, Liander, Liandro

Leary Ir. Gael. Anglicization of *laoghaire*, which means "herder." Dun Laoghaire is an important Irish port near Dublin.

Lebrun Fr. "Brown-haired one." The most common version of this descriptive name is Bruno, but Brunel and Burnett also come from the same source.

Labron, Labrun, Lebron

Lech Polish. "A Pole." An old name from the myth of the origins of the Slavic peoples. Three brothers, Czech, Rus, and Lech, were the ancestors of the Czechs, the Russians, and the Poles. Polish president Lech Walesa.

— **Lee** OE. Place name: "Pasture or meadow." One of the few truly unisex names. Usually a name becomes exclusively feminine once it is used for girls (Ashley, Leslie). The tenacious masculine hold on Lee may have been helped by tough-guy actor Lee Marvin. U.S. use seems to have been sparked by admiration for Confederate General Robert E. Lee. Peaked in the 1950s. Chrysler chairman Lee Iacocca; actor Lee Majors.

Lea, Leigh

Leggett OF. "One who is sent; delegate."

Legate, Leggitt, Liggett

Lehman Ger. "Tenant, renter." This name indicates a long-ago ancestor who was a tenant as opposed to an owner, probably of farmland.

Lehmann

Leif Scand. "Loved." Explorer Leif Ericsson.

Lief

Leighton OE. Place name: "Meadow settlement." Used as

a first name starting in the 19th century. Artist Frederick Leighton.

Layton, Leyton

Leith Scot. Gael. "Broad river."

Leland OE. Place name: "Meadow land." Philanthropist Leland Stanford; dramatic agent Leland Hayward.

Le, Leeland, Leighland, Leyland

Lemuel Heb. "Devoted to God." Old Testament name passed over in the wholesale Puritan revival of Biblical names, but given new life from around 1840 into the 1930s. Currently extremely rare.

Lem, Lemmie

Lenis Lat. "Mild."

Lennon Ir. Gael. "Small cloak or cape." Admiration for John Lennon has not inspired much use of this name, though some pop stars (Bob Dylan, Elvis Presley) have numerous namesakes.

Lennox Scot. Gael. "With many elm trees." This is the name of an aristocratic landowning family in Scotland that had huge influence in the 16th century.

Lenox

Leo Lat. "Lion." Common in Roman times, and the name of thirteen popes, but little used in the 18th and early 19th centuries. Perhaps it was the historical appeal of the name that made it more popular at the turn of the century. Astrological appeal notwithstanding, it is not much in fashion today. Author Leo Tolstoy; actor Leo G. Carroll.

Lee, Leon, Leoncio, Leonel, Leonello, Leontios, Lev, Lion, Lyon

Leomaris Lat. "Lion of the sea." An elaboration of Leo.

Leon Gk. Var. **Leo**. Very popular in the U.S., 1870–1890, and currently more familiar than Leo, but still very unusual. Author Leon Uris; football player Leon Lett.

Leoncio, Leone, Lioni, Lionisio, Lionni

Leonard OG. "Lion-bold." Name of a saint who was much venerated in the Middle Ages (as patron of prisoners, among others), but did not inspire many parents until the 18th century. Use grew gradually to 1930 and has diminished since. Artist Leonardo Da Vinci; composer Leonard Bernstein; actor Leonard Nimoy.

Lee, Len, Lenard, Lenn, Lennard, Lennart, Lennerd, Len-

nie, **Lenny, Leo, Leon, Leonardo, Leondaus, Leone, Leo-
nerd, Leonhard, Leonid, Leonidas, Leonides, Leonis,
Lonnard, Lonny**

Leonzio It. Var. Leo.
Leonce, Leontios, Leontius

Leopold OG. "People-brave." Use mainly British and European. The fact that it has been a royal or aristocratic name in Belgium, Austria, and Britain has not increased its sparse use.
Leo, Leupold

Leroy OF. "The king." Occupational name: one of the servants or pages of a king. Revived in the late 19th century, especially in America, but use today is minimal.
Elroi, Elroy, Lee, Leeroy, Leroi, Roy

Leslie Scot. Gael. Place name: Some sources suggest "The gray castle." Became a last name, then (in the 18th century) a first name used for boys and girls. Boys' use has been tied to admiration for actor Leslie Howard, and is more common in Britain. Not much used now, as Leslie has become a girls' name. Actor Leslie Nielsen.
Leslea, Leslee, Lesley, Lesly, Lezly

Lester OE. Place name: "From Leicester," an area in central England. First-name use dates from the mid–19th century, and its popularity lasted about 100 years. Georgia governor Lester Maddox.
Leicester, Les

Lev Rus. Var. Leo.

Levander Several sources are possible. May mean "From the Levant," i.e., the eastern Mediterranean. Equally possibly, the name is a variant of Leander, or Evander with an initial "L" added.

Levant Fr. "Rising." This is a place name, referring to the eastern Mediterranean where the sun rises, if you are in Italy, for instance.

Leverett OF. "Baby rabbit." May indicate an ancestor who hunted or trapped rabbits.
Leveret, Leverit, Leveritt

Leverton OE. "From the rush-farm."

Levi Heb. "Joined, attached." In the Old Testament, one of Jacob's sons, whose descendants (known as the Levites) were Israel's tribe of priests. After its revival by the Puritans, the name has been steadily used.

Levey, Levin, Levon, Levy

Leviticus Gk. "Beloning to the Levites." The name of the third book of the Old Testament, which contains religious and ethical laws that regulated the behavior of priests and believers.

Lewis Anglicization of Louis. Briefly popular in the late 19th century, but now takes a back seat to Louis, which is not particularly fashionable. Author Lewis Carroll.

Lew, Lewes, Lou, Louis

Lexer Ger. Dim. **Alexander** (Gk. "Man's defender"). May also come from Alexis.

Lex, Lexo, Lexus

Lexus Lat. "Law." To most people, this is now the name of a car.

Liam Ir. Var. **William** (OG. "Will-helmet"). Actor Liam Neeson.

Liberio Port. "Freedom." Other versions of this name, like the Spanish Liberato, are actually based on the Latin word that means "released" or "set free."

Liberato, Liberatus, Liberto

Lidio Port. "From Lydia." Lydia was an area of Asia famous for its two rich kings, Midas and Croesus. The female form, **Lydia**, is more common than the male.

Licio, Lydio

Lidon Heb. "Judgment is mine."

Ledon, Leedon

Lincoln OE. Place name: "Town by the pool." Surname transferred occasionally to a first name. The fame of Abraham Lincoln did not, surprisingly enough, encourage parents to use the name widely, and it is not a favorite today.

Linc, Link

Lindberg OG. Place name: "Linden tree mountain." Would probably be unknown as a first name without the career of flier Charles Lindbergh. Very scarce.

Lindbergh, Lindburg, Lindy

Lindell OE. Place name: "Linden tree valley."

Lindal, Lindall, Lindel, Lyndall, Lyndell

Lindeman Ger. "Dweller near the lindens."

Lindemann, Linder

Linden Nature name: a tall, handsome deciduous tree, also known as a lime tree or basswood. Its wood is particularly easy to carve.
Lindo, Lindon, Lynden, Lyndon

Lindhurst OE. "Linden village."
Lindenhurst, Lyndenhurst, Lyndhurst

Lindley OE. "Linden tree meadow."
Lindlea, Lindlee, Lindleigh, Lindly

Lindsay OE. Place name: "Island of linden trees." Originally a surname, used for boys until the middle of this century, but now quite popular as a girl's name. Film director Lindsay Anderson; New York mayor John Lindsay.
Lind, Lindesay, Lindsee, Lindsey, Lindsy, Lindy, Linsay, Linsey, Linzy, Lyndsay, Lyndsey, Lyndsie

Linford OE. Place name: "Linden tree ford" or "Flax ford." The elements meaning flax ("Lin-") and linden tree ("Lind-") are so similar that they have probably been confused over the years. Track star Linford Christie.
Lindford, Lynford

Link Possibly a diminutive of **Lincoln**. May also mean "An enclosure, paddock."

Linley OE. Place name: "Flax meadow."
Linlea, Linlee, Linleigh, Linly

Linn OE. May refer either to flax, as in Linus, or to linden trees, as in Lindsay. Rare, whatever its derivation, and will be greatly confused with the girl's name Lynn.
Lin, Linnie, Lyn, Lynn

Linton OE. Place name: "Flax settlement."
Lintonn, Lynton, Lyntonn

Linus Gk. "Flax." Flax is the fiber used to make linen. May have originated as a descriptive name, applied to someone with flaxen or extremely pale hair. This description does not apply to today's best-known Linus, the famous *Peanuts* character who is lost without his blanket. In Greek myth, Linus is a son of Apollo, and a musician who taught music to both Hercules and Orpheus.
Lino

Lionel Lat. "Young lion." Used in the Middle Ages and never resoundingly revived beyond a twinge of popularity in the 1920s and 1930s. Actor Lionel Barrymore; pop star Lionel Richie.

Léonel, Leonello, Lionell, Lionelo, Lionello, Lionnel, Lionnell, Lionnello, Lyonel, Lyinell, Lyonelo, Lyonnel, Lyonnell, Lyonnello

Liron Heb. "My song."
Leeron, Lyron

Lisle Place name: Lille, France, center of the French textile
industry. Lisle thread, a strong cotton used for gloves and
stockings, was originally made there. This name may also
be related to Lyle, which means "the island."
Lyall, Lyell, Lyle, Lysle

Litton OE. Place name: "Settlement on the hill." Author
Lytton Strachey.
Litten, Littonn, Lytten, Lytton

Livingston OE. Place name: "Leif's settlement." The Livingston family were prominent Hudson River landowners
in the 18th and 19th centuries.
Livingsten, Livingstin, Livingstone

Llewellyn Welsh. "Resembling a lion." This is the generally accepted meaning, though some scholars think the
origin relates to an element meaning "leader." Rare outside of Wales in any case.
Lew, Lewellen, Lewellyn, Llewellen, Llwewellin

Lloyd Welsh. "Gray" or "Sacred." One of the most common Welsh names in general use, perhaps because it is
one of the simplest. Particularly widespread in the 1940s.
Actor Lloyd Bridges; Senator Lloyd Bentsen; baseball
player Graeme Lloyd.
Floyd, Loyd

Lobo Sp. "Wolf." A well-known Latino pop group is
called "Los Lobos."

Lochner OG. Place name: "Dweller by the pond."
Lockner

Locke OE. Place name: "Woods" or "Fortified place," or
OG. "Pond." Possibly an occupational name for locksmiths, though locks were not in general use when English last names came into use. Philosopher John Locke.
Lock, Lockwood

Lockhart OE. Possibly "Deer from the forest."

Lockwood OE. Place name: "Forest near the fortified
place."

Lodge ME. "Shelter." U.S. Senator Henry Cabot Lodge.

Lodur Scand. Mythology name: Lodur was one o brothers.

Loeb Ger. "Lion." Seen as a last name, or occasionally a middle name.
Loeber, Loew, Loewe, Loewy

— Logan Ir. Gael. Place name: "Small hollow." For a name with no connections to a celebrity who might have brought it into public view, Logan is quite popular. Author Logan Pearsall Smith; playwright and director Joshua Logan.
Logen

Loki ONorse mythology name: Loki was the mischief-maker in the Norse pantheon.

Loman Ir. Gael. "Small bare one."

Lombard Lat. "Long-bearded." May also have origins as a place name: Lombardy is an area in northern Italy. Very rare as a first name. Football coach Vince Lombardi; bandleader Guy Lombardo.
Lombardi, Lombardo

Lon Dim. Alonzo (OG. "Ready for battle"). Mostly associated with sinister film actor Lon Chaney. Lonnie is actually the more popular form.
Lonn, Lonnie, Lonny

London Place name: the capital of Great Britain (the name was originally Londinium). The name may be used by anglophiles or admirers of American novelist (*Call of the Wild, White Fang*) Jack London.

Long OE. "Tall." Rare as a first name.
Lang

Longfellow OE. "Tall one." Used in admiration of poet Henry Wadsworth Longfellow, who wrote "Evangeline," "The Song of Hiawatha," and "Paul Revere's Ride," among other poems. His technical skill and his romantic view of early American history made him the best-loved— and bestselling—American poet of the 19th century.

Lonzo Dim. Alonzo (OG. "Ready for battle").

Lorcan Ir. Gael. "Small fierce one."

Lord OE. "Loaf-keeper," or, in more modern terms, someone with power and authority. Less common in the U.S. than Earl or Duke, which are higher ranks in England's aristocracy. Actor Jack Lord.

Loren Var. **Lawrence** via **Lorenzo**. A purely modern form, in use since the 1940s but not common, possibly because of potential confusion with the girl's name Lauren.
Lorin, Lorren, Lorrin, Loron

Lorenzo It. Var. **Lawrence** (Lat. "From Laurentium"). Substantially used in the U.S., most likely in Latino communities. Actor Lorenzo Lamas.
Laurencio, Loreno, Lorent, Lorento, Lorentz, Lorenzino, Nenzo

Lorimer Lat. Occupational name: "Harness maker." Probably related to Larrimore.
Lorrimer, Lorymer

Loring OG. "Renowned warrior's son." Related to **Louis**.
Lorring

Lorne Var. **Lawrence**. Also a Scottish place name, and more common in Scotland. Actor Lorne Green; TV producer Lorne Michaels.
Lorn

Lot Heb. "Veil, covering." In the Old Testament, as Lot and his wife fled the destruction of Sodom, his wife looked back and turned into a pillar of salt.

Lothar OG. "Famous army." A character called Lothario in an early 18th-century English play made this name synonomous for a while with a libertine or a careless seducer of women.
Lother, Lothair, Lothario, Lothur

Loukas Gk. "From Lucania," an area of southern Italy. This name and its variants are almost indistinguishable from various forms of Luke, Lucas, and Lucian.
Loukanos, Loukas, Loukianos

Louis OG./Fr. "Renowned warrior." The German form is Ludwig, and an early French variant was Clovis, a name borne by several Frankish kings. The later French kings (18 of them) who chose Louis as their name were no doubt harking back to those early monarchs, one of whom included the 13th-century saint. Lewis was the more common form in Britain until a mid–19th-century revival of Louis, which was very popular in the U.S. until the depression era. The name is still quite steadily used. Musician Louis Armstrong; scientist Louis Pasteur; archaeologist Louis Leakey; author Louis L'Amour; actor Lou Gossett, Jr.

Aloysius, Lew, Lewes, Lewis, Lodewick, Lodovico, Lou, Louie, Lucho, Ludovic, Ludovicus, Ludvig, Ludvik, Ludwig, Luigi, Luis

Lowell OF. "Young wolf." Mostly 19th-century use. The Lowell family of Massachusetts has produced poets, academics, and textile magnates. Lowell, Massachusetts, was named for an early 19th-century member of the family. Poet Robert Lowell.
Lovel, Lovell, Lowe, Lowel

Lubomir Polish. "Great love."

Lucan Lat. "From Lucania." Lucania was an area in southern Italy. It can be very difficult to sort out Lucan, Lucas, Luke, and their variants.
Loucan, Louccan, Lukan

Lucas Var. Luke. Generally a transferred last name, but gaining popularity in Britain as a first name, and quite popular in the U.S. as well. Actor Lukas Haas.
Loucas, Loukas, Lukas

Luce Lat. "Light." Scarce as a first name. Magazine publisher Henry Luce.

Lucian Lat. "Light." More unusual form of Lucius, which itself is quite rare. Artist Lucian Freud; opera star Luciano Pavarotti.
Luciano, Lucianus, Lucien, Lucio, Lucjan, Lukianos, Lukyan

Lucius Lat. "Light." Used by the Romans, but extremely scarce in the 20th century.
Luca, Lucas, Luccheus, Luce, Lucias, Lucio, Lukas, Luke, Lukeus

Lucky Modern name: descriptive. Lucky has usually been used as a nickname, but some parents, perhaps full of hope, use it as a given name.

Lucretius Lat. Clan name of uncertain meaning, though some sources suggest "wealth." Lucretius was the name of a Roman philosophical poet.

Ludlow OE. Place name: "Ruler's hill."
Ludlowe

Ludoslaw Polish. "Glorious people."

Ludwig Ger. "Renowned in battle." Very unusual in English-speaking countries, where Louis or Lewis are used instead. Composer Ludwig van Beethoven.
Ludo, Ludovic, Ludovico

Luis Sp. Var. **Louis** (Ger. "Renowned in battle"). More popular than the English spelling.
Luiz

Luke Gk. "From Lucanus," a region of southern Italy. Not, strictly speaking, a nickname for Lucius and Lucian, though it may be used that way. The most famous Luke is, of course, the author of the Gospel and of Acts. He was a physician, and is patron saint of doctors and artists. After medieval use, rather neglected, but the name is turning up quite frequently in preschools and hospital nurseries. It may be helped along by the appeal of actor Luke Perry.
Loukas, Luc, Lucas, Lucian, Lucien, Lucio, Lucius, Luck, Lucky, Lukacs, Lukas

Lundy Scot. Place name: "Grove near the island," or possibly Fr. "Monday's child." Generally a transferred surname.

Lunn Ir. Gael. "Strong, warlike."
Lon, Lonn

Luther OG. "Army people." Generally homage to Martin Luther, the German religious reformer, or to Martin Luther King, Jr., the civil rights activist. Botanist Luther Burbank.
Lotario, Lothair, Lothar, Lothario, Louther, Lutero

Lyle OF. Place name: "The island." First-name use was mostly in the middle of this century. May also come from Lille, the name of a city in northeast France (see Lisle). Musician Lyle Lovett.
Lisle, Lyall, Lyell, Lysle

Lyman OE. "Meadow-dweller."
Leaman, Leyman

Lynch Ir. Gael. "Mariner." One of the most common Irish last names, occasionally transferred for first-name use. Film director David Lynch; actor John Lynch.

Lyndell OE. Place name: "Linden tree valley."
Lindall, Lindell, Lyndall

Lyndon OE. Place name: "Linden tree hill." First-name use coincides with the 19th-century fondness for transferred surnames, but has been given extra renown by U.S. President Lyndon Baines Johnson.
Lin, Linden, Lindon, Lindy, Lyn, Lynden

Lynford OE. Place name: "Linden tree ford."
Linford, Linnford

Lynley OE. Place name: "Flax field."

Lyon Fr. "Lion." May be a place name, referring to the city of Lyons, in southern France.
Lyons

Lysander Gk. "Liberator." In Greek history, Lysander was a Spartan naval and military commander some 400 years before Christ. A character in Shakespeare's *A Midsummer Night's Dream* also bears this name.
Lesandro, Lisandro, Lizandro

Lytton OE. Place name: "Settlement on the hill." Author and critic Lytton Strachey.

LAW AND ORDER

In this country, you can name your child almost anything. Numbers are forbidden, as are obscene names, but from the very beginning, when Oceanus Hopkins was born on board the *Mayflower*, Americans have had great latitude in choosing names. Mister, Aladdin, even Messiah would be perfectly legal (if unwise) selections. Not so in many countries, though. There's a law on Argentina's books that forbids names "contrary to our customs." "Foreign" names have to be "Hispanicized." Aristobulo would be acceptable: Jack would not. France has also been historically concerned with maintaining Frenchness, and under Napoleon, the government created a list of French names with French spellings for parents to choose from. The list has been updated, but when you go to register the birth of your child in France, your name choice can be refused if it isn't considered acceptable. Saints' names are fine; names of American soap opera characters are not. Germany has a similarly strict approach: in 1900 their civil code embraced guidelines governing name choice. German parents have to choose names that are, well, *names*. Not descriptions (forget Precious) and not last names (good-bye, Madison). Most startling to American parents would be the ruling that a first name should indicate the child's gender. (So long Ashley, Leslie, Mackenzie, Taylor. . . .)

Mabon Welsh. "Son."

Mabry Origin unclear: Probably an Old English place name, however: the "-bry" ending is likely to be a contraction of "-bury," which ultimately comes from a Germanic word meaning "fortified place." The first syllable could be reference to the month of May, or even a contraction of "Mary."
Mabrey, Maybery, Mayberry, Maybrey, Maybury

Mac Scot. Gael. "Son of." Also used as a nickname for given names that begin with "Mac-," many of which are transferred last names.
Mack, Mackey, Mackie

Macadam Scot. Gael. "Son of Adam." The 19th-century engineer John McAdam gave his name to a method of paving roads that became very widespread.
MacAdam, McAdam

Macallister Scot. Gael. "Son of Alistair." Alistair is the Scottish version of Alexander.
MacAlister, McAlister, McAllister

Macardle Scot. Gael. "Son of great courage."
MacArdell, McCardell

Macarios Gk. "Blessed." The name of some seventy-three Catholic saints.
Macario, Macarius, Makar, Makari, Makario, Makarios, Makary

MacArthur Scot. Gael. "Son of Arthur." Some parents used this name in admiration of World War II General Douglas MacArthur.
McArthur

Macbride Ir. Gael. "Son of the follower of Saint Brigid," who was an influential 5th-century Irish nun.
Macbryde, McBride

Maccabee Arab. "Hammer." Other sources suggest the derivation comes from a Hebrew acrostic reading "Who is like unto thee among the gods, oh Lord?" Refers to a

group of Jewish patriots who overthrew Syrian rule in the
century before Christ; this was their battle cry. The Hannukah story took place during this struggle, making this
an appropriate name for boys born during the holiday.
Macabee, Makabee

Maccoy Ir. Gael. "Son of Hugh." The phrase "the real
McCoy" came from Scotland, where it referred to some-
thing of the highest quality.
MacCoy, McCoy

Maccrea Ir. Gael. "Son of grace." Actor Joel McCrea.
MacCrae, MacCray, MacCrea, Macrae, McCrea

Macdonald Scot. Gael. "Son of Donald." The McDonalds
were a powerful Scottish clan. One of their members,
Flora McDonald, smuggled Bonnie Prince Charlie to the
Isle of Skye when he was fleeing from the British who
had defeated him in his bid for the English throne.
MacDonald, McDonald

Macdougal Scot. Gael. "Son of Dougal." Since Dougal
means "dark foreigner," this may refer to an ancestor
who was a Viking invader (not all of whom were blond).
MacDougal, MacDowell, McDougal, McDowell

Mace ME. "Heavy staff or club." In the Middle Ages,
maces were often spiked, and used to break armor. May
also be a nickname for Mason.
Maceo, Macey

Macedonio Sp. from Gk. "From Macedonia." Macedonia
is a mountainous area to the north of Greece.

Macgowan Ir. Gael. "Son of the blacksmith."
**MacCowan, MacCowen, MacGowan, Magowan, Mc-
Gowan, McGowen, McGown**

MacHenry Scot. Gael. "Son of Henry." Fort McHenry was
part of the defenses of Baltimore in the War of 1812, and
it was the bombardment of this fort in 1814 that inspired
Francis Scott Key to write "The Star-Spangled Banner."
McHenry

Mackenzie Ir. Gael. "Son of the wise ruler." Currently
enjoying a minor vogue as a girl's name.
MacKensie, McKenzie, McKensie

Mackinac Place name: the strait between the peninsula of
Upper and Lower Michigan, and the name of the highly
picturesque resort island located there. The name is a
shortening of the Iroquois word *michilimackinac*.

Mackinley Ir. Gael. "Learned ruler." The highest peak in the U.S. is Mount McKinley, 20,300 feet high. In 1896 an Alaskan prospector named it after the Republican Presidential candidate. It is also known as Denali, its Athabaskan Indian name, which means "the big one." William McKinley, incidentally, was assassinated early in his second term. Vice-President Theodore Roosevelt thus became President.
MacKinlay, McKinlay, McKinley

Macmahon Ir. Gael. "Son of the bear." TV host Ed McMahon.
MacMahon, McMahon

Macmurray Ir. Gael. "Son of the seafarer." Actor Fred MacMurray.
MacMurray, McMurray

MacNeil Scot. Gael. "Son of Neil."
MacNeal, MacNeill, McNeal, McNeil, McNeill

Macon Place name: city in central France, in the center of the Burgundy wine district. Also a significant city in Georgia.

Macy OF. Place name: "Matthew's estate." This name, like Mackenzie, is also enjoying popularity among parents looking for an unusual girl's name. Department store founder R. H. Macy; actor William Macy.
Macey

Maddock Old Welsh. "Benevolent, charitable."
Madoc, Madock, Madog

Maddox Anglo-Welsh. "Benefactor's son." A contracted form of "Maddock's son." Novelist Ford Madox Ford.
Madocks, Maddocks, Madox

Madison OE. "Son of the mighty warrior." More common than many of these "son of" names, possibly because of admiration for U.S. President James Madison. There are towns or cities named Madison in at least fourteen states.
Maddison, Maddy, Madisson

Magal Heb. "Scythe."

Magee Ir. Gael. "Son of Hugh."
MacGee, MacGhee, McGee

Magni ONorse. "Tremendous might." In Norse myth, Magni was the son of Thor.

Magnus Lat. "Great." Appropriately enough, a royal name

in Norway and Denmark. It was transferred from Scandinavia to Scotland, where it is used somewhat.

Magnes, Magnusson, Manus

Maguire Ir. Gael. "Son of the beige one."

MacGuire, McGuire, McGwire

Magus Lat. "Sorcerer." The three kings, or wise men, who visited the baby Jesus, are supposed to have belonged to a tribe of priests from ancient Iran, who were thought to have power over demons. The name is the root of the word "magic."

Mahatma Sanskrit. "Great-souled." This was the title given to Mohandas Gandhi; it is used for those of great spiritual development.

Mahavira Hindi. "The great hero."

Mahavir

Mahesh Hindi. "Great ruler."

Mahir Arab. "Skillful."

Mahlon Heb. "Sickness." Old Testament name.

Mahmoud Arab. "Praiseworthy." Though it comes from the same root, this is not the same name as Muhammad. It is, however, popular in the Arab world.

Mahmood, Mehmood, Mehmud

Maimon Arab. "Dependable, faithful." Other sources suggest "Good fortune." This word is the root of Maimonides, the name of a great Jewish philosopher and scholar who lived in 12th-century Spain.

Maimun

Maitland OE. Place name: may refer to a meadow, or possibly to "Matthew's land."

Maytland

Majid Arab. "Glorious."

Majeed

Major Lat. "Greater." Use (which is sparing) probably harks back to the military title used in the British and American armies.

Majer, Mayer, Mayor

Makarios Gk. "Blessed."

Macario, Macarios, Macarius, Maccario, Maccarios, Mackario, Mackarios, Makar, Makkarios

Maks Var. Max (Lat. "Greatest").

Malachi Heb. "Angel, messenger." Name of one of the

minor prophets in the Old Testament, but not widely used. Author Malachi Martin.

Malachie, Malachy, Malaki, Malakie, Malaquias, Malechy, Maleki, Malequi

Malcolm Scot. Gael. "Devotee of Saint Columba." The name of the prince of Scotland who became king after Macbeth murdered his father, Duncan. Shakespeare's play was based on historical fact. The name has been used primarily in Scotland, but spread more widely in the middle of the 20th century. Black families may use it in honor of Malcolm X, who, upon his conversion to Islam, took the name El-Hajj Malik El-Shabazz. Publisher Malcolm Forbes.

Malcolum, Malkolm

Malden OE. Place name: possibly "Strong warrior's valley." Actor Karl Malden.

Maldon

Malik Arab. "Master." Malcolm X's Islamic name was El-Hajj Malik El-Shabazz. Actor Art Malik.

Maleek, Maleeq, Mallik, Maliq

Malin OE. "Little strong warrior."

Mallen, Mallin, Mallon

Malki Heb. "My king." Many variations of this name exist, with slightly different meanings in Hebrew; it is also the root of Melchior, one of the three kings' names. It is used as a girl's name as well.

Malcam, Malkam, Malkiel, Malkior, Malkiya, Mehlech

Mallory OF. "Unhappy, unlucky." Literally, *malheureux.* Originally a nickname, transferred to a last name and thus to a first name. Used quite often for girls now, though it was originally a man's name. Poet Sir Thomas Malory.

Mallery, Mallorie, Malory

Maloney Ir. Gael. "Pious, disciple of Sunday worship."

Malone, Malonee, Malonie, Malony

Malvin Var. Melvin. Could come from a number of sources: possibly Ir. Gael. "Polished chief," OE. "Council-friend," or an adaptation of **Melville**.

Malvinn, Malvyn

Mamun Arab. "Worthy of trust."

Mamoun

Manasseh Heb. "Making forgetfulness." This is the an-

glicized version, and is popular in Israel, while Hispanic variants also thrive. The Civil War battle of Bull Run was fought near the town of Manassas in Virginia.
Manassas, Manases, Manasio, Menashe, Menashi

Manchester OE. Place name: an important city in northern England. Its Latin name was Mancunium. In the 19th century, Manchester was the foremost city in the world for the manufacture of cotton fabric.

Mandan Native American: the name of a tribe indigenous to the upper Missouri River. The Mandan had developed high levels of material culture but were nearly wiped out by smallpox in 1837. A city in North Dakota is named after them.

Mandel Ger. "Almond."
Mandell

Manfred OE. "Man of peace." Seldom found in real life, but used by Byron for an antihero in an epic poem.
Manfredo, Manfrid, Manfried, Mannfred, Mannfryd

Mankato Native American place name: "Blue earth." A city in north central Kansas.

Mannheim Ger. Place name: "Swamp hamlet."
Manheim

Manley OE. Place name: "Man's meadow." Or originally a descriptive term meaning "masculine." Poet Gerard Manley Hopkins.
Manlea, Manleigh, Manly

Mann Ger. "Man." Author Thomas Mann.

Manning OE. "Son of the man."
Mannyng

Mannix Ir. Gael. "Little monk." An anglicized version of Munchin or Mainchin. Under English rule, many Gaelic names were very roughly anglicized, and often the correspondences are just approximate.

Manoach Heb. "Place of rest." Old Testament name: the father of Samson.
Manoa, Manoah

Manolo Var. **Manuel**. Shoe designer Manolo Blahnik.
Mano, Manollo

Mansel OE. "From the manse." A manse is a house occupied by a clergyman.
Mansell

Mansfield OE. Place name: "Field by the little river."

Mansur Arab. "Victorious."
Mansoor, Mansour

Manton OE. Place name: "Man's or hero's town."
Manten, Mannton

Manuel Dim. **Emanuel** (Heb. "God be with us"). Most widely used in Spanish-speaking countries, but it has a considerable presence in the U.S. as well. Shoe designer Manolo Blahnik; artist Manuel Ocampo.
Mano, Manolo

Manville OF. Place name: "Great town."
Mandeville, Manvel, Manvile, Manvill

Marcel Fr. Dim. **Marcellus** (Lat. "Little warrior"). One of the less common of a group of names that all have their root in the Roman god of war, Mars. Author Marcel Proust; pantomime artist Marcel Marceau.
Marceau, Marcelin, Marcellin, Marcellino, Marcello, Marcellus, Marcelo, Marcely

March OF. Place name: "Borderland, frontier." The Marches of western England border Wales: similarly, in Italy; *le marche* was a territory between two ancient kingdoms. The verb "march," meaning "to walk," comes from a slightly different root. The name may also, of course, be used to commemorate the month of birth. Actor Fredric March.
Marcio, Marzo

Marco It. Var. **Mark**. Italian explorer Marco Polo.
Marcos

Marcus Lat. "Warlike." The root of such names as Mark and Marcel, and based on the name of the Roman war god, Mars. Common enough in Roman times, but unknown in English-speaking countries until the 19th century. When Mark was hugely popular in the 1970s, Marcus also crept up the charts, possibly boosted by the hit TV series *Marcus Welby, M.D.* It may also be used in memory of civil rights activist Marcus Garvey.
Marc, Marco, Marko, Markus

Marden OE. Place name: "The valley with the pool."

Mariano Sp./Lat. "Of Marius." Possibly an old Roman clan name referring to Mars, possibly a reference to the Latin word for "manly." It is most likely used, however, as a reference to the Virgin Mary. Baseball play[er] iano Duncan, Mariano Rivera.

Marianos, Marianus, Marimo

Mario It. Var. **Mark**. New York Governor Mario Cuomo.

Marianus, Marius, Meirion

Marion Fr. Var. **Mary** (Heb. "Bitter or rebellious"). Almost always a girl's name, and likely to cause some confusion if given to a boy. The most famous male Marion, Marion Morrison, chose the unmistakably masculine "John Wayne" when he changed his name. Revolutionary war soldier Francis "Swamp Fox" Marion.

Mariano

Marino Gk./Lat. "The sea." A third-century Roman martyr named Marinus was canonized; another Saint Marinus, for whom the Italian republic of San Marino is named, seems to be legendary.

Marinos, Marinus

Mark Lat. "Warlike." The anglicized version of Marcus, and the most popular in this country. In spite of the automatic exposure given the name by the evangelist Saint Mark, it was not widely used in the Middle Ages, nor indeed was it really common until a sudden inexplicable flurry of use in the 1950s. The popular author Mark Twain (whose real name was Samuel Clemens) took his pseudonym from the call of Mississippi River boatmen: "Mark twain!" meant that the water they were navigating was two fathoms deep. Explorer Marco Polo; choreographer Mark Mitchell; New York Governor Mario Cuomo; swimmer Mark Spitz.

Marc, Marco, Marcos, Marcus, Marek, Mario, Marius, Marko, Markos, Markus, Marq, Marquus

Markham OE. Place name: "Mark's village."

Marland OE. Place name: "Land near the lake." Some sources suggest that the name means "famous land" and is the source of Marlon as well.

Marlin, Marlon, Marlond, Marlondo

Marley OE. Place name: "Meadow near the lake." Musician Bob Marley.

Marlea, Marleigh, Marly

Marlon OF. "Little hawk," or possibly a variation of **Mer**-

lin. Current use, which is scanty, is inspired by the career of actor Marlon Brando.
Marlen, Marlin, Marlinn, Marlonn

Marlow OE. Place name: "Hill near the lake." Rare as a first name, though classic film lovers might be reminded of Humphrey Bogart as Philip Marlowe in *The Big Sleep*. English playwright Christopher Marlowe.
Marloe, Marlowe

Marmaduke Old English name of uncertain derivation. It may be an adaptation of a Gaelic name. Has almost comical English upper-class connotations.
Duke, Marmeduke

Marmion OF. "Tiny one." Extremely rare, though used by Sir Walter Scott in a popular narrative poem of that title.
Marmeon, Marmionn, Marmyon

Marom Heb. "Height, peak."
Merom

Marquez Sp. "Nobleman." In the European nobility, Marquis is a lower rank than Duke, but higher than Earl (or Count), Viscount, or Baron, and means "lord of the marches or frontier." Of all these titles, Viscount alone has never made the transition to a first name, and Earl is the most common. Football player Marquez Pope; baseball player Marquis Grissom.
Markese, Markess, Markise, Markiss, Markize, Markwees, Markwess, Marques, Marquess, Marquis, Marquise, Marquiz

Marr OG. Place name: "Swamp."
Mar

Marriner Eng. "Mariner, sailor, seaman." This is not one of the old-style occupational names because, at the time when last names came into formation, being a mariner simply was not a possible career. Musician Neville Marriner.
Mariner, Marinor, Marrinor

Mars Mythology name: the classical god of war. Politically incorrect, despite its many well-used adaptations (Mark, Marcus, etc.).

Marsden OE. Place name: "Swampy valley." Painter Marsden Hartley.
Marsdin, Marsdon

Marsh OE. Place name: "Swamp or marsh." Like Marsden and Marston, more generally a last name, occasionally used as a first name. Nineteenth-century parents were particularly fond of transferring surnames as given names.

Marshall OF. Occupational name: "Horse-keeper." Also a military title of great honor, as in "field marshal." As a last name, common in Scotland, and used rather widely as a first name since the early 19th century. Department store founder Marshall Field; media theorist Marshall McLuhan; actor David Marshall Grant; Supreme Court Justice Thurgood Marshall; football player Marshall Faulk.
Marchall, Marischal, Marischall, Marschal, Marsh, Marshal, Marshell

Marston OE. Place name: "Town by the marsh."

Martell Fr. Dim. **Martin**.

Martin Lat. "Warlike." Like Marcus and its variants, Martin originates with the Roman war god, Mars. The 4th-century Saint Martin (most famous for dividing his cloak in two and giving half to a beggar) was much venerated, making his name popular in the Middle Ages. The influence of Protestant reformer Martin Luther may have added to the name's appeal, since it was used very steadily right into the 19th century, though there are comparatively few variants. The pattern since then has been of growing disuse, except for a spurt of popularity in the 1950s. Even the eminence of civil rights activist Martin Luther King, Jr. has not drawn parents to this name in great numbers. U.S. President Martin Van Buren; film director Martin Scorsese; actor Martin Short.
Marinos, Mart, Martel, Martell, Marten, Martenn, Martie, Martijn, Martinien, Martino, Martinos, Martinus, Marton, Marty, Martyn

Marvell OE. Derivation unclear: may be a diminutive of Marvin, formed as Martell was. Also possibly related to the verb "to marvel." Poet Andrew Marvell.
Marvel

Marvin Origin obscure, though many sources suggest OE. "Sea lover," while others claim that it is Welsh. Popular in America starting in the 19th century, peaking in the

, and now unusual. Actor Lee Marvin; songwriter Marvin Hamlisch; singer Marvin Gaye.

Marve, Marven, Marwin, Marwynn, Mervin, Mervyn, Merwin, Merwyn, Murvin, Murvynn

Marwood OE. Place name: "Lake near the woods."

Maryland Place name: the state of Maryland, which was named for English Queen Henrietta Maria, the wife of King Charles I, who was on the throne when the vast tract of land that now includes much of Pennsylvania, as well as Delaware and Maryland, was granted to Lord Baltimore. Football player Russell Maryland.

Mariland, Marilland, Marriland, Marryland

Masefield Eng. Place name: "Corn field." This name could not have developed in the early Middle Ages with many of the English place names because corn (or maize) is not native to England. It was not imported to Europe until after 15th-century exploration of the New World had begun. Poet John Masefield.

Maslin OF. "Little Thomas."

Maslen, Masling, Maslon, Masslen, Masslin, Masslon

Mason OF. Occupational name: "Stoneworker." Transferred from surname status starting in the mid–19th century, and used today quite steadily. Actor James Mason.

Masos Heb. "Gladness, happiness."

Massey Origin unclear. May go back to the German *Masse* which means "mass, measure," or it may be related to the Catholic Mass. Actor Raymond Massey; author Robert K. Massie.

Massie

Mataniah Heb. "Gift of God."

Matanya, Matanyahu, Mattania, Mattaniah

Mather OE. "Powerful army." The surname of a dynasty of 17th- and 18th-century Massachusetts theologians, Richard, Increase, and Cotton Mather.

Maither, Matther

Matthew Heb. "Gift of the Lord." Like Mark, Luke, and John, given great exposure by the author of one of the four Gospels. In more religious eras, parents would hear these names over and over again in the course of a year. Matthew began to be neglected in the 19th century and was little used early in the 20th until an enthusiastic re-

vival at midcentury. It is still one of the top ten boys'
names in the United States. Actors Matthew Broderick,
Matthew Modine; photographer Mathew Brady; poet Matthew Arnold; tennis star Mats Wilander.

**Madteo, Madteos, Madtheos, Mat, Mata, Mateo, Ma-
teusz, Mathé, Matheu, Mathew, Mathian, Mathias, Mathieu, Matias, Matico, Mats, Matt, Mattaeus, Mattaus,
Matteo, Matthaus, Mattheus, Matthias, Matthiew, Mattias, Mattie, Mattieu, Matty, Matvey, Matyas, Matz**

Matthias Ger. Var. Matthew.

Mathias, Mattias

Maurice Lat. "Dark-skinned, Moorish." Roman name
brought to Britain by the Normans and widely used into
the 17th century. A 19th-century revival faded around the
end of that century, but Maurice is still quite steadily used.
Actor Maurice Chevalier; writer Maurice Sendak; composer Maurice Ravel.

**Mauricio, Maurids, Maurie, Maurise, Maurits, Mauritius,
Mauritz, Maurizio, Maury, Maurycy, Morey, Morice, Mor-
icz, Moris, Moritz, Moriz, Morrel, Morrey, Morrice, Mor-
rill, Morris, Morriss, Moss**

Max Dim. Maxwell, Maximilian. Appeared at the turn of
the 20th century, fashionable by the 1930s, then faded,
but today's parents are showing strong interest in it again.
Writer Max Beerbohm; actor Max von Sydow.

Maks, Maxence, Maxson

Maximilian Lat. "Greatest." Appropriately enough, used
by the emperor of Mexico and the Holy Roman emperor,
though a bit of a mouthful for a child. Actor Maximilian
Schell.

**Mac, Mack, Maks, Maksim, Maksym, Maksymilian, Mas-
similiano, Massimo, Max, Maxey, Maxemilian, Maxemi-
lion, Maxie, Maxim, Maxime, Maximiliano, Maximilianus,
Maximilien, Maximillian, Maximino, Maximo, Maximos,
Maxy, Maxymilian, Maxymillian**

Maxwell OE. Place name: Maybe "Marcus's well," though
some sources also suggest "large well" or "important
man's well." Mostly Scottish last name, fairly common
as a first name. Parents who wish to call a son Max but
want to give him something a little more important-
sounding as a first name may turn to Maxwell. Editor

Maxwell Perkins; playwright Maxwell Anderson.
Maxwelle

Mayer Lat. "Larger." Var. **Major.** Also Ger. "Farmer,"
Heb. "Bright, shining." Banker Mayer Rotschild.
Maier, Meir, Meyer

Mayes English. Origin unclear; may be related to the month
of May, or to the cultivation of corn ("maize") or even
to veneration of the Virgin Mary. Baseball player Willie
Mays.
Mays

Mayfield OE. Place name: "Strong one's field."

Mayhew OF. Var. **Matthew** (Heb. "Gift of the Lord").

Maynard OE. "Hard strength." See **Meinhard.** Economist
John Maynard Keynes.
Mayne, Maynhard, Meinhard, Meinhardt, Menard

Mayo Ir. Gael. Place name: "Yew tree plain." Mayo is a
county in western Ireland. It is also most commonly the
short name for a condiment used in sandwiches, a fact
parents should bear in mind.

Mazor Heb. "Bandage."

Mead OE. Place name: "Meadow." General George Meade
was in charge of the Army of the Potomac in the Civil
War, and played a crucial part in the Union victory at
Gettysburg. Architect William Rutherford Mead.
Meade, Meed

Medad Heb. "Friend."
Meydad

Medford OE. Place name: "Ford at the meadow."
Meadford

Medwin OG. "Strong friend."
Medvin, Medwinn, Medwyn

Meged Heb. "Blessing, goodness."

Meilyr Welsh. "Chief ruler."

Meinhard Ger. "Hard strength." Maynard is the anglicized
form.
Mainard, Maynard, Meinhardt, Meino

Meinrad Ger. "Strong counsel."

Meir Heb. "Bright, shining." This name is currently popular in Israel, possibly in remembrance of Prime Minister
Golda Meir. More common forms in the U.S. include
some of the variant spellings.
Meiri, Mayer, Meyer, Myer

Mel Dim. **Melvin** and other "Mel-" names. Actor Mel Gibson; filmmaker Mel Brooks.

Melbourne OE. Place name: "Mill stream." Also the name of a prominent city in Australia, which was called Melbourne after the man who was Prime Minister of England in 1837, when Queen Victoria came to the throne. Occasional use.

Mel, Melborn, Melburn, Milbourn, Milbourne, Milburn, Millburn, Millburne

Melchior Pol. "King." The root of the name is actually the Hebrew Malki, which means King. One Hebrew version is Malkior. Traditionally the name of one of the Three Kings, along with Caspar and Balthasar. Opera singer Lauritz Melchior.

Malchior, Malkior, Melker, Melkior

Melchisedek Heb. "My king is righteousness." Old Testament name.

Melchisadak, Melchisadeck, Melchizadek

Meldon OE. Place name: "Mill hill."

Melden

Meldrick OE. "Mill ruler."

Melderick, Meldrake, Meldric

Melesio Sp. from Gk. "Careful, meticulous."

Melacio, Melasio, Melecio, Melicio, Meliseo, Milesio

Mellen Ir. Gael. "Small pleasant one."

Meldan, Mellan, Mellin, Mellon

Melville OE./OF. Place name: "Industrious one's town." Author Herman Melville.

Melvin Could come from a number of sources: possibly Ir. Gael. "Polished chief," OE. "Sword friend," or an adaptation of Melville.

Malvin, Malvyn, Malvynn, Mel, Melvyn, Melwin, Melwyn, Melwynn, Vinnie

Menachem Heb. "Comforter." Israeli statesman Menachem Begin.

Menahem, Nachum, Nahum

Mendel Semitic. "Wisdom, learning." The father of modern genetics, Gregor Mendel, was a 19th-century Austrian priest, abbot of an order of monks.

Mendell, Mendeley, Mendl

Mentor Gk. Myth name: in the *Odyssey*, Mentor was the name of a friend of Odysseus', who became his son Telemachus' tutor. To speak to Odysseus the goddess Athena assumed Mentor's guise. The name has been adapted as the current noun, meaning a wise and trusted guide.

Mercer ME. Occupational name: "Storekeeper." Choreographer Merce Cunningham.

Merce

Mercury Mythology name: the messenger of the gods. He corresponds to the Greek Hermes, and was usually depicted as a young man with winged sandals. He was the god of science and commerce, as well as the patron of travelers and thieves! A 6th-century priest named Mercury changed his name to John when he was elected to the papacy, since he felt that it was inappropriate for a pope to have the name of a pagan god. Football player Mercury Morris.

Mercuree, Mercurey

Mercator Lat. "Merchant." The Latinate name of Gerardus Kremer, the 16th-century cartographer whose projection for a map of the world was extremely useful to navigators.

Meredith Welsh. "Great ruler." More commonly a girl's name, but still clung to for boys in Wales. Composer Meredith Willson.

Meredyth, Merideth, Meridith

Merle Fr. "Blackbird." Very rare for boys. Singer Merle Haggard.

Merlin ME. "Small falcon." Also the name (via a mistranslation: see **Mervin**) of the wizard of the Arthurian legends. Use dates from the 20th century. Football player Merlin Olsen.

Marlin, Marlon, Merle, Merlen, Merlinn, Merlyn, Merlynn

Merrick Anglicization of a Welsh variant of **Maurice**. Used from time to time in this century. Theater producer David Merrick.

Merrik, Meyrick

Merrill Origin disputed, perhaps OF. "Famous." Its status as a surname probably depends on the medieval use of its antecedent, Muriel. Poet James Merrill.

Meril, Merill, Merrel, Merrell, Merril, Meryl

Merritt OE. "Little renowned one."
Merrett, Merit, Meritt

Mersey OE. Place name, meaning unclear. A river in western England that runs into the Irish sea and connects the industrial cities of Liverpool and Manchester.

Merton OE. Place name: "Town by the lake." Theologian Thomas Merton.
Merwyn, Murton

Mervin Old Welsh. "Sea hill." Mervyn is more common in Britain. Merlin the wizard of Arthurian legend was known in Welsh as Myrddin, translated into Latin as Merlin. The name was mildly popular around the turn of the century.
Merven, Mervyn, Mervynn, Merwin, Merwinn, Merwyn, Murvin, Murvyn

Meshach Heb. Meaning unknown. Old Testament name: one of three Hebrew men (along with Shadrach and Abednego) thrown into a fiery furnace by King Nebuchadnezzar and rescued by an angel. Used sparingly in the 19th century, even more rare today. Actor Meshach Taylor.

Methodios Gk. "Fellow traveler." Saint Methodius, a bishop of Constantinople, is venerated in the Orthodox church for his support of sacred images such as icons, which came under attack in the 9th century. Ironically, the term "fellow traveler" came to be used of communists, especially in England, in the 20th century.
Methodius

Methuselah Heb. Possibly "One who was sent." Biblical character Methuselah lived to be 969 years old. A name that would sit oddly on a baby.
Mathusela

Meyer Ger. "Farmer"; Heb. "Bringer of light." Architect Richard Meier; financier Mayer Rothschild.
Mayeer, Mayer, Mayor, Meier, Meir, Myer

Micah Heb. Var. **Michael**. Very easily confused with Michael when it is spoken. And though Michael is a perennial favorite among names and parents sometimes tinker with its spelling, they do not turn to this alternative in great numbers.
Mike, Mikey, Mikal, Mycah

Michael Heb. "Who is like the Lord?" In the New Testament, Michael is the name of the archangel who defeats the dragon. Usage was steady until a period of neglect that lasted from the early 19th to the early 20th century. The subsequent revival was immense, and Michael was, according to many listings, the most popular name for American boys in the 1970s and 1980s. Even as we move into the 21st century, this continues to be a favorite. Baseball star Mickey Mantle; actors Mickey Rooney, Michael Caine, Michael J. Fox; singers Michael Jackson, Mick Jagger; cartoon star Mickey Mouse; Soviet President Mikhail Gorbachev.

Micael, Mical, Michal, Micheal, Michel, Michele, Michiel, Mickey, Micky, Miguel, Mihail, Mihaly, Mikael, Mike, Mikel, Mikey, Mikhail, Mikhalis, Mikhos, Mikkel, Miko, Mikol, Miky, Mischa, Misha, Mitch, Mitchell, Mychal, Mykal, Mykell

Michelangelo Comb. form Michael (Heb. "Who is like the Lord?") and Angelo (Gk. "Messenger"). Use, mostly Italian, probably refers to the great Italian Renaissance artist Michelangelo Buonarroti.

Middleton OE. Place name: "Settlement in the middle" or possibly "Settlement near the meadow."

Midian Old Testament name: a son of Abraham who founded the tribe of Midianites, who continually oppressed the Israelites until their decisive defeat by Gideon.

Migdal Heb. "Tower." Photographer Herb Migdoll.
Migdahl, Migdoll

Miguel Sp. Var. **Michael** (Heb. "Who is like the Lord?").
Migelly

Milbank OE. Place name: "Mill on the bank."
Millbank

Milan Possibly a variant of **Miles**; also possibly reference to the northern Italian city of Milan (or Milano), which takes its name from a Celtic word meaning "mid-plain."
Milano

Miles Several possible origins, including Lat. "Soldier," OG. "Merciful," or variant of **Emil** (Lat. "Eager to please"). Since the end of the 18th century, it has been quite unusual. Pilgrim leader Miles Standish; musician Miles Davis.
Milan, Milo, Myles

Milburn OE. Place name: "Mill near the stream."
Milborn, Milborne, Milbourne, Millborn, Millborne, Millbourne, Millburne

Milford OE. Place name: "Mill-ford."
Millford

Millard OE. "Guardian of the mill." U.S. President Millard Fillmore.
Millerd, Millward, Milward

Millbrook OE. Place name: "Mill by the brook."
Milbrook, Milbrooke, Millbrooke

Miller OE. Occupational name. Use as a first name began in the late 19th century, is now sparing. Playwright Arthur Miller.
Millar, Myller

Mills OE. Place name "Near the mills," or possibly a contraction of "Miles's son."

Milo Ger. Var. **Miles**. Very unusual. Actor Milo O'Shea.

Milton OE. Place name: "Mill town" or perhaps "Middle town." One of the more commonplace names transferred to a first name, dating from the early 19th century. Now it sounds like a name for a man of a previous generation. Poet John Milton; comedian Milton Berle.
Milt, Millton, Milten, Miltin, Mylton

Miner Occupational name: "Miner."

Minor Lat. "Younger." It used to be the practice in English boarding schools, where boys were known by their last names, to call younger brothers Churchill and Churchill Minor, for instance. Photographer Minor White.
Menor, Miner, Meinor, Mynor

Minos Greek mythology name: the king of Crete who built the labyrinth. According to legend, Cretan civilization reached a peak under his reign.

Minster OE. Place name: "Church." It originally meant a church belonging to a monastery.

Miroslaw Slavic. "Great glory."
Mirek, Miroslav, Miroslawy

Misha Rus. Dim. **Michael** (Heb. "Who is like the Lord?"). Given some modern exposure as the nickname of superstar dancer Mikhail Baryshnikov.
Mischa

Mistral Provencal. "Masterful." The name of a cold, violent wind that blows seasonally in the South of France.

Mitchell ME. Var. **Michael** (Heb. "Who is like the Lord?"). The last name evolved in the Middle Ages, when surnames began to be regularly used, and it was transferred back to a first name in the 19th century. It was popular in the middle of the 20th century, and is now steadily used without being fashionable. Band leader Mitch Miller.

Mitch, Mitchel, Mitchill, Mytch

Mitford OE. Place name: probably "Middle ford."

Moab Old Testament name of uncertain meaning: Moab was one of the sons of Lot, and the tribe of Moabites was consistently in conflict with the Israelites.

Modesto Sp. from Lat. "Modest, humble."

Madesto, Medesto, Modestus

Modred OE. "Brave counselor." In the Arthurian legend, Modred is Arthur's illegitimate son who tries to claim his father's throne, and engineers his ultimate downfall.

Mordred

Mohajit Sanskrit. "Alluring, bewitching."

Mohammed Arab. "Highly praised." The name of the prophet and founder of Islam. There are many different forms of this name as it has been spelled in many different languages, many of which had little in common with Arabic. Boxer Muhammad Ali.

Mahmood, Mahmoud, Mahmud, Mahomet, Mehmood, Mehmoud, Mehmud, Mohammad, Muhammad, Muhammed

Mohandas Sanskrit. "Servant of Mohan." Mohan, which means "alluring," is one of the names of Krishna, one of the great Hindu gods. Mohandas was the first name of the Indian leader Ghandi, also known as Mahatma Ghandi. His use of passive resistance and civil disobedience were instrumental in gaining Indian independence from Britain.

Mohave American place name: the Mohave Desert covers about 15,000 miles in southern California. It takes its name from the Mohave Indians, related to the Yumans.

Mojave

Mohawk Native American name: the Mohawk Indians were a tribe of the Iroquois confederacy. Their name has been given to a river and also to a roadway, the Mohawk Trail, by which many settlers traveled from the eastern seabord to the area of the Great Lakes.

Mohegan Native American name: a tribe related to the Algonquins, indigenous to eastern Connecticut. They have also been known as Mahicans and Mohicans, and as such were subjects of the James Fenimore Cooper novel (made into a film in the 1990s), *The Last of the Mohicans*. They have been considered a division of the Pequot tribe, which has been so successful in pioneering gambling in Connecticut.

Mahican, Mohican

Monahan Ir. Gael. "Monk."

Monaghan, Monoghan

Monckton OE. Place name: "Monk's settlement."

Monkton

Monroe Ir. Gael. Place name: May mean "Mouth of the Roe River" or possibly "The red marsh." U.S. President James Monroe; novelist H.H. Munro.

Monro, Munro, Munroe

Montague Fr. Place name: "Sharply pointed mount." More common as first name in the 19th century.

Montagew, Montagu

— **Montana** Latinate place name: "Mountainous." The name is not true Latin, but is understood as if it were. This kind of pretentious naming was common in the 19th century, when to call a state simply "Mountain State" would have seemed undignified. Though the "-a" ending usually signifies a female name, the state itself is so rugged and the legend of the West so masculine that Montana, like Dakota, is sometimes used for boys. Fashion designer Claude Montana.

Montgomery OE. Place name: "Mount of the rich man." Unusual as a first name, and very likely to be shortened to "Monty." Actor Montgomery Clift.

Monte, Montie, Montgomerie, Monty

Monty Dim. "Mont-" names like Montague and Montgomery, used rarely as a given name. Given slightly ridiculous connotations by TV master of ceremonies Monty Hall and British comedy troupe Monty Python.

Moore OE. Place name: "The moors" or OF. "Dark-

skinned'' (as in ''Moorish''). Clement Clarke Moore was the author of the much-loved poem '' 'Twas the night before Christmas.''
More

Mordecai Heb. Meaning not clear, but possibly ''Follower of Marduk'' (who was a god of the Babylonians). An Old Testament name revived by the Puritans and neglected since the 19th century. Author Mordecai Richler.
Mordechai, Mordy, Mort

Moreland OE. Place name: ''Moor-land.'' Moor is a British term referring to a large, rolling expanse of scrubby, infertile wild land.
Moorland, Morland

Morgan Different sources give several meanings, including Welsh. ''Great and bright'' and OE. ''Bright or white sea dweller.'' The name is most common in Wales as both a first and a last name. It occurs infrequently in the U.S., though there has been some crossover use for girls. Actor Morgan Freeman; financier J.P. Morgan.
Morgen, Morgun, Morrgan

Moriel Heb. ''God is my teacher.''
Mori

Morley OE. Place name: ''Meadow on the moor.'' TV commentator Morley Safer.
Moorley, Moorly, Morlee, Morleigh, Morly, Morrley

Morris Anglicization of Maurice. Now more common as a surname, though it was once interchangeable with Maurice. Choreographer Mark Morris.
Morey, Morice, Moris, Morrey, Morrie, Morrison, Morrisson, Morry

Morse OE. ''Son of Maurice.'' Contracted from Morrison. Inventor Samuel F.B. Morse.
Morrison

Mortimer OF. Place name: ''Still water.'' Literally, ''Dead sea,'' *mort mer*. First-name use, as with so many of these place names, dates from the 19th century. Entrepreneur Mortimer Zuckerman.
Mort, Morty, Mortymer

Morton OE. Place name: ''Moor town.'' Like Mortimer, used as a first name since the 19th century, though probably more common.
Morten

Morven Scot. Gael. "Huge mountain." First-name use is mostly Scottish, and generally confined to girls.

Morfin, Morfinn, Morfyn, Morvyn

Moses History unclear. Some sources suggest Heb. "Savior," while others claim it means "Taken from the water." The latter definition clearly comes from the biblical story of the infant Moses afloat in the bulrushes, whence he was rescued by Pharaoh's daughter, later to become the great leader of the exiled Israelites. Always current in Jewish families, adopted by the Puritans in the 17th century, now uncommon. The fashion for Old Testament names that brought Jeremy and Joshua to popularity bypassed Moses completely, possibly because we tend to think of Moses as a great leader, the one who received the tablet of the Ten Commandments. It may seem like too big a name for a child. Israeli defense minister Moshe Dayan.

Mioshe, Mioshye, Mo, Moe, Moise, Moises, Mose, Moshe, Mosheh, Mosie, Moss, Moyses, Mozes

Moss Possibly OE. Place name describing a locale covered with moss, or perhaps an adaptation of Moses. Director and playwright Moss Hart.

Mostyn Welsh. Place name: "Mossy settlement."

Muhammad Arab. "Greatly praised." Name of the prophet and founder of Islam. There are some 500 variants of this name, and if they were all counted as one name, it would be the most popular name in the world. Many Muslims believe that angels pray with families which have a member named Muhammad. Converts to Islam (Cassius Clay being a notable example) often take a holy name when they convert: the boxer, of course, became Muhammad Ali.

Hamid, Hammad, Mahomet, Mehmet, Mihammad, Mohamet, Mohammad, Mohammed, Muhamet, Muhammed

Muir Scot. Gael. Place name: "Moor." Naturalist John Muir.

Muller Ger. Occupational name: "Miller."

Mueller

Munchin Ir. Gael. "Little monk." This is the anglicized version of Mainchin. Mannix is another form.

Mungo Scot. Gael. Some sources suggest "Most dear," while others dispute this meaning. Mungo (from *Munghu*) is a nickname for the ancient name Kentigern, and the 7th-century Scottish Saint Kentigern is sometimes referred to as Saint Mungo. The name appears from time to time in Scotland.

Munir Arab. "Shining, glowing."
Mouneer, Mouneir, Mounir, Muneer, Muneir

Munroe See Monroe.

Murdock Scot. Gael. "Sea fighter" or "Sailor." Generally Scottish usage; in the U.S., occurs mainly as a transferred surname. Media magnate Rupert Murdoch.
Murdo, Murdoch, Murtagh, Murtaugh

Muriel Ir. Gael. "Sea bright." Usually a female name.

Murphy Ir. Gael. "Sea fighter." A quintessentially Irish last name, in occasional use as a first name. Although, TV's Murphy Brown notwithstanding, it hasn't crossed over to become a girl's name, possibly because Murphy is a comic character.
Murfee, Murfey, Murfie, Murphee, Murphey, Murphie

Murray Scot. Gael. Place name, or possibly "mariner." Somewhat common as a first name in the 1930s and 1940s, but now little used.
Moray, Murrey, Murry

Murrow Celt. "Sea warrior." Journalist Edward R. Murrow.
Morrow, Morrowe, Murough, Murrough

Mustafa Arab. "Chosen." This is one of the names of Muhammad. It is also the name of the Turkish general who helped found modern Turkey.
Mustapha

Myron Gk. "Fragrant oil." Not, despite its sound, related to myrrh (as carried by the Three Kings). Like Murray, most common in the middle third of the 20th century.
Miron

Nabil Arab. "Highborn."
   Nabeel
Nachman Heb. "Comforter."
   Menachem, Menahem, Nacham, Nachmann, Nahum
Nachson Heb. "Adventurous person."
Nachum Heb. "Comfort."
   Nahum, Nechum, Nehum
Nadim Arab. "Friend."
   Nadeem
Nadir Arab. "Precious, scarce." Parents should bear in mind that in English the nadir of something is its lowest point, so this name may have negative connotations.
   Nadeer, Nadeir
Naftali Heb. "Wrestle, struggle, fight." Old Testament name: a son of Jacob and one of the ancestors of the Twelve Tribes of Israel.
   Naphtali, Naphthali, Neftali, Nefthali, Nephtali, Nephthali
Nagel Ger. Occupational name: "Maker of nails."
   Naegel, Nageler, Nagelle, Nagle, Nagler
Nagid Heb. "Ruler, leader."
Nahir Heb. "Clear, bright."
   Naheer
Naim Heb. "Sweet," Arab. "Contented."
   Naeem
Nairn Scot. Gael. Place name: "River with alder trees."
   Nairne
Nairobi African place name: the capital of Kenya.
Najib Arab. "Of highborn parentage."
   Nageeb, Nagib, Najeeb
Naldo Sp. Dim. **Reginald** (OG. "Powerful advice").
Nalin Hindi. "Lotus." The name signifies different plants in several different cultures: The Egyptians consider it a kind of water lily, while to the Greeks it is a shrub. It also has great significance in both Buddhism and the

Hindu religion, when the lotus, as a beautiful flower that flourishes in muddy waters, symbolizes enlightenment found in the most unpromising circustances. Buddha is frequently depicted sitting on a lotus blossom. In Homeric legend, by contrast, eating the lotus causes people to forget their homes and families and long for a life of idleness.

Naleen

Napier Scottish place name. Sixteenth-century Scottish mathematician Sir John Napier was very influential.

Neper

Napoleon OG. Meaning unclear, though tradition says it means "Lion of Naples." Another possibility is Greek "New town." Napoleon Bonaparte (who obviously inspired its use) came not from Naples, but from Corsica.

Leon, Leone, Nap, Napoleone

Narcisse Fr. "Daffodil." Not, as it would be in English, a flower name, but the name of a beautiful Greek youth who became enamored of his own reflection—hence "narcissism."

Narciso, Narcissus, Narkissos, Narses

Naren Sanskrit. "Superior man."

Nash OE. Meaning obscure, but "Headland, cliff" is one possibility. Poet Ogden Nash; architect Sir John Nash.

Nashua Place name: a city in New Hampshire at the conjunction of the Nashua and Merrimack rivers. This is also the name of a famous race horse who nearly won the Triple Crown in 1955. Despite its sound, this is not a Hebrew or Old Testament name.

Nasser Arab. "The winner." Egyptian President Abdel Nasser.

Nasir, Naser, Nasr

Nat Dim. **Nathan, Nathaniel**.

Natal Sp. "Birthday." Referring, of course, to the birthday of Jesus, or Christmas. This is also a place name, a province in South Africa. It is called Natal because explorer Vasco da Gama caught sight of the shore on Christmas Day 1497. Durban is its principal port.

Natale, Natalino, Natalio, Nataly

Nathan Heb. "Given." Old Testament name, revived in the 18th century and quite popular in the last forty years. It has now reached the top fifty boys' names in the U.S.

Nathan Hale was the American spy who declared, just before he was hanged by the British in 1776, "I regret that I have but one life to lose for my country." Critic George Jean Nathan; actor Nathan Lane; football player Nate Newton.

Nat, Natan, Nate, Nathen, Nathon

Nathaniel Heb. "Given by God." New Testament name of one of the apostles (who was also called Bartholomew). Used by the Puritans, and a steady presence ever since, though quite a bit less popular than Nathan. Author Nathaniel Hawthorne; musician Nat "King" Cole; slave insurrectionist Nat Turner.

Nat, Natanael, Nataniel, Nate, Nathan, Nathaneal, Nathanial, Nathanyal, Nathanyel, Nethanel, Nethaniel, Nethanyel, Thaniel

Naylor OE. Meaning obscure. This may come from an Old English name meaning "sea," or it may be an occupational name referring to a carpenter or "nailer."

Nailer, Nailor

Naveed Pers. "Auspicious news."

Navid

Nazaire Lat. version of Nazareth, the town where Jesus grew up. Saint Nazarius was an obscure 4th century Italian martyr. This is also the name of a town on the northwest cost of France.

Nasareo, Nasarrio, Nazario, Nazarius, Nazaro, Nazor

Neal Ir. Var. Neil.

Neale, Neall, Nealle, Neel

Neander Gk. "New man." In 16th-century Germany, many educated Germans or scholars changed their names by Latinizing them, substituting Faber for Schmidt, for instance. Neander is a translation of the German Neumann, a little bit of old-fashioned prententiousness. Johann Neander, a 19th-century German theologian, was born the Jewish David Mendel, and changed his name when he converted to Christianity.

Nebo Mythological name: a Babylonian god of wisdom who invented writing.

Nectarios Gk. "Of nectar." Nectar is the drink of the gods, in classical myth. Nektarios is the name of a Greek saint, canonized in 1961, who devoted his life to the restoration and organization of a convent on the Greek island of Aegina. He died in 1920.

Nectaire, Nectarius, Nektario, Nektarios, Nektarius

Ned Dim. **Edward** OE. ''Wealthy defender''; **Edmund** OE. ''wealthy protector.''

Negasi Amharic. ''He will wear a crown.'' Amharic is the language spoken in Ethiopia.

Nehemiah Heb. ''The Lord's comfort.'' Old Testament prophet, Puritan name, rare in this century.

Nechemia, Nechemiah, Nechemya

Neil Gael. ''Champion.'' Although the name of the most famous Celtic king of Ireland (Niall of the Nine Hostages), it has been used mostly in Scotland until the middle of this century. Astronaut Neil Armstrong; singers Neil Diamond and Neil Young; playwright Neil Simon; actor Sam Neill.

Neal, Neale, Neall, Nealle, Nealon, Neel, Neile, Neill, Neille, Neils, Nels, Nial, Niall, Niel, Niles

Nels Scand. Var. **Nicholas**.

Nelson Eng. ''Son of Neil.'' Established by parents who admired the exploits of English Admiral Nelson at the Battle of Trafalgar. Used consistently, if never widely, since then. Actor Nelson Eddy; New York Governor and U.S. Vice President Nelson Rockefeller; South African activist Nelson Mandela.

Nealson, Neils, Neilson, Neillson, Nels, Nelsen, Niles, Nils, Nilson, Nilsson

Nemesio Sp. ''Justice.''

Nemo Literary name: the captain in Jules Verne's adventure novel *20,000 Leagues Under the Sea.* In Latin, *nemo* can also mean ''nobody,'' which Verne (who enjoyed giving punning names to his characters) probably knew.

Neptune Roman god of the sea, and a fanciful name for sea-loving parents.

Ner Heb. ''Light, flame, candle.'' Appropriate name for boys with Hannukah birthdays.

Nereus Gk. Myth name: Nereus was the old man of the sea, father of the sea-nymphs, the nereids.

Nereo

Nesbit OE. Place name: ''Bend shaped like a nose.'' Refers to a bend in a road, or else to a plot of land.

Naisbit, Naisbitt, Nesbitt, Nisbet, Nisbett

Nestor Gk. "Traveler, voyager." In Greek legend, Nestor was the wise ruler of the kingdom of Pylos who, when he went to fight in the Trojan wars, was constantly called on for advice. Cinematographer Nestor Almendros.

Nester, Nesterio, Nestore, Nestorio

Neville OF. Place name: "New town." More common in Britain, but very rare in the U.S. Musical conductor Neville Marriner.

Nev, Nevil, Nevile, Nevyle

Nevin Anglicization of Gaelic names that mean "Holy, sacred," or "Little bone" or "Servant of the saint's disciple." Not very widely used, though it may profit from Kevin's popularity, since it has the same sound.

Nev, Nevan, Neven, Nevins, Nevon, Niven

Newbury ME. "New borough, new settlement."

Newbery, Newberry

Newcomb OE. Place name: "New valley." Combe is an old British term for a valley or the flank of a hill.

Newcombe

Newell OE. Place name: "New hall." "Hall" was often a term for the local manor in early England.

Newall, Newel, Newhall

Newland OE. Place name: "New land."

Newlin Old Welsh. Place name: "New pond."

Newman OE. "Newcomer." Began to be used as a first name in England in the 19th century, perhaps influenced by the fame of reforming cleric John Henry (Cardinal) Newman. People may think of the character on the popular TV show *Seinfeld*. Now scarce. Actor Paul Newman.

Neuman, Neumann, Newmann

Newport OE. Place name: "New port." In the U.S. the name has been given "cool" connotations by the Newport Jazz Festival and a brand of mentholated cigarettes. The resort of Newport, Rhode Island is one of ten cities or towns named Newport in America.

Newton OE. Place name: "New town." Like many place names turned last names, made the move to a first name in the 19th century, and has now drifted back to last-name status. Entertainer Wayne Newton; English mathematician Isaac Newton.

Heb. "Diadem, crown."

Niall Ir. Gael. "Champion." A less common variant of Neil, used chiefly in Ireland.
Nial

Niaz Per. "A presentation, a present."

Nicandro Sp. from Gk. "Man of victory."
Nicandreo, Nicandrios, Nicandros, Nikander, Nikandreo, Nikandrios

Nicholas Gk. "People of victory." A New Testament name given even greater fame by the 4th-century Saint Nicholas, patron saint of children and (via his Dutch name, Sinte Klaas) the original Santa Claus. The name was widespread in the Middle Ages through the 17th century, then had a long period of disuse which ended in the middle of the 20th century. This is now one of the top ten names for boys in the nation. Theater director Nikos Psacharapolous; Dickens novel *Nicholas Nickleby*; actors Nicholas Cage, Nickolas Grace, Nicol Williamson; composer Nicolai Rimsky-Korsakov; political philosopher Niccolo Machiavelli.
Claas, Claes, Claus, Colas, Cole, Colet, Colin, Collin, Klaas, Klaes, Klaus, Nic, Nicanor, Niccolo, Nichol, Nichole, Nicholl, Nichols, Nick, Nickey, Nickie, Nicklas, Nickolas, Nickolaus, Nicky, Nicol, Nicola, Nicolaas, Nicolai, Nicolas, Nicolao, Nicolay, Nicolet, Nicollet, Nicolis, Nicoll, Nicolls, Nicolo, Nik, Niki, Nikita, Nikki, Nikkolas, Nikkolay, Nikky, Niklaas, Niklas, Nikolai, Nikolas, Nikolaus, Nikolay, Nikolos, Nikos, Nilos

Nickleby OE. Place name: "Nicholas' village." Made famous by the Charles Dickens novel *Nicholas Nickleby*.

Nico Gk. Diminutive of any of the "Nico-" names.
Nicos, Niko, Nikos

Nicodemus Gk. "Victory of the people." New Testament name, very scarce.
Nicodemo, Nikodema

Nicomedes Gk. "Pondering victory." It is the mark of a fierce people that so many names should feature the word particle meaning "victory."
Nicomedo, Nikomedes

Niels Dan. Var. Neil.
Niel, Niles, Nils

Nigel Ir. Gael. "Champion." Related not, as many sources claim, to the Latin *niger* ("black"), but to the Latin form of Neil, Nigellus. Almost exclusively a British name, popular in the 20th century. Actor Nigel Havers.

Nikostratos Gk. "Army of victory."
Nicostrato, Nicostratos, Nicostratus

Niles Scand. "Son of Neil." Not common, but cool.
Nyles

Nimrod Heb. "We shall rise up, we shall rebel." Nimrod "the mighty hunter" is mentioned in Genesis.

Ninian Meaning unknown. An Irish saint of the 5th century A.D. Little used, possibly because it sounds so much like "ninny."

Nissan Heb. "Miracle." This is the name of the first month in the Jewish year, when Passover falls. The accent falls on the second syllable, differentiating this name from that of the Japanese car company.
Nisan

Nissim Heb. "Wondrous things."

Nixon OE. "Son of Nicholas." A contraction of "Nicolas's son," or "Nick's son." After the disgrace of President Nixon in the early 1970s, unlikely to be used as a first name.

Njord Scand. "North." In Norse myth, the god of the sea, patron of fishermen and seafarers.
Njorth

Noah Heb. Meaning unclear, possibly "Rest" or "Wandering." The latter would be appropriate for the patriarch who drifted in the ark for forty days. Steadily but not widely used since the 17th century. Lexicographer Noah Webster.
Noach, Noak, Noé

Noam Heb. "Pleasantness, charm, tenderness." Related to Naim. Critic Noam Chomsky.

Noble Lat. "Aristocratic." Use as a first name may derive from surnames, or from the use of the adjective as a name. Mostly 19th century.

Noel Fr. "Christmas." Used since the Middle Ages, but not very widespread. More likely to be used for girls. Playwright and actor Noel Coward.
Nata, Natal, Natale, Nowel, Nowell

Nolan Ir. Gael. "Renowned." A last name transferred to first name. Baseball star Nolan Ryan.
Noland, Nolen, Nolin, Nollan

Noor Arab. "Light, brilliance."
Nour, Nur

Norbert OG. "Renowned northerner." Saint's name that was mildly popular in the middle of the 20th century.
Bert, Bertie, Berty, Norberto

Norman OE. "Northerner." The Normans of France were originally from Scandinavia, or the North, but the name was also used in England even before the Norman Conquest. After medieval use, it was neglected until a substantial 19th-century revival, which has long since faded. Artist Norman Rockwell; authors Norman Vincent Peale, Norman Mailer; TV producer Norman Lear.
Norm, Normand, Normen, Normie

Norris OF. "Northerner." May also derive from the French word for "nurse." Modern use dates from the 19th century. Novelist Frank Norris.

Northcliff OE. Place name: "Northern cliff."
Northcliffe, Northclyff, Northclyffe

Northrop OE. Place name: "Northern farm." Critic Northrop Frye.
Northrup

Norton OE. Place name: "Northern town." Revived as a first name in the mid–19th century. The comical Norton on the TV show *The Honeymooners* made this name impossible for older baby boomers to use.

Norville OE./Fr. Place name: "Northern town."
Norval, Norvel, Norvell, Norvil, Norvill, Norvylle

Norvin OE. "Northern friend."
Norvyn, Norwin, Norwinn, Norwyn, Norwynn

Norward OE. "Warden of the north."
Norwerd

Norwell OE. "Northern well."

Norwood OE. "Woods in the north."

Nuncio It. "Messenger." Comes from the same root that gives us the word "announce."
Nunzio

Nuri Arab. "Light."
    Noori, Nur, Nuriel, Nuris
Nuriel Heb. "Light of God, fire of God." Obviously related to the Arab *nur*.
    Nooriel, Nuriya, Nuriyah, Nurya

Oakes OE. Place name: "Near the oak trees." Transferred surname. This is also sometimes an anglicization of the German **Ochs**, which means "ox."
    Oak, Oaks, Ochs
Oakley OE. Place name: "Oak-tree meadow." The equally unusual Ackerley and Acton also refer to landmark oak trees. Oakley is the name of a company that manufactures extremely fashionable (at the moment) sunglasses.
    Oak, Oakes, Oakleigh, Oaklee, Oakly
Obadiah Heb. "Servant of God." One of the lesser Old Testament prophets. The name has faded gradually from sight after its revival by the Puritans in the 17th century.
    Obadias, Obadya, Obed, Obediah, Obie, Ovadiah, Ovadiach, Oved
Oberon OG. "Highborn and bearlike." This is its more famous (though little-used) form, as used by Shakespeare for the King of the Fairies in *A Midsummer Night's Dream*. It also occurs (very rarely) as Auberon. Author Auberon Waugh.
    Auberon, Auberron, Oberron
Obert OG. "Wealthy and bright."
Obi Ibo (Nigerian). "Heart."
Octavius Lat. "Eighth child." In English-speaking countries the name had its heyday in the Victorian era of large families. It has survived slightly better in Latin countries, but it is used in America. Probably very few of today's Octaviuses, though, have seven elder sibliings. Mexican poet Octavio Paz.
    Octave, Octavian, Octavien, Octavio, Octavious, Octavo, Octavus, Ottavio

Odell Derivation disputed. Some sources relate it to either German "Rich" or Greek "Song," but the *Facts on File Dictionary of First Names* claims that it derives from an Old English place name: "Woad hill." Woad is a blue dye reputedly used by the ancient Druids in their religious rites.
Dell, Odall, Odie

Odilo OG. "Prospers in battle." The root name is Otthild, and the feminine form **Odile** is more common. Saint Odilo was an 11th-century monk who instituted the observation of All Souls' Day on November 2. Like Saint Odo (see below), he was abbott of the influential monastery at Cluny. French painter Odilon Redon.
Odilio, Odilon, Otildo, Ottild, Ottildo

Odin Norse mythology name. The meaning is unknown, but Odin was the principal god. He ruled over culture as well as giving life and souls to people. Finally, he reigned over the dead.

Odolf OG. "Prosperous wolf." In the Middle Ages, to allude to a man as a "wolf" was to compliment his fierceness and courage.
Odolff, Odulf

Odo Var. **Otto** (OG. "Prosperous"). The "-o" ending is most often found in Germanic and Scandinavian names. Saint Odo was a French saint of the 9th century who was abbott at the famous monastery of Cluny.

Odran Ir. Gael. "Little pale green one." It's hard to imagine what this name refers to: eye color? A greenish complexion?
Odhran, Oran

Odysseus Gk. Myth. name: the word particle "dys" means "hate." Odysseus is the wanderer in Homer's great epic poem *The Odyssey*. The Latin version of the name, Ulysses, is a little better known in America, because of the fame of President Ulysses S. Grant.
Odysse

Ofir Heb. "Gold." Ophir is an Old Testament place name. It is frequently mentioned as an exceptionally rich source of gold, sandalwood, precious stones, and other luxuries. Its actual location is a moot point: scholars can narrow it down no further than India, Africa, or Arabia. In the late 19th century one of the most productive mines in Cali-

fornia's Comstock Lode was called "Ophir."
Ofeer, Ophir

Ogden OE. Place name: "Oak valley." Launched as a first name in the 19th century, but never widely used. Poet Ogden Nash.
Ogdan, Ogdon

Ohad Heb. "Loved one."
Ohed

Oisin Gael. "Little deer." In Irish history this was the name of the son of a legendary Gaelic poet, Fionn MacCumhail. Oisin MacCumhail was a warrior and a bard in his own right. In its English form, Ossian, it is also the name of a famous literary hoax. A mid–18th century Scottish poet, James MacPherson, published a group of poems that he claimed he had translated from ancient sources. The purported author was Ossian, who was supposed to have lived late in the 3rd century. But after initial acclaim and great popularity, skeptics began to perceive the truth: that MacPherson had written much of the poetry himself.
Ossian, Ossin

Olaf Scand. "Ancestor." A royal name in Norway, as well as a saint's name, but when it came to the British Isles with Norse invaders, it did not catch on. There was a King Olaf of Dublin in the 10th century, but when the Irish finally succeeded in expelling the Norse from Ireland, this name did not stay behind. Novelist Ole Edvart Rölvaag.
Olaff, Olav, Olave, Ole, Olin, Olle, Olof, Olov

Oleg Rus. "Holy." Fashion designer Oleg Cassini.

Olexei Var. **Alexei**, Rus. Var. **Alexander** (Gk. "Defender of mankind").
Oleksei, Oleksey, Oleksi, Oleksiy, Olexey, Olexi, Olexiy

Olimpio "From Mount Olympus." Olympus was the legendary home of the Greek gods.
Olimpo, Olympios, Olympus

Olin Eng. Var. **Olaf**. Actor Ken Olin.
Olen, Olyn

Olindo Lat. "Scented."

Oliver Lat. "Olive tree" is the most common meaning assigned, but some scholars suggest ONorse. "Kindly" or "Ancestor," among other possibilities. It came to Britain from France, and the controversial Lord Protector Oliver

Cromwell made it unpopular for generations. A mild revival occurred in the late 19th century, and the name is infrequently used today. Charles Dickens's *Oliver Twist*; director Oliver Stone; comic actor Oliver Hardy.

Noll, Oliverio, Olivero, Olivier, Oliviero, Olivio, Olivor, Olley, Ollie, Olliver, Ollivor

Omar Arab. "Elevated; follower of the Prophet." Heb. "Expressive." Currently popular in Arab countries and among Muslims in the U.S. This is in fact the most popular of all the "O-" names for boys. Poet Omar Khayyam; actor Omar Sharif; General Omar Bradley.

Omer

Omri Heb. "My sheaf" (of grain, etc.) Another possible meaning is "Jehovah's servant."

Ondré Var. Andre (Gk. "Man").

Ohndrae, Ohndray, Ohndré, Ohndrei, Ohndrey, Ondrae, Ondray, On'drei, Onndrae, Onndrai, Onndray, Onndré

Onofrio It. from Ger. "Peace defender." Actor Vincent D'Onofrio.

Onofré, Onofrius, Onophrio

Onslow OE. Place name: "Enthusiast's hill."

Onslowe, Ounslow

Ophir Heb. "Gold." See **Ofir**.

Or Heb. "Light, brilliance." Related to Oran. This name is often used in combination with other names as in Or-Chaim ("Light of life") and Or-Zion ("Light of Zion").

Oran Ir. Gael. "Green." Also Aramaic. "Light."

Oren, Orin, Orran, Orren, Orrin

Orazio It. "Prayer." May also be a variant of Horace, an ancient Latin clan name of uncertain meaning.

Oratio

Oren Heb. "Pine tree"; Ir. Gael. "Fair, pale-skinned." Very unusual. U.S. Senator Orrin Hatch.

Orin, Orren, Orrin

Orestes Gk. "Man of the mountain." An important figure in Greek myth, the son of Agamemnon and the brother of Electra, with whose help he murdered his mother (to avenge his father, whom *she* had murdered). Orestes appears in eight of the classic Greek tragedies. Not a cheerful heritage, overall.

Aoresty, Aresty, Oreste

Orford OE. Place name: "Ford of cattle."

Orion Gk. "Son of fire or light." In Greek myth, Orion was a mighty hunter who was turned into the constellation of the same name.
Oryon

Orlando Sp. Var. **Roland** (OG. "Famous land"). Mostly literary and minor late–19th-century use. Virginia Woolf's novel *Orlando* is a gender-bending fantasy inspired by Woolf's friend Vita Sackville-West. Composer Orlando Gibbons; football player Orlando Pace.
Arlando, Land, Lanny, Orlan, Orland, Roland, Rolando

Orman OG. "Sea-man" or OE. "Spear-man."
Ormand

Ormond OE. Place name: "Mountain of bears," or "Spear or ship protector"; Ir. Gael. "Red." Irish last name, occasionally transferred.
Ormand, Ormonde

Oro Sp. "Golden."

Orpheus Gk. Myth. name. Orpheus' music gave him spellbinding power over all living things. He married a nymph, Eurydice, and went to the Underworld to find her after her death. The gods, enchanted by his music, permitted him to take her back to earth on the condition that he not glance at her as he led her upward to the lands of open sky. He could not resist glancing at her, and she vanished back into Hades. The story of Orpehus and Eurydice has been made into several operas.
Orfeo

Orrick OE. Place name: "Old oak tree." Poet Orric Johns.
Orric

Orson Lat. "Like a bear." In an old French story, a child named Orson is reared in the forest by a bear. The name is very unusual, though it may be used by ardent fans of director Orson Welles. Actor Orson Bean.
Orsen, Orsin, Orsini, Orsino, Orsis, Orsonio, Sonny, Urson

Orton OE. Place name: "Shore settlement." Playwright Joe Orton.

Orval OE. "Strength of a spear." Also a variant of **Orville**.

Orville OF. Place name: "Town of gold." Though the name translates this way, it may actually have been coined by an 18th-century novelist. Never widespread. Flight pioneer Orville Wright.

Orv, Orval, Orvell, Orvil

Orvin OE. "Spear-friend."

Orwin, Orwynn

Osage Name for a Native American tribe of the Plains. This name is probably a French version of their own name for themselves. They were displaced from Missouri and Arkansas into smaller land holdings in Oklahoma.

Osbert OE. "Divine and bright." Anglo-Saxon name revived mildly with the antiquarian craze of the 19th century, but now extremely rare. Poet Osbert Sitwell.

Osborn OE. "Divine bear." The 19th-century revival of this Anglo-Saxon name was followed by another small spurt of use in the middle of the 20th century. Rock star Ozzy Osbourne.

Osborne, Osbourn, Osbourne, Osburn, Osburne, Ozzie

Oscar Scand. "Divine spear." Anglo-Saxon name revived by 18th-century literary use, reaching substantial popularity by the late 19th century. Fans of *Sesame Street* might hesitate to name a baby for the curmudgeonly Oscar the Grouch, but some parents bravely persist. Lyricist Oscar Hammerstein II; playwright Oscar Wilde; fashion designer Oscar de la Renta.

Oskar, Osker, Ossie, Ozzy

Osei Ghanaian. "Honorable, worthy of respect."

Osgood OE. "Divine Goth." The Goths were a Germanic ethnic group that took over various parts of Europe after the fall of the Roman Empire. Since the Goths were not Christian until well into the 6th century, the meaning of this name is puzzling.

Osher Heb. "Happiness, good fortune."

Osier OE. Place name: "By the willows." Osier twigs or shoots have long been used to make baskets and wicker.

Osmar OE. "Divine and wonderful."

Osmond OE. "Divine protector." Anglo-Saxon name revived in the 19th century, but scarcely found now. Henry James named one of his most sinister characters (Isabel Archer's suitor in *The Portrait of a Lady*) Gilbert Osmond. Singer Michael Osmond.

Osman, Osmonde, Osmont, Osmund, Osmunde

Osred OE. "Divine counsel."

Osric OE. "Divine ruler."
Osrick

Osten Var. **Austin** (Lat. "Worthy of respect").
Austen, Austin, Ostin, Ostyn

Oswald OE. "Divine power." Another Anglo-Saxon name
that endured partially because of the fame of two saints
of the name. Use has been mostly 19th century, though
actor Ozzie Nelson's real name was Oswald. After President Kennedy's assasination was pinned on Lee Harvey
Oswald, this name became unusable in America. Fashion
designer Ossie Clark.
Ossie, Osvald, Osvaldo, Oswaldo, Oswell, Ozzie, Waldo

Oswin OE. "Divine friend."
Osvin, Oswinn, Oswyn, Oswynn

Othman OG. "Wealthy man."

Othniel Heb. "God's strength, God's lion."
Otniel

Otis OE. "Son of Otto." Use is mostly American. Maybe
because of associations with composer Otis Redding, this
name is currently quite cool, a rock star's child kind of
name. Actor Otis Skinner.
Oates, Otess

Ottfried OG. "Prosperous peace."
Ottfrid

Otto OG. "Prosperous." German name that was fairly
common in English-speaking countries until Otto von Bis-
marck's German armies became threateningly powerful at
the turn of the 20th century. The Second World War
against Germany further limited the name's use. The
slight vogue for names ending with "-o" may bring it
back to favor.
Odo, Othello, Otho

Oved Heb. "Worshiper, follower." Related to Obadiah.
Obed

Ovid Meaning disputed: some sources suggest "Shepherd,"
others offer "Egg" or "Obedient." This may be a Latin
clan name: it was the middle name of Publius Obidius
Naso, a Roman poet of the first century A.D. whose *Metamorphoses* has been a staple of the Western literary
canon.

Owen Welsh. Var. **Eugene** (Gk. "Wellborn"). Fairly common outside Wales since the 18th century. Owen Glendower was a 14th-century Welsh chieftain who battled unsuccessfully for Welsh independence from England. Author Owen Wister.
Ewan, Ewen, Owain, Owin

Oxford OE. Place name: "Ford of the oxen." To parents who grew up in the 1960s, this was either a kind of laced shoe (generally detested) or possibly a famous English university. To parents grappling with turn-of-the-century reality, it is a health care plan.
Oxxford

Oz Heb. "Power, force, courage."

Pablo Sp. Var. **Paul** (Lat. "Little"). Spanish names have now reached considerable popularity in the U.S. and may even be more popular than the English version of a name. This is not true with Pablo, however. Paul is somewhere in the top 5 percent of names in the U.S., while Pablo ranks with anomalies like Kiefer, Dontavius, and Quincy. Artist Pablo Picasso; cellist Pablo Casals; poet Pablo Neruda.
Pablos

Pace Possibly a variation of **Pascal** (Fr. "Easter"). Connotations of efficiency and speed may make this name appealing.
Paice, Payce

Paciano Sp. from Lat. "Peaceful."

Pacifico Sp. from Lat. "Calmed, tranquil." Obviously the root is the same as it is for Paciano: the Latin *pax*. This is, of course, where the (rather deceptive) name of the Pacific Ocean comes from.
Pacificus

Packard Origin disputed. Some sources give German, "Dweller at the brook," while others refer to a peddler's pack. Packard was a brand of car earlier in the 20th century. Author Vance Packard.
Packer, Packert

Paco Sp. Var. **Francis** (Lat. "From France"). A diminutive of **Francisco**. Fashion designer Paco Rabanne.
Pacorro

Paddy Ir. Var. **Patrick** (Lat. "Noble, patrician"). Unusual as a given name, though so common as a nickname that it used to be used as a generic term for Irishmen. Author Paddy Chayefsky.
Paddey, Paddie, Padraic, Padraig

Pagan Lat. "From the country, countryman." Pagan has come to mean heathen, someone not initiated into the true religion (which true religion depends on who is calling whom a pagan). The name Paine comes from this term.

Page Fr. Occupational name: a young boy in training as a personal assistant to a knight. Usually a transferred surname, possibly indicating an ancestor who was a page. In the U.S., this has become almost exclusively a girls' name, but some of the diminutives and variations, like Padgett, are still used for boys.
Padget, Padgett, Paget, Pagett, Paige, Payge

Pagiel Heb. "God disposes." Old Testament name.

Paine Lat. "Countryman." Thomas Paine, a political theorist of the 18th century, wrote many political pamphlets that were influential during the American Revolution, and his *The Rights of Man* supported the French Revolution.
Pain, Payne

Paisley Scottish place name: an industrial town west of Glasgow. The name "paisley" referring to a pattern on fabric comes from this town, since shawls with that pattern were made here in the 18th century. The characteristic elongated comma shape, however, is actually Indian, and based on a pine cone.

Paladio Sp. from Gk. "Follower of Pallas," which was another name for the Greek goddess Athena. Saint Palladius was the first bishop of the Christians in Ireland, in the middle of the fifth century A.D.
Palladius

Paley OE. Origin unclear: may relate to Paul, or may be a place name, with the "-ley" ending indicating a meadow. CBS founder William Paley.

Palmer OE. "One who holds a palm." Usually indicates a

im, who would have carried a palm branch on his pilgrimage.

Pallmer, Palmar, Palmerston

Palomo Sp. "Dove." More popular in the feminine form, Paloma.

Paltiel Heb. "God is my deliverance."

Platya, Platyahu

Paquito Sp. Dim. **Francis** (Lat. "From France").

Paco

Paris OE. Place name: "From Paris," the city. Also a key figure in Greek myth. Paris was a young man of staggering beauty, son of King Priam of Troy. He was chosen to judge a beauty contest of the goddesses by awarding to one of them a golden apple which bore the legend "For the fairest." Hera, the wife of Zeus, promised Paris greatness if he chose her. Athene offered him greatness in war, and Aphrodite the love of the world's most beautiful woman. He chose Aphrodite, who caused Helen of Troy to fall in love with him. The Trojan War was the outcome: Paris died an ignoble death in it. The Judgment of Paris has frequently been portrayed in European painting, probably as a good excuse to depict three scantily clad beauties. Use of the name is predominantly American and is beginning to cross over to use for girls.

Parris

Parker OE. "Park keeper." Occupational name turned surname, popular in the 19th century as a given name, but now more unusual. Also occasionally used for girls. Actor Parker Stevenson; musician Charlie Parker; historian Francis Parkman.

Parke, Parkes, Parkman, Parks

Parkin OE. "Little Peter."

Parken

Parmenio Sp. "Intelligent, studious."

Parmenios, Parmenius

Parnell OF. "Little Peter." Made famous by the 19th-century Irish politician Charles Parnell, who campaigned for home rule in Ireland.

Parrnell, Pernell

Parr OE. Place name: "Castle park."

Parrish OF. "Ecclesiastical locality." A parish is the area

under the care of one pastor or priest. This would [   ]
nally have been a last name based on a place name.

Parish, Parris, Parriss

Parry Old Welsh. "Son of Harry." Composer Hubert Parry.

Parrey, Parrie

Parsons OE. Occupational name: "Clergyman." This word originally meant "Man in charge of a parish," and it's the source of our word "person."

Parson, Person, Persons

Parthenios Gk. "Virginal." Difficult to use unless there are compelling familial reasons to do so. A very hard name for a child to explain to his peers!

Parthenius

Parton OE. Place name: possibly "Peter's settlement" or "Castle park settlement."

Parvaiz Pers. "Lucky, happy."

Parvez, Parviz, Parwiz

Pascal Fr. "Child of Easter." Used as a first name in English-speaking countries only since the 1960s, and very scarce. The little boy in *The Red Balloon* is named Pascal, which gives the name faintly poignant associations. Philosopher Blaise Pascal.

Pascale, Pascalle, Paschal, Paschalis, Pascuale, Pasquale

Patrick Lat. "Noble, patrician." A Roman name made famous by the 5th-century missionary (and patron of Ireland) Saint Patrick, whose feast day on March 17 is celebrated with parades in the U.S., an honor accorded to no other saint. The name spread outside of Ireland in the 18th century and was widely used by the middle of the 20th century. It is now steadily used and has lost its firm associations with Ireland. U.S. statesman Patrick Henry; actors Patrick Swayze, Jason Patric; playwright John Patrick Shanley; basketball player Patrick Ewing.

Paddey, Paddie, Paddy, Padhraig, Padraic, Padraig, Padriac, Pat, Patrece, Patric, Patrice, Patricio, Patrik, Patrizio, Patrizius, Patryk, Pats, Patten, Patton, Patty

Patterson OE. "Son of Peter."

Paterson, Pattison

Patton OE. Place name: "Fighter's town." Almost too appropriate a meaning for the name of General George Patton. Author Alan Paton.

Paten, Patin, Paton, Patten, Pattin

Paul Lat. "Small." Popular Roman and medieval name whose tremendously widespread modern use dates from the 18th century. For baby boomer parents, Paul is the name of the cute Beatle, as well as the name of the pope who spearheaded Vatican II. It is not fashionable in the current vogue for original names, but steadily used by parents seeking a familiar name that everybody knows how to spell. Artists Paul Cézanne, Paul Gauguin; actor Paul Newman; Revolutionary War hero Paul Revere; musician Paul Simon.

Paavo, Pablo, Paolo, Pauel, Paulie, Paulin, Paulinus, Paulus, Pauly, Pavel, Pawel, Pol, Poll, Poul

Pawnee Native American tribal name. The Pawnee were a Plains tribe, excellent horsemen, who by 1859 were already settled onto a reservation on the Platte River. Their chief enemies were the Sioux and Wichita tribes rather than European settlers.

Paxton Lat./OE. Place name: "Peace town." This kind of name that combines a Latin word with an Old English word is rare: usually compounds put together particles of the same language. Actors Paxton Whitehead, Bill Paxton.

Packston, Paxon, Paxten, Paxtun

Payne Lat. "Countryman." See **Paine**.

Paine

Pazel Heb. "God's gold." The simpler form, Paz, is also used for boys and girls alike. In Spanish the same word means "peace."

Paz

Peabody OE. Origin unclear. It may be related to a bird name (the pea bird, for instance) or to the familiar vegetable. It is a name to reckon with in Massachusetts, the home of 19th-century financier and philanthropist George Peabody and his numerous descendants, many of whom have been educators.

Peak Geography name: the top of a mountain. Good name for a climber's son.

Peale OE. Possibly occupational name referring to a bell-ringer: a "peal" is a bell-ringing pattern that dates from the Middle Ages. May also be a variant spelling of Peel. Painters Charles Willson Peale, Raphaelle Peale, Rembrandt Peale.

Peal, Peall, Pealle

Pedro Sp. Var. **Peter** (Gk. "Rock"). Filmmaker Pedro Almodovar.

Pedrio, Pepe, Petrolino, Piero

Pedahel Heb. "Redeemed by God."

Pedael, Pedayel

Peel OE. Probably a place name. A peel tower was a small fortified tower common in northern England that permitted a family and its livestock to shelter together in a massive building with limited access to enemies. The humans would live upstairs and withdraw all ladders when they were attacked. English statesman Sir Robert Peel.

Peele

Pelagios Gk. "Of the sea, from the sea."

Pelagius, Pelayo

Peleh Heb. "Miracle."

Pelham OE. Place name: possiby "Tanner's settlement" or "Clerk's settlement."

Pellam

Pell Middle English. "Skin, parchment." As in parchment that legal documents would be written on; this may be an occupational name, indicating an ancestor who was a clerk.

Pall

Pembroke Celt. Place name: "Bluff, headland."

Pembrook

Pendleton OE. Place name: "Overhanging settlement." May refer to an ancient town on a clifftop. Actor Austin Pendleton.

Penley OE. Place name: "Enclosed meadow."

Penlea, Penleigh, Penly, Pennlea, Pennleigh, Pennley

Penn OE. "Enclosure." In the U.S., tied to the eminent Quaker and founder of Pennsylvania, William Penn.

Pen

Pepper Plant name. Of course the common seasoning comes from a different kind of plant entirely than the jalapeños or serranos that season Latin and Indian food. This name has probably been used more generally as a nickname, to describe someone of a peppery temperament. Football player Pepper Johnson.

Percival OF. "Pierce the vale." Invented by a medieval poet for one of King Arthur's knights, and its meaning is not completely clear. Adopted with some enthusiasm, however, and particularly well used in the late 19th century, along with more genuinely ancient names. It may have become popular because Percival was the one Knight of the Round Table who actually caught a glimpse of the Holy Grail, the famously evasive chalice from Christ's Last Supper. Wagner's opera *Parsifal* is based on one version of this knight's story. The name is now scarce.
Parsafal, Parsefal, Parsifal, Perce, Perceval, Percevall, Percey, Percivall, Percy, Purcell

Percy Fr. "From Percy." A Norman place name that became associated with an immensely powerful aristocratic family in the north of England. Its greatest popularity coincided with that of Percival, and like that name, Percy is now widely neglected. Author Walker Percy; poet Percy Bysshe Shelley.
Pearcy, Percey, Percie

Perdido Sp. "Lost." The feminine version, **Perdita**, is occasionally used in English literature. This form is scarce.

Peregrine Lat. "Traveler, pilgrim." "Peregrinations" is a synonym for "wanderings." Peregrine is also the name of a kind of falcon. The name persists in a small way in Britain. English writer Peregrine Worsthorne.
Peregrin, Peregrino, Peregryn

Peretz Heb. "Breach, breakthrough." (As in a wall.)
Perez

Perfecto Sp. "Perfect." Refers to Jesus Christ, the only perfect man.

Peri Heb. "Fruit, result."

Pericles Gk. Uncertain meaning. Athenian statesman of Greece's golden age, the 4th century B.C. He promoted systematic democracy on the one hand, and the dominance of Athens on the other. In the 19th-century South, slave owners sometimes gave slaves classical names like Pericles or Aeneas, and they have been handed down in Southern families since then.

Perkin OE. "Little Peter."
    Perkins, Perkyn, Perrin
Perry Dim. **Peregrine** or OE. Place name: "pear tree." Modern use seems mostly to be inspired by fictional detective Perry Mason. Matthew Calbraith Perry was the American naval officer who established American trade relations with Japan in 1854, which for almost 200 years had been closed to Western trade or contact. Singer Perry Como; designer Perry Ellis.
    Parry, Perrie
Perseus Gk. Myth. name: the son of Zeus and Danaë (whom Zeus visited in the guise of a shower of gold). He killed the Medusa, a monster with snakes for hair who turned all who looked at her into stone. Then he rescued Andromeda from a sea monster, and later married her.
Pesach Heb. "Spared." The Hebrew name for the great holiday of Passover, which commemorates the fact that Jehovah spared the Israelites in a plague that killed many Egyptians.
    Pessach
Peter Gk. "Rock." New Testament name; the saint who, tradition has it, guards the gates to Heaven. The name's greatest popularity came in the first three-quarters of this century—prompted, some sources suggest, by the play *Peter Pan*. The numerous variants suggest how widespread this name has been. In the U.S. it is still a standby, though nowhere near fashionable. Artists Piero della Francesca, Peter Paul Rubens; Russian emperor Peter the Great; actor Peter O'Toole; storybook character Peter Rabbit; film director Peter Bogdanovich.
    Peadar, Pearce, Peder, Pedro, Peerus, Peirce, Per, Perkin, Pero, Perrin, Perry, Pete, Petey, Peto, Petr, Pierce, Piero, Pierre, Pierson, Piet, Pieter, Pietrek, Pietro, Piotr, Pjotr, Pyotr
Petuel Aramaic. "Vision of the Lord." Old Testament name.
Peverell OF. "Piper."
    Peverall, Peverel, Peveril
Peyton OE. Place name: "Fighting-man's estate." Probably related to Patton. Primarily American use, probably as a transferred last name, i.e., a mother's maiden name.

Football players Walter Payton, Peyton Manning; basketball player Gary Payton.

Payton

Phelan Ir. Gael. "Wolf." Mostly Irish use.

Felan, Phelim, Felim

Phelps OE. "Son of Philip."

Philander Gk. "Loving mankind." This word has come to mean "flirt" in English, but it still occurs as a name, especially in the South.

Philemon Gk. "Affectionate." Old Testament name: one of Saint Paul's epistles is addressed to Philemon.

Philip Gk. "Lover of horses." The name of one of the twelve apostles, and a staple since early Christian times, though it receded somewhat in the 19th century. A 20th-century resurgence peaked in the 1960s; like Peter, Philip is familiar but not common. Britain's Prince Philip; Crown Prince Felipe of Spain; painter Filippo Lippi; playwright Philip Barry; talk show host Phil Donahue; author Philip Roth; football player Phil Simms.

Felipe, Filip, Filippo, Fillip, Fyllip, Phil, Philipp, Philippe, Philippos, Philippus, Phillip, Phillips, Phyllip, Pip, Pippo

Philo Gk. "Loving." Regrettably similar in sound to phyllo pastry. This is the same root that we use in words like bibliophile and philanthropist (which, strictly translated from Greek, means "loving others").

Phineas Derivation and meaning unknown, though many sources offer Heb. "Oracle." Another possible meaning is "mouth of brass," which would be appropriate for showman Phineas T. Barnum. Violinist Pinchas Zuckerman.

Fineas, Phinehas, Pincas, Pinchas, Pinchos, Pincus, Pinhas, Pinkus

Phipps OE. "Son of Philip."

Philips, Philipson, Phips

Phoebus Gk. "Shining, brilliant." One of the epithets of Apollo, the sun god, was Phoebus Apollo, referring to the fact that he brought light. The feminine version, **Phoebe**, has always been much better established as a common name, perhaps because there is a Phoebe in the New Testament.

Phoibos

Phoenix Gk. "Dark red." In myth, the phoenix is an Arabian bird that periodically sets itself aflame and rises alive from the ashes. It is often considered a symbol of immortality. In our era, this is the last name of a family of young actors—Leaf, Joaquin, and the late River Phoenix.
Fenix, Phenix

Pickford OE. "From the ford at the peak."

Pierce Var. **Peter** (Gk. "Rock"). One of a group of Peter-derived names along with Piers, Pearson, etc. Actor Pierce Brosnan.
Pearce, Pears, Pearson, Pearsson, Peerce, Peirce, Piers, Pierson, Piersson

Pierre Fr. Var. **Peter** (Gk. "Rock"). Canadian Prime Minister Pierre Trudeau.

Piers Gk. "Rock." Peter is actually the Latin form of the name that the Normans took to Britain as Piers. This form, along with Pierce, has been an alternate form more popular in Britain than in America.
Pearce, Pears, Pearson, Pierce, Pierson, Piersson

Pike OE. Possibly a place name referring to a turnpike road where fees for use are collected at toll-gates. May also refer to a large freshwater fish. Zebulon Pike, for whom Pike's Peak in Colorado was named, was an early 19th-century soldier and explorer who first sighted Pike's Peak in his search for the source of the Mississippi River.
Pyke

Pio Lat. "Pious." A name used by twelve popes, but not found much among English-speaking children.
Pius

Piper Occupational name; one who plays the pipes.

Pitney OE. Place name: "Island of the stubborn one."
Pittney

Pitt OE. Place name: "Pit or ditch." Actor Brad Pitt.

Placido Sp. "Serene." Made famous currently by opera star Placido Domingo.
Placedo, Placidus, Placijo, Placyd, Placydo, Plasedo

Plantagenet OF. "Sprig of broom." Broom is an English flower. The Plantagenet family ruled England in the 13th and 14th centuries, and the name resonates, in England, with connotations of ancient high rank. Victorian novelist Anthony Trollope named his powerful English duke "Plantagenet Palliser."

Plato Gk. "Broad-shouldered." Its occasional use in English-speaking countries may be inspired by admiration for the famous Greek philosopher.
Platon

Platt OF. Place name: "Flat land."
Platte

Pluto Gk. "Rich." In Roman myth, the god of the underworld. In Disney myth, a dog who walks on his hind legs. Unlikely name for a child.

Pocano Pueblo Indian. "Arrival of the spirits."

Pollard ME. "Shorn head." "Poll" was originally a term for head, hence our expression "take a poll." A pollard tree's branches have been cut back to the trunk to promote a bushy growth at the top. Thus the name may either be a place name (for someone who lived near a pollard tree) or a descriptive name (for someone whose head had been closely cropped).
Poll, Pollerd, Pollyrd

Pollock OE. Var. **Pollux**. Also the name of a large fish. In German, *Pollak* is the term for someone from neighboring Poland. Artist Jackson Pollock.
Pollack, Polloch

Pollux Gk. "Crown." Along with Castor, one of the Heavenly Twins, the constellation also known as Gemini.

Pomeroy OF. Place name: "Apple orchard." The French word for apple is *pomme*.
Pommeray, Pommeroy

Pompey Lat. Meaning unclear. Pompey was a Roman statesman and military man, and Caesar's chief rival. This name was occasionally used as a slave name in the South, and also survived in Latin culture because of a saint whose feast day is April 10.
Pompeyo, Pompi, Pompilio, Pomponio

Ponce Sp. "Fifth." Made famous by Spanish explorer Ponce de Leon, but no more common than Quintus, its Latin equivalent.

Pope Gk. "Father." A transferred last name, and extremely unusual. English poet Alexander Pope.

Porat Heb. "Fruitful, productive."

Poriel Heb. "Fruit of God."

Porfirio Gk. "Purple stone." The English term is "porphyry." Very rare, but borne by one of the 20th century's great playboys, Porfirio Rubirosa, as well as a saint of the 4th century.
Porphirios, Prophyrios

Porter Lat. "Gatekeeper." Occupational name.

Porthos Literary name: along with Athos and Aramis, one of the three musketeers from Alexandre Dumas's novel of the same name. Dumas may have invented the name for the way it sounded with the two others.

Portland OE. Place name: "Land near the port."

Poseidon Gk. Myth. name: the sea god, corresponding to the Roman Neptune. He is usually depicted with a trident, with which he caused storms and earthquakes.

Potter OE. Occupational name: "Maker of pots."

Powell OE. Surname related to Paul. Author Anthony Powell.
Powel

Powhatan Algonquin Indian: "Powwow hill." As young Disney fans know, this is the name of the father of Pocahontas, who in history was a powerful chieftain in Virginia.

Pradeep Hindi. "Light."

Pratap Hindi. "Majesty, magnificence."

Pratt OE. Fairly common last name whose origin is cloudy. One early meaning of "prat" was the buttocks, as in the comedy term "pratfall." Another similar word, "prate," meant to babble or talk without meaning. Pratt may come from one of these two terms.

Prentice ME. "Apprentice."
Prentis, Prentiss

Prescott OE. Place name: "Priest's cottage." The middle name of President George Bush, but not widespread.
Prescot, Prestcot, Prestcott

Presley OE. Place name: "Priest's meadow." In the Middle Ages, when these names came into use, the priest was a very important figure in any community. Of course, in the late 20th century the name is associated with another important figure, Elvis Presley.

Presleigh, Presly, Presslee, Pressley, Prestley, Priestley, Priestly

Preston OE. Place name: "Priest's estate." Actor Robert Preston; film director Preston Sturges.

Prewitt OF. "Brave little one."
Prewet, Prewett, Prewit, Pruitt

Price Welsh. "Son of Rhys." Rhys is a common Welsh name meaning "ardent."
Brice, Bryce, Pryce

Priestley OE. Place name: "Priest's meadow."
Priestly

Primo It. "First; firstborn." Number names usually refer to children born with quite a number of older siblings (Quintus, Octavian), and tend to indicate exhaustion of the imagination, but Primo may allude to great pride in the firstborn, especially a son. Author Primo Levi.
Preemo, Premo, Prime

Prince Lat. "Prince." As a last name, it may have indicated someone who worked in a prince's household, and occasional first-name use is generally transferred from the last name. There are, of course, exceptions, like the artist formerly known as Prince, who undoubtedly cherished the name for its royal connotations. Comedian Freddie Prinze; theatrical producer Harold Prince.
Printz, Printze, Prinz, Prinze

Prior See Pryor.

Procopius Gk. "Forward-looking." Procopius was a saint who was beheaded in the early 4th century for refusing to worship pagan gods. The oldest restaurant in Paris, still in business on a picturesque street of the Left Bank, is called "Le Procope."
Procopio, Procopios

Proctor Lat. "Official, administrator." Occupational last name.
Prockter, Procter

Prosper Lat. "Fortunate," as in "prosperous." Poet Prosper Mérimée.
Prospero

Proverb Eng. "A short, pithy saying." The name usually comes from one of the books of the Old Testament, Proverbs. Unusual. Football player Proverb Jacobs.

Prudencio Sp. from Lat. "Caution, discretion." As "Prudence," this was one of the more popular and durable virtue names. The male version is rare.

Prudentius

Pryor Lat. "Monastic leader." A prior is the monk in charge of a monastery, so this might be an occupational name. On the other hand, the tradition of monastic chastity would seem to prevent such a name's being handed down to children.

Prior

Purvis Eng./Fr. "Purveyor." Originally indicated someone who provided food, or provisions.

Purves, Purviss

LAST NAME FIRST

Last names aren't necessary unless tracking a lot of people is important. In self-contained societies, a first name suffices. If you refer to Rufus ("red-haired" in Latin), everybody knows who you're talking about. As populations grow, last names get added on to avoid confusion: Rufus Miller grinds the flour, while Rufus Ford lives by the river ford.

The big change comes when last names are fixed. If Rufus Miller's son became a shepherd in 9th-century England, he would have been called Rufus Shepherd. But some time after the Norman Conquest in 1066, all of Rufus Miller's children would have shared his last name, and his grandchildren as well. In 1267, last names became officially hereditary.

This turning point arrived in different cultures at different times. The Irish reached it in the 10th century, before any other country in post-Roman Europe. The Chinese were way ahead of Europeans and adopted hereditary last names around the time of Christ. But the Ashkenazi Jews of Northern Europe didn't use hereditary last names until the 18th and 19th centuries, when they were required to do so by law.

Qadir Arab. "Capable, competent." This is one of the ninety-nine attribute names of Allah. Football player Qadry Ismail.
Qadar, Qadry

Qasim Arab. "Charitable, generous; one who gives to the people."

Quanah Native American: "Fragrant, sweet-smelling."

Quennell OF. Place name: "Small oak."
Quennel

Quentin Lat. "Fifth." Probably used without any consideration of its meaning, since so few families extend to five children any more. Author Quentin Crisp.
Quent, Quenten, Quenton, Quint, Quintin, Quinton, Quintus

Quigley Ir. Gael. Meaning disputed: possibly "Distaff," or "One with messy hair."

Quillan Ir. Gael. "Cub."
Quillen

Quiller OE. Possibly an occupational name: a "quiller" could have been a scribe, or someone who wrote with a quill pen.

Quimby ONorse. Place name: "Estate of the woman." A woman's estate would have been quite a rarity in the Old Norse era.
Quinby

Quincy OF. Place name: "Estate of the fifth son." Last name of a prominent Massachusetts family whose name is borne by a town and by the 6th U.S. President, John Quincy Adams. Musician Quincy Jones.
Quin, Quincey, Quinsy

Quinlan Ir. Gael. "Fit, shapely, strong."
Quindlen

Quinn Ir. Gael. Meaning unknown, though some speculate that it means "descendant of Con," which in turn means something like "intelligence." Very common Irish last name, occasionally transferred to first-name status, especially in the U.S. Actor Aidan Quinn.

Quinton OE. Place name: "Queen's settlement." This is now the most popular of the "Q" names, surpassing Quentin by a considerable margin. This spelling may be perceived as a variation of Quentin.
Quinntan, Quinnten, Quinntin, Quinnton, Quintain, Quintan, Quintyn, Quintynn

Rabi Arab. "Gentle wind."
  Rabbi, Rabee
Racham Heb. "Mercy, compassion."
  Rachim, Raham, Rahim
Rad OE. "Adviser." This word particle, which comes from Scandinavian and Slavic sources, occurs in many other names.

Radbert OE. "Bright adviser."

Radburn OE. Place name: "Red brook."
Radborn, Radborne, Radbourn, Radbourne, Radburne

Radcliff OE. Place name: "Red cliff." In America, most likely to be associated with the renowned women's college that is now part of Harvard.
Radcliffe, Radclyffe, Ratcliff, Ratcliffe

Radek Slavic Var. **Roderick** (OG. "Famous ruler").

Radford OE. Place name: "Red ford" or "Ford with reeds."
Radferd, Radfurd

Radimir Slavic. "Famous joy."

Radley OE. Place name: "Red meadow." As in Radford, the first element could also refer to reeds.
Radlea, Radlee, Radleigh, Radly

Radnor OE. Place name: "Red shore" or "Reedy shore."

Radwan Arab. "Pleasure, satisfaction."

Rafael Var. **Raphael** (Heb. "God has healed"). This is the form most often used in the United States. Now that the Ninja Turtles fad is over, it seems safe to give a child this name again. Baseball player Rafael Palmiero.
Rafe, Rafel, Rafello, Rafer, Raffaelo, Raffaello, Raphael

Rafferty Ir. Gael. "Prosperity wielder." Irish last name occasionally used as a first name.
Raferty, Raffarty, Raffertey

Rafi Arab. "Holding high." The name of the preeminent recording artist for children, which some parents may not consider a drawback.
Rafee, Raffi, Raffy

Rafiq Arab. "Friend" or possibly "Gentle."
Rafi, Rafik

Ragnar Nor. "Powerful army" or "Warrior of judgment." Though this ancient Scandinavian form is very rare in the U.S., the anglicized versions are seen from time to time. The most famous Rainier, of course, is the Prince of Monaco, husband of Grace Kelly.
Ragnor, Rainer, Rainier, Rayner, Raynor, Regner, Reiner

Raiden Mythology name: the Japanese god of thunder.

Rahim Arab. "Empathetic, merciful." This is one of the ninety-nine attributes of Allah which are considered by Muslims to be particularly auspicious names.
Raheem, Rahiem

Rainart Ger. "Mighty judgment."
Rainhard, Rainhardt, Reinart, Reinhard, Reinhardt, Reinhart, Renke

Raines English name of uncertain derivation. It may be yet another spinoff from Reginald/Reynold/Rainier, or come from a different English root that means "lord." Actor Claude Rains.
Rain, Raine, Rains, Rayne, Raynes

Rainier Fr. Var. **Reginald** (OE. "Counsel power"). A famous place name in the Pacific Northwest, where the peak of Mount Rainier, at 14,408 feet, is an important landmark. The peak was named for a British naval officer, but the Indian name was Tacoma or Tahoma, meaning "snowy peak." The nearby city took that name. Poet Rainer Maria Rilke.
Rainer, Rayner, Raynier

Rajiv Sanskrit "Striped." Familiar to non-Indians because of Rajiv Gandhi, son of Indira Gandhi and Prime Minister of India.

Raleigh OE. Place name: "Meadow of roe deer." Commemorates Sir Walter Raleigh, explorer and court favorite of Queen Elizabeth I. He is supposed to have spread his cape over a puddle so she could cross with dry feet. The city in North Carolina was named for him. Usually a boy's name, but the two-syllable "-leigh" form, based on the popularity of Ashley, is increasingly being considered appropriate for girls as well.

Ralegh, Rawleigh, Rawley, Rawly

Ralph OE. "Wolf-counsel." A name that has been steadily, if not enormously, popular for the last thousand years (though today's parents might not recognize it immediately in older forms like Rathulf or Radolphus). Its greatest vogue in the U.S. occurred at the turn of the century. Traditional Englishmen (actor Ralph Fiennes among them) pronounce it "Rafe," to the confusion of most Americans. Now uncommon. Poet Ralph Waldo Emerson; consumer activist Ralph Nader; actor Ralph Macchio.

Rafe, Raff, Ralf, Raoul, Raul, Rolf, Rolph

Ralston OE. Place name: "Ralph's settlement."

Ram Sanskrit. "Pleasing."

Rahm

Ramiro Port. "Great judge." Baseball player Manny Ramirez.

Ramirez

Ramon Sp. Var. **Raymond** (OG. "Counselor-protector"). Given its greatest exposure by the silent-movie star of the 1920s, Ramon Novarro. Baseball player Ramon Martinez.

Ramsay OE. Place name: "Raven island" or "Ram island." Originally a last name common in Scotland. English statesman Ramsay McDonald; U.S. Attorney General Ramsey Clark.

Ramsey

Ramsden OE. Place name: "Ram valley." Like most of these place names turned last names, this was transferred to a first name in the 19th century.

Ramses The name of several of the most prominent kings of ancient Egpyt.

Rameses, Ramesses

Rance Unusual name of uncertain derivation. It may come from an old Scottish term for a tool used to make holes, akin to a reamer, so perhaps it is an occupational name.

Rancel, Rancell

Rand OE. "Shield, fighter." Generally a diminutive of **Randolph** and related names.

Randall OE. "Shield-wolf." This is the medieval spoken form of Randolph. Enjoyed some popularity with parents in the baby boom era, and is steadily used today, without being particularly popular. Actor Tony Randall; football player Randall Cunningham; poet Randall Jarrell.

Rand, Randal, Randel, Randell, Randey, Randie, Randl, Randle, Randy

Randolph OE. "Shield-wolf." From the same root as Randall, which has been more popular in the U.S. English politician Lord Randolph Churchill.

Randal, Randall, Randell, Randolf, Randy

Randy Dim. **Randall, Randolph**. More popular now than either Randall or Randolph, which makes it an exception to the trend of parents overlooking nicknames in favor of longer, more formal names. In British slang, "randy" means "amorous," so this name is barely used there.

Randey, Randi, Randie

Ranger OF. "Forest guardian."

Rainger, Range

Ranjit Sanskrit. "Charmed, beguiled." Ranjit Singh was an important maharajah of the Punjab area of India in the late 18th and early 19th centuries.

Ranjeet

Rankin OE. "Little shield" or Celt. "Son of Francis." A last name found in Scotland and Ireland, rarely transferred as a first name.

Rankine, Rankinn

Ransford OE. Place name: "Raven ford."

Ransley OE. Place name: "Raven meadow."

Ransleigh, Ransly

Ransom Opinions differ: possibly OE. "Shield's son," possibly a diminutive of **Randolph**. It seems unlikely that the casual meaning of money paid to redeem a captive has anything to do with the name. First-name use is mostly a late-Victorian phenomenon.

Ransome

Raoul Fr. Var. **Ralph** (OE. "Wolf-counsel"). Uncommon among English-speaking parents. Actor Raul Julia.

Raul, Roul, Rowl

Raphael Heb. "God has healed." The name of one of the archangels, possibly (because of his name) the one who stirred the waters at the pool of Bethesda to give it healing powers. Most common in very religious eras (16th and 17th centuries) and the 19th century, which cherished the picturesque. May become more popular (as Gabriel has) in the current quest for the unique. Painter Raphael Sanzio; author Rafe Yglesias.

Falito, Rafal, Rafael, Rafaelle, Rafaelo, Rafaello, Rafe, Rafel, Rafello, Raffael, Raffaello, Raphaello, Raphello, Ravel

Rashad Arab. "Having good judgment." Related to Rashid, but much more popular in the U.S.

Rashaad, Rashod

Rashid Arab. "Righteous, rightly advised." Rashida is also used for girls.

Rasheed, Rasheid, Rasheyd

Rasmus Dim. **Erasmus** (Gk. "Loved, desired"). Used occasionally in German-speaking countries.

Rastus Dim. **Erasmus** (Gk. "Beloved").

Raven Name of the large black bird that is closely related to the crow. A fanciful name for a black-haired or dark-skinned baby. Probably more common for girls, owing to the fame of actress Raven Symone of *The Cosby Show*.

Ravinn, Rayven, Rayvin

Ravi Hindi. "Sun." Made familiar to today's parents by the eminent sitar player Ravi Shankar.

Ravee

Rawlins OF. Ultimately a diminutive of Roland. A name like this was originally an oral contraction (Rolandson to Rawlinson to Rawlins), then became a last name, and was revived in the late 19th century as a first name.

Rawlinson, Rawson

Ray Dim. **Raymond**. Quite firmly rooted as an independent name, used mostly in the 20th century. Singer Ray Charles; boxer Sugar Ray Leonard; author Ray Bradbury; actor Ray Liotta.

Rae, Rai, Raye, Reigh

Rayburn OE. Place name: "Roe-deer brook." Painter Henry Raeburn.

Raeborn, Raeborne, Raebourn, Raeburn, Rayborn, Raybourne, Rayburne

Raymond OG. "Counselor-protector." Old Teutonic name

that was used in the Middle Ages, then forgotten until a very strong 19th-century revival, especially in America. Though far from fashionable, it is steadily used in a quiet way. Author Raymond Chandler; actors Raymond Massey, Raymond Burr.

Raemond, Raemondo, Raimond, Raimondo, Raimund, Raimundo, Rajmund, Ramon, Ramond, Ramonde, Ramone, Ray, Rayment, Raymondo, Raymund, Raymunde, Raymundo

Raynor Nor. "Mighty army." An anglicized version of Ragnar, and a version of the better-known Rainier.

Ragnar, Rainer, Rainier, Rainor, Ranieri, Raynar, Rayner

Raziel Aramaic. "The Lord is my secret."

Read OE. "Red-haired." Descriptive name that long ago became a last name, and thence a first name, especially in the U.S.

Reade, Reed, Reid, Reide

Reading OE. "Son of the red-haired." Also a place name.

Redding, Reeding, Reiding

Redford OE. Place name: "Red ford." Hard to use today without invoking the ultrafamous blond actor Robert Redford.

Radford, Radfurd, Redfurd

Redley OE. Place name: "Red meadow."

Radley, Redlea, Redleigh, Redly

Redman OE. Obscure: could mean either "Man of counsel" or "Man who rides." Never a common choice for parents.

Redmond Ir. Var. **Raymond**.

Radmond, Radmund, Redmund

Reece Welsh. "Fiery, zealous." The native Welsh form is Rhys, and it is fairly common in Wales. Actor Roger Rees.

Rees, Reese, Rhys, Rice

Reed OE. "Red-haired." It is also perfectly possible that Reed comes from a place name referring to the reeds in a swampy place. This spelling of the name had a mild flourish of popularity in the baby boom era.

Read, Reade, Reid, Reyd

Reeve ME. Occupational name: "Bailiff." A reeve was an administrator for the king or someone of high position, who collected rents and maintained order on the lord's estates. Actor Christopher Reeve.

Reave, Reeves

Regan Ir. Gael. "Little king." Mostly 20th-century use.

Reagan, Reagen, Regen

Reginald OE. "Counsel power." Ronald and Reynolds are just two of the names that come from the same source; Reginald's popularity was mainly British and 19th century. But the name has clearly been used across Europe, to judge from the variety of spellings and pronunciations. Actor Judge Reinhold; baseball star Reggie Jackson.

Naldo, Raghnall, Rainault, Rainhold, Raonull, Raynald, Rayniero, Reg, Reggie, Regin, Reginalt, Reginauld, Reginault, Reginvald, Reginvalt, Regnauld, Regnault, Reinald, Reinaldo, Reinaldos, Reinhold, Reinold, Reinwald, Renaud, Renault, Rene, Reynaldo, Reynaldos, Reynold, Reynolds, Rheinallt, Rinaldo, Ronald

Regino Unusual name that may be a variation of Reginald or may be a way of making Regina (Latin for "queen") masculine. In the languages most closely related to Latin, the words for "king" are much shorter.

Regis Fr. "Kingly." This was a French last name transferred to a first name: literally, it is the Latin word for "of the king" and there are Catholic schools all over the country called "Regis" (the king, in this case, being Jesus). This is a very unusual name made familiar by talk show host Regis Philbin.

Reid OE. Place name: "Near the reeds" or descriptive name: "Red-haired." This is the most popular form at the moment.

Read, Reade, Reed

Remedio Sp. "Help, remedy." The feminine version, Remedios, is currently popular in South America.

Remington OE. Place name: "Raven-family settlement." Familiar to Americans as a brand of razors, and as the name of a TV action hero of the eighties, Remington Steele. Artist Frederick Remington.

Remy Fr. "From Rheims." Champagne, and the fine brandies made from champagne, are the principal product of Rheims, a town in central France. The name is used for both boys and girls. Author Remy Charlip.

Remee, Remi, Remie, Remmey, Remmy

Remus Lat. "Swift." The name of one of the legendary twins (the other was Romulus) who founded Rome. At the turn of the century Joel Chandler Harris's "Uncle Remus" stories (including the famous one about the Tar Baby) were very popular.
Remo

Ren Probably a nickname for Reginald or any of the "Ren-" names, or else a variant of René. It was used occasionally before the success of the cartoon "Ren and Stimpy."
Renne, Renny

René Fr. "Reborn." The modern form of Renatus, which did not survive as a male name. Unlike the female version, René has not really spread beyond French-speaking families, probably because it is well entrenched as a girl's name. Actor René Auberjonois.
Renat, Renato, Renatus

Renfred OE. "Powerful peace."

Renfrew Old Welsh. Place name: "Calm river."
Renfro

Renny Ir. Gael. "Small and mighty."

Reno Place name: the largest city in Nevada. It was named for a Confederate general, Jesse Lee Reno, and became prosperous as the silver mines of Nevada were exploited. It later became the divorce capital of the United States; Nevada had lenient divorce laws and required a short residency. Because it is now a gambling center, the name still has an aura of the rough-and-ready about it.

Renshaw OE. Place name: "Raven woods."
Renishaw

Renton OE. Place name: "Settlement of the roe deer."

Renwick OE. Place name: "Roe deer village" or "Raven village."
Renwyck

Renzo Dim. **Lorenzo** (Lat. "Laurel"). Interior designer Renzo Mongiardino.

Reuben Heb. "Behold, a son." Old Testament name that came into general use in the 18th century. Also a sandwich that features corned beef, sauerkraut, and Swiss cheese. Singer Rubén Blades.

Reuban, Reubin, Reuven, Rouvin, Rube, Rubén, Rubin, Rubino, Ruby

Reuel Heb. "Friend of the Lord."
Ruel

Rex Lat. "King." Mostly 20th-century use, possibly influenced by actor Rex Harrison. Probably most common as a name for a dog.

Rexford OE. Place name: "King's ford."

Rey Sp. "King." The Hispanic equivalent of Rex or Leroy. Not in general use.
Reyes, Reyni

Reynard OF. "Fox" or OG. "Powerful and courageous." Some of the variations (like Renaud) come close to variations of the Reynold/Reginald names, but are not as common. The French word for fox (*renard*) actually comes from a set of medieval European animal stories in which the cunning fox is known as "Reynard," no doubt to emphasize his cleverness.
Raynard, Reinhard, Reinhardt, Renard, Renaud, Renauld, Rennard

Reynold Var. **Reginald** (OE. "Counsel power"). Probably most familiar in America as a surname, though in the Middle Ages this was the most common form of Reginald. Painter Joshua Reynolds.
Reinaldo, Renado, Renaldo, Renato, Renauld, Renault, Reynaldo, Reynolds, Rinaldo

Rhett Var. **Rhys**. Modern parents can hardly use it without thinking of Margaret Mitchell's immortal Rhett Butler, and his great line, "Frankly, my dear, I don't give a damn!"

Rhinebeck Ger. Place name: "Brook of the Rhine." The Rhine is a major European river that serves as the boundary between France and Germany. The name of a picturesque town on the Hudson River.
Rheinbeck

Rhinelander Ger. Place name: "Dweller at the Rhineland."
Rheinlander

Rhodes Gk. "Where roses grow." The name of an important Greek island and an important British philanthropist, Cecil Rhodes. He gave his name to both a country (Rho-

a) and a scholarship fund that would allow outstand-
students from England's former colonies to study at
Oxford in England. Some famous former Rhodes scholars
are Senator Bill Bradley and President Bill Clinton.

Rhoads, Rhodas, Rodas

Rhys Welsh. "Fiery, zealous." This is the native Welsh
form of the name that appears more often in English-
speaking countries as Reece.

Rice Either an anglicization of Rhys or a respelling of a
German name, Reis, that has many meanings. The most
appealing of them for descendants is "Knight on
horseback," a far more attractive prospect as an ancestor
than "Gatherer of twigs," "Wood carver" or "Dweller
in the brush." This is generally a last name, and could
cause quite a few giggles among preschool children.

Richard OG. "Dominant ruler." Norman name that went
on to be a steady favorite for the last 900 years, with one
century (the 19th) of neglect. In the current hunger for
the unusual, it is somewhat overlooked, but plenty of parents still choose it. It is unfortunately short of nicknames
at the moment, given the slang meaning of Dick. English
Kings Richard I–III; rock star Little Richard; composer
Richard Rodgers; actors Richard Burton, Richard Kiley,
Richard Gere, Richard Chamberlain; photographer Richard Avedon; U.S. President Richard Nixon.

**Dick, Dickie, Dicky, Raechard, Ric, Richard, Ricardo, Ric-
cardo, Rich, Richardo, Richart, Richerd, Richie, Rick,
Rickard, Rickert, Rickey, Ricki, Rickie, Ricky, Rico, Ri-
kard, Riki, Rikki, Riocard, Ritchard, Ritcherd, Ritchie,
Ritchy, Ritchyrd, Ritshard, Ritsherd, Ryszard**

Richmond OG. "Powerful protector." Most frequently encountered in the U.S. as a place name, like the capital city
of Virginia.

Rick Dim. **Richard, Frederick**. Used independently,
though more common as a nickname, and one that isn't
often used today. Humphrey Bogart's character in *Casa-
blanca* was named Rick. Actors Rick Moranis, Rick Nelson.

Ric, Ricci, Rickey, Rickie, Ricky, Rik, Rikki, Rikky

Ricky Dim. **Richard, Frederick**. More common than Rick as an independent name. Baseball player Rickey Henderson.

Ricci, Rickey, Ricki

Rickward OE. "Mighty guardian."

Rickwerd, Rickwood

Rico It. Dim. **Henry** (OE. "home ruler") via Enrico, or dim. **Ricardo**.

Rider OE. "Horseman." Likely to be a transferred last name, for instance, a mother's maiden name. Author Rider Haggard.

Ridder, Ryder

Ridge OE. Place name: "Ridge." Referring to a geographical feature in a landscape, as do the "Ridg-" names below.

Rigg

Ridgeway OE. Place name: "Road on the ridge."

Ridgeley OE. Place name: "Ridge meadow."

Ridgeleigh, Ridgeley, Ridglea, Ridglee, Ridgleigh

Ridley OE. Place name: "Red meadow." Film director Ridley Scott.

Riddley, Ridlea, Ridleigh, Ridly

Rigoberto Sp. from Ger. "Brilliant and mighty." A number of German names survive only in Spanish forms. They may date back to the days when Spain and Germany formed part of the Holy Roman Empire, or even further back to when the Goths began to overrun Europe in the fifth century A.D., before dividing into tribes that occupied Germany and Spain.

Rigobert

Riley Ir. Gael. "Courageous." Irish last name used as a first name for the last 150 years.

Reilly, Ryley

Ring OE. "Ring." Very unusual, though given exposure by author Ring Lardner. Beatles fans will remember that Ringo Starr took his name from the jewelry he favored.

Ringo

Rio Sp. "River." Unusual place name. The Brazilian capital is Rio de Janeiro, which means "January river" in Portuguese. The Rio Grande is the boundary river between Texas and Mexico; its name means "big river" in Spanish.

Reo

dan Ir. Gael. "Bard, minstrel."

arden, Reardon

Rip Invented name: made famous by actor Rip Torn, who was actually named Elmore. Before his fame, the best-known American Rip was Rip van Winkle, the man who slept for twenty years in Washington Irving's tale.

Ripley OE. Place name: "Shouting man's meadow."

Ripleigh, Riply

Rishon Heb. "The first."

Risley OE. Place name: "Meadow with shrubs."

Rislea, Rislee, Risleigh, Risly, Wrisley

Riston OE. Place name: "Settlement near the shrubs." Financier Walter Wriston.

Wriston

Ritter Ger. "Knight." Actor John Ritter.

River Place name. As a last name, Rivers is more common, but this name was given a lot of exposure by the late actor River Phoenix. Born in 1970, he and one of his brothers (actor Leaf Phoenix) were given nature names. The third brother, also an actor, got away with Joaquin.

Rivers

Rives OF. Place name: "Dweller by the riverbank." Sounds the same as Reeves, but with a completely different history.

Riyad Arab. Place name: "Gardens." The name of the capital of Saudi Arabia.

Riyadh

Roald OG. "Famous and powerful" or "Famous ruler." Rare in English-speaking countries, though the immense popularity of author Roald Dahl keeps this name in the public eye. Polar explorer Roald Amundsen.

Roark Ir. Gael. "Illustrious and mighty." Usually occurs as a last name. Actor Mickey Rourke.

Roarke, Rorke, Rourke, Ruark

Rob Dim. **Robert**. The most common nickname for Robert is probably Bob, but Rob may be given more often as an independent name. Actor Rob Lowe.

Robb, Robbie, Robby

Robert OE. "Bright fame." Another staple male name, common for the last millennium and still in the American top twenty. Parents tend to be more conservative with boys' names, which explains why Michael, James, David, Andrew, and, yes, Robert are still top choices. Senator Robert Kennedy; poet Robert Burns; actors Robert DeNiro, Robert Duvall; author Robert Lawson; Confederate general Robert E. Lee; author Robert Ludlum; baseball players Roberto Alomar, Roberto Clemente.

Bert, Bertie, Bob, Bobbie, Bobby, Rab, Rabbie, Riobard, Rip, Rob, Roban, Robb, Robben, Robbin, Robbins, Robbinson, Robby, Robers, Roberto, Robertson, Robi, Robin, Robinson, Robson, Robyn, Robynson, Rupert, Ruperto, Ruprecht

Robin Dim. Robert. Usually a girl's name in America, though A.A. Milne immortalized his son as Christopher Robin in the "Winnie the Pooh" stories. Actor Robin Williams; TV personality Robin Leach.

Roban, Robben, Robbin, Robbyn, Robyn

Robinson OE. "Son of Robert." More commonly a last name. Singer Smokey Robinson; poet Robinson Jeffers; actor Paul Robeson.

Robbinson, Robeson, Robynson, Robson

Rocco Ger./It. "Rest." The most common form (in America, at least) of the name of a popular saint who cured plague victims. He was especially venerated in Italy, which may be why this version of the name is the most common. Rocky is usually a nickname.

Roch, Roche, Rochus, Rock, Rocko, Rocky, Roque

Rochester OE. Place name: "Stone camp or fortress."
Chester, Chet, Rock

Rocio Sp. "Dew." Alludes to the dew of Heaven.

Rock Var. Rocco. Actor Rock Hudson is the most important precedent for using this name. His original name was Roy Scherer.
Rocky

Rockley OE. Place name: "Rock meadow."
Rocklee, Rockleigh, Rockly

Rocklin Possibly OE. place name, a contraction of Rockland, for instance. May also be a continental name, something like "Little Rocco."

Rockwell OE. Place name: "Rock spring." Illustrators Norman Rockwell, Rockwell Kent.

Rocky Var. **Rocco**. Impossible to use today without invoking Sylvester Stallone's *Rocky* movies.

Rod Dim. **Roderick**. Used sparingly as an independent name. Actors Rod Steiger, Roddy McDowall.
Rodd, Roddie, Roddy

Rodeo Sp. "Roundup." A show of the skills used by cowboys in rounding up cattle: roping, riding bucking horses, and so forth. A name redolent of the Wild West.

Roderick OG. "Renowned rule." Most commonly used in Scotland and other parts of Britain; never a great favorite in America.
Broderick, Brodrick, Brodryck, Rhoderick, Rhodric, Rod, Rodd, Rodderick, Roddie, Roddrick, Roddy, Roderic, Roderich, Roderigo, Roderyck, Rodrick, Rodrik, Rodrigo, Rodrigue, Rodrigues, Rodriguez, Rodrique, Rodriquez, Rodryck, Rodryk, Roric, Rorick, Rory, Rurek, Rurik, Ruy

Rodman OG. "Renowned man." Unusable at the moment without reference to the flamboyant basketball player Dennis Rodman.
Rodmann

Rodney OE. Place name: "Island near the clearing." Like many last names, this one began intensive use as a first name in the mid–19th century. Consequent mild popularity has endured for some 150 years. Comedian Rodney Dangerfield.
Rodnee, Rodnie

Rodolfo Var. **Rudolph** (OG. "Famous wolf"). This was the original version of Rudolph Valentino's given name: the rest of the impressive string was Alfonzo Raffaelo Pierre Filibert Guglielmi.
Rodolf, Rodolphe, Rodolpho

Roe ME. "Roe deer." May originally have been an occupational name indicating an ancestor who hunted or trapped such deer.
Row, Rowe

Rogan Ir. Gael. "Red-head." Irish Gaelic has several names to indicate red hair; but then, the Irish people produce many redheads.

Roger OG. "Renowned spearman." At its most popular in the Middle Ages and the 19th and 20th centuries, but on the wane since the 1950s. Actors Rutger Hauer, Roger Moore; opera singer Ruggiero Raimondi.

Dodge, Hodge, Rodge, Rodger, Rog, Rogelio, Rogerio, Rogers, Rogiero, Rudiger, Ruggero, Ruggiero, Rutger, Ruttger

Roland OG. "Renowned land." Orlando is a more common variant in several European languages. Rowland was, for a long time, the preferred version in English. The name dates from the Dark Ages, and the most famous Roland was the valorous nephew of Charlemagne, about whom many romantic tales were written.

Lannie, Lanny, Orlando, Roeland, Rolando, Roldan, Roley, Rolland, Rollie, Rollin, Rollins, Rollo, Rolly, Rowe, Rowland

Rolf Var. **Rudolph** (OG. "Famous wolf"). Most common in Scandinavian countries.

Rolfe, Rolle, Rollo, Rolph, Rowland

Rollo Var. **Roland**. Used occasionally in continental Europe, where the "-o" ending for first names is more common. Author Rollo May.

Roman Lat. "From Rome." The name of several obscure saints and one short-lived pope. The significance of the name no doubt comes from the fact that Rome is the center of the Roman Catholic faith. Football star Roman Gabriel; film director Roman Polanski; author Romain Gary.

Romain, Romaine, Romanes, Romano, Romanos, Romanus

Romeo It. "Pilgrim to Rome." Cannot be used without reference to the famous romance, and sure to engender a lot of teasing.

Romney Old Welsh. Place name: "Winding river." Painter George Romney.

Romulus Lat. "Man of Rome." Along with Remus, the legendary founder of Rome, though Romulus actually murdered his twin brother in a quarrel over where to situate the city, which he then ruled for 37 years. A rare name. Playwright Romulus Linney.

Romolo

Ronald OE. "Counsel power." Also from the same source as Reginald and Reynold. Though it was fairly common in the 1940s and 1950s, most parents will associate Ronald with two-term President Ronald Reagan and with clown Ronald McDonald. In spite of these uncool connections, the name is used from time to time.

Ranald, Renaldo, Ron, Ronaldo, Roneld, Ronell, Ronello, Ronnie, Ronny

Ronan Ir. Gael. "Little seal." Mostly Irish use.

Ronson OE. "Son of Ronald."

Rooney Ir. Gael. "Red-haired." Yet another Irish name indicating the traditional Irish coloring. Actor Mickey Rooney.

Roone, Rowan, Rowen, Rowney

Roosevelt Old Dutch. Place name: "Rose field." A name that would be simply an ethnic curiosity if it hadn't been borne by two 20th-century presidents, Theodore and Franklin Delano Roosevelt (who were second cousins).

Roper OE. Occupational name: "Rope maker."

Rory Ir. Gael. "Red." Also occurs as a nickname for Roderick. Mostly Scottish use, but the name seems highly eligible for 21st century popularity, since it is unusual without being weird.

Rosario Port. "The rosary." Most common, for obvious reasons, among Catholic families.

Roscoe ONorse. Place name: "Woods of the female deer." This is a place name from northern England, where Norse influence may be more likely to have lingered in the language. Tennis star Roscoe Tanner.

Ross, Rosscoe

Roshan Pers. "Daybreak, dawn."

Roslin Scot. Gael. "Little redhead."

Roslyn, Rosselin, Rosslyn

Ross Scot. Gael. "Headland." A place name in Scotland. The name (like so many of the "R" names) may also come from the Gaelic word for "red." Entrepreneur Ross Perot.

Rosse, Rossell

Roswell OE. Place name: "Rose spring."

Roth OG. "Red." Could apply to hair or complexion, though England's flaxen-haired Teutonic invaders might have used it more for the former, in sheer surprise. Actor Tim Roth.

Rothe

Rothwell ONorse. Place name: "Red spring."

Rousseau OF. "Little red-haired one." A relative
sell. May be given to honor Jean Jacques Rousseau, the
18th-century French philosopher whose writings
influenced the French and American revolutions.
Roussell, Russo

Rover ME. "Traveler, wanderer." The term "roving"
turns up most often in poetry and songs (as in Byron's
poem "So, We'll Go No More A-Roving"), and the name
is most commonly given to dogs.

Rowan OE. Place name: "Rowan tree." The rowan is a
flowering tree that later produces red berries. Also possibly another Gaelic name meaning "red." Presumably,
since the term applied to so many people, variations in
the name were necessary to tell them apart.
Roan, Rohan, Rowe

Rowdy English "Boisterous." In England making a row
(rhymes with how) means making a lot of noise. Probably
used most often as a nickname. Diver Rowdy Gaines.

Rowell OE. Place name: "Roe deer well."

Rowley OE. Place name: "Roughly cleared meadow."
Rowlea, Rowlee, Rowleigh, Rowly

Roxbert OE. "Bright raven."

Roxbury OE. Place name: "Rook's town or fortress."
"Rook" may have referred to a large population of rooks
or crows.
Roxburghe

Roy Gael. "Red" or Fr. "King." Most popular earlier in
the 20th century, but hard to use because of the Roy Rogers chain of fast-food restaurants. Cowboy Roy Rogers;
actor Roy Scheider.
Rey, Roi, Ruy

Royal OF. "Kingly." Scarce as a name, though the merely
aristocratic names like Earl and Marquez occur much
more often.
Royall

Royce Meaning and origin unclear: some sources offer OF./
OE. "Son of the king"; others suggest OG. "Kind
fame." The most famous Royce is the man who, along
with Mr. Rolls, began turning out England's foremost luxury car.
Roice

Royden OE. Place name: "Rye hill."
Roydan, Roydon

Royston OE. Place name: not related to Roy at all, but a name whose original meaning varied geographically.

Rozen Heb. "Ruler."

Rubén Sp. Var. **Reuben** (Heb. "Behold, a son").
This form occurs more often than the anglicized Reuben or the original Hebrew, Reuven. Singer Rubén Blades.
Rube, Rubi, Rubin, Rubino

Rubio Sp. "Ruby."

Rudd OE. "Ruddy-skinned." Student leader Mark Rudd.

Rudiger Ger. "Spear fame." May refer to an ancestor's skill with a weapon.

Rudolph OG. "Famous wolf." Parents would have to have very strong feelings about the name to use it, given the enormous fame of Rudolph the red-nosed reindeer. Actor Rudolph Valentino; ballet star Rudolf Nureyev.
Dolph, Raoul, Rodolfo, Rodolph, Rodolphe, Rolf, Rolfe, Rollo, Rolph, Rolphe, Rudey, Rudi, Rudie, Rudolf, Rudolfo, Rudolphus, Rudy

Rudy Dim. "Rud-" names. Well established by singer Rudy Vallee, and more common than Rudolph, perhaps because of that pesky reindeer. Fashion designer Rudi Gernreich.
Rudee, Rudi

Rudyard OE. Place name: "Red paddock." Preempted by English poet and novelist Rudyard Kipling, though fans of the *Just So Stories* or *The Jungle Book* might want to use it.

Rufaro Shona (Zimbabwe). "Happiness, elation."

Rufino Lat. var. **Rufus**.
Ruffino

Ruford OE. Place name: "Red ford" or "Rough ford."
Rufford

Rufus Lat. "Red-haired." Another redhead name, though this one comes from Latin rather than Gaelic. Most common in the 19th century.
Ruffus, Rufous

Rugby OE. "Rook fortress." The name of a famous British school, which in turn gave its name to a famous game.

Rune ONorse. "Secret, whisper." Runes were the alphabet of the ancient Germanic peoples, dating from about the third century A.D. They carry the aura of mystery because they could not be translated until comparatively recently. Not related to Rooney, despite the sound.

Rumford OE. Place name: "Wide river-crossing."

Rupert Var. **Robert** (OE. "Bright fame"). Well established in Britain since the 18th century, but less used here, possibly because to Americans, it has a very English flavor. Actor Rupert Everett; publisher Rupert Murdoch.
Ruprecht

Rurik Rus. Var. **Roderick** (OG. "Famous king").

Rush OE. Place name: "Dweller by the rushes." Given great exposure by commentator Rush Limbaugh, but parents don't necessarily name their children after their favorite radio star.

Rushford OE. Place name: "Ford with rushes."

Ruskin OF. "Little red-haired one." Author John Ruskin.

Russell Fr. "Red-head; red-skinned." Originally a last name, but popular as a first name in the middle of the 20th century. Like most fashions of that era, the name is now somewhat neglected. Philosopher Bertrand Russell; author Russell Baker.
Roussell, Russ, Russel

Ruston OE. Place name: "Rust's estate," referring, once again, to that red-haired ancestor.
Russton

Rusty Fr. "Red-haired." Most commonly a nickname, given when the characteristic of red hair is well established (which may occur long after a bald baby is given a proper name).

Rutherford OE. "Cattle crossing." Most commonly a family name transferred to first-name use, since passionate admiration for U.S. President Rutherford Hayes seems unlikely to influence parental choice. Use may also be limited by the fact that there is no handy nickname.
Rutherfurd

Rutland ONorse. Place name: "Land of roots" or "Red land."

Rutledge OE./ONorse. Place name: "Root ledge" or "Red ledge."
Routledge

Rutley OE. Place name: "Root meadow" or "Red meadow."

Ryan Irish last name. Meaning is unclear, though some sources connect it with "king." Has been very popular in recent years, to the extent that boys named Ryan are numerous in elementary schools. Actor Ryan O'Neal; baseball player Ryne Sandberg.
Rian, Rien, Ryen, Ryne, Ryon, Ryun

Rycroft OE. Place name: "Rye field."
Ryecroft

Rye The name of a grain that is widely grown in northern Europe and the United States. It is used as a basis for bread and also for whiskey.

Ryland OE. Place name: "Land where rye is grown."
Ryeland

Saad Aramaic. "Aid, help."

Saahdia Aramaic. "The help of the Lord."
Saadya, Seadya

Saarik Hindi. Nature name: a kind of thrush, a small, drably feathered songbird.
Saariq, Sareek, Sareeq, Sariq

Saber Fr. "Sword." The kind of curved sword traditionally used by cavalrymen; also a weapon used in modern-day fencing. Slightly bloodthirsty as a first name.
Sabr, Sabre

Sabin Lat. "Sabine." The Sabines were a tribe living in central Italy around the time Romulus and Remus established the city of Rome. In an effort to provide wives for the citizens of Rome, Romulus arranged the mass kidnapping of the Sabine women, which came to be known (and frequently portrayed in art and literature) as the "Rape of the Sabines." The name is more common in the feminine form, **Sabina**.
Sabeeno, Sabino, Savin, Savino

Sable Old French animal name. In ancient heraldic terms, sable is black, even though the furry little creatures are actually golden-brown to brown. This is also the name of a popular model of station wagon, which need not be a deterrent to parents.

Sacha Rus. Dim. **Alexander** (Gk. "Defender of mankind"). Cropped up in English-speaking countries in the last twenty years. The "-a" ending in Russian is not necessarily feminine, and in fact this name is used for boys as well as girls in the U.S. French singer Sacha Guitry.
Sascha, Sasha

Sachar Heb. Var. **Yisachar** ("Reward").
Sacar

Sacheverell Old English name, possibly of Norman origins, meaning "Lost to time." Poet Sir Sacheverell Sitwell was known to his family as "Sachie."

Sachiel Heb. The name of the archangel whose job it is to watch out for people born under the sign of Sagittarius.
Sachiell

Sackville OE. "Saxon's town." Saxony is an area in northern Germany that sent many invaders to England (hence Anglo-Saxon).

Sadiki Swahili. "Faithful, loyal."
Sadeeki

Sadler OE. Occupational name: "Harness maker." Like most last names turned first names, this one was first transferred in the 19th century.
Saddler

Safford OE. Place name: "Willow river crossing."

Saffron Plant name: saffron refers to a substance (the dried stamens of saffron crocuses) used as a spice in Mediterranean and other Southern cuisines. It produces a bright orange-yellow color, and is sometimes used as a dye. Monks of some Eastern religions wear saffron robes, which may explain why the name was used occasionally in the 1960s, an era when saffron robes and Eastern religions went mainstream.
Saffran, Saffren, Saphron

Sage Plant name: a shrubby herb that grows widely in the West, and is also used for seasoning in cooking. It is considered to have healing properties, too. "Sage" is also sometimes used as to mean a wise man. Actor Sage Stallone; philanthropist Russell Sage.
Saige, Sayge

Sagiv Heb. "Great, sublime, mighty."
Segev

Saguaro The variety of tall, branched cactus that has become an icon for the American Southwest. They may grow as tall as 70 feet. Saguaro National Monument in Arizona is a wild area of almost 80,000 acres.
Seguaro

Sahil Hindi. "Leader."
Sahel

Said Arab. "Happy." Currently popular in Arabic countries and also used in northern and eastern Africa. Actor Saeed Jaffrey.
Saeed, Saiyid, Sayeed, Sayid, Syed

Sail Noun used as name. Appealing for parents who like its quintessentially outdoorsy connotations.

Sainsbury OE. "Saint's settlement." The name of a huge grocery store chain in the United Kingdom.
Sainsberry

Saint Lat. "Holy." This name is more readily used as a first name in Latin (and Catholic) cultures.

Sajan Hindi. "Loved one."

Saladin Arab. "The righteous faith." The name of an important Muslim sultan of the 12th century who captured Jerusalem from the Crusaders.
Saladdin

Salem Heb. "Peace." Related to Shalom, Solomon, etc. Used in the Psalms as an abbreviation for Jerusalem. In the U.S., this name has been used for some dozen cities and towns including the capital of Oregon and the historic coastal town in Massachusetts, site of the Salem witch trials and setting of Nathaniel Hawthorne's tale *The House of the Seven Gables*.

Salim Arab. "Tranquility."
Saleem, Salem

Salisbury ME. Place name: probably "Willow settlement." *Saule* is the French word for willow. In England, Salisbury is a picturesque and important cathedral town. This is also an American place name.
Salisbery, Salisberry, Saulsberry, Saulsbery, Saulsbury, Saulisbury

Salman Arab. "Safety." Author Salman Rushdie.

Salton OE. Place name: "Manor settlement" or "Willow settlement." The Salton Sea, in southern Calfornia, is a body of water 287 feet below sea level.

Salvatore It. "Savior." Used mostly by families of Latin descent. Salvador is an important place name in Latin America. Artist Salvador Dali.

Sal, Salvador, Salvator, Salvidor, Sauveur, Xavier, Xaviero, Zavier, Zaviero

Salvio Lat. "Saved." The feminine term is **Salvia**, which is the Latin word for the herb sage (see preceding).

Salvian, Salviano, Salviatus

Sam Dim. **Samuel** or **Samson**. Occasionally used on its own, more commonly a nickname. Playwright Sam Shepard; actor Sam Waterston.

Samm, Sammey, Sammie, Samy

Sami Arab. "On high, exalted." Pronounced "Sahmi."

Samson Heb. "Sun." In the Old Testament, Samson was the warrior whose strength ebbed away when his hair was cut by Delilah. The name was used in the Middle Ages, and the Puritans kept it current with their fondness for Old Testament names, but it has not been fashionable for several hundred years.

Sam, Sampson, Sansom, Sanson, Sansone, Shem

Samuel Heb. "Told by God." A judge and prophet in early Israel; two Old Testament books are named for him. The name was used, predictably, by the Puritans and has never really faded since then, though it peaked in the 19th century. Opera singer Samuel Ramey; lexicographer Samuel Johnson; playwright Samuel Beckett; author Samuel Clemens (Mark Twain).

Sam, Sammie, Sammy, Samuele, Samuello, Samwell, Shem

Sanborn OE. Place name: "Sandy stream."

Sanborne, Sanbourn, Sanburn, Sanburne, Sandborn, Sandbourne

Sancho Lat. "Sacred." Don Quixote's sidekick was called Sancho Panza, which is a little joke, since "Panza" is Spanish slang for "belly." When French-born journalist Sanche de Gramont took American citizenship, he changed his name to Ted Morgan.

Sanche, Sanctio, Sancos, Sanzio, Sauncho

Sandberg OE. Place name: "Sand village." Poet Carl Sanburg.
Sandbergh, Sandburg, Sandburgh

Sander Ger. Var. **Alexander** (Gk. "Defender of mankind"). Used in Europe.
Sandino, Sandor, Sender, Xan, Xander, Zander

Sanders ME. "Son of Alexander." (Gk. "Defender of mankind").
Sanderson, Sandor, Saunders, Saunderson, Sandros

Sandor Hung. Var. **Alexander** (Gk. "Defender of mankind").
Sandros, Xandros

Sanditon OE. "Sandy settlement."

Sandhurst OE. Place name: "Sandy thicket of trees." In England, the premier military academy is known as Sandhurst, for the village where it is located.
Sandhirst

Sandy Dim. **Alexander** (Gk. "Defender of mankind"). Sometimes also given as a nickname based on a person's coloring, like Rusty. Apparently red or reddish hair is unusual enough to warrant this kind of name, but corresponding names for blonds or brunets don't seem to exist.
Sandey, Sandie, Sandino

Sanford OE. Place name: "Sandy ford." Acting teacher Sanford Meisner.
Sandford, Sandfurd

Sanjay Sanskrit. "Conquering, triumphant."

Satchel Lat. "Sack, small bag." Made famous by baseball player Satchel Paige and, more recently, Woody Allen's child with Mia Farrow.
Satchell

Santiago Sp. "Saint James." Catholics are traditionally less reticent about using religious names than Protestants, routinely naming children Salvatore, Socorro, and even Jesús, as well as choosing the names of individual saints.
Sandiago, Sandiego, Santeago, Santiaco, Santigo

Santo It./Sp. "Holy." Also a nickname for full saints' names.
Santos

Sapir Heb. "Sapphire."
Safir, Saphir, Saphiros

Sargent OF. Occupational name: "Officer." Painter John Singer Sargent; politician Sargent Shriver.
Sarge, Sergeant, Sergent, Serjeant

Sassacus Native American: "Wild man" in the Massachuset language. This was the name of the last chief of the Pequot tribe of Connecticut. Though virtually exterminated in 1637, the Pequots have had the last laugh by building immensely successful casinos on their tribal lands in eastern Connecticut.

Saturnin Sp. "Saturn." A "saturnine" temperament is moody or sullen, and people born under the sign of Saturn (Capricorns) are generally considered painstaking, reliable, and reserved.
Saturnino

Saul Heb. "Asked for." The name of the first king of Israel, and also the name of the apostle Paul before his conversion to Christianity. Overlooked in the 16th-century revival of Old Testament names, at its peak in the late 19th century. Author Saul Bellow.
Saulo, Shaul, Sol, Sollie

Saville Fr. "Willow town." Savile Row, in London, is the worldwide source for fine men's tailoring.
Savil, Savile, Savill, Savylle

Saviero Sp. Var. **Xavier** (Basque "New house"). The wide use of Xavier and its variations is partly the result of veneration of Saint Francis Xavier, but it may also be influenced by the fact that Xavier and Savior sound so much alike that parents may take them to be related.

Savion Modern name, possibly derived from Xavier (Basque, "New house"). Brought to the public's eye by the fame of tapdance genius Savion Glover.
Xavion, Savionn

Savoy Place name: An area of southeastern France bordering Switzerland. There used to be a kingdom of Savoy, whose descendants ruled Italy into this century. The name's connotations of luxury go back to a palace in London built by Peter of Savoy in the 13th century. A famously lavish hotel was later built on its site.

Savyon Heb. Plant name: a low-growing shrubby groundcover.

Sawyer ME. Occupational name: "Wood-worker." Most familiar as the name of Mark Twain's boy hero of the eponymous *Tom Sawyer*.

Saxe OE. "From Saxony." Saxony was the area of northern German where the Saxon tribe originated.
Sachs, Sachsen

Saxon OE. "Knife, sword." Used for one of the Germanic tribes that fought with short-bladed weapons. The name may also describe origin in the German area of Saxony, which probably took its name from those effective daggers.
Saxe, Saxen

Sayer Welsh. "Woodworker." Football star Gale Sayers.
Sayers, Sayre, Sayres

Scanlon Ir. Gael. "Little trapper."
Scanlan, Scanlen

Schubert Ger. "Shoemaker." Made famous by 18–19th-century German composer Franz Schubert.
Shubert

Schultz Ger. "Village magistrate or administrator." A German occupational name.

Schuyler Dutch. "Shield, protection" or "Scholar." Harks back to the Dutch settlers who brought the name to America in the 17th century. Slightly fashionable for both boys and girls, often with different spelling.
Schuylar, Skuyler, Skylar, Skyler, Skylor

Scipio Ancient Roman name of uncertain meaning. Scipio Africanus was the Roman general who, in the Second Punic War (around 200 B.C.), defeated the Carthaginian general Hannibal. Western European culture has identified so strongly with Greco-Roman culture that for generations this was seen as the good guys defeating the bad guys, making Scipio a hero. Scipio was used in the south as a slave name (with an unpleasant note of irony) and has survived in some southern families.

Scirocco It. from Arab. "Warm wind." The word originally described the wind that blew over Italy from the Libyan deserts.
Cirocco, Sirocco

Scorpio Lat. "Scorpion." Zodiac sign, for people born be-

tween Oct. 21 and Nov. 21. Scorpions carry a v
sting in their tails, making this a startling name for a child.
Skorpios

Scott OE. "Scotsman." Use is emphatically 20th century,
and while the name is not fashionable, it certainly is fa-
miliar to parents and nursery school teachers in our era.
Actor Scott Glenn; authors Scott Peck, F. Scott Fitzgerald,
Scott Turow; musician Scott Joplin; basketball player
Scottie Pippen.
Scot, Scottie, Scotto, Scotty

Scout OF. "To listen." (French speakers will recognize the
word *écouter*.) Occupational name: someone who scouts,
gathers information quietly. When Bruce Willis and Demi
Moore named their daughter Scout after a character in *To
Kill a Mockingbird*, they gave the name a new credibility.
It is so unusual, though, that its gender is still up for grabs.

Scribner OE. Occupational name: "Scribe, copier." Or
"scrivener," to use the old term. Charles Scribner's Sons
was a prominent American publishing firm, now part of
a larger company.

Seabert OE. "Shining sea."
Seabright, Sebert, Seibert

Seabrook OE. Place name: "Stream near the sea."
Seabrooke

Seabury OE. Place name: "Settlement near the sea." Sam-
uel Seabury was the first Episcopal bishop of the United
States, appointed in 1789.
Seaberry, Seabry

Seal Animal name. Brought to prominence by a rock star
who uses only this name.

Seaman OE. Occupational name: "Mariner."

Seamus Ir. Var. **James** (Heb. "He who supplants"). "Shamus" is old-fashioned American slang for a detective,
possibly because the urban police force has traditionally
been heavily Irish.
Seumas, Seumus, Shamus

Sean Ir. Var. **John** (Heb. "God is gracious"). Spread outside of Ireland only in the 20th century. Quite heavily
used now, perhaps influenced by the popularity of actors

Sean Connery and Sean Penn. Basketball player Shawn Kemp.

Shane, Shaughn, Shaun, Shawn

Searle OE. "Armor."

Seaton OE. Place name: "Town near the sea."

Seeton, Seton

Sebastian Lat. "From Sebastia" (an ancient city). Saint Sebastian, an early Christian martyr, was killed in a hail of arrows, and was a favorite subject for Old Master painters. (He is now patron of soldiers.) The name has never been common, though the British have used it somewhat since the 1940s, possibly influenced by a character in Evelyn Waugh's popular *Brideshead Revisited*. To Americans, it may seem a little too rarefied, and it provides no handy nickname. Track star Sebastian Coe.

Bastian, Bastien, Seb, Sebastiano, Sebastien, Sebestyen, Sebo

Secondo It. "Second son." For parents who simply cannot agree on anything else?

Segundo

Sedgley OE. Place name: "Sword meadow." Could indicate a kind of coarse, sharp reedlike grass growing in a meadow, or that the meadow belonged to (or was frequented by) a swordsman. In all cases, refers to a long-ago meadow.

Sedgeley, Sedgely

Sedgwick OE. Place name: "Sword place." As with Sedgley, the sword could refer to grass or an actual weapon.

Sedgewick, Sedgewyck, Sedgwyck

Seeley OE. "Blessed." From the same Germanic root as Selig.

Sealey, Seely, Seelye

Seferino Sp. from Gk. "A soft, gentle wind." Another version of Zephyr, or Zefirino. Before he was the monkey in the Babar stories, Zephyr was the West Wind personified in Greek myth. He was married to Iris, the rainbow.

Cefirino, Sebarino, Sephirio, Zefarin, Zefirino, Zephir, Zephyr

Sefton OE. Place name: "Town in the rushes."

Seger OE. "Sea fighter." Musician Pete Seeger.

Seager, Segar, Seeger

Segundo Sp. "Second." Not common: parents usually have enough imagination to come up with at least two proper names.
Secondo

Sela Heb. "Boulder, cliff." This is also a word that occurs frequently in the Psalms, though its meaning is unknown. It may be an ancient musical notation.
Selah

Selby OE. Place name: "Manor village." As Shelby is appropriated by girls, Selby may lose its maleness.
Selbey, Shelbey, Shelbie, Shelby

Seldon OE. Place name: "Willow valley."
Selden, Sellden, Shelden

Selig OG. "Blessed."
Seligman, Seligmann, Zelig

Selkirk Scot. Gael. Place name: its meaning is unclear, though "kirk" means church. It is an area in Scotland. Scottish sailor Alexander Selkirk is thought to have been Daniel Defoe's inspiration for the novel *Robinson Crusoe*.

Sellers OE. "Marshland dweller." Actor Peter Sellers.
Sellars

Selwyn OE. "Manor-friend." Alternatively, an offshoot of Silvanus. Mostly 19th-century use.
Selwin, Selwinn, Selwynn, Selwynne

Seminole Native American name: the tribe, related to the Creeks, who settled in Florida and resisted European-American attempts to annex their land in the ten-year Seminole War. The football players of Florida State University are known as the "Seminoles."

Seneca Both the name of a Native American tribe (part of the Iroquois confederacy) and several New York State place names, and the name of a Roman philosopher and statesman around the time of Christ. He was Nero's tutor.

Senior OF. "Lord." Hard to use in these days when it has come to mean any individual older than 65.

Sennett Fr. "Elderly." Related to Senior. Comedian Mack Sennett.
Sennet

Septimus Lat. "Seventh." Most common in the 19th-century, when very large families were the norm.

Sequoia Cherokee: "Sparrow." The 19th-century Cherokee scholar who developed a form of written language for his tribe was named Sequoia. This is also the name of a kind of redwood tree named for him.

Sequoya, Sequoyah

Seraphim Heb. "Ardent." The seraphim are the highest-ranking angels in Heaven (above angels, archangels, cherubim, etc.). They have six wings and are noted for their zealous love. There have been two Saints Seraphim, one a 17th-century Italian, one an 18th-century Russian mystic.

Sarafino, Saraph, Serafín, Serafino, Seraph, Seraphimus

Sereno Lat. "Tranquil." Though the feminine form, **Serena**, is somewhat popular, the masculine version is very rare.

Cereno

Sergio Lat. "Servant, attendant." Strongly associated with Russia, perhaps because of composers Rachmaninoff and Prokofiev, yet it comes from a Latin name and was used by an early pope. This Spanish form is the most common one in the U.S. Impresario Serge Diaghilev; film director Sergio Leone.

Seargeoh, Sergei, Sergey, Sergi, Sergio, Sergios, Sergiu, Sergiusz, Serguei, Sirgio, Sirgios

Servas Lat. "Redeemed." Used in northern Europe.

Servaas, Servacio, Servatus

Sesame The seed and flavoring agent.

Sesamey, Sessame, Sessamee

Seth Heb. "Set, appointed." In the Old Testament, Adam and Eve's third son (after Cain and Abel). Passed over in the Puritan revival of biblical names, but included to some extent in the late–20th-century revival of the same.

Seton OE. Place name: "Sea settlement."

Severin Lat. "Severe."

Severino, Severinus, Seweryn

Severn OE. "Boundary." The Severn is an important river running through southern England.

Seward OE. "Sea guardian" or "Victory guardian." An 11th-century earl of Northumberland (in England), born in Denmark, was named Siward. Largely 19th century. Secretary of State under Lincoln and Johnson, William Henry Seward was responsible for the U.S. purchase of Alaska from Russia. It was known at the time as "Seward's Folly."

Sewerd, Siward

Sewell OE. "Sea strong."
Sewald, Sewall

Sexton ME. Occupational name: "Church custodian." The sexton (or sacristan) is charged with the upkeep of a church building.

Sextus Lat. "Sixth." Less common than Septimus or Octavius, though five popes have used it. The first one, oddly enough, was actually Christendom's seventh pope.
Sesto, Sixto, Sixtus

Seymour OF. "From Saint Maur." Indicates an ancestor who came from a village called Saint Maur, most probably in Normandy. Quite a popular name in the 19th century, but virtually invisible today.
Seamore, Seamor, Seamour, Seymore

Shabat Heb. "To finish, to stop." Related to the term "sabbath," for the end of the week.
Shabbat

Shachar Heb. "Dawn, sunrise."

Shadow OE. "Shade."
Shadoe

Shad Possibly dim. **Shadrach**. Also a nature name: the shad is a common food fish in both Europe and America.

Shadrach Heb. Meaning unknown. Old Testament name: one of three Hebrew men (along with Meshach and Abednego) thrown into a fiery furnace by King Nebuchadnezzar and rescued by an angel. Used steadily in the 16th to 19th centuries, but now rare.
Shad, Shadrack

Shafiq Arab. "Empathetic, merciful."
Shafeek, Shafik

Shafir Heb. "Handsome."
Shafeer, Shafer, Shefer

Shahzad Pers. "Son of the king." Shah is Persian for king.

Shai Heb. "Present, gift."

Shakil Arab. "Good-looking, well-developed." The root of Shaquille O'Neal's name, and more accurate than his parents could ever have predicted.
Shakeel, Shakill, Shakille, Shaqueel, Shaquil, Shaquille

Shakir Arab. "Gratitude, thanksgiving."
Shakeer, Shaqueer

Shalom Heb. "Peace." Related to Solomon. Not just a

but also a common greeting to speakers of Hebrew.

n, Solomon

Shamir Heb. "Flint, thorn." Shamir is a legendary material capable of cutting stone; Solomon used it in the building of the Temple. Israeli statesman Yitzhak Shamir.

Shameer

Shamus Var. **Seamus** (Ir. Var. **James**: Heb. "The supplanter").

Shanahan Ir. Gael. "Wise, clever." Football coach Mike Shanahan.

Shandy Possibly OE. "Boisterous, high-spirited." Name of a drink popular in Britain, half beer and half lemonade or ginger ale. Also used for girls, possibly because it sounds like the familiar Sandy or Mandy.

Shandey

Shane Var. **Sean** (Ir. Var. **John**: Heb. "The Lord is gracious"). Popularity in the 1950s and 1960s probably depended on the film *Shane*. Now losing ground to Sean, as those now-grown Shanes watch their children grow up. Screenwriter Shane Black.

Shaine, Shayn, Shayne

Shani Heb. "Crimson, bright red." Also used for girls.

Shanley Ir. Gael. "Small and ancient."

Shannley

Shannon Ir. Gael. "Old, ancient." The name of an important river, county, and airport in Ireland, used as a first name in this century. Most popular among families with Irish roots, and more common for girls. Football player Shannon Sharpe.

Shanan, Shanen, Shannan, Shannen, Shanon

Shaquille Modern respelling of Shakil (Arab. "Well-developed, good-looking"). Known the world over as the name of basketball megastar Shaquille O'Neal.

Shaq, Shaqeell, Shaqueel, Shaquil

Sharif Arab. "Honest." Actor Omar Sharif.

Shareef

Shashi Hindi. "Moonbeam." Indian movie star Shashi Kapoor.

Shasta Oregon mountain of some 14,000 feet that rises from nearly sea level. It is at the southernmost end of the Cascade Mountain range. Also the name of a brand of soda, though parents using this name are more likely to be evoking America's natural beauty. The "-a" ending may make Shasta more appealing to parents of girl babies.

Shavon Phonetic spelling of the Irish name Siobhan, which corresponds to the English Joan. Used as a boy's name in this context.
Shavonne, Shivaun, Shovon

Shaw OE. Place name: "Copse, grove of trees."

Shawn Var. **Sean**. This version is not as common as the Irish spelling, Sean. Basketball player Shawn Kemp.
Shawnel, Shawnell

Shawnee Name of a Native American tribe that originated in the eastern forests of the U.S. and gradually migrated westward. Shawnee Mission is the name of a town in Kansas. Also, possibly, a variant of Shawn.
Shawney, Shawnie

Shayan Phonetic spelling of Cheyenne, the name of a Native American tribe. See **Cheyenne**.

Shea Ir. Gael. "From the fairy fort." More commonly an Irish last name. Actor John Shea.
Shae, Shay, Shaye, Shays

Sheehan Ir. Gael. "Small and tranquil."

Sheffield OE. Place name: "Crooked meadow." Sheffield is the name of a city in England that was famous for manufacture of cutlery, and "Sheffield plate" is a term for silverplated copper, a product that originated there.

Shelby OE. Place name: "Village on the ledge." Author Shelby Foote.
Shelbey, Shelbie

Sheldon OE. Place name: "Steep valley," or possibly "Flat-topped hill." Most common in the middle of the 20th century. This is one of a group of Old English names (along with Seymour, Marvin, Irving) that were enthusiastically used by Jewish immigrants eager to assimilate to the U.S. Author Sidney Sheldon.
Shelden, Sheldin

Shelley OE. Place name: "Ledge meadow." Last name made famous by the poet Percy Bysshe Shelley. Much more commonly used for girls at the moment.
Shelly

Shelton OE. Place name: "Ledge village."

Shem Heb. "Fame." The name of Noah's eldest son in the Old Testament. (Ham and Japheth were the other two.) None of the sons' names are as popular as that of their father, and though the entire human race descends, according to the Bible, from these three men and their wives, the wives are never named at all.

Shenandoah Place name: a city in Iowa and a town in Pennsylvania, but most famously, a long, fertile, beautiful valley between the Allegehenies and the Blue Ridge Mountains in Virginia. There is a famous, wistful folk song that begins "Oh, Shenandoah, I long to hear you . . ." The name may be related to the Iroquois word for deer.

Shepherd OE. Occupational name: "Shepherd." Mostly 19th-century use, very uncommon now. *Pooh* illustrator Ernest Shepard.
Shep, Shepard, Shephard, Shepp, Sheppard, Shepperd

Shepley OE. Place name: "Sheep meadow."
Sheplea, Shepleigh, Shepply, Shipley

Sherborn OE. Place name: "Bright stream."
Sherborne, Sherbourn, Sherburn, Sherburne

Sheridan Ir. Gael. Unclear meaning, possibly "Wild man." Used mostly in Britain. Critic Sheridan Morley; playwright Richard Brinsley Sheridan; Civil War general Philip Sheridan.
Sheredan, Sheridon, Sherridan

Sherill OE. Place name: possibly "Bright hill." A common enough last name, but easily confused with Cheryl as a first name. Opera singer Sherrill Milnes.
Sherrill

Sherlock OE. "Bright hair." Irresistibly reminiscent of Arthur Conan Doyle's fictional detective, Sherlock Holmes.
Sherlocke, Shurlock

Sherman OE. Occupational name: "Shear man." Around the time when last names were coming into being, England's great export was wool. The wool business has given the modern world a number of occupational names, like Sherman, Shepherd, Fuller, and Weaver. Civil War general William Tecumseh Sherman.
Scherman, Schermann, Shearman, Shermann

Sherrerd Unknown origin. Possibly related to Sheridan.

Familiar-sounding enough, owing to the "Sher" component, to be used occasionally as a name, more often for
girls. There is no definitive spelling.

Sherard, Sherrard, Sherrod

Sherwin ME. "Bright friend."

Sherwind, Sherwinn, Sherwyn, Sherwynne

Sherwood OE. Place name: "Shining forest." Sherwood
Forest, a real forest in central England, was the home of
the legendary bandit/hero Robin Hood. Playwright Robert
Sherwood; author Sherwood Anderson.

Sherwoode, Shurwood

Shiloh Heb. Meaning disputed: possibly "His gift" or "He
who was sent." Biblical place name used for a small town
in Tennessee, the site of the bloodiest Civil War battle,
where both Confederate and Union armies had casualties
(men wounded and killed) of over 10,000 men.

Shilo, Shylo, Shyloh

Shipton OE. Place name: "Sheep village" or "Ship village."

Shiva Sanskrit. "Benign, bringing good fortune." This is
the name of one of the preeminent Hindu gods who takes
many forms with many different characteristics. His name
is used as part of many other names in India.

Shlomo Var. **Solomon** (Heb. "Peaceable").

Shelomi, Shelomo, Shlomi

Shomer Heb. "Watchman."

Shoshone Native American tribe, indigenous to eastern
Nevada, southern Idaho, and western Utah. These nomads
were also known as the Snake Indians. Sacajawea, Lewis
and Clark's guide on their Western explorations, was a
Shoshone.

Shoshoni

Shoval Heb. "Path." Old Testament name.

Shura Rus. Dim. **Alexander** (Gk. "Man's defender").
Used in Russia as a nickname for a man.

Schura, Shoura

Sicily Place name: large island off the tip of Italy's "boot."
Many Italian immigrants to the United States have roots
in Sicily.

Sicilly

Sidney OE. "From Saint Denis." Famous English last

name turned first name in the 18th century, very fashionable in the late 19th century, now little used for boys. It is getting a new lease on life as a girl's name, though. Author Sidney Sheldon; film director Sydney Pollack; actor Sidney Poitier.

Sid, Sydney

Sidonio Lat. "From Sidonia." Sidon was an area in the Middle East. Most often used as a girl's name in France.

Siegfried OG. "Victory peace." The hero of the last two operas of Wagner's Ring cycle, son of Siegmund, husband of Brunhilde.

Sigfred, Sigfrid, Sigfried, Sigfryd, Sigvard, Sygfried

Sigbjorn ONorse. "Victory bear."

Siegbjorn

Sigmund OG. "Victorious protector." Another character from the Ring cycle, son of the god Wotan. He fathers Siegfried on his own sister, Sieglinde. The other famous Sigmund is the father of psychoanalysis, Sigmund Freud. A name with many weighty connotations.

Seigmond, Segismond, Siegmund, Sigismond, Sigismondo, Sigismund, Sigismundo, Sigismundus, Sigmond, Szygmond

Signe Unknown Scandinavian meaning, though the word particle meaning "victory" may give us a clue.

Signy

Sigwald OG. "Victorious leader."

Siegwald

Sigurd ONorse. "Guardian of victory."

Silas A contraction of Silvanus. New Testament name used in the Puritan era and occurring since then. Has an old-fashioned air that may appeal to parents of the 1990s.

Silvan, Silvano, Silvanus, Silvaon, Silvio, Sylas, Sylvan

Sill OE. "Beam, threshold."

Sills

Silvanus Lat. "Wood dweller." Also a New Testament name, but never as widely adopted as its spinoff, Silas.

Silvain, Silvano, Silvio, Sylvanus, Sylvio

Silver Noun as name, or possibly a contraction of Silvester. Scarce.

Sylver

Silverman OG. Occupational name: "Silver worker."

Silberman, Silbermann

Silverton OE. Place name: "Silver settlement."
Silvertown

Silvester Lat. "Wooded." Original form of the name we know as **Sylvester**.
Silvestre, Silvestro, Sylvester

Simba Swahili. "Lion." It's reassuring to find that the Walt Disney Company does its research thoroughly, and that *The Lion King*'s lion hero is actually named "lion."

Simcha Heb. "Joy."
Simha

Simeon Heb. "Listening intently." In the New Testament, Simeon is a holy old man who has been promised that he would see the Messiah before he died; when the infant Jesus was presented at the temple Simeon recognized him instantly. Simon is the more common anglicized form.
Shimon, Simyon

Simmons OE. "Son of Simon." Music producer Russell Simmons.
Semmes, Sim, Simms, Simmonds, Symonds, Syms

Simon Heb. "Listening intently." Prominent New Testament name, one of the twelve apostles. A common name from the Middle Ages through the 18th century, then revived early in the 20th century. To Americans, it has a rather English air. Simeon has never been as common. Orchestra conductor Simon Rattle; Latin American freedom fighter Simón Bolívar.
Shimon, Si, Sim, Simen, Simeon, Simmonds, Simmons, Simms, Simone, Simonson, Simpson, Symms, Symon, Syms, Szymon

Simpson OE. "Son of Simon."

Sinbad A character in the *Arabian Nights* stories, a merchant from Baghdad who goes on seven adventurous voyages and, through wit and ingenuity, comes home rich. Adopted as the name of a comedian who no doubt started with similar aspirations.

Sinclair OF. Place name: "From Saint Clair." Still much more familiar as a last name. Authors Sinclair Lewis, Upton Sinclair.
Sinclare, Synclair

Sinjin Phonetic spelling of the English pronunciation of

Saint John, an unusual name in a widely Protestant culture.

Sion Heb. "Highest point." In the Christian religion, Sion is a symbolic name for heaven, and is used often in hymns and even the names of some churches.
　Zion

Siraj Arab. "Light, beam."

Sirius Star name: the brightest star seen from earth.

Sixtus Lat. "Sixth." See **Sextus.**

Sivney Ir. Gael. "Well-going." Rare Irish last name.
　Sivneigh, Sivnie

Skeet ONorse. "To shoot." Skeet shooting consists of shooting with a rifle at a clay "pigeon," or target tossed into the air mechanically to simulate the flight of a bird. A very rarefied sport. Actor Skeet Ulrich.

Skelly Ir. Gael. "Bard."
　Scully

Skerry ONorse. Place name: "Stony isle."

Skinner OE. Occupational name: "Skinner of hides." Actor Otis Skinner; psychologist B. F. Skinner.

Skip Scand. "Ship boss." The term that has come down to us is "skipper," for the captain of a ship or boat. Skip occurs more commonly as a nickname.
　Skipp, Skipper

Skiriki Pawnee. "Coyote." Nature name with Native American credibility.

Skye Scot. Place name: the name of a spectacular island off the west coast of Scotland. With the current trend toward nature and geography names, it may also refer to the big blue bowl overhead.
　Skie, Sky

Skyler Dutch. "Giving shelter." Probably an adaptation of the Dutch last name Schuyler, which was brought to New York by 17th-century settlers. Used for both boys and girls, in widely variant spellings.
　Schuyler, Schyler, Skielar, Skielor, Skylar, Skylen, Skyller

Slade OE. Place name: "Valley." Art collector Felix Slade.
　Slaide, Slayde

Slater OE. Occupational name: "Hewer of slates." Actor Christian Slater.

Slavin Ir. Gael. "Mountain man."
 Slawin, Slavin, Sleven
Slavomir Czech. "Renowned glory."
Slim English: "Slender." Most often, given as a nickname to someone who is notably thin.
Sloan Ir. Gael. "Man of arms." An Irish last name that has become well entrenched in Britain and the U.S. Sometimes makes the leap to first-name status, perhaps as a maternal maiden name. Given extra prominence by the fact that Britain's version of preppies are known as "Sloane Rangers," for Sloane Square, the area in London where they congregate.
 Sloane
Smedley OE. Place name: "Flat meadow."
 Smedleigh, Smedly
Smith OE. Occupational name: "Blacksmith." This extremely common last name occurs as a first name, but parents would be unlikely to use it unless it was a family name. Economist Adam Smith; Mormon leader Joseph Smith; Smithsonian founder James Smithson.
 Smithson, Smitty, Smyth, Smythe, Smythson
Smokey Descriptive name. Made famous by singer Smokey Robinson, which gives this name a very cool aura.
 Smoky
Snowden OE. Place name: "Snowy peak." The name of a mountain in Wales, and the title of Princess Margaret's ex-husband (the Earl of Snowdon).
 Snowdon
Snyder OG. Occupational name: "Tailor."
 Schneider, Snider
Socorro Sp. "Aid, help." Currently popular in Spain. Most likely refers to the aid or help provided by the Almighty.
Socrates Gk. Meaning unknown. The name of the great Greek philosopher, used mostly by Greek families.
 Sokrates
Sofus Gk. "Wisdom." The highly unusual masculine version of Sophie.
 Sophus
Sohan Hindi. "Charming, handsome."
 Sohil
Solomon Heb. "Peaceable." In the Old Testament, the

wise king of Israel. Used in the Middle Ages and the 18th century, but currently a far from common choice.
Salmon, Salomo, Salomon, Salomone, Shalmon, Sol, Solaman, Sollie, Soloman

Somerby ME. Place name: "Summer village."
Somerbie, Somersby, Sommersby

Somerley Ir. Gael. "Summer sailors." May refer to Vikings, who made their invading voyages in the summer.
Somerled, Sorley

Somers Probably short for an Old English place name having to do with summer, like Somerset. Actor Josef Sommer.
Sommers

Somerset OE. Place name: "Summer settlement." A county in England, and a last name given prominence as a first name by author and playwright Somerset Maugham.
Sommerset, Summerset

Somerton OE. Place name: "Summer town."
Somervile, Somerville

Somerville ME. "Summer town." Probably refers to settlements where grazing was particularly good in summer, not what we think of as summer resorts.
Somervil, Sommerville

Sonny Word as name, sometimes friendly and sometimes a little condescending. Sonny Bono, entertainer turned politician, seems to have lived down any disparaging connotations to the name.
Sunny

Sophocles Gk. Meaning unknown. Name of one of the greatest classical Greek playwrights, author of *Oedipus the King*.

Soren Meaning unclear: may be related to Severin (Lat. "Severe"). This is a Danish form, known to literati as the first name of gloomy philosopher Søren Kierkegaard.

Sorrell OF. "Red-brown." A term now used to describe the color of a horse, perhaps applied long ago to the color of an ancestor's hair.
Sorel, Sorrel

Sothern OE. Place name: "From the south."
Southern

Southwell OE. Place name: "South well."

Spalding OE. Place name: "Divided field." More commonly a last name, rarely transferred to first-name use. Sports-minded families already know this name as a manufacturer of athletic equipment. Performance artist Spalding Gray.
Spaulding

Spark Lat. "To scatter." Noun used as name: a scattered bit of fire. Has probably been used most often as a nickname. Baseball player Sparky Lyle.
Sparky

Spear OE. Occupational name: "Spear-man." Names are sometimes a window into the concerns of a former era, and a number of names from the war-torn Anglo-Saxon age have to do with weapons.
Speare, Spears, Speer, Speers, Spiers

Speed OE. "Good fortune." Long ago, the phrase "God speed" meant, "God bring you good fortune." Speed has come to mean swiftness.

Spencer ME. Occupational name: "Provisioner." Used for the person in a large household who dispensed food and drink. Usually a last name, but occurs as a first name, more commonly in Britain. Actor Spencer Tracy; poet Edmund Spenser.
Spence, Spenser

Spider Noun as name. Usually used as a nickname because of the slightly creepy connotations. Skier Spider Sabich.
Spyder

Spike Noun as name. Possibly because of sports connotations ("spiking" a ball means slamming it to the ground), Spike is a very cool name, though a bit hard-edged for a small child. Filmmaker Spike Lee.

Spiridon Gk. "Basket." The name of a 4th-century Cypriot sheep farmer who became a bishop and a popular Greek saint. The name is little used outside Greek communities. U.S. Vice President Spiro Agnew.
Speero, Spero, Spiridion, Spiro, Spiros, Spyridon, Spyros

Spud Derivation unclear, possibly related to the Middle English word for a spade (as in a shovel). In slang terms, a spud is a potato. The name occurs as a nickname, most often in sporting contexts.

Squire ME. Occupational name: "Knight's companion." In more modern terms, perhaps, an aide-de-camp. First-name use mostly 19th century.

Squier, Squiers, Squires, Squyre, Squyres

Stacy Dim. **Eustace** (Gk. "Fertile"). More common as a female name. Actor Stacy Keach.

Stacey, Stacie

Stafford OE. Place name: "Landing place ford." As with many of these place/last names, used mostly in the 19th century.

Stafforde, Staford

Stanbury OE. Place name: "Stone fortification."

Stanberry, Stanbery, Stanburghe, Stansberry, Stansburghe, Stansbury

Stancliff OE. Place name: "Stony cliff."

Stancliffe, Stanclyffe, Stanscliff, Stanscliffe

Standish OE. Place name: "Stony parkland." The Pilgrims' military leader was Miles Standish, whose courtship Longfellow immortalized in a poem.

Stanfield OE. Place name: "Stony field."

Stansfield

Stanford OE. Place name: "Stony ford." Familiar as the name of the great California railroad magnate Leland Stanford, who founded the university that bears his name. Probably because Stanford is thought of as California's answer to the Ivy League, the name has Waspy connotations. Composer Charles Stanford.

Stamford, Standford

Stanislaus Slavic. Possibly "Glorious camp or stand." The patron saint of Poland, Saint Stanislaus, was an 11th-century bishop and martyr.

Stana, Stanek, Stanicek, Stanislas, Stanislav, Stanislaw, Stannes, Stanousek, Stasio

Stanley OE. Place name: "Stony field." It is not clear why some place names, like Sidney and Stanley, became popular enough so that they made the transition to common first names, while others, like Stanford or Sinclair, remain primarily last names. As with Sidney, Stanley's transformation to a first name was the result of great popularity

at the turn of the century. Filmmaker Stanley Kubrick.
Stan, Stanlea, Stanlee, Stanly

Stanmore OE. Place name: "Stony lake." On the evidence of this group of "Stan-" names, stones seem to have occupied a great deal of Anglo-Saxon man's attention, perhaps because they had to be cleared from the earth before it could be farmed effectively.
Stanmere

Stanton OE. Place name: "Stony village."
Stanten, Staunton

Stanway OE. Place name: "Stony roadway."
Stanaway, Stannaway, Stannway

Stanwick OE. "Dweller at the rocky village."
Stanwicke, Stanwyck

Stanwood OE. Place name: "Stony woods."

Stark Ger. "Strong."
Starck, Starke

Starling Bird name. The starling is a fairly common bird with drab plumage, so the name's appeal may reside in its resemblance to the word "star."

Starr ME. "Star." Beatle Ringo Starr; football player Bart Starr.

Stavros Gk. "Crowned." Related to Stephen, and currently popular in Greece. Greek plutocrat Stavros Niarchos.

Steadman OE. Occupational name: "Farmstead occupant." To some parents, the name will recall Hope and Michael Steadman, characters on the TV series *thirtysomething*. Others will be reminded of sports entrepreneur and Oprah Winfrey love interest Stedman Graham.
Steadmann, Stedman

Steed OE. "Stallion, spirited horse." As in "the hero's trusty steed."

Steel OE. "Like steel." In the rough times when the name was coined, this would have been quite a compliment. TV character Remington Steele.
Steele

Stefan Scand. Var. **Stephen.** Quite widely used in the U.S. by parents who have no Northern European ties whatever. Sometimes variations on a very popular name will become popular themselves, as parents seek something just a little bit different from the hot name of the moment. Tennis star Stefan Edberg; basketball player Stephon Marbury.

Staffan, Stefanos, Steffen, Steffon, Stefonn, Stephonn

Stein Ger. "Stone." Skiing champion Stein Erickson.

Steen, Sten, Steno, Stensen, Stenssen

Steinar ONorse "Stone fighter."

Steinard, Steinart, Steinhardt

Stennis Scottish place name: a spot in the Orkneys, to the north of Scotland, where there are a set of standing stones, a prehistoric monument akin to Stonehenge.

Stephanus Gk. "Garland." Obviously related to Stephen, but a slightly different name. The popular blossom stephanotis (the name in Greek means "fit for a crown") is often used in bridal headpieces.

Stefanas, Stefanos, Stefanus, Stephanas, Stephanos

Stephen Gk. "Crowned." As the name of Christianity's first martyr (Saint Stephen, who was stoned to death), common until the late 18th century. A slow decline was reversed in the middle of the 20th century, and Steven is still going very strong after a long period of great popularity. Though the "ph-" spelling is traditional, the "v-" is much more common. Actors Stephen Collins, Steve Martin, Steve McQueen; songwriter Stephen Foster; physicist Stephen Hawking; author Stephen King; filmmaker Steven Spielberg; musician Stevie Wonder; computer entrepreneur Steven Jobs.

Esteban, Estefan, Estevan, Etienne, Staffan, Steban, Steben, Stefan, Stefano, Steffen, Steffon, Stephan, Stephanus, Stephens, Stephenson, Stephon, Stevan, Steve, Steven, Stevenson, Stevie, Stevy

Stepney OE. Place name: "Stephen's island."

Stepny

Sterling OE. "Genuine, first-rate." As in sterling silver. The derivation is not clear, but might come from stars engraved on early pennies. Since then it has come to refer to either the legal proportion of silver to alloy in sterling silver, or to the British currency, known as pounds sterling. Not common, but has potential for 21st-century popularity. Race-car driver Stirling Moss.

Stirling

Sterne ME. "Stern, unbending"; Ger. "Star." Authors

Laurence Sterne, Thomas Stearns Eliot; violinist Isaac Stern.
Stearn, Stearne, Stearns, Stern

Stetson Probably OE. surname meaning "Stephen's son." It has a certain rakish air, probably conveyed by the associations of the famous Stetson "ten-gallon" hat, worn by cowboys in the late 19th century.
Stetcyn, Stettson

Stewart OE. Occupational name: "Steward." An early variant of Stuart, which finally became the more popular form of the name. It is more common as a first name than many occupational names (Baker, Shepherd, Carpenter), but has never really become a standard first name either. Actor Jimmy Stewart.
Steward, Stuart

Stian ONorse. "Voyager, pilgrim." Used quite often in Scandinavia. Stig, though it sounds quite different, comes from the same source.
Stig, Styg, Stygge

Stiles See Styles.

Stillman OE. "Silent man." This name may also have to do with the process of distillation, or brewing liquor from grain, which is performed in a still. Filmmaker Whit Stillman.

Stockard Probably an Old English place name referring to a tree stump (the "stock-" particle). Used as a first name occasionally.
Stocker, Stockerd

Stockley OE. Place name: "Tree-stump field." Like the stones in the "Stan-" names, tree stumps would be a hindrance to efficient farming, and thus worthy of note and commemoration in last names.

Stockton OE. Place name: "Tree-stump settlement."

Stockwell OE. Place name: "Tree-stump well."

Stoddard OE. "Horse guard" or "Horse herder." Occupational name.
Stoddart

Stone Noun as name. It is a fairly common last name, very occasionally transferred to a first name. The connotations are a little harsh for a child, and might well invite teasing.
Stoner, Stones, Stoney

Storey OE. "Level of a house or building." Transferred last name. Sculptor William Wetmore Story.
Story

Storm OE. "Tempest; storm." The almost too appropriate name of meteorologist Storm Field.

Strahan Ir. Gael. "Minstrel, sage."
Strachan

Stratford OE. Place name: "Street river-crossing."
Strafford

Straus Ger. "Ostrich" or "Bouquet" or "Fight." Strange though it may seem, "ostrich" may be the most usual meaning for this common last name, because long-ago inns or taverns might have been named after an ostrich. Composers Johann and Richard Strauss; retailer Isidor Straus.
Strauss

Strickland OE. Place name: "Flax field."

Strom Ger. Place name: "Stream, brook." Politician Strom Thurmond.

Strong OE. "Powerful." Originally a name that would characterize its bearer. In the last name, the meaning is lost.

Struthers Ir. Gael. Place name: "Near the brook."
Struther

Stuart OE. Occupational name: "Steward." The steward would administer a large feudal household. This was the name of kings of Scotland and England, often considered the most romantic ruling family. (Long curls, a taste for luxury, a reputation for womanizing, and a couple of beheadings all added to the romance.) Most popular in the middle of the 20th century. Though not often used, this form is more popular than Stewart. Portrait painter Gilbert Stuart.
Steward, Stewart

Styles OE. Place name: "Stile." A stile is a set of stairs placed over a wall so it can be crossed easily on foot—an important feature in a rural landscape.
Stiles

Sudbury ME. Place name: "Southern settlement." In this case, unlike Suffield, the French form of "Sud-" has survived.
Sudbery, Sudberry, Sudborough

Suffield OE. Place name: "Southern field."

Suffolk OE. "People from the south." As opposed to Norfolk, people from the north. The name of a region (formerly a county) in England, south of London.

Sujay Hindi. "Good victory."
Sujit

Sulaiman Arab. "Peaceable." The Arabic version of Solomon. The Turkish sultan Suleiman the Magnificent brought civilization in his country to new heights, but contemporaneous Western rulers would never have characterized him as living up to his name.
Suleiman, Suleyman

Sullivan Ir. Gael. "Black-eyed." Composer Arthur Sullivan; TV host Ed Sullivan; architect Louis Sullivan.
Sullavan, Sullevan, Sully

Sully OE. Place name: "South meadow." Painter Thomas Sully.
Sulleigh, Sulley

Suman Hindi. "Clever, wise."

Sumner OE. Occupational name: "One who serves a summons." A medieval legal official. In Geoffrey Chaucer's famous *Canterbury Tales*, a summoner is one of the pilgrims headed to Canterbury. Entrepreneur Sumner Redstone.

Sunil Hindi. "Navy blue."

Sunny Word as name: most likely to be a nickname characterizing a child's temperament, or a respelling of Sonny.
Sunney, Sunnie

Sutcliff OE. Place name: "Southern cliff."
Sutcliffe

Sutherland Scand. "Southern land." Sutherland is the name of a county in northern Scotland, which was nevertheless to the south of the Nordic people who called it that.
Southerland

Sutton OE. Place name: "Southern settlement."

Svatomir Czech. "Renowned and holy."

Svatoslav Czech. "Holy glory." Sometimes these names reveal a great deal about the countries they come from:

in the Slavic languages, the word particle "Slav-" means "glory."

Sven Scand. "Youth." Currently popular in Sweden, but not much used in English-speaking countries.

Svein, Sveinn, Svend, Swain, Swen, Swensen, Swenson

Swahili Arab. "Coast people." Language spoken in much of East Africa.

Swaine OE. Occupational name: "Swineherd." Swine is an old term for pigs. Swain may also be related to Sven, though: the first Danish king of England (1013 A.D.) was named Swain.

Swain, Swayn, Swayne

Swanton OE. Place name: "Swan settlement." Swans were considered a great delicacy in the Middle Ages.

Sweeney Ir. Gael. "Small hero."

Sweeny

Swinburne OE. Place name: "Swine stream." Swine, or pigs, were also an important feature of life in the days when last names were being formed. Poet Algernon Swinburne.

Swinborn, Swinbourne, Swinburn, Swinbyrn, Swynborne

Swinford OE. Place name: "Swine ford."

Swynford

Swinton OE. Place name: "Swine settlement."

Swithin OE. "Quick, strong." Saint's name: Saint Swithin was a 9th-century bishop of Winchester in England, whose feast day, July 15, was a notable fixture on the calendar. It was said that whatever the weather on Saint Swithin's day, it would remain the same for the next forty days. Given England's changeable climate, this is hard to believe.

Swithinn, Swithun

Sylvester Lat. "Wooded." In spite of a distinguished past, the name is now associated with a cartoon cat and an extremely muscular actor, Sylvester Stallone.

Silvester, Sly

Syon Sanskrit. "Happy, fortunate."

FAMOUS INVENTED NAMES

Sometimes it seems that today's parents are awfully quick to invent names for their children. Conservative observers might wonder, "Why not just use a *real* name?" So it can be surprising to learn that many of what we *consider* real names (names that are somewhat familiar) have been made up, too—by some of the top wordsmiths of all time. They appeared in plays or books, and caught on. So the next time somebody objects to your choice because it's too innovative, trot out a couple of the following.

Cora	1826	in James Fenimore Cooper's *The Last of the Mohicans*
Dora	1850	in Charles Dickens' *David Copperfield*
Estelle	1861	in Charles Dickens' *Great Expectations*
Evangeline	1847	in Alfred Lord Tennyson's *Evangeline*
Gloria	1898	in G.B. Shaw's *You Never Can Tell*
Jessica	1595	in Shakespeare's *The Merchant of Venice*
Lorna	1869	in R.D. Blackmore's *Lorna Doone*
Miranda	ca. 1611	in Shakespeare's *The Tempest*
Pamela	1590	in Sir Philip Sidney's *Arcadia*
Thelma	1887	in Marie Corelli's *Thelma*
Vanessa	ca. 1700	in Jonathan Swift's *Cadenus and Vanessa*
Wendy	1904	in J.M. Barrie's *Peter Pan*

Tab Several origins are proposed, including OG. "Shining, brilliant" and ME. "Drummer." But the name would be merely a curiosity without the career of 1950s teen idol Tab Hunter, whose given name was Arthur.

Tabb, Taber, Tabor

Tabasco Place name: a state in southeastern Mexico. Also the name of a fiery pepper condiment. A jaunty choice.

Tabor Hung. "Encampment" or Heb. "Misfortune, bad luck." The name of a mountain in Israel.

Taber, Taibor, Tavor, Taybor, Tayber

Tabib Turkish. "Doctor."

Tabeeb

Tacitus Meaning unclear. The name of a celebrated Roman historian of about 100 A.D.

Tad Dim. **Thaddeus** (meaning unknown). Also Old Welsh. "Father." Also used as a nickname in the U.S., where "tad" is slang for "small," probably from "tadpole."

Tadd, Thad

Tadeo Sp. Var. **Thaddeus** (meaning unknown).

Taddeo, Tadzio

Tadi Native American: Omaha. "Breeze, wind."

Taft Meaning unknown, though some sources offer OE. "Marsh" or "River." William Howard Taft was 26th President of the United States and was also appointed Chief Justice of the Supreme Court after he had retired from politics.

Taggart Ir. Gael. "Son of the priest."

Taggert

Tahir Arab. "Pure, unsullied."

Taheer

Tahoe Native American. "Big water." A remarkably beautiful lake in Nevada and northern California, at some 6,000 feet above sea level. Good choice for the outdoorsy.

Tahoma Navajo. "Coast, edge of the water" or Pacific Northwest Indian, "Snowy mountain peak." The name is familiar in the latter form as the Native American name of the peak later renamed Mount Rainier, and also as the name of a city in Washington state.
Tacoma, Tekoma, Tocoma

Tait ONorse. "Cheerful, gay."
Tate, Tayte

Taj Sanskrit. "Crown." As in the Taj Mahal, the famous pleasure palace/mausoleum built in 17th-century India by Shah Jahan for his favorite wife, Mumtaz Mahal.

Takoda Sioux. "Considered friends." The basis for Dakota.

Tal Heb. "Rain, dew."
Tahl, Talor

Talbot Meaning unknown. An aristocratic last name in England, used as a first name since the 19th century. Tennis star Billy Talbert.
Talbert, Talbott, Talibot, Talbott

Talfryn Welsh. "High hill."
Talfrin, Talfrynn, Tallfryn

Talib Arab. "One who seeks wisdom."
Taleeb

Taliesin Welsh. Meaning unknown, but this was the name of a Welsh poet of around 550 A.D. The name has persisted into our era because architect Frank Lloyd Wright named his two residences Taliesin (in Wisconsin) and Taliesin West (in Arizona).

Tallis OE. Meaning unknown. This was the name of a great 16th-century English composer of church music, Thomas Tallis, some of whose tunes (notably "Tallis's Canon") are still familiar.
Tallys, Talys

Talmai Aramaic. "Hillock, mound."

Talmon Heb. "Oppressed, downtrodden." An Old Testament name.

Talon Noun as a name: the large claw of a bird of prey such as a hawk or an eagle. This name's meaning is probably less important than its sound, though, in recommending it to parents.
Talen, Talin, Tallan, Tallen, Tallin, Tallon

Tamarack Nature name: a common name for a tree also known as a larch.

Tamarisk Nature name: small shrubby flowering tree that flourishes in a great range of climates.

Tamerlane Possibly "Timur the Lame." This was the name of a Mongol warrior descended from Genghis Khan, who, like his ancestor, conquered huge tracts of Asia from Russia to India. His tale was retold by 16th-century English poet Christoper Marlowe as a romantic tragedy. Edgar Allan Poe also wrote about Tamerlane in an early poem.
Tamarlain, Tamarlayn, Tamberlain, Tamberlaine, Tamberlane, Tamburlaine, Tamburlane, Tamurlaine, Tamurlayn

Tamir Heb. "Erect, tall." or Arab. "One who owns many palm trees." Related to the girl's name Tamar, which means "Date palm."

Tammany Native American: Delaware. "Friendly, cheerful." The name of a Native American chief who was friendly to William Penn. After the American Revolution "Tammany Societies" sprang up. They were patriotic and social in nature at first, but by 1850 the members of New York's Tammany Society controlled New York politics.

Tamson OE. "Son of Thomas." The girl's forms, **Tamsin** and **Thomasina**, is more common, but still scarce.
Tamsen

Tancred OG. "Well-considered counsel or advice." Tancred was a Norman crusader who played a prominent part in the First Crusade, at the end of the 11th century. An epic poem by Tasso (*Gerusalemme Liberato*) and operas by Rossini and Monteverdi were based on his story and keep the name alive today, especially in Italy.
Tancredi, Tancredo

Tandie Modern name, possibly derived from a Scottish nickname for Andrew or from the Zulu name Thandiwe (see below). It may also be adapted from the name of an Irish patriot, James Napper Tandy, whose exploits are immortalized in the ballad "The Wearing of the Green."
Tandey, Tandy

Tanner OE. Occupational name: "Leather tanner." Hides need to be tanned (treated with a substance containing tannin) before they become leather. Use as a first name is increasing beyond the stage of a transferred last name. Artist Henry Ossawa Tanner.

Tan, Tanier, Tannen, Tanney, Tannie, Tannis, Tannon

Tannon Invented name, possibly based on Tanner or on Shannon, or on the German word for "fir tree," *tanne* (as in the famous Christmas carol "O Tannenbaum").

Tannan, Tannen, Tannin, Tansen, Tanson

Tanton OE. Place name: "Still river settlement."

Taos Place name: city and county in New Mexico. Located at 7,000 feet above sea level, it has long attracted artists for the quality of the light. There are also a famous Indian pueblo and a ski resort in Taos. Very hip.

Tarik Arab. "The one who knocks to enter."

Tareek, Tariq

Tarleton OE. "Thor's settlement." Margaret Mitchell fans will remember the Tarleton twins, admirers of Scarlett O'Hara, in the early pages of *Gone With the Wind*.

Tarquin Roman clan name of uncertain meaning. The Tarquins were early Etruscan kings of Rome, dating from around the 5th century B.C. The son of the last king was the perpetrator of the famous Rape of Lucretia, the Roman matron who killed herself rather than live with the shame. This unlovely episode led to the dethronement of the Tarquins and the installation of elected consuls to rule Rome instead. It has also been turned into poetry and drama in many languages.

Tarquinius, Tarquino

Tarrant Old Welsh. "Thunder."

Tarrent

Tarun Sanskrit. "Youthful."

Taroon, Taroun

Tasso It. "Cup." The name of a great Italian epic poet of the 16th century, Torquato Tasso.

Tate ME. "Happy, cheerful." Related to Norwegian Tait.

Tait, Taitt, Tayte

Tau Tswana (from Botswana). "Lion."

Taurus Lat. "Bull." Sign of the zodiac; the sun enters Taurus on April 20. Taurus is also the name of a constellation.

Tavaris Modern name, meaning and derivation unclear. The use of the name, which is showing up on some national lists at the same level as older names like Owen and Ralph, may be inspired by a 1970s band called Ta-vares. The band may have taken its name in turn from a town in Central Florida. Another possible source is a Spanish last name that may mean "Hermit's place."

Tavaress, Tavarious, Tavariss, Tavarous, Tevarus

Taverner OE. Occupational name: "Tavern-keeper."

Tavener, Tavenner, Tavernier

Tavi Aramaic. "Good."

Tavee

Tavish Ir. Gael. "Twin."

Tavis, Tevis

Tay Scottish place name: the largest river in Scotland, re-nowned for salmon fishing.

Taylor ME. Occupational name: "Tailor." Twelfth U.S. President Zachary Taylor served only one year of his term and died of typhus in 1850. Like many occupational names, this was first used as a given name in the 19th century. It has recently become much more popular, and though it is streaking up the charts as a girls' name, it is also still well used for boys. Film director Taylor Hack-ford; football player Lawrence Taylor; singers James and Livingston Taylor.

Tailer, Tailor, Tayler

Tayton Modern name, possibly a variant on Taylor or Pey-ton.

Tayten, Taytin, Teytan, Teyten, Teytin, Teyton

Taz Modern name. Probably promoted by the use of Chaz, and possibly also by a cartoon character, the Tasmanian Devil, known as Taz. The country of Tasmania was named for 17th-century Dutch explorer Abel Tasman, who discovered it.

Tasman, Tazman, Tazz

Teague Ir. Gael. "Bard, poet." This name and its variants are experiencing a little flicker of popularity among par-ents who want to be adventurous in their choice of names.

Teagan, Tegan, Teger, Teigan, Teige, Teigen, Teigue

Tecumseh Native American: Shawnee. "Traveling, mov-ing." Tecumseh was a prominent Shawnee chief of the 18th and 19th centuries who tried to unite various tribes to negotiate with the U.S. government. His name appeared again as the middle name of Union Army General William Tecumseh Sherman.

Ted Dim. **Theodore** (Gk. "Gift of God") or Edward (OE. "Wealthy defender"). Rarely used as an independent name. Parents tend to give the longer rather than the shorter version of a name, even if they have decided ahead of time to use the diminutive form. Newscaster Ted Koppel; actor Ted Danson.
Tedd, Teddey, Teddie, Teddy

Tedmund OE. "Protector of the land."
Tedmond

Teilo Welsh. Meaning unknown. The name of a prominent Welsh saint of the 6th century. There is a cathedral named after him (and three other saints) in the Welsh town of Llandaff.

Telford OF. "Iron-piercer."
Telfer, Telfor, Telfour, Tellfer, Tellfour

Temani Heb. "From the south." This is the Hebrew term for someone from Yemen, which is south of Israel. The word literally means "on the right side," which is, of course, to the south when you are facing east. Old Testament name.
Teman, Temeni

Tempest Fr. "Storm." Occurs as an aristocratic English last name, and occasionally as a first name, though few parents could wish for a baby's personality to fit the name.
Tempestt

Temple Lat. "Sacred place." Probably a place name transferred to first name.
Templar, Templer

Templeton OE. Place name: "Temple settlement." Also the name of the rat in *Charlotte's Web*, a point that the young are sure to seize on.
Temp, Temple, Templeten

Tempo It. "Time." In musical terms, how fast a piece of music is supposed to be performed.

Tennant OE. "Tenant, renter." Last name used as first name.
Tenant, Tennent

Tennessee Cherokee place name, used for the state. Made famous by playwright Tennessee Williams (whose given name was Thomas) and likely to be used by parents in homage, or perhaps in nostalgia for a childhood home.

Tennyson ME. "Son of Dennis." Used by 19th-century parents in homage to British Poet Laureate Alfred, Lord Tennyson.
Tenny

Teom Heb. "Twin." The basis of the name Thomas.

Terach Heb. "Old fool" or "Wild goat." A Biblical name: the father of Abraham.
Terah

Terence Lat. Clan name of unknown meaning, though some sources propose "Smooth" or "Polished." Early Christian name that was never widely adopted until the late 19th century, and even then did not become a standard choice. The most common spelling today is Terrance. Actor Terence Stamp; playwright Terence McNally; priest Terence Cardinal Cooke.
Tarrants, Tarrance, Tarrenz, Terance, Terencio, Terrance, Terrence, Terrey, Terri, Terris, Terrious, Terrius, Terron, Terronce, Terry

Tern Nature name: a marine bird smaller than a seagull. The Arctic tern migrates 11,000 miles twice yearly, from the Arctic to Antarctica and back. Clearly a creature with tremendous stamina.

Terrill OG. "Following Thor." Thor, the god of thunder, was a crucial figure in Norse mythology. The son of the chief god, Odin, Thor was the benevolent intercessor for mankind. His name is an element in many names that have come down to us, the most notable being "Thursday." Parents may think of this name as a variant of Terence, though it hardly matters. Football player Terrell Davis.
Tarrall, Terrall, Terrel, Terrell, Terryal, Terryl, Terryll, Tirrell, Tyrrell

Terron Modern name. Possibly a respelling of Darren, or a variation of Terence. Spellings are almost infinite in number.
Taran, Tarin, Taron, Tarran, Tarren, Tarrin, Tarron, Tarryn, Teran, Teron, Terrin, Terryn, Teryn

Terry Dim. **Terence.** Used for both boys and girls, almost as frequently as Terence itself. Football player Terry Bradshaw.

Terrey, Terri, Terrie

Teton Western American place name: a river and, more famously, a range of mountains on the border between Idaho and Wyoming. Grand Teton National Park is a favorite destination for hikers and climbers.

Tevon Modern name, Kevin or Devon with a "T-."

Tevan, Teven, Tevin, Tevinn, Tevonn

Tex Modern name of the Lone Star state, used occasionally as a first name. It has a rakish aura, no doubt from association with cowboys and the Wild West.

Thaddeus Aramaic. Meaning unclear, though "courageous" and "praise" have been suggested. Thaddeus was one of the more obscure of the twelve apostles, but even this distinction has not popularized the name. Jude is another form of the name.

Tad, Tadd, Taddeo, Taddeusz, Tadeo, Tadio, Tadzio, Thad, Thaddaeus, Thaddaios, Thaddaos, Thaddaus, Thadeus, Thady

Thandiwe Zulu. "Loved one."

Tandie, Tandy, Thandey, Thandie, Thandy

Thane OE. "Landholder." In Old England a thane fit, socially, between the serfs and the nobility. He held his own land, but owed service to his lord. Rare even as a last name.

Thaine, Thayne

Thatcher OE. Occupational name: "Roof thatcher." Soon this name will be free of any associations with British Prime Minister Margaret Thatcher. It will be interesting to see if it is taken up by parents as other occupational names (Hunter, Taylor, Tanner) have been.

Thacher, Thatch, Thaxter

Thaw OE. "Melt." Found more often as a last name.

Thayer Old English name of uncertain meaning: may be related to Thatcher.

Theobald OG. "Courageous people." Unusual, though some of its foreign variants like Thibault are more common in their countries of origin. Tybalt, another version of the name, is an important character in Shakespeare's *Romeo and Juliet*.

...ld, Dietbold, Ted, Teddy, Teobaldo, Thebault, ...Thibaud, Thibault, Thibaut, Tibold, Tiebold, Tiebout, Tybald, Tybalt, Tybault

Theodore Gk. "Gift of God." Early Christian name and saint's name, but only mildly popular until President Theodore Roosevelt brought it to prominence. (The teddy bear, of course, is named for him.) The name is now neither popular nor unpopular; a good choice for parents who want an unusual but not fashionable name. Authors Theodore Dreiser, Theodore Sturgeon; painter Théodore Rousseau.

Fedor, Feodor, Fyodor, Teador, Ted, Teddie, Teddy, Tedor, Teodoor, Teodor, Teodoro, Theo, Theodor, Theodorus, Theodosios, Theodosius, Todor, Tudor

Theodoric OG. "People's ruler." This is the original form of Dietrich and the more common Derek or Dirk. In this version it is extremely rare.

Derek, Derrick, Dieter, Dietrich, Dirck, Dirk, Rick, Ted, Teodorico, Thedric, Thedrick

Theophilus Gk. "Loved by God." A New Testament name that is very rare, though Thornton Wilder entitled one of his most popular novels *Theophilus North*. French author Théophile Gautier.

Teofil, Teofilo, Théophile

Theron Possibly derived from a Greek word meaning "hunter," but just as likely this is a modern name combining the popular "-on" ending with unusual "Ther-."
Tharon

Theseus Gk. Myth. name: the young hero who slew the Cretan Minotaur, among many other exploits. He was the son of King Aegeus, for whom the Aegean Sea around Greece is named. He figures in several of the classic Greek tragedies as well as in Chaucer's *Canterbury Tales* and Shakespeare's *A Midsummer Night's Dream*.

Thierry Fr. Var. **Theodoric**. Not, as one might suppose, the French version of Terry. Fashion designer Thierry Mugler.

Thomas Aramaic. "Twin." One of the apostles, known as Doubting Thomas because he refused to recognize the risen Christ unless he could see and feel the marks of the crucifixion. In spite of this skeptical example, the name has been hugely popular since the 12th-century martyr-dom of Thomas à Becket. Other Saints Thomas include Thomas Aquinas and Thomas More, but the name has been so widely used that it has no religious aura. The recent vogue for unusual names has somewhat eclipsed this old standard, but it is still one of the basic names for boys born in America. President Thomas Jefferson; inventor Thomas Edison; actors Tom Cruise, Tom Hanks; dancer Tommy Tune.

Tam, Tamas, Tamhas, Thom, Thoma, Thomason, Thomson, Thompson, Tom, Tomas, Tomaso, Tomasso, Tomasz, Tome, Tomek, Tomey, Tomie, Tomislaw, Tomkin, Tomlin, Tommaso, Tommey, Tommie, Tommy

Thor ONorse. ''Thunder.'' The Norse god of thunder, Thor, holds an important place in the Norse pantheon, but in the Anglo-Saxon world the name appears more often in derivative forms, as in Terrill. Explorer Thor Heyerdahl.

Thorin, Thorvald, Tor, Tore, Torre, Tyrus

Thorald ONorse. ''Follower of Thor.''

Terrell, Terrill, Thorold, Torald, Tyrell

Thorbert ONorse. ''Thor's brightness.''

Torbert

Thorburn ONorse. ''Thor's bear.''

Thorbern, Thorbjorn

Thoreau Possibly a Frenchified version of Thorald, but parents using this name would be invoking the 19th-century naturalist and author of *Walden*, Henry David Thoreau.

Thorley OE. Place name: ''Thor's meadow'' or ''Thorn meadow.''

Thorlea, Thorlee, Thorleigh, Thorly, Torley

Thormond OE. ''Defended by Thor.'' Senator Strom Thurmond.

Thurman, Thurmond, Thurmund

Thorndike OE. Place name: ''Thorny bank.''

Thorndyck, Thorndyke

Thorne OE. Place name: ''Thorn thicket.''

Thorn

Thornley OE. Place name: ''Thorny meadow.''

Thornlea, Thornleigh, Thornly

Thornton OE. Place name: ''Thorny village or town.''

Used as a first name since the 19th century. Writer Thornton Wilder.

Thornycroft OE. Place name: "Thorny field." "Croft" is an old British term for a small farm of five to ten acres, usually cultivated by a tenant farmer.
Thorneycroft

Thorpe OE. Place name: "Hamlet, village." Athlete Jim Thorpe.
Thorp

Thurgood Puritan virtue name. Supreme Court Justice Thurgood Marshall's name was probably originally "Thoroughgood," quite a mouthful and a lot to live up to.

Thurlow OE. Place name: "Thor's hill."
Thurloe

Thurman ONorse. "Defended by Thor." Probably the most common variant of **Thormond**. Baseball player Thurman Munson.
Thurmon

Thurston Scand. "Thor's stone." Parents who watched a lot of TV in the 1960s might shy away from a name that recalled Thurston Howell, the effete millionaire castaway on *Gilligan's Island*. Social critic Thorstein Veblen.
Thorstan, Thorstein, Thorsten, Thurstain, Thurstan, Thursten, Torsten, Torston

Tibor Slavic. "Sacred place."

Tiburon Sp. "Shark." California place name: a town on San Francisco Bay where presumably someone once saw a you-know-what in the water.

Tiernan Ir. Gael. "Lord."
Tiarnan, Tiarney, Tierney

Tiger Nature name. Given immense exposure recently by young golf phenomenon Tiger Woods, whose given name is actually Eldrick (see **Eldridge**).
Tige, Tigre, Tigris

Tilden OE. Place name: "Fertile valley." Statesman Samuel Tilden; tennis champion William Tilden.
Tillden, Tildon

Tilford OE. Place name: "Fertile ford."

Tillman OE. Occupational name: "One who plows the earth." Tilling the soil meant turning and lightening it before it was planted. An important process in an agricultural economy.

Tilghman, Tilman

Tilton OE. Place name: "Fertile estate." All of these "Til-" names were last names, used occasionally as first names starting in the 19th century.

Till Ger. "People's ruler." Another form of Theodoric, vaguely familiar to American ears from the German legends about Till Eulenspiegel, inspiration for an opera by Richard Strauss.

Thilo, Tillman, Tilmann

Timon Greek name of uncertain meaning. Shakespeare wrote a play, *Timon of Athens*, about a misanthropic Greek of the 4th century B.C., but most parents are more likely to be familiar with the meerkat Timon from Disney's movie of *The Lion King*.

Timothy Gk. "Honoring God." New Testament name, correspondent with Saint Paul. Scanty use until the 18th century, then increased gradually to the middle of the 20th. After a baby boom peak, it has faded to steady but unspectacular use. Radical thinker Timothy Leary; actors Timothy Hutton, Tim Allen.

Tim, Timmo, Timmy, Timmothy, Timo, Timofei, Timofeo, Timofey, Timon, Timoteo, Timothé, Timotheo, Timothey, Timotheus, Tymmothy, Tymon, Tymoteusz, Tymothy

Tino Sp. Dim. **Agostino** and other "-tin" names. Baseball player Tino Martinez.

Teeno, Teino, Tyno

Tipu Hindi. "Tiger."

Tippoo

Titus Lat. Unknown meaning. New Testament character. Use is mostly 18th and 19th centuries. Has nothing to do, in spite of its sound, with titans or giants.

Tito, Titos

Tobias Heb. "The Lord is good." Old Testament name that faded after the Puritans used it, and was revived in the 19th century. The diminutive, **Toby**, is slightly more common now, though still very unusual. Author Tobias Wolff.

Thobey, Thobie, Thoby, Tobe, Tobee, Tobey, Tobi, Tobia, Tobiah, Tobie, Tobin, Tobit, Toby, Tobyn

Toby Dim. **Tobias**.

Thobey, Thobie, Thoby, Tobe, Tobee, Tobey, Tobi, Tobie

Todd ME. "Fox." Used mostly in this century, and fashionable for a spell in the 1970s. Still quite steadily used; much more popular that Tobias, for instance.
Tod

Todhunter OE. Occupational name: "Foxhunter." Ralph Lauren should know about this name!

Togo Place name: a country on the Gulf of Guinea in western Africa, between Benin and Ghana.

Tom Dim. **Thomas**. Most common in the 19th century as an independent name.
Thom, Tomm, Tommy

Tomlin OE. "Little Tom."
Tomalin, Tomlinson

Tommy Dim. **Thomas** (Aramaic. "Twin"). Given with some regularity as a first name. Baseball player Tommy John.

Tompkins OE. "Little Thomas."
Tompkinson

Tony Dim. **Anthony** (Lat. "Beyond price"). Used independently only since the middle of the 20th century. Actors Tony Curtis, Tony Danza.
Toney, Tonie

Tor Nor. "Thunder." Var. **Thor**. Also, Hebrew for "Turtledove."
Thor

Torger ONorse. "Thor's spear."

Toril Hindi. "Character, temperament."

Torquil ONorse. "Thor's kettle." Refers to a cauldron used in sacrifice. Used in Scandinavian countries and a tiny bit in Britain.
Thirkell, Thorkel, Torkel, Torkel, Torkill

Torr OE. Place name: "Tower."
Tor

Torrance Ir. Gael. Place name: "Little hills."
Tore, Torin, Torr, Torrence, Torrens, Torrey, Torrin, Torry

Torrey ONorse. "Thor." With this spelling, a boy's name, though the same name spelled Tori is a girl's name derived from Victoria.

Toussaint Fr. "All saints." Used with some frequency in

Haiti, in honor of Haitian leader Toussaint L'Ouverture, a former slave who helped Haiti gain independence from France in the early 19th century. Also appropriate for babies born on November 1, All Saints' Day.

Tower OE. Place name. While nature names, even those of fierce animals or mountain peaks, are used as children's names, architectural features somehow seem a little too inanimate to be appropriate. Yet as a transferred last name, Tower may make sense.
Towers

Townley OE. Place name: "Town meadow."
Townlea, Townlee, Townleigh, Townlie, Townly

Townsend OE. Place name: "End of town."
Townshend

Trace Possibly the noun as name, equally possibly a variation of Tracy.

Tracy OF. Place name. Almost always a girl's name now.
Trace, Tracey, Treacy

Trahern Welsh. "Strength of iron."
Trahearn, Trahearne, Traherne

Trail Noun as name. Connotations of the outdoors, nature, mountains, and general ruggedness.
Traill

Traugott Ger. "Faith in God."

Travis OF. Occupational name: "Toll taker." Most common in the U.S., and quite steadily used without being trendy. Fictional detective Travis Magee.
Traver, Travers, Traviss, Travys

Tremain Celt. Place name: "Stone house." Popular among African-American families.
Tramain, Tramaine, Tramayne, Tremaine, Tremayne

Tremont Fr. Place name: "Three mountains."

Trent Lat. "Gushing waters." Name of an important river in England, thus a place name. U.S. Senator Trent Lott.
Trenten, Trentin, Trenton

Trenton OE. Place name. "Trent's town." Or an elaboration of Trent, with the fashionable "-on" ending. Probably not used much around Trenton, New Jersey.
Trenten, Trentin

Trevor Welsh. "Large homestead." Use expanded outside of Wales in the mid-Victorian era, but the name was most popular in the middle of the 20th century. Actor Trevor Howard.

Trefor, Trevar, Trever

Trey ME. "Three." Related to the French *trois* for "three." Very unusual. Actor Trey Hunt.

Trai, Traye, Tre

Tristan Welsh. The name's Welsh meaning is unclear, but since *triste* is French for "sad," that explanation is often given. Tristan, in medieval legends, is the knight who is in love with Isolde, wife of his uncle. The tale has been told in many forms, including an epic poem by Tennyson and an opera by Wagner.

Tris, Tristam, Tristram

Trowbridge OE. Place name: "Bridge by the tree."

Troy Ir. Gael. "Foot-soldier." The name of the famous Greek city where the Trojan wars were fought, and a fairly common place name in America (as in Troy, NY). Actor Troy Donahue may have been behind the name's surge of popularity in the 1960s and 1970s. Jane Fonda named one of her children Troy. Football player Troy Aikman.

Troi, Troye

True OE. "True." May be used for its emotional qualities.

Truesdale OE. Place name: "Honest man's valley."

Truman OE. "Loyal one." Unusual as a last name or a first name, in spite of the greatly admired author Truman Capote or U.S. President Harry S Truman.

Trueman, Trumaine, Trumann

Trumble OE. "Powerful."

Trumball, Trumbell, Trumbo, Trumbull

Tucker OE. Occupational name: "Fabric pleater." Another occupational name relating to one of medieval Britain's principal industries, the woolen trade.

Tuck, Tuckerman

Tudor Welsh. Var. **Theodore** (Gk. "Gift of God"). Famous as the name of the English dynasty of kings.

Tully Ir. Gael. "Mighty people."

Tulley, Tullie, Tullis

Tune English. "A melody." Dancer Tommy Tune.

Tupper OE. "Ram, male sheep." Tupper Lake is a resort in the Adirondack Mountains.

Turbo Lat. "Spinning object." Usually used to indicate the presence of a turbine engine in combination with something else, as in a turbopropellor. Connotations are of speed and great energy, making this a likely nickname for an extremely energetic child.

Turk English. "From Turkey."
Turck

Turner ME. Occupational name: "Wood-worker." "Turning" referred to use of a lathe, which provided the decorative elements on much furniture in the 16th and 17th centuries. Painter J. M. W. Turner.

Tuvyah Heb. "Goodness of the Lord." Related to Tobias, Toby, etc.
Tov, Toviach, Tovyah, Toviah, Tuviyahu

Twain ME. "Divided in two." The most famous bearer of this name, the American writer Mark Twain, took it from the calls of rivermen. His original name was Samuel Clemens.
Twaine, Twayn

Twyford OE. Place name: "Double river crossing."

Ty Diminutive or variant of the "Ty-" names below. Given credibility by child TV star Zachery Ty Bryan. Baseball player Ty Cobb.

Tychon Gk. "Accurate."

Tyler OE. Occupational name: "Maker of tiles." The name of one of the country's less memorable presidents (John Tyler, 1841–1845). Still, the name rocketed up popularity charts in the late 1990s, with no clear prompting from popular culture. It seems likely that thousands and thousands of parents just like the way it sounds.
Tilar, Ty, Tylar, Tylor

Tynan Ir. Gael. "Dark, dusky."
Tienan, Tynell, Tynen, Tynin, Tynnen, Tynnin, Tynon

Typhoon Chinese. "Great wind." The name of the tropical storms of the Asian coasts. Not predictive of a toddler's behavior, with any luck.

Tyquan Modern name composed of two fashionable elements.
Tyquahn, Tyquann, Tyquohn, Tyquonne

Tyr Ancient Norse god, the bravest and boldest of a warlike bunch.

Tyree Modern name. Possibly an elaboration of the fashionable "Ty-" sounds.

Tyrell Modern name. Could be related to Terrell, or may be another elaboration of "Ty-." The "-el" ending is fashionable with African-American families.
Tirell, Tyrel, Tyrrel, Tyrrell

Tyrone Ir. Gael. "Land of Owen." Given prominence almost entirely by the actors Tyrone Power, Sr. and Jr., around the middle of the 20th century. Football player Tyrone Wheatley.
Tirone, Tirohn, Tirown, Tyron

Tyson OF. Meaning unclear, though "spark, firebrand" has been suggested. Parents in the late 1980s may have used it in admiration of the boxing star Mike Tyson.
Thyssen, Tiesen, Tycen, Tyssen

Ubadah Arab. "Serves God."

Uberto It. Var. **Hubert** (OG. "Bright or shining intellect").

Udayan Hindi. "Rising, showing up."

Udi Heb. "My torch, burning stick."

Udell OE. Place name: "Valley of yew trees." Arizona politician Morris Udall.
Dell, Eudel, Udel, Udall, Yudale, Yudell

Udo Dim. **Ulric**.

Udolf OE. "Wolf-wealth."
Udolfo, Udolph

Ugo It. Var. **Hugh** (OG. "Mind, intellect").

Ukiah NAm Ind. "Deep valley." Place name: a town in Mendocino County in Northern California.

Ulf OG. "Wolf." Currently very popular in Sweden.

Ulick Ir. Gael. "Little Willliam." This is the anglicized version: the Gaelic, very hard for English-speakers to pronounce or spell, is Uilleog.

Ull ONorse. "Glory." One of the gods in the ancient Norse pantheon, whose special responsibility was winter. He was thought to created the aurora borealis, the northern lights.

Ulmer OE. "Fame of the wolf."
Ullmar, Ulmar

Ulric OG. "Power of the wolf " or "Power of the home."
Used in Britain before the Norman invasion, but barely
known in the last 900-odd years. Actor Skeet Ulrich.
Rick, Udo, Ullric, Ulrich, Ulrick, Ulrik

Ulysses Lat. Var. **Odysseus**, which may mean "wrathful."
American use was spurred by the presidency of Civil War
hero Ulysses S. Grant. Now rare.
Ulises, Ulisse

Umar Arab. "Prospering, thriving." A popular name in the
Arab world. In the U.S., as Omar, it is quite steadily used.
Omar, Omer, Umer

Umber Fr. "Shade." A brown mineral-derived pigment that
is a staple of the artist's palette. The word "umbrella"
comes from the same source.
Umbro

Umberto It. Var. **Humbert** (OG. "Renowned Hun"). A
royal name in Italy, though very scarce in English-
speaking countries. Author Umberto Eco.

Umed Hindi. "Desire, goal."

Umi African. (Yao.) "Life."
Umee

Uncas NAm Ind. (Mohegan.) "The fox." In James Fenimore Cooper's novel *The Last of the Mohicans*, Uncas is
the noble Mohican who rescues and falls in love with
Englishwoman Cora Munro. In the filmed version it is
Hawkeye, the Englishman raised by the Indians (and
played by heartthrob Daniel Day-Lewis) who gets the girl
and Uncas is demoted to sidekick.

Unwin OE. "Nonfriend."
Unwinn, Unwyn

Updike OE. Place name: "Upper bank." Author John Updike.
Updyke

Upshaw OE. Place name: "Upper thicket."

Upton OE. Place name: "Upper settlement." Mostly last-
name use. Author Upton Sinclair.

Upwood OE. Place name: "Upper forest."

Urban Lat. "From the city." We have a modern word,
"urbane," from the same root. Apparently in ancient

times city-dwellers had better manners than their rural contemporaries. Though the name was used by eight popes, it is scarce today in English-speaking countries.

Urbain, Urbaine, Urbane, Urbano, Urbanus

Uri Heb. "My light, my flame." Related to Uriah and Uriel.

Uriah Heb. "The Lord is my light." Prominent Old Testament name at its most popular in the 19th century, though literary parents will be reminded of the smarmy, hand-wringing Uriah Heep in Charles Dickens's *David Copperfield*. Dickens may have killed off the name, in fact; it is very scarce today.

Uri, Uria, Urias, Urija, Urijah, Urioh, Uriyah, Yuri, Yuria

Uriel Heb. "Flame of God." The Muslim version of the name is Israfil; he is the Muslim angel of music and appears in the Koran along with Gabriel and Michael. In Christian terms he is one of seven named archangels.

Usamah Arab. "Like a lion."

Urso It. "Bear."

Ursel, Ursino, Ursins, Ursinus

Usher Lat. "River mouth." By extension, a door-keeper. This is also an anglicization of an Irish place name that occurs occasionally as Ussery or Ossory.

Ussher

Uther Ancient English name of uncertain meaning. In legend, Uther Pendragon was the father of King Arthur.

Uziah Heb. "The Lord is my strength." Old Testament name: a King of Judah around 700 years before Christ. He was on the throne when Isaiah was prophesying.

Uzziah

Uziel Heb. "Strength, power."

Uzziah, Uzziel

Vachel OF. "Small cow." Something of a curiosity, brought to public notice by the poet Vachel Lindsay.
Vachell

Vail OE. Place name: "Valley." Famous now as a ski resort in Colorado. Generally a transferred last name.
Bail, Bale, Vaile, Vaill, Vale

Val Dim. Valentine. Perhaps because Valerie was such a popular name a number of years ago, Val still seems more like a girl's name, despite the fame and macho appeal of actor Val Kilmer.

Valdemar OG. "Renowned leader." A royal name in early Denmark.
Waldemar

Valentine Lat. "Strong." This name and Valerian come from the same root. Valentine is used for both boys and girls, although the early Christian martyr for whom the holiday is named was male. It seems likely that the hearts-and-flowers observations of this day actually belonged to a pagan feast day celebrating spring and fertility and all that stuff. Canny early churchmen probably combined the two feasts. Saint Valentine himself had nothing to do with romantic love.
Val, Valentijn, Valentin, Valentinian, Valentino, Valentinus, Valentyn

Valerian Lat. "Strong, healthy." Far less common than the feminine version, Valerie. Designer Valerian Rybar.
Valerien, Valerio, Valerius, Valery, Valeryan

Vali Old Norse mythology name; another warlike son of Odin.

Van Dutch. "Of." A particle of many Dutch names, as in Vandyke. Also possibly a nickname for Evan. Originally may have been used as a nickname for children with transferred Dutch last names, but it became generally popular ın the middle of the 20th century. Neglected now. Pianist Van Cliburn; actor Van Johnson.

Vann, Von, Vonn

Vance OE. Place name: "Marshland." Author Vance Packard; diplomat Cyrus Vance.

Vandan Hindi. "Salvation."

Vander Possibly a particle of a Dutch place name meaning "from the," as in Van der Meer or Van der Velt. Also possibly a shortening of Evander (Gk. "Good man"). An unusual name with a certain individualistic air.

Vandyke Dutch. Place name: "Of the dyke." The New York area was originally settled by Dutch colonists, and a few Dutch names survive, though not many are used as first names. A "vandyke" is also the name of a small beard or goatee, from the beards portrayed in portraits by the 17th-century Flemish painter Anthony Van Dyck. Actor Dick Van Dyke.

Vane OE. "Banner." A device usually attached to a mast or flagpole to indicate the direction of the wind. An aristocratic family name in England.

Vanya Rus. Dim. **John** (Heb. "The Lord is gracious") via Ivan. Rare outside of Russia.

Vardon OF. Place name: "Green knoll." The second half of the name comes from the French word that gives us "dune."

Varden, Verdon, Verdun

Varick OG. "Leader who defends."

Varrick, Warick, Warrick

Varun Hindi. "Water god."

Varoun

Vasilis Gk. "Royal, kingly." More familiar in its anglicized form, Basil.

Vasileios, Vasilij, Vasily, Vaso, Vasos, Vassilij, Vassily, Vasya, Wassily

Vaughn Welsh. "Small." Appeared as a first name at the turn of the 20th century, at its peak popularity in the baby boom era. Never especially common, though. Actor Robert Vaughn; composer Ralph Vaughan Williams.

Vaughan

Veltry Modern name, coined for euphony.

Venezio It. "Venice." The feminine forms like **Venetia** are more common, though still rare.

Venetziano, Veneziano

Venturo Sp. "Good fortune, good luck."
   Venturio
Vere Fr. Place name of unknown meaning. It was an upper-class last name in England, and took on near-caricature connotations of nobility, especially after Tennyson published "Lady Clara Vere de Vere," a poem praising the simple values of simple folk. (It contains the famous line "Kind hearts are more than coronets.") Vere has not been used much in the self-consciously democratic U.S.
Verlyn Modern name. Derivation not entirely clear. It may depend on Vernon, or else on the syllable "Ver-," which is often taken to mean "green." As with most modern names, the sound seems to be more important to parents than the meaning.
   Verle, Verlin, Verllin, Verlon, Verlyn, Virle, Vyrle
Vermont Fr. "Green mountain." Mountainous New England state, much loved by skiers and hikers for the recreational opportunities it provides. Author Vermont Royster.
Vernon OF. Place name: "Alder grove." A Norman name that took root as an English last name and, by the 19th century, a first name. Statesman Vernon Jordan.
   Lavern, Vern, Vernal, Verne, Vernen, Vernin, Verney
Verrier French. Occupational name: "Glassblower." Or possibly a variation on Farrier, which means "blacksmith."
Verrill OF. "Loyal" or OG. "Masculine."
   Verill, Verrall, Verrell, Verroll, Veryl
Vester Dim. **Sylvester** (Lat. "Wooded").
Vesuvio Italian place name: a large, active volcano near Naples.
Victor Lat. "Conqueror." Extremely common in Christian Rome, as was its female form, Victoria. Revived during the reign of Queen Victoria, but not extremely popular (except among her numerous descendants and godchildren). It was used most during the baby boom era, but not very widely. Cinematographer Vittorio Storaro; actor Victor Mature; author Victor Hugo.
   Vic, Vick, Victorien, Victorin, Vidor, Viktor, Vitorio, Vittorio, Vittorios
Vidal Sp. from Latin "Vigorous, lively." Related to Vito.

Author Gore Vidal; hairdresser Vidal Sassoon.
Bidal, Videl, Videlio

Vidar ONorse. Myth. name: a son of Odin, immensely strong, who did not speak.

Vijay Sanskrit. "Victory."
Bijay, Vijun

Villard Nineteenth-century invented name. Henry Hilgard of Bavaria changed his name to Villard when he came to the U.S. Since he later became a financier and railroad magnate, it has some connotations of wealth and grandeur, especially in New York, where he lived. Perhaps he chose this name with those aspirations in mind.

Villiers Fr. "Town-dweller." Aristocratic Franco-English name.

Vilmos Hung. "Determined fighter."

Vincent Lat. "Conquering." From the same root as Victor, but used much more steadily since early Christian days. It has not suffered neglect, but neither has it ever been truly popular. Saint Vincent de Paul, a 17th-century priest, founded an order of missionary brothers, and the Saint Vincent de Paul Society, an international charitable organization, was founded in his honor in the 19th century. Painter Vincent Van Gogh; film director Vincente Minnelli; actor Vincent Gardenia; football coach Vince Lombardi.
Vicente, Vicenzio, Vincenzo, Vin, Vince, Vincens, Vincentius, Vincents, Vincenty, Vincenz, Vincenzio, Vincenzo, Vincien, Vinicent, Vinnie, Vinny, Vinzenz, Wincenty

Vine OE. Occupational name: "Vineyard worker."

Vinson OE. "Son of Vincent."

Vinton OE. Place name: "Vine settlement" or "Vincent's settlement."

Vireo Nature name: a small, migratory, insect-eating bird with green plumage and a melodious song.

Virgil Lat. Clan name: possibly meaning "Staff bearer." (The staff would have been part of official insignia in ancient Rome.) The name is usually homage to the Roman author of *The Aeneid*.
Verge, Vergil, Vergilio, Virgilio

Virginius Lat. "Chaste." Masculine version of **Virginia**. Much less common, perhaps because chastity has historically been less prized for males. It occasionally occurs in old Virginia families, in which case it refers to the state known as the Old Dominion rather than to sexual experience or the lack of it.

Virginio

Vischer German. "Fisherman." Probably an occupational name.

Visscher

Vito Lat. "Alive." Generally used by Italian families. Saint Vitus was an early martyr whose legend held that he could cure epilepsy and another disorder known as "Saint Vitus' dance."

Vital, Vitale, Vitalis, Vitaly, Vitas, Vitus, Witold

Vivek Sanskrit. "Discernment, wisdom."

Vivian Lat. "Full of life." Used occasionally for boys in Britain, but an American infant named Vivian would be assumed to be a girl.

Viviani, Vivien, Vivyan, Vyvian, Vyvyan

Vladimir Slavic. "Renowned prince." Pianist Vladimir Horowitz.

Vladamir, Vladimeer, Wladimir, Wladimyr

Vladislav Old Slavic. "Splendid rule."

Volker Ger. "People's defender." From the German word that gives us "folk."

Volney OG. "Spirit of the folk."

Von ONorse. "Hope." Also a respelling of the Dutch-derived Van.

Vonn

TALK ABOUT TEMPESTUOUS

The National Hurricane Center began assigning names to hurricanes back in 1953. It created six rosters of names in alphabetical order, and cycled through them every six years, assigning a name to each storm once wind velocity reached 39 miles per hour. Names were all female until 1979, when they began alternating: girl, boy, girl, boy, one year; boy, girl, boy, girl the next. There are different lists for the Atlantic and Pacific storms. The names for Atlantic storms are drawn from French, English, and

Spanish, while the Pacific possibilities include some Hawaiian names. Every few years the Hurricane Center retires a name if a really fierce storm used it: Hurricane Hugo in 1989, for instance, wrought such havoc that there will never again be another Hugo. The Hurricane Center is apparently just as broad-minded as the American public in its choice of names: other names that have been retired are Cleo, Fifi, Klaus, and Ione.

Wade OE. Place name: "River ford." Transferred last name with a certain popularity in old Southern families, after Confederate general Wade Hampton.
Waddell, Wadell, Wayde

Wadham OE. Place name: "Ford village." At a river ford, of course, it was possible to wade across the water, hence all these names.

Wadley OE. Place name: "Ford meadow."
Wadleigh, Wadly

Wadsworth OE. Place name: "Village near the ford." Transferred last name of a family that has long been prominent on the American cultural scene. Poet Henry Wadsworth Longfellow.
Waddsworth

Wagner Ger. Occupational name: "Wagon-builder." New York City Mayor Robert Wagner; composer Richard Wagner.
Waggoner, Wagoner

Wahib Arab. "Giver, donor." One of Allah's ninety-nine attributes.
Waheeb

Wainwright OE. Occupational name: "Wagon-builder." Quite a mouthful as a first name, and most likely to be used when it's a family name, such as a mother's maiden name.
Wainright, Wainewright, Wayneright, Waynewright, Waynright

Waite Middle English. Occupational name: "Guard, watchman." In other words, one who waited for something to happen. Christmas carolers used to be known as "waits" because the custom of singing carols originated with bands of watchmen who would sing a tune to mark the passing hours of the night. Actor/musician Tom Waits.
Waights, Waits, Wayte

Wakefield OE. Place name: "Damp field."

Wakeley OE. Place name: "Damp meadow."
Wakelea, Wakeleigh, Wakely

Wakeman OE. Occupational name: "Watchman." Or one who was awake when others slept. All too appropriate for most babies.
Wake

Walcott OE. Place name: "Cottage by the wall." Could originally have referred to the great Roman wall that still stands in the north of England.
Wallcot, Wallcott, Wolcott

Wald Ger. Place name: "Woods, forest." Vast tracts of Europe were originally covered with dense, impenetrable forest.

Waldemar OG. "Renowned ruler." Many of these Old German names (William is another) are actually made up of two particles that are both nouns: in this case they are "fame" and "power." In German, two nouns are often joined to make a new word, but translations of some of these names into English are awkward and approximate.
Valdemar

Walden OE. Place name: "Wooded valley." Could also be another variant of one of the Old German names that include the "Wald-" ("power") element, like Walter. Many literature-loving parents may think of Thoreau's book and the pond *Walden*.
Waldenn, Waldi, Waldon

Waldo Dim. **Waldemar**, etc. The "-o" ending is a particularly Germanic diminutive. Possibly also a German place name: "Forest meadow." Though more common than some of the longer forms like Waldemar, it's still unusual and may retain a slightly comical aura from the *Where's Waldo* books that were popular among children in the 1990s. Poet Ralph Waldo Emerson.

Waldorf Ger. Place name: "Village in the woods."
   Waldorp
Waldron OG. "Powerful raven."
Waldwick Ger./OE. Place name: "Village in the forest."
   Waldwyck
Walford OE. Place name: "Brook ford." Composer Walford Davies.
Walfred OG. "Ruler of peace."
   Walfried
Walid Arab. "Just born."
   Waleed
Walker OE. Occupational name: "Cloth-walker." The era that saw the rise of last names was also the great English era of the wool trade, giving us such cloth-manufacturing names as Fuller, Dyer, and Weaver. In that medieval era, workers trod on the wool to clean it. Author Walker Percy; photographer Walker Evans.
Wallace OE. "Welshman." Originally a Scottish name, used to identify foreigners from the south. Like many last names, it was most popular as a first name in the 19th century. In this case the popularity could have been sparked by the Victorian passion for the past; Sir William Wallace was a Scottish patriot of the 13th century who struggled (in vain) against the English King Edward I. Poet Wallace Stevens; actor Wallace Beery.
   Wallach, Wallas, Wallie, Wallis, Wally, Walsh, Welch, Welsh
Waller OE. Occupational name: "Wall maker" or OG. "Powerful one."
Wally Dim. **Walter, Wallace,** etc. Actors Wally Shawn, Wally Cox.
Walsh OE. "Welsh." Also related to Wallace.
Walter OG. "People of power" or "Army of power." Norman name that took root strongly in Britain and has been used quite steadily for the last 900 years (with the occasional century of neglect). Not particularly fashionable now. Cartoonist Walt Disney; poet Walt Whitman; journalist Walter Cronkite; actors Walter Brennan, Walter Matthau.
   Gaultier, Gauthier, Gautier, Gualterio, Gualtiero, Valter, Valther, Walder, Wally, Walt, Walther, Wat, Watkins

Waltham OE. Place name: "Walt's village."

Walton OE. Place name: "Walled town." Composer William Walton; entrepreneur Sam Walton.

Walworth OE. Place name: "Walled farm."

Walwyn OE. "Welsh friend."
Walwin, Walwinn, Walwynn, Walwynne, Welwyn

Wanamaker Ger. Occupational name: "Basket maker." John Wanamaker was a merchant in 19th-century Philadelphia who founded one of the first American department stores.
Wannamaker

Wapiti Native American. "White, whitish." The name refers to the pale rump and tail of the American elk, a majestic member of the deer family usually seen in sizable herds in national parks.

Warburton OE. Place name: "Long-standing fortress town."

Ward OE. Occupational name: "Watchman." Like many of these occupational or place names turned last names, Ward was revived as a first name in the 19th century. It is still somewhat more common as a first name than most other occupational names (Smith, Baker, Turner, etc.). Author Ward Just.
Warde, Warden, Worden

Wardell OE. Place name: "Watchman's hill."

Wardley OE. Place name: "Watchman's meadow."
Wardlea, Wardleigh

Ware OE. "Watchful, aware."

Warfield ME. Place name: "Field by the weir." A weir was a kind of enclosure built into a stream to trap fish.

Warford ME. "Ford near the weir."

Warley ME. "Meadow near the weir."

Warner OG. "Fighting defender." Philosopher Wernher Erhardt; U.S. Senator John Warner.
Werner, Wernher

Warren OE. "Watchman" or Middle English "Park warden." A warren was originally an area devoted to breeding game, especially rabbits. By extension, the word is now used to describe human dwellings that resemble haphazard and overcrowded rabbits' tunnels. As a name, Warren was used in the late 19th century and given a

boost by the career of President Warren G. Harding. Actor Warren Beatty; U.S. Supreme Court Chief Justice Warren Burger.
Ware, Waring, Warrin, Warriner

Warton OE. Place name: "Town near the weir."
Wharton

Warwick OE. Place name: "Buildings near the weir." The town of Warwick in England was home for centuries to the very powerful Earls of Warwick.
Warick, Warrick

Washburn OE. Place name: "Flooding stream."
Washborn, Washbourne, Washburne

Washington OE. Place name: Possibly "Clever man's settlement." Author Washington Irving, born in 1783, was in all likelihood named for the first U.S. president, but the name has not been used as much as one might think, possibly because of its length. Educator Booker T. Washington.

Wasim Arab. "Good-looking, beautiful."

Waterford OE. Place name: "Ford over the water." Irish place name: a county in southern Ireland with two notable harbors.

Watkins OE. "Son of Walter, little Walter."

Watson OE. "Son of Walter." Last name used as a first name primarily in the 19th century. Most famous as the name of the sidekick to whom Sherlock Holmes perpetually condescended: "Elementary, my dear Watson." IBM founder Thomas Watson.

Watt Dim. **Walter** (OG. "People of power"). The watt, a unit of electrical power (as in the 60-watt bulb) was named after Scottish inventor James Watt, who refined and marketed the steam engine early in the 19th century.
Watts

Waunakee NAm Ind. (Algonquin.) "Peaceful one."

Waverley OE. Place name: "Meadow of quivering aspens." Sir Walter Scott's series of thirty-two historical novels, written in the mid–19th century, was known as the "Waverley novels" after the title of the first one.
Waverlee, Waverley

Wayland OE. Place name: "Land by the path." Singer Waylon Jennings.

Way, Waylan, Waylen, Waylin, Waylon, Weylin

Wayne OE. Occupational name: "Wagon builder or driver," as in Wainwright. Its period of greatest popularity coincided with the popularity of the actor Marion Morrison, better known as John Wayne. Still used from time to time, but uncommon. Performer Wayne Newton; hockey player Wayne Gretzky.

Wain, Wayn

Weaver OE. Occupational name: "Weaver." Most familiar as a last name.

Webb OE. Occupational name: "Weaver." Mostly 19th-century use. Actors Clifton Webb, Jack Webb.

Web, Weber, Webster

Webley OE. Place name: "Weaver's meadow."

Webbley, Webbly, Webly

Webster OE. Occupational name: "Weaver." As in weaving a web. Lexicographer Noah Webster produced America's first dictionary in 1828, and students today still depend on various editions of Webster's dictionaries. Statesman Daniel Webster.

Web, Webb, Webbster

Wedgwood OE. Place name: "Triangular woodland." The name of a famous English potter who produced blue and white china beginning in the 18th century. The company is still in existence.

Wedgewood

Weissman Ger. "White-haired man."

Weissmann

Welborne OE. Place name: "Spring-fed stream." Not, alas, indicative of patrician origins.

Welborn, Welbourne, Welburn, Wellborn, Wellbourn, Wellburn

Welby OG. Place name: "Well-farm." Many parents will think of the long-running TV serial *Marcus Welby, M.D.*

Welbey, Welbie, Wellbey, Wellby

Weldon OE. Place name: "Well-hill."

Welden, Welldon

Welford OE. Place name: "Well-ford."

Wellford

Wellington OE. Place name of unclear meaning. Has aristocratic connotations, no doubt from the famous Duke of

Wellington, who defeated Napoleon and gave his name to tall waterproof boots and filet of beef wrapped in pastry.

Wells OE. Place name: "Wells." The name of a famous cathedral town in western England. First-name use was mostly 19th century.

Welton OE. Place name: "Well-town."

Wenceslaus Old Slavic. "Glorious garland." King Wenceslas, the patron saint of the Czech Republic, was a 10th-century monarch of Bohemia and a martyr for the faith. The famous Christmas carol (written in the 19th century) refers to an entirely imaginary episode, but the name would be unknown to us without it.

Wenceslas, Wenzel, Wiencyslaw

Wendell OG. "Wanderer." Quite rare. Attorney Wendell Willkie.

Wendall, Wendel

Wentworth OE. Place name: "Pale man's settlement."

Werner OG. "Defense army." Closely related to Warner. Use is mostly confined to the U.S. Rocket scientist Werner von Braun.

Verner, Warner, Wernhar, Wernher

Wesley OE. Place name: "Western meadow." Used in honor of John and Charles Wesley, who founded the Methodist church in the 18th century. The name is quite steadily used, and despite the "-ley" ending that is so fashionable for girls, Wesley is still solidly masculine. Actor Wesley Snipes.

Wesly, Wessley, Westleigh, Westley

Westbrook OE. Place name: "Western stream." This group of place names illustrates one way last names came into use: They described the location of someone's dwelling. Fencer Peter Westbrook.

Brook, Brooke, Wesbrook, West, Westbrooke

Westby OE. Place name: "Western farmstead."

Westbey, Westbie

Westcott OE. Place name: "Western cottage."

Wescot, Wescott, Westcot

Westerly OE. "From the west, toward the west."

Westerley

Weston OE. Place name: "Western settlement." Photographer Edward Weston.

Westen, Westin

Wetherby OE. Place name: "Wether-sheep farm." A wether is a male sheep that has been castrated; a bellwether is a wether who wears a bell and leads a flock. Again, the importance of the wool trade in England when last names were formed gives these "Wether-" names unusual prominence.

Weatherbey, Weatherbie, Weatherby, Wetherbey, Wetherbie

Wetherell OE. Place name: "Wether-sheep corner."

Weatherell, Weatherill, Wetherill, Wethrill

Wetherly OE. Place name: "Wether-sheep meadow."

Weatherley, Weatherly, Wetherleigh, Wetherley

Wharton OE. Place name: "Shore or bank settlement." Author William Wharton.

Warton

Wheatley OE. Place name: "Wheat field." Football player Tyrone Wheatley.

Wheatlea, Wheatleigh, Wheatly

Wheaton OE. Place name: "Wheat settlement."

Wheeler OE. Occupational name: "Wheel maker."

Wheelwright OE. Occupational name: "Wheel maker." Corresponds to Wainwright.

Whistler OE. Occupational name: "Whistler or piper." Artist James Whistler.

Whitbeck OE. Place name: "White stream."

Whitby OE. Place name: "White farm." All of these "Whit-" names are more commonly last names, though some were used more regularly as first names in the 19th century.

Whitbey, Whitbie

Whitcomb OE. Place name: "White valley." Poet James Whitcomb Riley.

Whitcombe, Whitcumb

White OE. Descriptive name: "White or fair." Probably referred to complexion or hair color of an ancestor. Extremely unlikely to be used as a first name today. Architect Stanford White; baseball player Whitey Ford.

Whitey

Whitehead OE. Descriptive name: "Fair-headed."

Whitelaw OE. Place name: "White hill." Diplomat Whitelaw Reid.
Whitlaw

Whitfield OE. Place name: "White field."

Whitford OE. Place name: "White ford."

Whitley OE. Place name: "White meadow." Author Whitley Streiber.

Whitlock OE. "White lock of hair."

Whitman OE. "White man." The description would refer to hair or complexion. Poet Walt Whitman.

Whitmore OE. Place name: "White moor."
Whitmoor, Whittemore, Witmore, Wittemore

Whitney OE. Place name: "White island." Last name that was annexed as a girl's name in the 1980s. It became much more popular for girls than it ever was for boys. Even though the vogue for female Whitneys is fading, the name is almost never used for boys now. Railroad millionaire William Collins Whitney; inventor Eli Whitney.

Whittaker OE. Place name: "White field." The last part of the name may refer to an acre of land. Actor Forrest Whittaker.
Whitacker, Whitaker

Wickham OE. Place name: "Village paddock."

Wickley OE. Place name: "Village meadow."

Wilbert OG. "Brilliant and resolute." Not the same as Wilbur, despite the similar sound. Used sporadically in the 19th and 20th centuries.
Wilburt

Wilbur OG. Last name of obscure meaning. Probably confused with Wilbert over the years. E.B. White fans will associate it with the protagonist of *Charlotte's Web*, Wilbur the Pig. Aviator Wilbur Wright.
Wilber, Willbur

Wilder Ger. Occupational name: "Hunter." In other words, someone who traps or kills wild animals. A nonconformist choice for the heavily civilized 21st century. Playwrights Thornton Wilder, Oscar Wilde.
Wild, Wilde

Wiley OE. Place name: "Water meadow." Indicates a meadow that would be flooded from time to time.
Willey, Wylie

Wilford OE. Place name: "Willow-ford." Actor Wilford Brimley.

Wilfred OE. "Purposeful peace." Like Waldemar, another name whose two elements are both nouns (in this case "will" and "peace"), to the confusion of the translator. Neglected after the Norman invasion, but revived in the 19th century to some popularity, which never spread as far as the U.S. Author Wilfred Sheed.

Wilfredo, Wilfrid, Wilfried, Wilfryd, Will, Willfred, Will-fredo, Willfrid, Willfried, Willfryd

Wilkes OE. Probably a contraction of Wilkins. Presidential assassin John Wilkes Booth.

Wilkie, Willkes, Willkie

Wilkinson OE. "Son of little Will."

Wilkins, Willkins, Willkinson

Willard OG. "Bold will." Most common in the U.S., though far from a household word. TV weatherman Willard Scott.

Willerd

Willet OE. "Little Will."

Willets, Willett

William OG. "Will-helmet." Another two-noun name, more often translated as "resolute protection" or the like. Given a great boost in Norman England by William the Conqueror and succeeding English kings. Between the 17th and 20th centuries, one of the top handful of boy's names. Its popularity faded somewhat in the middle of the 20th century, but by the end, it was one of the top two dozen boys' names in America. Its popularity may have been partially prompted by the birth of Prince William of Wales. Just as boys named Robert are no longer called Bobby, boys named William are not nicknamed Billy. The usual diminutive is Will. Playwright William Shakespeare; actors William Hurt, Willem Dafoe; film director Wim Wenders; poet William Blake; author William Faulkner; U.S. Presidents William H. Harrison, William H. Taft, William McKinley, Bill Clinton.

Bill, Bille, Billie, Billy, Guglielmo, Guillaume, Guillermo, Liam, Vilhelm, Villem, Wilek, Wiley, Wilhelm, Wilhelmus, Wilkes, Wilkie, Wilkinson, Will, Willem, Willhelmus, Willi, Williamson, Willie, Willis, Willkie, Wills, Willson, Willy, Wilmar, Wilmot, Wilmott, Wilson, Wim

Willis OE. Dim. **William**. Basketball player Willis Reed.
Willes, Willess, Williss, Williston

Willoughby OE. Place name: "Willow farm." In the early English agricultural economy willows were important because their pliable branches could be woven into baskets.
Willoughbey, Willoughbie, Willughby

Wilmer OG. "Determined fame."
Wilmar, Willmar, Willmer, Wylmer

Wilson OE. "Son of Will." Last name turned first name, possibly in compliment to President Woodrow Wilson. Composer Robert Wilson; Beach Boy Brian Wilson.
Willson

Wilton OE. Place name: "Well settlement."

Windsor OE. Place name: "Riverbank with a winch." Famous from the town and castle of that name in England, and above all from the fact that this is the British royal family's last name. Until 1917 it had been Wettin, but during World War I emotions ran so high against Germany that it seemed more patriotic to adopt a staunch English name. Also the name of a standard way to tie a necktie, invented by the Duke of Windsor, who was a great dandy.
Wyndsor

Winfield OE. "Friend's field." Baseball player Dave Winfield; Civil War general Winfield Scott.
Winnfield, Wynfield, Wynnfield

Wingate OE. Place name: "Winding gate." May refer to a gate like a turnstile.

Winslow OE. Place name: "Friend's hill." Painter Winslow Homer.

Winsted OE. Place name: "Friend's farm."
Winstead

Winston OE. Place name: "Friend's town" or "Wine's town." For modern parents, recalls both English statesman Winston Churchill and a popular brand of cigarettes.
Winsten, Winstonn, Wynstan, Wynston

Winter OE. Season name. Musician Paul Winter.
Winters

Winthrop OE. Place name: "Friend's village." In the U.S., it hearkens back to the Puritan governor of Massachusetts,

John Winthrop, and his numerous Bostonian descendants.

Winton OE. Place name: "Friend's settlement." Closely related to Winston.

Winwood OE. Place name: "Friend's woods." Musician Steve Winwood.

Wistar Ger. Last name of uncertain meaning. Used with pride among Philadelphia families: Caspar Wistar was a very prominent doctor in late 18th–century Philadelphia, and taught at what became the University of Pennsylvania. An earlier Caspar Wistar (in all likelihood the doctor's father) founded a thriving glass factory in southern New Jersey in the 1740s. The flower wisteria was named after the doctor. Author Owen Wister.

Wister

Wolcott OE. Place name: "Wolf's cottage." Wolf, in this case, would be a first name. Oliver Wolcott of Connecticut signed the Declaration of Independence.

Wolfe OG. "Wolf." From the evidence of names and Grimm's fairy tales, it's clear that wolves occupied a big part in the medieval German imagination. They obviously posed a threat (remember "Little Red Riding Hood?"), but at the same time their qualities of fierceness and tenacity must have seemed admirable. It's an interesting window on the life of the times: would we name a son "Shark"? Irish patriot Wolfe Tone.

Wolf, Wolff, Wolfhart, Woolf, Wulf, Wulfe

Wolfert OG. "Wolf army."

Wolfgang OG. "Wolf gait." A very Germanic name that would not be considered by English-speaking parents without the fame of composer Wolfgang Amadeus Mozart. Film director Wolfgang Petersen.

Wolfram OG. "Wolf raven."

Wulfram

Woodrow OE. "Row by the woods." "Row" could refer to a row of houses or trees or bushes (as in a hedgerow). The name has been given prominence beyond the usual place name by admirers of U.S. President Woodrow Wilson.

Woody

Woodson OE. "Wood's son." Football players Rod Woodson, Darren Woodson.

Woodstock OE. "Wooden fence." As in stockade fencing. Also as in the rock festival of the 1970s, which the vast majority of today's parents were too young to go to.

Woodward OE. Place name: "Woods warden." Actor Edward Woodward.
  Woodard

Woody Dim. **Woodrow**, etc. A particularly American name adopted by actor Allen Konigsberg, now better known as Woody Allen. Folk singer Woody Guthrie.

Woolworth OE. "Wool farm." Famous as the name of a now-defunct chain of stores.

Worth OE. Place name: "Fenced farm." Used since the 19th century.
  Worthey, Worthing, Worthington, Worthy

Woyzeck Slavic. "Comforting soldier." Opera fans will recognize the variation Wozzeck as the name of an opera by Alban Berg.
  Wojtek, Wozzeck

Wray ONorse. Place name: "Dweller in the corner."

Wright OE. Occupational name: "Carpenter." This word occurs in names like Wainwright and Wheelwright. Again, mostly 19th-century use. The astounding feats of aviators Orville and Wilbur Wright apparently did not inspire parents to use their name in homage. Painter Joseph Wright of Derby; architect Frank Lloyd Wright.

Wyandanch Native American: Montauk. "Speaks with wisdom." The name of a town on Long Island in New York State.

Wyatt OF. "Small fighter." Last name occasionally used as a first name, notably by Wild West sheriff Wyatt Earp.
  Wiatt, Wye, Wyeth

Wyck OE. Place name: "Village." Occurs more often in combination with other names, like Wickham.
  Wick, Wyche

Wycliff OE. Place name: "White cliff."
  Wycliffe

Wyckoff OG. "Wine seller."
  Wykoff

Wycombe OE. Place name: "White valley."
  Wycomb

Wylie OE. "Clever, charming, full of wiles." Literary agent Andrew Wylie.
Wiley, Wye

Wyman OE. "Fair-haired man."

Wyndham OE. Place name: either "Wyman's hamlet" or "Hamlet near the winding way." Used as a first name in the 19th century and into the 20th, but very unusual today. Author Wyndham Lewis.
Windham, Wynndham

Wynn Welsh. "Fair, white" or OE. "Friend." Used more frequently for girls in the past few years, but still uncommon. Gambling entrepreneur Steve Wynn.
Win, Winn, Wynne

Wystan OE. "Battle stone." The first name of poet Wystan Hughes Auden. Otherwise obscure.
Wystann

Xan Dim. **Alexander**. Gk. "Defender of mankind."

Xanthus Gk. "Golden-haired."
Xanthos

Xavier Basque. "New house." Most often found as a middle name following Francis, in honor of Saint Francis Xavier, a 16th-century Jesuit missionary who took Christianity to the East Indies and Japan. Some of its popularity may be explained by the fact that it sounds a lot like the word "savior," a synonym for Jesus to Christians. Band leader Xavier Cugat; baseball player Javier Lopez.
Javier, Saviero, Savion, Savyon, Xaviell, Xayvion, Xever, Zavier

Xenophon Gk. "Foreign voice." Xenophon was a Greek historian of the 4th century B.C.
Xeno

Xenos Gk. "Hospitality."
Zeno, Zenos

Xerxes Per. "Monarch." Xerxes was the title of several Persian rulers. One (in the 5th century B.C.) made war on the Greeks and also appears in the biblical Apocrypha as Ahasuerus, husband of Esther.

Ximenes Sp. Var. **Simon** (Heb. "Listening intently").
Jimenes, Jimenez, Ximenez

Yaakov Heb. Form of **Jacob** ("he who supplants"). Comedian Yakov Smirnov.
Iago, Yaacob, Yachov, Yacov, Yago, Yakob, Yakov

Yaar Heb. "Forest."

Yakar Heb. "Precious."

Yakim Heb. Var. **Joachim** ("The Lord will set up").
Jachim, Jakim, Yacheem, Yachim

Yaholo Native American: Creek. "He who yells." Highly appropriate for most children.

Yale OE. Place name: "Fertile moor." Familiar as the name of one of the Ivy League universities, founded by Elihu Yale.
Yael

Yanai Aramaic. "He will answer." Old Testament name.

Yancy Origin unclear. Several sources suggest this was an Indian word for "Englishman," and propose that this was the origin of the word "Yankee." But the *Facts on File Dictionary of First Names* claims the name is used to honor a Southern proslavery politician of the 19th century. Rare, in any case. Football player Yancey Thigpen.
Yance, Yancey, Yantsey

Yann Fr. Var. **John** (Heb. "The Lord is gracious"). Comparable to the Dutch Jan. Tennis player Yannick Noah.
Yannic, Yannick

Yannis Gk. Var. **John** (Heb. "The Lord is gracious").
Ioannis, Yanni, Yannakis

Yaphet Heb. "Comely." Actor Yaphet Koto.
Japhet, Japheth, Yapheth

Yardley OE. Place name: "Fenced meadow."
Yardlee, Yardlea, Yardleigh, Yardly, Yarley, Yeardley

Yarrow Plant name: a strongly scented herb. Musician Peter Yarrow.

Yasahiro Jap. "Serene."

Yasir Arab. "Well to do." Palestinian leader Yasser Arafat.
Yaseer, Yasr, Yasser

Yates ME. Place name: "The gates." Poet W. B. Yeats.
Yeats

Yazid Arab./Swahili. "Becoming greater."
Yazeed

Yehudi Heb. "Praise." Related to the feminine Judith, and to the nearly obsolete Jude. Violinist Yehudi Menuhin.
Judah,   Yechudi,   Yechudit,   Yehuda,   Yehudah, Yehudit

Yeoman Middle English. "Attendant, servant."
Youman

Yevgeny Rus. Var. **Eugene** (Gk. "Wellborn").
Yevgeniy

Yishachar Heb. "Reward will come."
Issachar, Yisachar

Yitzhak Heb. Var. **Isaac** ("Laughter"). Violinist Itzhak Perlman.
Itzak, Izaak, Yitzchak

Ymir ONorse. Myth. name: the giant from whose body the earth was created.

Yochanan Heb. "The Lord is gracious." A form of **John**.
Johanan, Yohannan

Yoelvis Modern name: possibly, in Spanish, "I, Elvis." Or a variation of **Elvis** (Scand. "All-wise"). Olympic track athlete Yoelvis Quesada.

Yonas Heb. "Dove." The English form is Jonas.

Yorath Welsh. "Handsome lord."

Yorick OE. "Farmer." Related to George and Yuri. Most people have only heard this name in the context of Shakespeare's play *Hamlet*, in which Hamlet mutters to a skull, "Alas! poor Yorick."

York OE. Place name: "Boar settlement" or "Yew settlement." Used as a title (Duke of York) in the English royal family for several hundred years. Also familiar as an American place name, which makes it a bit difficult to use as a first name.
Yorick, Yorrick, Yorke

Yosemite Place name: a national park in eastern California on the western slope of the Sierra Nevada. The name may be a Native American term for grizzly bear.

Young Eng. Adjective as name: usually a transferred last name.

Yovanny Phonetic variant on Giovanni, It. form of John (Heb. "The Lord is gracious").
Yovanney, Yovanni

Yucatán Mexican place name: the peninsula that separates the Caribbean from the Gulf of Mexico, and a very popular vacation spot.

Yukon Canadian place name: territory between Alaska and the Northwest Territories, famous for its gold and its cold.

Yule OE. "Winter solstice." The time of year around Dec. 21, the pagan winter feast. Now, of course, it means Christmas. Rarely used, even for Christmas babies.
Euell, Ewell

Yuri Rus. Var. **George** (Lat. "Farmer")
Yurii, Yury

Yusuf Var. **Joseph** (Heb. "The Lord increases"). Currently very popular in Arabic-speaking countries. The "-uf" ending is more typically Arab, the "-ef" ending more often Hebrew.
Yosef, Yoseff, Yusef, Yusuff

Yves Fr. Var. **Ivo** (OG. "Yew wood"). Since yew wood was used for bows, the name may have been an occupational one meaning "archer." This form is almost exclusively found in France; its closest cognate in America is the feminine **Yvonne**. Singer Yves Montand; fashion designer Yves Saint Laurent.
Evo, Ives, Ivo, Yvo, Yvon

Zachariah Heb. "The Lord has remembered." Biblical name occurring in both Old and New Testaments. As might be expected, it was revived by the Puritans and found fairly constantly through the 19th century. The numerous phonetic variations hint at its current popularity.
Zacaria, Zacarias, Zacary, Zaccaria, Zacchariah, Zaccheus,

Zach, Zachaios, Zacharia, Zacharias, Zacharie, Zachary, Zacheriah, Zachery, Zacheus, Zack, Zackariah, Zackerias, Zackery, Zak, Zakarias, Zakarie, Zakariyyah, Zakery, Zecheriah, Zekariah, Zekeriah, Zeke

Zachary Heb. ''The Lord has remembered.'' The most popular form of Zachariah, one of the top two dozen names for boys in the country. Probably brought to fashion by the Old Testament names Jeremy, Jason, and Joshua. Parents tend to look for names similar to—but not exactly the same as—what's stylish. President Zachary Taylor; actor Zachery Ty Bryan

Zaccary, Zaccery, Zach, Zacharie, Zachery, Zack, Zackarey, Zackary, Zackery, Zak

Zaccheus Heb. ''The Lord has remembered.'' A variation of **Zachariah**. The name was borne by a tax collector in the New Testament who, being short, climbed into a tree to see Jesus in a crowd. Jesus spotted him in his perch, called to him by name, and visited his house. This is a story that has immense appeal to children.

Zachaios, Zacchaeus

Zadok Heb. ''Fair, righteous.''

Zadoc, Zaydok

Zafar Arab. ''Victory.''

Zaphar

Zahavi Heb. ''Gold.''

Zahir Arab. ''Flourishing, brilliant'' or Heb. ''Shining.''

Zaheer, Zahur

Zaki Arab. ''Full of virtue, pure.'' Likely to be mistaken for a variant of the popular Zachary/Zachariah.

Zale Gk. ''Sea-strength.''

Zayle

Zalman Heb. ''Peaceable.'' The more common form in English is Solomon. Author Salman Rushdie.

Salman, Zalomon

Zahir Arab. ''Brilliant.'' Currently popular in Arabic-speaking countries.

Zayyir

Zahur Arab./Swahili. ''Blossom.''

Zahour, Zahoor

Zan Dim. **Alexander** (Gk. ''Man's defender''). A trendy new form of a name that has been quite popular in recent years.

Xan, Zander, Zandro, Zandros, Zann

Zane Derivation and meaning unclear. May be a variation of John (Heb. "The Lord is gracious"), or a version of a Scandinavian last name. Made famous by author Zane Grey, who wrote many western novels, among them *Riders of the Purple Sage.*

Zain, Zayne

Zared Heb. "Trap."

Zarek Polish Var. **Belshazzar** (Babylonian "May Bal watch over the king"). In the Old Testament, the son of Nebuchadnezzar and the last king of Babylon. At a famous feast, handwriting appeared on the wall of the banqueting hall that was interpreted by Daniel as a warning of the king's doom. Hence our saying "the writing on the wall." Balthazar is a related name.

Zebediah Heb. "Gift of Jehovah." In the New Testament, the father of apostles John and James. The name is all but obsolete today.

Zeb, Zebedee, Zebediah

Zebulon Heb. "To give honor to." Old Testament name of one of Jacob's sons. Extremely rare. Explorer Zebulon Pike.

Zebulen, Zebulun, Zevulon, Zevulun

Zedekiah Heb. "The Lord is just." Name of an Old Testament king of Judah. Mostly 19th-century use.

Zed, Zedechiah, Zedekias

Zeke Heb. "Strength of God." Dim. **Ezekiel**. Ezekiel was an important Old Testament prophet.

Zelig Yiddish: "Blessed, holy." In German, "*selig*" means holy. Movie buffs will remember a Woody Allen movie in which a character named Zelig turns up at many different historic events.

Selig, Zeligman, Zelik

Zenas Gk: "Hospitable."

Zenios, Zenon

Zeno Name of a Greek philosopher. Derivation unclear.

Zenon, Zino, Zinon

Zenobios Gk. "Life of Zeus."

Zenobius, Zinov, Zinovi

Zephaniah Heb: "Precious to the Lord." A minor Old Testament prophet. Sparing 19th-century use.
Zeph, Zephan

Zephariah Modern name, apparently coined from Zephaniah and Zachariah.

Zephyr Gk. "West wind." A mythology name that has persisted in variations like Cefirino and Zephirine (for girls). Laurent de Brunhoff, in his *Babar* books, named the mischievous monkey Zéphir.
Zayfeer, Zayfir, Zayphir, Zefir, Zéphir, Zephiros, Zephirus, Zephyrus

Zerach Heb. "A lamp."
Zerah

Zero Arab. "Void." A rather daunting name for a baby. Actor Zero Mostel (originally Samuel Joel Mostel) adopted it as an adult.

Zeus Gk. "Living." The name of the chief of the Olympian gods, who was also father of many gods and goddesses including Athena, Ares, Apollo and Artemis.

Zikomo Ngono (Malawi). "Thank you."

Zimran Heb. "Holy."

Zindel Yiddish. Var. **Alexander** (Gk. "Defender of mankind").
Zindil

Zion Heb. "Highest point." In the Christian religion, Zion is a symbolic name for heaven, and is used often in hymns and even the names of some churches.
Sion

Zipkiyah NAm Ind. (Kiowa.) "Big bow." As in bow and arrow.

Ziv Heb. "Full of life, glorious, splendid."
Ziven, Zivon

Zoilo Sp. from Gk. "Life." The most common form of this name is Zoe.

Zoltan Hung. "Life." Composer Zoltan Kodaly.

Zuberi Swahili. "Strong."
Zooberi, Zubery

Zuhayr Arab. "Small blossoms."
Zuhair

Zuni Native American tribe: the Zuni live in New Mexico.
Zuriel Heb. "The Lord my rock."

COOL NAMES

In this ironic age, sometimes parents give their children names
that seem deliberately unfashionable, in the same way that they'd
wear odd-looking glasses or drive resolutely clunky cars. The uncool thus becomes cool. Movie stars aren't immune to this trend.
Check out the choices below:

Diane Keaton: Dexter
Tom Hanks and Rita Wilson: Chester and Truman
Roseanne and Ben Thomas: Buck
Robin Givens: Buddy
Melanie Griffith and Antonio Banderas:
Stella
Kate Capshaw and Stephen Spielberg: Saw-
yer
Nicolas Cage and Christina Fulton: Weston
Kyra Sedgwick and Kevin Bacon: Travis

If It's a

GIRL...

Abarrane (Fem. **Abraham**) Basque from Heb. "Father of many."
    Abame
Abebi Nig. "She came after asking."
Abelia (Fem. **Abel**) Fr. from Heb. "Sigh."
    Abella, Abelle
Abellona Dan. (Fem. **Apollo**) In Greek myth, Apollo is the sun god. See **Apolline**.
Aberdeen Place name: city in northeast Scotland.
Abina Ghanaian. "Born on Thursday."
    Abena
Abia Arab. "Great."
Abida Arab. "She who worships" or Heb. "My father knows."
Abiela Heb. "My father is the Lord."
    Abiela, Abielah, Aviela
Abigail Heb. "My father is joyful." Biblical name adopted by the Puritans and popular through the 18th century. Abigail was the wife of David and referred to herself as his "handmaid." Her name became widely used as a term for a ladies' maid by the early nineteenth century, which may have contributed to its fall from favor. After a hundred years of obscurity, it was revived with the trend toward old-fashioned names beginning in the 1970s. Still unusual, but a coming choice for parents seeking a distinctive but not outlandish name. Abigail Adams, wife of President John Adams; advice columnist Abigail Van Buren.
    Abagael, Abagail, Abagale, Abagil, Abaigeal, Abbe, Abbey, Abbi, Abbie, Abbigael, Abbigail, Abbigale, Abby, Abbye, Abbygael, Abbygail, Abbygale, Abegale, Abichayil, Abihail, Abigael, Abigal, Abigale, Abigall, Abigil, Abigayle, Avichayil, Avihail, Gael, Gail, Gaila, Gal, Gale, Gayel, Gayle

Abijah Heb. "God is my father."

Abeedja, Abeeja, Abeesha, Abisha, Abishah

Abilene Place name: town in Texas, and also, in early Christian times, an area in Lebanon near Damascus.

Abalene, Abalina, Abilena, Abiline

Abir Arab. "Scent."

Abeer

Abital Heb. "My father is dew." Currently popular in Israel.

Abeetal, Avital

Abra (Fem. **Abraham**) Heb. "Father of many" or Arab. "Example, lesson." King Solomon's favorite concubine was named Abra.

Abame, Abarrane, Abrahana

Acacia Gr. Name of a blossoming tree that symbolized resurrection. Uncommon even in Greece, though the derivatives like Casey occur often in the U.S.

Acasia, Acasiya, Acasya, Accacia, Accasie, Cacia, Cacie, Casey, Casha, Casia, Cassie, Cassy, Caysha, Kacey, Kacie, Kasey, Kasi, Kassja, Kassy

Acadia Place name: the French settlers of Nova Scotia called their region Acadia after the name of a river there. When the French settlers were driven out by the English in the 18th century, many of them settled in Louisiana and became known as "Cajuns."

Accalia Lat. In myth, the name of the human foster mother of Romulus and Remus, the twins who founded Rome. Legend has it that after their abandonment as infants, they were initially suckled by a she-wolf, whose name is not known. Accalia was her replacement.

Aceline (Fem. **Acelin**) Fr. "Highborn."

Asceline

Achsah Heb. "Ankle bracelet"

Achsa

Acima (Fem. **Acim**) Heb. "The Lord will judge."

Acimah, Achima, Achimah

Acquanetta Invented name related to the particle *aqua*, which is Latin for water. Possibly derived from the name of the hairspray "AquaNet."

Acquanette, Aquanette, Aquannette

Ada Ger. "Noble, nobility." Originated as a short form of names like Adelaide, and popular in the last quarter of the 19th century, though infrequently used now.

Adabella, Adabelle, Adalee, Adan, Adda, Adette, Addi, Addie, Addiah, Addy, Adey, Adi, Adia, Adiah, Adie, Aida, Aidah

Adah Heb. "Ornament, adornment." Biblical name. Unusual, but brought to prominence in the 19th century by American actress Adah Isaacs Mencken. It may also, of course, be considered a variation of **Ada.**

Adair Scottish last name, possibly based on Scots pronunciation of Edgar. Attractive, modern-sounding unisex name, currently scarce but appearing more often for girls.

Adare, Adayre

Adalgisa It. from OG. "Noble promise." The name of a priestess in Bellini's popular opera *Norma*, but exceedingly rare.

Adalgise, Adelgise, Adelvice

Adalia Heb. "God is my refuge" or OG. "Noble one." See also **Adelaide.**

Adal, Adala, Adalee, Adali, Adalie, Adalley, Addal, Addala

Adamina (Fem. **Adam**) Heb. "Child of the red earth." In the Bible God created Adam out of the "red earth" and breathed life into him. This unusual feminine version of the name is Scottish in origin.

Ada, Adameena, Adamine, Adaminna, Addie, Ademina, Ademeena, Mina, Minna

Adamma Nigerian. "Lovely child."

Adara Gk. "beauty" or Arab. "virgin."

Adra

Addie Dim. **Adelaide** or **Adeline**. A nostalgic-sounding nickname.

Addy

Addolorata It. "Full of grief." Refers to the Virgin Mary as Our Lady of Sorrows.

Adolorata, Dolorata

Addula Teut. "Noble cheer."

Adelaide OG. "Noble, nobility." First popular in England after the reign (1830–1837) of William IV and Queen Adelaide. She was a German princess who accepted the young prince after he'd been turned down by seven ladies.

The city of Adelaide, Australia, founded in 1836, was named for her.

Ada, Adalaide, Adalayde, Addala, Addalla, Addey, Addi, Addie, Addy, Adel, Adela, Adelaida, Adelais, Adele, Adelheid, Adelina, Adeline, Adelice, Adelicia, Adelis, Adelita, Adeliza, Adelka, Adelle, Adelvice, Adelvicia, Adey, Adi, Adlin, Adline, Ado, Ady, Asaide, Aline, Aliosha, Alline, Alyosha, Del, Della, Delle, Delli, Delly, Edeline, Eline, Heidi, Lady, Laidey

Adele OG. "Noble, nobility." See **Adelaide**. Nutritionist Adelle Davis; writer Adela Rogers St. John.

Adelia, Adell, Adella, Adellah, Adelle, Edelle

Adelinda Teut. "Noble, sweet." Com. form **Adele** and **Linda**.

Adele, Adeline, Adelinde, Linda

Adeline OG. "Noble, nobility." See **Adelaide**. Adelina enjoyed a burst of popularity during the career of operatic soprano Adelina Patti, in the late 19th century, and a well-known song called "Sweet Adeline" also gave the name exposure at the turn of the century. Perhaps too much exposure, for it fell into disuse.

Adalina, Adaline, Adallina, Adelina, Adelind, Adella, Adellah, Adlin, Adlina, Adline, Ahdella, Aline, Dahlina, Dalina, Daline, Dallina, Delina, Deline, Dellina, Delly, Delyne, Edelie, Lina

Adena Heb. "Decoration."

Adene, Adina, Adinah, Deena, Denah, Dina, Dinah

Adelpha Gr. "Beloved sister."

Adelfa

Adeola Nig. "Crown."

Adola, Dola

Adesina Nig. "She paves the way." Often used to mark a birth if a couple has had trouble conceiving, implying that this will be the first of many children.

Adiba Arab. "Cultured, refined."

Adeeba, Adibah

Adiella Heb. "The Lord's adornment."

Adima Teut. "Noble, renowned."

Adin Heb. Meaning unclear: possibly "Delicate and slender." Appears in the Old Testament as a male name.

Adina, Adeana

Adina Heb. Perhaps "Longing," also possibly "Gentle,

delicate." Easily confused by the ear with Edina, which is an English name.

Adeana, Adena, Adine

Adira Heb. "Noble, powerful."

Adeera, Edira

Aditi Hindi. "Boundless." In Hindu cosmology, Aditi is the mother of the gods.

Adiva Arab. "Agreeable, gentle."

Adlai Arab./Heb. "Just." More familiar to us as a man's name made famous by U.S. Senator Adlai Stevenson.

Adolpha (Fem. **Adolph**) Ger. "Noble wolf."

Adolfa, Adollfa

Adoncia Sp. "Sweet."

Doncia

Adonia (Fem. **Adonis**) Gr. In Greek myth Adonis was a young man so beautiful that Aphrodite, goddess of love, became enamored of him. The name Adonis has come to epitomize male beauty.

Adora Lat. "Adored." A rare but appropriate choice for parents who know themseves to be the doting types.

Adorabelle, Adorae, Adoray, Adorée, Adoré, Adoria, Adorlee, Dora, Dorae, Dori, Dorie, Dorri, Dorrie, Dorry, Dory

Adra Arab. "Virgin."

Adara

Adrian Lat. Place name: Adria was a North Italian city. First popular in the 1950s in Britain, and more common as a man's name. Hollywood costume designer Adrian (*Queen Christina, The Philadelphia Story*) and 12th-century Pope Adrian IV (the only English pope) both pre-date its use as a girls' name. Ripe for revival in this era of unisex names. Fashion designer Adrienne Vittadini.

Adrea, Adreea, Adria, Adriah, Adriana, Adrianah, Adriane, Adrianna, Adriannah, Adrianne, Adrie, Adrien, Adriena, Adrienah, Adrienne, Aydrian, Aydrienne, Hadria, Hadrienne

Aegina In Greek myth, the name of a nymph (one of many, of course) who was impregnated by Zeus. More familiar to travelers, perhaps, as one of the Greek islands close to the mainland.

Egina

Afra Arab. "Color of earth" or Heb. "Young deer" or "Dust." The first female professional writer in England was named Aphra Behn; she was a playwright and a novelist in the latter half of the 17th century.

Affera, Affery, Affra, Aphra

Afraima Arab./Heb. "Fertile."

Africa Place name; the continent. The word also means "pleasant" in Celtic languages, and occurred occasionally as a name in Scotland from the Middle Ages up to the 1700s. There was even a Celtic queen in the 12th century named Affrica. In the U.S. it is used among African-American parents to highlight their heritage.

Affrica, Affricah, Affrika, Affrikah, Africah, Afrika, Afrikah, Aifric, Aifrica, Aphria, Aphfrica, Apirka, Apirkah

Afton OE. Place name: There is a town called Afton in southern Scotland. Like so many place names that have become first names, this one was first a name for boys.

Affton

Afua Ghanaian. "Born on Friday."

Agapi Gk. "Love, affection."

Agape, Agappe

Agate OF. A semiprecious stone. Can be considered either one of the jewel names so popular in the 19th century, or a variant of **Agatha**. The agate, though not a particularly beautiful stone, was once believed to have numerous magical and curative powers.

Agatha Gk. "Good." Saint Agatha was a 3rd-century Christian who refused to marry a Roman consul. She was tortured and ultimately martyred. Her breasts were cut off as part of her torture and she is frequently depicted holding her breasts on a plate. Owing to their resemblance to bells, she is the patron saint of bell ringers. Her name was popular in the early years of the Christian Church, but not again until the late 19th century. It now has an unfashionable ring, but some of the international variants are pretty. Writer Agatha Christie.

Ag, Agace, Agacia, Agafia, Agafon, Agafya, Agapet, Agapit, Agasha, Agata, Agathe, Agathi, Agatta, Aggi, Aggie, Aggy, Aggye, Agi, Agie, Agota, Agotha, Agueda, Agy, Agye

Agave Gk. "Illustrious, noble."

Aglaia In Greek myth, one of the three Graces, epitomizing brilliance. Thalia (blossoming) is still sometimes used; Euphrosyne (joy) is obsolete.

Agnes Gk. "Pure, virginal." Another early Christian saint's name. She was a virgin martyr, and her emblem in art is a lamb (the Latin for "lamb" is *agnus*). Very popular in England between the 12th and 16th centuries, Agnes is uncommon now, perhaps because of its connotations of homeliness which were probably magnified by Patrick Dennis's portrait of a a frustrated spinster (Agnes Gooch) in *Auntie Mame*. Choreographer Agnes De Mille; actress Agnes Moorhead; writer Anaïs Nin; film director Agnieska Holland.

Ag, Agafi, Agafia, Agafon, Aggi, Aggie, Aggye, Aghna, Agi, Agie, Agna, Agnah, Agnella, Agnellah, Agnelle, Agnese, Agnesca, Agnesse, Agnessina, Agneta, Agnetta, Agnettah, Agnieska, Agniya, Agnola, Agnolah, Agot, Agota, Agote, Agoti, Agy, Agye, Aigneis, Aina, Ainah, Anaïs, Annais, Anneyce, Annis, Annisa, Annisah, Annise, Ina, Inah, Ines, Inessa, Inez, Nessa, Nessah, Nesi, Nessie, Nessy, Nesta, Nestah, Nevsa, Nevesah, Neysa, Oona, Oonagh, Oonah, Senga, Una, Unah, Ynes, Ynez

Agnola It. "Angel." Also a variant of **Agnes**.

Agnolla, Agnolle

Agraciana Sp. "Forgiving."

Agracianna, Agracyanna

Agrafina Rus. "Born feet first." See **Agrippa**.

Agrippa Lat. "Born feet first." The name of a 1st-century Roman Emperor, the son of Herod. A man's name possibly transferred to female use because of the "-a" ending.

Agrafina, Agrippina, Agrippine

Agrippina Lat. Sister of the corrupt Roman Emperor Caligula and mother of the equally unsavory Roman Emperor Nero, who had her murdered. Not a common name, for obvious reasons.

Ahava Heb. "Loved one."

Ahouva, Ahuva, Ahuda

Aibhlin Ir. Gael. form of **Evelyn** or **Helen**.

Aida Arab. "Reward, present." Name of an immensely popular opera by Giuseppe Verdi.

Aeeda, Ayeeda, Ieeda, Iyeeda

. Gael. "fire." Saint Aidan was a 7th-century Irish
. The name is more common for men than for
women.

Adan, Aden, Aiden, Aydan, Ayden, Aydenn

Aiko Jap. "Little loved one."

Ailbhe Ir. "Noble, bright."

Alva, Alvy, Elva, Elvy

Aileen Irish variant of **Helen** (Gk. "Light"). This form has
been most popular in Scotland as opposed to the variant
Eileen, which is more common in the U.S.

**Aila, Ailee, Ailene, Ailey, Ailli, Ailie, Aleen, Alene, Aline,
Alleen, Allene, Alline, Eileen, Eleen, Elleen, Ellene,
Ileana, Ileane, Ileanna, Ilene, Iliana, Iliane, Ilianna, Il-
leanne, Illene, Leana, Leanah, Leanna, Leannah, Lena,
Lenah, Liana, Lianna, Liannah, Lina, Linah**

Ailith OE. "Seasoned warrior."

Aldith, Eilith

Ailsa Scot. The name has two possible sources. As a homonym for **Elsa**, a diminutive of **Elizabeth**, it means
"Pledge from God." An alternate source is the tiny Scottish island Ailsa Craig, which has prompted a few home-
sick Scots to use the name in the U.S.

Ailis, Ailse, Elsa, Elsha, Elshe

Aimée Fr. "Beloved." This form of Amy is popular with
parents who are looking for a fanciful twist on an old
favorite. Evangelist Aimee Semple McPherson.

Aimie, Aimey, Amey, Amie

Aina Scand. "Forever."

Aine Celt. "Happiness."

Ainsley Scot. Gael. Place name: "One's own meadow." A
last name converted to a first name, used by both sexes,
though never with the frequency of the closely related
Ashley.

**Ainslea, Ainslee, Ainsleigh, Ainslie, Ansley, Aynslee, Ayn-
sley, Aynslie**

Airlea Gk. "Ethereal."

Airlia

Aisha Arab. "Woman" or Swahili "Life." Aisha was the
favored wife of Mohammed, hence the name's current
huge popularity among Muslim families all over the

world. It is also frequently used by African-Am
families, and just as often respelled or embroidered to
make interesting variations.

Aeesha, Aeeshah, Aesha, Aeshah, Aiesha, Aieshah, Ais-
hah, Aisia, Aisiah, Aixa, Asha, Ashah, Ashia, Ashiah,
Asia, Asiah, Ayeesa, Ayeesah, Ayeesha, Ayeeshah, Ay-
eisa, Ayeisah, Ayeisha, Ayeishah, Ayisa, Ayisah, Ayisha,
Ayishah, Ieasha, Ieashah, Ieashia, Ieashiah, Iesha, Ies-
hah, Ieesha, Ieeshah, Ieeshia, Ieeshiah, Yiesha, Yieshah

Aislinn Ir. Gael. "Dream."

Aisling, Ashling, Isleen

Aithne (Fem. **Aidan**) Ir. Gael. "Fire." Not to be confused,
despite its sound, with the name of the Sicilian volcano.

Aine, Aithnea, Eithne, Ena, Ethnah, Ethnea, Ethnee

Aiyana Native American. "Forever flowering."

Aja Hindi. "Goat." Also possibly used as a phonetic variation on **Asia**.

Azha

Ajua Ghanaian. "Born on Monday."

Akela Haw. "Noble." A form of **Adele**.

Akilina Gk./Rus. "Eagle."

Acquilina, Acuqileena, Aquilina

Akiva Heb. "Protect, shelter."

Akeeva, Keeva, Keevah, Kiba, Kibah, Kiva, Kivah, Kivi

Akosua Ghanaian. "Born on Sunday."

Alaia Arab. "Sublime."

Alaine (Fem. **Alan**) Fr. from Gael. Possibly "Rock" or
"Comely." Not actually used in France, where it would
be very easily confused with Hélène.

Alaina, Alayna, Alayne, Aleine, Alenne, Aleyne, Allaine,
Allayne, Alleine, Allene

Alala Gk. In Greek mythology, the sister of Ares, the god
of war.

Alamea Haw. "Ripe, precious."

Alanna (Fem. **Alan**) Gael. "Rock" or "Comely." Also a
possible derivative of Elaine (OF. "Bright, shining") or
Helen (Gk. "Light"). Singer Alanis Morrissette; actress
Lana Turner.

Alaina, Alaine, Alana, Alane, Alanis, Alannah, Alayne,
Alène, Aleyna, Aleynah, Aleyne, Alleen, Allena, Allene, Al-

lyna, Alleynah, Alleyne, Allina, Allinah, Allyn, Lana, Lanah, Lanna, Lannah

Alaqua Native American. "Sweet gum tree."

Alarice (Fem. **Alaric**) OG. "Noble king." Alaric was a king of the Visigoths who sacked Rome.

Alarica, Alaricka, Alarieka

Alastair Scot. Var. of **Alexander** (Gk. "Man's defender"). More generally used as a man's name, though the feminizations sometimes crop up in Scotland.

Alasdair, Alastrina, Alastriona, Alistair

Alaula Haw. "Light of daybreak."

Alba Lat. "White." See **Albinia**.

Albane, Albina, Albine, Albinia, Albinka, Alva

Alberga Lat. "White" or OG. "Noble." Also closely related to the French and Italian word for "inn."

Alberge, Elberga, Elberge

Alberta OE. "Noble-shining." Rare and old-fashioned now, it was most widely used during the lifetime of Queen Victoria's Prince Consort, Albert. Also the name of a western Canadian province, and a very popular strain of peach.

Alberthine, Albertina, Albertine, Ali, Alli, Allie, Ally, Auberta, Auberte, Aubertha, Auberthe, Aubine, Berrie, Berry, Bert, Berta, Berte, Berti, Bertie, Berty, Elberta, Elbertha, Elberthina, Elberthine, Elbertina, Elbertine

Albinia (Fem. **Alban, Albin**) Lat. "White, fair." From the same root as "albino."

Alba, Albina, Alva, Alvina, Aubine

Albreda (Fem. **Aubrey**) OG. "Counsel from the elves."

Alcestis Gk. In Euripides' play of the same name, Alcestis descends to Hades in place of her husband, and is then rescued by Hercules.

Alcina Gk. In Greek myth, a sorceress who rules over a magical island. When she tired of her lovers, Alcina turned them into animals, trees, or stones. Despite this startling role model the name occurs from time to time.

Alcine, Alcinia, Allcine, Allcinia, Alseena, Alsina, Alsinia, Alsyna, Alzina

Alcinda Possibly an adaptation of **Lucinda** (Lat. "Light") or a variant of **Alison** (OG. "Noble, nobility").

Alacinda, Alicinda, Alicynthia, Allcinda

Alda (Fem. **Aldo, Otto**) OG. "Old, prosperous."
Aldabella, Aldea, Aldina, Aldine, Aleda, Alida

Aldara Gk. "Winged gift."

Aldis OE. "Battle-seasoned."
Aldith, Ailith

Aldonza Sp. "Sweet."

Aleeza Heb. "Joy."
Aleezah, Alieza, Aliezah, Aliza, Alizah, Alitza

Alegria Sp. "Happiness, joy." For related names, see **Hilary, Felicity, Bliss**. A charming choice for a much-wanted child.
Alagria, Alegrya, Allegra, Allegria

Alena Rus. Var. **Helen** (Gk. "Light").

Alesia Gk. "Help, aid."
Alessia

Aleta Gk. "Footloose."
Aletta, Alette, Alletta, Allette, Eletta, Elletta, Ellette, Lettee, Lettie, Letty

Alethea Gk. "Truth." Unusual name that first appeared in Britain in the 17th century.
Alathea, Alathia, Aleethia, Aleta, Aletea, Aletha, Alethia, Aletta, Alette, Alithea, Alithia, Elethea, Elithia

—**Alexandra** (Fem. **Alexander**) Gk. "Man's defender." Became very popular in Britain after the Prince of Wales (later Edward VII) married the Danish Princess Alexandra. Still used in the English royal family and its many branches. Possibly this aristocratic connection has fueled the name's recent surge in popularity. Ballet dancer Alexandra Danilova; fashion designer Zandra Rhodes.
Alastrina, Alastriona, Alejanda, Alejandra, Alejandrina, Aleka, Aleki, Alesandare, Alesandere, Alessanda, Alessandra, Alessandre, Alessandrina, Alessandrine, Alessia, Alex, Alexa, Alexanda, Alexandere, Alexanderia, Alexanderina, Alexanderine, Alexandre, Alexandrea, Alexandreana, Alexandrena, Alexandrene, Alexandretta, Alexandria, Alexandrina, Alexandrine, Alexea, Alexena, Alexene, Alexia, Alexina, Alexine, Alexis, Ali, Aliki, Alissandre, Alissandrine, Alista, Alix, Alla, Allejandra, Allejandrina, Allessa, Allessandra, Alle, Allexa, Allexandra, Allexandrina, Allexina, Allexine, Alli, Allie, Allix, Ally, Anda, Cesya, Elena, Ellena, Lesy, Lesya, Lexi, Lexie, Lex-

ine, Lissandre, Lissandrine, Sanda, Sande, Sandi, San-
die, Sandra, Sandrina, Sandrine, Sandy, Sandye,
Sanndra, Sasha, Sashenka, Shura, Shurochka, Sohndra,
Sondra, Xandra, Zahndra, Zanda, Zanndra, Zohndra,
Zondra

Alexis Gk. "Helper." Usually thought of as a short form
of Alexandra, though it has a different etymological root.
Originally a name for both genders, it is now almost exclusively female. Actress Alexis Smith; TV character
Alexis Carrington.

Alessa, Alessi, Alexa, Alexi, Alexia, Lexi, Lexie, Lexy

Alfonsine (Fem. **Alfonso**) OG. "Noble and ready for battle."

Alfonsa, Alfonsia, Alonza, Alphonsina

Alfreda (Fem. **Alfred**) OE. "Elf power." Actress Alfre
Woodard.

**Alfi, Alfie, Alfre, Alfredah, Alfredda, Alfreeda, Alfri, Al-
fried, Alfrieda, Alfryda, Alfy, Allfie, Allfreda, Allfredah,
Allfredda, Allfrie, Allfrieda, Allfry, Allfryda, Allfy, Elfie,
Elfré, Elfrea, Elfredah, Elfredda, Elfreeda, Elfrida, El-
frieda, Elfryda, Elfrydah, Ellfreda, Ellfredah, Ellfredda,
Ellfreeda, Ellfrida, Ellfrieda, Ellfryda, Ellfrydah, Elva, El-
vah, Freda, Freddi, Freddie, Freddy, Fredi, Fredy,
Freeda, Freedah, Frieda, Friedah, Fryda, Frydah**

— **Alice** OG. "Noble, nobility." See **Adelaide**. An old
standby name since the Middle Ages that became enormously popular after the 1865 publication of Lewis Carroll's *Alice's Adventures in Wonderland*. Its popularity
waned in the 1930s, and it now has a pleasantly old-
fashioned air. A good choice for parents seeking an unusual but not startling name. Ballerina Alicia Markova;
writer Alice Walker; actresses Ali McGraw, Ally Sheedy.

**Adelice, Ailis, Ala, Aleceea, Alecia, Aleetheea, Aleethia,
Ali, Alica, Alicah, Alicea, Alicen, Alicia, Alidée, Alie, Alika,
Alikah, Aliki, Alis, Alisa, Alisah, Alisann, Alisanne, Al-
isha, Alison, Alissa, Alisz, Alitheea, Alitia, Aliz, Alla, Al-
lecia, Alleece, Alleeceea, Alles, Alless, Alli, Allice, Allicea,
Allie, Allis, Allison, Allissa, Allisun, Allisunne, Allsun,
Ally, Allyce, Allyceea, Allys, Allyse, Allysia, Allysiah, Allyson, Allyssa, Allysson, Alyce, Alyceea, Alys, Alyse, Alysia, Alyson, Alyss, Alyssa, Elissa, Elli, Ellie, Ellissa, Ellsa,**

Elsa, Illyssa, Ilysa, Ilysah, Ilyssa, Ilysse, Leece
cha, Lichah, Lissa, Lyssa, Talicia

Alickina (Fem. Alick) Scot. Var. Alexander (Gl. defender'').

Aleckina

Alida Lat. "Small winged one." Another possible etymology traces the name to the Greek for "well dressed."

Adela, Adelina, Adelita, Adellyna, Adellyta, Adelyna, Adelyta, Alaida, Alda, Aldina, Aldine, Aldona, Aldonna, Aldyne, Aleda, Aleta, Aletta, Alette, Alidah, Alidia, Alita, Allda, Alldina, Alldine, Alldona, Alldonna, Alldyne, Alleda, Allida, Allidah, Allidia, Allidiah, Allyda, Allydah, Alyda, Alydah, Dela, Della, Dila, Dilla, Elida, Elita, Leda, Ledah, Lida, Lidah, Lita, Lyda, Lydah, Oleda, Oleta, Oletta, Olette

Aliki Variant of Alice (OG. "Noble, nobility''). Author Aliki.

Aleeki, Alliki

Alima Arab. "Cultured."

Alina Slavic. Var. Helen (Gk. "Light'').

Aleen, Aleena, Alena, Alenah, Alene, Aline, Alleen, Allena, Allene, Alline, Allyna, Allynah, Allyne, Alyna, Alynah, Alyne, Leena, Leenah, Lena, Lenah, Lina, Linah, Lyna, Lynah

Alinda Elaboration of Linda (Sp. "Pretty'').

Alindea, Alindia, Allinda, Allindie, Alynda

Alisa Heb. "Great happiness." Easily confused with Elisa, which is a variation of Elizabeth. Another similar name, Alyssa, is much more popular.

Alisah, Alissa, Alissah, Alitza, Alitzah, Aliza, Allisa, Allisah, Allissa, Allissah, Allysa, Allysah, Alyssa, Alyssah

Alison Dim. Alice (OG. "Noble, nobility'').

Ali, Alisann, Alisanne, Alisoun, Alisun, Allcen, Allcenne, Alli, Allicen, Allicenne, Allie, Allisann, Allisanne, Allison, Allisoun, Allsun, Ally, Allysann, Allysanne, Allyson, Allysoun, Alysan, Alysann, Alysanne, Alyson, Alysoun

Alix OG. "Noble." See Alexandra. The ill-fated Alexandra, last Empress of Russia, was known to her family as Alix.

Alex, Alexa, Alexis, Aliki, Alissandre, Alissandrine, Lissandre

liya Arab. "Highborn."
Alia, Aliah Aliyah, Aliye, Allia, Alliah

Alla Numerous possible origins: a variant of **Ella**, a shortening of any of the myriad "Al-" names, even, possibly, a reference to Allah.
Ala, Alah, Allah

Allegra It. "Joyous." The musical term "allegro" means "quickly, with a happy air." Ballerina Allegra Kent.
Alegra, Allegretta, Alegria, Legra, Leggra

Allena (Fem. **Allen, Alan**) Ir. Possible meaning "Rock" or "Comely." See **Alanna.**
Alana, Alanice, Alanis, Alanna, Alena, Alene, Allana, Allene, Alleyne, Allynn, Allynne, Allynn, Alynne

Allura OF. "To entice, attract." Based on the noun, which means "power of attraction."
Alloura, Alura

Allyriane Fr. from Gk. "Lyre." The lyre was a stringed instrument, a predecessor of today's harp or guitar.

Alma Lat. "Giving nurture"; It. "Soul"; Arab. "Learned." Also the name of a river in the Crimea where a famous 19th century battle was fought, bringing it into prominence as a first name. The more common usage, of course, is "alma mater" for a college or university. Composer's wife Alma Mahler.
Almah, Allma

Almarine OG. "Work ruler."
Almeria, Almerine

Almeda Lat. "Goal-directed, ambitious."
Allmeda, Allmedah, Allmeta, Allmetah, Allmida, Allmidah, Allmita, Allmitah, Almedah, Almeta, Almetah, Almida, Almidah, Almita, Almitah, Maelle

Almera (Fem. **Elmer**) Arab. "Aristocratic lady." Popular in Arabic countries.
Allmeera, Allmeria, Almeera, Almeeria, Almeria, Almire, Almirah, Almyra, Ellmera, Ellmeria, Elmeera, Elmeeria, Elmera, Elmeria, Elmira, Elmyra, Elmyrah, Mera, Meera, Mira, Mirah, Myra, Myrah

Almodine Lat. "Precious stone."

Almond Plant name. May refer to skin tone, or to the shape of a baby's eyes.
Almandina, Almandine, Almondine, Amande, Amandina

Aloe Plant name. The aloe plant grows in hot climates, and its fleshy leaves, though often equipped with thorns, are full of sap that is widely considered to have healing qualities.

Aloha Haw. "Love, kindness, affection." The familiar Hawaiian greeting.

Aloisia (fem. **Aloysius**) OG. "Famous fighter."
Aloysia, Eloisia, Eloysia

Alona Heb. "Oak tree." The many different spellings of this name attest to its use all over Europe.
Allona, Allonia, Alonia, Elona, Ilona, Ilonka

Alonsa (fem. **Alonso**) Sp./OG. "Ready for battle."
Alonsina, Alonza

Alouette Fr. "Lark." Bird name. Familiar from the children's song, "*Alouette, gentille alouette, je te plumerai,*" which is actually a threat to pluck all the feathers from the poor bird.
Allouette, Alouetta, Alowette

Alpha Gk. First letter of Greek alphabet, corresponding to *A*. Appropriate for a first daughter.
Alfa

Alphonsine (Fem. **Alphonse**) Fr. from OG. "Ready for battle."

Alta Lat. "Elevated."
Allta

Altagracia Sp. Elaboration of "grace." Also commemorates the feast of "Our Lady of Altagracia."
Allagracia, Altagrazia

Altair Arab. "Bird." Also the name of the brightest star in the constellation Aquila. It is about ten times as bright as the sun.

Althea Gk. "With healing power." Tennis star Althea Gibson.
Altha, Althaia, Altheda, Althelia, Althia, Eltha, Elthea, Thea

Altheda Gk. "Like a blossom."

Aludra Gk. "Virgin." Can be used for babies born under the sign of Virgo.

Alufa Heb. "Leader."

Aluma Heb. "Maiden" or "Sheaf" (as in a sheaf of grain at the harvest).
Alumice, Alumit

a Mineral name: oxygen and aluminium form the substance called "corundum," which is the basis of such gems as ruby, sapphire, and amethyst. *Lumina*, the source of the name, is the Latin word for light.

Allumina

Alura OE. "Godlike adviser." Same sound as Allura, but completely different source.

Alurea, Allura, Ellura

Alva Sp. "Blond, fair-skinned." See **Alba, Albina.** Also Heb. "Foliage." Better-known as a man's name, as in Thomas Alva Edison.

Alba, Albina, Albine, Albinia, Alvah, Alvit

Alvar OE. "Army of elves." Also used as a man's name, but very unusual.

Alverdine OE. "Counsel from the elves." A rare feminine variant of **Alfred.** Alfreda is more common.

Alvina (Fem. **Alvin**) OE. "Noble friend" or "Elf-friend."

Alveena, Alveene, Alveenia, Alvine, Alvineea, Alvinia, Alwinna, Alwyna, Alwyne, Elveena, Elvena, Elvene, Elvenia, Elvina, Elvine, Elvinia, Vina, Vinni, Vinnie, Vinny

Alvita Lat. "Lively."

Alysia Gk. "Entrancing."

Alyssa Gk. "Rational." Also the name of a bright yellow flower, alyssum, and its use may have been influenced by the 19th-century vogue for flower names. Also see the variants of **Alice.** Currently quite popular among American parents.

Alissa, Allissa, Alysa, Elissa, Ilyssa, Lyssa

Alzena Arab. "Woman."

Alzeena, Alzeina, Alzina, Elzeena, Elzina

Ama Ghanaian. "Born on Saturday."

Amabel Lat. "Lovable, amiable." Somewhat popular in the 19th century.

Ama, Amabelle, Belle, Mab, Mabel

Amada Lat. "Loved one."

Amata

Amadea (Fem. **Amadeus**) Lat. "God's beloved." Amadeus was Mozart's middle name, given great prominence by Peter Shaffer's play and the subsequent film.

Amadée, Amédée

Amadore It. "Gift of love."
Amadora
Amal Arab. "Hope."
Amahl, Amahla, Amala
Amalfi Place name: spectacular Italian town and section of coastline overlooking the Gulf of Salerno.
Amalfey, Malfie
Amalida OG. "Hardworking woman." See **Amelia**.
Amaleeda, Amelida
Amalthea In Greek myth, the name of the mountain goat that nursed the infant Zeus. Her horns were the basis for the cornucopia, the horn of plenty spilling over with fruits and vegetables.
Amaltheia
Amana Heb. "Loyal, true, established." A Biblical place name.
— **Amanda** Lat. "Much-loved." Regularly used since the 17th century, and by 1990, the number four choice of American families. In fact, Amanda has had a strikingly long run: it has been in the top five names since 1983 and maintained its huge popularity in many cities as late as 1995. For some reason the name has never seemed trendy, like Ashley or Tiffany. Actress Amanda Plummer.
Amandi, Amandie, Amandine, Amandy, Amata, Manda, Mandaline, Mandee, Mandi, Mandie, Mandy
Amapola Sp. from Arab. "Poppy."
Ama, Ammapola, Pola, Poli
Amara Gk. "Lovely forever."
Amargo, Amargoe, Amargot, Amarinda, Amaris, Amarra, Amarrinda, Mara, Marra
Amarantha Gk. "Deathless." Also the name of both a mythical and a real plant. The mythical one was supposed to be immortal.
Amarande, Amaranta, Amarante
Amarilla Ger. "Shiny" or Sp. "Yellow." There is a city in Texas called Amarillo.
Amaris Heb. "Pledged by God."
Amariah, Amarit
Amaryllis Gk. "Fresh." Also the name of a flower. Used in 18th-century poetry to refer to an unspoiled rural beauty like an idealized shepherdess.
Amarilis

Amber OF. Name of the gold-brown semiprecious stone. Jewel names were popular in the 19th century, but Amber came to prominence again in the 1960s, prompted by the Kathleen Winsor novel and film *Forever Amber*. Possibly because it is a good descriptive name for a golden-skinned baby, Amber is quite fashionable today.

Ambar, Amberetta, Amberly, Ambur

Amberly Com. form **Amber** and **Kimberly**. Or perhaps simply the popular Amber with the also popular "-ly" ending.

Ambarlie, Amberlea, Amberleigh, Amberlie, Amberley

Ambika Hindi. "Mother." Also one of many names for the goddess Devi, wife of Shiva. She has both positive and negative forms, with names for each.

Ambeeka, Ambeika

Ambrosine (Fem. **Ambrose**) Gk. "Ever-living." Like other names with an "-ine" ending, this one has a French air.

Ambrosia, Ambrosina, Ambrosinetta, Ambrosinette, Ambrosiya, Ambrozetta, Ambrozia, Ambrozine

Amelia OG. "Industrious." See **Emily**. An 18th-century Princess Amelia brought the name to Britain, where it was popular in the 19th century. Unusual now, but ripe for a revival. Dress reformer Amelia Bloomer; aviatrix Amelia Earhart.

Aimiliona, Amalea, Amalee, Amaleta, Amalia, Amalie, Amalija, Amalina, Amaline, Amalita, Amaliya, Amalya, Amalyna, Amalyne, Amalyta, Amela, Amelcia, Ameldy, Amélie, Amelina, Ameline, Amelit, Amelita, Ameliya, Amelyna, Amelyne, Amelyta, Amilia, Amy, Em, Emelie, Emelina, Emeline, Emelita, Emma, Emmeline, Emmie, Emmy, Mali, Malia, Malika, Melia, Meline, Millie, Milly

Amelinda Lat./Sp. Com. form "Beloved" and "Pretty."

Amalinda, Amalynda, Amelindah, Amellinda

Amethyst Gk. "Precious wine-colored jewel." An unusual jewel name, though appropriate for a February baby, since amethyst is that month's birthstone.

Amathyst, Amatista, Amethist, Amethiste

Amica Lat. "Friend." Very unusual. Closely related to

Spanish *amiga* or Italian *amica*, the everyday words for "friend" in those languages.

Amicah, Amice, Amika

Amilia Lat. "Amiable." Also possible variant spelling for Amelia or Emilia, though it comes from a different root than the latter.

Amiliya, Amillia, Amilya

Amina Arab. "Honest, trustworthy." Mother of the prophet Muhammad.

Ameena, Aminah, Amineh, Amna, Amyna

Aminta Lat. "Protector." Aminta was the heroine of a well-known pastoral play of the Renaissance, but her name was not much used in real life.

Amintah, Amynta, Eminta, Minta, Minty

Amira Arab. "Highborn girl." Currently popular in the Arabic-speaking countries.

Ameera, Ameerah, Amera, Amerah, Amirah, Amyra, Amyrah, Meera, Meerah, Mera, Merah, Mira, Mirah

Amisa Heb. "Companion, friend."

Amissa

Amita Heb. "Truth" or It. "Friendship." See **Amica, Amy**.

Amit

Amitola Native American. "Rainbow."

Amity Lat. "Friendship, harmony." Could be promoted to the 21st-century version of the virtue names (Prudence, Charity) so popular with the Puritans.

Amitie

Amor Sp. "Love."

Amora, Amore, Amorra

Amorette Fr. "Little love."

Amoretta

Amy Lat. "Loved." In spite of the prominence given the name by Louisa May Alcott's *Little Women*, it didn't become a favorite until the 1950s. Hugely popular (along with Jennifer) in the 1970s. High-achieving Amys of that generation like Olympic swimmer Amy Van Dyken and actress Amy Madigan are now becoming famous. The popular 1995 film of the book may inspire some parents to name daughters Amy. Poet Amy Lowell; evangelist

...ee Semple McPherson; singer Amy Grant; actress Amy Irving; author Amy Tan.

Aime, Aimée, Aimie, Amada, Amata, Amatia, Amé, Amecia, Ami, Amia, Amiah, Amice, Amie, Amii, Amiya, Ammy, Amye, Esma, Esmé

Anafa Heb. "Heron."

Analilia Comb. form **Ana** and **Lilia**.

Analillia, Analiliya, Analillya, Analilya, Annalilia

Ananda Hindi. "Bliss."

Anda

Anastasia Gk. "Resurrection." Indelibly associated with the daughter of Czar Nicholas II who was rumored to have escaped death when her family was assassinated during the Russian Revolution. The 1956 film starring Ingrid Bergman popularized her story, but the name is still something of a mouthful. Short forms like Stacey are much more common. Actress Nastassja Kinski.

Ana, Anastaïse, Anastase, Anastasie, Anastasija, Anastasiya, Anastassia, Anastay, Anasztaizia, Anasztasia, Anestassia, Anstass, Anstice, Asia, Nastassia, Nastassiya, Nastassja, Nastassya, Nastya, Stace, Stacey, Stacia, Stacie, Stacy, Stasiya, Stasja, Stasya, Taisie, Tasenka, Tasia, Tasiya, Tasja, Tasya

Anat Heb. "To sing."

Anath

Anatola Gk. "From the east." Anatolia is a region of Turkey, Greece's nearest neighbor to the East. In fact the ancient city of Troy, site of the legendary Trojan War, is actually in Turkey.

Anatolia, Anatolya

Ancelote Fr. Feminine form of **Lancelot**, the famous knight of the Round Table.

—**Andrea** (Fem. **Andrew**) Gk. "A man's woman." Used very steadily without ever becoming truly fashionable. Actresses Andie MacDowell, Andrea McArdle.

Aindrea, Andee, Andelis, Andere, Anderea, Andi, Andie, Andis, Andra, Andrae, Andre, Andreana, Andreas, Andrée, Andreena, Andreina, Andrel, Andresa, Andretta, Andrette, Andrewena, Andrewina, Andri, Andria, Andriana, Andricka, Andrietta, Andrina, Andrine, Andy, Aun-

drea, Ohndrea, Ohndreea, Ohndria, Ondrea, Ondreea, Ondria, Onndrea, Onndreea, Onndria

Andromeda Gk. In Greek myth, the beautiful daughter of Cassiopeia (now famous as a constellation). She was chained to a rock as a sacrifice to a sea monster until Perseus rescued her. She, too, became a star. Also the name of a spring-blooming shrub.

Anemone Gk. "Breath." In Greek myth, Anemone was the name of a nymph who was turned into a flower, which is also called a windflower.

Anemona, Ann-Aymone, Anne-Aymone

Angela Gk. "Messenger from God, angel." Angel was originally used as a name for men, and in Latin countries Angelo is still popular. Angela came into frequent use in the early 20th century, and is still used often enough to be very familiar. Actresses Angela Lansbury, Angie Dickinson; Olympic swimmer Angel Martino.

Aingeal, Andzela, Anela, Anelja, Ange, Angel, Angèle, Angelene, Angeleta, Angelia, Angelic, Angelica, Angelika, Angeliki, Angelina, Angeline, Angélique, Angelita, Angelle, Angellina, Angie, Angil, Angiola, Angy, Angyola, Anhelina, Anjali, Anjel, Anjela, Anjelica, Anjelika, Anngela, Anngil, Anngilla, Anngiola, Annjela, Annijilla, Anyelle, Gelya, Ohngel, Ohnjella, Onngelle, Onnjelia

Angelica Lat. "Angelic." See **Angela**. Actress Anjelica Huston.

Angelika, Angélique, Angelisa, Angelissa, Angyalka, Anjelica, Anjelika, Anyelika

Angharad Welsh. "Beloved."

Anice Var. **Agnes**. Also possibly a variant of **Ann**, or even of **Anise**.

Anicka, Annice, Annick, Anis, Annis, Annys

Aniceta Sp. from Ger. "Unconquerable." Saint Anicetus was a 2nd-century pope and a martyr. The name also sounds a great deal like Anisette, which has an utterly different source.

Anicetta, Anniceta, Annicetta

Anina Aramaic. "Let my prayer be answered."

Aninna, Annina

Anise Plant name. The source of licorice flavoring. This name may also be used as a variant of **Agnes** or **Anne**.

Aneese, Anis, Anisette

Anisah Arab. "Friendly, congenial."
Anisa, Annissa

Anita Sp. form of **Ann**. Most common in 1950s, possibly because of the popularity of Swedish actress Anita Ekberg. Writers Anita Loos, Anita Brookner.
Anitra, Annita, Annitra, Annitta

Anitra Elaboration of Anita, invented by the playwright Henrik Ibsen for his 1867 drama *Peer Gynt.*
Annitra

Ann Anglicization of **Hannah** (Heb. "Grace"). One of the most frequently used names for girls until the mid–19th century, when it became less popular. When Elizabeth II of England named her daughter Anne in 1950, it became more prominent, but is still more common as a middle name (Betty Ann, etc.). Though the name Ann may seem plain to many, its numerous derivatives offer plenty of variety. The European form Anna is now much more popular than plain old Ann in the United States. Saint Anne (mother of the Virgin Mary); Anne Boleyn, Queen of England; ballerina Anna Pavlova; Wild West sharpshooter Annie Oakley; actresses Anouk Aimée, Anne Bancroft; writers Ayn Rand, Anne Tyler, Anna Quindlen; diarist Anne Frank.
Aine, Ana, Anazizi, Anci, Anechka, Anel, Anell, Anet, Anett, Anette, Ania, Anica, Anika, Aniko, Anissa, Anita, Anitra, Anka, Anke, Anki, Anna, Annabel, Annabella, Annabelle, Annaelle, Annajee, Annella, Annelle, Annelore, Annetta, Annette, Anney, Anni, Annice, Annick, Annie, Annimae, Annina, Annis, Annise, Annora, Annus, Annuska, Anny, Anona, Anouche, Anouk, Anoushka, Anouska, Anushka, Anuska, Anya, Anyi, Anyoushka, Anyshka, Anyu, Asya, Ayn, Hajna, Hana, Hanja, Hanka, Hanna, Hannah, Hanneke, Hannelore, Hanni, Hannie, Hanny, Nan, Nana, Nance, Nancee, Nancey, Nanci, Nancie, Nancy, Nanete, Nanette, Nanice, Nanine, Nanni, Nannie, Nanny, Nanon, Nanor, Neti, Nettia, Nettie, Netty, Nina, Ninette, Ninon, Ninor, Nita, Nona, Nonie

Annabel Possibly com. form **Anna** and **Belle**: "Graceful" and "Beautiful." Also a mutation of Amabel. Most famous bearer was Edgar Allan Poe's Annabel Lee, in the poem of the same name.

Anabel, Anabella, Anabelle, Annabal, Annabelinda, Annabell, Annabella, Annabelle

Annamaria Comb. form **Ann** and **Mary**. Annemarie is the most popular variation, especially since the 1950s. The reverse form, Marianne, is also frequently used. The popularity of the pairing may originate in Roman Catholic veneration of Saint Anne and Saint Mary, mother and daughter.

Annamarie, Annemarie, Annmaria

Annalise Comb. form **Ann** and **Lise**.

Analeisa, Analiesa, Analiese, Analise, Anelisa, Anelise, Annaleisa, Annalie, Annaliesa, Annaliese, Annalise, Annelie, Anneliese, Annelisa, Annelise, Annelisse, Annelyse, Annissa

Annemae Comb. form **Ann** and **May**.

Annamae, Annamay, Annemie

Annette Dim. **Ann**. Most baby boomers will always associate this name with Mouseketeer Annette Funicello. Elaborated forms like Annetta may also be considered variations of **Agnes**.

Anet, Anett, Anneth, Anetta, Annetta

Annis Gk. "Finished, completed." See also variants of **Ann**. Also easily confused by the ear with Agnes, Anice, and Anise, a point prospective parents might keep in mind.

Anissa, Annes, Annice, Annys

Annora Lat. "Honor." A phonetic version of **Honora**.

Anora, Anorah, Honor, Honora, Onora, Nora, Norah

Annwyl Welsh. "Loved one."

Annwyll, Anwylle

Anona Lat. from Sp. "Pineapple." A name likely to be used for its pretty sound rather than for its meaning.

Annona, Anonna

Anouska Rus. var. **Ann**.

Annouska, Annuskha, Anuska, Anyoushka

Annunciata Lat. Allusion to the Annunciation, when the Virgin Mary learned she would be Jesus' mother. Some times given to a girl born in March, the logical month for such an announcement.

Anonciada, Annunziate, Anunciacion, Anunciata, Anunziata

Annot Heb./Scot. "Light."

Anonna Lat. Name of the Roman goddess of the annual harvest. An appropriate name for an October or November baby.
Anona, Nona

Anselma (Fem. **Anselm**) OG. "Godly helmet." The short forms are much more common.
Selma, Zelma

Ansley OE. Place name: "The awesome one's meadow." Probably not, in spite of the way it sounds, "Ann's meadow" because women so rarely owned property in the days when last names were coming into existence. An alternative to Ashley.
Annesleigh, Annslea, Annsleigh, Anslea, Ansleigh, Anslie

Ansonia (Fem. **Anson**). Unclear origin and meaning. Possibly "Son of Ann," though "Son of the divine" seems more likely. It can even be considered a combined form of **Ann** and **Sonia**.
Annesonia, Annsonia, Annsonya, Ansonya

Anstice Var. **Anastasia** (Gk. "Resurrection").
Anstiss, Anstyce

Antalya Rus. from Gk. "From the East." A variant of **Anatola**. Also an anagram of the popular Russian Natalya, which means Christmas.
Antaliya

Anthea Gk. "Flowerlike." Used by English 17th-century poets to symbolize spring, but occurring infrequently in real life. Slightly more popular in England, where it has an upper-class aura.
Annthea, Anthe, Antheia, Antheya, Antia, Thia

Anthemia Gk. "In bloom." From the same Greek root as Anthea.
Antheemia, Anthemya, Anthymia

Antje Ger. form of **Ann** (Heb. "Grace"). Currently popular in Germany.

Antigone Gk. In myth, the daughter of Oedipus.

Antoinette (Fem. **Anthony**) Lat. "Beyond price, invaluable." Also a diminutive of **Ann**. Irresistibly associated with the ill-fated French Queen Marie Antoinette. Ballerina Antoinette Sibley.
Antonetta, Antonia, Antonie, Antonieta, Antonietta, Antonina, Antonine, Antwahnette, Antwanetta, Antwinett,

Antwohnette, Netta, Netti, Nettie, Netty, Toinette, Toni, Tonia, Tonie, Tony, Tonye

Antonia Lat. "Beyond price, invaluable." Also a diminutive of **Ann**. The increasing popularity of dignified Latinate names may bring this one to greater prominence. Willa Cather novel *My Antonía;* English writer Antonia Fraser.

Antoinette, Antonetta, Antonie, Antonietta, Antonija, Antoniya, Antonina, Antonya, Netta, Nettie, Netty, Toinette, Tonechka, Tonette, Toni, Tonia, Tonie, Tony, Tonya

Anwen Welsh. "Very fair."

Anwyn, Anwynne

Anwar Arab. "Rays of light." Most familiar as a man's name borne by Egyptian president Anwar Sadat.

Aphra Heb. "Dust." The English Puritans actually used both Dust and Ashes as first names in the 17th century. Early female playwright Aphra Behn.

Affera, Affery, Afra

Apia Lat. "Pious, prayerful." The parallel is the name borne by numerous popes, Pius.

Apphia

Apolline (Fem. **Apollo**) Gk. The god of the sun in Greek mythology. Saint Apollonia was an early Christian martyr. Her teeth were knocked out as part of her martyrdom. In art she is often portrayed with a pair of tongs and an outsized molar.

Abbeline, Abbelina, Appoline, Appolinia, Apollinia, Apollonia, Apollyne, Appolonia

Aponi NAm. Ind. "Butterfly."

Aponee

Apple Fruit name. For no very clear reason, fruits are underrepresented among names: Cherry is the only one in common usage. Yet we say that a much loved person is "the apple of my eye."

April Lat. "Opening up." First used as a name in the 20th century, and occurs most often for a girl born in that month. However the sidekick of the hugely popular Ninja Turtles was named April, which will give it an undesirable cartoony resonance for a few years. Curiously, only the months April, May, and June are used for names, with June the most popular.

Aipril, Aprilete, Aprill, Aprille, Averel, Averell, Averil, Averill, Averyl, Averyll, Averylle, Avril, Avrill

Aquilina (Fem. **Aquilino**) Sp. "Like an eagle."

Ara Arab. "Brings rain."

Ari, Aria, Arria

Arabella Lat. "Answered prayer." Unusual name that occurs most frequently in England, where it has an upper-class aura. A ship named the *Arbella* brought a group of Puritan English aristocrats to the Massachusetts Bay Colony in 1630; many socially prominent Boston families are descended from this group.

Ara, Arabel, Arabela, Arabele, Arabelle, Arbela, Arbell, Arbella, Arbelle, Bel, Bella, Belle, Orabel, Orabella, Orabelle, Orbel, Orbella, Orbelle

Araceli Sp. from Lat. "Altar of heaven."

Aracelis, Ariceli, Aricelly

Arachne Gk. In myth, a young maiden who challenged the goddess Athena to a weaving contest and was turned into a spider for her presumption. Spiders, as a biological group, are known as "arachnids."

Arakne, Archna

Araminta Comb. form **Arabella** and **Aminta**. Invented by an 18th-century English playwright, and very unusual.

Arameta, Areminta

Arava Heb. "Willow" or "Arid land." The willow is one of the four kinds of wood used at Sukkoth, the Jewish harvest festival.

Aravah

Arcadia Gk. Originally the place name of a region in Greece which eventually came to stand for the home of simple pastoral happiness, and later still for Paradise itself.

Arcadie

Arcangela Gk. "High-ranking angel." Archangels rank above angels in the celestial hierarchy (which also includes seraphim, cherubim, thrones, principalities, and powers).

Arcangel, Archangela, Archangella

Arcelia Sp. "Treasure chest."

Aricelia, Aricelly

Arda Heb. "Bronze."

Ardah, Ardath

Ardelle Lat. "Burning with enthusiasm." See **Arden**.
   Arda, Ardalia, Ardeen, Ardelia, Ardelis, Ardella, Ardene, Ardia, Ardine, Ardis, Ardra
Arden Lat. "Burning with enthusiasm." The Forest of Arden in Shakespeare's *As You Like It* was a magically beautiful place. Most famous in modern times as the surnames of cosmetics queen Elizabeth Arden and actress Eve Arden. Great potential for a 21st century girls' name.
   Ardeen, Ardena, Ardenia, Ardin, Ardis
Arella Heb. "Messenger from God, angel."
   Arela, Arelle
Arete Gk. "Woman of virtue." Singer Aretha Franklin has put an indelible stamp on her version of this name.
   Areta, Aretha, Arethusa, Aretina, Aretta, Arette, Oreta, Oretha, Oretta, Orette, Retha
Arethusa Greek mythology. Arethusa was a nymph being pursued by a river god, who was changed by Artemis into a stream to avoid a fate worse than death.
Argenta Lat. "Silvery." The country of Argentina is named for the silver its early Spanish settlers hoped to find there, but did not.
   Argentia, Argentina
Aria It. "A melody." In the classical operatic form, arias are solos performed by the leading characters.
Ariadne Gk. The mythological daughter of Cretan King Minos, who gave Theseus a thread to guide him out of the mazelike prison known as the Labyrinth. Theseus married, then abandoned, her. Also the subject and title of a Richard Strauss opera. TV commentator Arianna Stassinopoulos Huffington.
   Arène, Ariadna, Ariagna, Ariana, Ariane, Arianie, Arianna, Arianne, Aryana, Aryane, Aryanie, Aryanna, Aryanne
Ariana Welsh. "Like silver." This is also the Italian version of **Ariadne**.
   Ariane, Arianna
Arianwyn Welsh. "Woman of silver."
   Arianwen, Arianwynn, Arianwynne, Aryanwen
Ariel Heb. "Lioness of God." In Shakespeare's *The Tempest*, Ariel is a sprite who can disappear at will. The name has the connotation of something otherworldly, and

though Shakespeare's Ariel is male, the name is used mostly for girls.

Aeriel, Aeriela, Aeriell, Ariela, Ariella, Arielle, Ariellel

Arista Gk. "The best." The root of our word "aristocrat."

Aristella, Aristelle

Arizona Place name: southwestern U.S. state. The name comes from an Indian word thought to mean "small spring."

Arlene Derivation unclear. Possibly Dim. **Charles** (OE. "Man"); possibly Fem. **Arlen**, related to Gael. "Pledge." The name first appeared in the mid–19th century and was popular by the 1930s, though it is hardly ever used now. Actresses Arlene Francis, Arlene Dahl.

Arla, Arlana, Arlee, Arleen, Arlen, Arlena, Arleta, Arlette, Arleyne, Arlie, Arliene, Arlina, Arlinda, Arline, Arluene, Arly, Arlyn, Arlyne, Arlynn, Lena, Lene, Lina

Arlette Fr. from **Charles** (OE "Man").

Arlet, Arletta

Arlise (Fem. **Arliss**) Heb. "Pledge."

Arlyse, Arlyss

Armande (Fem. **Armand**) Fr. from OG. "Army man."

Armanda, Armonde, Ormonde

Armida Lat. "Little armed one."

Armina It. from OG. "Army man." Both Armande and Armina are versions of **Herman**.

Armantine, Armeena, Armine, Arminie, Armyne, Erminia, Erminie, Ermyne

Armona Heb. "Chestnut brown."

Armonit

Arnalda (Fem. **Arnold**) OG. "Eagle-strength."

Arnolda

Arnett OE. "Small eagle."

Arnette, Ornett, Ornetta, Ornette, Orrnett

Arnina (Fem. **Aaron**) Heb. "On high."

Arna, Arona, Arnice, Arnit

Arsenia Fem. **Arsenio** (Sp. from Gk. "Manly"). This name was little known outside the Spanish-speaking community until Arsenio Hall became famous.

Arcenia, Arsania, Arsemia

Artemisia Gk./Sp. "Perfect." Also a version of **Artemas**,

a man's name that occurs in the Bible. Better know
days as the name of a shrub fairly common in the U.S.

Artemasia, Artemesia

Artha Hindi. "Riches."

Arthuretta (Fem. **Arthur**) Celt. Possibly "Bear" or
"Rock." A 19th-century version of the man's name that
was very popular until about 1920. The feminine versions
never really caught on.

Artheia, Arthelia, Arthene, Arthurene, Arthurette, Arthurina, Arthurine, Artia, Artice, Artina, Artis, Artlette, Artrice

Arza Heb. "Panels of cedar." The walls of Solomon's temple were lined with cedar.

Ariza, Arizit, Arzice, Arzit

Asención Sp. Literally "ascension," marking Christ's ascension into heaven, which is commemorated forty days
after Easter. The capital of Paraguay is Asunción.

Asunción

Ashanti Af. Area in West Africa where many American
slaves came from. Used in modern American black families as a link to the African past. The "-i" ending, which
is so close to the English diminutives "-ie" or "-y,"
seems to make it more popular for girls.

Ashanta, Ashantae, Ashantay, Ashante, Ashantee, Ashaunta, Ashaunte, Ashauntee, Ashaunti, Ashuntae, Shantee, Shanti, Shauntae, Shauntee

Ashira Heb. "Rich" or "I will sing."

Asheera, Ashirah

Ashra (Fem. **Asher**) Heb. "Fortunate, felicitous."

Ashera, Asherit

Ashby OE. Place name: "Ash tree farm." The meaning of
all of these "Ash-" names is virtually irrelevant, since
the popularity of Ashley has long since eclipsed any
meaning the name once had. Related names may gain
popularity from it, or the backlash may already have begun, and the tide of fashion may be moving on to distinctly non-Ashley names.

Ashbea, Ashbie

Ashley OE. Place name: "Ash-tree meadow." Originally a
surname that migrated to first-name status, possibly
helped along by Ashley Wilkes in Margaret Mitchell's

Gone With the Wind. Though originally used for boys, it is now tremendously popular for girls, especially on the East Coast. In Florida, for instance, Ashley was the number one name in 1995. It is probably the Waspy nature of the name, with its lingering upper-class aura, that continues to make it such a hit. The immense TV exposure of *Full House*'s Ashley Olsen probably doesn't hurt.

Ashely, Ashla, Ashlay, Ashlan, Ashlee, Ashleigh, Ashlen, Ashli, Ashlie, Ashly

Ashlynn Var. **Aisling** (Ir. Gael. "Dream"). Strictly speaking, this name is a Gaelic adaptation, but parents who use it are more likely to be mentally combining Ashley and Lynn.

Ashelynn, Ashlin, Ashlinne, Ashlynne

Ashton OE. Place name: "Eastern town."

Asia Name of the continent. The feminine "-ia" ending lends itself to adaptation as a girl's name, while the panglobal connotations may give it a boost in the next decade.

Aja, Asiah, Azha

Asima Arab. "Guardian."

Asma Arab. "Of high standing." Currently popular in the Arab-speaking community.

Aspasia Gk. "Welcoming." The famous Athenian statesman Pericles had a mistress named Aspasia, who was noted for her beauty and wit. Surprisingly the name enjoyed mild popularity in the straitlaced 19th century. Almost unknown now.

Aspen Tree name: a kind of poplar familiar in the West, with heart-shaped leaves that quiver in the lightest breeze, hence its nickname, the "quaking" or "trembling" aspen. Also a chic ski resort and town in Colorado.

Asphodel Gk. "Lily." Flower name, albeit an unusual one. The asphodel is a member of the lily family.

Asfodel, Asfodelle, Asphodelle

Assunta It. "Raised up." From the Assumption of the Virgin Mary, the day she was raised up to heaven. The feast of the Assumption is celebrated on August 15. Asunción, the Spanish term, is also used as a girl's name.

Asta Gk. "Like a star." Also short form of **Anastasia, Astrid, Augusta**, etc. The most famous Asta is probably the terrier owned by Nick and Nora Charles in the famous Thin Man movies of the 1930s.

Astera, Asteria, Asti, Astra, Estella, Esther, Estrella, Étoile, Hadassah, Hester, Stella

Asteria Greek mythological name: Asteria was a woman whom Zeus took a fancy to. She was changed into a quail to escape him.

Astra Lat. "Starlike, of the stars." First appeared in the 1940s, though other "star names," like Estella, have been around longer.

Asta, Astera, Asteria, Asterina, Astraea, Astrea, Astri, Astria

Astraea Gk. The goddess of justice in classical mythology. When she retired from the earth, according to legend, she became the constellation Virgo. A clever name for a girl born under that sign.

Astraeia

Astrid ONorse. "Beautiful like a god." Unusual in English-speaking countries, but occurs in the royal families of Norway and Belgium. Brazilian singer Astrud Gilberto.

Assi, Astra, Astri, Astride, Astrud, Astryr, Atti

Asunción Sp. Marking the Virgin Mary's ascent into Heaven, which is commemorated on August 15. Also the name of the capital city of Paraguay.

Asención

Atalanta (Fem. **Atlas**) Gk. "Immovable." In Greek myth, Atalanta was an extremely athletic young maiden who refused to marry any man who couldn't beat her in a foot race. In the end, she was defeated by a ruse involving three golden apples.

Atlanta, Atlante

Atara Heb. "Diadem."

Atera, Ateret

Athalia Heb. "The Lord is exalted." In the Old Testament, Athalia was wife of the King of Judah. She murdered forty-two princes to win the throne for herself, and after a reign of six years, was ultimately killed by a mob. A pretty name if you can overlook the history.

Atalee, Atalia, Atalie, Atha, Athalee, Athalie, Attalie

Athanasia (Fem. **Athanasius**) Gk. "Immortal."

Atanasia, Atanasya, Athenasia

Athena Gk. The goddess of wisdom in Greek myth. She was a virgin goddess who sprang fully armed from Zeus's

head, and Homer, in the *Odyssey*, frequently refers to her
as "gray-eyed Athena." A daunting name to live up to.
Athenaïs, Athene, Athie, Athina, Attie

Atifa Arab. "Empathy, affection."
Ateefa, Ateefah, Atifah

Aubrey OF. "Elf ruler." Originally a man's name that arrived in England with the Norman Conquest. For a girl,
the ear will readily confuse it with Audrey, which may
explain why the name has not caught on as readily as
some other previously male names like Ashley.
**Aubary, Aubery, Aubree, Aubreigh, Aubrette, Aubrie, Au-
bry, Aubury**

Auda OF. "Prosperous."
Aud, Aude

Audrey OE. "Noble strength." Also the root, via Saint Audrey, for the word "tawdry." (In England gaudy neck
laces used to be sold at Saint Audrey's Fair.) Most popular in the 1920s and 1930s, now out of fashion. Actress
Audrey Hepburn.
**Audi, Audie, Audra, Audré, Audree, Audreen, Audria, Au-
drie, Audry, Audrye, Audy**

Audris OG. "Lucky."
Audriss

Augusta (Fem. **Augustus**) Lat. "Worthy of respect." Imported to England by the German mother of George III.
Though common enough in the 18th and 19th centuries,
it is little used now. P. G. Wodehouse's foppish hero Bertie Wooster had a terrifying Aunt Augusta, and she may
be responsible for the slightly intimidating connotations
of the name. It can't help that the most logical diminutive
is "Gussie."
**Auguste, Augustia, Augustina, Augustine, Augustyna,
Augustyne, Austina, Austine, Austyna, Austyne, Gus,
Gussie, Gusta, Tina**

Aura Gk. "Soft breeze" or Lat. "Gold." Most familiar
now, perhaps, in its psychic sense, meaning the atmo-
sphere surrounding an individual.
Aure, Aurea, Auria, Oria

Aurelia Lat. "Gold." Originally a name used by Roman
clans, it resurfaced as a first name in the 19th century, but
is seldom seen now.

Aranka, Aural, Auralia, Aurea, Aurel, Aureliana, Aurélie, Aurelina, Aurita, Ora, Oralia, Orel, Orelee, Orelia

Auriel Lat. "Golden." Not to be confused with Ariel. A name used for slaves in the Roman Empire, possibly as a descriptive term. The 19th-century penchant for unusual names brought it back to occasional use, but it is rare now.

Aureola, Aureole, Auriol, Oriel, Oriole

Aurora Lat. "Dawn." Aurora was the Roman goddess of sunrise. Used by 19th-century poets such as Byron and Browning, but never common. In some version of the fairy tale *Sleeping Beauty*, the princess's name is Aurora.

Aurore, Ora, Rora, Rory, Zora, Zorica

Austine (Fem. **Austin** or **Augustine**) Lat. "Worthy of respect."

Autumn Season name, only recently used as a first name.

Ava Lat. "Like a bird." May have originated as a form of **Eva**. Actress Ava Gardner.

Avis

Avalon Celt. "Island of apples." In Celtic myth, Avalon is an island paradise. In Arthurian legend, it is the island where King Arthur took refuge after his final defeat, and whence he will reappear.

Ave Lat. "Hail."

Avena Lat. "Field of oats."

Avichayil Heb. "Strong father." The anglicized version is Abigail.

Abichail, Avigail, Avigayil

Aviela Heb. "My father is God."

Aviella

Aviva Heb. "Springlike, fresh, dewy."

Auvit, Avivah, Avivi, Avivit, Viva

Avril A French version of April, the month name. Also possibly a version of the name of a 7th-century saint, Everild.

Averel, Averell, Averil, Averill, Averyl

Axelle (Fem. **Axel**) OG. "Father of peace."

Axella

Aya Heb. "Bird."

Ayla

Ayanna Recently invented name that may be considered an elaboration of Anna, or of the typically feminine "-ana" ending. Probably popular because it sounds pretty.

Aiyana, Aiyanna, Ayana, Ayania, Ayannia, Iana, Ianna

Ayesha Per. "Small one."

Aza Arab. "Comfort."

Azalea Lat. "Dry earth." More familiar to us as the name of the shrub that produces brilliant blooms in the spring.
Azaleia, Azalia

Azelia Heb. "Aided by God."

Azhar Arab. "Flowers."

Aziza Heb. "mighty"; Arab. "precious."

Azuba Meaning unknown. Biblical name, used occasionally from the 17th through 19th centuries.
Azubah, Zuba, Zubah

Azucena Sp. from Arab. "White lily."
Asucena, Asusena, Ayscena, Azusayna, Azusena, Azuzena

Azura OF. "Azure, sky blue." A good attribute name for a blue-eyed baby.
Azor, Azora, Azure, Azzura, Azzurra

FORMERLY KNOWN AS

You can name your child almost anything in this country, but the freedom to chose a name doesn't stop there. It's also relatively easy to change your name. Many immigrants to this country, both slaves and European newcomers, had new names arbitrarily assigned when they reached these shores. But plenty of Americans have also opted to shed, streamline, or simply rethink what they're called.

This process has been most notable in the entertainment industry, where names have been changed to add allure (Mary Pickford was originally Gladys Smith) or to present a WASP face to a xenophobic public (Judy Holliday was named Judith Tuvim by her parents). No one bothers much with this anymore, unless to reverse the trend, as Martin Sheen's son Emilio Estevez did. Young actress Renee Zellwegger came to Hollywood with a name that the moguls of the 1940s and '50s would have transformed in an instant. But she stood her ground, saying, "If Arnold Schwarzenegger can keep his name, I can darn well keep mine."

Babe Dim. **Barbara** (Gk. "Foreign"). Also short for "baby," as in "See ya, babe," and a term for an attractive woman. The latter politically incorrect usage will probably limit the number of Babes on birth certificates for the time being. Socialite Babe Paley.

Babette Fr. Dim. **Barbara** (Gk. "Foreign").

Baila Sp. "Dance."
> Beyla, Byla

Bailey OE. "Law enforcer, bailiff." A surname that metamorphosed into a first name in the 19th century, though uncommon. Used more often for boys than for girls though that balance seems to be shifting.
> Bailee, Baily

Baja Geography name: the peninsula attached to the southernmost end of California, which forms part of Mexico. The word comes from the Spanish and means "lower."

Bakura Heb. "A ripe fruit."

Balbina Lat. "Little stutterer."
> Balbine

Ballade Name of a musical or poetic form, usually one that tells a story.

Bambi It. "Child." Short for bambina. Of course, the most famous Bambi is Walt Disney's cartoon deer, who happens to be male.
> Bambalina, Bambie, Bambina, Bamby

Baptista Lat. "One who baptizes."
> Baptiste, Batista, Battista, Bautista

Bara Heb. "To select."
> Barah, Bari, Barra, Barrie

Barbara Gk. "Foreign." The adjective was originally applied to anyone who did not speak Greek; it has the same root as "barbarian." The early Christian martyr Saint Barbara was imprisoned in a tower by her father; she is patroness of engineers and architects. The name

413

had its greatest popularity in the 19th and 20th centuries, peaking around 1925, when in the U.S. it was second only to Mary. Use since then has dropped off dramatically, and in one 1989 poll it didn't even make the top 100. Many people may associate this name with the popular doll Barbie. Actress Barbara Stanwyck; singer Barbra Streisand; writer Barbara Tuchman; First Lady Barbara Bush.

Bab, Baba, Babara, Babb, Babbett, Babbette, Babbie, Babe, Babett, Babette, Babita, Babs, Baibin, Bairbre, Barb, Barbary, Barbe, Barbee, Barbette, Barbey, Barbi, Barbie, Barbra, Barbro, Barby, Barra, Basha, Basia, Baubie, Bauby, Beba, Berbera, Berberia, Berberya, Berbya, Bobbe, Bobbee, Bobbi, Bobbie, Bobby, Bonni, Bonnie, Bonny, Varvara, Varina

Barcelona Geography name: the second largest city in Spain, and the site of the 1992 summer Olympics. It was named for its founder, Carthaginian leader Hamilcar Barca. This is also the name of an influential modern chair designed by Ludwig Mies van der Rohe in 1929.

Barinda Modern name: probably combined from **Barbara** and **Lucinda.**

Barra Var. **Barrie** or dim. **Barbara**.

Barrie A place name (Barry Islands, Wales) turned into a surname turned into a first name used by both sexes. Possibly influenced by the fame of Sir James Barrie, author of *Peter Pan*, since it first appeared as a given name during the height of his renown. It can also be considered a more feminine version of **Barry**.

Bari, Barri

Bartha OG. "Shining, brilliant." Var. of **Bertha**.

Barta

Basha Pol. "Stranger." From the same root as Barbara.

Basia

Basilia (Fem. **Basil**) Gk. "Royal, regal." Common in the Middle Ages, but very unusual now.

Baseele, Baseelia, Baseelle, Bazeele, Bazeelia, Bazeelle, Basile, Basilie, Basille, Bazile, Bazille, Bazilia

Basma Arab. "A smile."

Basima

Bathilda OG. "Woman warrior." Saint Bathild was a young English girl who became queen of the Franks in the 7th century. She was apparently canonized for opposing the then-flourishing slave trade, and also for founding a convent.

Bathild, Bathilde, Batilda, Batilde, Berthilda, Berthilde, Bertilda, Bertilde

Bathsheba Heb. "Daughter of the oath." Biblical name: Bathsheba was the mistress and later the wife of King David. Surprisingly (given her history), the name was used often by the Puritans. Now rare.

Bathseva, Bathshua, Batsheba, Batsheva, Batshua, Batya, Bethsabée, Sheba, Sheva

Bathshira Arab. "Seventh girl-child." Unlikely to be appropriate in this age of small families.

Batya Heb. "God's daughter."

Bitya, Basha

Bay Geographic name (to describe an indentation of land in a coastline) or plant name. The term "bay" is used for several different kinds of trees, including the bay laurel, whose leaves are used as an herb and were also twined into wreaths by the Greeks, to crown victors. The name is equally unusual for girls or boys, and is usually a family name.

Beata Lat. "Blessed." First word of the Latin version of the famous "beatitudes" of the biblical Sermon on the Mount: "Blessed are the poor in spirit. . . ." A popular name in northern Europe.

Bea, Beate

Beatrice Lat. "Bringer of gladness." The original form, Beatrix, was often found in the Middle Ages in England, then forgotten until its Victorian revival as Beatrice. Its popularity was no doubt boosted by Queen Victoria's naming one of her daughters Beatrice. It fell out of fashion after the 1920s, but may become more popular again following the Duke and Duchess of York's use of it for their elder daughter. Heroine of Dante's *Divine Comedy* and of Shakespeare's *Much Ado About Nothing*; entertainer Beatrice Lillie; writer Beatrix Potter; actress Bea Arthur; Queen Beatrix of the Netherlands.

Bea, Beah, Beatrisa, Beatrix, Bebe, Bee, Beea, Beeatrice, Beeatris, Beeatrisa, Beeatriss, Beeatrissa, Beeatrix, Beitris, Beitriss, Trix, Trixi, Trixie, Trixy

Bebba Heb. "God's pledge."

Bechira Heb. "The chosen one."

Becky Dim. **Rebecca** (Heb. "Noose"). Often used as an independent first name. Becky Sharp, heroine of William Thackeray's novel *Vanity Fair*.

Beda OE. "Battle maid."

Bedelia Ir. variant of **Bridget** (Ir. Gael. "Strength, power") by way of Biddy. There is a popular series of children's books featuring an excessively literal-minded maid named "Amelia Bedelia." Actress Bonnie Bedelia.

Bedeelia, Bidelia, Delia

Bee Dim. **Beatrice** (Lat. "Bringer of gladness"). Also the name of an obscure 7th-century English saint. There is an English village called Saint Bees.

Begonia Flower name: the showy houseplant with fleshy leaves and white, yellow, pink or red blossoms. The plant was named for Michel Begon, an 18th-century governor of Santo Domingo.

Behira Heb. "Shining, bright."

Belinda Unclear origin; possibly com. form **Belle** and **Linda**. Since the name first occurs in 18th-century English poet Alexander Pope's *The Rape of the Lock*, that derivation seems unlikely. It may be related to the Old German for "dragon." Has upper-class English connotations. Rock star Belinda Carlisle.

Bel, Belle, Bellinda, Bellynda, Belynda, Linda, Lindie, Lindy

Belita Sp. "Little beauty."

Bellita

Bell Dim. **Isabel** (Heb. "Pledged to God"). Also, surname used as a first name.

Bella Lat. "Beautiful." Dim. **Isabella** (Heb. "Pledged to God"). Used as early as the Middle Ages, but not popular until the 18th century. Politician Bella Abzug.

Bell, Belle, Bellette

Bellanca It. "Blond."

Bianca, Blanca

Belle Fr. "Beautiful." Enjoyed a brief fad in the
almost unheard-of since then except as the na
of Disney's most popular heroines. This is probably not
a recommendation to parents. Author Belva Plain.

Belinda, Belisse, Bell, Bella, Bellina, Belva, Belvia, Billie, Billy

Bellona Lat. "Goddess of battle." From the same root that
gives us the English word "bellicose."

Ballona, Belona

Belva Possibly a variant of **Bell**, though some sources suggest the name has a Latin root and means "beautiful
view." It would be very obscure without the fame of author Belva Plain.

Bellva

Bena (Fem. **Ben**) Heb. "Wise."

Benedicta (Fem. **Benedict**) Lat. "Blessed." Extremely
rare. Benita is the more common form.

**Benedetta, Bénédicte, Benedictine, Benedikta, Benetta,
Benita, Benoîte, Bennie, Dixie**

Benicia Place name: town in northern California.

Benigna Lat. "Kindly, benevolent."

Benita Sp. Var. **Benedicta**. More common than Benedicta,
but very unusual in English-speaking countries. Soprano
Benita Valente.

**Bendite, Benedetta, Benedicta, Benedikta, Benetta,
Benni, Bennie, Benny, Benoîte, Binnie, Binny**

Benjamina (Fem. **Benjamin**) Heb. "Son of the right
hand." Not one of the more common feminizations, despite the recent popularity of Benjamin for boys.

Benyameena, Benyamina

Bentley OE. "Meadow of ben (grass)." Place name become surname become first name, more common for boys.
Irresistibly linked in most minds with the luxurious English cars.

Bentlea, Bentlee, Bentleigh, Bently

Bera Teut. "Bear."

Beracha Heb. "A blessing." The male name from the
same root is Baruch.

Barucha, Berucha, Bracha

Berdine "Bright or glowing maiden."

Berengaria OE. "Maiden of the bear-spear." The wife of English King Richard the Lion-Heart.

Berit Scan. "Gorgeous, splendid, magnificent." Currently popular in Sweden.

Beret

Bernadette (Fem. **Bernard**) Fr. "Bear/courageous." Made famous by Saint Bernadette of Lourdes, a miller's daughter who in 1858 repeatedly saw visions of the Virgin Mary. By the time she was canonized in 1933, Lourdes had become a world-famous destination for pilgrims. The name was popular among Catholic families especially after the 1943 movie *Song of Bernadette*, but is now unusual in English-speaking countries. Actress Bernadette Peters.

Benadette, Bennie, Benny, Berna, Bernadeena, Bernadene, Bernadett, Bernadetta, Bernadina, Bernadine, Bernadyna, Bernardina, Bernardine, Bernee, Berneta, Bernetta, Bernette, Bernie, Bernina, Bernita, Berny

Bernice Gk. "She who brings victory." From the same root as Veronica. The name appears in the New Testament and first occurred in Britain in the 16th century, but its only real popularity came at the end of the 19th century. Little used today.

Barri, Barrie, Barry, Beranice, Beraniece, Beranyce, Bereniece, Berenice, Berenyce, Berneece, Bernelle, Bernetta, Bernette, Bernee, Berni, Bernie, Berniece, Berny, Bernyce, Berri, Berrie, Berry, Bunni, Bunnie, Bunny, Nixie, Veronica, Veronika, Veronike, Veronique

Berry Nature name. Also diminutive of **Bernice**, **Bernadette**, etc. Flower names enjoyed a vogue, especially in Britain, in the 1880s. Berry is also used for men, in that case more often as a transferred surname or a diminutive for Bernard. Photographer Berry Berenson.

Berree, Berrie

Bertha OG. "Bright." Also related to the name of a Teutonic goddess. Very popular in the late 19th century, but almost unheard of since 1920. This disuse may be explained by the fact that a German cannon used in World War I was nicknamed "Big Bertha" after Bertha Krupp, daughter of the family that manufactured the weapon.

Berrta, Berrte, Berrti, Berrtina, Berrty, Berta, B
the, Berti, Bertie, Bertina, Bertine, Bertuska, B
Birdie, Birdy, Birta, Birtha

Bertilde OG. "Bright warrior maiden."

Bertina Ger. "Bright, shining." Dim. **Bertha**.

Bertrade OE. "Bright adviser."

Bertrice Com. name, possibly **Bertha** and **Bernice.**

Berura Heb. "Pure."

Beruria Heb. "God-selected."

Beryl Gk. "Pale green gemstone." The beryl was considered a token of good luck. The name first appeared with the fashion for jewel names in the late 19th century. Its popularity peaked in the 1920s, and it is now rare. Author Beryl Markham.

Berri, Berrie, Berry, Beryle, Berylla, Beryn

Beta Gk. Second letter of the Greek alphabet. Also a middle-European variant of **Beth**.

Beth Heb. "House." Dim. **Elizabeth** (Heb. "pledged to God"), **Bethany**. In Louisa May Alcott's *Little Women*, Beth is the sweet, gentle sister who dies young.

Bethany Biblical: the name of the village near Jerusalem where Lazarus lived with his sisters Mary and Martha. Because the New Testament includes some vivid descriptions of life in their house, the name has rather domestic, cozy connotations. In some cases a variant on the combined form Beth-Ann. Possibly because it sounds like the phenomenally popular Brittany, Bethany has inched into the top 100 American names for girls.

Bethanee, Bethaney, Bethanie, Bethanne, Bethannie, Bethanny, Betheney, Betheny

Bethell Heb. "House of God." Another biblical place name: the spot where Abraham built an altar. Unusual as a first name.

Bethel, Bethell, Bethelle, Bethuel, Bethuna, Bethune

Bethesda Heb. "House of mercy." Bethesda pool in Jerusalem was supposed to have healing powers after being stirred by an angel.

Bethia Heb. "Daughter of Jehovah." Popular in the eras, such as the 17th century, when Old Testament names have been intensively used.

Betia, Bithia

Betsy Dim. **Elizabeth** (Heb. "Pledged to God"). An old nickname for Elizabeth, made famous by Betsy Ross, who supposedly made the first American flag.
Bets, Betsey, Betsie, Betts

Bettina Dim. **Elizabeth** (Heb. "Pledged to God"). Spanish or Italian in origin, and briefly popular in the sixties. One of photographer William Wegman's canine models was named Battina.
Battina, Betiana, Betina, Bettine

Betty Dim. **Elizabeth** (Heb. "Pledged to God"). A nickname with great popularity in its own right. It first be came common in the 18th century, and after a spell of disuse, by the 1920s was one of the top names in every English-speaking country. Now it appears most often in combination with other names—Betty Lou, Betty Ann, etc.—and rarely at that. Today's parents seeking a diminutive for Elizabeth are more likely to use Liza or possibly Beth. Actresses Betty Grable and Bette Davis; singer Bette Midler; First Lady Betty Ford.
Bett, Betta, Bette, Bettey, Betti, Bettie, Bettina, Bettine

Beulah Heb. "Married." Also used to refer to Israel, and in John Bunyan's *Pilgrim's Progress*, Beulah is the promised land. It first became a girls' name in the late 16th century. References to "Beulah land" appear in American spirituals.
Beula, Bewlah, Byulah

Beverly OE. Place name: "Beaver-stream." Originally an English place name and a surname, then used for both sexes as a first name. Probably still most famous as a place name, referring to Beverly Hills. The English spelling is usually Beverley. Singer Beverly Sills.
Bev, Beverle, Beverlee, Beverley, Beverlie, Beverlye, Bevlyn, Bevverlie, Bevverly, Bevvy, Buffy, Verlee, Verlie, Verly, Verlye

Bevinn Ir. Gael. "Singer." More commonly a man's name, although Ireland's famous 11th-century king Brian Boru had a daughter with the name.
Bevan

Bianca It. "White." The meek younger daughter in Shakespeare's *The Taming of the Shrew*, and subject of a song in the spin-off musical *Kiss Me, Kate*. The most famous

Bianca in recent times is former Rolling Stone wife
Bianca Jagger. A good name for a fair-haired baby.
Biancha, Bianka, Blanca, Blancha

Bibi Arab. ''Lady.''
Bebe, Beebee

Bibiana Sp. Var. **Vivian** (Lat. ''Alive'').
Bibiane, Bibianna

Biddy Dim. **Bridget** (Ir. Gael. ''Strength, power'').
Biddie, Bidou

Bienvenida Sp. ''Welcome.''

Billie OE. Dim. **Wilhelmina** (OG. ''Will-helmet''). Femi-
nine use of what is generally considered a man's name;
more popular in the South, though uncommon now.
Singer Billie Holliday; actress Billie Burke; tennis player
Billie Jean King.
Billa, Billee, Billi, Billina, Billy, Willa

Bina Heb. ''Knowledge, perception.'' Also dim. **Albina,
Sabina**, etc.
Binah, Buna

Bird Eng. Unusual nature name. May also be a nickname
for Bertha.
Birdey, Birdie, Byrd, Byrdie

Birgit Nor. ''Splendid.'' Var. **Bridget**. The Irish popularity
of Bridget is based on the appeal of an Irish saint of that
name. There was also a Saint Birgitta, who was the patron
saint of Sweden.
Birget, Birgetta, Birgitt, Birgitta, Birgitte, Byrget, Byrgitt

Bithron Heb. ''Daughter of song.''

Blaine Ir. Gael. ''Slender.'' Surname now used as a first
name, more usually for boys. Cropped up as a first name
in the 1930s. Socialite Blaine Trump.
Blane, Blayne

Blair Scot. Gael. Place name referring to a plain or flat area.
Surname now used as a first name, again more common
for boys. Like many similarly transferred names, Blair
was used for girls in greater numbers starting in the early
1980s and may become even more visible in the 21st century. Actress Blair Brown.
Blaire, Blayre

Blaise Lat. ''One who stutters.'' Used for both sexes,
though more common for men. The alternate spelling of

Blaze probably refers to fire instead. French philosopher Blaise Pascal.

Blaize, Blase, Blasia, Blaze

Blake OE. Paradoxically, could mean either "Pale-skinned" or "Dark." Surname used as a first name for either sex, but more common for boys.

Blakelee, Blakeley, Blakely, Blakenee, Blakeney, Blakeny

Blanche Fr. "White, pale." Very popular in America at the end of the 19th century, but unusual now. Blanche DuBois in Tennessee Williams' *A Streetcar Named Desire* does not provide an encouraging role model.

Bellanca, Bianca, Blanca, Blanch, Blanka, Blinny, Branca

Blanchefleur Fr. "White flower."

Blanda Lat. "Smooth, seductive." Saint Blandina was a 2nd-century martyr, a slave girl who was gored to death by a bull.

Blandina, Blandine

Blasia Var. Blaise (Lat. "One who stutters").

Blaise, Blaisia, Blasya, Blaysia

Blessing OE. "Consecration."

Blimah Heb. "Blossom."

Blimah, Blime

Bliss OE. "Intense happiness."

Blisse, Blyss

Blodwen Welsh. "White flower." Literal translation into Welsh of Blanchefleur. Little used outside Wales.

Blodwyn, Blodwynne

Blondelle Fr. "Little pale one."

Blondell, Blondie, Blondy

Blossom OE. "Flowerlike." Generic flower name, used mostly at the turn of the 20th century.

Bluebell Flower name popular in the 19th century, though when it became the typical name for a cow (like Rover for a dog), it dropped out of human use.

Blythe OE. "Happy, carefree." Made famous by the opening lines of Shelley's poem "To a Skylark" ("Hail to thee, blithe spirit!") and Noel Coward's play *Blithe Spirit*. Actress Blythe Danner.

Blithe

Bo Chinese. "Precious." More often used as a masculine diminutive for names like Robert. Actress Bo Derek.
Beau

Boadicea Name of a heroic queen of early Britain, who led a massive army against Roman invaders. Has rather intimidating connotations.

Bobbie Dim. **Roberta** (OE. "Bright renown"). Like Billie, a feminine version of a man's nickname, often used in combination with a monosyllabic second name, and more common in the South. Also derives from Barbara (Gk. "Stranger"). Author Bobbie Ann Mason.

Bogdana Pol. "Gift from God."
Bogna, Bohdana

Bolade Nig. "The coming of honor."

Bolanile Nig. "This house's riches."

Bonfilia It. "Good daughter."

Bonita Sp. "Pretty." Popular in the early 1940s, but unusual now.
Bo, Bonie, Bonnie, Bonny, Nita

Bonnie Scot. "Good, fair of face." The Scots adopted the French word *bonne*, meaning "good." Its most common use as an adjective is the fond nickname "Bonnie Prince Charlie." The old nursery rhyme claims that "the child born on the sabbath day/Is bonny and blithe and good and gay," which makes this an appropriate name for a Sunday's child. Literary types may also remember that Scarlett O'Hara's daughter by Rhett Butler was named "Bonnie Blue." Singer Bonnie Raitt.
Bonne, Bonnebell, Bonnee, Bonni, Bonnibel, Bonnibell, Bonnibelle, Bonny, Bunni, Bunnie, Bunny

Borbala Hung. "Foreigner." Var. **Barbara** (Gk. "Stranger").
Bora, Boriska, Borka, Borsala, Borsca

Bracken Plant name: a large, coarse fern. Lovers of English literature are familiar with the word, if not the plant itself.

Bradley OE. Place name: "Broad field." Surname now used as a first name for either sex, though more common for boys. Little seen outside America.
Bradlea, Bradlee, Bradleigh, Bradly

Brandy Name of a liquor. In the early 1980s, one of the most popular names for American girls, reaching the top some surveys. Like most trendy names, it has lost favor rather rapidly.

Brandais, Brande, Brandea, Brandee, Brandess, Brandi, Brandice, Brandie, Brandye, Branndais, Brannde, Branndea, Branndi, Branndie

Branice Modern invention: possibly a variation of **Janice** (Heb. "The Lord is Gracious").

Braulia Sp. from Ger. "Glowing, one who burns." More familiar in the masculine form, **Braulio**.

Brenda (Fem. **Brendan**) OE. "Burning." One source translates the Irish as "stinking hair," though the origin may also be a Norse word for "sword." Brenda was originally a Scottish name and was particularly fashionable in the 1940s. Actresses Brenda Vaccaro and Brenda Blethyn; comic strip heroine Brenda Starr.

Bren, Brenn, Brennda, Brenndah

Brenna Ir. Gael. "Raven; black-haired." Also dim. **Brendan**.

Bren, Brenn, Brenne, Brennah, Brinna, Brynna, Brynne

Brett Lat. "From Britain." Surname transferred to first name. Still more common for boys, but may be boosted by the huge popularity of Brittany in the late 1980s.

Brette, Britt

Briana (Fem. **Brian**) Ir. Gael. Meaning obscure, possibly "Strong" or "Hill."

Brana, Breana, Breanne, Breeann, Breeanna, Breeanne, Breena, Bria, Brianna, Brianne, Brina, Briney, Brinn, Brinna, Briny, Bryana, Bryann, Bryanna, Bryanne, Bryn, Bryna, Brynne

Brice Obscure origin, possibly OE. "Noble" or Celt. "Swift." Originally a surname. This is the kind of brisk unisex name that seems slated for greater popularity in the next few years.

Bryce

Bridget Ir. Gael. "Strength, power." May also derive from the name of a goddess of ancient Ireland. Very popular name in Ireland from the 18th century to the 1950s, so much so that in the late 19th century in the U.S. the stock figure of the Irish housemaid (in plays, cartoons, etc.) was frequently called Bridget. Saint Brigid of Kildare, patroness of Ireland; opera star Birgit Nilsson; actresses Brigitte Bardot, Brigitte Nielsen, Bridget Fonda; super̶̶̶̶̶del Bridget Hall.

Beret, Berett, Berget, Bergett, Bergette, Biddie, Biddy, Birget, Birgett, Birgit, Birgitt, Birgitta, Birgitte, Birkita, Birkitta, Birkitte, Birte, Bitta, Breeda, Bride, Bridee, Bridey, Bridgett, Bridgette, Bridgit, Bridgitt, Bridgitta, Bridgitte, Bridie, Bridy, Brietta, Briget, Brigett, Brighid, Brigid, Brigida, Brigidine, Brigit, Brigitt, Brigitta, Brigitte, Brijet, Brijit, Brijitte, Brita, Britt, Britta, Britte, Brydie, Brydget, Brydgit, Brydgitta, Brydgitte, Brydjette, Brydjitt, Bryget, Brygette, Brygid, Brygit, Brygitte, Bryjet, Bryjit

Brie Fr. Place name for a region in France most famous for the production of its cheese. The name is also sometimes considered a feminine adaptation of **Brian**.

Bree, Briette

Brier Fr. "Heather." Unusual botanical name. Though the personal name derives from the French term for heather, the word in English usually describes a wild rose with small, prickly thorns. In some versions of *The Sleeping Beauty*, Prince Charming has to cut through a hedge of briers to reach the princess.

Briar, Bryar

Brigantia Poss. Celtic, "Strength." The name of a legendary goddess of springs. Oddly, the word "brigand," a kind of pirate, comes from the same source.

Brina (Fem. **Brian**) Slavic. "defender."

Brinn, Bryn, Bryna, Brynn, Brynna, Brynne

Brit Celt. "Spotted, freckled." Also a diminutive of **Brittany**.

Britt

Britannia Lat. "Britain." Personification of Britain or the British Empire. She first appeared on a coin in the 2nd century A.D. For zealous Anglophiles.

Brites Port. "Power."

Brittany Lat. "From England." According to one 1989 survey, the third most fashionable name for American girls, behind Sarah and Katherine. It may have derived some of its popularity from associations with England, which held tremendous glamor in the 1980s in America. Lists of popular girls' names these days are dominated by similar choices, including Ashley, Courtney, Lindsay, Kelsey, Whitney, and Casey.

Brett, Brit, Briteny, Britiney, Britney, Britni, Britny, Britt, Britta, Brittan, Brittaney, Brittani, Britteny, Brittin, Brittiny, Brittnee, Brittney, Brittni, Brittny, Britton

Bronwyn Welsh. "Fair breast." Use of Welsh-language names such as Bronwyn, Blodwyn, and the like may be related to periodic surges of separatist or nationalistic feeling in Wales.

Bronnie, Bronny, Bronwen, Bronya

Brooke OE. Place name: "Small stream." Also a surname, and originally more common for boys. But in recent years (perhaps influenced by the fame of actress Brooke Shields), this has become a clearly feminine name, and a rather popular one at that. The final "-e" seems to contribute to that perception. Actress Brooke Adams; philanthropist Brooke Astor.

Brook, Brookie, Brooks, Brooky

Brucie (Fem. **Bruce**) OF. "Thicket of brushwood." The man's name was first common in Scotland, after a 14th-century king. The feminine variant is little used.

Brucina, Brucine

Bruna (Fem. **Bruno**) It. "Brown-skinned, brown-haired."

Brunella OF. "Little one with brown hair."

Brunelle, Brunetta, Brunette

Brunhilda OG. "Armor-wearing fighting maid." Heroine of the Siegfried legend popularized in the Ring cycle of operas by Richard Wagner. Brunhilda is one of the Valkyrie, maidens who ride into battle. The name naturally has connotations of great physical strength, slightly comical in nature.

Brinhild, Brinhilda, Brinhilde, Brunhild, Brunhilde, Brunnhilda, Brunnhilde, Brynhild, Brynhilda, Brynhilde, Brynnhild, Brynnhilda, Brynnhilde, Hilda, Hilde, Hildi, Hildie, Hildy

Bryony Botanical name. Bryony is a vine native to Europe that has large leaves and small flowers.

Bryonie, Briony

Bryn Welsh. "Mount." Another place name converted to a Christian name in the 20th century. Along with other

''Br-'' names like Brianna and Brenna, Bryn has seen increased use in the last ten years.

Brinn, Brinna, Brinne, Brynn, Brynna, Brynne

Buena Sp. ''Good, excellent.''

Bunny Nickname deriving from a number of ''B'' names such as Barbara or Bernice. Has come to be a child's name for a rabbit, of course. Likely to be associated with the famous Playboy Bunnies, the now defunct mid–20th-century emblem of a slightly licentious good time.

Bunnee, Bunni, Bunnie

Cabalina Sp. from Lat. ''Having to do with horses.'' From the same root as the Spanish word *caballero*.

Cadence Lat. ''With rhythm.''

Cadena, Cadenza, Kadena, Kadence, Kadenza

Cadette Fr. ''Younger.'' The French word is also the source of the term for students at West Point and other military schools.

Cady OE. Last name of uncertain meaning. It may have been successfully adopted as a girl's first name because of its resemblance to other popular girls' names like Katie. The new acceptability of Cody for boys may also boost Cady in the next few years. Women's rights pioneer Elizabeth Cady Stanton.

Cade, Cadee, Cadey, Cadi, Cadie, Cadye, Caidie, Kade, Kadee, Kadi, Kadie, Kady, Kadye

Cai Viet. ''Feminine.''

Caitlin Ir. See **Catherine**. Along with Megan, Caitlin has been very popular recently among families with no Irish ties whatsoever. In fact, both names have been among the top ten girls' names as recently as 1990. Parents who find the name appealing but want to choose something a little more distinctive tend to opt for one of the many phonetic variations.

Caitilin, Caitlan, Caitlann, Caitlinn, Caitlyn, Caitlynn, Catelan, Catelinn, Catelynn, Catlin, Catlinn, Cayelin, Cay-

lin, **Kaitlan, Kaitlann, Kaitlin, Kaitlinn, Kaitlyn, Kaitlynn, Katelan, Katelin, Katelynn, Kayelin, Kayelyn**

Cala "Castle, fortress."

Calandra Gk. "Lark."
Cal, Calandre, Calandria, Calendre, Callee, Calley, Calli, Callie, Cally, Kalandra

Calantha Gk. "Lovely flower."
Cal, Calanthe, Callee, Calley, Calli, Callie, Cally, Kalantha

Caledonia Lat. "From Scotland." Place name adapted to first name, probably because of its typically feminine "-ia" ending. The Caledonian Canal runs through northern Scotland, while New Caledonia consists of a group of tiny islands in the South Pacific.

Calida Sp. "Heated, with warmth."
Calla, Calli, Callida

California Geography name: the state on the West Coast. The original meaning of the name is unclear, but it has distinct connotations in modern American life: palm trees, surfing, the sun setting over the Pacific. . . .

Calla Gk. "Beautiful." Also the name of a flower, though the calla lily, with its smooth, sculptured lines, was not fashionable at the same time as the general vogue for flower names.

Callidora Gk. "Gift of beauty."

Callie Gk. There are many Greek names with the "Cal-" prefix, which means "beautiful" or "lovely." This diminutive (which can also be considered a diminutive of Caroline or even Carol), which is less of a mouthful, is somewhat more accessible and may coast on the coattails of currently fashionable "Hallie" to greater exposure. Screenwriter Callie Khoury.
Callee, Calley, Calli, Kallee, Kalley, Kalli, Kallie

Calligenia Gk. "Daughter of beauty." A subtle compliment to the baby's mother.

Calliope Gk. Muse of epic poetry. See **Clio**. Also the name of a musical instrument typically seen at circuses and carnivals.
Callia, Callyope, Kalliope

Callista Gk. "Most beautiful." Actress Callista Flockhart.
Cala, Calesta, Calista, Calla, Callesta, Calli, Callie, Cally,

Callysta, Calysta, Kala, Kalesta, Kalista, Kalla, Kallesta, Kalli, Kallie, Kallista, Kally, Kallysta

Callula Lat. "Small beauty."

Calpurnia Lat. Probably from a clan name of uncertain meaning. The name of Julius Caesar's last wife, the one who appears in Shakespeare's play *Julius Caesar.*

Caltha Lat. "Golden flower."

Calvina (Fem. **Calvin**) Lat. "Hairless." Very unusual.
Calvine

Calypso Gk. "She who hides." In Greek myth the nymph Calypso held Odysseus captive on an island for seven years. The name is also applied to the lilting music of the West Indies, perhaps because it could make visitors reluctant to leave.
Calipso, Callypso, Kallypso

Cambria Geography name: Cambria is both a term for Wales and the name of a period of prehistoric time (part of the Paleozoic era, to be precise).
Cambaria

Camellia Flower name first used in the 1930s, when the rather exotic blooms were quite fashionable. Its root is actually distinct from the more common Camille. The confusion arises not from the similarity of the words, but from the fact that Alexandre Dumas's famous 19th-century play *La Dame aux Camélias* was known in America as *Camille.* The heroine (whose name is Marguerite Gauthier) suffers from tuberculosis and can tolerate only camellias, because they have no scent.
Camelia, Cammelia, Kamelia

Cameo It. from Middle French. "Skin." A stone or shell (frequently pinkish), carved with a picture, often a tiny portrait. Cameos have been very popular as jewelry at various periods, most recently the Victorian era.
Cammeo

Cameron Scot. Gael. "Crooked nose." Clan name derived from the facial feature. Little used as a first name, even for boys, until the middle of this century. Now, with the huge push to use previously masculine names for boys, Cameron may well be co-opted. The fame of actress Cameron Diaz may not directly inspire parents, but puts the name in the public eye.

Camaran, Camie, Camren, Camron, Kameren, Kameron, Kamren

Camilla Lat. Meaning unclear, though some sources trace it to the young girls who assisted at pagan religious ceremonies. The heroine of Alexandre Dumas's famous play *Camille* was actually named Marguerite (see **Camellia**, above). The name has been used consistently since the 19th century. Camille has been more common in the U.S., and some sources predict it will be popular in France during the upcoming decade. Friend of royalty Camilla Parker-Bowles.

Cam, Cama, Camala, Cami, Camila, Camile, Camille, Cammi, Cammie, Cammilla, Cammille, Cammy, Cammylle, Camyla, Camylla, Camylle, Kamila, Kamilka, Kamilla, Kamille, Kamyla, Milla, Mille, Millee, Milli, Millie, Milly

Canada Geographic name: the large country just to the north of the United States. Its name comes from an Iroquois word meaning ''horizon.''

Candace Possibly Lat. ''Brilliantly white.'' Historically the name was the ancient title of the queens of Ethiopia before the 4th century. Not much used until the mid–20th century. Actress Candice Bergen; writer Candace Bushnell.

Candaice, Candase, Candayce, Candee, Candi, Candie, Candis, Candiss, Candy, Candyce, Dace, Dacee, Dacey, Dacie, Dacy, Kandace, Kandice, Kandiss, Kandy

Candelaria Sp. Relates to the Feast of Candlemass, on February 2, commemorating Christ's presentation at the Temple.

Candelara, Candelarea, Candeloria

Candida Lat. ''White.'' Popular in the early Christian era, then very rare until this century, when it has been used occasionally. Journalist Candida Crewe.

Candi, Candide, Candie, Candy

Candra Lat. ''Glowing.''

Cantara Arab. ''Little bridge.''

Caparina Fauna name: like the much more famous Vanessa, Caparina is the name of a type of butterfly.

Caprina

Caprice It. ''Ruled by whim.''

Capreece, Capricia, Caprise

Capucine Fr. "Cowl." French form of an Italian word for a cloak with a deep collar, characteristic of a certain order of Franciscan monks. A French actress who worked in Hollywood in the 1960s gave the name some exposure in the U.S., but it is rare.

Cara Lat. "Darling." Began to be fashionable from the 1970s onward.

Caralie, Caretta, Carina, Carine, Carrie, Carry, Kara, Karina, Karine, Karra, Karrie, Karry

Carabelle Com. form **Cara** and **Belle**. Much more common is Clarabelle.

Carabel, Carabell, Carrabelle

Carden ME. "One whom combs wool." Wool must be carded, or combed smooth, before it can be spun. Carding was one of the important occupations in the Middle Ages, when the economy of southern England relied heavily on the wool trade; names like Fuller and Weaver have survived even when the occupations are virtually defunct. As a name, Carden is rare among both boys and girls.

Cardin, Cardon

Carey Welsh. Place name: "Near the castle." A name used for both men and women. In this form it is a transferred surname, but especially for women, it may be considered a diminutive of Caroline.

Carrey, Cary

Carina It. "Dear little one." Dim. **Cara**. Often used in Italy in the exclamation *"Che carina!"* meaning "How darling!" or even "How cute!"

Careena, Caren, Carena, Carin, Carine, Kareena, Karena, Karina, Karine

Carinthia Place name: an idyllic region of southern Austria.

Carissa Gk. "Grace." See **Charis**. Also possibly another variation of **Cara**.

Caresa, Caressa, Carisa, Charissa, Karisa, Karissa, Kharissa

Carita Lat. "Beloved." Also possibly derived from the Latin word for charity, *caritas*. Occasionally used in the last hundred years.

Caritta, Karita

Carla (Fem. **Carl**) Dim. **Caroline** (OG. "Man"). A European-sounding version of the many names that derive from Charles.

Carlah, Carlana, Carlette, Carlia, Carlla, Karla, Karlla

Carlie (Fem. **Charles**) Dim. **Caroline, Charlotte** (OG. "Man"). The form Carleen (or Carlene) was primarily a product of the 1960s; this shorter version is now more popular. Singer Carly Simon.

Carlee, Carleen, Carleigh, Carlene, Carley, Carli, Carline, Carlita, Carly, Carlye, Carlyne, Carlyta, Karlee, Karlene, Karli, Karlie, Karline, Karlita, Karly, Karlyta

Carlin Gael. "Little champion."

Carling

Carmel Heb. "Garden." Biblical place name: Mount Carmel is in Israel, and is often referred to as a kind of paradise. The name has been used by Catholic families for some hundred years, though the form Carmen is much more common. Editor Carmel Snow.

Carma, Carman, Carmania, Carmanya, Carmela, Carmeli, Carmelina, Carmelit, Carmelita, Carmia, Carmie, Carmiela, Carmina, Carmine, Carmit, Carmiya, Carmy, Karmel, Karmela, Karmelit, Karmen, Lina, Lita, Melina, Melita, Mina

Carmen Lat. "Song." A derivation of **Carmel**. One of the titles of the Virgin Mary is Santa Maria del Carmen (meaning Saint Mary of Mount Carmel), and this form of the name honors her. The most famous Carmen, of course, is the ill-fated heroine of Bizet's opera. Dancer Carmen Miranda.

Carma, Carmelia, Carmelina, Carmelita, Carmencita, Carmia, Carmie, Carmina, Carmine, Carmita, Carmyna, Carmyta, Charmaine, Karmen, Karmia, Karmina, Karmita, Lita, Mina

Carna Lat. "Horn." See **Cornelia**.

Carniela, Carniella, Carnyella, Karniela, Karniella, Karnyella

Carnation Lat. "Becoming flesh." Unusual flower name.

Carol (Fem. **Carl, Charles**) OG. "Man." Originally a short form of Caroline, not an adoption of "Christmas carol." It first appeared about a hundred years ago, and by mid–20th century was enormously popular, possibly influenced by the career of actress Carole Lombard. It is sometimes paired with a monosyllabic second name, most commonly Ann, as in Carol-Ann. The popularity of the name peaked in the mid-sixties, and it is now out of style. Actresses Carol Burnett, Carol Channing; skater Carol Heiss.

Carel, Carey, Cari, Carla, Carleen, Carlene, Carley, Carlin, Carlina, Carline, Carlita, Carlota, Carlotta, Carly, Carlyn, Carlynn, Carlynne, Caro, Carola, Carole, Carolena, Carolin, Carolina, Carolinda, Caroline, Caroll, Caroly, Carolyn, Carolynn, Carolynne, Carri, Carrie, Carroll, Carrolyn, Carry, Cary, Caryl, Caryll, Charla, Charleen, Charlena, Charlene, Charlotta, Charmain, Charmaine, Charmian, Charmion, Charyl, Cheryl, Cherlyn, Ina, Karel, Kari, Karla, Karleen, Karli, Karlie, Karlina, Karlinka, Karlote, Karlotta, Karole, Karolina, Karyl, Karyll, Karryl, Karryll, Kerril, Kerryl, Keryl, Lola, Loleta, Lolita, Lotta, Lotte, Lotti, Lottie, Sharleen, Sharlene, Sharline, Sharmain, Sharmian

Caroline (Fem. dim. **Carl, Charles**) OG. "Man." A rather stately diminutive with royal connotations. The name was brought to England by George II's queen and was popular until the end of the 19th century. It is now enjoying a revival among parents who like its formal, aristocratic, old-fashioned aura. Princess Caroline of Monaco; fashion designers Carolina Herrera, Carolyne Roehm, Caroline Charles.

Caraleen, Caraleena, Caraline, Caralyn, Caralyne, Caralynn, Carla, Carleen, Carleena, Carlen, Carlene, Carley, Carlin, Carlina, Carlita, Carlota, Carlotta, Carly, Carlyn, Carlyna, Carlyne, Carlynn, Carlynne, Carol, Carola, Carole, Carolin, Carolina, Carolyne, Carolynn, Carolynne, Carri, Carrie, Caroll, Carollyn, Cary, Charla, Charleen, Charleena, Charlena, Charlene, Charline, Charlyne, Ina, Karaleen, Karaleena, Karalina, Karaline, Karalyn, Karalynna, Karalynne, Karla, Karleen, Karlen, Karlena, Karlene, Karli, Karlie, Karlina, Karlinka, Karolina, Karoline, Karolinka, Karolyn, Karolyna, Karolyne, Karolynn, Karolynne, Leena, Lina, Sharla, Sharleen, Sharlena, Sharlene, Sharline, Sharlyne

Caron Var. Karen.

Caren, Carin, Carren, Carron

ndelet Geography name: street name in New Orleans. The street was named for a Spanish governor of New Orleans from 1791 to 1807. He was such an inept statesman that he almost managed to bring Spain to war with the U.S.

Carondalay, Carondella

Carrington OE place name: possibly "Charles's town." Any historical meaning the name might have had was buried by the Carrington family of the famous 1980s TV series *Dynasty*. Despite the current trend toward unisex names, this one is probably too long for widespread acceptance.

Carington

Carys Welsh. "Love." A Welsh name dating from the 1960s.

Casey Ir. Gael. "Watchful." Made famous by the song about the engineer of the *Cannon Ball Express*, Casey Jones. Used for both boys and girls, though it is increasingly a girls' name. Can be considered a diminutive of **Acacia**.

Cacey, Cacie, Caisee, Caisey, Caisi, Caisie, Casee, Casi, Casie, Caycee, Caycey, Cayci, Caycie, Caysee, Caysey, Caysi, Caysie, Kacey, Kacie, Kacy, Kacyee, Kasey, Kaycee, Kaycey, Kayci, Kaycie, Kaysee, Kaysey, Kaysi, Kaysie, Kaysy, Kaysyee

Casilda Lat. "Dwelling place." Also Sp. from Ger., "Warlike, a fighter." Saint Casilda is the patron saint of Burgos, a town in Spain.

Cassilda

Casiphia Heb. "Gleaming, silvery white." An Old Testament place name.

Cassandra Gk. Perhaps a version of Alexander. In Greek myth, she was the daughter of King Priam of Troy. Apollo gave her the gift of foresight, but because she spurned his advances, decreed that her prophecies would never be believed. In vain she warned the besieged Trojans against accepting the gift of a gigantic wooden horse presented by their Greek enemy; it was full of Greek soldiers, who took the city captive. The name now indicates someone who is always prophesying doom and gloom. Not a cheerful name for a child, unless a beloved relative named Cassandra erases the name's woeful connotations.

Casandera, Casandra, Cass, Cassandre, Cassandry, Cassaundra, Cassi, Cassie, Cassondra, Cassy, Kasandera, Kassandra, Kassi, Kassie, Kassy, Sande, Sandee, Sandera, Sandi, Sandie, Sandy, Saundra, Sohndra, Sondra, Zandra

Cassia Gk. "Cinnamon."

Cassidy Ir. "Clever." Surname transferred to male first name transferred to girl's name. The name is very trendy in the late '90s, part of the movement toward chosing surnames as first names for girl babies. The fact that Kathie Lee and Frank Gifford named their daughter Cassidy is both a symptom and a cause of this trendiness.

Cassady, Cassidey, Kassadey, Kassidy, Kassodey

Cassiopeia Name from Greek myth: Cassiopeia was the mother of Andromeda, the maiden who was chained to a rock and rescued by Perseus. Both mother and daughter were placed among the stars after death, according to legend, and there are constellations named after them.

Cassiopia, Kassiopeia, Kassiopia

Castalia Yet another nymph from Greek myth who met a bad end: Castalia was being pursued by Apollo and fell into a spring on Mount Parnassus.

Castallia, Kastalia

Catalina Sp. Var. **Catherine**. An island off the coast of southern California is named Catalina.

Catherine Gk. "Pure." One of the oldest recorded names, with roots in Greek antiquity. Almost every Western country has its own form of the name, and phonetic variations are endless. It has been borne by such illustrious women as Saint Catherine of Alexandria, the early martyr who was tortured on a spiked wheel; Empress Catherine the Great of Russia; and three of Henry VIII's six wives. It is currently very popular in England and France, and was one of the top ten American girls' names in the 1980s, though it has skidded since. The fashion in diminutives for Catherine have changed completely in thirty years: if the name is shortened now, it is almost always Katie instead of Cathy. Actresses Catherine Oxenberg, Catherine Deneuve, Katharine Hepburn.

Cait, Caitey, Caitie, Caitlin, Caitlinn, Caitrin, Caitrine,

Caitrinn, Caitriona, Caitrionagh, Caity, Caren, ⟨Cari,⟩
Carin, Caron, Caronne, Carren, Carri, Carrin, Carron,
Caryn, Carynn, Cass, Cassey, Cassi, Cassie, Cassy, Cat,
Cataleen, Cataleena, Catalin, Catalina, Cataline, Catar-
ina, Catarine, Cate, Cateline, Caterina, Catey, Catha,
Cathaleen, Cathaline, Catharin, Catharina, Catharine,
Catharyna, Catharyne, Cathe, Cathee, Cathelin, Cathel-
ina, Cathelle, Catherin, Catherina, Catherinn, Catheryn,
Cathi, Cathie, Cathirin, Cathiryn, Cathleen, Cathlene,
Cathline, Cathlyne, Cathrine, Cathrinn, Cathryn, Cath-
rynn, Cathy, Cathye, Cathyleen, Cati, Catia, Catie, Ca-
tina, Catlaina, Catreena, Catrin, Catrina, Catrine,
Catriona, Catrionagh, Catryna, ⟨Caty,⟩ Cay, Caye, Cazzy,
Ekaterina, Kait, Kaitey, Kaitie, ⟨Kaitlin,⟩ Kaitlinne, Kaitrin,
Kaitrine, Kaitrinna, Kaitriona, Kaitrionagh, Kaity, Karen,
Karena, Kari, Karin, Karon, Karri, Karrin, Karyn, Ka-
rynn, Kasia, Kasienka, Kasja, Kaska, Kass, Kassey, Kas-
sia, Kassy, Kasya, Kat, Kata, Kataleen, Katalin, Katalina,
Katarina, Katchen, Kate, Katee, Katell, Katelle, Katenka,
Katerina, Katerinka, Katey, Katinka, Katha, Katharine,
Katharyn, Katharyne, Kathee, Kathelina, Katheline,
Katherin, Katherina, Katherine, Katheryn, Katherynn,
Kathi, Kathie, Kathileen, Kathiryn, Kathleen, Kathlene,
Kathleyn, Kathline, Kathyleen, Kathrine, Kathrinna,
Kathryn, Kathryne, Kathy, Kathyrine, Kati, Katica, Katie,
Katina, Katka, Katla, Katlaina, Katleen, Katoushka, Ka-
trena, Katrine, Katrina, Katriona, Katrionagh, Katryna,
Katushka, Katy, Katya, Kay, Kaye, Kit, Kittee, Kittie,
Kitty, Trina, Trine, Trinette, Yekaterin, Yekaterina

Cathleen Ir. Var. **Catherine**, Gk. "Pure." The "K-" spelling of Kathleen is more common, and parents today seem
to turn to Caitlin as a more fashionable version of Catherine.
Cathaleen, Catleen, Catline, Catlin

Cavanaugh ME. "Chubby." Meaning aside, this is the
kind of name that is increasingly popular for girls in the
late nineties.
Cavanagh, Kavanagh, Kavanaugh

Cayley Fashionable modern name, probably made up of
elements from the trendy Kayla and Ashley, though a
scholar could probably trace the name back to Catherine

via the hugely popular Caitlin. Since this is not a traditional name there is no "correct" spelling: any one of the many variants will do.

Caileigh, Cailey, Cailie, Caleigh, Caylee, Cayleigh, Caylie, Kaileigh, Kailey, Kailie, Kaleigh, Kaylee, Kayleigh, Kayley

Cecilia (Fem. **Cecil**) Lat. "Blind one." From a Roman clan name. Saint Cecilia is the patroness of music. The name was used in Roman times, then resurfaced in the Victorian era, possibly given a boost by the fame of industrialist (and founder of Rhodesia) Cecil Rhodes. The form Cecily was briefly popular in the 1920s, but neither name has been used much since. With very feminine names like Amanda, Jessica, and Stephanie among the top ten nationwide, Cecilia seems a good candidate for rediscovery. Actress Cicely Tyson; soprano Cecilia Bartoli.

Ceceley, Cecely, Cecil, Cecile, Ceciley, Ceciliane, Cecilija, Cecilla, Cecily, Cecilyann, Cecyl, Cecyle, Cecylia, Ceil, Cela, Cele, Celia, Celie, Celli, Cellie, Cesia, Cesya, Cicely, Cicily, Cile, Cilka, Cilia, Cilla, Cilly, Cissie, Kikelia, Kikylia, Sacilia, Sasilia, Sasilie, Seelia, Seelie, Seely, Sesilia, Sessaley, Sesseelya, Sessile, Sessilly, Sessily, Sheila, Sile, Sileas, Sisely, Siselya, Siseel, Sisile, Sisiliya, Sissela, Sissie, Sissy

Celandine Gk. Botanical name: a yellow-blossomed wild-flower.

Celadonia, Celida, Cellandine, Selodonia, Zeledonia

Celena Gk. Goddess of the moon, later identified with Artemis. A version of the more common Selina, although neither name is frequently used.

Cela, Celeena, Celina, Celinka, Cesia, Cesya, Saleena, Salena, Salina, Selena, Selina

Celeste Lat. "Heavenly." Unusual in any of its forms, and probably most familiar through the fame of actress Celeste Holm. Baby boomers may associate the name with Queen Céleste, wife of Jean and Laurent de Brunhoff's children's book character Babar, the Elephant. Casting agent Celestia Fox.

Cela, Celesta, Celestena, Celestene, Celestia, Celestijna, Celestina, Celestine, Celestyne, Celia, Celie, Celina, Celinda, Celine, Celinka, Celka, Celleste, Celyna, Saleste,

Salestia, Seleste, Selestia, Selestina, Selestine, Selestyna, Selestyne, Silesta, Silestena, Silestia, Silestijna, Silestina, Silestyna, Silestyne, Tina, Tinka

Celinda Gk. Var. **Celeste**.
Celinde, Salinda, Salinde, Selinda, Selinde

Celosia Gk. "Aflame."

Cendrine Dim. of **Cendrillon**, the French name for Cinderella. Also a phonetic respelling of Sandrine, which is derived from **Alexandra** (Gk. "Man's defender.").

Cenobia "Power of Zeus." A Spanish form of the slightly more common Zenobia.

Cerelia Lat. "Relating to springtime." A nice name for a spring baby.
Cerella, Sarelia, Sarilia

Ceres Roman mythology name: the goddess of the harvest, known in Greek myth as Demeter. She is the mother of Persephone, who was kidnapped by Pluto. Ceres' name is the root of our word "cereal."

Cerise Fr. "Cherry." See **Cherry**.
Cerisse, Cherise, Sarese. Sherise

Cesarina (Fem. **Caesar**) Lat. Probably "hairy, hirsute."
Cesarea, Cesarie, Cesarine, Kesare

Cézanne Name of the French painter Paul Cézanne. Acceptable as a girl's name, perhaps, because of its resemblance to Suzanne.

Chamania Heb. "Sunflower."
Chamaniah, Hamania

Chanah Heb. "Grace." See **Hannah**.
Chaanach, Chaanah, Chana, Chanach

Chanina Heb. "Gracious."
Chaninah, Hanina, Haninach, Haninah

Chanya Heb. "Grace of the Lord."
Chania, Chaniach, Chanyah, Hania, Haniah, Hanyah

Chandelle Fr. "Candle." Sounds familiar enough (like Chantal and its variants) to seem like a "real" name.
Chantelle, Shandelle, Shantelle

Chandler OE. Occupational name: "Candle maker." In an era when Taylor is one of the top ten names for girls, can Chandler be far behind?

Chandra Sanskrit. "Like the moon." The greatest Hindu goddess Devi is also known as Chandra.
Candra, Chandi, Shandra

Chanel Fr. Surname of the legendary fashion designer Coco Chanel, and by extension, the name of a number of famous perfumes. Began to be used as a first name in the 1980s, usually in a phonetic variation, probably because of its elegant and luxurious connotations.

Chanelle, Channelle, Shanel, Shanell, Shanelle, Shannel, Shannelle, Shenelle, Shynelle

Chaney Dim. **Chandler** (OE ''Candle maker'') The ''-ey'' ending is enough to make this sound like a girl's name in the late nineties.

Chainey, Chayney

Chantal Fr. Originally a place name meaning ''Stony spot,'' but possibly also derived from the verb *chanter*, ''to sing.'' Not uncommon in France, but unusual in the U.S.

Chantalle, Chantel, Chantelle, Chantele, Shantal, Shantalle, Shantel, Shantell, Shantelle, Shontel, Shontelle

Chappell OE. Place name: ''Near the chapel.'' Another place name turned last name, adopted as a girl's first name, but scarce so far.

Chapell, Chappel

Charlesetta Fem. **Charles** (OG. ''Man''). The more common feminizations are Caroline and Charlotte.

Charlesette, Charlesina, Charlice

Charis Gk. ''Grace.'' One term for the mythological Three Graces often depicted in classical art, who embodied charm. Taken individually, the graces were Aglaia (brilliance), Thalia (flowering), and Euphrosyne (joy). Not to be confused with those other legendary female gangs the Fates (also three, who controlled destiny) or the Muses (nine, who inspired the arts and sciences).

Chareesse, Charisse, Charysse, Karas, Karis, Karisse

Charity Lat. ''Brotherly love.'' One of the three cardinal virtues, along with Faith and Hope. They have survived better than many of the other virtue names (Temperance, Fortitude, Humility, Chastity, Mercy, Obedience) popular among the Puritans in the 17th century.

Carissa, Carita, Chareese, Charis, Charissa, Charisse, Charita, Charitee, Charitey, Charitye, Chariza, Charty, Cherri, Cherry, Sharitee, Sharitey, Sharity, Sharitye

Charlotte Fr. "Little and womanly." One of the most popular feminine forms of Charles. Like Caroline, Charlotte was popularized in England by a queen (George III's wife) and was much used from the 18th century to the beginning of the 20th. In the U.S. its use peaked in the 1870s, but with the recent return to "old-fashioned" names, it has been dusted off for a reappearance. In E. B. White's *Charlotte's Web*, the heroine of the title is a spider. Novelist Charlotte Brontë; actress Charlotte Rampling.

Carla, Carleen, Carlie, Carline, Carlota, Carlotta, Carly, Carlyne, Char, Chara, Charill, Charla, Charlaine, Charleen, Charlene, Charlet, Charlette, Charline, Charlot, Charlotta, Charly, Charlyne, Charmain, Charmaine, Charmian, Charmion, Charo, Charty, Charyl, Cherlyn, Cheryl, Cheryll, Karla, Karleen, Karlene, Karli, Karlicka, Karlie, Karlika, Karline, Karlota, Karlotta, Karlotte, Karly, Karlyne, Lola, Loleta, Loletta, Lolita, Lolotte, Lotta, Lottchen, Lotte, Lottey, Lotti, Lottie, Lotty, Sharel, Sharil, Sharla, Sharlaine, Sharleen, Sharlene, Sharlet, Sharlette, Sharline, Sharlot, Sharmain, Sharmayne, Sharmian, Sharmion, Sharyl, Sheri, Sherie, Sherrie, Sherry, Sherye, Sheryl

Charmaine From a Latin clan name; also possibly related to Carmen and Caroline. Enjoyed bursts of popularity in the 1920s and 1950s.

Charmain, Charmane, Charmayne, Charmian, Charmion, Charmyan, Charmyn, Sharmain, Sharman, Sharmane, Sharmayne, Sharmian, Sharmion, Sharmyn

Charmian Gk. "Joy." A distinctly separate name from Charmaine, though they are often confused. Because of its Greek origin, Charmian should be pronounced with a hard *C*, but it rarely is.

Charmin, Charmiane, Charmyan, Charmin, Sharmian, Sharmiane, Sharmyan, Sharmyane

Chasidah Heb. "Devout woman." From the same root that gives its name to the very devout sects of Jews known as the Hasidim.

Chasina Aramaic. "Strong, mighty."

Chastity Lat. "Purity." A virtue name that has, for obvious reasons, fallen out of favor, though Cher used it for her daughter.

Chasaty, Chasity, Chassity, Chastitee, Chastitey

Chava Heb. "Life."

Chabah, Chaya, Chayka, Eva, Hava, Haya, Kaija

Chaviva Heb. "Beloved."

Eva

Chazona Heb. "Oracle, prophetess."

Chazonah, Hazona, Hazonach

Chermona Heb. "Sacred mountain." The mountain referred to is probably Mount Hermon, in what is now southern Syria.

Chermonah, Hermona, Hermonach, Hermonah

Chelsea OE. "Port or landing place." Place name; possibly owes some of its appeal to British pop culture of the late 1960s and songs like Joni Mitchell's "Chelsea Morning." It seems likely that the name's current huge popularity depends on its aura of English stuffiness rather than English bohemianism. First Daughter Chelsea Clinton.

Chelcie, Chelsee, Chelseigh, Chelsey, Chelsie, Chelsy

Chepzibah Heb. "My delight is in her." See **Hepzibah**.

Cher Fr. "Beloved." For most people, inseparable from the singer and actress who uses this name alone, without a surname, though the heroine of the movie and TV series *Clueless* has put a new spin on it. Somewhat popular in the late 1960s and early 1970s.

Chere, Cherée, Cherey, Cheri, Cherice, Cherie, Cherise, Cherish, Cherrie, Cherry, Chery, Cherye, Cherylee, Cherylie, Sher, Sherelle, Sherey, Sheri, Sherice, Sherie, Sherry, Sheryll

Cherry OF. "Cherry." The 19th-century vogue for botanical names did not usually extend to fruit, so when Cherry occurs, it is most likely a variant of Charity or Cheryl.

Chere, Cheree, Cherey, Cherida, Cherise, Cherita, Cherrey, Cherri, Cherrie

Cheryl Familiar form of **Charlotte** or **Cherry**. A 20th-century development that first became popular in the 1940s, and increased in use into the 1960s. Like most thirty-year-old fashions, it is now quite dated.

Charil, Charyl, Cheriann, Cherianne, Cherryl, Cheryll, Cherylle, Cherilynn, Chryil, Chyrill, Sharil, Sharyl, Shar-

yil, Sheral, Sherianne, Sheril, Sherill, Sheryl, Shyril, Shyrill

Cherilyn Form of **Cheryl**. Names that are modern developments seem more susceptible to widely variable spellings, as this one is.

Charalin, Charalyn, Charalynne, Charelin, Charelyn, Charelynn, Charilyn, Charilynn, Cheralin, Cheralyn, Cherilin, Cherilynn, Cherilynne, Cherralyn, Cherrilin, Cherrilyn, Cherrylene, Cherrylin, Cherryline, Cherrylyn, Cherylin, Cheryline, Cheryllyn, Cherylyn, Sharalin, Sharalyn, Sharelyn, Sharelynne, Sharilynn, Sheralin, Sheralynne, Sherilin, Sherralin, Sherrilyn, Sherrylene, Sherryline, Sherrylyn, Sherylin, Sherylyn

Chesleigh OE. ''Camp on the meadow.'' Can also be taken as a variation on **Chelsea** and **Ashley**.

Cheslea, Chesley, Cheslie, Chesli, Chesslea, Chessley, Chesslie, Chessli

Chesney OE. Place name referring to a camp. Close enough to Kelsey and Chelsea to be a reasonable choice.

Chesnea, Chesneigh, Chesnie, Chesni, Chessnea, Chessney, Chessni, Chessnie

Chesna Slavic. ''Peaceful.''

Chessa, Chessy

Cheyenne Name of a Native American tribe. The Cheyennes originated in what is now Minnesota, and were famous for their courage in battle. They fiercely resisted the Anglo takeover of the Plains. Several features of the Western states were named after the tribe, including the city that is now the capital of Wyoming. Possibly because of the familiar ''-enne'' ending, this name seems more acceptable as a girl's name than a tribal name like Algonquin would be.

Chayan, Chayanne, Shayan, Shayanne, Chyanne, Shyann, Shyanne

Chiara It. ''Light.'' See **Claire**. Some potential for use in the late '90s by enthusiastic Italophiles.

Chiarra, Kiara, Kiarra

China Geography name. After all, why not name a daughter for the most populous nation on earth?

Chiquita Sp. ''Little one.'' Most parents will probably associate this name with the heavily advertised Chiquita banana.

Chickie, Chicky, Chiqueeta, Chiquin

Chloë Gk. "Young green shoot." Appears in the Bible, and as a name in literature, especially in the tale of Daphnis and Chloë, set to music by Ravel. Since the late seventies, it has been gaining popularity in England, and is occasionally used in the U.S. Candice Bergen has a daughter named Chloë. Actress Chloë Webb.

Clo, Cloe, Cloey, Khloe, Khloey, Kloe

Chloris Gk. "Pale." Another name from Greek mythology, though an obscure one. Actress Cloris Leachman.

Chloress, Cloris, Khloris, Kloris

Cholena Delaware Indian. "Bird."

Christabel Lat./Fr. "Fair Christian." Use has been primarily literary, as in Samuel Taylor Coleridge's poem of the same name, in which the heroine is an example of innocent purity. Used occasionally in Britain.

Christabella, Christabelle, Christobel, Chrystabel, Chrystabelle, Chrystobel, Cristabel, Cristabella, Cristabelle, Crystabel, Crystabella

Christina (Fem. **Christian**) Gk. "Anointed, Christian." Christian was used for women in medieval times, but by the 18th century Christina was the more common form. It was superseded in the 1930s by the French form Christine, which was very popular in the fifties and sixties, but the cycle of fashion has now brought Christina back to solid but not trendy popularity. Christiane is currently very popular in Germany. Queen Christina of Sweden; poet Christina Rossetti; tennis star Chris Evert; model Christie Brinkley.

Chris, Chrissie, Chrissy, Chrissta, Chrisstan, Chrissten, Chrissti, Chrisstie, Chrissty, Christa, Christan, Christeen, Christel, Christen, Christi, Christian, Christiana, Christiane, Christianna, Christie, Christin, Christine, Christini, Christinn, Christmar, Christy, Christyna, Chrystal, Chrystalle, Chrystee, Chrystel, Chrystelle, Chrystle, Cris, Crissey, Crissie, Crissy, Crista, Cristal, Cristel, Cristelle, Cristen, Cristena, Cristi, Cristie, Cristin, Cristina, Cristine, Cristiona, Cristy, Crysta, Crystena, Crystene, Crystie, Crystina, Crystine, Crystyna,

Khristeen, Khristena, Khristina, Khristine, Khristya, Kirsten, Kirstin, Kit, Kris, Krissy, Krista, Kristeen, Kristel, Kristen, Kristi, Kristijna, Kristin, Kristina, Kristy, Krysta, Krystka, Krystle, Stina, Teena, Teyna, Tina, Tiny

Christmas OE. Name of the holiday, used occasionally through the 19th century for December 25 babies, but now more usually replaced by the French, and somewhat subtler, form Noel.

Chryseis Lat. "Golden daughter." A very beautiful young girl named Chryseis appears in Homer's *Iliad*.
Chrysilla

Chuma Aramaic. "Warmth, heat."

Chumani Sioux. "Drops of dew."

Ciara Modern name, created for its sound. Can be traced either to Chiara (It. "Light") or to the increasingly popular Sierra (Sp. "Saw").
Ceara, Ciarra, Cieara, Searra, Siara

Cilia Scientific term: tiny hairs that project from some cells. The name can also be considered a variation on Celia, or a diminutive of Cecilia.
Silia, Sillia

Cilicia Biblical place name: a province mentioned in both Old and New Testaments. It is in Southeast Asia Minor.
Cilicea, Salicia

Cimarron Place name: a city in western Kansas and a river that runs 650 miles across the Great Plains from New Mexico to Oklahoma. It was made famous by an Edna Ferber novel that was the basis for movies made in 1933 and 1961.
Cimeron, Simarron, Simeron

Cinderella Fr. "Little ash-girl." The name from the fairy tale. Very rare.
Cendrillon, Cenerentola, Cindie, Cindy, Ella

Cindy Originally a nickname for **Cynthia** (Gk. "Goddess from Mt. Cynthos") or **Lucinda** (Lat. "Light"). Popular for children born in the fifties and sixties, but rarely used for *their* children of the eighties and nineties. Singer Cyndi Lauper; model Cindy Crawford.
Cindee, Cindi, Cindie, Cyndee, Cyndi, Cyndie, Cyndy, Sindee, Sindi, Sindie, Sindy, Syndi, Syndie, Syndy

Cinnabar The ore that produces mercury. It is a deep brownish red in color.

Cinnamon Familiar spice that has been grown in tropical climates for thousands of years. It is the inner bark of a small evergreen tree, and has been used by cultures from China to the Netherlands for flavoring food, for scenting fabrics and household goods, and for medical purposes.
Cynnamon, Sinemmon, Sinnamon

Cipriana It. "From Cyprus."
Chipriana, Chiprianna, Cipriane, Ciprianna, Cypriana, Cyprienne, Sipriana, Sipriane, Siprianne, Sypriana, Syprianne

Cithara Ancient musical instrument resembling both the lyre and the zither. The name is probably the root of the word "guitar."
Citara, Kitara, Kithara

Claire Lat. "Bright." The original form was Clare, as in Saint Clare, 13th-century founder of a Franciscan order of nuns. In the 19th century Clara became fashionable, but since the 1960s, the French form Claire has dominated. Writer Clare Booth Luce; actresses Clara Bow, Claire Bloom.
Ceara, Cearra, Cheeara, Chiara, Ciara, Ciarra, Clair, Claire, Claireen, Clairene, Claireta, Clairette, Clairey, Clairice, Clairinda, Clairissa, Clairita, Clairy, Clarabel, Clarabelle, Clare, Clarene, Claresta, Clareta, Claretta, Clarey, Clari, Claribel, Claribella, Claribelle, Clarice, Clarie, Clarinda, Clarine, Clarissa, Clarisse, Clarita, Claritza, Clarrie, Clarry, Clary, Claryce, Clayre, Clayrette, Clayrice, Clayrinda, Clayrissa, Clerissa, Cliara, Clorinda, Klaire, Klara, Klaretta, Klarissa, Klaryce, Klayre, Kliara, Klyara, Seara, Searra

Clara Lat. "Bright." Another version of Claire, but one that has been very rare for some time. It was at its most popular in the 19th century.
Clarabelle, Claretha, Claribel, Clarice, Clarie, Clarinda, Clarine, Clarita, Claritza, Clarry, Klara, Klarra

Claramae Eng. A compound form of Clara, probably dating from the late 19th century, when May was also a popular name.
Claramay

Clarice Variant of **Claire** that enjoyed a flurry of popularity around the turn of the 20th century. Clarissa is a Latinized version made famous by Samuel Richardson's 18th-century novel *Clarissa Harlowe*.

Claris, Clarise, Clarisse, Claryce, Clerissa, Clerisse, Cleryce, Clerysse, Klarice, Klarissa, Klaryce

Clarimond Lat./Ger. "Shining defender."

Claramond, Claramonda, Claramonde, Clarimunde

Claudia (Fem. **Claude, Claudius**) Lat. Clan name probably meaning "Lame." The name has never been very popular in English-speaking countries in any of its forms, in spite of the exposure given it by Colette's novels (*Claudine at School*, etc.) and the career of actress Claudette Colbert. It is currently used quite a bit in Germany. Actress Claudia Cardinale; supermodel Claudia Schiffer.

Claude, Claudella, Claudelle, Claudetta, Claudette, Claudie, Claudina, Claudine, Claudey, Claudy, Clodia, Klaudia, Klodia

Clea Unknown derivation, but possibly invented by author Lawrence Durrell, for a character in his famous Alexandria Quartet. See also **Cleopatra, Clio.**

Claea, Klea

Clelia Lat. "Glorious." A maiden who figures in the legendary history of Rome. Her story was retold (in ten volumes!) by the 17th-century French novelist Mlle. de Scudery.

Clematis Gk. "Vine or brushwood." Flower name, from the blossoming vine with white or purple blooms.

Clematia, Clematice, Clematiss

Clementine Lat. "Mild, giving mercy." Clemence and Clemency were both Puritan virtue names, but are now unheard-of. Clementia was used until the 19th century, when it was replaced by Clementina. The well-known song "My Darling Clementine" would make it hard to use that version of the name with a straight face. Winston Churchill's wife was named Clementine.

Clem, Clemence, Clemency, Clementia, Clementina, Clementya, Clementyna, Clementyn, Clemmie, Clemmy, Klementijna, Klementina

Cleopatra Gk. "Her father's renown." There were actually generations of Egyptian princesses of this name, but the most famous is the intriguer who enthralled both Caesar and Antony. Very rare.

Clea, Cleo, Cleona, Cleone, Cleonie, Cleta

Cleva (Fem. **Cleve, Clive**) Middle English. "Hill-dweller." Place name transferred to a surname and thence to a first name used for men. This feminine form is unusual.

Cliantha Gk. "Glory-flower."

Cleantha, Cleanthe, Clianthe, Kliantha, Klianthe

Clio Gk. Mythological name of the muse of history. There are nine muses, the daughters of Zeus and Mnemosyne, and each represents an art or science. Calliope (epic poetry), Terpsichore (choral song and dance), and Thalia (comedy) have survived as first names.

Klio

Clorinda Lat. Literary name coined by 16th-century Italian poet Tasso. Possibly derived from Claire or Chloe.

Chlorinda

Clotilda Ger. "Renowned battle." Saint Clothilde was the wife of Frankish King Clovis I in the 6th century, and supposedly went into battle by his side. One of Paris's most fashionable churches is named for her.

Clothilda, Clothilde, Clotilde, Klothilda, Klothilde

Cloudy Weather name. Could be used to describe a baby's delicate coloring, or to refer to the weather on the day of birth.

Clove Name of the spice. It comes from the Latin word for "nail," which whole cloves resemble. Can also be a diminutive for **Clover**.

Clover OE. Flower name. Perhaps because of the modest nature of the flower, the name occurred in the 19th century more commonly as a nickname.

Clymene Gk. "Renowned one." In Greek myth, most notably the daughter of Oceanus and mother of Atlas and Prometheus, though several other legendary figures also bear this name.

Clytie Gk. "Lovely one." Another mythological figure. Her unrequited love for the sun god resulted in her being changed into a heliotrope, or sunflower, which turns to follow the sun's path.

Cochava Heb. "Star."

Cody OE. "Pillow." This is an example of the kind of

unisex name that has been recently popular for girls in the U.S., though unlike most of these names, Cody remains more usually masculine.

Codee, Codey, Codi, Codie, Kodee, Kodey, Kodie, Kody

Colette Dim. **Nicole** (Gk./Fr. "People of victory"). Used mostly since the 1940s, though never widespread. Probably made familiar by the French writer Colette, whose last name it was.

Coletta, Collet, Collete, Collette, Nicolette

Coline (Fem. **Colin**, derived from **Nicholas**) Gk. "People of victory."

Colena, Colene, Coletta, Colina, Collina, Colline, Nicoleen, Nicolene, Nicoline, Nicolyne

Colleen Ir. Gael. "Girl." In use since the 1940s in English-speaking countries *except* Ireland. A vogue in the early 1960s faded rapidly. Actress Colleen Dewhurst; writer Colleen McCullough.

Coleen, Collie, Colline, Colly, Kolleen, Kolline

Collis OE. Occupational name: "Coal miner." Scarce for boys and girls.

Collice, Colliss

Columba Lat. "Dove." Saint Columba, 6th-century Irish saint, founded an influential monastery on the Scottish island of Iona, and is supposed to have exorcised the River Ness of a monster. Though the Irish Columba was a man, two other saints of that name were both women. The dove, of course, is a Christian symbol for the Holy Spirit.

Collie, Colly, Colombe, Columbia, Columbine

Columbine Lat. "Dove." Columbine is also a literary character who appears in traditional Italian comedy and English pantomime as Harlequin's beloved. Also a flower name for a delicate two-colored blossom.

Comfort Fr. "To strengthen and comfort." In the Bible the Holy Ghost is referred to as the "Comforter." It was a surname in the Middle Ages, then popular among the Puritans. Almost unused since the 18th century.

Concepción Lat. "Conception." Used mostly in Latin American countries to honor the Immaculate Conception and, by extension, the Virgin Mary.

Cetta, Chiquin, Chita, Concetta, Concha, Concheta, Conchissa, Conchita

Conchita Dim. Concepción.

Conchata, Conchissa

Concordia Lat. "Peace, harmony." In classical myth, Concordia was the goddess of peace succeeding a battle. The concept is memorialized in several place names like Concord, Massachusetts and Paris's *Place de la Concorde*.

Concord, Concorde

Conradine (Fem. **Conrad**) OG. "Brave counsel."

Connee, Connie, Conny, Conrada, Conradeen, Conradina

Constance Lat. "Steadfastness." Used often in the early Christian and medieval eras, then by the Puritans (usually as Constant or Constancy). After a brief revival at the beginning of this century, it lapsed back into obscurity. Singer Connie Francis.

Con, Conetta, Connee, Conney, Conni, Connie, Conny, Constancia, Constancy, Constanta, Constantia, Constantija, Constantina, Constantine, Constantya, Constanz, Costanza, Konstance, Konstantija, Konstantina, Konstanze, Kosta, Kostatina, Tina

Consuelo Sp. "Consolation, comfort." Honors Santa Maria del Consuelo. In 1842 George Sand, a popular French author, published an historical novel called *Consuelo*. The heroine, a gypsy, became a successful opera singer.

Chela, Chelo, Consolata, Consuela

Cora Gk. "Maiden." Though some sources trace the name to classical myth, its modern form was probably coined by American writer James Fenimore Cooper in *The Last of the Mohicans* (1826). It grew in popularity through the 19th century, but now its variant forms are more often used. A simple, pretty name with an old-fashioned air. Civil rights activist Coretta Scott King.

Corabel, Corabella, Corabelle, Corabellita, Coree, Corella, Corena, Corene, Coretta, Corey, Cori, Corie, Corilla, Corine, Corinna, Corinne, Corita, Correen, Corrella, Correlle, Correna, Correnda, Correne, Correy, Corri, Corrie, Corrina, Corrine, Corrissa, Corry, Corynna, Corynne, Coryssa, Kora, Korabell, Kore, Koreen, Korella, Koretta, Korey, Korilla, Korina, Korinne, Korry, Koryne, Korynna, Koryssa

Coral Lat. Nature name: first appeared as a name during the Victorian vogue for jewel names, usually in England, though of course coral is not a mineral, but the deposits left by tiny aquatic creatures. Actress Coral Browne.

Coralee, Coralena, Coralie, Coraline, Corallina, Coralline, Coraly, Coralyn, Coralyne, Koral, Korall, Koralie, Koralline

Corazón Sp. "Heart." Corazón Aquino, president of the Philippines.

Cordelia Derivation unclear, but probably related to Latin *cor* or "heart." In Shakespeare's *King Lear*, Cordelia is the youngest and only lovable daughter of the tragic king.

Cordélie, Cordella, Cordelle, Cordey, Cordi, Cordie, Cordy, Delia, Delie, Della, Kordelia, Kordella, Kordelle

Cordis Lat. "Of the heart."

Cordiss

Cordula Ger. from Lat. "Of the heart" or possibly from Welsh, "Sea jewel."

Cordulla, Kordula, Kordulla

Corey Ir. Gael. Place name: "The hollow." Place name transferred to surname. It is still much more popular for boys. Author Corrie ten Boom.

Cory, Cori, Corrie, Corry, Cory, Korie, Korrey, Korri, Korry

Corin Lat. "Spear." The name, which refers both to a male saint and to an early Roman god of war, is more commonly given to boys. As a girl's name, it may even be a variant of **Corinne**.

Coren, Corrin, Cyran, Korin

Corinne French form of **Cora**, used since the 1860s.

Carinna, Carinne, Carine, Carynna, Carynne, Corenne, Corin, Corina, Corinda, Corine, Corinn, Corinna, Correna, Corrianne, Corrienne, Corrinda, Corrine, Corrinn, Corrinna, Karinne, Karynna, Koreen, Korina, Korinne, Korrina

Corinthia Place name: from Corinth, an ancient Greek city that had a very early Christian church. Saint Paul wrote two Epistles to the Corinthians that form part of the New Testament.

Korinthia

Corisande Gk. "Chorus-singer." Disraeli used this name for a character in his play *Lothair*.
  Corisanda, Corissande, Corrisande
Corliss OE. "Benevolent, cheery."
  Corlee, Corless, Corley, Corlie, Corly
Cornelia (fem. **Cornelius**) Lat. "Like a horn." Comes from a famous Latin clan name, and was often used in the Roman Empire. Modern use is sparing, dating from mid-19th century.
  Cornalia, Corneelija, Cornela, Cornelija, Cornelya, Corelie, Cornella, Cornelle, Cornie, Korneelia, Korneelya, Kornelia, Kornelija, Kornelya, Neel, Neely, Nela, Nelia, Nell, Nella, Nellie, Nelly
Corona Sp. "Crown." A spate of English use occurred around the coronation of King Edward VII in 1902, but this sentimental homage to royalty was not repeated at subsequent coronations. Also the name of a very popular Mexican beer, which would seem to limit its further use as a given name.
  Coronetta, Coronette, Coronna
Corvina Lat. "Like a raven." A good name for a dark-haired baby.
  Corva, Corveena, Corvetta
Cosette Fr. Probably a feminine diminutive of **Nicholas** (Gk. "People of victory"). Given new exposure in recent years by the immensely popular musical *Les Miserables*, whose female romantic lead is named Cosette.
  Cosetta
Cosima (Fem. **Cosmo**) Gk. "Order." Very unusual in English-speaking countries. The composer Richard Wagner married (as his second wife) Cosima Liszt, daughter of the composer Franz Liszt. Two of their children were named Siegfried and Isolde, after characters in two of his operas.
  Cosma, Cosmé, Kosma
Courtney OE. "Court-dweller." Surname transferred to first name; usually feminine in the U.S. Immensely popular, probably owing to upper-class connotations, though when a name or group of names (in this case, Ashley, Whitney, Brittany, and the like) becomes this fashionable the sheer glamor of popularity probably eclipses any pre-

vious connotations the name may have had. Actress Courteney Cox.

Cordney, Cordni, Cortenay, Corteney, Cortland, Cortnee, Cortneigh, Cortney, Cortnie, Cortny, Courtenay, Courteneigh, Courteney, Courtland, Courtnay, Courtnee, Courtnie, Courtny, Kordney, Kortney, Kortni, Kourtenay, Kourtneigh, Kourtney, Kourtnee, Kourtnie

Creola Fr. from Port. "Of American birth but European descent." Used to describe natives of the West Indies and Louisiana who were the offspring of European-born colonists.

Créole, Creolla, Criolla

Crescent OF. "Increasing, growing." Also, by extension, the shape of the crescent moon.

Crescence, Crescenta, Crescentia, Cressant, Cressent, Cressentia, Cressentya

Cressida Gk. Heroine of a tale (*Troilus and Cressida*) that has been told by Boccaccio, Chaucer, and Shakespeare, among others.

Crisanta Sp. from Gk. "Golden flower, chrysanthemum."

Chrisanta, Chrisantha, Chrissanta, Chrissantha, Chryssantha

Crispina (Fem. **Crispin**) Lat. "Curly-haired."

Cristina Lat. "Anointed, Christian." See **Christina.**

Crystal Gk. "Ice." Transferred use of the word, mostly modern, and increasing since the 1950s. The TV series *Dynasty* brought the name to great prominence in the 1980s, though that character spelled it "Krystle." Phonetic variants probably outnumber the original spelling. Curiously enough, Crystal was considered a man's name in Scotland hundreds of years ago, where it was a diminutive of Christopher. See **Christina**.

Christal, Christalle, Chrystal, Chrystalle, Chrystel, Chrystle, Cristal, Cristel, Cristle, Crysta, Crystel, Khristalle, Khrystle, Kristle, Krystal, Krystalle, Krystle

Csilla Hung. "Defenses."

Cyanea Gk. "Sky blue."

Cybele Gk. Asian goddess, also known in Greek myth as Rhea, and in Rome as "Great Mother of the Gods." In legend she was originally bisexual, but made female by the Olympian gods.

Cymbeline Possibly Gk. "Hollow" (which relates to the hollow percussion instrument, the cymbal) or Celt. "Sun lord." The title of one of Shakespeare's lesser-known plays, whose protagonist is a 12th-century king of Britain.
Cymbaline

Cyma Gk. "Flourishing."
Syma

Cynara Gk. "Thistly plant." Made famous by the late–19th-century English poet Ernest Dowson, who is in turn largely remembered by the line *"I have been faithful to thee, Cynara! in my fashion."*
Zinara

Cynthia Gk. "Goddess from Mount Cynthos," i.e., Artemis, the moon goddess, who was supposed to have been born there. Used as a literary name in the 17th century, and by American slave owners in the early 19th century. Enjoyed a period of popularity from the 1920s to 1950s, then was replaced by its nickname, Cindy, which is now rare. Although many polysyllabic names ending in "-a" (Alexandra, Olivia, Antonia) are becoming more popular, Cynthia may sound too much like the early 20th century to attract 21st-century interest. Many of the diminutives are also variants of Lucinda. Ballerina Cynthia Gregory.
Cinda, Cindee, Cindi, Cindie, Cindy, Cinnie, Cinny, Cinthia, Cintia, Cinzia, Cyn, Cynda, Cyndee, Cyndia, Cyndie, Cyndra, Cyndy, Cynnie, Cynthea, Cynthie, Cynthya, Cytia, Kynthia, Kynthija, Sindee, Sindi, Sindy, Sindya, Sinnie, Sinny, Synda, Syndee, Syndi, Syndy, Syntha, Synthee, Syntheea, Synthia, Synthie, Synthya

Cypris Gk. "From the island of Cyprus."
Cipriana, Cypriane, Ciprienne, Cyprianne, Cyprien, Cyprienne, Sipriana, Siprianne

Cyra (Fem. **Cyrus**) Per. "Sun" or "Throne." Author Cyra McFadden.

Cyrilla (Fem. **Cyril**) Lat. "Lordly."
Ciri, Cirilla, Siri, Sirilla, Syrilla

Cytherea Gk. "From the island of Cythera," i.e., Aphrodite or Venus, who is supposed to have come ashore there after being born of seafoam.

Dabney OF. place name: "From Aubigny." This is an old Virginia name, given with pride to establish a connection with a 1649 immigrant to the New World named Cornelius d'Aubigny. It is used for both boys and girls.

Dabnie, Dabny

Dacey Ir. Gael. "From the south."

Dacee, Dacia, Dacie, Dacy, Daicee, Daicy, Daisey

Dacia Lat. Place name: Dacia was a Roman province which existed where Romania is now.

Dada Nig. "Curly-haired."

Daffodil OF. Flower name for the familiar yellow blossom; an inventive name for a spring baby.

Dagmar OG. Meaning unclear; possibly "Day's glory." In Denmark Dagmar is a royal name; Czarina Marie, wife of Czar Alexander III of Russia, was Princess Dagmar of Denmark. The name appears only rarely in English-speaking countries.

Dagny ONorse. "New day." Probably etymologically related to Dagmar.

Dagna, Dagne

Dahlia Scand. Flower name of fairly recent vintage, first used in numbers since the 1920s. The flower itself was named in honor of the 18th-century Swedish botanist Anders Dahl.

Dahiana, Dayha, Daleia, Dalia, Dalla

Dai Jap. "Great."

Daira Sp. from Gk. "Knowing, informed." Extremely rare.

Daeira, Danira, Dayeera

— **Daisy** OE. "Eye of the day." One of the most popular of the 19th-century flower names. It was often used as a nickname for Margaret, since in France the flower is called a *marguerite*. It was such a popular name that, when Henry James was writing the story of the typical

American girl in Europe, he named her Daisy Miller. Little used in the modern era, but this is the kind of name that nostalgia may resurrect. The old song "Bicycle Built for Two" (which begins "Daisy, Daisy, give me your answer, do . . .") is probably so obscure that it shouldn't prevent parents from selecting the name. Actress Daisy Fuentes.

Daisee, Daisey, Daisie, Dasie

Dakota American place name: the word may be Sioux for "Allies," though another source suggests "Forever smiling." Despite its "-a" ending, this is used (perhaps because of the percussive consonants or the ruggedness it evokes) as a name for both boys and girls.

Dakoda, Dakotah

Dale OE. Place name: "Valley." Originally a surname meaning "One who lives in the valley." The term "dale" is still used in parts of England. Most popular as a first name in the 1930s. Actress Dale Evans.

Dael, Dail, Daile, Dalla, Dayle

Dalia Heb. "Slender branch, tendril."

Daliah, Dalit, Daliya, Dalya, Dalyah

Dalila Swahili. "Delicate."

Lila

Dallas Scot. Gael. Place name of a village in northeastern Scotland, used as a first name since the 19th century. Apparently unrelated to Dallas, Texas, which was named for a U.S. Vice President, but few modern Americans will fail to make the connection between the name and the city.

Dalles

Dalmace Lat./Fr. Place name: Dalmatia is a region of northeastern Italy, extending down into coastal Yugoslavia, and the supposed origin of dalmatian dogs, white-haired with black spots.

Dalma, Dalmassa, Dalmatia

Damaris Gk. "Calf" is the most commonly suggested meaning though another source suggests "to tame." A Damaris in the New Testament was converted by Saint Paul, and the Puritans adopted the name with enthusiasm, if not uniformity in spelling. Many variants exist, though the name is very unusual.

Damalas, Damalis, Damalit, Damalla, Damara, Dama-

ss, Dameris, Damerys, Dameryss, Damiris, Damris, Demaras, Demaris, Demarys, Mara, Mari, Maris

Damia Gk. Meaning not clear; possibly "To tame," although the Greek root is also close to the word for "Spirit." The masculine form, Damian, is more often seen.

Damian, Damiana, Damiane, Damienne, Damya, Damyan, Damyana, Damyen, Damyenne

Damita Sp. "Little noblewoman." From the root that gives us "dame."

Dama

Dana OE. "From Denmark." Also a surname, used as a boy's first name in the 19th century, but now almost exclusively a girl's name, and a specifically American one. Actress Dana Delany.

Danaca, Danay, Dane, Danet, Dania, Danica, Danna, Danya, Dayna, Donnica

Danaë Gk. A character in Greek myth whom Zeus visited in the form of a shower of gold (a popular subject for Old Master painters). The child of this union was the heroic Perseus who rescued Andromeda.

Dee, Denaë, Dené, Dinae, Dinay, Diné, Donnay

Dangelis Modern elaboration of Angela, perhaps suggested by the Italian last name D'Angelo.

Dangela, Dangellis, Deangelis, Diangelis

Danica Lat. "From Denmark." There is a famous (and phenomenally expensive) Royal Copenhagen china pattern known as "Flora Danica," or "Flowers of Denmark." Actress Danica McKellar.

Danaca, Danika, Donika, Donnica

— **Danielle** (Fem. **Daniel**) Heb. "God is my judge." Uncommon until the middle of the 20th century, when, following a revival of Daniel, it became more fashionable. It was one of the top ten names in New York City in 1994. Novelist Danielle Steele.

Daanelle, Danee, Danele, Danella, Danelle, Danelly, Danette, Daney, Dani, Dania, Danica, Danice, Danie, Daniela, Daniella, Danijela, Danila, Danit, Danita, Danitza, Danna, Dannette, Danney, Danni, Danniella, Dannielle, Danny, Dannyce, Dany, Danya, Danyell, Danyella, Danyelle

Daphne Gk. "Laurel tree." In Greek myth Daphne was a nymph who, attempting to flee an amorous Apollo, was turned into a laurel tree. Though used under the Roman Empire, the name disappeared until the 18th century. It came to the U.S. as a slave name, and enjoyed a brief English vogue between 1900 and 1930. Pretty, unusual, but not trendy, Daphne is ripe for revival. Author Daphne du Maurier.

Daffi, Daffie, Daffy, Dafna, Dafné, Dafnee, Dafneigh, Dafnie, Daphna, Daphney, Daphnie, Danfy

Dara Heb. "Nugget of wisdom." In the New Testament, a man's name, but its occasional modern use is for girls. Its resemblance to the familiar Sarah and Farrah probably works in its favor. Olympic swimmer Darra Torres.

Darda, Daria, Darian, Darragh, Darrah, Darya

Daralis OE. "Beloved."

Daralice, Darelis

Darby OE. Place name: "Park with deer." Derived from Derby, a surname used as a first name, almost exclusively for boys. Darby is also usually masculine.

Darb, Darbee, Darbey, Darbie, Darrbey, Darrbie, Darrby

Darcie Ir. Gael. "Dark." Also Norman place name, "From Arcy." In Britain, usually a boy's name, but in the U.S., more likely to be feminine. Ballerina Darci Kistler.

D'Arcy, Darcee, Darceigh, Darcey, Darcy, Darice, Darsee, Darseigh, Darsey, Darsie, Darsi

Darenda Invented name, composed of compatible elements to achieve a pretty sound. Though this trend may seem particularly current, parents have been making up names for hundreds of years.

Daria (Fem. **Darius**) Gk. "Rich."

Dari, Darian, Darice, Darien, Darya, Dhariana, Dorian, Doriane

Darice Modern feminization of Darius. The "-ice" ending has a real mid-twentieth century flavor.

Dareece, Dareese

Darlene Modern adaptation of "darling" used for a given name. First used in the late 1930s and extremely fashionable by the 1950s in the U.S. Now out of style, and unlikely to be revived soon.

Dareen, Darelle, Darla, Darleen, Darlenny, Darline, Dar-

linn, Darlyn, Darlyne, Darrelle, Darryleen, Darrylene, Darryline

Daron (Fem. **Darren**) Modern use. Darren may be a transferred Irish surname, first used widely in the 1950s as a given name. Daron can be considered a feminine form because of its similiarity to Sharon (also popular in that era).

Daryl Transferred surname, possibly originated as a French place name, like Darcy. Its use was probably influenced by names that were fashionable mid-century, like Cheryl. Actress Daryl Hannah.

Darel, Darille, Darrel, Darrell, Darrelle, Darrill, Darrille, Darrylene, Darryline, Darryl, Darrylin, Darryline, Darrylyn, Darylin, Daryline, Darylyne, Derrill

Datya Heb. ''Belief in God.''

Datia, Datiah, Datyah

Davina (Fem. **David**) Heb. ''Loved one.'' The most commonly used feminine variant of the hugely popular masculine name.

Daveen, Daviana, Daviane, Davida, Davidina, Davine, Davinia, Davita, Devina, Divina, Divinia

Dawn OE. ''Dawn.'' Modern use of the word for a name. Aurora, the Latin term, dates back some 1500 years, but Dawn first appeared in the late 1920s. Its popularity has waned considerably as taste turns back to the more stately polysyllabic names of the 19th century. Opera singer Dawn Upshaw.

Daun, Dawna, Dawnita, Dawnyelle, Dawnysia, Dowan, Duwan, Dwan

Day OE. ''Day.'' Possibly use of the word as a name, like Dawn, but more likely to be a transferred surname.

Daya Heb. ''Bird of prey.'' Specifically, a kind of hawk known as a kite.

Dayah

Dea Lat. ''Goddess.''

Deanna OE. Place name ''Valley'' or occupational name ''Church leader.'' Feminine of Dean, which only came into use as a first name in the 1950s. Could also be considered a version of Diana. Actress Deanna Durbin.

Deana, Deann, Deanne, Deeann, Deeanna

Debonnaire Fr. ''Urbane, nonchalant.'' Perhaps a Norman family name: it could have meant ''of good lineage.'' To

moderns, debonair is the word you use to describe Fred
Astaire.
Debonair, Debonaire
Deborah Heb. "Bee." One of the few significant women's
names to figure in the Old Testament; in the Book of
Judges, she was an important prophetess and judge. Predictably, the Puritans latched on to the name, but it was
not widely used until the 1950s, possibly influenced by
the career of actress Deborah Kerr. Like most names popular fifty years ago, it is little used for children now. Actresses Debbie Reynolds, Debra Winger; Olympic figure
skater Debi Thomas; TV journalist Deborah Norville.
**Deb, Debb, Debbee, Debbera, Debbey, Debbi, Debbie,
Debbra, Debby, Debee, Debera, Deberah, Debi, Debor,
Debora, Debra, Debrah, Debs, Devora, Devorah, Dobra**
Decca Possibly from the Greek root meaning "Ten." Most
famous perhaps as the Mitford family nickname for the
journalist sister Jessica, and as a defunct American record
label.
Decka, Deka
Decembra Month name. A way to refer to the holiday sea-
son without using Noel.
Decima Lat. "Tenth girl." Unlikely to be used in these
days of small families.
Decia
Dee Welsh. "Swarthy." Dim. **Deirdre, Diana, Delia**, etc.
Dede, Dedie, DeeDee, DeeAnn, Didi
Deifilia Lat. "God's daughter."
Deiondra Fem. **Dion**, dim. **Dionysus**. Dionysus is the
Greek god of wine. The name Dion is used occasionally,
most notably now by football star Deion Sanders, who
named his daughter Deiondra.
Deionna, Diondra, Dionna
Deirdre Ir. Possible meanings are "Fear" or "Raging
woman." In Irish myth, Deirdre was the most beautiful
woman in Ireland, whose tragically complex love life
caused several deaths, including her own. The name, currently popular in Britain, has been in use only since the
1920s. Actress Deidre Hall.
**Dede, Dedra, Dee, DeeDee, Deedre, Deidra, Deidre, Dei-
drie, Derdre, Didi, Dierdrey**

Delana Adaptation of Delano, Franklin D. Roosevelt's middle name. Usage (it has never been anything but rare) coincided with FDR's presidential career.

Delancey French place name. There is a Delancey Street in New York City, named for long-ago owners of nearby land.
Delancie, Delancy

Delaney Ir. Gael. "Offspring of the challenger."
DeLaina, Delaine, Delainey, Delainy, Delane, Delanie, Delany, DeLayna

Delia Gk. "From Delos." In Greek myth, the goddess Artemis was born in Delos, so Delia could be an allusion to her. It may also be a diminutive of **Cordelia** or **Adelaide**. Though it has never had a period of great popularity, it has never faded from sight either. Author Delia Ephron.
Deelia, Delya

Delicia Lat. "Delight." Used in the Roman Empire, and occasionally since then, but never common. Nowadays it might be considered an elaboration of Alicia.
Dalicia, Dalise, Dalisha, Dalisse, Dee, DeeDee, Dela, Delice, Delis, Delise, Delisha, Delissa, Deliz, Della, Dellis, Dellise, Delyse, Delysia, Didi

Delight OF. The emotion as a name. Scarce.

Delilah Heb. "Lovelorn, seductive." In the Old Testament, mistress of Samson. The familiar story of how she cuts off his hair to sap his strength probably limits use of her name.
Dalila, Delila, Lila, Lilah

Della Short for **Adelle, Adeline, Adelaide**. Used as an independent name since the 1870s. Singer Della Reese.
Delle, Dellene, Delline

Delores Sp. "Sorrows." Var. **Dolores**.

Delphine Gk. "Dolphin." This is a French form of a name with a complex origin. It alludes to the Greek town of Delphi, home of a famous oracle. The Greeks believed that Delphi was the earth's womb; the dolphin's shape resembles that of a pregnant woman. The larkspur flower, whose center resembles a dolphin, is also known as delphinium, so in some respects this is a flower name. French actress Delphine Seyrig.
Delfa, Delfin, Delfine, Delfyne, Delpha, Delphina, Delphinea, Delphinia

Delta Fourth letter of the Greek alphabet, thus a name for a fourth child. May also be a place name, as in the Mississippi Delta. Actress Delta Burke.

Delta

Demetria Gk. In Greek myth, Demeter was goddess of corn, and mother of Persephone, whose abduction to Hades led to the cycle of seasons. Her Roman name is Ceres, from the word root that gives us "cereal."

Demeter, Demetra, Demetria, Demetris, Dimitra, Dimitria

Demelza Cornish. "Fort on the hill." First used as a given name in the 1950s, probably because of its pretty sound.

Demi Fr. "Half." As virtually everyone in America must know, the name of a certain shapely actress who pronounces it in the "French" way, with the accent on the last syllable.

Demee, Demie

Dena OE. Place name: "Valley." Use of Dena followed the popularity of Dean in the 1950s.

Deana, Deane, Deanna, Deena, Dene, Denna, Denni, Dina

Denelle Modern name: perhaps a simplification of the popular Danielle, or an elaboration of Nell.

Danell, Denell, Dinelle, Donell, Donella, Donelle

Denise (Fem. **Dennis**) Fr. "Follower of Dionysius." Though there is an ancient Latin form of the name (Dionysia), this variation dates back only to the 1920s. It was very popular in the 1950s, but since the mid-1960s has been eclipsed. Singer Deniece Williams.

Deneigh, Denese, Dennet, Dennette, Deney, Deni, Denice, Deniece, Denisse, Denize, Denni, Dennie, Dennise, Denny, Denyce, Denys, Denyse, Dinnie, Dinny

Deolinda Port. "Beautiful God."

Deora Place name: a tiny town in northeastern Colorado.

Derinda Modern name, probably formed from **Derek** and **Linda**.

Darinda, Dorinda

Derora Heb. "A bird, a swallow."

Derorit, Drora, Drorah, Drorit, Droriya

Deryn Welsh. "Bird." Dates from the 1950s, and its popularity mirrors names like Karen and Sharon. Unusual after the 1970s.

Derran, Deren, Derhyn, Deron, Derrin, Derrine, Derron, Derrynne

Desdemona Gk. "Wretchedness." In Shakespeare's *Othello*, Desdemona is the beautiful, innocent heroine, wrongly accused of adultery by her husband, who then murders her and commits suicide in a fit of remorse. Little used, for obvious reasons.

Desmona

Desirée Fr. "Much desired." The Puritans used Desire as a given name, though its connotations in the 17th century were religious rather than erotic. The French form is more usual today. An immensely popular novel published in the 1960s traced the biography of the French Desirée Clary from poverty in Marseilles to the throne of Sweden. The name is quite steadily used.

Desarae, Deseray, Desideria, Desir, Desirae, Desirat, Desiray, Desirea, Desiri, Disirae, Dezirae, Deziray

Desma Gk. "Binding oath."

Desmé

Destiny OF. "Fate." Not exactly popular, but the name occurs in the top 150 girls' names.

Desta, Destanay, Destianay, Destinay, Destinee, Destiney, Destinie, Destyni

Detta Dim. **Benedetta** (Lat. "Blessed").

Deva Hindi. "Godlike." In Hindu myth, Deva is another name for the moon goddess.

Devi

Devin Ir. Gael. "Poet." Also an alternative spelling for Devon (see below).

Deva, Devinne, Devvin, Devyn

Devon OE. Place name: a county in Southern England. More common for girls than for boys. **Devin** may also be considered a variant.

Devan, Deven, Devenne, Devona, Devondra, Devonne, Devvon

Devri Dim. **Devora**, var. **Deborah** (Heb. "Bee").

Dextra (Fem. **Dexter**) OE. "Dyer" or Lat. "Right-handed." Dexter, like most occupational names, was originally a surname. Dextra could also mean "skillful, dextrous."

Dextera

Deyanira Sp. from Gk. "Devastating, capable of great destruction." In Greco-Roman myth, the wife of Hercules, who managed by trickery to kill him.

Daianira, Dayanira, Deianira, Dellanira, Diyanira, Neera, Nira

Diamond Unusual jewel name, first used in the 1890s but not as common then as Ruby, Emerald, etc. In 1994, however, Diamond was the seventh most popular name given to African-American girls; Darryl Strawberry's daughter is named Diamond. The gem is the birthstone for April.

Diamanta, Diamanté

Diana "Divine." The Roman goddess of the moon, corresponding to the Greek Artemis. Used steadily since the 16th century, though the French version Diane eclipsed it in the mid–20th century. The vogue for Diane faded after the 1960s, and the apotheosis of Lady Diana Spencer as Princess of Wales in 1980 gave Diana new charm for prospective parents, especially in Britain. Her tragic death in 1997 and the subsequent outpouring of grief in its wake will undoubtedly add to the popularity of this name in years to come. French courtesan Diana de Poitiers; actresses Diahann Carroll, Dyan Cannon, Diane Keaton, Dianne Wiest.

Danne, Dayann, Dayanna, Dayanne, Deana, Deane, Deandra, Deanna, Dede, Dee, DeeDee, Deeana, Deeane, Deann, Dena, Di, Diahann, Diahanne, Dian, Diandra, Diane, Diann, Dianna, Dianne, Didi, Dyan, Dyana, Dyane, Dyann, Dyanna, Dyanne

Diandra Possibly an elaboration of Diana. Another interpretation goes back to Greek word particles: "di-" means "two" and "-andra" means "male." The name could refer to flowers with two stamens, for instance.

Deandra, Dyandra

Dianthe Gk. "Flower of the gods."

Diandra, Diandre, Diantha

Didi Var. **Diana, Deirdre**. Actress Didi Conn.

DeeDee

Didiane Fr. Feminine form of **Didier**, which is in turn a form of Desirée, through the Latin **Desideratus**. They all mean "desired." In America this name is likely to be heard as "Didi Ann."

Didiana, Didianna, Didiere

Dido Gk. In Virgil's *Aeneid*, the queen of Carthage who falls in love with the wandering Aeneas, and commits suicide when he leaves her. The name's origins are obscure: Virgil may have coined it.

Didrika (Fem. **Dietrich**) OG. "People's ruler."
Diedericka, Diedricka, Diedrika

Dielle Fr. "God." Probably a female version of the French *dieu*, for "God." Unusual.
Diella

Digna Lat. "Worthy."
Deenya, Dinya

Dillian OE. "Idol, god." Pretty and very unusual name.
Diliana, Dilli, Dilliana, Dillianna

Dilys Welsh. "Reliable." Somewhat older than many names now popular in Wales, since it dates from the mid–19th century.
Dillys, Dylis, Dyllis, Dylys

Dimitra (Fem. **Demetrius**) Gk. "Follower of Demeter." Can also be considered a variant of Demetria (see above).
Demetra, Demetria, Dimitria

Dimity Name of an unpretentious sheer cotton fabric that is textured with checks or stripes in the weaving.
Dimitee, Dimitey, Dimitie

Dimona Heb. "South."
Demona, Demonah, Dimonah

Dinah Heb. "Justified." Old Testament name. In the U.S., has been popular in the South. Dina may also be considered a diminutive of names like **Claudina**. Actresses Dina Merrill, Dinah Shore.
Dina, Dyna, Dynah

Dinya Heb. "Judgment of the Lord."
Dinia, Diniah, Dinyah

Dionne Two possible sources: Dione, in Greek myth, is the mother of Aphrodite. The name can also be a feminine version of **Dion** (Gk. "Follower of Dionysus"). It is also a homonym for the French pronunciation of Diane. Singer Dionne Warwick.
Deiondra, Deonne, Dion, Diona, Diondra, Dione, Dionetta, Dionis, Dionna

Dionysia Lat. Form of **Denise** (Gk. "Follower of Dionysus)."
Deonisia, Deonysia, Dinicia, Dinisha, Dinitia, Dionisia

Dita Var. **Edith**. OE. "Prosperity/battle."

Ditza Heb. "Joy."
  Ditzah, Diza

Divina It. "Divine, heavenly." Also var. **Davina** (Heb. "Loved one").
  Divine, Divinia

Dixie Fr. "Tenth." The term "Dixie" for the Southern states, made popular by the song, is mysterious. It might come from the Mason-Dixon line, or from Louisiana dollars printed in French with the word *dix* on them (hence, "the land of dixies"). Actress Dixie Carter.
  Dix, Dixee

Docila Lat. "Biddable."

Dodie Heb. "Well loved." Familiar form of **Dora**, **Dorothy** (Gk. "Gift of God"). Author Dodie Smith.
  Doda, Dodee, Dodey, Dodi, Dody

Dolly Familiar form of Dorothy. As an independent name, it was most popular at the turn of the century, but never a favorite. First Lady Dolly Madison; country singer Dolly Parton.
  Dollee, Dolley, Dollie

Dolores Sp. "Sorrows." An allusion to the Virgin Mary, Santa Maria de los Dolores. During the 1920s and '30s the name crossed over strongly into the Anglo world, possibly sparked by the career of actress Dolores Del Rio.
  Dalores, Delora, Delores, Deloria, Deloris, Dolorcita, Dolorcitas, Dolorita, Doloritas, Lola, Lolita

Domina Lat. "Lady."

Dominique (Fem. **Dominic**) Lat. "Lord." French form of a Latin name, rather fashionable in the last twenty-five years. Could be used for a child born on Sunday, "the Lord's day." Olympic gymnasts Dominique Dawes, Dominique Moceanu.
  Domaneke, Domanique, Domenica, Domeniga, Domenique, Dominga, Domineek, Domineke, Domini, Dominica, Dominie, Dominika, Dominizia, Domino, Domitia, Meeka, Mika, Domorique

Domitilla Latin clan name: the second-century saint Flavia Domitilla allowed her gardens in Rome to be used as a Christian cemetery.
  Domicia, Domitila, Domitilia

Dona Sp. "Lady." Unusual variation on **Donna**.

Donalda Scot. Gael. "World mighty." One of many attempts to form a feminine of Donald, a Scottish name particularly popular in the first half of the 20th century.
Dona, Donaldette, Donaldina, Donaline, Donelda, Donetta, Donia, Donita

Donata Lat. "Given." From the same root that gives us "donate."
Donatila, Donatilia

Donna It. "Lady." The original meaning is closer to "lady of the home." Strictly modern use as a given name, dating from the 1920s. Very popular in the 1950s, but little used now. Actress Donna Reed; swimming champion Donna DeVarona; fashion designer Donna Karan; singer Donna Summer.
Dona, Donalie, Donella, Donelle, Donetta, Donia, Donica, Donielle, Donita, Donnell, Donnella, Donnelle, Donni, Donnica, Donnie, Donnisse, Donny, Ladonna

Dora Gk. "Gift." Probably originated as a diminutive of names like **Theodora**, and introduced as an independent name by a character in Charles Dickens's *David Copperfield*. Its heyday in the U.S. came at the turn of the century, but it is currently popular in Greece. Good potential for revival as it is quaint and dignified but not unwieldy for a small child.
Dodee, Dodi, Dodie, Dody, Doralee, Doraleene, Doralia, Doralice, Doralicia, Doralina, Doralisha, Doralyn, Doralynn, Dore, Dorea, Doree, Doreen, Dorelia, Dorelle, Dorena, Dorene, Doretta, Dorette, Doreyda, Dori, Dorie, Dorita, Dorrie, Dory

Dorcas Gk. "Gazelle." New Testament name, Greek version of *Tabitha*. Saint Peter raised her from the dead. Predictably, well used by the Puritans, but uncommon since.
Dorcass, Dorcia, Dorkas

Dorée Fr. "Gilded."
Dorae, Doraie, D'Oray, Doré, Dorey, Dorie, Dory

Doreen Several possible origins, including Ir. Gael. "Brooding," Fr. "Gilded," and an elaboration of Dora. In the top ten in Britain in the 1920s, now unusual.
Dorene, Doreyn, Dorine, Dorreen, Doryne

Doretta Gk. "Gift from God." Variant of **Dora** or **Theodora**.

Doria Gk. Place name: "From Doris," an area in Greece. Also feminine of **Dorian**; var. **Dorothy, Theodora** (Gk. "Gift from God").

Dori, Dorian, Doriane, Dorianne, Dorria, Dory

Dorinda Gk./Sp. Var. **Dora**. English poets in the 18th century coined a number of names with the "-inda" suffix. This one has enjoyed a small revival in this century.

Derinda, Dorrinda, Dyrinda

Doris (Fem. **Dorian**) Gk. Place name: "From Doris," an area in Greece. This form is more common than Doria, having been hugely popular between 1900 and the 1930s, when it subsided. To most people having children these days, "Doris" is the name of a much older woman. Actress Doris Day; writer Doris Lessing.

Dori, Doria, Dorice, Dorisa, Dorita, Dorrie, Dorry, Dorrys, Dory, Dorys, Doryse

Dorma Lat. "Sleeping." As in "dormitory." Equally possibly, a variation on the familiar **Norma**.

Dorrma

Dorona Heb. "Gift."

Doran, Dorran

Dorothy Gk. "Gift of God." Theodora, never as popular, simply reverses the order of the Greek words. Has had two periods of popularity, around 1500 to 1700, and 1900 to the mid-1920s. The latter vogue may have been inspired by the heroine of Frank Baum's *The Wonderful Wizard of Oz*, published in 1900. The success of the film version (1939) and its perennial popularity ensure that most people, upon first meeting a child named Dorothy, cannot help thinking of Judy Garland. Writers Dorothy Parker, Dorothy Sayers; actresses Dorothy Gish, Dorothy Lamour.

Dasha, Dasya, Dodie, Dody, Doe, Doll, Dolley, Dolli, Dollie, Dolly, Doortje, Dora, Doretta, Dori, Dorika, Dorinda, Dorit, Dorita, Doritha, Dorlisa, Doro, Doronit, Dorota, Dorotea, Doroteya, Dorothea, Dorothée, Dorrit, Dorthea, Dorthy, Dory, Dosha, Dosya, Dot, Dottey, Dottie, Dotty, Tea, Thea

Dorrit Dim. **Dorothy**. Another example of the influence of popular culture on names, as it probably stems from Charles Dickens's novel *Little Dorrit*.
Dorita, Doritt

Dorsey Place name: possibly French, "From Orsay," or related to Dorset, a county on the southern coast of England.
Dorcie, Dorsay, Dorsea, Dorseigh, Dorsie

Dory Fr."Gilded." Also dim. **Dorothy, Isadora**.

Douce Fr. "Sweet."

Dove Bird name. The dove, of course, symbolizes peace, God's covenant with Noah, and the Holy Spirit.
Dova

Doveva Heb. "Graceful."
Dova, Dovit

Dreama As in what happens when you go to sleep.

Drew Dim. **Andrew** (Gk. "Masculine"). More commonly used for boys. When used as a girl's name, it is probably a transferred surname, though it has been given new exposure by the career of actress Drew Barrymore.

Drusilla Lat. Feminine version of a Roman clan name which appears in the New Testament. Very unusual nowadays. Philanthropist Drue Heinz.
Drewsila, Dru, Drucella, Drucie, Drucilla, Drucy, Drue, Druesilla, Druscilla, Drusella, Drusy

Duane Ir. Gael. "Swarthy." Dates from the 1940s. More common for boys, but use for girls may increase with the trend toward unisex names. Socialite Duane Hampton.
Duana, Duna, Dwana, Dwayna, Dwayne

Duena Sp. "Chaperone."

Dulcie Lat. "Sweet." Roman name revived for some years at the turn of the 20th century, but extremely unusual now. Cervantes used a slightly different form when he named the heroine of *Don Quixote* Dulcinea.
Delcina, Delcine, Delsine, Dulce, Dulcea, Dulci, Dulcia, Dulciana, Dulcibella, Dulcibelle, Dulcine, Dulcinea, Dulcy, Dulsea, Dulsia, Dulsiana, Dulsibell, Dulsine

Dumia Heb. "Silent."
Dumiya

Duscha Rus. "Happy."
Duschenka, Duschinka, Dusica, Dusa

Dusty (Fem. **Dustin**). An English place name transferred to first name. Probably popularized in this century by English singer Dusty Springfield. Today's parents are more likely to simply use Dustin.
Dustan, Dustee, Dustie, Dustin

Dylana (Fem. **Dylan**) Welsh. "Born from waves." Use of Dylan tends to be a tribute to the poet Dylan Thomas, and most parents today would not hesitate to use the original masculine name for a girl. The name is quite popular for boys.
Dillan, Dillon, Dylane, Dyllan

Dympna Ir. Gael. Saint's name of obscure origin. Many cures of epilepsy and other mental disturbances were attributed to her, and she became known as patroness of the insane. A medieval mental hospital in Belgium, in the town where her bones were discovered, is still going strong.
Dymphna

SPELL THAT, PLEASE

Many parents like to put a twist on their baby's name by spelling it in an unusual way. They may be hoping to add a bit of individuality to the name, or make it memorable. Experts tend to see this as a bad idea: by the time your child reaches school age, the inconvenience of having to spell "Emylee" to every stranger (and correct the ones who get it wrong) tells you why. What's more, you take the chance that their innovative spelling may be seen as pretentious or even illiterate. So think long and hard if you're considering writing "Nickolaus" on the birth certificate. Your child will probably thank you.

Earla (Fem. **Earl**) OE. "Nobleman, leader." Several English aristocratic titles such as Duke, Earl, and Baron have been turned into proper names, a sterling example of wishful thinking. Feminine variants are more uncommon.

Earldena, Earldene, Earldina, Earleen, Earlene, Earletta, Erlette, Earley, Earlie, Earline, Erla, Erlene, Erletta, Erlette, Erlina, Erline, Erlinia, Ireleen, Irelene, Irelina, Irelene

Eartha OE. "Earth." Used by the Puritans in the 17th century, but obsolete since then. New Age, environmentally conscious parents may bring this name back to a degree of popularity. Singer Eartha Kitt.

Erda, Ertha, Herta, Hertha

Easter Name of the holiday, transferred to use as a Christian name predominantly in the 19th century. (Some sources trace it to a variation of Esther.) A more common Eastertide name is the French Pascale.

Ebba OE. "Fortress of riches" or ONorse, "Strength of a boar." There was a 7th-century saint in northern England named Edburga, which was probably contracted to Ebba.

Ebbe

Eberta Teut. "Bright."

Ebony Name of the wood, which is prized for its black color. Popular since the 1970s with African-American families, who also favor other descriptive names like Amber and Tawny.

Ebboney, Ebbony, Ebonee, Eboney, Ebonney, Ebonni, Ebonny, Eboni, Ebonie, Ebonyi

Echo Gk. Name of a mythological nymph who was a disembodied voice. One version of her story holds that she pined away of love for Narcissus until only her voice was left. A pretty choice for lovers of Greek culture, though it might turn out to be a little too appropriate for a chatty child.

Eda OE. "Wealthy, happy." Also possibly a variation of Edith.

Ede

Edana (Fem. **Aidan**) Gael. "Fire." Saint Aidan was a 7th-century Irish monk.

Aidana, Aydana

Edeline OG. "Noble, nobility." Var. **Adeline**.

Edelina

Edelmira Sp. from Ger. "Admired for nobility."

Eden Heb. "Pleasure, delight." It is a short step from the Hebrew meaning of the word to its general association with Paradise. The name is used, infrequently, for boys as well as girls, though its brisk rhythm and alluring meaning could bring it new prominence in the next few years.

Eaden, Eadin, Edenia, Edin

Edina OE. Possibly a form of Edwina, or a literary term meaning "From Edinburgh," the capital city of Scotland. One of the characters in the dotty British sitcom *Absolutely Fabulous* is called Edina: she is not what most parents would consider a good role model. Fashion designer Edina Ronay.

Adena, Adina, Edeena, Edyna

Edith OE. "Prosperity/battle." Anglo-Saxon name that continued to be used after the Norman Conquest, and was revived along with other ancient names in the 19th century. By the 1870s it was one of the ten most popular girls' names in Britain, but it has been steadily displaced since the 1930s. At the moment associations with characters like Edith Bunker make it seem dated but not pleasantly old-fashioned. Writer Edith Wharton; singers Eydie Gorme and Édith Piaf; actress Dame Edith Evans.

Dita, Eadie, Eadith, Eda, Ede, Edi, Edie, Edita, Editha, Édithe, Ediva, Edy, Edyth, Edytha, Edythe, Eidith, Eidyth, Eidytha, Eyde, Eydie, Eydith

Edlyn OE. "Small noble one."

Edelynn, Edlin, Edlinn, Edlinna, Edlynn

Edmonda (Fem. **Edmund**) OE. "Wealthy defender." A popular, and sainted, king of the East Angles in the 9th

century gave the masculine version of the name enough
popularity to survive the Norman Conquest. The feminine
variants are unusual.

Edma, Edmée, Edmonde, Edmunda

Edna Heb. "Pleasure, enjoyment." Perhaps arising from
the same root as Eden. First used in the 18th century, but
very popular in the last half of the 19th century, especially
in America. Now almost unheard-of. Poet Edna St. Vincent Millay; novelist Edna Ferber.

Eddi, Eddie, Eddna, Eddnah, Eddy, Ednah

Edrea OE. "Wealthy, powerful."

Edra, Eidra, Eydra

Edris (Fem. **Edric**) Anglo-Saxon. "Wealthy, powerful."
The masculine version was an Old English name revived
slightly in the 19th century; feminine variants are uncommon.

**Edrice, Edriss, Edryce, Eidris, Eidriss, Eydris, Edrys, Id-
rice, Idris, Idrys**

Edwardine (Fem. **Edward**) OE. "Wealthy defender."
Rare and slightly awkward variant of a steadily well-used
masculine name.

**Edwarda, Edwardeen, Edwardene, Edwardina, Edwar-
dyne**

Edwige Fr. from OG. "Happy battle."

**Eduvigis, Edvig, Edvigis, Edwig, Hedvig, Hedwig, Hed-
wige**

Edwina (Fem. **Edwin**) OE. "Wealth/friend." Feminine
variant of an Anglo-Saxon name revived in the 19th century, but never hugely popular.

**Edina, Edweena, Edwiena, Edwena, Edwine, Edwinna,
Edwyna, Edwynne**

Effie Gk. "Pleasant speech." Short version of Euphemia,
used as an independent name starting in the 1860s. Popularity faded after the 1930s.

**Efffemie, Effemy Effi, Effy, Efthemia, Ephie, Eppie, Eu-
phemia, Euphemie, Euphie**

Efrata Heb. "Fertile, fruitful; honored." An Old Testament
name: Efrata was the second wife of Caleb.

Efrat, Ephrata

Egberta (Fem. **Egbert**) OE. "Brilliant sword."

Egbertha, Egbertina, Egbertine, Egbertyna, Ebgertyne

Egeria In Roman myth, a wise nymph who helped one of

the early kings of Rome draft legislation. In more literate times, wise women who advised statesmen were sometimes referred to as "Egeria."

Aegeria, Ejeria, Igeria

Egidia Latinized feminine form of **Giles** (Gk. "Kid, young goat"). Mostly Scottish use.

Aegidia, Egidiana

Egelina OG. from Lat. "Eagle." In the variations on this name you can trace the evolution of the word, from the Latin *aquilina* to the English "eagle."

Agilina, Eaglin, Egilina

Eglantine OF. Poetic-sounding botanical name for the shrub also known as "sweetbrier."

Eglantyne

Eibhlin Ir. Gael. "Shining, brilliant." Form of Evelyn, the English phonetic version, or Helen. More commonly anglicized as Eileen or Aileen.

Aibhlin

Eila Dim. **Ilana** (Heb. "Tree, oak tree") or **Eileen** (Ir. "Shining, bright"). Names as short as this are sometimes impossible to trace accurately, because very similar word particles may have different meanings in different languages.

Eilah, Eilona, Ela, Elah, Ila

Eileen Ir. "Shining, brilliant." Form of Helen. Irish names were fashionable in England around 1870, when the issue of Irish Home Rule was being hotly debated in Great Britain. By the 1920s (when the Irish Free State was finally formed) Eileen was one of the most popular girls' names in Britain. It has never been quite as fashionable in the U.S. Fashion designer Eileen Fisher; actress Eileen Brennan.

Aileen, Ailene, Alene, Aline, Ayleen, Eila, Eilah, Eilean, Eilleen, Eiley, Eily, Ileana, Ileanna, Ileene, Ilene, Iliana, Ilianna, Leana, Lena, Lianna, Lina

Eilish Ir. Gael. Var. of **Elizabeth** (Heb. "Pledged to God").

Eilis, Elis, Elish

Eiluned Welsh. "Idol." Var. **Lynette**.

Eluned

Eir ONorse. "Peacefulness/mercy."

Eira Welsh. "Snow." Mostly 20th-century use; a pretty name for a winter baby.

Eirian Welsh. "Silver." Another modern Welsh name.

Eithne Ir. "Fire." See **Aithne,** feminine version of **Aidan.**
Aine, Aithnea, Eithne, Ena, Ethnah, Ethnea, Ethnee

Ekaterina Slavic Var. of **Catherine** (Gk. "Pure"). Olympic figure skater Ekaterina Gordeeva.
Yekaterina

Elaine OF. "Bright, shining, light." Form of **Helen.** In the King Arthur myths, Elaine is a maiden who desperately loves Lancelot. Tennyson's version of the tale has her dying of this love, but in an earlier telling, she actually has a son—Galahad—by Lancelot. Tennyson's poetry may have contributed to the 19th-century revival of the name. It is now strongly associated with the character on *Seinfeld.* Film director Elaine May.
Alaina, Alayna, Alayne, Allaine, Elaina, Elana, Elane, Elanna, Elaene, Elayne, Ellaina, Ellaine, Ellane, Ellayne, Lainey, Layney

Elata Lat. "Lofty, elevated."

Elba Dim. **Elberta.** Also a place name: the island off the coast of Italy to which Napoleon was first exiled, and from which he escaped. The Elbe, similar in sound, is an important river in Germany and the Czech Republic.
Elbe, Ellba

Elberta (Fem. **Elbert**) OE. "Highborn/shining." Var. **Alberta.**
Elbertha, Elberthe

Eldora Sp. "Covered with gold." The Indian legend about the land of the Golden Man (*El Dorado*) kept explorers and conquistadores like Coronado and Pizarro combing the South American jungles and mountains through the 16th century.
Eldorada, Eldoree, Eldoria, Eldoris

Eleanor Possibly a form of Helen (Gk. "Light"), or from a different Greek root meaning "Clemency, mercy." The queen of Henry II of England, Eleanor of Aquitaine, introduced the name to England in the 13th century, and it has been used steadily since, especially in the U.S. under the influence of much-loved First Lady Eleanor Roosevelt. Charles II's mistress Nell Gwynn; Italian actress Eleonora Duse; women's rights activist Eleanor Smeal.
Aleanor, Alenor, Aleonore, Aline, Allinor, Eileen, Elaine,

Eleanora, Eleanore, Elen, Elena, Elenor, Elenora, Ele-nore, Eleonora, Eleonore, Elianora, Elianore, Elienora, Elienore, Elinor, Elinore, Ella, Elladine, Elleanor, Elleanora, Elle, Ellen, Ellene, Ellenora, Ellenore, Elleonor, Elli, Ellie, Ellin, Ellinor, Ellinore, Elly, Ellyn, Elna, Elnora, Elyn, Enora, Heleanor, Heleonor, Helen, Helena, Hélène, Helenora, Leanora, Lena, Lenora, Lenore, Leonora, Léonore, Leora, Lina, Nelda, Nell, Nelle, Nelley, Nelli, Nellie, Nelly, Nonnie, Nora, Norah, Norina

Electra Gk. "Shining, bright." Though the name is derived from the same roots as the word "electricity," many people will associate it with the Greek tragedies of the house of Atreus, told by Aeschylus, Euripides, and Sophocles and retold by Eugene O'Neill in the play *Mourning Becomes Electra*. All versions involve incest, murder, and vengeance, themes not usually associated with babies.

Alectra, Elektra, Elettra, Ellectra, Ellektra, Ilectra

Elena Sp. Var. **Helen** (Gk. "Light").

Elaina

Eleuthera Gk. "Freedom, liberty." Also a place name: an island in the Bahamas.

Eleftheria, Elefteria, Elesteria, Eleutheria, Eleutherya

Elfrida OE. "Elf power." See **Alfreda**. Uncommon.

Alfrida, Alfrieda, Elfie, Elfre, Elfredah, Elfredda, El-freeda, Elfrida, Elfrieda, Elfryda, Elfrydah, Ellfreda, Elva, Elvah, Freda, Freddi, Freddy, Freeda, Frieda, Friedah, Fryda

Elga Slavic. "Sacred." See **Olga**.

Elgiva, Ellga, Helga

Eliane (Fem. **Elias**) Fr. from Heb. "Jehovah is God."

Elia, Eliana, Elianna, Eliette, Elice, Eline, Elyette

Elidi Gk. "Gift of the sun."

Elinda Var. **Belinda**.

Eliora Heb. "The Lord is my light."

Eleora, Eliorah, Elleora, Elliora

Elise Fr. Var. **Elizabeth** (Heb. "Pledged to God").

Eliese, Elisa, Elisee, Elize, Elyce, Elyse, Liese, Liesel, Lie-selotte, Liesl, Lise, Lison, Lize

Elisheva Heb. "The Lord is my pledge."

Eliseva, Elisheba

Elissa Form of **Alice** or **Elizabeth**. First appeared around the 1930s, and is now fairly common in all its various spellings, though by far the most popular is Alyssa.

Alissa, Allissa, Allyssa, Alyssa, Elissia, Ellissa, Elysa, Elyssa, Elyssia, Ilissa, Ilysa, Ilyssa, Lissa, Lissie, Lissy, Lyssa

Elita Lat. "The elect, chosen."

Elitta, Ellita, Lita

Eliza Dim. **Elizabeth**. Frequently used in its own right from the 18th century onward, and probably most famous as the name of the escaping slave in *Uncle Tom's Cabin* and Cockney flower girl Eliza Dolittle in *My Fair Lady*. Especially popular in the first decade of this century. The recent fondness for nostalgic-sounding names has brought it to some prominence.

Aliza, Alizah, Elizah, Elyza, Elyzza, Liza

Elixyvett Modern name. This combination of elements from **Alexandra** (Gk. "Man's defender") and **Yvette** (OG. "Yew wood") ends up sounding remarkably like Elizabeth. Few portmanteau names end up being as compact and elegant. The variations below are just a few of the ways parents could elect to spell this name.

Alixevette, Alixyvetha, Elixevetta, Elixyvetha, Elixyvette

Elizabeth Heb. "Pledged to God." One of the thirty most popular girls' names in the U.S.; in the top five in Australia, Canada, and Great Britain. Used in full, it has a pleasant, old-fashioned ring, though some research attaches a "seductive" connotation to it (perhaps by association with actress Elizabeth Taylor). It is a source of endless diminutives and nicknames, which keeps it a perennial favorite. Saint Elizabeth, mother of John the Baptist; poet Elizabeth Barrett Browning; Queens Elizabeth I and II of England; actresses Elizabeth Ashley, Elizabeth Montgomery; politician Elizabeth Dole; suffragist Elizabeth Cady Stanton; model/actress Elizabeth Hurley.

Alixyveth, Babette, Belita, Bell, Bella, Belle, Bess, Bessie, Bessy, Beth, Betsey, Betsie, Betsy, Bett, Betta, Bette, Betti, Bettina, Bettine, Betty, Bettye, Buffy, Elisa, Elisabet, Elisabeth, Elisabetta, Elise, Elissa, Eliza, Elizabet, Elizabetta, Elizabette, Elixyveth, Elle, Elliza, Ellsa, Ellse, Ellsee, Ellsey, Ellsi, Ellspet, Ellyse, Ellyssa, Ellyza, Elsa, Else, Elsee, Elsie, Elspet, Elspeth, Elsy, Elyse, Elyssa,

Elyza, Elyzza, Elzbieta, Helsa, Ilsa, Ilse, Isabel, Isabella, Isabelle, Isobel, Leesa, Leeza, Lib, Libbey, Libbi, Libbie, Libby, Libbye, Lilibet, Lisa, Lisabeth, Lisbet, Lisbeth, Lisbett, Lisbetta, Lisbette, Lise, Lisette, Lissa, Lissi, Lissy, Liz, Liza, Lizabeth, Lizbeth, Lizette, Lizzi, Lizzy, Lusa, Lysa, Lysbet, Lysbeth, Lysbette, Lyssa, Lyssie, Lyza, Lyzbet, Lyzbeth, Lyzbette, Lyzette, Ylisabet, Ylisabette, Ysabel, Ysabella, Yzabelle

Elkana Heb. "God has made." More commonly used by men, and a man's name in the Old Testament.
Elkanah, Elkanna

Elke Ger. Var. **Alice** (OG. "Noble, nobility"). Possibly introduced to the English-speaking world by actress Elke Sommer.
Elka, Ellke, Ilka

Ella OG. "All, completely." Also possibly derived from **Alice, Eleanor, Ellen**. Common in the Middle Ages and revived in America in the late 19th century, but now unusual. Singer Ella Fitzgerald.
Alla, Ela, Elladine, Elletta, Ellette, Elley, Elli, Ellie, Ellina, Elly

Ellamae Comb. form **Ella** and **May**, two very popular 19th-century names.
Ellamay

Ellen Var. **Helen** (Gk. "shining, brightness"). Both forms have been popular, but rarely at the same time. In America Ellen has dominated since the 1950s, but neither version is much used now. English actress Ellen Terry; American actresses Ellyn Burstyn, Ellen Barkin, Ellen DeGeneres.
Elan, Elen, Elena, Elene, Eleni, Elenita, Elenyi, Elin, Ellan, Ellin, Ellene, Ellie, Ellon, Elly, Ellyn, Elon, Elyn

Ellice (Fem. **Elias**) Gk. "The Lord is God." Also possibly variant of **Alice** or **Ellis**.
Elice

Elma Dim. of names like **Wilhelmina** (OG. "Will-helmet") or variant of **Alma** (Lat. "Soul").
Ellma

Elmina Dim. **Wilhelmina** (OG. "Will-helmet"). Mildly popular in the 19th century.
Almeena, Almena, Almina, Elmeena, Elmena

Elmira Arab. "Aristocratic lady." See **Almera**. Also possibly a feminization of **Elmer** (OE. "Highborn and renowned").

Allmera, Allmeera, Almeria, Almira, Almyra, Ellmera, Ellmeria, Ellmeera, Elmeeria, Elmera, Elmeria, Elmerya, Elmyrah, Mera, Meera, Mira, Mirah, Myra, Myrah

Elodie Fr. from Gk. "Marsh flower."

Elodea, Elodia, Helodea, Helodia, Helodie

Eloise Fr. form of **Louise** (OG. "Renowned in battle"). Made famous in the 12th century by the love letters between Heloise and Abelard, but modern parents are more likely to think of the madcap six-year-old denizen of the New York Plaza Hotel made famous by Kay Thompson's book for children.

Aloysia, Eloisa, Elouisa, Elouise, Heloise

Elpida Gk. "Hope."

Elrica OG. "Ruler over all."

Elsa Dim. **Elizabeth**. Now rare, in spite of the lingering fame of actress Elsa Lanchester. Baby boomers may remember Joy Adamson's famous lion Elsa in the book and movie called *Born Free.*

Else, Elsie, Elssa, Elsy, Ilsa, Ilse

Elsie Var. **Elizabeth** via its Scottish form, **Elspeth**. Independently used since the 18th century, and extremely popular in the U.S. by the late 19th. After the 1920s, its use faded.

Ellsey, Ellsi, Ellsie, Elsea, Elsee, Élsey, Elsi

Elspeth Scot. var. **Elizabeth**. Unusual outside Scotland. Author Elspeth Huxley.

Elsbeth, Elsbet, Elspet, Elspie

Eluned Welsh. "Idol, image." Used mostly in Wales. The French version, Lynette, is more common in the U.S.

Elined, Eiluned, Lanet, Lanette, Linet, Linette, Luned, Lynette, Lynnette

Elva Ir. Meaning unclear. Phonetic anglicization of the unusual Irish name Ailbhe.

Ailbhe, Elfie, Elvia, Elvie

Elvina (Fem. **Elvin**) OE. "Noble friend" or "Elf friend."

Alveena, Alvina, Alvine, Alvinia, Elvena, Elveena, Elvene, Elvenia, Elvine, Elvinia, Vina, Vinni, Vinnie, Vinny

Elvira Sp. Meaning unclear, possibly a place name. An Elvira figures in several versions of the story of Don Juan, as well as in other operas. The name seems to be used more in art than in life, however.

Ellvira, Elva, Elveera, Elvera, Elvina, Elvire, Elvyra, Elwira, Lira

Elysia Lat. From "Elysium," the mythical home of the blessed, also known as the "Elysian fields." Dates from the 1940s. Such modern borrowings from the classical world are unusual, but this name is sufficiently like the familiar Elise not to sound peculiar. It also sounds exactly like one pronunciation of the more common "Alicia."

Aleesyia, Eleese, Eliese, Elise, Elisia, Elyse, Ileesia, Ilise, Ilysa, Ilysia, Ilyse

Emeline OG. Possibly "Industrious." Possibly also a variant of Emily or Amelia. Norman name revived in the 18th century, now extremely rare despite its numerous variants.

Emaleen, Emalene, Emaline, Emalyn, Embline, Emblyn, Emelen, Emelyn, Emiline, Emlyn, Emmalee, Emmalene, Emmaline, Emmalyn, Emmalynne, Emmeline, Emmiline, Emylin, Emylynn

Emerald Jewel name, less common than Pearl or Ruby, and most frequently used in its Spanish form, Esmeralda. It is the birthstone for May. English socialite Emerald Cunard.

Emeralda, Emeraldina, Emeraude, Esmeralda

Emily Lat. Clan name. In spite of the similarity of form, it has a different root from Amelia. Naturally, many of the variants are very close. A hugely popular name in the 19th century, which lost status after 1900 and is now in favor again. Emily was on the top-ten list of several states, including Texas and Florida, in the mid-1990s. Poet Emily Dickinson; novelist Emily Brontë; etiquette maven Emily Post.

Aemiley, Aemilie, Aimil, Amalea, Amalia, Amalie, Amelia, Amelie, Ameline, Amelita, Amy, Eimile, Em, Emalee, Emalia, Emelda, Emelea, Emeli, Emelia, Emelie, Emelina, Emeline, Emelita, Emelly, Emely, Emelyn, Emelyne, Emera, Emila, Emilea, Emilee, Emiley, Emili, Emilia, Emilie, Emiline, Emilla, Emillea, Emilley, Emillie, Emilly, Emlyn, Emlynn, Emlynne, Emmalee, Emmalie, Emmaline, Emmalyn, Emmalynn, Emmalynne, Emmelee, Emmely, Emmey, Emmi, Emmie, Emmilee, Emmilie, Emmily, Emmlee, Emmy, Emmye, Emyle, Emylee, Milka

Emina Lat. "Eminent."

Emma OG. "Embracing everything." Royal name in medieval England, and hugely popular at the end of the 19th
century. Brought back to notice by Emma Peel in the popular TV series and film *The Avengers*, and now one of the
top girls' names in England. Still less common in America,
but gaining favor among literate parents, who have a host
of historical and artistic Emmas to name their daughters after. Lady Emma Hamilton, Lord Nelson's mistress; Emma
Bovary of *Madame Bovary*; Jane Austen's novel *Emma*;
actresses Emma Samms, Emma Thompson.

**Em, Ema, Emelina, Emeline, Emelyne, Emmaline, Emma-
lyn, Emmalynn, Emmalynne, Emme, Emmeleia, Emmeline, Emmelyn, Emmelyne, Emmet, Emmett, Emmette,
Emmi, Emmie, Emmot, Emmott, Emmy, Emmye**

Emmanuelle (Fem. **Emmanuel**) Heb. "God is among us."
Fashion designer Emmanuelle Khanh.

**Emanuela, Emanuella, Emanuelle, Emmanuella, Emon-
ualle, Emonualle**

Empress The title used as name. An empress, of course,
ranks even higher than a queen. Queen Victoria took the
title Empress of India in 1877.

Emperatriz, Imperatrice, Imperatrix

Ena Short for names like Georgina, Regina, etc. Queen Victoria's granddaughter Princess Victoria Eugenie, who became queen of Spain, was known as Princess Ena.

Eena, Ina

Engracia Sp. from Lat. "Endowed with God's grace."

Enid Welsh. "Life, spirit." Name from the King Arthur
myths revived mildly in the early 19th century and quite
popular in England by the 1920s. Never much used in
America. Author Enid Bagnold.

Eanid, Ened, Enedd, Enidd, Enyd, Enydd

Enjoli Invented name for a perfume. "*Joli*" is French for
"pretty," though to describe a girl it would have to be
spelled "*jolie*."

Enjolie

Ennis Irish place name: the principal town of County Clare.
Also a variant of **Angus** (Scot. Gael. "Sole or only
choice").

Ennish, Innis

Enrica (Fem. Henry) It. "Home ruler."
Enricka, Enricketta, Enriqueta, Enriquette

Enya Var. Eithne, Ir. Gael. "Fire." Other sources suggest "kernel" as a meaning. Enya is the name of an Irish pop singer.
Aenya, Ennya

Erga Heb. "Yearning, craving."

Erica (Fem. Eric) Scan. "Ruler forever." Though a staple in Scandinavia, it wasn't used in the English-speaking world until the late 19th century. It still has a strongly European flair. Writer Erica Jong; singer Rickie Lee Jones; actress Ricki Lake.
Aerica, Aericka, Airica, Airicka, Airika, Enrica, Enrika, Eraca, Ericka, Erika, Erricka, Errika, Eryca, Erycka, Eyrica, Rickee, Ricki, Rickie, Ricky, Rikki, Rikky

Erin Ir. Gael. "From the island to the west." Erin is a literary name for "Ireland," hence the name's popularity among Irish-descended families. Ironically, it is not used in Ireland. Cosmetics executive Aerin Lauder.
Aeran, Aerenne, Aerin, Airin, Eire, Eirin, Eirinn, Eiryn, Eirynn, Erina, Erinn, Eryn, Erynn

Eris In Greek myth, the sister of Ares (god of war) and the goddess of destruction.
Aeress, Eriss, Erys, Eryss

Erlinda Heb. "Spirited."

Erma Var. Irma. OG. "Universal, complete." Enjoyed a brief period of use from around 1890 to 1940; now almost unknown. Humorist Erma Bombeck.
Ermina, Erminia, Erminie, Irma, Irminia, Irminie, Hermia, Hermine, Herminie, Hermione

Ermine OF. "Weasel." Has come to be synonymous with the trappings of royalty, since the robes of royalty are typically trimmed with the fur and tails of ermine, a variety of weasel that turns white in winter.
Ermin, Ermina, Erminia, Erminne

Erna Var. Ernestine. Also possibly derived from an Irish root meaning "to know." Modern use.
Ernaline, Ernalynn

Ernestine (Fem. Ernest) OE. "Sincere." Use at the end of the 19th century follows Ernest's enormous popularity for boys at that period. A bit dated now, and possibly rendered silly by Lily Tomlin's inspired sketches featuring the obstructive telephone operator Ernestine.

Erna, Ernaline, Ernesta, Ernestina, Ernestyna

Eroica The name of Beethoven's Third Symphony, the "heroic" symphony, which the composer originally intended as a tribute to Napoleon.

Eroiqua, Eroïque, Heroica

Ersilia Sp. from Gk. "Delicate." Roman myth name: the wife of Romulus, Rome's founder, originally one of the famous Sabine women carried off to provide wives for the new citizens of Rome.

Ercilia, Ersila, Erzilia, Hersila, Hersilia

Erwina (Fem. **Erwin**) OE. "Boar/friend."

Irwina

Esma Var. **Esmé**. Possibly short form of Esmeralda.

Esmée Fr. "Esteemed." Originally a male name brought to Scotland by a French cousin of James VI. Now used more for girls, though scarce. J. D. Salinger titled a short story "For Esmé with Love and Squalor."

Esmae, Esmay, Esmé, Ismé

Esmeralda Sp. "Emerald." Jewel name first used in the 1880s, and more common than Emerald. Now, of course, subject to the fame brought by inclusion in a Disney cartoon extravaganza, *The Hunchback of Notre Dame*. Unlike some of the characters in the film, Esmeralda does actually appear in Victor Hugo's original novel.

Em, Emmie, Emerald, Emerant, Emeraude, Esma, Esmaralda, Esmarelda, Esmaria, Esmie, Esmiralda, Esmiralde, Esmirelda, Ezmeralda

Esperanza Sp. "Hope." One of the three cardinal virtues, along with Faith and Charity.

Esperance, Esperantia

Esta Var. **Esther**.

Estelle OF. "Star." See **Astra, Esther, Stella**. French form of a name apparently coined by Charles Dickens for a character in his 1861 novel *Great Expectations*. Her name is Estella, and perhaps because she's such an unhappy creature, Estelle is the more common form of the name. Actresses Estelle Getty, Estelle Parsons.

Essie, Estel, Estele, Estell, Estella, Estrella, Estrellita, Stella, Stelle

Esther Per. "Star." More particularly, the planet Venus. Esther in the Bible was an orphan named Hadassah who became wife of King Ahasuerus under her new name. Her story is told in the Old Testament Book of Esther. In the U.S. the name reached its peak of popularity around 1900, and is now unusual. Swimming actress Esther Williams; actress Esther Rolle; cosmetics pioneer Estée Lauder.

Essie, Essy, Esta, Estée, Ester, Ettey, Etti, Ettie, Etty, Hester, Hesther, Hettie, Hetty, Hittie

Etana (Fem. **Ethan**) Heb. "Strength of purpose."

Ethel OE. "Noble." A short form of various old-fashioned names like Etheldreda. First appeared on its own in the 1840s, and by the 1870s was very popular. This is one 19th-century name, however, that is unlikely to be revived in the 1990s, least of all by parents to whom "Ethel" will always be Lucy's sidekick from the TV series *I Love Lucy*. Actresses Ethel Barrymore, Ethel Merman.

Ethelda, Ethelin, Ethelinda, Etheline, Ethelyn, Ethelynne, Ethill, Ethille, Ethlin, Ethlyn, Ethlynn, Ethyll

Etheldreda OE. "Noble power." Saint's name from the 7th century, occasionally used in Britain. Audrey is the more common modern form.

Ethelinda OG. "Noble serpent." Not a composite, but an old name revived in the 19th century, along with many variants.

Athelina, Ethelenda, Ethelene, Ethelind, Ethelinde, Etheline, Ethlin, Ethlinda, Etholinda, Ethylind

Etta Feminine diminutive suffix (Georgette, Henriette) that has attained the status of an independent name.

Ettie, Etty

Eudocia Gk. "Well thought of."

Docia, Docie, Doxie, Doxy, Eudokia, Eudosia, Eudoxia

Eudora Gk. "Generous gift." Unusual name from Greek mythology (Eudora was a minor goddess) that was somewhat popular at the turn of the 20th century. Writer Eudora Welty.

Dora, Dorey, Dorie, Eudore

Eugenia (Fem. **Eugene**) Gk. "Wellborn." The French form, Eugenie, was made famous by Napoleon III's beautiful empress, and has persisted in the European royal houses. Used in Britain for the second daughter of the Duke and Duchess of York. Actresses Gena Rowlands, Geena Davis.

Eugénie, Evgenia, Geena, Gena, Gene, Genia, Genie, Gina, Janie, Jeena, Jenna, Jennie

Eulalia Gk. "Sweet-speaking."

Eula, Eulalee, Eulalie, Eulaylia, Eulaylie, Lallie, Lally

Eunice Gk. "Victorious." Biblical name: In the New Testament, Eunice is the mother of Timothy. Occasionally used in the modern era. Philanthropist Eunice Kennedy Shriver.

Eunices, Eunike, Euniss, Eunisse, Unice, Uniss

Euphemia Gk. "Favorable speech." Early Christian name borne by a 4th-century virgin martyr, but more common in its short forms, like Effie, through the 19th century. Rare since the 1930s. The word "euphemism" comes from the same roots.

Effam, Effie, Effy, Ephan, Ephie, Eufemia, Euphémie, Euphenia, Euphie, Phemie, Fanny, Mia

Eurydice Gk. In mythology, the wife of the musician Orpheus. She was poisoned by a snake, and Orpheus went to the underworld to find her. His music so charmed Hades that he was allowed to bring her back to life, if he could lead her to the upper world without looking at her. He failed, and she returned to Hades. Not surprisingly, the tale is the subject of numerous musical works.

Euridice, Euridiss

Eustacia (Fem. **Eustace**) Lat. "Giving fruit." The male form was used a bit in the 19th century, but the feminine form is rare.

Eustacie, Stacey, Stacia, Stacie, Stacy

Eva Form of **Eve** (Heb. "Life"). More common in Europe. Actress Eva Gabor; dictator Eva Peron.

Eeva, Evita

Evadne Gk. Meaning unclear, but may mean something like "Enjoying good fortune" or "Pleasing one."

Evadney, Evadnie, Evanne

Evangeline Gk. "Good news." Derived from "evangel," the term that came to be used for the Gospels, or the four

Old Testament accounts of Christ's life. First used in English by Alfred Tennyson in his 1847 poem "Evangeline."

Engie, Eva, Evangelia, Evangelina, Evangelista, Evangeliste, Eve, Vangie, Vangy

Evania Gk. "Peaceful."

Evanne, Evannie, Evanny

Evanthe Gk. "Good flower."

Evanthey, Evanthie

Eve Heb. "Life." In the form Eva, somewhat popular from the mid–19th century, usually as a shortened version of Evangeline. Eve, the French form of the name, is used steadily, but not in great numbers. A clever name for the first girl in a family of boys. Actress Eve Arden.

Aoiffe, Eba, Ebba, Eva, Evaleen, Evelina, Eveline, Evelyn, Evetta, Evette, Evey, Evie, Evita, Evlyn, Evonne, Evvie, Evvy, Evy

Evelina OG. or OF., possibly "Hazelnut." Norman import to Britain, where it was brought to prominence by Fanny Burney's popular novel *Evelina* in the 18th century. Gradually overwhelmed by Evelyn.

Eveleen, Evelene, Eveline, Evelyne

Evelyn OG. Obscure meaning, from the same root as Evelina. Not, as it would seem, a combination of Eve and Lynn, but originally a surname and later a boy's name. Its greatest popularity came in the first quarter of the 20th century in both Britain and the U.S. Track star Evelyn Ashford.

Aveline, Evaleen, Evalyn, Evalynn, Evalynne, Eveleen, Evelene, Eveline, Evelyne, Evelynn, Evelynne, Evilyn, Evlin, Evline, Evlyn, Evlynn

Evette Fr. Variant form of **Yvette**, in turn a diminutive of **Yvonne**. Also used as a diminutive for **Eve**, though the roots are different.

Eevette, Evetta, Eyvetta, Eyvette

Evonne Fr. Var. **Yvonne**. Tennis star Evonne Goolagong.

Evon, Eyvonne

Fabia (Fem. **Fabian**) Lat. clan name. Possibly meaning "One who grows beans." Today's Queen Fabiola of Belgium was a Spanish princess.
Fabiana, Fabiane, Fabianna, Fabienne, Fabiola

Fabrizia It. "Works with the hands."
Fabrice, Fabricia, Fabrienne, Fabriqua, Fabritzia

Faida Arab. "Plentiful."
Fayda

Faith Middle English. "Loyalty." One of the most common of the virtue names used by the Puritans, along with Hope and Charity. Modern use is sparing. Actress Faith Prince.
Fae, Faithe, Fay, Faye, Fayth, Faythe, Fé

Faline Lat. "Like a cat." Unusual spelling of a familiar term. Second-time parents may recognize this as the name of Bambi's girlfriend in the Disney cartoon.
Faeleen, Fayline, Felina, Feyline

Fallon Ir. Gael. "Descended from a ruler." Surname brought to public notice and some popularity by a character on the TV serial *Dynasty*.
Fallan, Fallen

Fanny (Dim. **Frances**) Lat. "From France." This form became extremely popular in the early 19th century and remained a favorite until around 1910, when its inexplicable adoption as a term for the buttocks extinguished it as a first name. Cookbook author Fannie Farmer; author Fannie Flagg; actress Fanny Ardant.
Fan, Fania, Fannee, Fanney, Fannie

Farica (Dim. **Frederica**) OG. "Peaceful ruler."
Faricka, Fericka, Flicka

Farina Lat. "Flour." Farina is still sometimes available on supermarket shelves.
Fareena

Farrah ME. "Lovely, pleasant." Unknown as a first name until the enormous fame of actress Farrah Fawcett. In the aftermath of her stardom, has a rather dated air.
Fara, Farah, Farra

Fatima Arab. Meaning unclear, though Fatima was Mohammed's favorite daughter. According to the Koran, she was one of only four perfect women in the world, and the name is consequently well used among Muslims. Fatima is also the name of Bluebeard's last wife in some versions of that tale.
Fateema, Fateemah, Fatimah, Fatma, Fatmah

Fauna Roman mythology name: the goddess of nature and animals.
Faune, Fauniel, Fauniella, Fawna

Faustine (Fem. **Faust**) Lat. "Fortunate, enjoying good luck." There is some irony to the name, since the Faust of legend sold his soul to the devil. Two Roman empresses were called Faustina, and the name was common under the Roman Empire, but is little used today.
Fausta, Fauste, Faustina

Fawn OF. "Young deer." Names for girl children have been drawn from various segments of the natural world—flowers, gems, seasons, months—but animal names, for some reason, are rarer. Biographer Fawn Brodie.
Faina, Fanya, Faun, Fauna, Faunia, Fawna, Fawne, Fawnia, Fawnya

Fay OF. "Fairy." Dim. **Faith**. First used in significant numbers in the 1920s, probably inspired by the fame of actresses Fay Wray and Fay Compton. Actress Faye Dunaway.
Fae, Fay, Faye, Fee, Fey

Fayette OF. "Little fairy."
Fayetta

Fedora Gr. Var. **Theodora** (Gk. "gift of God"). In this form, also a kind of soft felt hat with a modest brim, much favored by men until the early 1960s.
Fadora

Felda OG. "From the field."

Felicia (Fem. **Felix**) Lat. "Lucky, fortunate, happy." Felice was used in Britain until the early 19th century, when it was replaced by Felicia, which has since been supplanted by Felicity. None of them is very common. Actress Phylicia Rashad.

Falecia, Faleece, Falicia, Falisha, Falishia, Felice, Feliciana, Felicidad, Felicie, Felicienne, Félicité, Felicity, Felis, Felisa, Felise, Felisha, Feliss, Felita, Feliz, Feliza, Felysse, Filicia, Filisha, Phalicia, Phalisha, Phelicia, Phylicia, Phyllicia, Phyllisha

Fenella Ir. Gael. "White shoulder." Var. **Fionnula**. This is the anglicized form.
Finella, Fynella

Fenia In Scandinavian myth, a giantess enslaved by the Danish king Frodi, who reigned peacefully for thirty years.
Fenja, Fenya

Fern OE. "Fern." Also, diminutive of **Fernanda**. Unusual botanical name immortalized by E.B. White in *Charlotte's Web*.
Ferna, Ferne

Fernanda (Fem. **Ferdinand**) OG. Possibly "Peace/courage" or "Bold voyager." Very rare feminine of an equally rare male name.
Anda, Annda, Ferdinanda, Ferdinande, Fern, Fernande, Fernandina, Fernandine, Nan, Nanda

Fernley OE. Place name. "Fern meadow." In Britain, has been used as a first name since the turn of the century for both sexes. Little heard in the U.S.
Fernlea, Fernlee, Fernleigh, Fernlie, Fernly

Fiammetta It. "Little fiery one." The word *fiamma* means flame: it may refer to the flames of the Holy Spirit that descended on the apostles on the day Christians commemorate as Pentecost.
Fiamma

Fiby Sp. Var. **Phoebe** (Gk. "Shining, brilliant").

Fidelity Lat. "Loyalty." Latin form of Faith. In the U.S., use of the word for large financial institutions diminishes its appeal as a proper name. The Cuban track star Ana Fidelia Quirot was named in honor of Fidel Castro.
Fedila, Fideila, Fidela, Fidele, Fidelia, Fidelita, Fidella

Fidelma Old Irish name of obscure meaning. A princess named Feidhelm was one of Saint Patrick's first converts to Christianity.
Fedelma

Fifi Fr. Dim. **Josephine** (Heb. "Jehovah increases"). The stereotypical name for a French poodle, which would seem to limit its human use.

Fifine

Filia Gk. "Friendship." Currently popular in Greece.

Philia

Filippa Var. **Philippa** (Gk. "Lover of horses").

Filomena It. Var. **Philomena** (Gk. "Loved one").

Filis Sp. Var. **Phyllis** (Gk. "Leafy bough").

Fina Sp. Dim. **Josefina** (Heb. "Jehovah increases").

Fiona Ir. Gael. "Fair, pale." Apparently coined by an English author at the turn of the 20th century, and its popularity in Britain has been growing since the 1930s, especially in Scotland. Rare in the U.S.

Fee, Ffiona, Ffyona, Fione, Fionna, Fyona

Fionnula Ir. Gael. "White shoulder."

Fenella, Finella, Finola, Fionnuala, Fionnualagh, Nola, Nuala

Flaminia Lat. "Priest."

Flana Ir. Gael. "Russet hair." Flannery is probably the most common form of this very unusual name. Author Flannery O'Connor.

Flanagh, Flanna, Flannerey, Flannery

Flavia Lat. "Yellow hair." Originally a Latin clan name, and common enough in the Roman Empire, but never revived in an English-speaking country.

Flavie, Flaviere, Flavyere

Fleur Fr. "Flower." In John Galsworthy's *The Forsyte Saga*, one of the principal characters is called Fleur, which brought the name to some prominence. The BBC adaptation of the 1970s also provoked a spate of use.

Fleurette, Fleurine

Flora Lat. "Flower." The name of the Roman goddess of springtime, and of a 9th-century martyred saint. Flora Macdonald is a Scottish heroine who helped Bonnie Prince Charlie escape the English. The name was naturally popular in Scotland, and throughout England in the last half of the 19th century. Now little used, but a good option for parents searching out a quaint, pretty name.

Fiora, Fiordenni, Fiore, Fiorella, Fiori, Fleur, Flo, Flor, Floralia, Flore, Florella, Florelle, Florentia, Florentina,

Florenza, Florenzia, Floria, Florida, Florie, Florine, Floris, Florise, Florrie, Florry, Flory

Flordeperla Sp. "Flower of pearl."

Florence Lat. "In bloom." Used for both men and women until the 17th century, when it faded from sight. Modern use is almost entirely inspired by the fame of Florence Nightingale, who was actually named for the Italian city where she was born. (Her less fortunate sister was born in Naples, and given the Greek name of that city: Parthenope.) Like many names popular in the Victorian era, it fell out of fashion by the 1930s. Athlete Florence "Flo Jo" Griffith Joyner.

Fiorentina, Fiorenza, Flo, Floellen, Flor, Flora, Florance, Flore, Florenca, Florencia, Florencita, Florentia, Florentina, Florentyna, Florenza, Florenzia, Flori, Floria, Floriane, Floriana, Florie, Florina, Florincia, Florinda, Florine, Floris, Florrance, Florrie, Florry, Florynce, Floss, Flossey, Flossie, Flossy

Flower OF. "Blossom."

Florida Lat. "Flowery." Spanish variant of **Florence**. Spanish explorer Ponce de Leon dubbed the southern state "Florida" for the many flowers he found there. In frequent current use as a first name probably refers to the state.

Fortney Lat. "Strong." Similar enough to the hugely popular Courtney to warrant consideration.

Fortnea, Fortnee, Fortneigh, Fortnie, Fortny

Fortune Lat. "Good fate." Garden-variety name in the Roman Empire; Fortuna was the goddess of happiness. Revived somewhat by the Puritans but almost unknown today.

Fortuna, Fortunata

Forsythia Flower name: the brilliant yellow shrub that is one of the first signs of spring in a chilly climate. Named for William Forsythe, the 18th-century botanist who classified it.

Fran (Dim. **Frances**) Lat. "From France." Used as a given name on its own. Actress Fran Drescher.

Frani, Frannee, Franni, Frannie, Franny

Frances (Fem. **Francis**) Lat. "From France." Until the 17th century, Francis was used for both sexes. Spelled with an "e," it was a very popular choice in the first quarter of the 20th century, but has been little used since then. Writer Fran Lebowitz; actresses Fanny Brice, Frances McDormand.

Fan, Fancey, Fanchette, Fancie, Fancy, Fanechka, Fania, Fanney, Fannie, Fanny, Fanya, Fran, Francee, Franceline, Francene, Francesca, Francess, Francetta, Francette, Francey, Franchesca, Franci, Francie, Francine, Francisca, Franciska, Françoise, Francyne, Frania, Franie, Frank, Frankie, Franky, Franni, Frannie, Franny, Fransabelle, Fransabella, Franzetta, Franzi, Franziska, Fronia

Franisbel Elaboration of Fran, influenced by Isabel (Sp. from Heb. "Pledged to God").

Franisbella, Franisbelle

Frayda Yid. "Joy." The German word, *Freude*, is quite similar.

Frayde, Fraydel, Freyda, Freyde, Freydel

Freda OG. "Peaceful." Dim. **Alfreda, Frederica, Winifred.** Most popular at the end of the 19th century, when Fred was fashionable for men. Artist Frida Kahloo.

Freada, Freeda, Freida, Frida, Frieda, Frydda

Fredella Comb. form Freda and Ella.

Fredelle

Frederica OG. "Peaceful ruler." Following the popularity of Frederic, substantially used in the late 19th century, but now unusual. Opera singer Frederica von Stade.

Farica, Federica, Flicka, Fred, Fredalena, Freddee, Freddey, Freddi, Freddie, Freddy, Fredericha, Fredericka, Frederickina, Frederine, Frédérique, Fredi, Fredia, Fredie, Fredricia, Fredrika, Frerika, Friederike, Rica, Ricki, Rickie, Ricky, Rikki, Rikky

Freya Scan. "Highborn lady." In Norse myth, the goddess of love, corresponding perhaps to the Roman Venus. Friday is named for her.

Fraya

Friedelinde Ger. "Gentle peace." The word particle "Fried-" appears in so many German-based names that peace appears to have been a very lively concern in the era when these names were formed.

Friedalinda

Fritzi (Fem. **Fritz**) OG. "Peaceful ruler." German form of Frederick.

Fructuosa Lat. "Fruitful."

Fuensanta Sp. "Holy fountain."
    Fuenta

Fulgencia Lat. "Glowing, giving off light."

Fulvia Lat. "Blond one."

Fruma Yid. "Pious, deeply religious."

Fuchsia Plant name: the brilliant pink blossoms of this popular plant have even given their name to the color. The plant was named for the German botanist Leonhard Fuchs.
    Fusha

Gabrielle (Fem. **Gabriel**) Heb. "Heroine of God." Used in English-speaking countries for the last ninety years, though the Italian form, Gabriella, has been popular since the 1950s. Gabriel is an archangel who appears in Christian, Jewish, and Muslim texts. Tennis star Gabriela Sabatini; fashion designer Gabrielle "Coco" Chanel.
    Gabbe, Gabbi, Gabbie, Gabi, Gabriel, Gabriela, Gabriella, Gabriell, Gabriellen, Gabriellia, Gabrila, Gabryel, Gabryelle, Gabryella, Gaby, Gabysia, Gavi, Gavra, Gavraila, Gavrielle, Gavrila, Gavrilla, Gavrina

Gada Heb. "Fortunate."

Gaea Gk. "The earth."
    Gaia, Gaiea, Gala

Gaetana It. Place name. Gaeta is a region in southern Italy; the Gulf of Gaeta is just north of Naples.
    Gaetane

Gafna Heb. "Vine."

Gail Heb. "My father rejoices." A diminutive of **Abigail** with an unusually strong life of its own, dating from around 1940, with special popularity in the 1950s in the U.S. Authors Gael Greene, Gail Sheehy, Gail Godwin; track star Gail Devers.

Gael, Gahl, Gaila, Gaile, Gaill, Gal, Gale, Gayel, Gayelle, Gayla, Gayle, Gayleen, Gaylene, Gayline, Gayll, Gaylla, Gaylle

Gala OF. "Merrymaking, festivity." More associated with late-night parties than babies. Salvador Dali's wife was named Gala.

Galla

Galatea Gk. "White as milk." In Greek myth the sculptor Pygmalion fell in love with his ivory statue of Aphrodite, and prayed to the goddess to bring the statue to life. When his prayer was answered, he married his creation. The myth, via G. B. Shaw's play *Pygmalion*, is the source of the musical *My Fair Lady*.

Galatée, Galathea

Galiena OG. "High one."

Galiana, Galianna, Galliena, Galyena

Galila Heb. "Rolling hills." The root of this word is the source of the place name Galilee.

Galilah, Gelila, Gelilah, Gelilia, Gelilya, Glila, Glilah

Galina Rus. Var. **Helen** (Gk. "Shining brightly").

Galya

Gallia Lat. "Gaul." The Latin term for the country that would later be known as France; a name used from time to time for French babies.

Gala, Galla

Galya Heb. "The Lord has redeemed."

Galia, Gallia, Gallya

Gambhira Hindi. "Well born, of great dignity."

Gana Heb. "Garden."

Ganah, Ganit

Gardenia Flower name. The powerfully sweet-smelling flower is named for the 18th-century Scottish naturalist Alexander Garden, who first classified it.

Gardeenia

Garland OF. "Garland, wreath."

Garlande, Garlandina

Gardner Middle English. Occupational name: "Gardener." In the eastern U.S., reminiscent of two distinguished families, known as the "blind" Gardners (the name has no *i*) or the "sighted" Gardiners. The former are famous for the Isabella Stewart Gardner Museum in Boston, the latter

for Gardiner's Island on Long Island Sound. Where this occurs as a name for girls, it is usually a family name. Poet Gardner McFall.
Gardener, Gardie, Gardiner

Garnet ME. Jewel name, appropriate for January, since it is the birthstone for that month. Comes from the Old French for "pomegranate," which garnets very closely resemble.
Garnette, Granata, Grenata, Grenatta

Gauri Hindi. "Fair, pale." One of the names of a Hindu goddess; in this guise she is thought of as "Gauri the brilliant."
Gawri, Gori, Gowri

Gavrila Var. **Gabrielle** (Heb. "Heroine of God").
Gavrilla, Gavryla, Gavrylla

Gay OF. "Glad, lighthearted." A surname in the Middle Ages, used as a first name very heavily in the mid–20th century. The widespread informal use of the word to mean "homosexual" has limited its current use as a name.
Gae, Gai, Gaye

Gaynor Welsh "White and smooth, soft." Var. **Guinevere**. Used primarily in Britain.
Gaenor, Gayna, Gayner

Gazella Lat. "Gazelle." Unusual use of the animal name as a given name. Gazelles are traditionally thought of as very graceful creatures.
Gazelle

Geena Var. **Gina**. Made famous by movie star Geena Davis.

Geila Heb. "Joy."
Geela, Geelah, Geelan, Geila, Geiliya, Geiliyah, Gila, Gilah, Gilana

Gelsomina Italian plant name: the plant in question is a kind of jasmine.
Jelsomina

Gemini Gk. "Twin." Appropriate for either a child born under the sign of Gemini, or for one of a pair of twins.
Gemella, Gemelle, Gemina

Gemma It. "Precious stone." Did not, curiously, come into fashion with other jewel names in the late 19th century, but is slightly popular now. Probably helped along by the

1940 canonization of an Italian Saint Gemma, an ordinary young woman whose religious life included manifestations of the stigmata, or the marks of Christ's wounds. In the 1980s this was one of the top ten names in England.
Jemma, Jemsa

Gene Dim. **Eugenia** (Gk. "Wellborn") or Var. **Jean** (Heb. "The Lord is gracious"). More common for boys; actress Gene Tierney may have pioneered use of this spelling for girls.
Genie

Genesis The name of the first book of the Bible. In some favor among African-American parents.
Genesies, Genesiss, Gennesis, Gennesiss, Jenesis, Jenesyss, Jennasis

Geneva OF. "Juniper tree." There is considerable confusion about the sources of a constellation of names that include Geneva, Ginevra, and Genevieve. Use of Geneva may refer to the Swiss city; on the other hand, it may also be reference to the juniper tree, whose old Dutch name was *genever* (hence "gin," which is flavored with juniper berries). Various forms of Genevieve also overlap.
Gena, Genever, Genevia, Genevra, Genèvre, Genovefa, Genoveffa, Genoveva, Ginebra, Ginevra, Ginèvre, Janeva, Janevra, Jenovefa, Jineeva, Jineva, Joneva, Jonevah

Genevieve A name whose origin is unclear, but sources suggest possibly OG. "White wave" or Celt. "Race of women." Saint Genevieve, the patroness of Paris, was a 5th-century virgin who defended Paris against the depredations of Attila the Hun, among others. Use in English-speaking countries has tended to simmer along at a low level. Actress Geneviève Bujold.
Gena, Genavieve, Geneva, Geneveeve, Genivieve, Gennie, Genny, Genovera, Genoveva, Gina, Janeva, Jenevieve, Jennie, Jenny

Genista Plant name. The Latin name for broom (a shrub like heather) is *planta genista*.
Geneesta, Ginista, Jenista

Georgette Fr. from Lat. "Farmer." The French form of George, in mild use since the 1940s. A purposely wrinkled fabric called georgette was named after its French creator. Author Georgette Heyer; socialite Georgette Mosbacher.

Georgetta, Georjetta, Jorjetta, Jorjette

Georgia (Fem. **George**) Lat. "Farmer." The preferred feminine of George in the U.S. A long-ago farmer in Connecticut is reputed to have named each of his ten daughters for a state, and presumably Georgia was one of the eldest, along with Virginia and Carolina. Painter Georgia O'Keefe.

George, Georgeann, Georgeanne, Georgeina, Georgena, Georgene, Georgetta, Georgette, Georgiana, Georgianna, Georgianne, Georgie, Georgienne, Georgina, Georgine, Georgyann, Georgyanne, Georgyana, Giorgia, Giorgina, Giorgyna, Jorgina

Georgina (Fem. **George**) Lat. "Farmer." The form currently most common in England, replacing Georgiana, which has also been much used.

Georgeina, Georgena, Georgene, Georgejean, Georgiana, Georgianna, Georgianne, Georgienne, Georgine, Georgyana, Giorgina

Geraldine (Fem. **Gerald**) OG./Fr. "Spear ruler." Though the form was coined in the 16th century, its real popularity followed the fashion for Gerald, in the mid–19th century through the 1950s. Actresses Geraldine Chaplin, Geraldine Fitzgerald; politician Geraldine Ferraro.

Deena, Dina, Dyna, Geralda, Geraldeen, Geraldene, Geraldina, Geralyn, Geralynne, Gerdene, Gerdine, Geri, Gerianna, Gerianne, Gerilynn, Gerri, Gerrilyn, Gerroldine, Gerry, Giralda, Jeraldeen, Jeraldene, Jeraldine, Jeralee, Jere, Jeri, Jerilene, Jerrie, Jerrileen, Jerroldeen, Jerry

Geranium Flower name, though the name of the flower itself derives from the Greek for "crane."

Gerardine (Fem. **Gerard**) OE. "Spear brave."

Gerarda, Gerardina, Gerardyne, Gererdina, Gerrardene

Gerda ONorse. "Shelter."

Garda, Geerda

Germaine Fr. "From Germany." Use today may reflect admiration for the famous author and feminist Germaine Greer.

Germain, Germana, Germane, Germayn, Germayne, Jarmaine, Jermain, Jermaine, Jermane, Jermayn, Jermayne

Gertrude OG. "Strength of a spear." An old name (there was a 7th-century Saint Gertrude) revived to immense popularity with the late 19th–century fashion for the antique. Became so common that it suffered the corresponding fall from favor, and is now resoundingly out of style. Writer Gertrude Stein; actress Gertrude Lawrence.

Geertruide, Geltruda, Geltrudis, Gerda, Gert, Gerta, Gerte, Gerti, Gertie, Gertina, Gertraud, Gertrud, Gertruda, Gertrudis, Gerty, Traudl, Trude, Trudi, Trudie, Trudy

Gerusha Heb. "Sent away."

Geulah Heb. "Redemption."

Gevira Heb. "High-ranking lady."

Ghaliya Arab. "Sweet-smelling."

Ghislaine Fr. Unusual name of unclear origin and meaning.
Gillan, Gislaine

Ghita It. Dim. **Margherita** (Gk. "Pearl").
Geeta, Gita

Giacinta It. "Hyacinth."
Giacintha, Jacinta, Jacintha, Jacynth, Jiacintha, Yacinta, Yacintha

Gianina (Fem. **John**) It. from Heb. "God is gracious." The age-old favorite boy's name has spawned endless variants, both masculine and feminine.
Cinetta, Gianetta, Giannina, Giannine, Ginetta, Ginette, Ginnette, Janina, Janine, Jeannine, Jeeanina

Gigi Dim. **Georgina, Virginia**, etc. For a somewhat older generation of parents the name was given a glamorous gamine charm by Audrey Hepburn's performance in the 1951 Broadway production of *Gigi*, based on a short story by Colette. (In the 1958 musical film starring Maurice Chevalier, the ingenue role was taken by Leslie Caron.) Tennis star Gigi Fernandez.
GeeGee, G.G.

Gila Heb. "Joy." See **Geila**.
Gilah, Gilana

Gilia Heb. "Joy of the Lord."
Giliah, Giliya, Giliyah

Gilberte (Fem. **Gilbert**) OG. "Shining pledge." French variant of a Norman name that was fairly popular in the north of Britain.

Berta, Bertie, Berty, Gigi, Gilberta, Gilbertha, Gilberthe, Gilbertina, Gilbertine, Gill, Gillie, Gilly

Gilda OE. "Gilded." More scholarly sources trace Gilda to Ermengilda, a now obsolete Anglo-Saxon name, while others propose "God's servant." Actress Gilda Radner.

Gillian Lat. "Youthful." Anglicization of **Juliana**. A standard name in the Middle Ages in England, and revived for about forty years in this century, but fading since the sixties. Never widespread in the U.S., though its diminutive, Jill, had quite a fashionable spell.

Ghilian, Ghiliane, Ghillian, Gilian, Giliana, Gill, Gillan, Gillianna, Gillianne, Gillie, Gillyanne, Jillian, Jillianne, Jillyan, Jyllian

Gina Dim. **Regina, Angelina,** etc. Also could be considered a feminization of **Gene,** or a variant of **Jean**. Independent use dates from the 1920s, concentrated in the 1950s. Actresses Gina Lollobrigida, Geena Davis, Gena Rowlands.

Geena, Geina, Gena, Ginette, Ginna, Jena, Jeena, Jenna

Ginger Lat. "Ginger." Also can be a diminutive of **Virginia** (Lat. "Virgin"). Not to be confused with the usual botanical names, for it depends almost completely on the fame of actress Ginger Rogers, whose given name was Virginia.

Gingee, Gingie, Jinger

Ginny Dim. **Virginia** (Lat. "Virgin").

Ginnee, Ginnie, Jinnee, Jinnie, Jinny

Gioia It. "Joy." Unusual form in this country.

Gioya, Joya

Gioconda It. "Delight." The painting most Americans know as the *Mona Lisa* is also referred to as *"La Gioconda."*

Geoconda, Jeoconda

Giovanna (Fem. **John**) It. from Heb. "God is gracious."

Giovana, Jovana, Jovanna, Jovanne

Giselle OG. "Pledge/hostage." Use may reflect a fondness for the famous 19th-century ballet whose tragic heroine is a peasant girl betrayed by a noble suitor.

Ghisele, Ghisella, Gisela, Gisèle, Gisella, Giza, Gizela, Gizella

Gita Sanskrit. "Song."

Geeta, Gitika

Gitana Sp. "Gypsy."
   Gitane, Gitanna, Jeetanna
Gitta Dim. **Brigitte** (Ir. Gael. "Strength, power").
   Gitte
Giulia (Fem. **Giulio**) It. from Lat. "Youthful."
   Giula, Giuliana, Giulietta, Giullia, Jiulia, Jiuliana, Jiuliya, Jiyulia, Julia, Juliana, Julie, Juliet, Julietta, Juliette, Jullia, Julliana, Julliane
Giuseppina (Fem. **Giuseppe**) It. from Heb. "The Lord adds."
   Giuseppa, Josefina
Giustinia (Fem. **Justin**) It. from Lat. "Just, fair."
   Giustina, Justina, Justine, Justiniana
Glade OE. Place name: "clearing in the woods."
Gladys Welsh. Var. **Claudia** (Lat. "Lame'). Suddenly glamorous in the late 19th century, and used in several Edwardian romantic novels, which further heightened its appeal. The chic way to pronounce it was with a long "a." By the 1930s, beginning to be dated, and now rare. Singer Gladys Knight.
   Glad, Gladdis, Gladdys, Gladi, Gladyss, Gwladys, Gwyladyss
Glenda Welsh. "Fair and good." Mildly popular from the 1930s to the 1960s. Actress Glenda Jackson.
   Glennda
Glenna (Fem. **Glenn**) Ir. Gael. "Glen." A glen is a narrow valley between hills. Actresses Glenn Close, Glenne Headley.
   Gleana, Glenda, Gleneen, Glenene, Glenine, Glen, Glenn, Glenne, Glennene, Glennette, Glennie
Glenys Welsh. "Holy." Etymologically unrelated to the similar-sounding Glynis.
   Glenice, Glenis, Glennice, Glennis, Glennys
Gloria Lat. "Glory." Apparently coined by playwright George Bernard Shaw, in 1898's *You Never Can Tell*; the form Gloriana had earlier been used to refer in flattering fashion to Queen Elizabeth I. The exposure given the name by actress Gloria Swanson was probably crucial to its popularity from the 1920s through the 1960s. Now a bit passé. Writers Gloria Steinem, Gloria Naylor; singers Gloria Estefan, Gloria Gaynor.

Glaura, Glaurea, Glora, Glorea, Gloree, Glorey, Gloreya, Glori, Glorie, Gloriana, Gloriane, Glorie, Glorra, Glorria, Glory, Glorya, Gloryan, Gloryanna, Gloryanne

Glynis Welsh. "Small glen." Related to Glenn and its variants. Popular in the middle of the 20th century, but mostly in Britain. Actress Glynis Johns.

Glinnis, Glinyce, Glinys, Glinyss, Glynnis

Godfreya Fem. Godfrey, OG. "God-peace."

Godfreyda, Gotfreya

Godiva OE. "God's gift." The famous story runs that in the 11th century Lady Godiva rode through the town of Coventry naked, covered only by her long hair. Her motive (generally forgotten) was a pact with her husband, the Earl of Mercia, who relieved the townsfolk of certain taxes after her ride. In this era the name is probably more familiar as a brand of premium chocolates.

Golda OE. "Gold." Use is frequently a tribute to the late Israeli Prime Minister Golda Meir. Actress Goldie Hawn.

Goldarina, Goldarine, Goldee, Goldi, Goldie, Goldina, Goldy, Goldia

Grace Lat. "Grace." Originally had nothing to do with physical grace, but rather with divine favor and mercy. Used in that sense by the Puritans and taken to America, where it was very fashionable at the turn of the century. Periods of popularity followed in England (in the twenties) and Scotland (through the fifties). Little used now, but ripe for revival. Actress and princess Grace Kelly; singer Grace Jones; choreographer Graciela Daniele.

Engracia, Eugracia, Gracee, Gracey, Gracia, Graciana, Gracie, Graciela, Graciella, Gracija, Gracina, Gracious, Grata, Gratia, Gratiana, Gratiela, Gratiella, Grayce, Grazia, Graziella, Grazina, Graziosa, Grazyna

Grainne Ir. Gael. "Love." Popular in Ireland.

Grainnia, Grania

Granada Spanish place name. Granada was a Moorish kingdom in the southwestern part of what is now Spain, from the 700s until 1492, when Ferdinand and Isabella conquered it and drove the Moors definitively out of Europe. The capital city, also called Granada, is home to the famous Moorish fortress the Alhambra.

Granadda, Grenada, Grenadda

Greer Scot. Dim. **Gregory** (Lat. "Alert, watchful"). Given fame by actress Greer Garson, whose mother's maiden name it was.

Grier

Gregoria (Fem. **Gregory**) Lat. "Alert, watchful."

  Gregoriana, Gregorijana, Gregorina, Gregorine, Gregorya, Gregoryna

Greta Ger. Dim. **Margaret** (Gk. "Pearl"). Most used during the 1930s, clearly inspired by Greta Garbo. Marathon runner Greta Waitz.

  Greeta, Gretal, Gretchen, Grete, Gretel, Gretha, Grethe, Grethel, Gretna, Gretta, Grette, Grietje, Gryta

Gretchen Ger. Dim. **Margaret** (Gk. "Pearl"). Used on its own in English-speaking countries in this century.

Griselda OG. "Gray fighting maid." In a famous tale told by both Boccaccio and Chaucer, "Patient Griselda" is a meek wife who submits to numerous trials devised by her husband to test her submissiveness. The name has long since been eclipsed by its short form, Zelda.

  Chriselda, Gricely, Grisel, Griseldis, Griselly, Grishelda, Grishilde, Grissel, Grizel, Grizelda, Gryselde, Gryzelde, Selda, Zelda

Gudrun Scand. "Battle." D.H. Lawrence gave this name to one of the characters in his 1920 novel *Women in Love*, and Glenda Jackson won an Academy Award for playing her in the 1969 film.

  Gudren, Gudrid, Gudrin, Gudrinn, Gudruna, Gudrunn, Gudrunne, Guthrun, Guthrunn, Guthrunne

Guida It. "Guide."

Guinevere Welsh. "White and smooth, soft." The name of King Arthur's ill-fated queen, who betrayed him with his best buddy, Lancelot. The most common form today is Jennifer.

  Gaenna, Gaynor, Genever, Geneviève, Genevra, Geniffer, Geniver, Genivra, Genna, Gennie, Gennifer, Genny, Ginevra, Guenever, Guenevere, Gueniveer, Guenna, Guennola, Guinever, Guinna, Gwen, Gweniver, Gwenn, Gwennie, Gwennola, Gwennora, Gwennore, Gwenny, Gwenora, Gwenore, Gwyn, Gwynn, Gwynna, Gwynne, Janifer, Jen, Jeni, Jenifer, Jennee, Jenni, Jennie, Jenni-

fer, Jenny, Wendee, Wendie, Wendy, Win, Winne, Winnie, Winny

Gulielma (Fem. **Wilhelm**) It. from OG. "Will-helmet."
Guglielma

Gunhilda ONorse. "Battle-maid."
Gunhilde, Gunilda, Gunilla, Gunna, Gunnel, Gunnhilda

Gustava (Fem. **Gustav**) Swed. "Staff of the gods." Gustav is a royal name in Sweden.
Gustha

Gwen Dim. **Gwendolyn, Guinevere**. Often given as an independent name. Singer Gwen Stefani.
Gwenn, Gwyn, Gwynn

Gwenda Welsh. "Fair and good." Rare since the 1960s, even in Wales.
Gwennda, Gwynda

Gwendolyn Welsh. "Fair bow." In some legends, Merlin the magician has a wife named Gwendolyn. The old Welsh name was revived in the late 19th century, and is now rare, though its diminutive, **Wendy**, lingers on.
Guendolen, Guendolin, Guendolinn, Guendolynn, Guenna, Gwen, Gwenda, Gwendaline, Gwendolen, Gwendolene, Gwendolin, Gwendoline, Gwendolynne, Gwenna, Gwenette, Gwenndolen, Gwenni, Gwennie, Gwenny, Gwenyth, Gwyn, Gwyneth, Gwynn, Gwynna, Gwynne, Wendi, Wendie, Wendy, Win, Winne, Wynne

Gwladys Welsh. Var. **Gladys**.

Gwyneth Welsh. "Happiness." Most popular in Wales and Britain in the 1930s and 1940s, but never a strong name in America. Actress Gwyneth Paltrow.
Gweneth, Gwenith, Gwenyth, Gwineth, Gwinneth, Gwinyth, Gwynith, Gwynna, Gwynne, Gwynneth, Winnie, Winny, Wynne, Wynnie

Gwynn Welsh. "Fair, blessed." Also dim. **Gwendolyn** or **Gwyneth**.
Gwin, Gwinna, Gwinne, Gwyn, Gwynna, Gwynne

Gypsy OE. The tribe of Romany was originally called "gypsy" because it was thought that they had originated in Egypt. Use of the name, as in the case of Gypsy Rose Lee, is more often a nickname.
Gipsee, Gipsey, Gipsy

Habibah Arab. "Loved one."

Habiba, Haviva, Havivah, Hebiba

Hadar Heb. "Beauty, splendor."

Hadara, Hadarit, Haduraq

Hadija Arab. "Precious gift."

Hadley OE. Place name: "Heather meadow."
Has a certain rakish air, perhaps, because one of Ernest
Hemingway's four wives was named Hadley.

**Hadlea, Hadleigh, Hadly, Hedlea, Hedleigh, Hedley, Hed-
lie, Hedly**

Hadria Lat. Place name: "From Adria." Var. **Adrian**.

Hadriana, Hadriane, Hadrianna, Hadrien, Hadrienne

Hafsa Old Arabic name of unknown meaning or derivation.
A 7th-century figure named Hafsa was chosen, after Muhammad's death, to be the keeper of the first written copy
of the Koran.

Hafsah, Hafza

Hagar Heb. "Forsaken." In the Old Testament, Hagar is
the handmaid of Abraham's barren wife Sarah, and Sarah
sends her away when she has a son by Abraham. A similar
Muslim name (which also means "forsaken") is Hajar.
The same Hagar who was cast out by Sarah is considered
the mother of the Arabic race. Though the Puritans tended
to scour the Old Testament for feminine names, this was
not one they popularized, and its sparing use has dwindled
further since early in the 20th century.

Haggar, Hagir

Haidée Gk. "Modest." The name was brought to public
attention by Byron, who used it in his poem "Don Juan."
It has never really caught on.

Jaidee, Hadee, Hyday

Hala Arab. "Halo."

Halah

Halcyone Gk. "Kingfisher." In ancient myth, the kingfisher laid its eggs on the sea, and they floated on the

503

water for the two weeks preceding the winter solstice. During this time the waves were always calm, hence the expression "halcyon days" to mean a time of tranquil happiness.
Halcyon, Halcyona

Haldana ONorse. "Half-Danish." The name takes on real significance when you consider that in ancient Britain, the Danes were fierce and frequent invaders.
Haldane, Haldanna

Haley OE. "Hay meadow." Var. **Hayley**. This name and Hallie, in their various spellings, have become very popular recently. This is probably the least common form of Hayley.
Halea, Haleigh, Hailey, Hayley

Halfrida OG. "Peaceful heroine" or "Peaceful home."

Halimah Arab. "Gentle, soft-spoken."
Haleema, Haleemah, Haleima, Halima, Helima

Halimeda Gk. "Thinking of the sea."
Halameda, Halette, Hali, Hallie, Meda, Medie

Halleli Heb. "Greatly praised." Feminine of **Hillel**, the name of a great Talmudic scholar. The elaborated version of the name, Halleliya, is obviously very close to the Christian expression of praise, "Hallelujah."
Alleluia, Halleliya, Halleluja, Hallelujah, Hilly

Hallie Fem. **Henry** OG. "Ruler of the home or estate." Hallie is considered a form of Harriet, as Hal is a nickname for Harry. It is increasingly popular with the trend toward old-fashioned names. Actress Halle Berry.
Hali, Halle, Hallee, Halley, Halli

Hamida Arab. "Giving thanks."
Hameedah, Hameida, Hamidah

Hana Jap. "Flower." Fashion designer Hanae Mori.
Hanae, Hanako

Hania Heb. "A place to rest" or Arab. "To be happy."
Chania, Chaniya, Chaniyah, Chanya, Haniya, Haniyah, Hannia, Hanniah, Hanniya, Hanniyah, Hannya, Hannyah

Hanita Hindu. "Grace of the gods."

Hannah Heb. "Grace." In the Old Testament, Hannah is the mother of the prophet Samuel. The name was steadily popular from around 1600 through the 19th century, peaking around 1800. Though the European forms of the name—Ann, Anne, Anna, etc.—used to be more common, Hannah is now nearly as popular as the most fashionable of these (which happens to be Anna). Writer Hannah Arendt; sportscaster Hannah Storm.

Ann, Anna, Anne, Annie, Chana, Chanah, Chanha, Channach, Channah, Hana, Hanna, Hanne, Hannele, Hannelore, Hannie, Hanny, Honna, Nan, Nanney, Nannie, Nanny

Hansika Hindi. "Small swan."

Hansa, Hansila

Hansine Dan. Fem. **John** (Heb. "The Lord is gracious") by way of **Hans**.

Hanseen, Hansina

Happy Eng. "Cheerful, lighthearted." Though it was common enough in the 19th century, Felicity or Hilary are now more likely to be used, though Happy occurs as a nickname. The most famous Happy is the late Nelson Rockefeller's wife.

Haralda ONorse. "Army ruler" or "Army power." This form was coined during the great 19th-century popularity of Harold, but (as with many feminine variants, like Arthuretta) never really caught on.

Halley, Hallie, Hally, Harolda, Haroldene, Haroldina

Harela Heb. "The Lord's mountain."

Charela, Charrela, Harrela, Harrella, Harrellah

Harley OE. Place name: "The long field." Familiar to most people as half of the name of a great motorcycle, the Harley-Davidson. This would have considered a drawback to any other generation of parents, but turn-of-the-century hipsters seem to find it appealing.

Arlea, Arlee, Arleigh, Arley, Harlea, Harlee, Harleigh, Harlie, Harly

Harmony Lat. "Harmony." Great name for New Age parents seeking just that. A variant is **Harmonia**, the name of the Greek goddess of order.

Harmonee, Harmoney, Harmonia, Harmonie

Harolyn Var. **Carolyn** (OG. "Man"). To add some interest to a name, or sometimes to commemorate a beloved relative, families often substitute one consonant for another at the beginning of a name. Singer Harolyn Blackwell.

Harriet (Fem. **Henry**) OG. "Ruler of the home or estate." An informal version of Henrietta, very popular in the 18th and 19th centuries, and after nearly 100 years of obscurity, ready for a revival. Older parents may be put off by memories of '50s TV sitcom *Ozzie and Harriet*, however. Avid readers are more likely to associate the name with the children's book *Harriet the Spy*, which was introduced to a new generation in the 1996 movie. Author Harriet Beecher Stowe; civil rights leader Harriet Tubman.

Hallee, Hallie, Harrie, Harrietta, Harriett, Harrietta, Harriette, Harriot, Harriott, Harriotte, Hatsee, Hatsey, Hatsie, Hatsy, Hattie, Hatty

Hava Heb. "Life." This is the word that the Anglicized name Eve is based on, because of course Eve gave life to the rest of the human race.

Chaba, Chaya, Chayka, Eva, Eve, Hava, Haya, Kaija

Haviva Heb. "Well-loved."

Havivah, Havviva, Havvivah

Hayfa Arab. "Slender, well-shaped."

Haifa

Hayley OE. Place name: "Hay meadow." Other sources suggest derivation from a Norse word, *haela*, which means "hero." Probably neither meaning nor history contributes much to the recent popularity of this name, which was made famous by actress Hayley Mills in the 1960s, and thirty years later was one of the top fifty names given to American girls.

Haeley, Haelie, Haely, Hailea, Hailee, Haileigh, Haily, Haleigh, Halie, Hally, Haylea, Haylee, Hayleigh, Hayley

Hazel OE. Tree name. The late–19th-century vogue for botanical names tended to concentrate on flowers rather than trees; Hazel is an exception. A long-running comic strip about a maid called Hazel has given it connotations that will be tough to escape.

Hazal, Hazell, Hazelle, Hazle

Heather ME. Flower name. Introduced with other botanical names in the late 19th century, but really took off in the late 20th century, especially in the U.S., where its association with Scotland may lend it an upper-class aura. Anglo names like Heather are also emblematic of assimilation for families new to the US. Actress Heather Locklear.

Heath, Hether

Heaven Place name. Use is scarce but may be inspired by a V. C. Andrews book with that title.

Hebe Gk. "Youth." In Greek legend, Hebe was the goddess of youth and also cupbearer to the gods. Her name was used mostly in the late 19th century.

Hedda OG. "Warfare." The more common anglicized version of Hedwig. Mid–20th-century gossip queen Hedda Hopper.
Heda, Heddi, Heddie, Hedi, Hedvig, Hedvige, Hedwig, Hedwiga, Hedy, Hetta

Hedia Heb. "Jehovah's echo."
Hediah, Hedya, Hedyah

Hedwig OG. "Warfare, struggle, strife." Almost unknown in English-speaking countries. Actress Hedy Lamarr (née Hedwig Kiesler).
Hadvig, Hadwig, Hedvig, Hedviga, Hedvige, Hedwiga, Hedwige, Hedy

Hedy Gk. "Delightful, sweet" or Heb. "My echo." Use is more likely to reflect the glamorous Hedy Lamarr's popularity.
Heda, Hedia, Hediah, Hedyla

Heidi Dim. **Adelaide** (OG. "Noble, nobility"). Made popular by Johanna Spyri's famous novel of 1881, first in German-speaking countries, later in the U.S. Its surge of popularity in the 1970s may have been influenced by a highly publicized TV production of the late 1960s. The show went down in sports history as well, since NBC executives chose to begin showing "Heidi" rather than showing the final fifty seconds of a suspenseful football game, known ever since as "the Heidi game." (Two touchdowns were scored in the final minute that sports fans didn't see.)
Heida, Heide, Heidey, Heidy, Hydee

Heladia Sp. from Ger. "Greek." Greece is often known as the land of the Hellenes.
Eladia

Helen Gk. "Light." The most famous Helen is probably Helen of Troy, the daughter of Zeus by Leda. Her phenomenal beauty was, in some versions, the root cause of the Trojan War; hers was "the face that launched a thousand ships." The name has been understandably popular through the ages, and has spawned many variants, of which Ellen is the most popular. Still, for a simple, pretty name with many attractive variants and positive associations, it is underused. Writer Helen Keller; actresses Helen Hayes, Helen Hunt; publisher Helen Gurley Brown; singer Helen Reddy.

Aileen, Ailene, Aleanor, Alene, Aline, Eileen, Elaina, Elaine, Elana, Elayne, Eleanor, Eleanore, Elena, Eleni, Elenora, Elenore, Eleonora, Elianora, Elinor, Ella, Elladine, Elleanora, Elle, Ellee, Ellen, Ellenora, Ellette, Ellie, Ellin, Elliner, Ellinor, Elly, Ellyn, Galina, Halina, Heleanor, Helenore, Helena, Helenann, Hélène, Helia, Hella, Hellen, Hellena, Hellene, Hellenor, Hellia, Ileana, Ilene, Ilona, Jelena, Lana, Leanora, Lena, Lenore, Leonora, Leonore, Leora, Lienor, Lina, Nelda, Nell, Nellette, Nelliana, Nellie, Nelly, Nonnie, Nora, Yelena

Helga OG. "Holy, sacred." Var. Olga.
Helge, Hellga, Hellge

Helice Gk. "Spiral." An unusual name that comes from the same Greek root as helix, or double helix, the shape of the DNA molecule.
Helica, Helike

Helma OG. "Helmet." See Wilhelmina.
Hillma, Hilma

Heloise Fr. Var. Louise (OG. "Renowned in war"). The 12th-century French philosopher Pierre Abelard fell in love with and seduced his student Heloise. Her uncle and guardian had him emasculated, even though he married Heloise. She became a nun, he a monk. Today the name has housekeeping resonance, however, owing to the reach of the popular *Hints From Heloise* series of books.
Aloysia, Eloisa, Eloise, Heloisa, Lois

Helsa Dan. Var. Elizabeth. Heb. "Consecrated to God."
Hellsa

Hemali Sanskrit. "Gilded, gold-covered."

Henrietta (Fem. Henry) OG. "Ruler of the house." More formal version of Harriet that briefly became popular at the turn of the century. A bit of a mouthful for today's parents.
Enrichetta, Enrichette, Enriqueta, Etta, Ettie, Etty, Hat-

sie, Hatsy, Hattie, Hatty, Hendrika, Henia, Henie, Henka, Hennie, Henrie, Henrieta, Henriette, Henrika, Henryetta, Hetti, Hettie, Yetta, Yettie

Hepzibah Heb. "My delight is in her." Old Testament name widely used by the Puritans, but by the 20th century it had almost died out, in part because of its lack of euphony.

Chepziba, Chepzibah, Eppie, Hefzia, Hefziba, Hephzia, Hephziba, Hepsie, Hepsibah, Hepzi, Hepzia

Hera Gk. "Queen." In Greek myth, Hera was the wife (and sister) of Zeus, ruler of the gods. She is usually portrayed as a jealous woman who persecutes her husband's numerous mistresses. Her equivalent in the Roman pantheon is Juno.

Hermia Gk. "Messenger." This is a feminine version of Hermes, the name of the Greek messenger god (he is often depicted with wings on his heels). One of the characters in Shakespeare's *A Midsummer Night's Dream* is named Hermia.

Hermla, Hermilda

Hermione Gk. "Earthly." Very rare. Actress Hermione Gingold.

Erma, Herma, Hermia, Hermina, Hermine, Herminia

Hermosa Sp. "Beautiful."

Herodias Gk. "To monitor, watch over." In the Bible, Herodias is the wife of Herod Philip and mother of Salome. She divorced her husband to marry his brother, the governor of Judea, an act that John the Baptist denounced. When Salome performed her famous dance for her new stepfather, he was so thrilled that he promised her whatever she wanted: it was Herodias who suggested that John's head on a platter would be an appropriate reward. The story has been retold in a play by Oscar Wilde, an opera by Richard Strauss, and a short story by Gustave Flaubert, among others.

Hersilia Sp. from Gk. "Delicate." Roman myth name: the wife of Romulus, Rome's founder, originally one of the famous Sabine women carried off to provide wives for the new citizens of Rome.

Ercilia, Ersila, Ersilia, Erzilia, Hersila

Hertha OE. "Earth." The name of the German or Scandinavian Earth Mother.
Eartha, Erda, Ertha, Herta

Hesper Gk. "Evening or evening star." The Greeks referred to Italy as Hesperia, since the sun set and the evening star rose there. It is also, fittingly enough, the name of a town in California.
Hespera, Hesperia

Hester Gk. "Star." Var. **Esther**. The most famous Hester is probably the adulteress in Hawthorne's *The Scarlet Letter*, Hester Prynne.
Hesther, Hestia, Hettie, Hetty

Hibernia Lat. Place name for Ireland.

Hibiscus Lat. Botanical name for the plant colloquially known as the marsh mallow.

Hilary Gk. "Cheerful, happy." The name comes from the same root as the word "hilarious." There were a 4th-century saint and a 5th-century pope named Hilary, and the name was used for boys until the 17th century. The late–19th-century revival, though, made it generally a girls' name, which was especially fashionable in the 1950s. Parents can't consider the name now without reference to First Lady Hillary Clinton.
Hilaria, Hilarie, Hillary, Hillery, Hilliary

Hilda OG. "Battle woman." One of the Valkyrie of Teutonic legend was named Hilda. A medieval name with a Victorian revival that lasted through the 1930s. Now unusual.
Hilde, Hildie, Hildy

Hildegarde OG. "Battle stronghold." Rare in English-speaking countries. Saint Hildegarde of Bingen was a learned 12th-century abbess who left a considerable body of writing. Opera star Hildegarde Behrens.
Hellee, Hilda, Hildagard, Hildagarde, Hilde, Hildegard, Hildegaard, Hildegunn, Hille

Hildemar OG. "Battle-renowned."
Hildemarr

Hildreth OG. "Battle counselor." Briefly used at the turn of the 20th century in Britain.
Hildred

Hilma Dim. **Wilhelmina** (OG. "Will-helmet").
Halma, Helma
Hinda Heb. "Doe, female deer."
Hynda
Hippolyta Gk. Meaning not entirely clear, but alludes to horses. In Greek legend, she was a queen of the Amazons (a warlike race of women) who was finally bested by Hercules or, depending on the version, by Theseus. She is also a character in Shakespeare's *A Midsummer Night's Dream.*
Hippolita
Holda OG. "Hidden."
Holde, Holle, Hulda
Holiday Originally, "Holy day," which presumably meant some respite from the daily drudgery of pre-industrial Europe to honor the calendar of the Christian church. Now, it has taken on the aura of jollity and mirth.
Holladay, Holliday
Hollis OE. Place name: "Near the holly bushes." The usual transference of a masculine to a feminine name may be accelerated in this case because Hollis sounds like Holly.
Hollace, Holles, Holless, Holliss, Holyss
Holly OE. Botanical name. First used at the turn of the 20th century and newly popular in the 1960s, possibly inspired by Truman Capote's novel *Breakfast at Tiffany's*, which was made into a film in 1961. Audrey Hepburn starred as the heroine, Holly Golightly. Obviously a seasonal favorite most intensively used in December. Actress Holly Hunter; singer Holly Near.
Hollee, Holleigh, Holley, Hollie, Hollye
Honey OE. The word used as a name. May be as a diminutive of Honora, but is more likely to be a transference of the endearment.
Honeah, Honee
Honora Lat. "Woman of honor." As Honour, used by the Puritans (along with other abstract concepts like Constance). Honoria was more common in the 18th century. No version of the name is widely used now. Actress Honor Blackman; model Honor Fraser.
Honor, Honorah, Honorata, Honoria, Honorine, Honour, Nora, Norah, Norine, Norry

Hope OE. "Hope." One of the three cardinal virtues, along with Faith and Charity, and probably the one that has survived best, particularly in the U.S. Actress Hope Lange.

Horatia Lat. Clan name, possibly meaning "Timekeeper." The name was coined by the 18th-century admiral Lord Horatio Nelson, for his daughter.
Horacia, Horaisha, Horasha

Hortense Lat. Clan name. A related word means "of the garden." *Hortensia* is the French term for the hydrangea shrub.
Hartencia, Hartinsia, Hortensia, Hortenspa, Hortenxia, Hortinzia, Ortensia

Hosanna Gk. from Heb. "Save now, we pray!" An expression of praise interjected into worship.
Hosana, Osana, Osanna

Huberta (Fem. Hubert) OG. "Brilliant mind."
Hubertina, Hubertine, Uberta, Ubertina

Huette (Fem. Hugh) OG. "Mind, intellect." A feminization of a name that has never had a particular vogue.
Huela, Huella, Huetta, Hugette, Hughette, Hughina, Ugetta

Hulda OG. "Loved one." or Heb. "Mole." Very unusual, occurs in Scandinavian or English-speaking countries.
Huldah, Huldie

Hyacinth Gk. Flower name. There was a 3rd-century saint of this name, which was used for boys as well as girls. In Greek legend, Apollo loved a beautiful youth of the name; the hyacinth flower sprang up from his blood when he died.
Cintha, Cinthia, Cinthie, Cinthy, Giacinta, Giacintia, Hyacintha, Hyacinthe, Hyacinthia, Hyacinthie, Hyacintia, Jacenta, Jacinda, Jacinta, Jacintha, Jacinthe, Jackie, Jacky, Jacynth

Hypatia Gk. "Highest."
Hypacia, Hypasia

Iantha Gk. "Purple flower." Popular in the later 19th century, possibly influenced by Romantic poets earlier in the century.
Ianthe, Ianthia, Ianthina, Janthia

Iberia Poetic name for the country of Spain.
Ibeeria

Ida Meaning unclear: possibly OE. "Prosperous, happy" or OG. "Hardworking." Very fashionable at the turn of the 20th century in America, but little used in modern times.
Eida, Eidah, Idaleen, Idalene, Idalia, Idalina, Idaline, Idalya, Idalyne, Ide, Idelfa, Idelfia, Idell, Idella, Idelle, Idetta, Idette

Idina Var. **Edina**. OE. "from Edinburgh, Scotland."

Idona Possiby ONorse. "Renewal," or an elaboration of Ida.
Idonah, Idone, Idonea, Idonie, Idonna, Iduna

Idra Aramaic. "Fig tree." In the parched lands where Aramaic was spoken long ago, a fig tree was a symbol of wealth.

Idris Welsh. "Hotblooded lord." This is a masculine name in Wales.
Edris, Eedris

Iduna ONorse. "Loving one."
Idonia, Idunna

Ieesha Var. **Aisha**. Arab. "Woman" or Swahili. "Life."
Eyeesha, Ieasha, Ieashia, Ieashiah, Ieeshah, Iesha, Yeesha

Ignacia (Fem. **Ignatius**) Meaning unclear, though some sources suggest Lat. "Ardent, burning." Usage tends to commemorate Saint Ignatius Loyola, founder of the Society of Jesus, more commonly known as the Jesuits.
Ignatia, Ignazia, Iniga

Ila OF. Place name: "Island."
Eila, Ilanis, Ilanys, Isla

Ilana Heb. "Tree." Several names come from the Hebrew root and are also spelled several different ways.

Elana, Elanit, Eleana, Eleanna, Ileana, Ileanna, Iliana, Ilianna, Ilanit

Ilaria It. Var. **Hilary** (Gk. "Cheerful, happy").

Ilene Modern variant of **Aileen** (Gk. "Light").

Ilean, Ileen, Ileene, Ilene

Ilesha Hindi. "Earth lord."

Iliana Gk. "Trojan." The poetic name for the ancient city of Troy was "Ilion." Ileana has been used by the Greek royal family. Actress Ileanna Douglas.

Ileana, Ileane, Ileanna, Ileanne, Illeanna, Illia, Illiana

Ilka Slavic. "Flattering, hardworking." Writer Ilka Chase.

Ilke, Milka

Ilona Hung. Var. **Helen** (Gk. "Light"). Also carries the connotation of "beautiful," no doubt because of the legendary beauty of Helen of Troy.

Elona, Ellona, Elonna, Illona, Ilone, Ilonka, Ilonna, Yllona, Ylonna

Ilsa Ger. Var. **Elizabeth** (Heb. "Pledged to God"). Mostly limited to Germany, especially in the 19th century.

Ellsa, Elsa, Else, Illsa, Ilsae, Ilsaie, Ilse

Iluminada Sp. "Lit up."

Illuminada, Illuminata, Iluminata, Yluminata

Ima Var. **Emma** (OG. "Embracing everything").

Iman Arab. "Belief, faith." Model Iman.

Eman, Imani

Imelda OG./It. "All-consuming fight." A name occasionally used (especially in Catholic families, after a virgin saint) until the explosive fame of Philippine First Lady Imelda Marcos. Now it seems slated for a long period of neglect.

Amelda, Himalda, Imalda, Ymelda

Immaculada Sp. "Without stain." A reference to the Immaculate Conception, the doctrine that the Virgin Mary, from the moment of her conception, was free of the original sin that tainted humankind. It was not proclaimed dogma until 1854.

Imacolata, Imaculada, Immaculata, Immacolata

Imogen Lat. Some sources claim it means "Last-born," while others suggest "Image," while still another traces it back to "Innocent." Despite Shakespeare's use of the name, it was obscure until the 20th century. Still highly unusual. Actresses Imogene Coca, Imogen Stubbs.

Emogen, Emogene, Imogene, Imogenia, Imogine, Imojean, Imojeen

Imperia Lat. "Imperial."

Empress, Imperatrix

Ina Lat. Suffix to make male names feminine, as in Clementina or Edwina. Used independently since the Victorian era.

Ena, Yna

Inaya Arab. "Taking care, concerned."

Inayah

India Country name. Like any pretty geographic name, could be used by parents who have a special attachment to the country. Model India Hicks.

Indya

Indiana Lat. "From India." Also the name of a Middle Western State, of course.

Idiana

Indigo A deep blue dye derived from the indigo plant.

Indira Sanskrit. "Beauty." Name of longtime Indian Prime Minister Indira Ghandi.

Indeera

Indu Hindi. "Moon."

Inez Sp.Var. **Agnes** (Lat. "Pure"). Unusual in English-speaking countries. Designer Inès de la Fressange.

Ines, Inesita, Inessa, Ynes, Ynesita, Ynez

Inga Scand. "Guarded by Ing." Ing, in Norse mythology, was a powerful god of fertility and peace. His name is an element in several modern names like Ingrid and Ingmar. Actress Inger Stevens.

Ingaberg, Ingaborg, Inge, Ingeberg, Ingeborg, Inger, Innga, Inngeborg

Ingrid Scand. "Beautiful." The most popular of the "Ing-" names, and the only one to be widely used in non-Scandinavian cultures, doubtless because of the fame of Swedish actress Ingrid Bergman.

Inga, Inge, Inger, Ingmar

Inocencia Sp. "Innocence."

Innocencia, Innocenta, Inocenta, Inocentia, Ynocencia

Io Name from Greek mythology. Io was yet another maiden

who caught Zeus's eye and was transformed to elude him: this time, into a cow.

Eyo

Ioanna Gk. Var. **Hannah** (Heb. "Grace").

Ioana, Ioanah, Ioannah, Joanna, Yohanna

Ionia Place name: the Ionian Sea separates western Greece from Italy, and the Ionian Islands, on the west coast of Greece, include Corfu.

Eionia, Ionija, Ionya

Iola Gk. "Cloud of dawn."

Iole

Iolani Haw. "Hawk of royalty."

Iolanthe Gk. "Violet flower." The more common form is the Spanish variant, Yolanda. Gilbert and Sullivan's 1882 operetta *Iolanthe* did little to popularize this form.

Iolanda, Iolanta, Iolantha, Jolantha, Jolanthe, Yolantha, Yolanthe, Yolley, Yollie

Iona Gk. Place name. Island off the coast of Scotland, site of an early monastery. Use as a name is mostly Scottish.

Ione Gk. "Violet." Flower name in an exotic, little-used form. Actress Ione Skye.

Ionia, Ionie

Iphigenia Gk. "Sacrifice." In Greek myth, the daughter of Agamemnon. Her father sacrificed her to gain advantage in the Trojan War, though in most versions of the story, she is saved by Artemis. This savage tale inspired plays by Euripides, Goethe, and Racine.

Efigenia, Ephigenia, Ephigenie, Ifigenia, Iphigeneia, Iphigenie, Genia

Irene Gk. "Peace." Very common under the Roman Empire, but first appeared in English-speaking countries in the mid–19th century. It caught on quickly and was very popular in the first quarter of the 20th century. Actresses Irene Dunne, Irene Worth.

Arina, Eireen, Eiren, Eirena, Eirene, Erena, Erene, Ira, Ireen, Iren, Irena, Irenea, Irenée, Irenka, Irina, Irine, Iryna, Orina, Oryna, Rena, Rene, Renie, Rina, Yarina

Iris Gk. "Rainbow." Also (and this is probably the source of its popularity) the name of a flower. Its use was established and faded with other flower names, from around 1890 to the 1920s. Novelist Iris Murdoch.

Irida, Iridiana, Iridianny, Irisa, Irita

Irit Heb. Plant name: the asphodel.

Irma OG. "Universal, complete." Rare now, but somewhat used in the first part of this century.

Erma, Ermengard, Irmina, Irmine, Irmgard, Irmgarde

Irvette (Fem. **Irving**) OE. "Seafriend." Also Scot. place name. A rather awkward transformation of a name that was never immensely popular.

Earvette, Earvina, Ervette, Ervina, Irvina

Isabel Sp. Var. **Elizabeth** (Heb. "Pledged to God"). Most fashionable in the last quarter of the 19th century. Belle and Bella are also independently used, probably because of their own attractive meaning ("beautiful") in French and Spanish. Henry James named the heroine of his *Portrait of a Lady* Isabel Archer. Actresses Isabella Rossellini, Isabelle Adjani.

Bel, Belia, Belicia, Belita, Bell, Bella, Belle, Bellita, Ib, Ibbie, Isa, Isabeau, Isabele, Isabelita, Isabell, Isabella, Isabelle, Ishbel, Isobel, Isobell, Isobella, Isobelle, Issie, Issy, Izabella, Izabelle, Izzie, Izzy, Sabella, Sabelle, Ysabeau, Ysabel, Ysabella, Ysobel, Yzabelle, Yzobel, Yzobelle

Isadora (Fem. **Isidore**) Lat. "Gift of Isis." Isis was the principal goddess of ancient Egypt, and Isidore was a popular name among the ancient Greeks. The most famous Isadora was, of course, modern dance pioneer Isadora Duncan.

Isidora, Ysadora

Isaura Greek place name: Isauria was an ancient country in Asia Minor.

Aura, Isa, Isaure

Ishana Hindi. "Desire."

Ishani

Isis Egypt. The supreme goddess of ancient Egypt, Isis ruled with her brother/husband, Osiris, and her son, Horus.

Isla Name of a Scottish river, used in Britain as a first name.

Islay

Ismay Var. **Esmé**, French "Esteemed."

Isolde Meaning unclear, though some sources offer Welsh "Fair lady." In legend Isolde is an Irish princess loved by Tristan, but she marries his uncle, King Mark. There are many versions of the tale, the most famous of which is probably Wagner's opera *Tristan und Isolde*. Use of this version of the name probably reflects admiration for the opera.

Iseult, Iseut, Isold, Isolda, Isolt, Isolte, Isota, Isotta, Isotte, Yseult, Yseulte, Yseut, Ysolda, Ysolde, Ysotta, Ysotte

Ita Ir. Gael. "Thirst." Name of a 6th-century Irish saint. Rare outside of Ireland.

Ivana (Fem. **Ivan**) Slavic var. **John** (Heb. "Jehovah is gracious"). Most recently in the news with Ivana Mazzuchelli, the ex-wife of Donald Trump.

Iva, Ivanka, Ivanna

Ivory Lat. Word used as name, possibly related to the vogue for jewel names in the late 19th century.

Ivoreen, Ivorine

Ivy OE. Botanical name. Most popular in the first quarter of the 20th century. Author Ivy Compton-Burnett.

Ivee, Ivey, Ivie

THEY NAMED THE BABY *WHAT?*

Unless you've been hibernating for the past few years, you know that Bruce Willis and Demi Moore have chosen, well, *unusual* names for their daughters (Rumer, Scout, and Tallulah Belle). Presumably if your name is Demi you feel perfectly comfortable with startling names. Then again, sometimes it's hard to believe that celebrity parents have spared a thought for their children: film director Jonathan Demme named a daughter Brooklyn because he liked the way the name sounded—forget the borough, forget the Dodgers, forget the accent. Or do they reason that Chastity Bono and Moon Unit Zappa seem all right, so it's fine to name your child anything? Look at the following remarkable names:

Kim Basinger and Alec Baldwin: Ireland Eliesse
Kim Falconer and Robert Downey, Jr.: Indio
Sting and Trudie Styler: Giacomo Luke
Robby Benson and Karla DeVito: Zephyr

John Mellencamp: Speck
John Travolta and Kelly Preston: Jett
Cecil Fielder: Prince
Nick Nolte: Brawley
Sylvester Stallone and Talia Shire: Sage and Seargeoh
Brian de Palma and Gale Ann Hurd: Lolita

The winner in the preposterous names stakes, however, seems to be English musician Paula Yates. When married to Bob Geldof, she named one daughter Fifi Trixibelle and another Peaches. With singer Michael Hutchence, she recently had a baby who rejoices in the name of Heavenly Hiraani Tiger Lily.

Jacaranda Flower name: a tree with highly scented purple blossoms that flourishes in warm climates.

Jacarannda, Jacarranda, Jakaranda

Jacinda Sp. Var. **Hyacinth** (Gk. Flower name). There was a 3rd-century Saint Hyacinth, and the name was used for boys as well as girls. In Greek legend, Apollo loved a beautiful youth of the name; the hyacinth flower sprang up from his blood when he died.

Giacinda, Giacintha, Giacinthia, Jacenda, Jacenta, Jacey, Jacie, Jacindia, Jacinna, Jacinta, Jacinth, Jacintha, Jacinthe, Jacinthia, Jacy, Jacynth, Jacyntha, Jacynthe, Jacynthia

Jackie Dim., usually of **Jacqueline**. Used as an independent name in the 20th century, most notably in emulation of Jacqueline Kennedy Onassis.

Jackee, Jackey, Jacki, Jacky, Jacquey, Jacqui, Jacquie

Jacobina (Fem. **Jacob**) Heb. "He who supplants." James is an anglicization of Jacob, and has always been a favorite name in Scotland, which may account for the Scottish use of this feminization. It may also be related to the Scottish Jacobite movement of the 17th and 18th centuries that sought to keep Stuart kings on the throne of England—a lost cause, but a highly romantic one.

Jackee, Jackie, Jackobina, Jacky, Jacoba, Jacobetta, Jacobette, Jacobine, Jacobyna, Jakobina, Jakobine

Jacqueline Fr. Dim. **Jacob** (Heb. "He who supplants"). Existed in Britain as early as the 17th century, but used in numbers only from the beginning of the 20th century. Grew quickly, and was quite a favorite by mid-century. In the U.S., parents may have been inspired by the glamorous First Lady Jacqueline Kennedy, who put an indelible stamp on the name. It is, like most fashions of the early sixties, in a period of neglect, though the recent death of Jacqueline Kennedy Onassis may prompt a nostalgic surge of use. Actresses Jaclyn Smith, Jacqueline Bisset.

Jacalin, Jacalyn, Jackalin, Jackalinne, Jackelyn, Jacketta, Jackette, Jacki, Jackie, Jacklin, Jacklyn, Jacklynne, Jackqueline, Jacky, Jaclin, Jaclyn, Jacolyn, Jacqualine, Jacqualyn, Jacquel, Jacquelean, Jacquelin, Jacquella, Jacquelle, Jacquelyn, Jacquelynne, Jacquenetta, Jacquenette, Jacquetta, Jacquette, Jacqui, Jacquine, Jaculine, Jaquelin, Jaqueline, Jaquelyn, Jaquith, Zakelina, Zacqueline, Zhakelina, Zhaqueline

Jade Sp. Jewel name, for the semiprecious green stone. Perhaps because the jewel comes from the Orient, the name has a vaguely exotic air. Mick and Bianca Jagger used this name for their daughter. Actress Jada Pinkett.

Jada, Jadra, Jaida, Jayda, Jayde, Jaydra, Zhade

Jadwige Pol. "Safety in battle."

Jadwiga

Jael Heb. "Mountain goat." An Old Testament name: Jael was a heroic woman who killed a Canaanite captain, Sisera, with a tent peg. The name occurred from time to time among the Puritans and again in the 19th century. Now rare.

Jaelle, Jayel, Jayil

Jaffa Heb. "Beautiful." Also a place name: an ancient city that served as the port for Tel Aviv. It was probably most famous for its oranges, though it was also the setting for legendary and Old Testament dramas like those of Andromeda and Jonah.

Jafit, Joppa

Jaime Sp. Var. **James** (Heb. "He who supplants"). The use of variations on Jamie as a girl's name has increased recently, and parents use this and other creative spellings to indicate the gender of the child. Some parents, however, may prefer to consider it as French for "I love", *J'aime*, in which case they should be prepared to insist on the "Zh-" pronunciation.

Jamee, James, Jamey, Jamie, Jayme, Jaymee

Jaleesa Modern name: Lisa with "Ja-" prefix. Probably invented by a TV writer for a character on *A Different World*, and popular enough to be quite widely used.

Geleexa, Jaleisa, Jaliza, Jilleesa, Jilleisa, Joleesa, Joleisa

Jamaica Place name: nation in the Caribbean. Its name comes from an Indian word meaning "Isle with many springs." Author Jamaica Kincaid.

Jamaeca, Jamaika, Jemaica, Jemayka

Jamesina (Fem. **James**) Heb. "He who supplants." An old-fashioned form that has been abandoned in favor of the less formal Jamie, etc.

Jamesetta, Jamesette

Jamie (Fem. Var. **James**) Heb. "He who supplants." Also used as a boy's name, but once a name becomes entrenched as a feminine choice, parents tend to avoid it for their male children. Jamie may be headed in this direction since it has moved into the top fifty names for girls in the U.S. Actresses Jamie Lee Curtis, Jami Gertz.

Jaime, Jaimee, Jaimey, Jaimi, Jaimie, Jaimy, Jama, Jamee, Jamei, Jamese, Jami, Jammie, Jayme, Jaymee, Jaymie, Jaymse

Jamila Arab. "Lovely." Currently popular among Moslem families.

Jameela, Jameila, Jamelia, Jamilah, Jamilla, Jamille, Jamillia

Jan (Fem. **John**) Heb. "The Lord is gracious." This version of Jane has been completely eclipsed by other feminizations of John. Author Jan Morris.

Jana, Janah, Janina, Janine, Jann, Janna, Jannah

Jana (Fem. **John**) Heb. "The Lord is gracious." This Slavic variation of Jane is now more popular than the

Anglicized name that many of today's parents grew up with. Tennis star Jana Novotna.

Iana, Janaya, Janayah, Janna, Jannah, Yana, Yanna

Janae Modern name probably based on Jane or Jan.

Janay, Janea, Jenae, Jenay, Jennae, Jennay, Jinae, Jinnea

Jancis Modern name: probably a combination of **Jan** and **Francis** (Lat. "Frenchman").

Jances, Jancess

Jane (Fem. **John**) Heb. "The Lord is gracious." This is the simplest current variant of John (though Joan predates it), popular since the 16th century. It has been a tried-and-true standby like Mary or Katherine, as its number of variants demonstrate. When many women at a time shared the same name, variants sprang up to differentiate them from one another, hence Janet, Janine, Janelle, etc. At the moment, American parents are so hungry for the exotic that Jana and Janae outstrip Jane in popularity. Perhaps the connotations of "plain Jane" work against it, and the many parents who learned to read with Dick and Jane may be reluctant to use the name for their own children. Author Jane Austen; actresses Jane Fonda, Jane Seymour, Jane Wyman, Janeane Garofalo; newsreader Jane Pauley.

Gene, Gianina, Giovanna, Iva, Ivana, Ivancka, Ivanka, Ivanna, Jaine, Jainee, Jan, Jana, Janaya, Janaye, Jandy, Janeczka, Janeen, Janel, Janela, Janelba, Janella, Janelle, Janean, Janeane, Janene, Janerita, Janessa, Janet, Janeta, Janeth, Janetta, Janette, Janey, Jania, Janica, Janice, Janie, Janina, Janine, Janique, Janis, Janise, Janit, Janka, Janna, Jannel, Jannelle, Janney, Janny, Jany, Jayne, Jaynell, Jean, Jeanette, Jeanie, Jeanne, Jeannette, Jeannine, Jenda, Jenella, Jenelle, Jenica, Jeniece, Jeni, Jenie, Jensina, Jensine, Jess, Jinna, Joana, Joanna, Johanna, Johnetta, Johnna, Johnetta, Jonella, Jonelle, Joni, Jonie, Juana, Juanita, Sheena, Shene, Sinead, Vania, Vanya

Janelle (Fem. **John**) Heb. "The Lord is gracious." Parents seem to want to use names based in some way on John, but the fashions in these names change widely. Janelle appeared in the middle of this century and is now far more widely used than Janet.

**Janelba, Janell, Janellie, Janely, Janiella, Janielle, Je-
nell, Jenelle, Jinelia, Jinelle, Johnelle, Jonelle**

Janet (Fem. **John**) Heb. "The Lord is gracious." The currently common diminutive form of Jane is Janet, but other
forms such as Janeta and Jonet preceded it. Janet was
originally mostly Scots, and was very popular in the
1950s. Like most fifties favorites, it is now out of style.
Actresses Janet Leigh, Janet Gaynor; singer Dame Janet
Baker; swimmer Janet Evans; figure skater Janet Lynn.

**Gianetta, Janeta, Janeth, Janetta, Janette, Jannet, Jan-
netta, Janit, Janot, Jenetta, Jenette, Jennet, Jennette,
Jinnet, Jinnett, Johnetta, Johnette, Jonette**

Janice Var. **Jane**. Coined at the turn of the 20th century,
in general circulation by the thirties, and popular in the
fifties. Like Janet, now out of favor. Singer Janis Joplin.

**Janess, Janessa, Janesse, Janessia, Janiece, Janique,
Janis, Janiss, Jannice, Janyce, Jency, Jenice, Jeniece,
Jenise, Jennice**

Janoah Heb. "Quiet, calm." An Old Testament place
name. With two familiar names as its components (though
they have nothing to do with its meaning), this could be
a good choice for parents seeking an unusual but not peculiar name.

Janowa

Jardina Possibly a variant of **Jordan** (Heb. "Descend")
or an adaptation from the Spanish word for garden, *jardin.*

**Giardeena, Giardena, Giardina, Jardeena, Jardeina, Jar-
dyna**

Jarica Modern name made up of two euphonious elements.
Since Jessica is such a popular name at the turn of
the century, we can expect to see more names with the
"-ica" ending.

Gerrica, Jareeca, Jareika, Jarika, Jarrica, Jerrica

Jasmine Per. "Jasmine flower." Flower name with exotic
connotations. The turn-of-the-century vogue for flower
names had its source in the English upper class, but was
usually confined to temperate-zone specimens. (England's
Queen Mother, for instance, had sisters named Rose and
Violet Hyacinth.) Jasmine became fashionable a bit later,
in the 1930s. It was gaining popularity in the 1990s even
before the film *Aladdin* brought Princess Jasmine into mil-

lions of households. Now Jasmine is in the top ten in some cities, especially among Hispanic and African-American families. Author Jessamine West; model Yasmeen Ghauri.

Ismenia, Jaslyn, Jaslynn, Jasmin, Jasmina, Jasminda, Jassamayn, Jazan, Jazmin, Jazmon, Jazzmin, Jazzmine, Jazzmon, Jazzmyn, Jazzmynn, Jess, Jessamine, Jessamy, Jessamyn, Jessie, Jessimine, Jessimine, Yasmeen, Yasmin, Yasmina, Yasmine, Yasminia

Jay Lat. "Jaybird." A medieval name that has survived in a small way, especially in the U.S., where it is given to boys and girls alike. Its use may be inspired by a great American jurist, John Jay. It is sometimes used in combination with other names. Gymnast Jaycie Phelps.

Jae, Jaya, Jaycie, Jaye, Jaylene, Jeh, Jey, Jeyla

Jean Var. **Jane** (Heb. "The Lord is gracious"). Scottish origin, unusual elsewhere until the turn of the 20th century; most popular in the 1930s. Now unusual. Actresses Jean Arthur, Jean Harlow.

Gene, Genie, Jeana, Jeane, Jeanee, Jeaneen, Jeanelle, Jeanene, Jeanette, Jeanie, Jeanine, Jeanique, Jeanna, Jeanne, Jeanneen, Jeannetta, Jeannette, Jeannie, Jeannine, Jeannique, Jenette, Jenica, Jennet, Jennetta, Jennine

Jeannine (Fem. **John**) Var. **Jean**. Modern usage.

Janine, Jeanine, Jenine, Jannine, Jennine

Jearl Modern name: probably Pearl with a "J-." Track star Jearl Miller.

Jerle

Jecolia Heb. "The Lord has prevailed." Old Testament character: the mother of King Uzziah.

Jecholia, Jekolia

Jedida Heb. "Beloved." Another old Testament personage, this one the mother of Josiah.

Jeddida, Jedidah

Jelena Rus. Var. **Helen** (Gk. "light").

Galina, Yelena

Jemima Heb. "Dove." Old Testament name: Jemima was one of the three beautiful daughters of the persecuted Job. The Puritans brought the name to the U.S., where it is now probably most familiar because of the "Aunt Jemima'' brand name for pancake mix and syrup, as well as Beatrix Potter's foolish heroine of *Jemima Puddleduck*. Still, a good candidate for revival with the late nineties interest in old names.

Jamima, Jemimah, Jemmimah, Jemmie, Jemmy, Mima, Mimma

Jena Arab. ''Little bird.''

Jenna

Jenara Sp. from Lat. ''January.'' A good name for a January baby.

Genara, Gennara, Jennara

Jenessa Com. form **Jennifer** and **Vanessa**. Can also be considered an elaboration of Janice, though the current popularity of Vanessa makes it more likely that this is the primary influence.

Gianessa, Janessa, Jinessa

Jenilee Com. form. **Jenny** and **Lee**.

Jenilea, Jennielee, Jennylee

Jenna Dim. **Jennifer**. Made famous by a character on *Dallas* played by Priscilla Presley.

Jena

Jennie Dim. **Janet** or **Jennifer**. Given as an independent name since the 19th century. Swedish soprano Jennie Lind, talk show host Jenny Jones; actress Jenny McCarthy.

Jenee, Jennee, Jenney, Jenni, Jenny

— **Jennifer** Welsh. ''White and smooth, soft.'' The modern and most popular form of Guinevere, originally a Cornish variant. Its immense 20th-century popularity began in the 1920s and grew to a 1950s peak in Britain. In the U.S. the name reached the number one spot in the early eighties, and is now slipping down the charts though it is still very heavily used. Actresses Jennifer Gray, Jennifer Jones, Jennifer Jason Leigh, Jennifer O'Neill.

Genna, Genni, Gennie, Gennifer, Geniffer, Genniver, Genny, Jen, Jena, Jenefer, Jeni, Jenifer, Jeniffer, Jenn, Jenna, Jennee, Jenni, Jennica, Jennie, Jenniver, Jenny

Jeremia (Fem. **Jeremiah**) Heb. ''The Lord is exalted.''

Jeree, Jeremee, Jeremie, Jeri, Jerri, Jerrie, Jerry

Jerioth Heb. ''Curtains.'' Another Old Testament character.

Jerrie OG./Fr. "Spear ruler." Dim. **Geraldine.**
Jeree, Jeri, Jerree, Jerrey, Jerri, Jerry, Jery

Jerusha Heb. "Married, a possession." In the Old Testament, the wife of King Uzziah. The name was used by the Puritans and revived slightly in the 19th century. The heroine of James Michener's *Hawaii* is named Jerusha.
Jarusha, Jeruscha, Jerushah

Jessenia A variant spelling of **Yesenia**, a name that's very popular in the Hispanic community.
Jesenia, Jesenya, Yesenia, Yessenia, Yessenya

Jessica Heb. "He sees." Coined by Shakespeare from the Old Testament Iscah or Jesca. His Jessica was the daughter of Shylock in *The Merchant of Venice*. Popular in the U.S. in the 1970s, and one of the top three names in the nation for girls in the late 1990s, well used by every ethnic group. Curiously for a name with this kind of popularity, there are not many variant spellings, but that may be the next step in its development. Actresses Jessica Lange, Jessica Tandy.
Jess, Jessa, Jessaca, Jessaka, Jessalin, Jessalyn, Jesse, Jesseca, Jessey, Jessie, Jessika, Jessy

Jessie Dim. **Jessica.** Also, in Scotland, a diminutive of Janet.
Jess, Jessa, Jesse, Jessey, Jessi, Jessy

Jesusa Sp. Derived from Mary de Jesus, a name for the Virgin Mary.

Jethra Heb. "Plenty, abundance." A feminine form of **Jethro.**
Jeth

Jette Dan. "Black as coal." Currently popular in Denmark; also used in Germany.
Yette

Jewel OF. Word used as first name. Though the vogue for jewel names occurred at the turn of the 20th century (along with the flower-name fashion), Jewel came into use a little later, in the 1930s. Pop singer Jewel.
Jewell, Jewella, Jewelle

Jezebel Heb. "Pure, virginal." An Old Testament name that carries strong connotations that contradict its meaning: it was used as a term for a "painted lady" or a brazen hussy as portrayed by Bette Davis in the film *Jezebel.*

Jessabell, Jetzabel, Jezabel, Jezabella, Jezebelle, Jezibel, Jezibelle, Jezybell

Jezreel Heb. "The Lord sows." An Old Testament place name.

Jesreel

Jill Dim. of **Gillian**, ultimately of **Juliana** (Lat. "Youthful"). Jill was popular before the 17th century, and revived to widespread use after the 1920s. Now quite scarce. Actresses Jill St. John, Jill Eikenberry, Jill Ireland; English novelist Jilly Cooper; fashion designer Jil Sander.

Jil, Jilian, Jilana, Jillan, Jillana, Jillane, Jillayne, Jilleen, Jillene, Jilli, Jillian, Jillianne, Jillie, Jilly, Jillyan, Jyl, Jyll

Jillian Var. Gillian. Dim. **Juliana** (Lat. "Youthful"). In this age of elaboration, now much more popular than blunt, monosyllabic Jill.

Jilian, Jiliana, Jilan, Jillana, Jillane, Jilliana, Jillianne, Jillyan, Jillyanna, Jilliyanne

Jimena Sp. "Heard."

Jinny Dim. **Virginia** or Var. **Jenny**. Mostly 19th-century use in this form.

Jinna, Jinnee, Jinni, Jinnie

Jinx Lat. "Spell."

Jinxx, Jynx

Jo Dim. **Joan, Josephine**, etc. Often used in combination, as in Jo Ann, Betty Jo. The second daughter in Louisa May Alcott's *Little Women* was called Jo, short for Josephine, and was played by Katharine Hepburn and Winona Ryder in successive film versions of the novel. Still, the usage hasn't caught on widely, and is not likely to do so in an era when the top ten list does not include one monosyllabic girls' name.

Joakima (Fem. **Joachim**) Heb. "God will judge."

Joaquina, Joaquine

Joan (Fem. **John**) Heb. "The Lord is gracious." The medieval feminine version of **John**; Jeanne d'Arc's first name, for instance, was translated as Joan, Jeanne's popular English equivalent. It was neglected for Jane by the 17th century. A brief intense revival occurred early in the 20th century for a score of years, but Joan is again widely neglected. Actresses Joan Crawford, Joan Collins; comedienne Joan Rivers; musicians Joan Baez, Joni Mitchell; marathon runner Joan Benoit.

Joane, Joanie, Joannie, Jone, Jonee, Joni

Joanna Var. **Jane** or **Joan**. Its 19th-century use increased with the revival of Joan, and continued to grow until around 1950 in the U.S. Joanne, the French form, was hugely popular in Britain in the 1970s. Today Joanna is much more heavily used than Joanne in America, just as Anna is much more popular than Anne. Actresses Joanna Lumley, Joanne Woodward.

Jo, Joana, Joann, Jo Ann, Joanne, Jo Anne, Joeann, Johanna, Johannah

Jobeth Com. form **Jo** and **Beth**. Unusual, found mostly in the 1950s. Actress JoBeth Williams.

Joby (Fem. **Job**) Heb. "Persecuted." Unusual version of an Old Testament name widely used by the Puritans and their descendants well into the 19th century.

Jobey, Jobi, Jobie, Jobina, Jobyna

Jocasta It. "Lighthearted." In spite of its pleasant meaning, the name is little used because of its history. In Greek myth, Jocasta is the mother of Oedipus; he later unwittingly marries her, unleashing a series of gruesome tragedies. Interior design writer Jocasta Innes.

Jokasta

Jocelyn Derivation unclear; possibly Old German, possibly Lat. "cheerful." It was a man's name in the Middle Ages, revived as a girl's name in the early 20th century.

Jocelin, Joceline, Jocelinda, Jocelyne, Josaline, Joscelin, Josceline, Joscelyn, Joselina, Joseline, Joselyn, Joselyne, Josiline, Josline, Jossline, Josselyn, Josslyn, Joycelin

Jocosa Lat. "Joking."

Giocosa

Jody Dim. **Joan, Judith**. Used mostly since the 1950s in the U.S.; in the Canadian top ten in the 1970s. Actress Jodie Foster.

Jodee, Jodey, Jodi, Jodie

Joelle (Fem. **Joel**) Heb. "Jehovah is the Lord." Probably popularized by a vogue for combined forms beginning with "Jo," like Joanne and Jolene. Reached its peak in the 1960s. Actress Joely Richardson.

Joela, Joelin, Joell, Joella, Joelliane, Joellin, Joelly, Joely, Joelynn, Joetta, Jowella, Jowelle

Johanna (Fem. **Johann**) Ger. Var. **John** (Heb. "The Lord is gracious"). A European-sounding choice among the numerous feminizations of John.

Giovanna, Joanna, JoeHannah, Johana, Johannah, Jovanna

Johnna (Fem. **John**) Heb. "The Lord is gracious." May also be considered a contraction of Johanna.

Giana, Gianna, Giovanna, Jana, Janna, Johna, Johnetta, Johnette, Jovanna

Joie Fr. Var. **Joy**. Actress Joie Lee.

Joi

Jolan Gk. "Violet flower." This is a Middle-European form of Iolanthe. The most popular form in the U.S. is Yolanda.

Jola, Jolaine, Jolande, Jolanne, Jolanta, Jolantha, Yolanne

Jolene Comb. form "**Jo**" and "**lene**." In the 1940s names ending in "lene" (Darlene, Marlene, etc.) began to be fashionable, and a form beginning with "Jo" was a natural result. These names are now little used.

Joeline, Joeleen, Jolean, Joleen, Jolena, Jolina, Joline, Jolyn, Jolyna, Jolyne, Jolynn

Jolie Fr. "Pretty." Used mainly since the 1960s.

Joely, Jolee, Joley, Joli, Joliet, Jolietta, Joliette, Joly

Jonquil Flower name. Unlike most flower names, this one did not appear until the 1940s, and its two decades of popularity were mostly limited to Britain. The jonquil is a variety of narcissus closely related to a daffodil.

Jordan Heb. "Descend." Named after the River Jordan. First used in the Middle Ages by Crusaders returning from the Holy Land. Revived slightly in the 19th century, mostly for boys. Substantially popular now for girls, which lessens the likelihood of its being a boy's name again.

Jardena, Johrdan, Jordain, Jordana, Jordane, Jordanka, Jordanna, Jorden, Jordena, Jordenn, Jordie, Jordin, Jordyn, Jorey, Jori, Jorie, Jorrdan, Jorry, Jourdan

Josephine (Fem. **Joseph**) Heb. "Jehovah increases." Napoleon's famous Empress Josephine's real name was Marie Josephe (for the parents of Jesus), but Josephine was used as a diminutive. It did not become fashionable until the mid–19th century, and it has never caught on widely in the U.S. It probably does not help that author Jacqueline Susann's first book, a memoir of life with her dog published in 1963, was entitled *Every Night, Josephine!* For its million readers, Josephine will forever be a black miniature French poodle. Cabaret star Josephine Baker.

Fifi, Fifine, Fina, Finetta, Finette, Guiseppina, Jo, Joette, Joey, Joline, Josana, Josanna, Josanne, Josee, Josefa, Josefena, Josefene, Josefina, Josefine, Josepha, Josephe, Josephene, Josephina, Josephyna, Josephyne, Josetta, Josette, Josey, Josiane, Josianna, Josianne, Josie, Josy, Jozsa

Jovita Lat. "Made glad."

Giovita

Joy Lat. "Joy." Used in the Middle Ages and sparingly by the Puritans, then revived at the turn of the 20th century. Unusual after the height of its popularity in the 1950s.

Gioia, Gioya, Jioia, Jioya, Joi, Joice, Joie, Joya, Joyann, Joye

Joyce Lat. "Joyous." Used in the Middle Ages, but nearly died out until the early years of the 20th century, when it had a spurt of immense popularity, especially in Britain. Advice columnist Dr. Joyce Brothers; writer Joyce Carol Oates.

Joice, Joycelyn, Joyse, Joyous

Juanita Sp. Var. Joan.

Janita, Juana, Juniata, Junita, Juwaneeta, Juwanita, Nita, Wahnita, Wahnna, Wanna, Waneeta, Wanita

Jubilee Heb. "Ram's horn." Term for a fiftieth-year celebration, marked in Old Testament times by the blowing of a ram's horn. A great festival was held to mark each fiftieth anniversary of the liberation from Egypt. European monarchs in the 19th century took up the tradition, and Queen Victoria celebrated silver (twenty-fifth), golden (fiftieth), and diamond (sixtieth) jubilees. A nice name to mark great celebration.

Jubalee

Judith Heb. "Jewish." Old Testament name overlooked by the Puritans in their quest for girls' names, but fashionable from the 1920s through the 1950s. In the Apocrypha, Judith is a Jewish heroine who decapitates the Assyrian general Holofernes and shows his head to the Hebrew army, inciting them to victory. Actress Dame Judith Anderson; movie critic Judith Crist; chess champion Judit Polgar.

Giuditta, Jodie, Jody, Judee, Judi, Judie, Judit, Judita, Judite, Juditha, Judithe, Judy, Judye, Jutta

Judy Dim. **Judith**. Dates back to the 18th century, but its true popularity follows that of Judith in the 20th century. **Jody** is another frequently used diminutive. Actresses Judy Garland, Judy Holliday; singer Judy Collins.

Judee, Judey, Judi, Judie, Judye

Julia (Fem. **Julius**) Lat. Clan name: "Youthful." Along with Juliana, used among the early Christians, but it was rare in the Middle Ages. Since the 1700s it has gone mildly in and out of fashion without ever being a tremendous favorite. Julie, in this century, has been much more popular, but the European form with the "-a" ending is just as commonly used by now, and will probably surpass Julie soon. Chef Julia Child; opera star Julia Migenes; actresses Julia Ormond, Julia Roberts; pop singer Julee Cruise.

Giulia, Giuliana, Giulianna, Giulianne, Giulietta, Jiulia, Joleta, Joletta, Jolette, Julee, Juley, Juli, Juliaeta, Juliaetta, Juliana, Juliane, Juliann, Julianne, Julie, Julienne, Juliet, Julieta, Julietta, Juliette, Julina, Juline, Julinka, Juliska, Julissa, Julita, Julitta, Julyana, Julyanna, Julyet, Julyetta, Julyette, Julyne, Yulia, Yuliya

Juliana (Fem. **Julian**) Lat. Clan name: "Youthful." Appeared in the early Christian era, and medieval use contracted it to Gillian (and from there to Jill). Although a royal name in the Netherlands, it is unusual now, possibly seeming too stately. Contracted forms like Liana may eclipse it. Actress Julianne Phillips.

Giuliane, Giulianne, Juliane, Julianna, Julianne, Julieanna, Julieanne, Juline, Julinda, Julyana, Julyane, Julyanna, Julyanne

Julie Fr. Dim. **Julia**. Lat. Clan name: "Youthful." Imported from France in the 1920s and fashionable very quickly, especially in the 1970s. It had earlier taken root on the Continent, as evidenced by Strindberg's 1888 trag-

edy *Miss Julie*. Actresses Julie Andrews, Julie Harris, Julie Walters, Julie Kavner; cookbook author Julee Rosso.
Jooley, Joolie, Julee, Juley, Julienne, Jullee, Jullie, July, Jully

Juliet Lat. Clan name: "Youthful." Dim. **Julia**. Can scarcely be used without reference to Shakespeare's famous tragic heroine. Girls named Juliet can expect a certain amount of teasing about Romeo. Dancer Juliet Prowse.
Giulietta, Juliaetta, Julieta, Juliett, Julietta, Juliette, Julyet, Julette

Jumana Arab. "A silver pearl."
Jumanah, Jumanna

Juniata Place name: a county in central Pennsylvania.

June Month used as name, dating from the 20th century but most popular in the 1950s. It is more often used than April or May, the other most common month names. Actress June Allyson.
Junella, Junelle, Junette, Junia, Juniata, Junieta, Junina, Junine, Junya, Jyune

Juno Lat. "Queen of heaven." Juno was the Roman equivalent of Hera in classical mythology: Jupiter's wife, and the gods' queen. Not widely used in any era; in modern times the adjective "Junoesque" has come to be used for tall women with curvy figures, possibly because of the way Juno is often portrayed in Old Master paintings.
Juneau, Juneaux, Junot

Justice Virtue name for the 21st century. The cardinal virtues are prudence, fortitude, temperance, and justice, as opposed to the theological virtues of faith, hope, and charity. The last three have been more often used as names.
Justyce, Justiss

Justine Lat. "Fair, righteous." Justina was the original form, but the French version took over in the 1960s, probably aided by Lawrence Durrell's famous novel *Justine*. Actress Justine Bateman.
Giustina, Justa, Justeen, Justene, Justie, Justina, Justinn, Justy, Justyna, Justyne, Tina

Kadenza Lat. "With rhythm." Modern variant of **Cadence**.

    Cadenza, Kadena, Kadence

Kaitlin Var. **Caitlin**, Irish form of **Catherine** (Gk. "Pure"). A name as popular as Catherine has produced endless variations over the years, and recently Caitlin and its variants have become just as popular as the more familiar form, which is still in the top fifteen or twenty names used in most regions of the U.S.

    Caitlin, Caitlyn, Kaitlyn, Katelyn, Katelynn, Katelynne, Kathlin, Kathlinne, Kathlyn

Kala Var. **Kali**.

Kali Sanskrit. "Black one." This is the name of a Hindu goddess in her role as the essence of destruction, which includes a very grisly component (her worshippers, known as "thugs," strangled people to propitiate her).

    Kala, Kalli

Kalila Arab. "Beloved."

    Cailey, Cailie, Caylie, Kailey, Kalie, Kalilah, Kayllie, Kaly, Kaylee, Kylila, Kylilah

Kalliope Gk. myth name. Calliope was the muse of epic poetry. Many of the "C" names that come from the Greek are spelled with a "K" in their original forms.

    Kallyope

Kallista Gk. "Most beautiful."

    Cala, Calesta, Calista, Callie, Cally, Kala, Kalesta, Kalista, Kalli, Kallie, Kally, Kallysta

Kama Sanskrit. "Love" or Heb. "Ripe."

Kamilah Arab. "Perfect."

    Kamila, Kamilla, Kamillah

Kamilla European var. **Camilla**. Some sources trace Camilla to the young girls who assisted at pagan religious ceremonies.

    Camilla, Cammie, Kamella, Kamila, Kamilka, Kamilla, Kamille, Kamyla, Kemilla, Milla, Millie

Kandace Var. **Candace** (Lat. "Glowing white"). Historically the name was the ancient title of the queens of Ethiopia before the 4th century. Not much used before the middle of the 20th century.
Candie, Candy, Dacie, Kandice, Kandiss, Kandy

Kanara Heb. "Little bird, canary."
Kanarit, Kanarra

Kanga Short for kangaroo: sometimes given as a nickname to an Australian far from home.

Kanisha Very popular invented name, probably an adaptation of the fashionable Tanisha.
Kaneesha, Kanicia, Kenisha, Kinicia, Kinisha, Koneesha

Kara Var. **Cara** (Lat. "Dear one"). Principally used from the 1970s onward.
Cara, Carina, Carita, Karina, Karine, Karita, Karrah, Karrie, Kera

Karen Dan. Var. **Katherine** (Gk. "Pure"). Took hold in the 1930s in English-speaking countries, and blossomed to great popularity in the 1950s and 1960s. A mother who was one of four Karens in her kindergarten, however, is unlikely to use the same name for her daughter, so it is unusual today. Writer Karen Blixen (Isaak Dinesen); singer Karen Carpenter; actress Karen Allen.
Caren, Carin, Caron, Caronn, Carren, Carrin, Carron, Carryn, Caryn, Carynn, Carynne, Kari, Karin, Karna, Karon, Karryn, Karyn, Kerran, Kerrin, Kerron, Kerrynn, Keryn, Kerynne, Taran, Taren, Taryn

Karimah Arab. "Giving." Currently popular among Arabic-speaking parents.
Kareema, Kareemah, Kareima, Karima

Karla Var. **Carla** (OG. "Man"). One of the endless names that derive from Charles. Fans of John Le Carré's novels will remember that George Smiley's Russian nemesis used the code name Karla.
Karlah, Karlla, Karrla

Karlotta Ger. Var. **Charlotte** (Fr. from OG. "Man").
Karlota, Karlotte, Lotta, Lottee, Lottey, Lottie

Karma Hindi. "Destiny, spiritual force." A New Age name if ever there was one.

Karolina Slavic. Var. **Caroline** (Lat. "Little and womanly").

**Karaline, Karalyn, Karalynna, Karalynne, Karla, Kar-
leen, Karlen, Karlena, Karlene, Karli, Karlie, Karlina,
Karlinka, Karolina, Karoline, Karolinka, Karolyn, Karolyna, Karolyne, Karolynn, Karolynne, Leena, Lina, Lyna**

Kasmira (Fem. **Casimir**) Old Slavic. "Bringing peace."
Very unusual.

Kasha Var. **Katherine**. Also, coincidentally, the name of a
grain used in Middle European cooking.

Kassandra Var. **Cassandra** (Gk. Possibly Fem. **Alexander**).

Kataniya Heb. "Small."

Kate Dim. **Katherine**. Long-standing independent name,
especially popular in the late 19th century. Well used
without being trendy. Writer Kate Chopin; actresses Kate
Capshaw, Kate Jackson, Kate Nelligan; German artist
Kaethë Kollwitz.

**Cait, Caitie, Cate, Catee, Catey, Catie, Kaethë, Kait,
Kaite, Kaitlin, Katee, Katey, Kathe, Kati, Katie**

Katherine Gk. "Pure." One of the oldest recorded names,
with roots in Greek antiquity. Almost every Western
country has its own form of the name, and phonetic variations are endless. It has been borne by such illustrious
women as Saint Catherine of Alexandria, the early martyr
who was tortured on a spiked wheel; Empress Catherine
the Great of Russia; and three of Henry VIII's six wives.
It is currently very popular in England and France, and is
still in or near the top ten American girls' names. One of
the reasons it is so popular is that parents can name a
child the solid, conservative Katherine, and call her anything from Kathy to Katt. Actresses Catherine Oxenberg,
Catherine Deneuve, Katharine Hepburn; skater Katarina
Witt.

**Cait, Caitlin, Caitlinn, Caitrin, Caitrine, Caitriona, Cai-
trionagh, Caity, Caren, Cari, Carin, Caron, Caronne, Carren, Carri, Carrin, Carron, Caryn, Carynn, Cass, Cassey,
Cassi, Cassie, Cat, Cataleen, Cataleena, Catalin, Catalina, Cataline, Catarina, Catarine, Cate, Cateline, Caterina, Cathaleen, Cathaline, Catharin, Catharina,
Catharine, Catharyna, Catharyne, Cathee, Cathelina,
Catherine, Catherina, Catheryn, Cathie, Cathirin, Cathiryn, Cathleen, Cathline, Cathlyne, Cathrine, Cathrinn,**

Cathryn, Cathrynn, Cathy, Cathye, Cati, Catie, Catina, Catlaina, Catreen, Catreina, Catrin, Catrina, Catrine, Catriona, Catrionagh, Catryna, Caty, Cay, Caye, Ekaterina, Kaatje, Kait, Kaitee, Kaitie, Kaitlin, Kaitlinn, Kaitrin, Kaitrine, Kaitrinn, Kaitrinna, Kaitriona, Kaity, Karen, Karena, Kari, Karin, Karon, Karri, Karrin, Karyn, Karynn, Kasia, Kasienka, Kasja, Kaska, Kasya, Kass, Kassi, Kassia, Kassie, Kas, Kat, Kata, Kataleen, Katalin, Katalina, Katarina, Katchen, Kate, Katee, Katell, Katelle, Katenka, Katerina, Katey, Katha, Katharine, Katharyn, Kathee, Kathelina, Katheline, Katherin, Katherina, Katheryn, Katheryne, Kathi, Kathie, Kathileen, Kathirin, Kathiryn, Kathirynn, Kathleen, Kathlene, Kathleyn, Kathline, Kathlyne, Kathrene, Kathrine, Kathrinna, Kathryn, Kathryne, Kathy, Kathyrine, Kati, Katia, Katie, Katica, Katina, Katinka, Katka, Katla, Katlaina, Katleen, Katline, Katoushka, Katouska, Katrena, Katrien, Katrina, Katrine, Katriona, Katrionagh, Katryna, Katushka, Katuska, Katy, Katya, Kay, Kaye, Kit, Kittey, Kitti, Kittie, Kitty, Rina, Trina, Trinchen, Trine, Trinette, Yekaterin, Yekaterina

Kathleen Ir. Var. **Katherine**. Its use outside of Ireland began in the 1840s, and may have been influenced by the great wave of Irish emigration sparked by the potato famines of those years. U.S. popularity peaked in the 1950s. Actress Kathleen Turner.

Cathaleen, Cathaline, Cathleen, Kaitlin, Kaitlinn, Katha, Kathaleen, Kathaleya, Kathaleyna, Kathaline, Kathelina, Katheline, Kathleyn, Kathlin, Kathline, Kathlyn, Kathlyne, Kathyline, Katleen, Katlin, Katline, Katlyne

Kathy Diminutive, usually of **Katherine**. Rarely used as a given name by itself. TV host Kathie Lee Gifford; actress Kathy Najimy; fitness expert Kathy Smith.

Cathie, Cathy, Kathee, Kathey, Kathie

Katrina Var. **Katherine**. Appealing for its European sound.
Caitrionagh, Catreena, Catreina, Catrina, Catriona, Catrionagh, Kaitrina, Kaitrona, Katreena, Katreina, Katriona, Katrionagh, Katryna, Ketreina, Ketrina, Ketryna, Kotrijna, Kotryna

Kay Dim. **Katherine**. First appeared at the turn of the 20th century, but widespread in the middle of the century. Ac-

tress Kaye Ballard; author Kay Thompson; journal.... ....
Marton.

Caye, Kai, Kaye

Kayla Modern variant of **Katherine** (Gk. "Pure") or Dim.
Michaela (Heb. "Who is like the Lord?"). Has seen a
huge spurt of usage in recent years, vaulting up to the top
ten girls' names in the U.S. in 1991. It is now losing a
bit of steam, but was still the tenth most popular girl's
name in Florida in 1995.

Cayla, Caylie, Kaela, Kaila, Kaylyn

Kayley Could be considered a combination of perennials Kay
and Lee, but is more likely a variant of fashionable Kayla,
with the also popular "-ley" ending. Some sources even
give a Gaelic derivation and meaning: "Slender." Spelling
is up to the parents, since there is no traditional form.

**Caleigh, Cayleigh, Cayley, Kaeleigh, Kailee, Kaileigh,
Kailey, Kaili, Kaleigh, Kaley, Kaylea, Kaylee, Kaylie,
Kaylleigh, Kaylley**

Kaylin Variant of **Caitlin** or of **Kayla/Kayley**. Often names
from different traditions may resemble each other very
closely.

**Kailyn, Kaylan, Kaylanne, Kaylinn, Kaylyn, Kaylynn, Kay-
lynne**

Keely Ir. Var. **Kelly** ("Battle maid"). Not yet in the Kayla/
Kayley league, but has all the qualifications.

**Kealey, Kealy, Keeley, Keeli, Keelia, Keelie, Keighley,
Keighly, Keili, Keilie, Keyley, Keylie, Keylley, Keyllie**

Kefira Fem. **Kefir** (Heb. "Young lion").

Kefeera, Kefeira, Kefirah, Kefirra

Keila Heb. "Citadel." Old Testament place name; a town
in the kingdom of Judah.

Keilah

Keisha Modern name, possibly formed as a short version
of Lakeisha, which, in turn, may be a variant of Aisha
(Arab. "Woman"). Very popular with African-American
families.

Keasha, Keesha, Keeshah, Keicia, Keishah, Keshia, Kicia

Keitha Fem. **Keith** (Scot. Gael. "Forest").

Keithana

Kelby OE. Place name: "Farmhouse near the stream."

Kelbea, Kelbeigh, Kelbey, Kellbie

Kelda ONorse. ''Spring, fountain.''
Kellda

Kelila Heb. ''Crowned.''
Kayla, Kayle, Kaylee, Kelula, Kelulah, Kelulla, Kyla, Kyle

Kelly Ir. Gael. ''Battle maid.'' Originally a very common Irish last name, and very popular as a girl's first name from about the 1950s, peaking in the 1970s in America. Actress Kelly McGillis.
Kellee, Kelley, Kelli, Kellie, Kellina

Kelsey OE. Place name, incorporating a word particle that means ''island.'' Mostly recent usage, for boys as well as girls. As formerly masculine names like Ashley, Taylor, and Schuyler become first fashionable and then trendy, Kelsey seems likely to follow.
Kelcey, Kelcie, Kelcy, Kellsey, Kellsie, Kelsea, Kelsee, Kelseigh, Kelsi, Kelsy

Kempley Middle English: ''Fighter's meadow.''
Kemplea, Kempleigh, Kemplie, Kemply

Kendall OE. Place name: ''The valley of the Kent,'' a river in western England. Some sources also suggest ''The bright river valley.'' In either case, a transferred surname used as a first name since the 19th century, and occasionally adapted for girls.
Kendal, Kendell

Kendra Origin unclear: some sources suggest OE. ''Knowing,'' while one proposes a modern combination of Ken and Sandra. Modern, in any case.
Kendrah, Kenna, Kindra, Kinna

Kenna Fem. Kenneth (Ir. Gael. ''Handsome'' or ''Sprung from fire'').
Kenina, Kennina, Kennette

Kenya Place name used as first name, an increasingly popular trend in the late 1990s. Since Kenya is a country in eastern Africa this is an especially logical choice for an African-American family.
Kenia, Kennya

Kerensa Cornish. ''Love.'' Unusual name that has spread a bit from Cornwall since the 1970s, but still of limited popularity.
Karensa, Karenza, Kerenza

Kerry Ir. Place name: Kerry is a county in southwestern

Ireland. Also, according to some sources, Ir. Gael. "Dark-haired."

Kera, Keree, Keri, Kerrey, Kerri, Kerria, Kerridana, Kerrie

Ketura Heb. "Incense." Old Testament name: Keturah was Abraham's second wife. Revived by the Puritans and used with some steadiness through the 19th century.

Katura, Keturah

Kevyn (Fem. Kevin) Ir. Gael. "Handsome."

Kevina, Kevinne, Kevynn, Kevynne

Kezia Heb. "Cassia." Cassia is the generic name for a variety of trees and shrubs, one of which produces cinnamon. One of the three daughters of Job (along with Jemima; though their existence is mentioned in the Old Testament, their names are apocryphal). The name was adopted by the Puritans and brought to the U.S. in the 18th century, when it was popular. Use has declined gradually since then.

Kazia, Kessie, Kessy, Ketzia, Ketziah, Keziah, Kezzie, Kissie, Kizzie, Kizzy

Khadija Arab. "Premature baby." The name of Muhammad's first wife, the mother of his children, and the first convert to Islam. The name is understandably widely used in the Muslim world.

Kadija, Kadiya, Khadiya, Khadyja

Kiana Modern name of unclear origin; one scholarly source links it to Anna, but fashion mavens who lived through the 1970s will link it to the then-fashionable synthetic fiber Qiana.

Kia, Kiah, Kianna, Quiana, Quianna

Kiara Var. **Chiara** (It. "Light"). A modern looking phonetically spelled variation on **Claire**.

Keearra, Kiarra

Kiley More traditional spelling of the popular Kylie.

Kyley

Kim Dim. **Kimberly**. Used as an independent name from the mid–20th century, influenced by the careers of actresses Kim Novak, Kim Basinger.

Kimana, Kimm, Kym, Kymme

Kimberly OE. Place name. The "-ly" suffix indicates a meadow. The *Facts on File Dictionary of First Names* traces the masculine use of the name to the Boer War, when many English soldiers were fighting in the South African town of Kimberley. It was used for girls after 1940 and became a great favorite in the 1960s and 1970s, now declining but still plenty familiar to nursery school teachers. Judge Kimba Wood.

Kim, Kimba, Kimber, Kimberlee, Kimberleigh, Kimberley, Kimberli, Kimberlie, Kimberlyn, Kimblyn, Kimm, Kimmie, Kimmy, Kym, Kymberleigh, Kymberley, Kymmberly, Kymbra, Kymbrely

Kineta Gk. "Active one." From the same root as "kinetic."

Kinetta

Kinneret Heb. "Harp." Also a place name in Israel.

Kinsey OE "King's victory." Last name transferred to first name. The immense popularity of Ashley has generated interest in a host of Old English names like Courtney, Lindsay, and Macy. The desirable quality these names provide seems to be an aristocratic, anglophile aura, softened by the more feminine vowel ending. Kinsey in particular gets a lot of exposure from Sue Grafton's highly successful series of murder mysteries whose heroine is named Kinsey.

Kinnsee, Kinnsey, Kinnsie, Kinsee, Kinsie, Kinzee

Kinsley OE "King's meadow." Although parents may waver between Kinsley and Kinsey as if they were variants of the same name, the derivation is different. This is not likely to matter much in the ninth month of pregnancy.

Kingslea, Kingslee, Kingslie, Kinslea, Kinslee, Kinslie, Kinsly, Kinzlea, Kinzlee, Kinzley, Kinzly

Kira Var. Kyra (Gk. "Lady").

Keera, Kiera, Kierra, Kiria, Kiriah, Kirya, Kirra

Kirsten Scand. Var. **Christine** (Gk. "Christian"). Used generally from 1940, though the Scots had adopted this form long ago (possibly because of their geographical proximity to Scandinavia). Kristen is the most popular form of the name. Actress Kirstie Alley.

Keerstin, Keirstin, Kersten, Kerstin, Kiersten, Kierstin, Kierstynn, Kirsteen, Kirsti, Kirstie, Kirstin, Kirsty, Kirstynn, Kjerstin, Kristen, Kristin, Kristyn, Krystin

Kismet Arab. "Fate." Often used in connection with affairs

of the heart, so why not for a child?
Kismat

Kitty Dim. **Katherine** (Gk. "Pure"). Used independently before the 16th century and during the 18th and 19th. In the intervening 200 years it was a slang term for a woman of dubious morals. Author Kitty Kelley.
Kit, Kittee, Kittey

Kizzy Var. **Keziah** (Heb. "Cassia"). Adopted enthusiastically by parents after it was publicized in Alex Haley's *Roots* as a traditional African name. Spoilsport scholars, however, point out that Keziah and its variants were common slave names as early as the 18th century.
Kissie, Kizzie

Klara Hung. Var. **Clara** (Lat. "Bright").
Klari, Klarice, Klarika, Klarissa, Klarisza, Klaryssa

Klaudia Pol. Var. **Claudia** (Lat. "Lame").

Klementina Var. **Clementia** (Lat. "Mild, giving mercy").
Clemence, Clementine, Klementijna, Klementine, Klementyna

Klotild Hung. Var. **Clothide** (Ger. "Renowned battle").
Klothild, Klothilda, Klothilde, Klotilda, Klotilde

Konstanze Ger. Var. **Constance** (Lat. "Steadfastness").
Constancia, Constantijna, Constantina, Konstance, Konstantia, Konstantijna, Konstantina, Kosta, Kostatina, Kostya, Tina, Stanze

Kora Var. **Cora** (Gk. "Maiden"). Though some sources trace the name to classical myth, its modern form was probably coined by American writer James Fenimore Cooper in *The Last of the Mohicans* (1826). It grew in popularity through the 19th century, but now its variant forms are more often used. The "K" spelling is a particularly 20th-century twist.
Cora, Corabel, Corabella, Corabelle, Corabellita, Corella, Corena, Coretta, Corey, Cori, Corilla, Corrie, Corry, Coryna, Korabell, Koree, Koreen, Korella, Korena, Korenda, Korette, Korey, Korilla, Korina, Korinna, Korinne, Korissa, Korrina, Korrine, Korynna, Koryssa

Kornelia Var. **Cornelia** (Lat. "Like a horn").
Cornelia, Kornelija, Kornelya

Kristen Com. form **Kirsten** and **Kristina**, var. **Christine** (Gk. "Anointed, Christian"). Looks Scandinavian, but isn't. Popular in the last fifty years, along with similar forms like Kristin and Kristine; this is the most often used spelling. Actress Kristin Scott Thomas.

Khristin, Krissie, Krissy, Krista, Kristan, Kristeen, Kristel, Kristelle, Kristi, Kristijna, Kristin, Kristina, Kristine, Kristyn, Kristyna, Krisztina, Krysia, Krysta, Krystyna

Krystal Var. **Crystal** (Gk. "Ice"). Transferred use of the word, mostly modern, and increasing since the 1950s. The "K" spelling is a recent variation. Some parents may have been influenced by Krystle Carrington, a character on TV's *Dynasty*.

Cristalle, Cristel, Crysta, Khristalle, Khristel, Khrystle, Khrystalle, Kristle, Krystal, Krystaline, Krystalle, Krystalline, Krystle

Kyle Scot. Place name. "Narrow spit of land." Well-traveled parents may have crossed the Kyle of Lochalsh to reach the Isle of Skye. Traditionally used more often for boys than for girls, and quite popular as a boy's name in the 1990s. For girls, the more elaborate forms like Kylie or Kyla are fashionable.

Kyall, Kyel

Kylie (Fem. **Kyle**) Possibly derived from an Irish Gaelic word meaning "graceful." Well used in Australia in the 1970s and a candidate for great popularity in the U.S. Singer Kylie Minogue.

Keyely, Kilea, Kiley, Kylee, Kyley

Kynthia Gk. Var. **Cynthia** (Gk. "From Mount Cynthos").

Kyra Gk. "Lady." A contraction of "Kyria," the Greek title of respect. Ballerina Kyra Nichols; actress Kyra Sedgwick.

Kaira, Keera, Keira, Kira, Kyreena, Kyrene, Kyrha, Kyria, Kyrina, Kyrra

Lacey OF. Place name of obscure meaning, used as a boys' name in the 19th century and increasingly for girls today. The fact that the name resembles the adjective "lacy" gives it a feminine connotation missing in many old place names now adopted as first names. Substantially well used. Country singer Lacy J. Dalton.

Lace, Lacee, Laci, Lacie, Lacy, Laicee, Laicey, Laisey

Ladonna Modern elaboration of Donna (It. "Lady").

LeDonna

Lady OE. "Bread kneader." By extension, someone in charge of a household; by further extension, a woman of high rank.

Ladey, Laidy

Lainey Dim. Elaine (OF. "Bright, shining, light").

Laney

Laila Arab. "Night." See **Leila**. Usually taken to indicate dark hair or a dark complexion. Actress Laila Robbins.

Laela, Lailah, Lailie, Laily, Laleh, Layla, Laylah

Lake Geography name; inland body of water. Single-syllable names are not currently fashionable for girls, so Lake is less likely to become popular than geography names Sierra or Savannah.

Laiken, Laken

Lakeisha Popular modern name made up of elements in vogue in the 1980s, the fashionable "La-" prefix attached to Aisha (Arab. "woman"). There are numerous forms, most of them phonetic variations.

Lakeesha, Lakecia, Laketia, Lakeysha, Lakicia, Lakisha, Lakitia, Lekeesha, Lekeisha, Lekisha

Lakshmi Sanskrit. "Good sign, good omen." Lakshmi is the goddess of abundance, plenty, beauty, prosperity, etc.

Laxmi

Lala Slavonic. "Tulip."

Gk. "Babbler, prattler." Extremely unusual, though it occurs in literature.
Lalia

Lalia Lat. "Speaking well."
Lallia, Lalya

Lalika Hindi. "Lovely woman."

Lalla Poetic name. In 1817 poet Thomas Moore published a series of four verse tales called *Lalla Rookh*. The heroine was the daughter of the Emperor of Delhi. To several generations of readers, the name Lalla spelled Eastern glamor.

Lallie Dim. **Lalage**. More common than its source, though still rare. Journalist Lally Weymouth.
Lalia, Lally

Lana Var. **Helen** (Gk. "Light") or **Alanna** (Gael. "Rock" or "Comely"). The name also resembles the romance languages' term for wool: *laine* or *lana*. Made famous by actress Lana Turner (whose real name was Judy), but not widely used.
Lanae, Lanette, Lanna, Lanny

Lanai Haw. "Porch." Also the name of one of the Hawaiian islands.
Lenai

Lane Middle English. Place name. More common for boys than for girls, though still unusual for both. This is the kind of name that is likely to be a mother's maiden name transferred to a first name, though parents are increasingly using last names for first names regardless of family precedent.
Laine, Lainey, Laney, Lanie, Layne

Langley OE. Place name: "Long meadow."
Langlea, Langlee, Langleigh

Lani Haw. "Sky."

Lantana Place name: county in Florida. Also the name of a pungent-smelling flower with tiny clusters of orange or purple blossoms.
Lantanna

Lara Unclear origin. Some sources suggest Lat. "Famous"; others trace the name to the Gk. **Larissa**. Today's parents may be reminded of the famous "Lara's Theme" from the 1965 film *Dr. Zhivago*.
Larina, Larra

Laraine Var. **Lorraine** (Fr. "From Lorraine"). Actress Laraine Newman.
Laraene, Larayne, Lareine, Larina, Larine

Lareina Sp. "The queen." Compares to Leroy, Fr. "The king." Uncommon.
Larayna, Larayne, Lareine, Larena, Larrayna, Larreina

Larissa Gk. "Lighthearted." From the same root as Hilary. Unusual, even in times like the 18th century, when more elaborate names were the norm.
Larisa, Laryssa, Lerissa, Lissa, Lorissa, Lyssa

Lark ME. Nature name, used since the 1950s mostly in the U.S. Larks are usually thought of as playful, lighthearted songbirds.

Larkspur Flower name: a kind of delphinium with spur-shaped blue blossoms.

Larsen Scand. "Son of Lars." Lars is in turn the Scandinavian version of Lawrence. Even though this is explicitly a boy's name, it has been used for baby girls as part of the fashion for unisex names.
Larson, Larssen, Larsson

Lassie ME. "Little girl." "Lass" is a Scottish and northern English term for a girl, but the association for most parents is more likely to be a highly intelligent collie as seen on a popular TV series in the 1960s and again in the 1990s.
Lassey

Lata Hindi. "Beautiful vine."

Latanya Modern combined form: the "La-" prefix added to Tanya.
Latania, Latanja, Latonia, Latonya

Latifah Arab. "Gentle, pleasant." Singer Queen Latifah.
Lateefa, Lateefah, Lateifa, Lateiffa, Latifa, Latiffa

Latisha Var. Letitia (Lat. "Happiness").
Laticia, Latitia, Letisha, Letticia, Lettisha

Latona Myth name: in the Roman pantheon, mother of Apollo and Diana. Closely resembles some of the modern names like Latoya and Latonya, but predates them by some two thousand years.

Latoya One of the most famous of the modern "La-" names, probably because of Latoya Jackson's renown. Derivation and meaning are mysterious.
Latoyah, Latoia, Latoyla, Letoya

᥊e Modern combined form: Patricia (Lat. "Noble") with the "La-" prefix.

Latrecia, Latreece, Latreese, Latreshia, Latricia, Leatrice, Letreece, Letrice

Lauda Lat. "Praise." Also a medieval Italian form of dramatic song.

Laudomia It. "Praise to the house."

Laufeia Norse. "Wooded or leafy island." In Norse myth Laufeia is the mother of Loki, the Norse god of destruction and evil.

Laura Lat. "Laurel." In classical times, a crown made from the leaves of the bay laurel was given to heroes or victors. Two famous Lauras are the unknown woman to whom the poet Petrarch addressed his sonnets, and the heroine of the 1940s film *Laura*. The greatest popularity of the name came at the mid– to late 19th century, and it has remained quite a steady favorite ever since. A series of children's books were written by and about Laura Ingalls Wilder of *Little House on the Prairie* fame. Actress Laura Dern; singer Laura Branigan.

Laranca, Larea, Lari, Lauralee, Laure, Laureen, Laurel, Laurella, Lauren, Laurena, Laurence, Laurene, Laurentia, Laurentine, Laurestine, Lauretha, Lauretta, Laurette, Lauri, Lauriane, Laurianne, Laurice, Lauricia, Laurie, Laurina, Laurinda, Laurine, Laurnea, Lavra, Lawra, Lollie, Lolly, Lora, Loree, Loreen, Loren, Lorena, Lorene, Lorenza, Loretta, Lorette, Lorey, Lori, Lorie, Lorinda, Lorine, Lorita, Lorna, Lorretta, Lorrette, Lorri, Lorrie, Lorry, Lory

Laurel Lat. "Laurel tree." Nature name whose popularity has coasted on the coattails of Laura, especially in the 20th century.

Laural, Lauralle, Laurell, Loralle, Lorel, Lorelle

Lauren Var. **Laura** or fem. of **Lawrence** (Lat. "From Laurentium"). Introduced to the public by Lauren Bacall, and immediately popular probably because the streamlined "modern" character of the name struck a chord in the 1940s. It might be fading from sight by now, but has been given extended popularity by the influential designer Ralph Lauren (né Ralph Lifshitz), who has endowed it with fashionable associations and can probably be credited with keeping the name in the top twenty U.S. girls' names. Model Lauren Hutton.

Laren, Larentia, Larentina, Larenzina, Larren, Laryn, Larryn, Larrynn, Larsina, Larsine, Laurence, Laurin, Lauryn, Laurynn, Loren, Lorena, Lorene, Lorenza, Lorin, Loryn, Lorne, Lorren, Lorrin, Lorrynn, Lourenca, Lourence, Lowran, Lowrenn, Lowrynn, L'Wren

Laurence Fr. Fem. **Lawrence** (Lat. "From Laurentium"). Lauren is the most common feminization in English, but some of the European variants are quite commonly used in their own countries.

Larenzina, Larsina, Larsine, Laurentia, Laurentina, Laurentine, Laurentyna, Laurentyne, Lorenza, Lourenca, Lourence

Laveda Lat. "Cleansed."

Lavella, Lavelle, Laveta, Lavetta, Lavette

Laverne Lat. Classical goddess of minor criminals, though the parents who made this name mildly popular in the 20th century probably didn't know that. It sounds enough like the romance languages' word for "green" (*vert, verde*) to have acquired misplaced connotations of green trees or springtime.

Laverine, Lavern, Laverna, Laverrne, Leverne, Loverna, Verne

Lavinia Lat. "Women of Rome." Classical name. Revived in the Renaissance, again used in the 18th century, rather neglected for the last 200 years, but a pretty option for parents seeking a rather feminine name.

Lavena, Lavenia, Lavina, Lavinie, Levenia, Levinia, Livinia, Louvenia, Louvinia, Lovina, Lovinia, Luvena, Luvenia, Luvinia, Vinnie

Lavonne Modern combined form, probably "La-" attached to Yvonne (OF. "Yew wood"). Popular somewhat earlier (1950s–1980s) than most of the other "La-" names.

Lavonda, Lavonna, Lahvonne, Levonne, Levonda

Leah Heb. "Weary." Old Testament name: Leah was the wife of Jacob, married to him by a ruse in the place of her sister Rachel. Follows the typical usage pattern of the Old Testament names: revived by the Puritans, and still used with considerable steadiness. In a 1990 analysis of U.S. naming patterns, Leah ranked number seventy-two for girls. Actress Lea Thompson.

Lea, Lee, Leia, Leigh

Leala OF. "Loyal."
   Lealia, Lealie
Leandra (Fem. **Leander**) Gk. "Lion man." A spurt of use in the 1960s and 1970s has faded.
   Leanda, Leiandra, Leodora, Leoine, Leoline, Leonelle
Leanne Com. form **Lee** and **Ann**.
   Leana, Leeann, Leanna, Lee-Ann, Leianne, Leyanne, Leigh-Anne, Leighanna, Lianne
Leatrice Com. form **Lee** and **Beatrice**.
Leda Gk., possibly Dim. **Letitia** (Lat. "Joy, gladness"). In classical myth Leda was visited by Jupiter in the form of a swan, and produced four children, among them the beautiful Helen of Troy.
   Leida, Leta, Lida
Lee OE. Place name: "Pasture or meadow." One of the few truly unisex names. Usually a name becomes exclusively feminine once it is used for girls like Ashley or Leslie. The tenacious masculine hold on Lee may have been helped by tough-guy actor Lee Marvin. U.S. use seems to have been sparked by admiration for Confederate general Robert E. Lee. Peaked in the 1950s. Actress Lee Remick; Princess Lee Radziwill.
   Lea, Leigh
Lehava Heb. "Flame."
   Lehavit
Leila Arab. "Night." Used by authors in the early 19th century for exotic female characters, and more widely by U.S. parents later in the century. It is in wide use in the Middle East. American pronunciation of the first syllable varies, as the different spellings make clear.
   Layla, Leela, Leelah, Leilah, Leilia, Lela, Lelah, Lelia, Leyla, Lila, Lilah
Leilani Haw. "Flower from heaven."
Leith Scot. Gael. "Broad river." An alternative spelling, Lethe, is the river of forgetfulness in Greek myth.
   Leithe, Lethe
Leland OE. Place name: "Meadow land."
Lelia Lat. Clan name of unknown meaning, used in Britain and the U.S. in the late 19th century.
   Leelia, Lilia

Lemuela (Fem. **Lemuel**) Heb. "Devoted to God." Feminization of a name that was mildly popular in the 19th century.
Lemuelah, Lemuella, Lemuellah

Lena Lat. Diminutive of names like **Helena, Caroline, Marlene**. Independent use dates from the mid–19th century. Actress Lena Olin; singer Lena Horne; director Lina Wertmuller.
Leena, Leina, Lina

Lenis Lat. "Mild, soft, silky." Very rare.
Lene, Leneta, Lenice, Lenita, Lennice, Lenos

Lenna (Fem. **Leonard**) OG. "Lion's strength."
Lenda, Leonarda

Lenore Gk. "Light." Var. **Eleanor**.
Lenor, Lenora, Lenorah, Lenorr, Lenorra, Lenorre, Leonora, Leonore

Leoda OG. "Of the people."
Leota

Leona (Fem. **Leon**) Lat. "Lion." American version; Léonie is more popular in Europe. Use since the 1940s has grown, but the notorious Leona Helmsley has probably put a stop to its popularity. Singer Leontyne Price.
Leeona, Leeowna, Leoine, Leola, Leone, Leonelle, Leonia, Léonie, Leontine, Leontyne, Leowna

Leonarda (Fem. **Leonard**) OG. "Lion's strength."
Lenarda, Lenda, Lennarda, Leonarde

Léonie (Fem. **Leon**) Lat. "Lion." The French form of the name, more common in Britain than Leona.
Leoline, Leone, Leoni, Leonine, Leontine, Leontyne

Leonora Gk. "Light." Var. **Eleanor**. Name used for the heroine of three major operas (*Fidelio, Il Trovatore*, and *La Favorita*), but like many literary names, uncommon in real life.
Leanor, Leanora, Leanore, Lenora, Lenore, Leonore, Nora, Norah

Leopoldine (Fem. **Leopold**) OG. "Bold people."
Leopolda, Leopoldina

Leora Gk. "Light." Dim. **Eleanor**.
Leeora, Liora

Leslie Scot. Gael. Place name. Some sources suggest "The gray castle." Became a last name, then (in the 18th cen-

tury) a first name used for boys and girls. Boys' use has
been tied to admiration for actor Leslie Howard, and is
more common in Britain. Not much used now despite the
rage for comparable names like Ashley or Kelsey. Actresses Leslie-Ann Down, Lesley Ann Warren.
**Leslea, Leslee, Lesleigh, Lesley, Lesli, Lesly, Lezlee, Le-
zley, Lezlie**

Leta Lat. "Glad, joyful." Classical name mildly revived at
the turn of the 20th century.
Leeta, Lita

Letha Gk. "Forgetfulness." In Greek myth, a river in Hades that causes the dead to forget their lives on earth.
Leitha, Leithia, Lethe, Lethia

Letitia Lat. "Joy, gladness." In medieval England, the form
was Lettice, which survived into the 20th century. (The
name's resemblance to the principal ingredient of salad
cannot have helped its popularity.) Current use, which is
rare, is usually of the Latinized form, Letitia. Etiquette
expert Letitia Baldrige.
**Laetitia, Laetizia, Latashia, Latia, Latisha, Leda, Leta, Le-
tha, Letice, Leticia, Leticja, Letisha, Letizia, Letta, Lettice,
Lettie, Lettitia, Letty, Letycja, Tish, Tisha**

Levana Lat. "To rise." In Roman mythology, the goddess
of newborn babies, whose fathers accepted them as legitimate in a ceremony involving lifting the infant from the
ground.
Levania, Levanna, Levona, Livana, Livanna

Levina Lat. "Lightning bolt."

Levona Heb. "Frankincense."

Lewana Heb. "Shining white one: the moon."
Levana, Levanna, Lewanna, Livana

Lexia Dim. **Alexandra** (Gk. "Defender of mankind").
Lexa, Lexie, Lexina, Lexine, Lexya

Leya Sp. "The law."

Lia It. Dim. **Evangelia** ("Bringer of the gospel"). Used
independently in Italy. Author Lia Matera.
Leeya, Liya

Liana Fr. "To twine around." Liana is the name of a vine
common to tropical rain forests. Can also be a diminutive
of Italianate names like **Ceciliana** or **Silviana**.
Leana, Leiana, Liahna, Liane, Lianna, Lianne

Liane Diminutive of French variants like **Juliane, Lilliane**. Also a spelling variant of **Lee-Ann**.
Leeanne, Leeahnne, Liahne, Lianne

Libby Dim. **Elizabeth** (Heb. "Pledged to God"). Even if they intend to use a nickname, parents are more likely to put the full name down on a birth certificate, so officially the numbers of names like Libby are very small.
Lib, Libbee, Libbey, Libbie, Libet, Liby, Lilibet, Lilibeth

Liberty ME. "Freedom." Unusual, but occurs in "revolutionary" times like the 1970s.

Licia Dim. **Alicia, Felicia**, etc. used as an independent name.
Leecea, Leecia, Lesia, Lisia

Lida Slavic. "Loved by the people."
Leida, Lidah, Lyda

Lidwina Scand. "Friend of the people."
Lidweena, Lidweina

Liese Dim. **Elizabeth** (Heb. "Pledged to God"). Mostly found in Germany.
Liesa, Liesel, Liesl

Lieselotte Com. form **Liese** and **Charlotte** (Fr. "Little feminine").

Ligia Gk. "Musical."
Lygia

Liguria Place name: area of western coastal Italy. Genoa is the principal city.

Lila Arab. "Night." Can be a diminutive of **Delilah** (Heb. "Lovelorn, seductive"). Inching toward trendiness. Philanthropist Lila Acheson Wallace.
Layla, Leila, Lilah, Lyla, Lylah

Lilac Flower name. Not very common.
Lilach

Lilias Scot. Var. **Lillian** (Lat. "Lily").
Lilas, Lillas, Lillias

Lilibet Dim. **Elizabeth** (Heb. "Pledged to God"). The unlikely pet name of Her Majesty Queen Elizabeth II of England.
Lilibeth, Lillibet, Lilybet

Lilith Arab. "Ghost, night demon." One Old Testament translation refers to her as "the night hag." She was supposed to descend on sleepers and suck their blood. In

some legends she was Adam's first wife, who was expelled from Eden because she refused to be subservient to him. Connotations of the name are so fearsome that it is rarely used.
Lillis

Lillian Lat. "Lily." Very common variation of the flower name, flourishing at the turn of the 20th century. Actress Lillian Gish and First Mother Lillian Carter were born during the name's peak of fashion, which faded after the 1930s. Pretty as it is, it carries a rather dated aura. Writer Lillian Hellman; mail order entrepreneur Lillian Vernon.
Lila, Lili, Lilia, Lilian, Liliana, Liliane, Lilias, Lilli, Lillia, Lillianne, Lillie, Lilly, Lillyan, Lillyanne, Lily, Lilyan, Lilyann

Lily Lat. Flower name. Possibly because the lily plays such a large part in Christian iconography, this has been one of the most popular of the flower names and has produced many variants. The "-y" ending, usually thought of as feminine, has probably also boosted its use, though it has not been popular since 1900. Ripe for a revival among parents with a taste for nostalgia. Actresses Lillie Langtry, Lili Taylor, Lily Tomlin.
Lil, Lila, Lilas, Lili, Lilia, Lilian, Liliana, Liliane, Lilias, Lilie, Lilla, Lilley, Lilli, Lillia, Lillianne, Lillie, Lillika, Lillita, Lilly, Liliosa, Lily, Lilyan, Lilyanne

Limor Heb. "Myrrh."
Leemor

Lina Diminutive of names ending with "-line," like **Caroline, Helena, Marlene**. Var. **Lena**. Given as an independent name from the 1850s.
Leena, Leina

Linda Sp. "Pretty." Though the name existed as a particle of other English names (Belinda, Melinda) by the time of its great vogue in the 20th century (late 1930s to 1960s), it was probably interpreted as "pretty." Rather neglected now, probably as a direct result of its commonness back then. President's daughter Lynda Bird Johnson; actresses Linda Evans, Linda Hunt; singer Linda Ronstadt; journalist Linda Ellerbee; fashion designer Lindka Cierach.
Lin, Lindee, Lindey, Lindi, Lindie, Lindira, Lindka, Lindy, Linn, Lynda, Lynde, Lyndy, Lyn, Lynn, Lynne, Lynnda, Lynndie

Linden Tree name: a tall, graceful tree with heart-shaped leaves that grows in temperate climates. Also known in Europe as a lime tree, though unrelated to the tree that produces sour green citrus fruit.

Lindenn, Lindley, Lindon, Lindynn, Lyndon

Lindsay OE. Place name: "Island of linden trees." Originally a surname, used for boys until the middle of this century, but now quite popular as a girl's name. Phonetic variants occur frequently. Actress Lindsay Wagner.

Lind, Lindsea, Lindsee, Lindseigh, Lindsey, Lindsy, Linsay, Linsey, Linsie, Linzi, Linzy, Linzee, Linzy, Lyndsay, Lyndsey, Lyndsie, Lynnsey, Lynndsie, Lynnzey, Lynsey, Lynzey, Lynzi, Lynzy

Linette Welsh. "Idol" or OF. "Linnet" (a small bird). In historical terms, probably a variant of Lynette, which is not, surprisingly enough, a form of Lynn. These names and their variations were most popular from the 1940s into the 1960s.

Lenette, Lanette, Linet, Linnet, Linnetta, Lonette, Lynette, Lynnet, Lynnette

Linnea Scand. "Lime or linden tree" is the meaning given by most sources, but an informal network of people named Linnea trace the name to a mountain flower growing in northern climates that botanist Carl Linnaeus named for himself. A popular series of children's books by Christian Bjork featuring a character named Linnea has given the name greater exposure.

Linea, Linnaea, Lynea, Lynnea

Liora Heb. "I have a light."

Leeor, Leeora, Lior, Liorit

Lirit Heb. "Musical."

Leerit, Liri

Lisa Dim. **Elizabeth** (Heb. "Pledged to God"). Used in numbers only since the 1950s, and reached the U.S. top ten in the 1970s. The name is now undergoing that period of disuse that usually follows serious popularity. Actress Lisa Bonet; talk show host Leeza Gibbons.

Leesa, Leeza, Liesa, Liesebet, Lise, Liseta, Lisetta, Lisette, Liszka

Lissa Dim. **Melissa**. Gk. "Bee." May also be considered a variation of **Lisa**. Unusual.

Lissette, Lyssa

Lissandra Var. **Alexandra** (Gk. "Man's defender").

Liv ONorse. "Defense." Also short for Olivia, or even Lavinia. Use in this country probably derives from the fame of actress Liv Ullman. Actress Liv Tyler.

Livia Dim. **Olivia** (Lat. "Olive"). Though the historical connotations of Olivia should concern peace and harmony, in the modern era it is hard not to think of the little green morsel at the bottom of a martini glass. Joyce fans, on a higher plane, may use the name to pay homage to the character Anna Livia Plurabelle from *Finnegan's Wake*.

Livija, Livvy, Livy, Livya, Lyvia

Liya Heb. "I am the Lord's."

Leeya

Liz Dim. **Elizabeth** (Heb. "Pledged to God"). Too humdrum for today's parents unless used in one of the elaborated forms.

Lizanne, Lizette, Lizz, Lyz, Lyzz

Liza Diminutive of **Elizabeth** and more particularly of **Eliza**. The vogue for Lisa gave Liza some reflected popularity, but the immense fame of entertainer Liza Minnelli must account for a great deal of its use.

Litsea, Litzea, Liz, Lizette, Lizzie, Lyza

Logan Ir. Gael. Place name: "Small hollow." As Logan is more widely used as a boy's name, parents of girls may cast a favorable eye on it.

Logann

Loelia Var. **Leila** (Arab. "Night"). Unusual form used occasionally at the turn of the 20th century.

Loire Place name: river in France. Travelers know this area as being full of beautiful chateaux and producing pleasant white wine.

Loir, Loirane

Lois Var. **Louise** (OG. "Renowned in battle" though some sources suggest Gk. "Better"). Also, surprisingly enough a biblical name. Use peaked early in the 20th century. Superman's consort Lois Lane.

Lola Dim. **Dolores** (Sp. "Sorrows"). The most famous Lola has been the 19th-century courtesan Lola Montez, which has given the name a slightly racy aura. It is fairly well used regardless.

Loela, Lolla

Lolita Dim. **Lola** (Sp. "Sorrows"). Made famou[s]
dimir Nabokov's 1958 novel about a twelv[e]
nymphet and her much older admirer, Humbert Humbert.
So famous were the book and the movies adapted from it
that the name has become a generic term for a sexually
precocious young girl.

Lona Var. **Leona** (Lat. "Lion"). Uncommon. Actress Loni
Anderson.

Lonee, Lonie, Lonna, Lonnie

Lora Var. **Laura** (Lat. "Laurel"). Not, as it might seem, a
modern phonetic variant, but a throwback to the 14th century, when this was the usual spelling of the name.

**Lorabelle, Loree, Lorenna, Lorey, Lori, Loribelle, Lorra,
Lorree, Lorrie, Lory, Lowra**

Lorelei Ger. Place name. Derives from the name of a dangerous rock jutting into the Rhine. Though popularly supposed to be an old myth, the tale of a siren perched on
the rock to lure ships to destruction actually dates from a
novel of 1801. The name, however, carries connotations
of risky allure.

**Laurelei, Laurelie, Loralee, Loralie, Loralyn, Lorilee, Lor-
ilyn, Lura, Lurette, Lurleen, Lurlene, Lurline**

Lorelle Dim. **Laura** or **Laurel** (Lat. "Laurel tree").

Laurelle, Lorrella, Lowrelle

Lorenza (Fem. **Lorenzo**) Lat. "From Laurentium." Very
unusual in English-speaking countries, being primarily an
Italian name.

Laurença, Laurenza

Loretta Dim. **Laura** (Lat. "Laurel"). A name that cropped
up with the 19th-century taste for elaboration and became
famous with actress Loretta Young. Country singer Loretta Lynn; actress Loretta Swit.

**Laretta, Larretta, Lauretta, Laurette, Leretta, Lorretta,
Lowretta**

Lori Dim. **Laura** (Lat. "Laurel"). Unlike Lora, this is a
modern spelling and was very popular in the 1960s. The
rage for the "-i" ending on names has diminished considerably since then, replaced by a fondness for "-ey."

Loree, Lorri

Lorna Scot. Place name converted into a female name for
the 19th-century romantic novel *Lorna Doone*. Used oc-

casionally, but to most North Americans, is probably the name of a cookie. Entertainer Lorna Luft.

Lorrna

Lorraine Fr. "From Lorraine." Lorraine is an area in eastern France, but this is not just your average place name: it was often used for Joan of Arc (who was from Lorraine), and for the style of quiche with bacon and Gruyère cheese. It can also be considered an elaboration of Lora. Was well used from the 1930s, and in the U.S. its vogue peaked in the 1940s. Rare now. Actress Laraine Newman.

Laraine, Larayne, Laurraine, Leraine, Lerayne, Lorain, Loraine, Lori, Lorine, Lorrayne

Lottie Dim. **Charlotte** (Fr. "Little, womanly"). Mostly 19th-century use. Singer Lotte Lenya.

Lotta, Lotte, Lotie, Lotti, Lotty

Lotus Gk. "Lotus flower." The name signifies different plants in several different cultures: The Egyptians consider it a kind of water lily, while to the Greeks it is a shrub. It also has great significance in the Indian religions and in Homeric legend, where eating the lotus causes people to forget their homes and families and long for a life of idleness.

Lou Dim. **Louise.** Used mostly in America, and in combined forms such as Louann, Mary Lou, Louella, etc.

Louanna, Louanne, Louella, Lu, Loulou

Louise (Fem. **Louis**) OG. "Renowned in battle." Actually a French (and more euphonious) version of **Ludwig.** Louisa was the preferred form in the 18th and 19th centuries, eclipsed by Louise at the turn of the century. Currently experiencing a revival in Britain, but rare in the U.S. Author Louisa May Alcott; actresses Louise Brooks, Louise Lasser.

Aloisa, Aloise, Aloysia, Eloisa, Eloise, Heloisa, Heloise, Lois, Loise, Lola, Lolita, Lou, Louisa, Louisetta, Louisette, Louisina, Louisiana, Louisiane, Louisine, Louiza, Lovisa, Lowise, Loyise, Lu, Ludovica, Ludovika, Ludwiga, Luisa, Luise, Lujza, Lujzika, Lula, Lulita, Lulu

Lourdes French place name: the town where, in 1858, a young girl named Bernadette had visions of the Virgin Mary. Lourdes has since become a major pilgrimage site and a fairly common name among Catholics. Since Madonna named her baby Lourdes, the name will have an entirely different level of exposure. Ballerina Lourdes Lopez.

Lourdecita, Lourdetta, Lourdette, Lurdes

Love OE. "Love." Unromantically enough, probably not the name of the emotion but a transferred surname. Singer Courtney Love.

Loveday, Lovey

Luana OG. Com. form **Louise** and **Anne**. One of many possible phonetic versions of the name. Also used in Italy, inspired by a film of the 1930s.

Lewanna, Lou-Ann, Louanna, Louanne, Luane, Luann, Luannah, Luannie, Luwana

Luba Yiddish. "Dear."

Liba, Lubah, Lyuba, Lyubah

Lucerne Lat. "Lamp." Also the name of a city in Switzerland; parents have occasionally named children for the cities where they were born—or, in the modern era of frankness, conceived.

Lucerna

Lucetta Dim. **Lucy** (Lat. "Light"). Mostly 19th century, now very unusual.

Loucetta, Loucette, Lucette

Lucia It. Var. **Lucy** (Lat. "Light"). Uncommon form in English-speaking countries. Ballet patron Lucia Chase.

Lucille Fr. Var. **Lucy** (Lat. "Light"). As Lucilla, used by the Romans and revived in the 19th century. Lucille came into greater use at the turn of the 20th century, and its considerable popularity (roughly 1940–1960) seems to have been inspired by comedienne Lucille Ball. For now, the name has a rather dated air.

Loucille, Luseele, Lusile, Lucila, Lucile, Lucilla, Lucyle

Lucinda Var. **Lucy** (Lat. "Light"). Popular along with the other "-inda" names of the 18th century (Clarinda, Belinda), and boosted by the fondness for Lucille. In spite of an increasing interest in longer girl's names (Amanda, Stephanie), late–20th-century parents have not yet turned to the "-inda" names in significant numbers.

Cindy, Loucinda, Lusinda

Lucita Sp. Dim. **Lucy** (Lat. "Light"). Also an allusion to the Virgin Mary as Santa Maria de Luz.

Lusita, Luzita

Lucretia Lat. Clan name of uncertain meaning, though some sources suggest "Wealth." The famous story of the rape of Lucretia concerns a Roman matron who, having been raped, stabbed herself rather than live with the shame.

Loucrecia, Loucresha, Loucretia, Loucrezia, Lucrece, Lucrecia, Lucreecia, Lucreisha, Lucreesha, Lúcresha, Lucrezia

Lucy Lat. "Light." The vernacular form of Lucia, and more widely used in modern times, peaking in the U.S. at the turn of the century. The 4th-century martyr Saint Lucy, patroness of sight, is often depicted with a pair of eyes in a dish, though her martyrdom did not involve being blinded. The Lucy in Charles Schulz's much-loved *Peanuts* comic strip is the prototypical bossy little girl. For a pretty name with few negative connotations, it is surprisingly little-used.

Lou, Loulou, Lu, Luce, Lucetta, Lucette, Luci, Lucia, Luciana, Lucida, Lucie, Lucienne, Lucile, Lucilia, Lucilla, Lucille, Lucina, Lucinda, Lucine, Lucita, Lucyna, Lucyja, Lucza, Lulu, Lusita, Luz, Luzija

Ludmilla Slavic. "Beloved of the people."

Ludmila, Lyuba, Lyudmila

Luella OE. Com. form **Louise** (OG. "Renowned in battle") and **Ella** (OG. "All"). Can also be said to come from Lucy; it's often not possible to trace a name's roots accurately. Columnist Louella Parsons.

Loella, Lou, Louella, Lu, Luelle, Lula, Lulu

Lulu Dim. **Louise** (OG. "Renowned in battle").

Luminosa Sp. from Lat. "Brilliant, giving off light."

Lumina

Luna Lat. "Moon."

Luneth, Lunetta, Lunette, Lunneta

Lupe Sp. Allusion to the Virgin Mary as she miraculously appeared to a peasant boy in Guadalupe, Mexico.

Lupelina

Lurleen Modern variant of **Lorelei** (Ger. place name).

Lura, Lurette, Lurlene, Lurline

Luz Sp. "Light." Another name for the Virgin Mary: Santa Maria de Luz.

Lycia Gk. "From Lycia." A New Testament place name, in southwest Asia Minor.

Lydia Gk. "From Lydia." Lydia was an area of Asia famous for its two rich kings, Midas and Croesus. The name (biblical in origin) was used heavily in the 18th and 19th centuries, less so in the 20th. Cookbook author Lydie Marshall.

Lidia, Lidie, Lidija, Lyda, Lydie

Lynette Welsh. "Idol." Though it looks like a modern elaboration of Lynn, this is actually a French version of the Welsh Eiluned, and was popularized by the English poet Tennyson. However, its use (middling, since the 1940s) has certainly depended on the appeal of Lynn.

Lanette, Linett, Linette, Lynett, Lynetta

Lynn Dim. **Linda** (Sp. "Pretty"). This is one of those names that, along with its variations, is so popular as to virtually swamp its source. Most used in the 20th century. Actress Lynn Redgrave.

Lin, Linell, Linn, Linnell, Lyn, Lynae, Lyndel, Lyndell, Lynelle, Lynette, Lynna, Lynne, Lynell, Lynnelle, Lynnett, Lynette

Lyris Gk. "Lyre." The lyre is a small stringed intrument that is played by plucking: it is a predecessor of the harp.

Lyra, Lyria

Lysandra Var. **Alexandra** (Gk. "Man's defender").

Lisandra, Lisandrina, Lisandrine, Lissandra, Lissandrina, Lissandrine, Lyssandra

Mab Ir. Gael. "Joy, hilarity." or Welsh. "Baby." In old English, Welsh, and Irish stories, Queen Mab is monarch of the fairies.
Mave, Mavis, Meave

Mabel Dim. **Amabel** (Lat. "Lovable"). Very popular at the turn of the 20th century, but uncommon now, perhaps because it has the air of being a period artifact. Singer Mabel Mercer.
Amabel, Amable, Amaybel, Amaybelle, Amayble, Mab, Mabelle, Mable, Maible, Maybel, Maybelle, Mayble

Macaria Sp. from Gk. "Blessed."
Macarisa, Macarria, Maccaria, Makaria, Makarria

MacKenna Ir. Gael. "Son of the handsome one." Influenced by the popularity of Mackenzie.
Mackendra, McKenna

Mackenzie Ir. Gael. "Son of the wise ruler." A testament to the power of television. This was a last name and occasional male first name but actress Mackenzie Phillips has brought it to prominence at a time when masculine names for girls have been very much in vogue.
Mackenzey, Makensie, Makenzie, McKenzie, M'Kenzie

Macon Place name: a town in France, and later a town in Georgia.

Macy OF. Place name: "Matthew's estate." Obscure as a name for either sex, but a character on soap opera *The Bold and the Beautiful* introduced its use for girls. Its similarity to Lacy, currently slightly fashionable, will probably help promote it.
Macey, Macie, Maicey, Maicy

Madeline Gk. Place name: Magdala was a town on the Sea of Galilee, the home of Saint Mary Magdalen, whom Jesus healed and who was present at his crucifixion. Magdalen was the common form in the Middle Ages, but the "g" was dropped, leaving Madeline as the standard form. The French version, Madeleine, became more popular in the 1930s, but the name, pretty as it is, has never been a standard. Many people may be familiar with this name from Ludwig Bemelmans's books featuring French school girl Madeline in her wide-brimmed hat. Actresses Madeline Kahn, Madeleine Stowe .

Dalanna, Dalenna, Lena, Lina, Lynn, Mada, Madalaina, Madaleine, Madalena, Madalyn, Maddalena, Maddie, Maddy, Madel, Madelaine, Madelayne, Madeleine, Madelena, Madelene, Madelina, Madella, Madelle, Madelon, Madge, Madlen, Madlin, Madlyn, Mady, Madzia, Magda, Magdala, Magdalen, Magdalena, Magdalene, Magdalina, Magdaline, Magdalini, Magdeleine, Magdelina, Magdolna, Maidel, Maighdlin, Mala, Malena, Malina, Marleah, Marleen, Marlen, Marlena, Marlene, Marline, Marlyne, Maud, Maude

Madeira Place name: a group of volcanic islands in the North Atlantic off Morocco. The principal island, also called Madeira, is famous for the fortified wine made there.
Madera, Madira

Madge Dim. Madeline, Margaret (Gk. "Pearl").

Madison OE. "Son of the mighty warrior." Another obscure masculine name that has crossed over into fashionable use for girls, prompted by media exposure. In this case the transfer may have been sparked by the mermaid called "Madison" in Ron Howard's movie *Splash*. But Madison also sounds like the fashionable Addison and the even more popular Madeline, lending it a reassuring tinge of familiarity.
Maddison, Madisen, Madisson

Madonna Lat. "My lady." Used mostly by devout Catholic families, like the parents of rock star Madonna Louise Ciccone.
Madona

Madra Sp. "Mother."

Maeve Ir. Gael. Possibly "Delicate, fragile." Name of a 1st-century queen of Ireland, and used mostly in that country.

Mafalda Sp. Var. Matilda (OG. "Battle-mighty"). Also a royal name in Italy.
Maffalda

Magali Var. **Margaret** (Gk. "Pearl").
Magaley, Magalie, Maggali
Magda Ger. Var. **Madeline** (Gk. "From Magdala") or
Maida (OE. "Maiden").
Maggie Dim. **Margaret** (Gk. "Pearl"). Used as an inde-
pendent name in the late 19th century. Although babies
are more likely to be given the full name these days, Mag-
gie is precisely the kind of nostalgic-sounding nickname
that we'll probably see more of. Dance impresario Maguy
Marin; actress Maggie Smith.
Magali, Maggey, Maggi, Maggy, Magli, Maguy
Magnilda OG. "Strong in warfare."
Magnhilde
Magnolia Lat. Flower name. The tree was named after
17th-century French botanist Pierre Magnol. Because of
the tree's popularity on old Southern plantations (the magnolia is the state flower of Mississippi), the name is red-
olent of Dixie.
Maggie, Maggy, Nola
Mahala Heb. "Tender affection." Old Testament name that
was well used in the 19th century. Singer Mahalia Jackson
is keeping it alive today.
**Mahalah, Mahalath, Mahalia, Mahaliah, Mahalla, Mahe-
lia, Mehalia**
Maia Gk. "Mother." In Greek myth, a nymph who became
mother of Hermes; also the Roman goddess of the springtime, for whom the month of May is named. Writer Maya
Angelou.
**Maaja, Maiah, Maj, Maja, May, Maya, Mayah, Moia, Moja,
Moya, Mya**
Maida OE. "Maiden." Used with some frequency in the
19th century, often in the diminutive form **Maidie**.
**Maddie, Maddy, Mady, Magda, Maidel, Maidie, Mayda,
Maydena, Maydey**
Maisie Dim. **Margaret** (Gk. "Pearl"). Originally a Scottish
variation by way of Margery, it became more widespread
early in the 20th century. Literary parents may be re-
minded of Henry James's novel *What Maisie Knew*.
Maisey, Maisy, Maizie, Mazey, Mazie
Majesta Lat. "Majesty."

Majidah Arab. "Splendid."
Majida
Malcolmina Fem. **Malcolm** (Scot. Gael. "Devotee of Saint Columba"). Rather clumsy feminization of an uncommon name.
Malcolmeena
Malka Heb. "Queen."
Malcah, Malkah, Malke, Malkia, Malkie, Milcah, Milka, Milke
Mallorca Place name: an island off Spain in the Mediterranean. Mallorca is the larger island; nearby Minorca is smaller.
Majorca
Mallory OF. "Unhappy, unlucky." Literally, *malheureux*. Originally a nickname, transferred to a last name and thus to a first name. Used for boys as well, until some television scriptwriter on *Family Ties* named a girl Mallory and it crept into fashionable use for female children.
Mallary, Mallerey, Malloreigh, Mallorey, Mallorie, Malorey, Malorie, Malory
Malva Gk. "Slender, delicate." Also a flower name, for plants commonly known as mallows.
Melva, Melvina
Malvina Literary name invented by a romantic poet of the 18th century: it may come from the Gaelic words for "smooth brow." Sculptor Malvina Hoffman.
Mal, Malva, Malvie, Maveena, Mavina, Mel, Melva, Melvie, Melvina, Melvine
Mamie Dim. **Margaret** (Gk. "Pearl") or **Mary** (Heb. "Bitter"). The most famous fictional character to bear the name, of course, is Patrick Dennis's eccentric *Auntie Mame*, central character of a book, a Broadway musical, and a movie. First Lady Mamie Eisenhower.
Maime, Mame, Mayme
Manda Dim. **Amanda** (Lat. "Much-loved").
Mandee, Mandie, Mandy
Mandisa South African. "Sweet."
Mandoline Name of a stringed instrument in the lute family. The name also sounds like a combination of Amanda and Lynn.
Mandalin, Mandalyn, Mandalynn, Mandelin, Mandellin, Mandellyn, Mandolin, Mandolyn, Mandolynne

Mandy Dim. **Amanda** (Lat. "Much-loved"). Popular in Great Britain a generation ago.

Mandee, Mandie

Mansi Hopi. "Plucked flower."

Manuela (Fem. **Emmanuel**) Sp. from Heb. "The Lord is among us."

Manuelita

Mara Heb. "Bitter." In the Old Testament, Naomi says, "Call me Mara, for the Almighty has dealt very bitterly with me." This is widely considered to be the root of that all-time favorite, Mary.

Mahra, Marah, Maralina, Maraline, Mari, Marra

Maravilla Sp. from Lat. "Miracle, something to marvel at."

Marvel, Marvella, Marvelle, Marivel, Marivella

Marcella (Fem. **Marcellus**) Lat. "Warlike." First cropped up at the turn of the 20th century. Very unusual.

Marcela, Marcele, Marcelle, Marcellina, Marcelline, Marchella, Marchelle, Marcie, Marcile, Marcilee, Marcille, Marcy, Maricel, Marquita, Marsalina, Marsella, Marselle, Marsellonia, Marshella, Marsiella

Marcene (Fem. **Mark**) Lat. "Warlike." An American variant that occurred in the 1940s and 1950s, following on the popularity of Marcia.

Marceen, Marcena, Marcenia, Marceyne, Marcina

Marcia (Fem. **Mark**) Lat. "Warlike." Used in Imperial Rome and not revived until the late 19th century. It gradually became a great favorite in the middle of the 20th century, but was passé by the 1970s. Actress Marsha Mason.

Marcelia, Marcene, Marchita, Marci, Marciane, Marcie, Marcile, Marcille, Marcilyn, Marcilynn, Marcina, Marcita, Marcy, Marquita, Marsha, Marseea, Marsia, Martia

Marcy Dim. **Marcella** (Lat. "warlike"). This is the most common form of Marcella's diminutives.

Marcee, Marcey, Marci, Marcie, Marsee, Marsey

Mare Ir. Var. **Mary** (Heb. "Bitter"). Actress Mare Winningham.

Mair, Maire

Marelda OG. "Renowned battle maid."

Marilda, Marrelda

Margaret Gk. "Pearl." One of the standard female names of the Western world. In the Middle Ages the virgin martyr Saint Margaret (swallowed by a dragon) was hugely popular, keeping the name current. An 11th-century queen of Scotland was also a saint, and the name is especially common in Scotland. It has been neck and neck with Mary from the 17th century until the 1970s, when more novel names have moved to the forefront. Margaret is now less popular than upstart names like Tara, Sierra, and Haley. Britain's Princess Margaret and Prime Minister Margaret Thatcher; actress Margaret Sullavan; anthropologist Margaret Mead; writer Margaret Mitchell.

Greta, Gretal, Gretchen, Gretel, Grethel, Gretta, Grette, Gretl, Madge, Mag, Maggi, Maggie, Maggy, Maiga, Maighread, Mairead, Maisie, Maisy, Malgorzata, Marcheta, Marchieta, Marga, Margalit, Margalo, Margareta, Margarete, Margaretha, Margarethe, Margaretta, Margarette, Margarida, Margarit, Margarita, Margarite, Margaruite, Marge, Marged, Margeret, Margeretta, Margerie, Margerita, Margery, Marget, Margette, Margey, Marghanita, Margharita, Margherita, Marghretta, Margie, Margies, Margisia, Margit, Margize, Margo, Margot, Margred, Margret, Margreth, Margrett, Margrid, Marguarette, Marguarita, Marguerita, Marguerite, Marguita, Margy, Marjery, Marjey, Marji, Marjie, Marjorey, Marjorie, Marjory, Marketa, Marketta, Markie, Markita, Marquetta, Meg, Megan, Meggi, Meggie, Meggy, Meghan, Meta, Metta, Mette, Meyta, Peg, Pegeen, Peggie, Peggy, Rita

Margery Fr. Dim. Margaret. Imported to England in the 12th century and steadily used there until a late–19th-century revival that lasted into the 1930s, usually as Marjorie. Because it is unusual but not outlandish, a good candidate for a 21st century revival. Novelists Margery Allingham, Margery Sharp.

Marchery, Marge, Margeree, Margerey, Margerie, Margey, Margi, Margie, Margy, Marje, Marjerie, Marjery, Marjie, Marjorey, Marjori, Marjorie, Marjory, Marjy

Margo Fr. Dim. Margaret. Another import that never matched the popularity of Margery. Actress Margaux Hemingway changed the spelling of her name to match that of a famous Bordeaux wine, Château Margaux. Ballet star Dame Margot Fonteyn.

Margaux, Margot

Marguerite Fr. Var. **Margaret**. Also botanical, the French name for Daisy, and popular at the same time (late 19th century to mid-20th) as that flower name. French writers Marguerite Duras, Marguerite Yourcenar.

Margarite, Margaruite, Marghanita, Margherita, Margherite, Marguerita, Margurite

Maria Lat. Var. **Mary** (Heb. "Bitter"). Launched in English-speaking countries in the 18th century as a welcome alternative to the all-too-common Mary. Faded after some 200 years, but revived in the middle of the 20th century, particularly after the popularity of *West Side Story*, with its famous ballad "Maria." The explosive popularity of singer Mariah Carey has brough her spelling and pronunciation (with a long "-i") of the name to new prominence. Singer Maria Muldaur; TV journalist Maria Shriver.

Mariah, Marie, Marja, Marya, Mayra, Mayria, Moraiah, Moriah

Marian Fr. com. form **Mary** (Heb. "Bitter") and **Ann** (Heb. "Grace"). Var. **Mary**. Actually an anglicization of Marion. Common in the Middle Ages, and after a period of neglect, revived in the early Victorian era, when medieval history was very popular. Singer Marian Anderson; Robin Hood's love interest Maid Marian.

Mariam, Mariana, Mariane, Marion, Maryann, Maryanne

Marianne Fr. com. form **Marie** (Heb. "Bitter") and **Anne** (Heb. "Grace"). Like Annemarie, combines the names of the Virgin Mary and her mother, thus appealing powerfully to Catholic families. In English-speaking countries Mary Ann is the standard form, though Marianne has had moments of fashion, in the early 19th and mid-20th centuries. Marianne is the name of the official symbol who personifies the spirit of France.

Mariana, Mariane, Mariann, Marianna, Maryann, Maryanna

Maribel Com. form **Mary** (Heb. "bitter") and **Belle** (Fr. "beautiful"). This is a modern name.

Maribelle, Marybelle, Meribel, Meribella, Meribelle

Marie Fr. Var. **Mary**. Also the earliest English spelling of the name, revived in the 19th century, and in the 1970s nearly as popular as Mary. Now much less in vogue. Scientist Marie Curie; singer Marie Osmond.

Maree

Mariel Dutch.var. of **Mary** (Heb. "Bitter"). Actress Mariel Hemingway.

Marella, Marelle, Marial, Marieke, Mariela, Mariele, Mariella, Marielle, Mariet, Marijke, Marilla

Marietta Fr. Dim. **Mary** (Heb. "Bitter") via **Marie**. Current since the mid-19th century. Philanthropist Marietta Tree.

Maretta, Maryetta

Marigold Flower name. The golden yellow flower, whose name is a combination of Mary and gold. It cropped up in the 20th century, a bit later than the 19th-century craze for flower names.

Maragold, Marrigold

Marika Dutch. Var. **Mary**. (Heb. "Bitter").

Marieke, Marijke, Marike, Mariska, Mariske, Maryk, Maryka

Marilyn Dim. **Mary** (Heb. "Bitter"). Possibly also a combination of **Mary** and **Ellen**. In any case, a modern name promoted by show business, not in the person of Marilyn Monroe (whose career in the 1950s paralleled the name's decline), but by an earlier star, Marilyn Miller. As is often the case with modern names, there are numerous phonetic variations. Author Marilyn French; opera star Marilyn Horne.

Maralin, Maralynn, Marelyn, Marilee, Marilin, Marillyn, Marilynne, Marralynn, Marrilin, Marrilyn, Marylin, Marylyn

Marin Geography name: a bucolic county just north of San Francisco, on the shore of the Pacific Ocean.

Marinn, Marrin

Marina Lat. "From the sea." Also possibly, in the distant mists of time, related to the Latin god of war, Mars. The name was brought into the junior branches of the English royal family in the mid-1930s by Marina, Duchess of Kent, born a Princess of Greece.

Mareina, Marena, Marine, Marinell, Marinella, Marinna, Marna, Marne, Marnetta, Marnette, Marni, Marnie

Marion Fr. Dim. **Mary** (Heb. "Bitter"). Though it was turned into Marian when it arrived in Britain in the Middle Ages, this form was revived as well in the 19th century and is now just as common. It is occasionally used for s well, and was in fact the given name of John Wayne.

Marian, Maryon, Maryonn

Mariposa Sp. "Butterfly."

Marriposa

Maris Lat. "Of the sea." Comes from the phrase *stella maris*, or "star of the sea," which refers to the Virgin Mary.

Marisa, Marise, Marissa, Marisse, Marris, Marys, Maryse, Meris

Marisa Var. **Maris, Marissa**. Somewhat eclipsed by Marissa. Actresses Marisa Berenson, Marisa Tomei.

Mareesa, Mareisa, Marysia, Moreisa, Morisa, Morysa

Marisela Com. form **Mary** (Heb. "Bitter") and "-ela" from **Isabella, Graciela**, etc.

Maresella, Maricella, Marisella, Maryzela

Marisol Com. form **Mary** (Heb. "Bitter") and *sol* (Sp. "Sun"). A modern name particularly favored in Puerto Rico.

Marissa Var. **Maris** (Lat. "Of the sea"). The "-issa" ending is growing ever more popular, with names like Melissa and Alyssa quite frequently used.

Maressa, Marisa, Marisse, Marrissa, Merissa, Meryssa, Morissa

Maristela Sp. com. form **Mary** (Heb. "Bitter") and **Stella** (Per. "Star").

Marjolaine Fr. "Marjoram." Unusual botanical name.

Marjorie Var. **Margery**, Dim. **Margaret** (Gk. "Pearl"). Imported to England in the 12th century as Margery, and steadily used there until a late–19th-century revival that lasted into the 1930s. This is currently the most common form, though the name is infrequently given. Immortalized in Herman Wouk's novel *Marjorie Morningstar*.

Marcharie, Marge, Margeree, Margerey, Margerie, Margery, Margey, Margi, Margie, Margy, Marje, Marjerie, Marjery, Marjie, Marjorey, Marjori, Marjory, Marjy

Marla Var. **Marlene**. Appeared in the 1940s, but hard to find since the 1970s. Even the famous Marla Maples Trump doesn't seem to have inspired parents to choose her name for their baby. Actress Marla Gibbs.

Marlah, Marlla

Marlene Com. form **Mary** (Heb. "Bitter") and **Magdalene** (Gk. "From Magdala"). Marlene Dietrich introduced the name in the 1920s, and it was widespread by the 1940s, but is now rare. Actress Marlee Matlin.

Marla, Marlaina, Marlane, Marlayne, Marlea, Marlee, Marleen, Marlen, Marlena, Marley, Marlie, Marlin, Marline, Marlyn, Marlynne, Marna

Marlin Modern name: com. form **Mary** (Heb. "Bitter") and **Lynn** (Sp. "Pretty"). In cases like this, names are chosen for the sound alone rather than for meanings which are insignificant unless particularly unpleasant. The advantage of choosing a modern name is that it does not have the weight of cultural associations, making it a blank slate.

Marlen, Marlenn, Marrlen, Marlinn, Marlyn, Marrlin

Marlo Modern name, possibly a variation of the last name Marlow, or a diminutive of **Marlene**. Briefly popular in the 1970s, perhaps following the TV career of comedienne Marlo Thomas. The "-o" ending, which is becoming faintly popular for boys' names, seems dated for girls, but if the name is spelled with the "w" it suddenly seems more up to the moment.

Marlon, Marlow, Marlowe

Marmara Gk. "Sparkling, shining." The Sea of Marmara is a body of water in Turkey, between the Black Sea and the Mediterranean.

Marmee

Marna Origin disputed. May be a diminutive of **Marina** or of **Marlene**.

Marne, Marney, Marni, Marnia, Marnie, Marnja, Marnya

Marquesa Name of a rank in the Spanish nobility, and of a group of islands in the South Pacific. The name is not actually used in Spain.

Marchesa, Marchessa, Markaisa, Markessa, Marquessa

Marsala Place name: city in Sicily that produces a sweet fortified wine.

Marsalla

Marseilles Place name: city on the Mediterranean coast of France. Marseilles is the second largest city in France, and the oldest one. The French national anthem is also known as "La Marseillaise."

Marsha Var. **Marcia** (Lat. "Warlike"). The more common form in America.

Marsia, Marsita, Martia

Martha Aramaic. "Lady." In the New Testament, Martha is the woman who bustles around resentfully getting dinner ready while her sister Mary listens to Jesus. She is patron saint of the helping professions. The name has been very widely used since the Puritans revived it, though it is less common in the last forty years. Lifestyle maven Martha Stewart has become so famous that she is often known merely as "Martha;" the woman who bustles about getting dinner ready. First Lady Martha Washington; dancer Martha Graham; Martha "Calamity" Jane Burke; author Martha McPhee.

Maarva, Marfa, Mariet, Marit, Mart, Marta, Martella, Martelle, Marth, Marthe, Marthena, Marthine, Marthini, Marti, Martie, Martina, Martita, Martta, Marty, Martynne, Martyne, Marva, Mata, Matti, Mattie, Pat, Pattie

Martina (Fem. **Martin**) Lat. "Warlike." Tennis star Martina Navratilova.

Marta, Marteena, Marteina, Martie, Martine, Marty, Tina, Tine

Marvel OF. "Something to marvel at."

Maravilla, Maraville, Marivel, Marivella, Marivelle, Marva, Marvela, Marvele, Marvella, Marvelle

Mary Heb. Though "bitter, bitterness" is the most commonly accepted meaning, the *Facts on File Dictionary of First Names* disputes this. "Rebellious" is also sometimes suggested. Mary is the Greek version of Miriam. Although until the Middle Ages it was considered too sacred to use, it gradually became the most common female name. The numerous variants, both English and foreign, cropped up as a result of the name's great popularity. In the modern era it is frequently combined with other names (Mary Jo, Mary Lou, Mary Beth). Ironically, the name once thought of as commonplace is now unusual among young children, though this is still the most common form in America, surpassing both Maria and Marie in popularity. Actresses Mary Pickford and Mary Martin; Queens Marie Antoinette and Mary of Scots; artist Mary Cassatt; writer Mary Shelley; political strategist Mary Matalin.

Mair, Marie, Mal, Malia, Mallie, Mame, Mamie, Manette, Manon, Manya, Mara, Marabel, Marabelle, Mare, Maree, Marella, Marelle, Maren, Maretta, Marette, Maria, Mar-

iam, Marian, Mariann, Marianna, Marianne, Marice, Maridel, Marie, Mariel, Mariella, Marielle, Marietta, Mariette, Marilee, Marilin, Marilla, Marilyn, Marin, Marion, Mariquilla, Mariquita, Mariska, Marita, Maritsa, Maritza, Marja, Marje, Marla, Marlo, Marya, Maryann, Maryanne, Marylin, Marysa, Maryse, Marysia, Masha, Maura, Maure, Maureen, Maurene, Maurine, Maurise, Maurita, Maurizia, Mavra, May, Mayme, Maymie, Mayra, Mayria, Meridel, Meriel, Mimi, Minette, Minnie, Minny, Miriam, Mitzi, Moira, Moire, Moll, Mollie, Molly, Morag, Moya, Muire, Murial, Muriel, Murielle, Poll, Polly

Maryweld OE. "Mary of the woods."

Masada Heb. "Foundation." Also place name in the Jordan Valley.

Mason OE. Occupational name: "Stoneworker." Transferred from surname status starting in the mid–19th century. Has not yet been widely adapted as a girl's name.

Maison, Maysen

Massima It. from Lat. "The greatest." From the word root that gives us "maximum" and Maximilian.

Maxima

Matana Heb. "Gift."

Matilda OG. "Battle-mighty." William the Conqueror's wife took the name to Britain in the 11th century, when it was pronounced Maud. It was revived in the 18th century, but faded again in the 19th, and was never a real favorite in the U.S. Even with today's taste for nostalgic-sounding names, Matilda remains neglected, familiar only from the famous Australian song "Waltzing Matilda" and from a novel by Roald Dahl.

Mafalda, Maffalda, Maitilde, Maltilda, Maltilde, Mat, Matelda, Mathilda, Mathilde, Matilde, Matti, Mattie, Matty, Maud, Maude, Maudie, Tilda, Tilde, Tildie, Tildy, Tilli, Tillie, Tilly

Matriona Rus. from Lat. "Married woman, matron."

Matrena, Matresha, Matrina, Matryna, Motreina

Mattea (Fem. Matthew) Heb. "Gift of God."

Mathea, Mathia, Matthea, Matthia, Mattia

Maud Var. Matilda (OG. "Battle-mighty"). Although a common enough name after the Middle Ages, its period of real popularity was from 1840 to 1910, especially in Britain. Now rare. Actress Maude Adams.

Maude, Maudie

Maura Ir. Var. **Mary** (Heb. "Bitter").

Moira, Mora, Morah

Maureen Ir. Var. **Mary** (Heb. "Bitter"). Popular in the baby boom era, but not among baby boomers who are now parents. Actresses Maureen O'Sullivan, Maureen O'Hara.

Maura, Maurene, Maurine, Maurise, Maurita, Maurizia, Mavra, Moira, Mora, Moreen, Morena, Morene, Moria, Morine

Mauve Fr. "Mallow plant." The petals of the mallow are purple, hence the use of this word for a color.

Malva

Mavis Fr. "Thrush." Popular mostly in Britain from the turn of the 20th century into the thirties.

Maxine Lat. "Greatest." A modern name that had its moment from the fifties through the seventies, when it conferred a cherished air of Continental sophistication on a family.

Massima, Max, Maxeen, Maxena, Maxence, Maxene, Maxie, Maxime, Maxina, Maxy

Maxwelle Fem. **Maxwell** (OE. Place name). In this era, parents are more likely to do without the final "feminine" "-e" and just call a little girl Maxwell.

May Several possible sources: a medieval form of Matthew (Mayhew), a nickname form of Mary, or an anglicization of Maia. It was very fashionable in the U.S. in the 1870s, some fifty years before month names (April and June) became current, and was also tacked onto several names in combination, as in Anna Mae, Mary May, etc. This practice has been somewhat more common in the South. Actress Mae West; writer Maya Angelou; poet May Sarton.

Mae, Maia, Maj, Mala, Maya, Mayana, Maye, Mei

Mazarine Fr. Color name: a deep blue. Probably commemorates an influential 17th century cleric Cardinal Mazarin.

Mazine

Mazhira Heb. "Glistening, shining."

Mead OE. Place name: "Meadow." This is more common

as a last name, and is a bit stark to join the cavalcade of popular last names turned first names like Mallory and Lacy.

Meade

Meara Ir. Gael. "Jollity."

Mecca Place name: the holiest city of Islam. All Muslims are urged to make a pilgrimage to Mecca at least once, and because of its status as a destination in the Near East, the term has come to stand for a gathering point. Followers of Islam would not use either Mecca or Medina (below) as names.

Medea Gk. "Ruling." Since the Medea of Greek myth was a witch who left a trail of dead bodies behind her (including those of her two children), the name has gruesome connotations and is rarely used.

Madora, Medeia, Media, Medora, Medorah

Medina Arab. "City." The city of Medina in Saudi Arabia is the site of the tombs of Muhammad and his daughter Fatima.

Mdina

Meg Dim. **Margaret** (Gk. "Pearl"). Rarely given as an independent name. Actresses Meg Tilly, Meg Ryan.

Megan Welsh. Dim. **Margaret** (Gk. "Pearl"). Fairly widespread in the 20th century, and surged into popularity in the early '90s, when it hit the top ten in the U.S. Despite its Gaelic sound and popular opinion, the name has nothing Irish about it. It has been losing popularity recently, replaced in the top ten by more flowery names like Jessica and Samantha.

Maegan, Meagan, Meaghan, Meg, Megen, Meggi, Meggie, Meggy, Meghan, Meghann, Meghanne, Meighan

Mehitabel Heb. "Benefited by God." Old Testament name rarely used, except by writer Don Marquis in his tales of the great friends *archy and mehitabel*, a cockroach and a cat.

Mehetabel, Mehitabelle, Hetty, Hitty

Meira Heb. "Light."

Meiriona Welsh name of uncertain meaning and origin. Its use probably depends on its resemblance to the cluster of names derived from Mary.

Melanie Gk. "Black, dark-skinned." Uncommon until the

publication of *Gone with the Wind*, whose Melanie Wilkes launched it into fashion. Scarlett, though the more memorable character, did not inspire parents in the same way. Actresses Melanie Mayron, Melanie Griffith.

Malaney, Malanie, Mel, Mela, Melaina, Melaine, Melainey, Melaney, Melani, Melania, Melanney, Melannie, Melantha, Melany, Mella, Mellanie, Melli, Mellie, Melloney, Melly, Meloni, Melonie, Melonnie, Melony, Milena

Melantha Gk. "Dark flower."
Mallantha

Melba Name coined in honor of the Australian operatic soprano Nellie Melba (the dessert peach Melba and thin Melba toast was also named after her). She, in turn, took her name from her hometown, Melbourne, having been born Helen Mitchell. Actress Melba Moore.
Malva, Mellba, Melva

Melia Dim. **Amelia** (OG. "Industrious").
Meelia, Melya

Melina Gk. "Honey." Use was mostly 19th century. Actress Melina Mercouri.
Melibella, Melibelle, Malina, Mallina, Meleana, Meleena, Mellina

Melinda Lat. "Honey." Names ending in "-inda" (Belinda, Clarinda) were very fashionable in the 18th century, when this name was coined. It became more widespread in the 19th century, but is still far from common.
Linda, Lindy, Linnie, Lynda, Maillie, Malina, Malinda, Malinde, Mallie, Mally, Malynda, Mandy, Melina, Melinde, Meline, Mellinda, Melynda

Meliora Lat. "Better." Unusual Roman name used by the Puritans, but now rare.

Melisande Fr. Var. **Melissa**.
Lisandra, Malisande, Malissande, Malyssandre, Melesande, Melisandra, Melisandre, Melissande, Melissandre, Mellisande, Melysande, Melyssandre

Melisha Modern name: combination of Melissa and any of the -cia names like Alicia or Felicia. Spelling is up to the parental whim.
Malicia, Malisha, Malitia, Melicia, Melitia, Mellicia, Mellisha

Melissa Gk. "Bee." A name that existed in ancient Greece and occurred steadily through the 19th century, but had no real vogue in English-speaking countries until the 1970s. Now somewhat neglected. Singer Melissa Manchester; actress Melissa Gilbert; dancer Molissa Fenley.

Lissa, Malissa, Mallissa, Mel, Melesa, Melessa, Melicent, Melicia, Melisa, Melisande, Melise, Melisenda, Melisent, Melisha, Melisse, Melita, Melitta, Mellicent, Mellie, Mellisa, Melly, Melosa, Milli, Millicent, Millie, Millisent, Millissent, Milly, Misha, Missie, Missy

Melita Gk. "Honey."

Malita, Malitta, Melida, Melitta, Melyta

Melody Gk. "Song." Though it occurred as early as the 13th century, common usage didn't develop until the 1940s, and didn't endure.

Melodee, Melodey, Melodia, Melodie

Melvina Celt. "Chieftain." A variation of Malvina, itself a literary name coined in the 18th century. Melva is the most common variant, but all forms are rare.

Malvina, Melva, Melvena

Menemsha Place name: town in Martha's Vineyard, a resort island off the coast of Massachusetts.

Menora Heb. "Candlestick." To most U.S. Jews, the menora is the candelabrum with seven branches used at Hannukah, the Festival of Lights. An appropriate name for a baby born during that season.

Menorah

Mercedes Sp. "Mercies." Refers to Santa Maria de las Mercedes, or Our Lady of the Mercies, rather than to the German luxury car, though the car itself was named for a little girl named Mercedes. Mostly Catholic use. Actresses Mercedes McCambridge, Mercedes Ruehl.

Merced, Mercede, Mercedez

Mercia OE. Place name: Refers to the English Kingdom of Mercia, which comprised much of central England in the 6th through 9th centuries. The name has been used mostly in the 20th century, perhaps under the assumption that it was a variant of Mercy.

Mercy ME. "Mercy." One of the names of virtues that were so popular among the Puritans (who, since they were very pious but couldn't use saints' names, were often hard put to find appropriate names for their children).

Mercey, Merci, Mercie, Mersey

Meredith Old Welsh. "Great ruler." Occasionally used for boys, especially in Wales. Elsewhere a girl's name, used with some frequency. Actress Meredith Baxter; newscaster Meredith Vieira.

Meradith, Meredithe, Meredyth, Meridith, Merridie, Merry

Meriel Var. **Muriel** (Ir. Gael. "Sea-bright").

Merial, Merielle, Meriol, Merrill, Meryl

Merle Fr. "Blackbird." Use probably inspired by actress Merle Oberon, whose middle name it was. Little used recently.

Merl, Merla, Merlina, Merline, Merola, Meryl, Myrle, Myrleen, Myrlene, Myrline

Merona Aramaic. "Sheep."

Marona, Merrona

Merrill Var. **Meryl** (Ir. Gael. "Sea-bright"). An anglicized spelling of a name that was popular at the turn of the century. Humorist Merrill Markoe.

Merill, Merrall, Merril, Meryl

Merry OE. "Lighthearted, happy." Also dim. **Meredith, Mercy.** May also be considered a variant of its homonym **Mary**.

Marrilee, Marylea, Marylee, Merree, Merri, Merrie, Merrielle, Merrile, Merrilee, Merrili, Merrily

Mersera Com. form. **Mercedes** and **Sarah** (Heb. "Princess").

Meryl Var. **Muriel** via **Meriel**. Strictly a 20th-century name, which in the U.S. is strongly associated with actress Meryl Streep (who was actually christened Mary Louise).

Meral, Merel, Merrall, Merrell, Merril, Merrill, Merryl, Meryle, Meryll

Mesa Geographic name: flat-topped hill found in the southwestern United States. The word *mesa* means table in Spanish. The popularity of Savanna and Sierra as names, and the legendary beauty of American's landscape, have opened the door to the use of geographic features as proper names.

Maisa, Maysa

Messina Lat. "Middle." Also a place name: Messina is a town in Sicily.

Massina, Mussina

Meta Ger. Dim. **Margaret** (Gk. "Pearl"). Use is mostly German.

Mia It. "Mine." Also a Scandinavian variant of Mary. Probably owes much of its use to the career of actress Mia Farrow.

Mea, Meya

Mica Heb. var. **Michael**.

Meeca, Meica, Mika, Myka, Mykah

Michaela (Fem. **Michael**) Heb. "Who is like the Lord?" The most common feminine form of Michael is the French Michelle, but Michaela is gaining ground. It is an example of a name that may seem clumsy to one generation but intriguing to another. Probably the late '90s affinity for three-syllable names adds to its appeal. Phonetic variants are legion. Actress Michael Learned.

Macaela, MacKayla, Makayla, Makyla, Mechaela, Meeskaela, Mekea, Micaela, Michal, Michael, Michaelina, Michaeline, Michaila, Michalin, Michele, Michelina, Micheline, Michelle, Mickee, Mickie, Miguela, Miguelina, Miguelita, Mahalya, Mihaila, Mihalia, Mihaliya, Mikaela, Mikhaila, Mikhayla, Mishaela, Mishaila, Miskaela

Michelle (Fem. **Michael**) Fr. Variant. Heb. "Who is like the Lord?" Spelled with one or two "l"'s, fashionable right from its 1940s appearance in English-speaking countries. The Beatles' famous song "Michelle" gave the name even more of a boost, putting it on some top-ten lists in the 1970s. Now past its prime but still well used. Actress Michelle Pfeiffer.

Chelle, Machelle, Mashelle, M'chelle, Mechelle, Meechelle, Meshella, Mia, Micaela, Michaela, Michaelina, Michaeline, Michaella, Michal, Michele, Michelina, Micheline, Michell, Micki, Mickie, Midge, Miguela, Miguelita, Mikaela, Miquela, Misha, Mishaelle, Mishelle, M'shell, Mychelle, Myshell, Myshella

Michiko Jap. "The righteous way." The name of the first commoner ever to become empress of Japan.

Michee, Michi

Migdalia Possibly variant of **Madeline** (Gk. "From Magdala").

Magdala, Migdalla

Mignon Fr. "Cute." First used as a name by the German poet Goethe, and has spread from literary to real-life use, but not with great frequency. Opera singer Mignon Dunne.
Mignonette, Mignonne, Mingnon, Minyonne, Minyonette

Milada Czech. "My love."

Milagros Sp. "Miracles." Another name actually referring to the Virgin Mary as Santa Maria de los Milagros.
Mila, Milagritos, Miligrosa

Mildred OE. "Gentle strength." An Anglo-Saxon name that was revived in the 17th century, but its real popularity came in the U.S. from 1900 to 1930. By the time of the 1945 film *Mildred Pierce*, it was already slightly dated.
Mildrid, Millie, Milly

Milena Czech. "Love, warmth, grace." Popular in the Czech Republic: also used elsewhere in Europe perhaps because it can be considered a combination of **Milagros** (Sp. "Miracles") and **Elena** (Gk. "Light"). Costume designer Milena Canonero.
Milada, Milana, Miladena, Milanka, Mlada, Mladena

Milka Heb. "Queen, counselor."
Malka, Malke, Malkia, Malkiela, Malkit, Malkiya

Millicent OG. "Highborn power." Norman name that has been used mostly in Britain, at its most fashionable around 1900, but never a standard. U.S. Congresswoman Millicent Fenwick.
Lissa, Mel, Melicent, Melisande, Melisenda, Mellicent, Mellie, Mellisent, Melly, Milicent, Milissent, Millie, Millisent, Milly, Milzie, Missie

Mimi Dim. **Mary, Miriam**, etc. First used by parents after the appearance of Puccini's famous opera *La Bohème*, whose tragic heroine is named Mimi. Actress Mimi Rogers.
Meemee, Mim

Min Dim. **Araminta, Wilhelmina, Mignon**. Magazine editor Min Hogg.
Mina

Mindy Dim. **Melinda** (Lat. "Honey").
Mindee, Mindie

Minerva The name of the Roman goddess of wisdom. Those great revivalists the Victorians brought it back for their daughters, but by the Jazz Age it was obsolete.
Min, Minette, Minnie, Myna

Minna Dim. **Wilhelmina** (OG. "Will-helmet"). Most common at the turn of the 19th-20th century.
Min, Mina, Minetta, Minette, Minne, Minnie, Minny

Minnie Dim. **Mary, Wilhelmina**. Enjoyed a great vogue as an independent name around the 1870s for no very clear reason. Most parents now will associate it with Mickey Mouse's girlfriend. Actress Minnie Driver.
Minnee

Minorca Place name: island off Spain in the Mediterranean. Mallorca is the larger, Minorca the smaller in a trio known as the Balearic Islands.
Mini, Menorca

Minta Dim. **Araminta**. An 18th-century literary name.
Minty

Minuit Fr. "Midnight." Also the last name of the Dutch explorer who purchased Manhattan Island from the Canarsee Indians in the 17th century.

Mira Lat. "Admirable." Dim. **Miranda** or var. **Myra**, although it is usually pronounced with a short "i." In Spanish *mira* spelled this way means "Look!" The name was most used in the 19th century. Fashion designer Myrène de Premonville.
Mireille, Mirella, Mirelle, Mireya, Mirielle, Mirilla, Mirra, Myra, Myrella, Myrène, Myrilla

Mirabel Lat. "Wonderful." In this case the "-bel" ending does not mean "beautiful," though the variations often spell it "-belle." In fact, it was at one period a man's name. Very rare.
Meribel, Meribelle, Mira, Mirabella, Mirabelle

Miranda Lat. "Admirable." Another name contributed to us by Shakespeare, this time directly from the Latin: He used it for the heroine of *The Tempest*. Use has been steady until the early '90s, when it began increasing dramatically. Actress Miranda Richardson.
Maranda, Meranda, Mira, Miran, Mirandah, Mireille, Mirella, Mirra, Mirranda, Myra, Myranda, Myrella, Myrilla, Myrrilla, Randa, Randi, Randie, Randy

Mireio Provençal var. **Miriam** (Heb. "Bitter"). More frequently seen in the form Mireille. Singer Mireille Mathieu.
Mireilla, Mireille, Mireya

Sp. from Lat. "Admired."

Miraya, Mirella

Miriam Heb. Possibly "Bitter" or "Rebellious." This is the source of Mary, which is its Latin form, and its translation is not quite clear, though "bitter" is very widely accepted. Overlooked by the Puritan fervor for Old Testament names, but revived in the 18th century and quite common for some 250 years, peaking around 1900 in the U.S. Now unusual. Singer Miriam Makeba.

Mariam, Maryam, Meriam, Meryam, Mimi, Mirham, Mirjam, Mirjana, Mirriam, Miryam, Mitzi, Mitzie, Miyana, Miyanna

Mirta Sp. from Gk. "Crown of thorns."

Meerta, Meertha, Mirtha, Mitra

Missy Dim. **Melissa** (Gk. "Bee") or **Millicent** (OG. "Highborn power").

Missie

Misty OE. "Mist." Briefly popular in the U.S. in the middle of the 20th century.

Mysti

Mitzi Ger. Var. **Mary** (Heb. "Bitter"). Actress Mitzi Gaynor.

Mitzee, Mitzie

Modesty Lat. "Modesty." As Modesta, used by the Romans, but very rare ever since, even during the Puritan craze for virtue names.

Modesta, Modestia, Modestina, Modestine

Moira Ir. Var. **Mary** (Heb. "Bitter"). Found mostly in Scotland. Dancer Moira Shearer.

Moire, Moyra

Molly Dim. **Mary** (Heb. "Bitter"). Not Irish, in spite of the famous song "Cockles and Mussels" about Dublin's "sweet Molly Malone." Since a "moll" has meant, at various times, a prostitute or a gangster's girlfriend, the name has had long periods of disuse, but now that these slang terms are obsolete, only the pleasantly nostalgic aura remains, and the name has found its way into the top 100 in the U.S. Actress Molly Ringwald; author Mollie Hardwick.

Moll, Mollee, Molley, Mollie

Mona Ir. Gael. "Aristocratic." Spread from Ireland in the mid–19th century. Never widespread, but common enough not to be outlandish.

Moina, Monah, Monna, Moyna

Monet Adaptation of the last name of Impressionist painter Claude Monet. Also a brand of costume jewelry.

Monay, Moné

Monica Possibly Lat. "Adviser" or "Nun." Established by Saint Monica, the mother of Saint Augustine, and favored by Catholic families.

Mona, Monca, Monicka, Monika, Monike, Moniqua, Monique, Monnica

Montana Sp."Mountainous." Geographic name: the northernmost western state that the Rocky Mountains run through.

Montanna

Morela Pol. "Apricot."

— **Morgan** Different sources give different meanings, including Welsh "Great and bright" and OE. "Bright or white sea dweller." Morgan is common in Wales as both a first and a last name, for both sexes. The current trend toward unisex names suggests that the feminizations are in for a spell of disuse, and that any Morgan encountered in a nursery school—and there will be some, for the name is rather well used—is likely to be a girl. Actress Morgan Fairchild.

Morgana, Morgance, Morgane, Morganica, Morganne, Morgen, Morgin

Moriah Heb. "The Lord is my teacher." May also be arrived at as a variant of **Mariah/Maria/Mary**.

Moraia, Moraiah

Morwenna Welsh. Perhaps "Maiden," perhaps "White seas."

Morwena, Morwina, Morwinna, Morwyn, Morwynna

Moselle (Fem. **Moses**) Heb. Possibly "Savior." Also a variety of delicately sweet white wine.

Moiselle, Moisella

Mouna Arab. "Wish, desire."

Mounia, Muna, Munira

Moya Nor. var. **Maia** (Gk. "Mother").

Moja

Muriel Ir. Gael. "Sea-bright." Some names, like this one, seem rooted in a certain period (in this case, the first half of the 20th century), but Muriel actually dates back to the Middle Ages. Perhaps the children of the 21st century will find it nostalgic enough to use for *their* children. Novelist Muriel Spark.

Merial, Meriel, Merrill, Muireall, Murial, Muriella, Murielle

Musetta "Little bagpipe." Musette came to be the term for a dance tune that employed the musette, an instrument fashionable in the 18th century.

Musette

Musidora Gk. "Gift of the Muses."

Myra (Fem. **Myron**) Lat. "Scented oil." Literary name coined in the early 17th century, but real-life use dates from the 19th century. Harpsichordist Dame Myra Hess; author Maira Kalman.

Maira, Mira, Myree

Myrna Ir. Gael. "Tender, beloved." Popularity, in the 1930s and 1940s, spans the career of actress Myrna Loy.

Meirna, Merna, Mirna, Moina, Morna, Moyna, Muirna

Myrtle Botanical name. The myrtle is a dark green shrub with pink or white blossoms. The name first appeared in the 1850s, before the true vogue for flower names, but it became more popular along with those other names in the 1880s. Now dated.

Mertice, Mertis, Mertle, Mirtle, Myrta, Myrtia, Myrtice, Myrtie, Myrtis

Mystique The air of mystery surrounding someone.

Mistique

NICE NORMAL NAMES

Not all celebrities choose unusual names. Some of them seem to be swayed by the very same winds of fashion as the rest of us. For the children below, it's not their first names that are going to attract attention: it's the last names of their very famous parents.

Annette Bening and Warren Beatty: Kathlyn, Benjamin

Isabelle Adjani and Daniel Day-Lewis: Gabriel

Marlee Matlin: Sarah

Jamie Lee Curtis and Christopher Guest: Annie, Thomas

Kevin Costner: Annie, Joseph

Vanna White: Nicholas

Natasha Richardson and Liam Neeson: Michael, Daniel

Katie Couric: Caroline, Elinor

Amanda Pays and Corbin Bernsen: Henry, Angus,
Oliver

Rob Lowe and Sheryl Berkoff, as well as Michelle
Pfeiffer and David Kelley, should get extra "common
sense" points for naming sons the old
standby, John.

N

Naavah Heb. "Lovely."
  Nava, Navit
Nabila Arab. "Highborn."
  Nabeela, Nabilah
Nadette OG. "Bear/courageous." Dim. **Bernadette.**
Nadia Rus. "Hope." Nada appeared in English-speaking countries at the turn of the 20th century, but Nadia had taken root by the 1960s. Though not outlandish, it has a pleasantly foreign sound. Gymnast Nadia Comaneci; poet Nadezhda Mandelstam.
  Nada, Nadège, Nadejda, Nadezhda, Nadie, Nadija, Nadiya, Nadja, Nady, Nadya, Nadyenka, Nadzia, Nata, Natka
Nadine Fr. Var. **Nadia.** Author Nadine Gordimer.
  Nadeen, Nadena, Nadene, Nadie, Nadina, Nadyna, Nadyne, Naydeen
Nadira Arab. "Precious, scarce."
  Nadirah, Nadra
Nagida Heb. "Wealthy."
  Negida
Nahara Aramaic "Light."
Naida Gk. "Water nymph."
  Naia, Naiad, Naiada, Nayad, Niada, Nyad, Nyada

Naima Arab. "Satisfied, contented."
Naeema, Naimah

Nairobi Place name: capital of Kenya, in east Africa. Occasionally used by African-American parents.

Nalani Haw. "Serenity of the skies."
Nalanee

Nan Var. **Ann** (Heb. "Grace"). At its most common in the 18th century, but now occurs most often as a nickname for Ann. Its diminutives (**Nana, Nanny**) have come to mean grandmother or person who looks after children.
Nana, Nance, Nanci, Nancie, Nancy, Nanella, Nanelle, Nanette, Nania, Nanine, Nanna, Nannette, Nannie, Nanny, Nanon, Nettie, Ninon

Nancy Var. **Ann** (Heb. "Grace"). Also originally a nickname whose use as a given name began at roughly the same time as Nan, in the 18th century. Nancy, however, took root more firmly (perhaps because it had not acquired any other meanings) and was very popular in the U.S. in the middle of the 20th century. First Lady Nancy Reagan, skater Nancy Kerrigan; writer Nancy Miford.
Nainsey, Nainsi, Nance, Nancee, Nanci, Nancie, Nancsi, Nanice, Nanncey, Nanncy, Nannie, Nanny, Nansee, Nansey

Nanette Fr. Dim. **Nan.**
Nannette, Nettie, Netty, Ninon

Naomi Heb: "Pleasant." Old Testament name; the mother-in-law of Ruth, who, after her sons died, said, "Do not call me Naomi, call me Mara, for the Almighty has dealt very bitterly with me." Naomi came into English-speaking use not with the Puritan revival of biblical names, but in the 18th century.
Naoma, Naomia, Naomie, Nayomi, Navit, Noami, Noémi, Noémie

Narcissa Gk. "Daffodil." Not actually a flower name, but the unusual feminine version of the masculine (and equally unusual) **Narcisse**, which comes from the legend of the beautiful Greek youth who became enamored of his own reflection—hence "narcissism."
Narcisa, Narcisse, Narcyssa, Narkissa, Narsissa

Narda Lat. "Scented ointment."

Nastasia Gk. "Resurrection." Dim. **Anastasia**. Actress Nastassja Kinski.

Nastassia, Nastassija, Nastassja, Nastassiya, Nastassya

Nasya Heb. "The Lord's miracle."

Nasia

Nata Lat. "Swimmer."

Natalie Lat. "Birth day." More specifically, the Lord's birthday, or Christmas. This is probably the most common of all the Christmas names, and certainly the only one that is used for babies born at other times of the year (unlike Noel). Though there was a 4th-century Saint Natalia, this Frenchified form did not crop up until the late 19th century. Actress Natalie Wood.

Nat, Nata, Natala, Natalee, Natalene, Natalia, Natalja, Natalina, Nataline, Nataly, Nataliya, Natalya, Natasha, Natelie, Nately, Nathalia, Nathalie, Nathaliely, Nathalija, Natilie, Natividad, Nattilie, Nattie, Nettie, Talia, Talya, Tasha

Natana Heb. "He gave." A feminine form of **Nathan**.

Nataniela

Natasha Rus. Var. **Natalie**.

Nastaliya, Nastalya, Natacha, Natascha, Natashenka, Natosha, Natucha

Nathania (Fem. **Nathan**) Heb. "A gift or given of God."

Natania, Nataniella, Nataniya, Natanya, Natanyah, Nathaniella, Nathanielle, Netanella, Netania, Netanya, Nethania

Nathifa Arab. "Immaculate, pure."

Nathifah, Natifa, Natifah

Natividad Sp. "Christmas." See **Natalie**.

Natura Sp. "Nature."

Nausicaa Character from *The Odyssey*: a princess who treats the shipwrecked Odysseus with courtesy and consideration, unlike most of the women he meets on his voyage.

Nausikaa

Neala (Fem. **Neal**) Gael. "Champion." Unusual feminization of the male name that was quite popular in the middle of the 20th century.

Neale, Nealla, Neila, Neile, Neilla, Neille

Nebraska Place name. The name of the state comes from a Sioux Indian word meaning "Flat water."

Nebula Lat. "Mist." Used by astronomers to describe hazy masses around stars.

Nechama Heb. "Comfort, solace." The most common masculine version of the name is Nahum, one of the minor prophets in the Bible. Nehemiah is also related.
Nachmanit, Nachuma, Nechamah, Nechamit, Nehamah

Neda (Fem. **Edward**) OE. "Wealthy defender" via the nickname Ned, or Rus. "Born on Sunday." In any case, very unusual.
Nedda, Neddie, Nedi

Nedra OE. "Underground."
Neddra, Needra

Nefertiti Queen of Egypt around 1350 B.C. She has an aura of glamor because several portrait sculptures of her have survived, and she is strikingly beautiful, even by the standards of a world some 2400 years later than hers.

Nehara Heb. "Light of day."
Nehira, Nehora, Nehura

Neila Heb. "Closing, locking." The final service on Yom Kippur is called Neila.
Neilla

Neilina Scot. feminization of **Neil** (Ir. Gael. "Champion").
Neala, Neale, Neel, Neelle, Neille

Neima Heb. "A melody."

Neka Native American. "Goose, wild goose."

Nelia Dim. **Cornelia** (Lat. "Horn").
Neelia, Neelie, Neelya, Nela, Nila

Nell Dim. **Eleanor** (Gk. "Light"). Used sparingly as an independent name, though some of its variants like Nellie have had periods of popularity. Suitably nostalgic-sounding (but perhaps not elaborate enough) to be favored in the late '90s. Charles II's mistress Nell Gwynn; opera star Nellie Melba.
Nel, Nella, Nellene, Nellie, Nellwen, Nellwin, Nellwyn, Nelly

Nelsey Modern name: the popular Kelsey/Chelsea with an "N." Also reminiscent of Nell.
Nellsea, Nellseigh, Nellsey, Nellsie, Nelsea, Nelseigh, Nelsie, Nelsy

Nemera Heb. "Leopard."

Neneca Sp. var. **Amelia** (OG. "Industrious").
Nenica, Nenneca, Nennica

Neola Gk. "Young one." Comes from the same root as the widely used prefix "neo-."

Neoma Gk. "New moon."
Neomah, Nioma

Nera Heb. "Light of a candle." An appropriate name for a daughter born during Hannukah.
Nerit, Neriya

Nereida Sp. from Gk. "Sea nymph."
Nireida

Nerine Gk. "Sea nymph."
Narine, Narice, Narissa, Nerice, Nerida, Nerina, Nerissa, Neryssa

Nerissa Unusual name possibly derived from *nereid*, the Greek term for a sea nymph. Shakespeare wrote a character named Nerissa into *The Merchant of Venice*. The name is just as likely, though, to be a modification of the popular Marisa/Marissa.
Narissa, Naryssa, Neryssa

Nerola It. "Orange flower."
Nerolia, Nerolie, Neroly

Nerys Welsh. "Master, lord."
Neris, Neriss, Neryss

Nessie Dim. **Agnes** (Gk. "Lamb"). Also the name of the Loch Ness Monster, which might limit its appeal.
Nesha, Nessa, Nessia, Nessya, Nesta, Neta, Netia

Nesta Dim. **Ernesta, Agnes**.
Nest

Nettie Diminutive of "-ette" names like **Henriette** or **Nanette**. Use as an independent name mostly around the turn of the 20th century.
Netta, Netty

Neva Sp. "Snowy." Nevada, which means "covered with snow," is one of the American state names (like Florida) that adapts nicely to use as a girl's name. Actress Neve Campbell.
Nevada, Nevara, Neve, Nieves

Nia Swahili. "Goal, purpose."
Nea, Nya

Niagara Place name: home of the famous falls. Niagara Falls used to be a premier honeymooning destination. The falls are 186 feet high.

Nichele Modern name: com. form **Michele** and **Nicole**.
Nichelle, Nishell, Nishelle, N'Shell

Nicia Dim. of ''-nice'' names such as **Eunice** and **Berenice**.
Neecia, Nicija

Nicole (Fem. **Nicholas**) Gk. ''Victory of the people.'' Nicola, the Italian form, is more common in Britain (though its vogue peaked there in the 1970s). This French version has been more popular in other English-speaking countries, reaching the top ten in the U.S. in the 1980s. Still quite widely used, but it has lost its trendiness. Singer Nicolette Larson; actress Nicole Kidman.
Colette, Cosetta, Cosette, Nichelle, Nichola, Nicholassa, Nichole, Nicholette, Nicholl, Nicholle, Nicia, Nicki, Nickola, Nickole, Nicky, Nico, Nicola, Nicolasa, Nicolea, Nicolene, Nicoleen, Nicolette, Nicolie, Nicolina, Nicoline, Nicolla, Nicolle, Nika, Niki, Nikita, Nikki, Nikky, Niko, Nikola, Nikole, Nikoleta, Nikoletta, Nikolia, Niquole, Niquolle, Nychole, Nycholl, Nykia, Nycole, Nykole, Nykolia, Nyquole, Nyquolle

Nicosia Capital city of Cyprus. Similar enough to Nicole and other derivatives of Nicholas to be considered one of them.
Nicotia

Nidia Sp. from Gk. ''Graceful, sweet.''
Nibia, Nydia

Nikita Gk. ''Unconquered.'' Those who remember Nikita Khruschev may think of this as a masculine name, but it is often used as a variant of **Nicole**.
Nakeeta, Nikeeta, Niquita

Nilda Dim. **Brunhilda** (OG. ''Battle woman''). A surprising proportion of Spanish names are directly adapted from the German, possibly going back to the days when Spain and Germany were alllied as part of the Holy Roman Empire. Nilda is often used as an independent name.
Nillda

Nike Gk. ''Victory.'' Also, and more commonly to most Americans, the name of a very popular athletic shoe.
Nika

Nikki Var. **Nicole**. Used mostly in the 1960s.
Nickie, Nicky, Nikkey, Nikky

Nila Geography name, based on the River Nile. Logical choice for Egyptophiles.
Naila, Nyla

Nilsine Scand. Fem. **Nils** or **Neil** (Ir. Gael. "Champion").
Nilsa, Nilsina

Nina Sp. "Girl." Dim. **Ann** (Heb. "Grace"). History buffs will remember that Nina was the name of one of Christopher Columbus's three ships. The name is rather uncommon. Ballerina Dame Ninette de Valois.
Neena, Neina, Nenna, Neneh, Ninacska, Nineta, Ninete, Ninetta, Ninette, Ninnette, Ninon, Ninochka, Ninoska, Ninotchka, Nyna

Ninfa Sp. from Gk. "Nymph."

Ninon Fr. Dim. **Ann** (Heb. "Grace"). A famous 17th-century Parisian belle was named Anne de Lenclos, better known as Ninon de Lenclos.
Ninette

Niobe Gk. "Fern." In myth, Niobe was a boastful queen of Thebes whose children were all killed as a reprimand for her arrogance. In her resulting misery she asked Zeus to turn her to stone. In art she is usually depicted weeping.

Nira Heb. "Plowed field."
Niran, Nirela, Nirit

Nissa Two possible sources, Heb. "Sign" or Scand. "Elf." May also be independently arrived at as an attractive-sounding pair of syllables, vaguely reminiscent of Vanessa.
Nissana, Nissanit, Nyssa

Nita Sp. Dim. **Juanita, Anita**, etc. Unusual.

Nitsa Ger. Dim. **Irene** (Gk. "Peace").

Nituna Native American. "My daughter."

Nitza Heb. "Bud."
Nitzana, Nitzaniya

Nixie OG. "Water sprite." Usually beautiful and antagonistic to men, unlike pixies, which, though mischievous, are content to share the world with humans.

Noel Fr. "Christmas." Though used since the Middle Ages for both boys and girls, it is more common for the latter.
Noela, Noeleen, Noelene, Noeline, Noeliz, Noella, Noëlle, Noelleen, Noelynn, Nowel, Noweleen, Nowell

Nokomis NAm. Ind. "Daughter of the moon." The source is Longfellow's famous poem *The Song of Hiawatha*.

Nola Dim. **Finola.** Gael. "White shoulder." Related to Nuala but not, as many parents think, to Nolan.
Nowla

Nolan Ir. Gael. "Renowned." A last name transferred to first name and generally used for boys.
Noland, Nolanda, Nolen, Nolin, Nolynn, Nollan

Noleta Lat. "Unwilling."
Nolita

Nona Lat. "Ninth." Although it was originally used for a family's ninth baby, it would hardly have survived to this day if parents had not been willing to overlook its meaning.
Nonah, Noni, Nonie, Nonna, Nonnah

Nora Dim. **Eleanor, Honora.** Gk. "Light." Used independently, especially for the half century around 1900. Well-read parents will remember Nora as the heroine of Ibsen's *A Doll's House*; she sets a discouraging precedent, however. Writer Nora Ephron.
Norah, Norella, Norelle

Norberta (Fem. **Norbert**) OG. "Renowned northerner." Occurs in Germany.

Nordica Lat. "From the North." Familiar to skiers as a manufacturer of ski boots, and to opera fans as the last name of turn-of-the-century soprano Lillian Nordica, who was actually born Lillian Norton in Farmington, Maine. In those days, a plain Anglo-Saxon name was insufficiently exotic for an opera star.
Norda

Noreen Ir. Dim. **Nora.** Originated in Ireland.
Norene, Norina, Norine

Norma Lat. "Pattern." From the same root that gave us "normal" or "the norm." Launched by Bellini's 1831 opera of the same name, and boosted in the 1920s by popular actress Norma Shearer. Out of fashion for the last couple of generations. Fashion designer Norma Kamali.
Norm, Normie, Normina

Normandie Place name: the province of Normandy in northeastern France. Famous as the area that launched the Norman Invasion of England in the 11th century, and the

Allied invasion of German-dominated Europe, in 1944. Sometimes used as a girl's name, especially to compliment a relative named Norman, if Norma seems too out of date. After all, if Brittany (another French province) can reach the top ten . . .

Normandee, Normandey, Normandy

Norna Scand. goddess of time.

Norne

Novia Lat. "New"; Sp. "Girlfriend."

Nova

Nova An exploding star that temporarily becomes extraordinarily bright. Typically, a nova loses only a tiny part of its matter in the explosion. Chevrolet used to make a small car called a "Nova," which might dissuade parents who owned one from using this name for a baby.

Nuala Dim. **Fionnula** (Ir. Gael. "White shoulder").

Nola, Noola, Nualla, Nula

Nubia Place name: a region in ancient Africa, in part of what is now Sudan.

Nunzia It. "Messenger." See **Annunciata**.

Nunciata

Nur Arab. "Light." The Arabic name adopted by the current queen of Jordan, an American woman known formerly as Lisa Halaby.

Noor, Nour, Noura, Nureen, Nurine

Nurit Heb. "Buttercup."

Nydia Lat. "Nest." Also Sp. from Gk. "Graceful."

Nidia, Needia

Nysa Gk. "Goal, ambition." Currently used in Greece.

Nyssa

Nyx Gk. "Night."

Nix, Nixe

Oba Nig., the name of a goddess of rivers.

Ocarina A small simple wind instrument shaped like a jug with a spout.

Oceana Gk. "Ocean." In Greek myth Oceanus was a river that flowed around the earth. Oceania is a collective name for the islands in the Pacific.

Oceania

Octavia Lat. "Eighth." Used most often in the Victorian era of large families.

Octaviana, Octavianne, Octavie, Octiana, Octoviana, Ottavia, Tavia, Tavie, Tavy

Odele Derivation disputed. Some sources relate it to either German "Rich" or Greek "Song," but The *Facts on File Dictionary of First Names* claims that it derives from an Old English place name: "Woad hill." Woad is a blue dye reputedly used by the ancient Druids in their religious rites. Yet another possibility is that it is a variation of **Adele**.

Odela, Odelet, Odelette, Odelina, Odeline, Odell, Odella, Odelle, Udele, Udelia, Udilia

Odelia Heb. "I will praise the Lord." Possibly also related to Odele.

Oda, Odeelia, Odele, Odelinda, Odella, Odellia, Odilia, Udele, Udelia, Udilia

Odessa Gk. "Long voyage." As in "odyssey," more specifically Homer's epic poem about the wandering Odysseus. The Russian port of Odessa was supposedly named to honor *The Odyssey*.

Odissa, Odyssa, Odyssia

Odette Fr. from Ger. "Wealthy." In the famous ballet *Swan Lake*, the same ballerina usually dances as both Odette, the good swan, and Odile, the evil black swan. Folk singer Odetta.

Odetta

592

Odile Fr. Var. **Otthild** (OG. "Prospers in battle"). Related to Odette and also to Odelia. For balletomanes, the malevolent alter ego of Odette.
Odila, Odilia, Odolia, Udelia, Udile, Udilia

Ofra Heb. "Fawn." Another form of the name that is most famous as **Oprah**. See **Orpah**.
Ofrat, Ofrit, Ophra

Ogenya Heb. "God is my help."

Oksana Rus. from Heb. "Praise to God." Popular in what used to be the USSR, and made familiar world-wide by Ukrainian figure-skating champion Oksana Baiul.
Oksanna

Ola Var. **Olesia** (Gr. "Man's defender").
Olla

Olathe Native American. "Lovely."

Oleisa Var. **Elise**, Fr. Var. **Elizabeth** (Heb. "Pledged to God").
Oleesa, Olisa

Olena Rus. var. **Helen** (Gk. "Light").
Alena, Elena, Lena, Lenya, Olinia, Olinija, Olenya Olina, Olinia, Olinija

Olesia Gr. "Man's defender."
Ola

Olethea Var. **Alethea** (Gk. "Truth").
Oleta

Olga Rus. "Holy." The Russian form of Helga, and perhaps more common than Helga in English-speaking countries. The Russian Saint Olga was a princess from Kiev and a 10th-century Christian convert; the name was favored in the ill-fated Russian imperial family. Gymnast Olga Korbut.
Elga, Helga, Ola, Olenka, Olia

Oliana Polynesian. "Oleander."
Oleana, Olianna

Olinda Lat. "Scented."

Olivia Lat. "Olive tree." The most common form of the name today, though Olive had a flurry of popularity with other nature names at the turn of the 20th century. It would be hard to use Olive today given the fame of Popeye's scrawny girlfriend, Olive Oyl. This form, though, is gradually becoming more common, probably influenced by our turn-of-the-century fondness for three-syllable girl's names. Actresses Olivia de Havilland, Olivia Hussey; singer Olivia Newton John.

Liv, Liva, Livia, Livvie, Livvy, Olia, Oliff, Oliffe, Oliva, Olive, Oliveea, Olivet, Olivette, Olivija, Olivine, Olivya, Ollie, Olva

Olwen Welsh. "White footprint." Along with Bronwen, one of the best known Welsh-language first names. Nevertheless, it is very unusual outside Wales.

Olwenn, Olwin, Olwyn, Olwynne

Olympia Gk. "From Mount Olympus," the home of the gods. Slightly more common in Europe, where it may avoid the faintly commercial connotation of the Olympic Games. Actress Olympia Dukakis.

Olimpe, Olimpia, Olimpiada, Olimpiana, Olypme, Olympie

Oma Arab. "Leader." Infrequent use.

Omega Gk. "Last." It would seem to be tempting fate to use this name for a youngest child.

Omyra Var. **Myra** ("Scented oil").

Omeira

Ondine Lat. "Little wave." In myth, Undine is the spirit of the waters. Edith Wharton created a heroine in *The Custom of the Country* who was named Undine for the hair curling tonic that had made her father rich.

Ondina, Ondyne, Undine

Oneida NAm Ind. "Long awaited." In the U.S. probably most familiar as a brand of silverware, which was originally manufactured by a utopian colony that was disbanded in the 19th century because its residents practiced polygamy.

Onida, Onyda

Onella Gk. "Light."

Oneonta Place name: town in Central New York State.

Onnjel Var. **Angela** (Lat. "Angel").

Onjella

Onora Var. **Honoria** (Lat. "Honor").

Onnora, Onoria, Onorine, Ornora

Oona Ir. Var. **Una** (Lat. "Unity").

Oonagh, Una

Opal Sanskrit. "Gem." One of the less common of the

jewel names, but a logical choice for an October baby, since this is the birthstone for that month.

Opalina, Opaline, Opall

Ophelia Gk. "Help." Most famously, the young girl in Hamlet who goes mad. Mostly used in the late 19th century, but its connotations are far from happy.

Availia, Filia, Ofelia, Ofilia, Ophelie, Ophelya, Ophilia, Ovalia, Ovelia, Phelia, Ubelia, Uvelia

Ophira Fem. **Ophir**, Biblical place name. In the Old Testament, Ophir is frequently mentioned as an exceptionally rich source of gold, sandalwood, precious stones, and other luxuries. Its actual location is a moot point: scholars can narrow it down no further than India, Africa, or Arabia. In the late 19th century one of the most productive mines in California's Comstock Lode was called "Ophir."

Ofeera, Ofira

Ora Lat. "Prayer." Homonym for Aura, which means "Gold" or "Breeze."

Orabel, Orabelle, Orareeana, Orarariana, Orra

Oracia Sp. Fem. **Horace** (Lat. clan name). This name may also be taken as something to do with prayer or with gold, since the latinate roots are all very similar.

Orasia, Oratia, Orazia

Oralee Heb. "My light."

Orali, Oralit, Orlee

Oralie Fr. Var. **Aurelia** (Lat. "Golden").

Aurelie, Oralee, Oralia, Orélie, Oriel, Orielda, Orielle, Orlena, Orlene

Orane Fr. "Rising." From the same Latin source as Oriana.

Orania, Oriane

Orange Name of the fruit.

Orangetta, Orangia, Orangina

Orela Lat. "Announcement from the gods." Related to "Oracle."

Orelda, Orella, Orilla

Orfea Fem. **Orpheus**. In Greek myth, Orpheus was a brilliant musician. He married a dryad, Eurydice, who was poisoned by a snake, and he descended into the underworld to find her. His music so charmed Hades that he was allowed to bring her back to life, if he could lead her to the upper world without looking at her. He failed, and she returned to Hades.

Orfeya, Orfia, Orphea, Orpheya, Orphia

Oriana Lat. "Dawning." From the same root as Aurora. Italian journalist Orianna Falacci.

Oria, Oriane, Orianna

Oriel Lat. Dim. of "Golden." The more usual spelling for these "gold" names is "Au-." An oriel is also an architectural feature, an elaborate bay window.

Auriel, Auriella, Aurielle, Oriella, Orielle

Orinda Place name: town in California. Possibly related to the Spanish for gold (*oro*) or a variant of the Spanish for pretty (*linda*).

Orinthia Fem. **Oren** (Heb. "Pine tree" or Ir. Gael. "Fair-skinned").

Orenthia, Orna, Ornina, Orrinthia

Oriole Lat. "Golden." Most commonly the name of a bird with golden markings, or the name of the Baltimore baseball team.

Auriel, Oreolle, Oriel, Oriella, Oriola, Oriolle

Orit Heb. "Light."

Ora, Orah, Orya

Orla Ir. Gael. "Golden lady."

Orlagh, Orrla

Orlanda Fem. **Orlando**, Sp. Var. **Roland** (OG. "Famous land"). Very unusual.

Orpah Heb. "A fawn." Old Testament name, rarely used. Talk show star Oprah Winfrey's unusual name is the result of a misspelling of this name.

Afra, Aphra, Ofrit, Ophrah, Oprah, Orpa

Orquidea Sp. "Orchid."

Orsa Var. **Ursula** (Lat. "Bear").

Orsalina, Orsaline, Orsel, Orselina, Orseline, Orsola, Orssa, Ursa

Osaka Place name: Japanese city known as both a commercial and cultural center.

Orszebet Hung. Var. **Elizabeth** (Heb. "Devoted to God").

Ortensia It. Var. **Hortense** (Lat. clan name).

Ortensa, Ortensija, Ortensya

Osma Fem. **Osmond** (OE "Divine protector"). Avid readers of the entire series of Oz books by Frank Baum will remember Ozma of Oz.

Ozma

Ostia Place name: the original port for the city of Rome, now some distance inland because of silt deposited by the Tiber.

Otamisia Var. Artemisia, Gk/Sp. "Perfect."

Otameesia, Ottamisia

Otthild OG. "Prospers in battle." Odile is perhaps the most common form.

Otthilda Ottila, Ottilia, Ottilie, Ottiline, Ottoline, Otylia

Ottilie Fr. var. Otthild.

Ottalia, Ottilia, Ottilie, Ottolie

Otzara Heb. "Treasure, wealth."

Otzarah, Ozara

Ouida Pen name of a Victorian romantic novelist named Marie Louise de la Ramée. It originated as a childish version of Louisa.

Pacifica Sp. "Peaceful." Geography name, for the ocean bounding the West Coast of the U.S. Good choice for surfers and peaceniks.

Pasifica

Padma Hindi. "Lotus."

Page Fr. A young boy in training as a personal assistant to a knight. Usually a transferred surname, possibly indicating an ancestor who was a page. Use as a girl's name is quite recent, but fits in well with the current rage for masculine-sounding girls' names.

Padget, Padgett, Paget, Pagett, Paige, Payge

Pallas Gk. "Wisdom." Another name for the Greek deity Athena, goddess of wisdom.

Paladia, Palladia, Palles

Palma Lat. "Palm tree." Also a place name used in several countries, no doubt to indicate locales where palm trees grew.

Pallma, Pallmirah, Pallmyra, Palmeda, Palmeeda, Palmer, Palmira, Palmyra

Paloma Sp. "Dove." Little known until the recent fame of designer Paloma Picasso, daughter of the artist.
Palloma, Palometa, Palomita, Peloma

Pamela Gk. "All honey." Literary name coined at the end of the 16th century, growing gradually more common until a distinct vogue in the 1950s and 1960s. Likely to be neglected by the current generation of parents, precisely because it was popular among their parents. Actresses Pam Dawber, Pamela Anderson Lee, Pamela Reed; tennis star Pam Shriver.
Pam, Pama, Pamala, Pamalla, Pamelia, Pamelina, Pamelin, Pamelina, Pamella, Pamelyn, Pamelynne, Pamilla, Pammela, Pammie, Pammy, Permelia

Pamina Name of Italian origin, meaning unknown: a character in Mozart's famous opera *The Magic Flute*.

Pandora Gk. "All gifted." In Greek myth Pandora was the first woman, endowed with gifts by all the gods. She is famous for the box that was her dowry; it contained all the world's evils, which flew out when the box was opened. One of the more common of the Greek names in English-speaking countries, but still highly unusual.
Dora, Doura, Panndora, Pandorra, Pandoura

Pangiota Gk. "All is holy."

Pania Dim. **Stepania** (Gk. "Crowned"). The most familiar version of this name right now is Stephanie, which is hugely popular in the U.S.
Paniya, Panya

Panphila Gk. "All loving." A pleasant notion, though the name might require a lot of explanation.
Panfila, Panfyla, Panphyla

Pansy Flower name from the late 19th century: the name of the flower originally came from the French word for thought, *pensée*, possibly because the petals of the flower are thought to resemble wise little faces.
Pansey, Pansie

Panthea Gk. "All the gods." An early Middle Eastern queen was named Panthea, but the name is more familiar from its close relative "pantheon," which means a temple to all gods.
Pantheia, Pantheya, Panthia

Paquita Sp. Dim. **Frances** (Lat. "From France"), via Paco.

Paradisa Gk. "Garden, orchard." Paradise is the ancient name of the home of the blessed. In the Old Testament "paradise" refers to the Garden of Eden, while in the New Testament it refers to heaven.

Paris Place name: the capital city of France. Also the name of a character in Greek myth who was Helen of Troy's lover, but most modern parents using this name are likely to be thinking of the French City of Light.
Parris, Parrish

Parker OE. "Park keeper." Occupational name turned last name, borrowed for a girl's first name. Rare, but possibly appealing to parents looking for a WASPy first name. Actress Parker Posey.

Parmenia Sp. "Intelligent, studious."
Parmenya, Permenia

Parrish OF. "Ecclesiastical locality." A parish is the area under the care of one pastor or priest. The name would originally have been a last name based on a place name. Used primarily for boys.
Parish

Parthenia Gk. "Virginal." Used most often at the turn of the 20th century, when the attributes of the virgin were particularly highly valued.
Partheenia, Parthenie, Parthinia, Pathina, Pathinia

Parthenope Name from Greek mythology: she was one of the Sirens, who threw herself into the sea when she failed to lure Odysseus to his death. Also the original name for the Italian city of Naples. Florence Nightingale's sister was named Parthenope.

Pascale (Fem. **Pascal**) Fr. "Easter." Despite some English-speaking use in the last thirty years, still primarily a French name.
Pascalette, Pascaline, Pascalle, Pascha, Paschale, Pashelle, Pascua, Pascuala

Pat Dim. **Patricia.** Used as an independent name, but neglected with the recent leaning toward the nostalgic and elaborate.

Patches Occurs rarely as a family name. Scholars consider it a distant derivative of Peter.
Patch

Patience Virtue name. One of the more popular of the 16th century names, though eclipsed in the 20th century by Hope. Patience, after all, is not a very modern virtue.

Paciencia, Patient, Patienzia, Pazienza

Patricia (Fem. **Patrick**) Lat. "Noble, patrician." Obscure until it was used for one of Queen Victoria's grand daughters, which launched its enormous popularity for close to fifty years. It has now returned to near-neglect. Singers Patti LaBelle, Patsy Cline, Pat Benatar; choreographer Trisha Brown; actresses Patty Duke, Patricia Neal; First Lady Pat Nixon; Congresswoman Pat Schroeder.

Pat, Patreece, Patreice, Patrica, Patrice, Patricka, Patrizia, Patsy, Patte, Pattee, Pattey, Patti, Pattie, Patty, Tricia, Trish, Trisha

Paula (Fem. **Paul**) Lat. "Small." Roman name that cropped up in English-speaking countries in this century and was rather well used in the Baby Boom era. Actress Paulette Godard; singer Paula Abdul.

Paola, Paolina, Paule, Pauletta, Paulette, Paulie, Paulina, Pauline, Paulita, Paulla, Paullette, Pauly, Pavia, Pavla, Pola, Polina, Pollie, Polly

Pauline (Fem. **Paul**) Fr. from Lat. "Small." Popular earlier than Paula, having peaked at the turn of the 20th century in the U.S. Model Paulina Porizkova.

Pauleen, Paulina, Polline, Paulyne

Paxton Lat./OE. "Peace town." A place name.

Paxten

Payne Lat. "Countryman." The Spanish word is *paisano*, the French word *paysan*. "Peasant" is probably the closest English cognate.

Paine

Paz Sp. "Peace."

Pazia Heb. "Golden."

Paza, Pazit

Peace ME. Word used as a name. Though not strictly a virtue name, this is the kind of abstract quality celebrated by the Puritans in their choice of names.

Peachy From the fruit. Very much a modern name, used perhaps to describe an infant's complexion or temperament.

Peach

Peale Unusual former last name. May refer to a landmark like a "peel tower," a stronghold common in northern Britain, or may be related to the Latin word *pax*, which means "peace."
Peall, Pealle, Peele

Pearl Lat. "Pearl." Probably the most common of the jewel names, though of course it is not a gemstone. The Greek form, Margaret, is far more widespread and has been used for centuries, while Pearl only appeared in the late Victorian era. Writer Pearl S. Buck; singer Pearl Bailey.
Pearla, Pearle, Pearleen, Pearlette, Pearline, Perl, Perla, Perle, Perlette, Perley, Perline, Perlline

Peggy Dim. **Margaret** (Gk. "Pearl"). Used as an independent name since the 18th century, and parents who choose it today probably do so without thinking of Margaret. Its greatest vogue came in the first third of the 20th century. Skater Peggy Fleming.
Peg, Pegeen, Pegg, Peggie

Pelagia Gk. "Ocean, sea."
Palasha, Pasha, Pelage, Pelageia, Pelageya, Pélagie, Pellagia

Pelia Heb. "Marvel of God."
Peliah

Penelope Gk. "Bobbin worker." The bobbin probably refers to part of the equipment for weaving, since the Penelope of Greek myth was the wife of Odysseus. To put off the many suitors who courted her when it seemed that the wandering Odysseus must be dead, she told them she couldn't marry until she finished the tapestry she was weaving. She would work all day and unravel her work at night, hoping that her husband would come home. The name was most popular in the middle of the 20th century, in Britain. Model Penelope Tree; parenting expert Penelope Leach; actress Penelope Ann Miller.
Pen, Penelopa, Penina, Penna, Pennelope, Penney, Pennie, Penny

Peninah Heb. "Pearl."
Pnina

Penny Dim. **Penelope.** Gk. "Bobbin worker." Given as an independent name mostly in the 20th century.
Penee, Pennee, Penney, Pennie

Penthea Gk. "Fifth." Related to "pentagon."

Peony Unusual flower name.

Pepita Sp. Dim. **Joseph** (Heb. "Jehovah increases") via Pepe.
Pepa, Peppie, Peppy, Peta

Pepper Plant name. Because of the spicy nature of its namesake plant, children with spunky temperaments sometimes end up with Pepper as a nickname. Used very infrequently, for both boys and girls.

Perdita Lat. "Lost." Coined by Shakespeare, and rarely used since his day.

Perfecta Sp. "Perfect, flawless." A daunting name to give any child.

Peri Heb. "Outcome, result."

Pernella (Fem. **Peter**) Fr. from Gk. "Rock."
Parnella, Pernelle, Pernilla, Pernille

Perpetua Lat. "Forever, perpetual." Saint Perpetua, whose feast day is March 6, was one of the early Christian martyrs.

Perrin Fem. Var. **Peter** (Gk. "Rock") or **Peregrine** (Lat. "Voyager"). Names with "-in" or "-en" have been very fashionable recently.
Perran, Perren, Perrine, Perryn

Perry Fr. "Pear tree." Dim. **Peregrine** (Lat. "Voyager"). Originally a boy's name and common as a last name, but also used in America as a girl's name. The masculine names with "-y" or "-ie" endings (Leslie, for instance) seem more susceptible to feminine appropriation, which is irreversible. Author Perri Klass.
Perrey, Perri, Perrie

Persia Place name: the Middle Eastern country now known as Iran.

Persis Lat. "From Persia."
Perssis, Persys

Petaluma Place name: town in northern California.

Petra (Fem. **Peter**) Gk. "Rock." The simplest feminization of a name that seems to resist being feminized: but not for want of trying, as the variants below demonstrate.
Pella, Pernilla, Pernille, Perrine, Pet, Peta, Peterina, Peternella, Petria, Petrina, Petrine, Petronela, Petronella,

Petronelle, Petronia, Petronija, Petronilla, Petronille, Petrova, Petrovna, Piera, Pierette, Pierrette, Pietra

Petula Derivation unclear: may be a version of Peter, may come from a Latin word meaning "to seek." The name might even be an adaptation of the flower name Petunia. Its use is based entirely on the fame of singer Petula Clark.
Petulah

Petunia Flower name, for the rather humble trumpet-shaped flower with white or bright pink blossoms.

Phaedra Gk. "Bright." In Greek myth, the daughter of King Minos, who was married to the hero Theseus and fell in love with her stepson Hippolytus. When he spurned her advances, she committed suicide. One of those pretty Greek names with a not-so-pretty history.
Faydra, Phaedre, Phaidra, Phedra, Phèdre

Phemia Gk. "Language." Euphemia, while still rare, is the most common name containing this particle.
Femia, Femie, Phemie

Pheodora (Fem. **Theodore**) Rus. from Gk. "Gift of God."
Fedora, Feodora, Fyedora

Phila Gk. "Loving." This particle is the basis for many more common names.
Fila

Philadelphia Gk. "Loving people." The City of Brotherly Love was founded by Quakers with very high ideals: it was tradition among the Friends (as they were known) to name the eldest daughter in each family after the city. Possibly a little difficult to pull off in the waning days of the 20th century.

Philana Gk. "Loving mankind."
Filania, Filanna, Phila, Philena, Philene, Philina, Philine, Phillane, Phillina

Philantha Gk. "Lover of flowers."
Filanthia, Philanthia, Philanthie

Philiberta OE. "Very brilliant." Feminine of **Filbert**, which is the unusual modern form of Philibert, an Anglo-Saxon saint's name.
Filberta, Filiberta, Philberta, Philberthe

Philippa (Fem. **Philip**) Gk. "Horse lover." Another unusual feminization, though it was used somewhat in the

19th century. Something of a curiosity today.

Felipa, Filipa, Filipina, Filippa, Flip, Pelipa, Pelippa, Phil, Philipa, Philippe, Philippine, Phillie, Phillipa, Phillipina, Philly, Pippa, Pippie, Pippie, Pippy

Philomela Gk. "Lover of song." In Greek myth, Philomela is a princess who, after becoming entangled in a bloody and vengeful love triangle with her sister and brother-in-law, is turned into a nightingale, a bird renowned for its musical call.

Philomella

Philomena Gk. "Loved one." Name of a saint worshiped enthusiastically, especially in Italy, in the 19th and 20th centuries. However, her cult was based on nothing more than a set of bones discovered in Rome in 1802, which linked up very vaguely with a Roman inscription. It was assumed that she was a virgin martyr, and many miracles were attributed to Saint Philomena after a shrine was established to her. But in 1961, after archaeologists proved the bones in the shrine could not have been those of a young girl, her veneration was forbidden by Rome.

Filimena, Filomena, Filomène, Filumena, Philomène, Philomina

Philopena Fem. Var. **Philip** (Gk. "Lover of horses").

Felipina, Filipina, Filippina, Filippine, Philippina

Philothea Gk. "Lover of God." The elements are the same as in Theophilus, but reversed.

Filothea, Filotheya, Phillothea, Philotheia

Philyra Gk. "Lover of music."

Fillira, Phillira, Phillyra

Phoebe Gk. "Shining, brilliant." One of the epithets of Apollo, the sun god, was Phoebus Apollo, referring to the fact that he brought light. A Phoebe appears in the New Testament, but the name didn't gain ground until the 8th century. Reached a peak in the last part of the 19th century, now pleasantly old fashioned and ripe for revival. Singers Phoebe Legere, Phoebe Snow.

Febe, Pheabe, Phebe, Pheby, Phoebey, Phoeboe

Phoenix Gk. "Red as blood." The name of the mythical bird that, after a long life, set itself aflame and arose recreated from its own ashes. A common symbol of renewal or immortality.

Feenix, Fenix, Phenice

Phyllida Var. **Phyllis** (Gk. "Leafy bough"). Rare name that appeared in the 16th century; mostly literary use. Actress Phyllida Law.

Fillida, Phillida, Phillyda

Phyllis Gk. "Leafy bough." Name of a mythological woman, taken up by generations of poets to stand for the idealized country lass. Parents applied it to babies increasingly through the 19th century, but it died out after the 1930s. Poet Phyllis McGinley; comedienne Phyllis Diller.

Filis, Fillis, Fillys, Fyllis, Philis, Phillis, Philys, Phylis, Phyllida, Phyllie, Phylliss, Phyllys

Pia Lat. "Pious." More common in Europe than in English-speaking countries. Singer/actress Pia Zadora.

Picabo Place name: small town in Idaho that gave its name to one of America's top female skiers, Picabo Street. She pronounces it "Peekaboo."

Piedad Sp. "Piety, devotion."

Pierette Fr. Dim. **Peter** (Gk. "Rock"). Quite a few of Peter's feminizations come from the Continental form Pierre/Piero/Piers.

Piera, Pierina, Pietra

Pilar Sp. "Pillar." An allusion to the Virgin Mary, in her role as a "pillar" of the Church. Used mostly by Spanish-speaking parents.

Pima Place name: county in Arizona.

Piper OE. Occupational name: "Pipe player." Transferred to last name, and occasionally used as a first name, probably inspired, however indirectly, by actress Piper Laurie.

Pippa Dim. **Philippa** (Gk. "Lover of horses"). Almost exclusively British use.

Pippi, Pippy

Placidia Lat. "Calm, tranquil." From the word that gives us "placid." It seems a bit dangerous, however, to make predictions about a baby's temperament at birth.

Placida, Plasida

Pleasant Fr. "agreeable to the senses." Unusual, but occurs now and then for men as well. Entrepreneur Pleasant Rowland.

Pleasance

Pléiade Gk. The group of stars called the "Seven Sisters."

They are named after seven sisters in Greek myth, the daughters of Atlas and Pleione.

Pocahontas NAm Ind. ''Playful.'' The real Pocahontas's given name was Matoaka: Pocahontas was a nickname. For those who have not seen the Disney version, Pocahontas was the daughter of an Native American chief in Virginia, who is said to have rescued the English settler John Smith and who did marry John Rolfe, and later visited England.

Polly Var. **Molly**, Dim. **Mary** (Heb. ''Bitter''). Independent name, used especially in the 19th century. Another old-fashioned choice that should be appealing to parents of the 1990s, especially after the success of the rhyming Molly. Actress Polly Bergen.
Poll, Pollee, Polley, Polli, Pollie

Pomona Lat. ''Apple.'' The Roman goddess of fruit trees.

Poppy Lat. Flower name that reached its peak in the 1920s.

Porsha Possibly a phonetic variation of **Portia**, below, but more likely a feminization of **Porsche**, the glamorous German sports car.
Porscha

Portia Lat. Clan name, obscure meaning. The heroine of Shakespeare's *The Merchant of Venice*, an enterprising woman who disguises herself as a lawyer to save her husband's life. In spite of this worthy prototype, the name is uncommon.

Prairie Geography name, for that unique American feature, miles of fertile rolling grassland. Parents considering the name should remember that there is a blonde pig-tailed Muppet named ''Prairie Dawn.''

Precious Lat. ''Of great worth, expensive.'' Adjective used as name.

Priela Heb. ''Fruit of God.''
Priella

Prima Lat. ''First.''
Primalia, Primetta, Primina, Priminia

Primavera It. ''Spring.'' Pretty name for a spring baby.

Primrose ME. ''First rose.'' The primrose does not actually belong to the rose family, but it is one of the flowers that blooms early in spring. A 19th century flower name.
Primarosa, Primorosa, Primula

Princess Word as a name. Every little girl has the potential to live up to this name.
Princella, Princessa, Princesse, Principessa

Priscilla Lat. "Ancient." New Testament name and common in the early Christian era, then revived strongly by the Puritans. After generations of neglect, it was taken up in the 19th century, but has been scarce in the last half of the 20th century, possibly because the most natural nickname is "Prissy." Actress Priscilla Presley.
Cilla, Pris, Prisca, Priscella, Prisilla, Prissie, Prissy, Prysilla

Provence Place name: a picturesque area in southeastern France, brought special attention recently by Peter Mayle's bestselling book, *A Year in Provence.*

Prudence Lat. "Caution, discretion." Virtue name most common in the 19th century after its first popularity in the 16th and 17th centuries. Use now is mostly British.
Pru, Prudencia, Prudie, Prudy, Prue

Prunella Lat. "Small plum." Actress Prunella Scales.
Prunelle

Psyche Gk. "Breath" and, by extension, life or soul. In myth, Psyche was a mortal girl whom Cupid loved. In post-Freudian times, someone's psyche is his innermost soul or mind.

Purity Middle English. The word as name; a virtue name comparable to Chastity.
Pureza

Qiturah Arab. "Incense, scent." The name is more familiar in its Hebrew cognate form, Keturah.
Qeturah, Quetura, Queturah

Queen OE. "Queen."
Quanda, Queena, Queenette, Queenie

Quenby OE. Place name: "Queen's settlement."
Quenbie, Quinbie, Quinby

Querida Sp. "Dear, beloved."

Questa Fr. "One who seeks."

Quiana Possibly a variant of **Hannah**, but more often, a variation on **Ayanna**. A synthetic fabric very popular in the 1970s was called Qiana.
Qiana, Qianna, Quianna, Quiyanna

Quilla ME. ''Feather.'' As in a quill pen.
Quylla

Quinn Ir. Gael. Meaning unknown. Very common Irish last name, occasionally transferred to first-name status, though less often for girls. Actress Quinn Cummings.
Quin

Quincey OF. Place name: ''Estate of the fifth son.'' Last name of a prominent Massachusetts family whose name is borne by a town and by the 6th U.S. President, John Quincy Adams.
Quinci, Quincie, Quincy, Quinsy

Quintana Place name: Quintana Roo is a state on the east coast of Mexico.

Quintina Lat. ''Fifth.''
Quentina, Quintana, Quintessa, Quintona, Quintonette, Quintonice

Quirina Lat. ''Warrior.'' In Roman myth, Romulus (one of the founders of Rome) was deified as Quirino.

NAMES OF THE NINETIES

Donald Trump and Marla Maples named their daughter Tiffany because it seemed like the classiest possible name to them: never mind that its vogue is ten years past and teenagers named Tyffani (or Tiffenie, or Typhanny) are now turning up in beauty pageants all over the country. There are some names that will always carry with them a whiff of their era. Unfortunately, it's not usually clear what they are until your child reports to nursery school and discovers that he is one of four boys named Josh. The following celebrities may have fallen into the fashionable name trap: in any event, these are names that may very well appear dated in years to come.

Michael J. Fox and Tracy Pollan: Schuyler (a girl)
Pamela Lee: Brandon
Donna Mills: Chloë

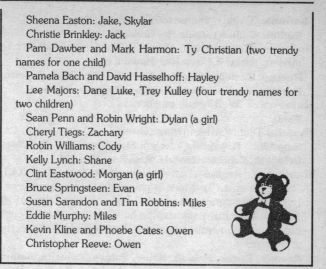

Sheena Easton: Jake, Skylar

Christie Brinkley: Jack

Pam Dawber and Mark Harmon: Ty Christian (two trendy names for one child)

Pamela Bach and David Hasselhoff: Hayley

Lee Majors: Dane Luke, Trey Kulley (four trendy names for two children)

Sean Penn and Robin Wright: Dylan (a girl)

Cheryl Tiegs: Zachary

Robin Williams: Cody

Kelly Lynch: Shane

Clint Eastwood: Morgan (a girl)

Bruce Springsteen: Evan

Susan Sarandon and Tim Robbins: Miles

Eddie Murphy: Miles

Kevin Kline and Phoebe Cates: Owen

Christopher Reeve: Owen

Rabab Arab. "Pale cloud."

Rabiah

Rabiah Arab. "Gentle wind."

Rachel Heb. "Ewe, female sheep." In the Old Testament Rachel is the wife of the patriarch Jacob. Like many Old Testament names, this one was taken up by the Puritans in the 17th century and remained current but not fashionable until parents of the late sixties and seventies used it in great numbers. It is still solidly popular, ranking in the top twenty names for girls in the early '90s. Actresses Raquel Welch, Rachel Ward; author Rachel Carson.

Rachael, Racheal, Rachelce, Rachele, Racheli, Rachelle, Rachil, Rae, Raechell, Rahel, Rahil, Rakel, Raquel, Raquela, Raquella, Raquelle, Ray, Raychel, Raychelle, Rashell, Rashelle, Rechell, Shell, Shelley, Shellie, Shelly

Radha Sanskrit. "Success." In the Hindu religion, the name of one of Krishna's consorts.

Radmilla Slavic. "Industrious for the people."
   Radilla, Radinka, Radmila, Redmilla
Rae Dim. **Rachel** (Heb. "Ewe"). Used independently in modern times. Actress Rae Dawn Chong.
   Raeann, Raelaine, Raeleen, Raelene, Ray, Raye, Rayette, Raylene, Raylina, Rayma, Rayna, Raynelle, Rayona
Rafa Arab. "Well-being, prosperity."
   Rafah
Ragnild Teut. "All-knowing power."
   Ragnhild, Ragnhilda, Ragnhilde, Ragnilda, Ranillda, Reinheld, Renilda, Renilde, Reynilda, Reynilde
Raina Var. **Regina** (Lat. "Queen") or fem. **Ray** (OG. "Wise guardian"). Modern name of several possible origins, including allusion to the wet stuff that falls out of the sky. Like many names that have appeared in this century, it has numerous variations, none of which is clearly a favorite.
   Raenah, Raene, Rainah, Raine, Rainey, Rainelle, Rainy, Raleine, Raya, Rayann, Rayette, Rayleine, Raylene, Raylina, Rayline, Rayna, Rayne, Rayney, Raynelle, Raynetta, Reyna, Reyney
Rainbow The phenomenon as a name. The rainbow, in Old Testament terms, is a symbol of the convenant between God and Noah that God will sustain his people. Loosely, it is also seen as a symbol of hope and (more recently) of ethnic and gender-preference tolerance.
Raissa Yid. "Rose."
   Raisa, Raisabel, Raisse, Raizel, Rayzel
Raja Arab. "Hope."
Raleigh OE. Place name: "Meadow of roe deer." Commemorates Sir Walter Raleigh, explorer and court favorite of Queen Elizabeth I, who is supposed to have spread his cape over a puddle so she could cross with dry feet. The city in North Carolina was named for him. Usually a name for boys, but the two-syllable "-leigh" form popularized by Ashley is prompting parents to look at many formerly masculine names as potential girls' names.
   Raileigh, Railey, Raley, Rawleigh, Rawley
Ralphina Fem. **Ralph** (OE. "Wolf-counsel").
   Ralphine
Rama Heb. "On high, exalted." The Hindu deity Vishnu

(a kindly god in the pantheon) appears in two forms as Rama.

Ramona (Fem. **Raymond**) Sp. "Wise guardian." A 19th-century historical novel of the same title was immensely successful, and brought the name to wide attention, but it is scarce now. Character in a very popular series of children's book of the same name by Beverly Cleary.

Mona, Ramoena, Ramohna, Ramonda, Ramonde, Ramonna, Ramowna, Romona, Romonda, Romonde

Ramsay OE. Place name: "Raven island" or "Ram island." Originally a last name common in Scotland, used only rarely as a first name for boys.

Ramsey

Randy Dim. **Miranda** (Lat. "Admirable"). Mostly U.S. use, and infrequent at that.

Randa, Randee, Randelle, Randene, Randi, Randie

Rana Arab. "Beautiful thing, eye-catching."

Rani Sanskrit. "Queen."

Raine, Rana, Ranee, Rania, Ranice, Ranique, Ranit, Rayna, Raynell

Ranielle Modern name: Danielle with an "R."

Ranita Heb. "Song."

Ranice, Ranit, Ranite, Ranith, Ranitra, Ranitta

Raoule Fem. **Raoul** (Fr. var. **Ralph**, OE "Wolf-counsel").

Raoula, Raula

Raphaela (Fem. **Raphael**) Heb. "God heals." The feminization is very unusual in English-speaking countries, though Italian parents use it with some frequency.

Rafa, Rafaela, Rafaelia, Rafaella, Raffaela, Raffaele, Raffaella, Rafella, Rafelle, Raphaella, Raphaëlle, Raphayella, Raphella, Refaella, Refella, Rephaela, Rephayelle

Rashida (Fem. **Rashid**) Turkish. "Righteous, rightly advised."

Rasheda, Rasheeda, Rasheida, Rashidah, Rashyda

Raven Name of the large black bird that is closely related to the crow. A fanciful name for a black-haired or dark-skinned baby. Actress Raven Symone's appearance on *The Cosby Show* has sparked a great deal of popularity for the name among African-American parents.

Ravenne, Rayven, Rayvinn

Ravenna Place name: city in Italy renowned for its Byz-

antine mosaics. Does not actually have anything to do with ravens, despite the sound.
Ravena, Ravinia, Ravinna

Rawnie Romany. "Lady." This is an English Gypsy term.

Raziah Aramaic. "The Lord's secret."
Razi, Raziela, Raziella, Razili

Ray Variant spelling of **Rae**, thus Dim. **Rachel** (Heb. "Ewe"). This spelling may look a little more "masculine," but short names like this are out of style anyway.
Raye, Rayla, Raylene

Reba Dim. **Rebecca**. Singer Reba McEntire.
Reyba, Rheba

Rebecca Heb. "Joined." A prominent Old Testament name; Rebecca is the wife of Isaac and mother of Jacob and Esau. Predictably, the name was taken up by the Puritans and remained fairly common through the 19th century. Subsequent revivals (in the thirties in the U.S., in the late sixties in Britain) may have been prompted by literary and cinematic use of the name, especially in the novel and film *Rebecca*. It is still used very steadily, as a familiar name in the currently fashionable three-syllable category. Philanthropist Rebekah Harkness; author Rebecca West; actress Rebecca De Mornay.
Becca, Becka, Beckee, Beckey, Beckie, Becky, Bekka, Bekki, Bekkie, Reba, Rebeca, Rebecka, Rebeka, Rebekah, Rebekkah, Rebeque, Ree, Reeba, Rheba, Revekka, Ribecca, Riva, Rivah, Rivalee, Reveka, Revekah, Rivekka, Rivi, Rivka, Rivkah, Rivy

Reed OE. "Red-haired." This is the most common spelling for masculine use of this name, which rarely crosses over to girls. The slightly less conventional spellings, however, may seem more feminine.
Read, Reade, Reid, Reida

Reese Var. **Rhys** (Welsh "Fiery, zealous").
Reece

Regan Ir. Celt. "Son of the small ruler." Use for girls may hark back to Shakespeare's play *King Lear*, but the king's daughter of that name is so cruel that this seems unlikely. Where Regan occurs it is more likely to be a family name adapted to a girl's name.
Reghan

Regina Lat. "Queen." Cropped up at the end of torian era, possibly encouraged by the fact that esty was often known as Victoria Regina. It may also be used as an allusion to the Virgin Mary, Regina Coelis ("Queen of the Heavens"). Nightclub founder Régine.
Gina, Raina, Raina, Raine, Regan, Reggi, Reggie, Régine, Reginette, Reginia, Reginna, Reina, Reine, Reinetta, Reinette, Reyna, Rina, Riona, Rionagh

Reina Sp. "Queen." See also **Raina**, for other spellings.
Reinella, Reinelle, Reinette, Reyna, Reynelle

Rella Var. Ella, OG. "All, completely."

Remedios Sp. "Help, remedy." Currently popular in South America.

Remy Fr. "From Rheims." Champagne, and the fine brandies made from champagne, are the principal product of Rheims, a town in central France.
Remi, Remie, Remmy, Rhemy

Rena Heb. "Melody," or Dim. **Irene** (Gk. "Peace").
Reena, Rina

Renata Lat. "Reborn." The Latin (and less popular) form of Renée. It was used in this guise by the Puritans. Author Renata Adler.
Ranae, Ranay, Renae, Renate, René, Renée, Renelle, Renetta, Renette, Renie, Renisa, Renita, Renise, Rennae, Rennay, Rennie

Rene Dim. **Irene** (Gk. "Peace"). Used on its own, primarily around the turn of the 20th century.
Reney, Renie, Rennie

Renée Fr. "Reborn." The French form of Renata, more common (though not really widespread) in modern times. Tennis star Renee Richards.
Ranae, Ranay, Ranée, Renae, René, Renell, Renelle, Renie, Rennie, Renny, Rhinaye, Rrenae

Renita Lat. "Resistant." Has come into use since the 1980s.
Reneeta, Renyta

Reseda Latin term for a flower more commonly known as mignonette.

Reta Var. **Rita**, Dim. **Margaret** (Gk. "Pearl").
Reda, Reeda, Reeta, Rheta, Rhetta

Rexana It is possible to translate this name by its parts,

with *rex* the Latin for "King," and *anna* a variant of the Hebrew word for "Grace." Or it may be a feminization of **Rex**, or a variant of **Roxane** (Per. "Dawn").
Rexanne, Rexanna, Rexalla, Rexella, Rexetta, Rexina, Rexine

Reza Hung. Dim. **Teresa** (Gk. "Harvest").
Rezi, Rezka, Riza

Rhea Gk. "Earth." In Greek myth, Rhea was an earth mother who bore Zeus, Demeter, Hera, and Poseidon, among other gods. Actress Rhea Perlman.
Rea, Rhia, Ria

Rheta Gk. "A speaker, eloquent." From the same root as the word "rhetoric."

Rhiannon Welsh. "Witch, goddess."
Rhianna, Rhianon, Rianon, Riannon

Rhoda Gk. "Rose," Lat. "From Rhodes." Rhodes is a Greek island originally named for its roses. The name is found in the New Testament, and was used mostly in the 18th and 19th centuries.
Rhodeia, Rhodia, Rhodie, Rhody, Roda, Rodi, Rodie, Rodina

Rhodanthe Gk. "Rose blossom."
Rhodante

Rhona ONorse. "Rough island." A form of Rona more common in Britain.
Rhona, Roana

Rhonda Welsh place name: the Rhondda Valley is a significant landmark in southern Wales, named for the river that runs through it. (In Welsh, the name means "noisy.") Today's parents will probably associate it with the Beach Boys' song "Help Me, Rhonda!"
Rhonnda, Ronda

Ria Dim. **Victoria** (Lat. "Victory"). Used occasionally as an independent name.
Rea

Riane (Fem. **Ryan**) Ir. last name. Uncommon, but analogous to the more widely used Briana.
Rhiane, Rhianna, Riana, Rianna, Rianne, Ryann, Ryanne

Rica Familiar form of **Erica**, Scand. "Ruler forever"; **Frederica** (OG. "Peaceful ruler"), or Sp. "Rich."

Rhica, Ricca, Ricki, Rickie, Ricky, Rieca, Riecka, Rieka, Riki, Rikki, Riqua, Rycca

Ricarda (Fem. **Richard**) OG. "Powerful ruler." One of many feminine forms of a very popular man's name, none of which has been adopted in large numbers.

Richanda, Richarda, Richardella, Richardene, Richardette, Richardina, Richardyne, Richel, Richela, Richele, Richella, Richelle, Richenda, Richenza, Richette, Richia, Richilene, Richina, Richmal, Richmalle

Rickie Dim. **Frederica** (OG. "Peaceful ruler"). Also possibly a feminine version of Richard, and certainly more popular than the longer forms. Occurred most often in the middle of the 20th century. Singer Rickie Lee Jones; actress Rickie Lake.

Rickie, Ricki, Ricky, Ricquie, Rika, Riki, Rikki, Rikky, Ryckie

Rihana Arab. Plant name: "Basil."

Riley Ir. Gael. "Courageous." Irish last name used as a first name for the last 150 years. Occasionally occurs as a girl's name.

Reilley, Reilly, Ryley

Rilla Middle German. "Small brook."

Rella, Rilletta, Rillette

Rima Arab. "Antelope."

Rimona Heb. "Pomegranate."

Riona Ir. Gael. "Like a queen."

Rionach, Rionagh, Rionna, Rionnagh

Risa Lat. "Laughter." A pretty name, but very unusual in English-speaking countries. Opera singer Risë Stevens.

Riesa, Risë, Rysa

Rita Dim. **Margaret** (Gk. "Pearl"). Comes via the Spanish form, Margarita. First used on its own some hundred years ago, and quite popular for fifty years. Actresses Rita Hayworth, Rita Moreno; authors Rita Mae Brown, Rita Dove.

Reeta, Reita, Rheeta, Rida, Riet, Rieta, Ritta

Ritsa Dim. **Alexander** (Gk. "Man's defender").

Riva Var. **Rebecca** (Heb. "Joined"). Also possibly from the French for "Shore," but the Jewish families who use it most often probably have the Old Testament associations in mind.

Ree, Reeva, Reevabel, Reva, Rifka, Rivalee, Rivi, Rivka, Rivke, Rivkah, Rivy

Roanna Var. Roseanne.

Ranna, Roanne, Ronni, Ronnie, Ronny

Roberta (Fem. **Robert**) OE. "Bright fame." While Ricarda, another simple feminization of an Old German name, never caught on, Roberta was rather widespread between its introduction in the late 19th century and its fall from favor some eighty years later. The name's similarity to the familiar Alberta probably promoted its acceptability. Singers Roberta Peters, Roberta Flack.

Berta, Bertie, Berty, Bobbe, Bobbee, Bobbette, Bobbie, Bobby, Bobbye, Bobette, Bobi, Bobina, Bobine, Bobinette, Reberta, Roba, Robbee, Robbey, Robbi, Robbie, Robby, Robeena, Robella, Robelle, Robena, Robenia, Robertena, Robertene, Robertha, Robertina, Robetta, Robette, Robettina, Robin, Robina, Robinett, Robinette, Robinia, Robyn, Robyna, Robynna, Ruperta, Rupetta

— **Robin** Dim. **Robert** (OE "Bright fame"). Originally a boy's nickname (as in Winnie the Pooh's friend Christopher Robin), but appropriated for girls in increasing numbers starting in the middle of the 20th century. Now out of fashion for both sexes. Actresses Robin Givens, Robin Wright.

Robee, Robbey, Robbi, Robbie, Robbin, Robby, Robbyn, Robena, Robene, Robenia, Robi, Robina, Robine, Robinet, Robinett, Robinette, Robinia, Robyn, Robyna, Robynette

Rochelle Fr. Place name: "Little rock." Enthusiastically used as a first name starting in the 1940s, but rare now.

Roch, Rochell, Rochella, Rochette, Roschella, Roschelle, Roshelle, Shell, Shelley, Shelly

Roderica (Fem. **Roderick**) OG. "Renowned ruler."

Rica, Roddie, Roderiga, Roderiqua, Roderique, Rodriga

Rohana Sanskrit. "Sandalwood."

Rohanna

Rolanda (Fem. **Roland**) OG. "Famous land."

Orlanda, Orlande, Rolande, Rollande

Roline Dim. **Caroline** (OG. "Man"). Unusual diminutive that appears from time to time in the South. It may also be a feminization of **Roland**.

Roelene, Roeline, Rolene, Rollene, Rolleen, Rollina, Rolline, Rolyne

Roma It. Place name: the capital city, Rome. Rather widely used since it first appeared in the late 19th century, though of course, it never approached the popularity of Florence.
Romelle, Romilda, Romina, Romma

Romaine (Fem. **Romain**) Fr. "From Rome." A pretty name that might be associated with a common variety of lettuce.
Romayne, Romeine, Romene

Romola Lat. "Roman woman."
Romala, Romella, Romelle, Rommola, Romolla, Romula

Romney OWelsh. Place name: "Winding river."

Romy Dim. **Rosemary** (Lat. "Dew of the sea"), or related to **Roma**. Actress Romy Schneider.

Rona ONorse. "Rough island." In Britain, used interchangeably with Rhona. Both versions cropped up at the turn of the century and have occurred steadily without ever being fashionable. Gossip columnist Rona Barrett.
Rhona, Ronella, Ronelle, Ronna

Ronni (Fem. **Ronald**) OE. "Strong counsel" or Dim. **Veronica** (Lat. "Image").
Ronalda, Ronee, Ronette, Roni, Ronna, Ronnee, Ronnelle, Ronnella, Ronney, Ronnie, Ronny

Rosabel Com. form **Rose** and **Belle**. A combination that appeared in the mid–19th century. Its meaning ("Beautiful rose") probably appealed as much to parents of the era as the name itself, which lost favor in the unsentimental 20th century. As Isabel becomes more popular, though, Rosabel may seem more appealing.
Rosabella, Rosabelle

Rosae Modern name: Rose with the innovative "-ae" ending. Also sounds like rosé wine: this spelling guarantees the right pronunciation.
Rosai, Rosay, Rosé, Rosée, Rosey

Rosalba Lat. "White rose." Artist Rosalba Carriera.

Rosalie Fr. Var. It. **Rosalia**. Possibly "Rose garden." Mostly 19th-century use.
Rosalee, Rosaleen, Rosaley, Rosalia, Rosalina, Rosaline, Rosalyne, Roselia, Rosella, Roselle, Rozalia, Rozalie, Rozele, Rozelie, Rozely, Rozella, Rozelle, Rozellia

Rosalind Sp. "Pretty rose" is the most common interpretation, though the name was actually coined in 16th-century Britain. A German form also existed, formed of words that meant "horse" or "renown" and "shield" or "snake." It has been used since the mid–19th century, with a surge in the middle of the 20th century. Today's parents considering the name may be haunted by the memory of Rosalyn Carter, a worthy but not exactly glamorous personage. Actress Rosalind Russell.

Ros, Rosalen, Rosalin, Rosalina, Rosalinda, Rosalinde, Rosaline, Rosalinn, Rosalyn, Rosalynd, Rosalynda, Rosanie, Roselin, Roselina, Roselind, Roselinda, Roselinde, Roseline, Roselinn, Roselyn, Roselynda, Roselynde, Rosina, Roslyn, Roslynn, Roslynne, Roz, Rozali, Rozalia, Rozalin, Rozalind, Rozalinda, Rozalynn, Rozalynne, Rozelin, Rozelind, Rozelinda, Rozelyn, Rozelynda

Rosalyn Com. form. **Rose** and **Lynn** (Sp. "Pretty"). The most common of the modern variants of Rosalind. First Lady Rosalyn Carter.

Rosalin, Rosalynn, Roselynn, Roslyn, Rozlynn

Rosamond OG. "Renowned protector." Also translatable (from the Latin) as "Rose of the world." More popular in the 19th century than it is today. Author Rosamond Bernier.

Ros, Rosamonde, Rosamund, Rosamunda, Rosemond, Rosemonda, Rosmund, Rosmunda, Roz, Rozamond

Rose Lat. Flower name. Scholars actually trace the name (which the Normans imported to Britain in the 11th century) to an Old German name meaning something like "Renown," but the flower meaning has had much more currency, particularly given the Christian symbolic meaning of the rose. (The "rosa mystica" is the Virgin Mary.) It reached its peak use at the turn of the 20th century, along with other flower names.

Rasia, Rasine, Rasja, Rasya, Rhoda, Rhodea, Rhodia, Rhody, Rosa, Rosaleen, Rosalia, Rosalie, Rosalin, Rosalina, Rosalind, Rosaline, Rosalinn, Rosalynn, Rosanie, Roselia, Roselina, Roseline, Rosella, Roselle, Rosena, Rosenah, Rosene, Rosetta, Rosette, Rosey, Rosheen, Rosie, Rosina, Rosita, Roslyn, Rosy, Roza, Rozalie, Rozaline, Rozalyne, Roze, Rozele, Rozella, Rozene, Rozina,

Rozsa, Rozsi, Rozsika, Rozy, Ruza, Ruzena, Ruzenka, Ruzha, Ruzsa, Zita

Roseanne Com. form. **Rose** and **Anne**. The pairing of the two names appeared in the 18th century, and various forms have drifted in and out of popularity. In our era, the name will inevitably summon associations with outspoken actress Roseanne Barr. Actress Rosanna Arquette.
Ranna, Roanna, Roanne, Rosanagh, Rosanna, Rosannah, Rosanne, Roseann, Roseanna, Rosehannah, Rozanna, Rozanne, Rozeanna

Rosemary Lat. "Dew of the sea" is the correct meaning, though the name gained great currency with the flower name fad of the late 19th century. The fact that most parents read it as a combination of Rose and Mary (both already popular, and with strong religious resonance for Catholics) can't have hurt. Singer Rosemary Clooney.
Rosemaree, Rosemarey, Rosemaria, Rosemarie, Rosmarie, Rozmary, Romy

Ross Scot. Gael. "Headland." A place name in Scotland. The name (like so many of the "R" names) may also come from the Gaelic word for "red."
Rosse

Rowena Welsh. "Slender and fair." This meaning is an approximation. The name was actually brought to public notice by novelist Sir Walter Scott with his immensely popular *Ivanhoe*, in the early 19th century.
Roweena, Roweina, Rowina

Roxanne Per. "Dawn." In history, the wife of Alexander the Great was named Roxane, but 20th-century parents may be more familiar with the Roxanne who is the heroine of Rostand's play *Cyrano de Bergerac*, or the character played by Daryl Hannah in Ron Howard's film adaptation. Favored in the U.S.
Oksana, Oksanna, Roksanne, Roxana, Roxane, Roxann, Roxanna, Roxene, Roxey, Roxiane, Roxianne, Roxie, Roxine, Roxy, Roxyanna, Ruksana, Ruksane, Ruksanna

Royale OF. "Regal one." Something of a curiosity in the democratic U.S.
Royalla, Royalene, Royalina, Royall, Royalle, Royalyn, Royalynne

Royce Meaning and origin unclear: some sources offer OF./

OE. "Son of the king"; others suggest OG. "Kind fame." The most famous Royce is the man who, along with Mr. Rolls, began turning out England's foremost luxury car. Very scanty use for girls.

Roice

Rubena Fem. **Reuben** (Heb. "Behold, a son").

Reubena, Reubina, Rubina, Rubine

Ruby Jewel name. Launched in the 1870s with other jewel names, but passé by the mid–20th century. Dancer Ruby Keeler.

Rubee, Rubetta, Rubey, Rubi, Rubia, Rubie, Rubina, Rubinia, Rubyna

Rudelle OG. "Renowned." From the same root that produces the male name Rudolph.

Rudella

Rufina Lat. "Red haired." Can be considered a feminine version of **Rufus**, which is given to boys regardless of their hair color.

Rufeena, Rufeine, Ruffina, Ruphyna

Ruta Lith. "Rue." The name of a plant.

Ruth Heb. "Friend, companion." The Old Testament Book of Ruth is about the widowed Moabite woman who refuses to leave her Hebrew mother-in-law, Naomi, and says, "Whither thou goest, I will go." Her sentiments appealed greatly to Victorian poets. The name has been consistently used ever since the 17th century, peaking at the turn of the century. Actresses Ruth Gordon, Ruth Buzzi; author Ruth Rendell.

Ruthe, Ruthelle, Ruthetta, Ruthi, Ruthie, Ruthina, Ruthine

Ruthann Com. form. **Ruth** and **Ann** (Heb. "Grace").

Ruthanna, Ruthanne

Ryan Irish last name. Meaning is unclear, though some sources connect it with "King." It has been very popular as a boy's name in recent years (well into the top twenty names on some lists) and is beginning to cross over as a girl's name.

Rian, Ryen, Ryenne

S

Saba Gk. "From Sheba" or Arab. "Morning." The queen of Sheba is mentioned in the Old Testament as having been hugely rich and very ostentatious.
Sabah, Sheba, Shebah

Sabina Lat. "Sabine." The Sabines were a tribe living in central Italy around the time Romulus and Remus established the city of Rome. In an effort to provide wives for the citizens of Rome, Romulus arranged the mass kidnapping of the Sabine women, which came to be known (and was frequently portrayed in art and literature) as the "Rape of the Sabines." The name was used among the ancient Romans and in English-speaking countries after the 17th century, but has been very rare lately.
Bina, Byna, Sabine, Sabinna, Sabiny, Sabyna, Sahbina, Savina, Savine, Sebina, Sebinah

Sabra Origin disputed: may be Heb. "To rest," or possibly "Cactus." It is now used as a term for a native-born Israeli.
Sabrah, Sebra, Sabrette

Sabrina Lat. Place name: the Latin term for the Severn River in England. Though Milton (among others) writes about a Sabrina, she appeared most vividly in modern culture as *Sabrina Fair* in the play and movie. The name was used in the 19th century and cropped up again in the last part of the 20th century. A popular choice for turn-of-the-century parents, perhaps.
Brina, Sabreena, Sabrinna, Sabryna, Sebreena, Sebrina, Zabrina

Sachi Jap. "child of joy."
Sachiko

Sadie Dim. **Sarah** (Heb. "Princess"). Use as an independent name occurred mostly at the turn of the 20th century. The trend toward folksy old-fashioned names has not

quite reached Sadie: it may be the wrong kind of old-fashioned. Actress Sada Thompson.
Sada, Sadah, Sadelle, Saida, Saidee, Saidey, Saidie, Saydie, Sydell, Sydella, Sydelle

Sadira Per. "Lotus tree." The lotus has great significance in several of the Eastern religions.

Saffron Flower name: saffron refers to a substance (the dried stamens of saffron crocuses) used as a spice in Mediterranean and other cuisines. It produces a bright orange-yellow color, and is sometimes used as a dye. Monks of some Eastern religions wear saffron robes, which may explain why the name was used occasionally in the 1960s, an era when saffron robes and Eastern religions went mainstream. This usage was mocked in the comic TV series *Absolutely Fabulous.*
Saffran, Saffren, Saffronia, Saphron

Sagara Indo-Pakistani. "The sea."

Sage Lat. "Wise, healthy." More likely to be a boy's name, perhaps via associations with sagebrush, cowboys, and the Wild West. Highly unusual, but this is the kind of allusive, genderless name that seems very popular at the moment.
Saige, Sayge

Sahara Arab. "Desert." Place name: desert in North Africa. The Sahara is the legendary desert, exceedingly inhospitable to mankind.
Saharra

Sakura Jap. "Cherry blossom."

Salena Var. Selina (Gk. "Moon goddess").
Salina

Salama Arab. "Peace." Related to Solomon, which is Hebrew for "Peace" or "Peaceful." Also related to Salome, but without the racy connotations.
Sallama, Saloma, Soloma

Salamanca Place name: city in western Spain, seat of an ancient university. It has been occupied by Hannibal, the Goths, the Moors, the French, and the English.

Salimah Arab. "Healthy, sound." Currently popular in Arabic countries. This was the name adopted by the English wife of the current Aga Khan when she married him; appropriate, since her English name was Sally.
Salima, Selima

Sally Dim. **Sarah** (Heb. "Princess"). A popular student name in the 18th century and again in [...] Though today's parents are largely ignoring nicknames, Sally has the same kind of honest, all-American appeal as Jack, which is becoming fashionable. Talk-show host Sally Jessy Raphael; actress Sally Field; astronaut Sally K. Ride.

Sal, Salcia, Saletta, Sallee, Salletta, Sallette, Salley, Sallianne, Sallie, Sallyann

Salome Heb. "Peace." Possibly from the same root that gives us the greeting "Shalom." The most famous biblical Salome is the woman who danced for King Herod and demanded, as her reward, the head of John the Baptist on a platter. In spite of this unsavory antecedent, the name was used somewhat in the 19th century, but its connotations make it an unlikely choice.

Sahlma, Salima, Salma, Salmah, Saloma, Salomea, Salomey, Salomi, Selima, Selma, Selmah, Solome, Solomea

Salvadora Sp. "Savior." Referring, of course, to Jesus Christ.

Salvia Lat. "Whole, healthy." The Latin name for the herb known as sage, which has mild healing powers and is an aromatic used in cooking.

Sallvia, Salvina

Samala Heb. "Requested of God."

Samale, Sammala

Samantha (Fem. **Samuel**) Heb. "Told by God." Also contains the Greek form "-antha," which means flower. Occasionally used in the 17th to 19th centuries, but truly popular in the 1960s and 1970s, possibly triggered by the TV series *Bewitched*. Unlike many names that were current when today's parents were children, Samantha is also popular now, climbing into the top ten in the early '90s. Actress Samantha Eggar.

Sam, Samey, Sami, Samentha, Sammantha, Sammee, Sammey, Sammie, Semantha, Semanntha, Simantha, Symantha

Samara Heb. "Under God's rule."

Samaria, Samarie, Sammara, Semara

Samuela (Fem. **Samuel**) Heb. "Told by God." Very scarce, particularly compared with Samantha.

Samella, Samelle, Samuella, Samuelle

Sancia Lat. "Sacred."
Sancha, Sanchia, Santsia, Sanzia

Sandra Dim. **Alexandra** (Gk. "Defender of mankind") via It. **Alessandra**. Popular in the middle of the 20th century, but today's parents are more inclined to prefer the full four syllables of the original name. Comedienne Sandra Bernhard; actresses Sandrine Bonnaire, Sondra Locke, Sandra Dee, Sandra Bullock; Supreme Court Justice Sandra Day O'Connor.
Sahndra, Sanda, Sandee, Sandie, Sandreea, Sandrella, Sandrelle, Sandretta, Sandrette, Sandria, Sandrina, Sandrine, Sandy, Sanndra, Sanndria, Sauhndra, Saundra, Sohndra, Sondra, Sonndra, Wysandria, Zandra

Sandy Dim. **Sandra**. Mostly used post-1950.
Sandee, Sandi, Sandie, Sanndi

Sanna Dim. **Susanna** (Heb. "Lily"). Used as an independent name in Scandinavia.
Sana, Zanna

Santana Sp. "Holy." May remind prospective parents more of a rock band that was famous in the '60s and '70s.
Santa

Santuzza It. "Holy." This is a diminutive form.

Sapphire Heb. Jewel name. Unusual biblical name, and the birthstone for September. One of the least used of the jewel names.
Safira, Saphira, Sapphira, Sephira

Sarah Heb. "Princess." In the Old Testament, the wife of the patriarch Abraham. Came into vogue with other biblical names in the 16th century and was enough of a staple for 400 years to have spawned a variety of nicknames (though not as many as the multisyllabic Elizabeth, for instance). Ranked number five in a 1990 nationwide survey of babies born in the United States. More recent polls show it continuing in top ten positions in San Francisco, Texas, and Florida, with heaviest use among Asian-American and European-American families. Actresses Sarah Bernhardt, Sarah Siddons, Sarah Jessica Parker; singer Sarah Vaughan; poet Sara Teasdale; Sarah Ferguson, Duchess of York.
Sadee, Sadella, Sadelle, Sadellia, Sadie, Sadye, Saidee, Sal, Sallee, Salley, Sallie, Sally, Sara, Sarai, Saraia, Sar-

een, **Sarely, Sarena, Sarette, Sari, Sarika, Sarina, Sarine, Sarita, Saritia, Sarka, Sarolta, Sarotta, Sarotte, Saroya, Sarra, Sarrah, Sasa, Sera, Serach, Serah, Serita, Shara, Sorcha, Sydel, Sydelle, Zahra, Zara, Zarah, Zaria, Zarita**

Sardinia Place name: mountainous island off the west coast of Italy. Sardines probably take their name from this island.
Sardegna

Saril Turkish. "Noise of flowing water."

Sasha (Fem. and Dim. **Alexander**) Rus. The "-sha" ending is not necessarily feminine in Russia, and Sasha is more commonly a male nickname.
Sacha, Sasa, Sascha, Saschenka, Zsazsa

Saskia Dutch name of unknown meaning. It would probably have been forgotten, but it was the name of Rembrandt's wife, who is depicted in some of his finest canvases. Actress Saskia Reeves.

Sato Jap. "Sugar."

Savanna Sp. "Treeless." Originally familiar as a place name, as in the city in Georgia, or name of a geographical feature: a wide, treeless plain. But its pretty sound and fashionable three-syllable "-a" ending form have made it increasingly fashionable among sophisticated parents. With the current trend toward geography names, this popularity will probably continue.
Savana, Savannah, Sevanna

Scarlett ME. "Scarlet." Given its fame by the inimitable Scarlett O'Hara, heroine of *Gone With the Wind*. Not hugely popular, possibly because the young lady in the novel is so headstrong. She probably came by the name from the family tree, but it does carry connotations of a "scarlet woman," a lady of easy virtue. It is nevertheless the middle name of one of Mick Jagger's children with Jerry Hall.
Scarlet, Scarletta, Scarlette

Scirocco It. from Arab. "Warm wind." The word originally described the wind that blew over Italy from the Libyan deserts.
Cirocco, Sirocco

Scotia Latin term for Scotland. Before the Irish invaded the country in 258 A.D., it was known as Caledonia.

Scout OF. "To listen." Occupational name: someone who scouts, gathers information quietly. When Bruce Willis and Demi Moore named their daughter Scout after a character in *To Kill a Mockingbird*, they gave the name a new credibility.
Scoutt

Season Lat. "Time of sowing." The word used as a name. Cropped up in the 1970s (along with Spring and Summer), when children were given counterculture names, but seems unlikely to endure. Actress Season Hubley.

Sedona Place name: city in Arizona much cherished for its natural beauty and tranquil ambiance.
Sadona, Sedonah, Sedonia

Seema Heb. "Precious thing, treasure."
Cima, Cyma, Seemah, Sima, Simah, Sina

Sebastiane (Fem. **Sebastian**) Lat. "From Sebastia." Unusual feminization of a name that is very uncommon in America.
Bastia, Bastiana, Sebastiana, Sebastienne

Secunda Lat. "Second."

Sefarina Sp. from Gk. "Gentle wind." This is the Spanish form of Zephyr.
Sefirina, Sepharina, Zefarina, Zepharina, Zephirina

Segovia Place name: province and city in central Spain. The name is most familiar to Americans through the fame of guitar player Andrés Segovia.

Selby OE. Place name: "Manor village." Likely to ride on the coattails of the increasingly common Shelby.
Selbea, Selbee, Selbeigh, Selbey, Selbie

Selena Gk. "Moon goddess." Most popular in the 19th century, though the immense fame of the late Tejana pop star of this name may promote its use.
Celene, Celie, Celina, Celinda, Celine, Cellina, Celyna, Saleena, Salena, Salina, Sela, Selene, Selia, Selie, Selina, Selinda, Seline, Sena

Selima Heb. "Tranquil." Another version of Salome.
Saleema, Saleemah, Selimah

Selma (Fem. **Anselm** by way of **Anselma**) OG. "Godly helmet." Selma is the more common form, though it is far from an everyday choice.
Anselma, Sellma, Selmah, Zelma

Semele Gk. In Greek myth, the mother of Dionysus by Zeus. Her name may come from the name of a very early Greek earth goddess. English composer G. F. Handel composed a secular oratorio about her.
Samelle, Semelle

Semiramis Heb. "Highest heaven." Semiramis was an Assyrian queen who, myth has it, built Babylon and turned into a dove after death. Her legend inspired both Voltaire and Rossini.
Semira

Senalda Sp. "A sign."

Seneca Name with both Native American and ancient Roman resonance. The Seneca tribe of Iroquois lived in the Finger Lakes region of western New York state and gave their name to a lake, a river, and a town. Entirely coincidentally, Seneca was also the name of an important Roman philosopher and tragedian, who was the Emperor Nero's tutor.
Senecca, Seneka, Senneca

Senga Var. Agnes (Gk. "Pure"). A rare Scottish name; it is Agnes spelled backward.

September Month name. Much less common than April, May, or June.

Septima Lat. "Seventh." If one has a seventh child, why not celebrate with her name?

Sequoia Tree name. The great sequoia is an ancient and immense tree native to northern California. The tree was named for a Cherokee Indian of the early 19th century who invented a system for writing down the Cherokee language.
Sacoya, Secoya, Saquoia, Saquoya, Sequoya

Seraphina Heb. "Ardent." The seraphim are the highest-ranking angels in Heaven (above angels, archangels, cherubim, etc.). They have six wings and are noted for their zealous love.
Sarafina, Serafina, Sérafine, Seraphe, Séraphine, Serofina, Serophine

Serena Lat. "Tranquil, serene." Used by Roman Christians, and periodically popular since, though never in a big way.
Cerena, Reena, Sarina, Saryna, Serene, Serenna, Serina, Serenity, Seryna

Serilda OG. "Armed warrior woman."
Sarilda, Serhilda, Serhilde, Serrilda
Sesame The seed and flavoring agent.
Sesamey, Sessame, Sessamee
Sesheta Name from Egyptian mythology: Sesheta was the goddess of the stars and the patroness of writing and literature.
Sevilla Sp. Var. **Sibyl** (Gk. "Seer, oracle"). Also the name of an ancient Spanish city, home of painter Diego Velazquez, and the setting of Bizet's famous opera *Carmen*.
Shadow OE "Shade."
Shadoe
Shandy Derivation unknown. Name of a drink popular in Britain, half beer and half lemonade or ginger ale. Possibly adapted as a girl's name because it sounds so much like the familiar Sandy and Mandy.
Shandea, Shandee, Shandeigh, Shandey, Shandie
Shaina Heb. "Beautiful."
Shaine, Shana, Shanee, Shani, Shanie, Shayna, Shayne
Shaka Modern name: "Sha-," like "La-," is a very fashionable prefix, attached to any number of other particles to form names that have no specific meaning but sound attractive.
Shakeela, Shakeita, Shakeera, Shakette, Shakila, Shakina, Shakira, Shakitra, Shaquina, Shaquita
Shalimar Name of a Guerlain perfume, which in turn was named for the famous Shalimar Gardens, eighty acres of gardens near what is now Lahore, Pakistan. The gardens were laid out by Shah Jahan, who also had the Taj Mahal built.
Shalamar, Shalemar, Shallimar
Shalom Heb. "Peace." Not a name, but a greeting to speakers of Hebrew. Nevertheless adapted by some parents for its meaning. Model Shalom Harlow.
Shalome, Shalva, Shalvah, Shelom, Shilom, Sholome
Shamira Heb. "He who defends."
Shamirah, Shameera, Shemira
Shana Dim. **Shannon**, or anglicization of **Shaina**, or diminutive of **Shoshana**. Uncommon, but kept in the public eye by journalist and biographer Shana Alexander.
Shanah, Shanna, Shannah

Shaneika Modern U.S. Another elaboration of the ["Sha-" prefix. Some of the more common of these names are the ones that sound like "Ashanti," which is an important name in western Africa, where many American slaves originally came from. Other "Sha-" names, like the "La-" names, are limited in form only by parental imagination.

Shandee, Shandeigh, Shandey, Shandeya, Shanecka, Shaneese, Shaneikah, Shanequa, Shaneyka, Shaniece, Shanika, Shanique, Shanisse, Shanneice, Shanta, Shantee, Shanteigh, Shantella, Shantelle, Shantey, Sheniece, Shenika, Sheniqua, Shonyce

Shanelle Modern U.S. name which is a phonetic spelling of "Chanel," the name of the great French couturier. It has double-barreled appeal, since it combines the "Sha-" prefix with an evocation of great feminine elegance.

Shanel, Shanella, Shanelly, Shannel, Shaney, Shanilly, Shanisse, Shanita, Shenell, Shenelle, Shinella, Shonelle, Shynelle

Shani Heb. "Scarlet." Refers to a metaphorical "scarlet thread" or theme of a story.

Shanit

Shannon Ir. Gael. "Old, ancient." The name of an important river, county, and airport in Ireland, used as a first name in this century. Most popular among families with Irish roots, but little found in Ireland. Actress Shannen Doherty; gymnast Shannon Miller.

Channa, Shana, Shandy, Shane, Shani, Shanna, Shannae, Shannen, Shannin, Shanon

Shantal Var. **Chantal** (Fr. place name). Its popularity may be associated with both Shanelle and the other "Sha-" names, rather than with the rather obscure French first name.

Shanta, Shantahl, Shantay, Shantalle, Shante, Shantella, Shantelle, Shontal, Shontalle, Shontelle

Sharlene (Fem. and Dim. **Charles**) OG. "Man." Var. **Caroline**. One of the numerous variations that were popular in the 1950s and 1960s.

Sharleen, Sharleyne, Sharlina, Sharline, Sharlyne

Sharon Heb. Place name: "A plain." In the Old Testament, refers to flat land at the foot of Mount Carmel. Not picked up by the 16th-century Puritans, probably since it wasn't a personal name, but by mid–20th century it was quite popular in America. Now much less common. Actresses Sharon Gless, Sharon Stone.

Charin, Cheron, Shara, Sharan, Sharen, Sharene, Shari, Sharie, Sharla, Sharolyn, Sharona, Sharonda, Sharren, Sharrin, Sharronne, Sheran, Sheron, Sherri, Sherry, Sheryn, Sherynn

Shashi Hindi. "Moonbeam."

Shasta Oregon mountain of some 14,000 feet that rises from nearly sea level. It is at the southernmost end of the Cascade Mountain range. Also the name of a brand of soda, though parents using this name are more likely to be evoking America's natural beauty.

Shahsta, Shastah

Shavonne Phonetic var. **Siobhan** (Ir. Gael. var. **Joan**, fem. **John**) Heb. "The Lord is gracious."

Shevon, Shevonne, Shivonne, Shyvon, Shyvonne

Shawn (Fem. var. **Sean**, Ir. var. **John**) Heb. "The Lord is gracious." Use of Sean and its variants, feminine and masculine, is on the wane since the late 1970s. Actress Sean Young.

Sean, Seana, Seanna, Shana, Shanna, Shaun, Shauna, Shaunee, Shaunie, Shawna, Shawnee, Shawneen, Shawnette, Sianna

Shawnee Name of a Native American tribe that originated in the eastern forests of the U.S. and gradually migrated westward. Shawnee Mission is the name of a town in Kansas. Also, possibly, a variant of **Shawn**.

Shawney, Shawnie

Shayla Var. **Sheila** (Ir. from Lat., "Blind") or dim. **Michaela** (Fem. **Michael**, Heb. "Who is like the Lord?").

Shaela, Shae-Lynn, Shaila, Shailagh, Shaylah

Shayna Var. **Shaina** (Heb. "Beautiful").

Shaina, Sheina

Shea Ir. Gael. "From the fairy fort." More commonly an Irish last name.

Shae, Shay, Shaye, Shayla, Shaylyn

Sheba Heb. "From Sheba." Also a short version of Bathsheba (Heb. "Daughter of the oath"). The Queen of

Sheba is mentioned in the Old Testament as having been hugely rich and very ostentatious.

Saba, Sabah, Scheba, Shebah, Sheeba, Shieba

Sheena Ir. Var. **Jane** (Heb. "The Lord is gracious"). Many of the "Sh" names are Gaelic versions of Jane, Jean, and Joan, which are in turn variations on that old staple, **John**. Rock star Sheena Easton.

Sheenagh, Sheenah, Sheina, Shena, Shiona, Shionagh, Sina, Sine

Sheherezade Arab. "Dweller in cities." Sheherezade was the famous teller of tales, married to a sultan who had resolved to marry a woman a day and strangle her at dawn. Sheherezade told him stories for 1,001 nights, after which he relented.

Scheherezade, Sheherazade, Sharazad, Sharizad

Sheila Ir. Var. **Cecilia** (Lat. "Blind"). Popular in mid–20th century in Britain and the Commonwealth; in Australian slang, a "sheila" is a woman.

Seila, Selia, Shayla, Shaylah, Sheela, Sheelagh, Sheelah, Sheilagh, Sheilah, Shela, Shelagh, Shelia, Shiela

Shelby OE. Place name: "Estate on the ledge." Used to occur infrequently as a man's name, but it has recently been taken up by parents, reaching into the top 100 U.S. girls' names by the early 1990s.

Shelbea, Shelbee, Shelbeigh, Shelbey, Shelbie, Shellby

Shell Several possible sources: diminutive for **Michelle** or **Shelley**, or use of the object as a name.

Chell, Chella, Chelle, Shella, Shelle

Shelley OE. Place name: "Meadow on the ledge." Last name made famous by the poet Percy Bysshe Shelley. Use as a feminine first name seems to have been related to Shirley. Actresses Shelley Winters, Shelley Duvall, Shelley Long.

Schelley, Shellee, Shellie, Shelly

Shera Aramaic. "Brightness."

Sheridan Ir. Gael. Unclear meaning, possibly "Wild man." Used mostly in Britain as a male name, but the "Sher-" element sounds enough like Cheryl or Sharon to make use for girls possible.

Sheredon, Sheridan, Sheridawn, Sheriden, Sheridon, Sherridan, Sherriden, Sherrydan

Sherrerd Unknown origin. Possibly related to Sheridan. Familiar sounding enough, owing to the "Sher-" component, to be used occasionally as a girl's name. There is no definitive spelling.

Sherard, Sherrard, Sherrod

Sherry Var. **Cher** (Fr. "Dear"), **Sharon** (Heb. "The plain"), or **Cheryl** (var. **Charlotte**, OG. "Man"). In the 1950s and 1960s these three names and their variants were all popular, giving rise to a parade of further forms, spellings, and elaborations. Tracing the exact origin of any of them is difficult. Puppeteer Shari Lewis.

Cheray, Sharee, Shari, Sharie, Sharrie, Sherae, Sheraie, Sheray, Sheree, Sherey, Sheri, Sherice, Shericia, Sherie, Sherina, Sherissa, Sherita, Sherree, Sherrey, Sherri, Sherryn, Sherye, Sh'rae

Sheryl Var. **Cheryl** (var. **Charlotte**, OG. "Man"). Actress Sherilyn Fenn.

Cheralin, Cheralyn, Cheralynne, Cherilynn, Sheralyn, Sheralin, Sherileen, Sherill, Sherilyn, Sherilynne, Sherrell, Sherrill, Sherryl, Sheryll

Shiloh Biblical place name. Also the name of a Civil War battle in Tennessee.

Shilo, Shylo

Shifra Heb. "Lovely."

Schifra, Shifrah

Shiri Heb. "My song."

Shira, Shirah, Shirit

Shirley OE. Place name: "Bright meadow." Originally a last name, brought to immense fame and popularity as a girl's name with the career of child star Shirley Temple. Now widely neglected. At the moment, almost any name with an "-ley" ending is considered suitable for girls. The popularity of first Shirley, then Ashley and Kelly, paved the way for this fashion. Actress Shirley MacLaine; politician Shirley Chisholm.

Sherlee, Sherli, Sherlie, Sherrlie, Sheryl, Shirely, Shirl, Shirlea, Shirlee, Shirleen, Shirleigh, Shirlene, Shirlinda, Shirline, Shirlley, Shirly, Shirlyn, Shurlee

Shona Ir. Gael. Var. **John** (Heb. "The Lord is gracious"). While Sinead is a Gaelic form of Janet, Shona is the equivalent form of Joan.

Shonagh, Shonah, Shone, Shuna, Shunagh

Shoshana Heb. "Lily." The more common form is the anglicized Susan or Susanna.
Shosha, Shoshanah, Sosanna, Sosannah

Shoshone Native American tribe, indigenous to eastern Nevada, southern Idaho, and western Utah. These nomads were also known as the Snake Indians. Sacajawea, Lewis and Clark's guide on their Western explorations, was a Shoshone.
Shoshoni

Shulamith Heb. "Peace." Composer Shulamit Ran; writer Shulamith Firestone.
Shula, Shulamit, Sula, Sulamith

Shura Rus. dim. **Alexander** (Gk. "Man's defender"). Used in Russia as a nickname for a man.
Shurka

Sian Welsh var. **John** (Heb. "The Lord is gracious"). Actress Sian Phillips.

Sibyl Gk. "Seer, oracle." In ancient myth, sibyls interpreted the messages from oracles devoted to particular Gods, but their legend was also taken up and Christianized, and the name was common in the Middle Ages. Use dropped off and was revived at the turn of the 20th century, but the name (more commonly spelled Sybil) now has a slightly dated aura. Actress Cybill Shepherd.
Cybele, Cybil, Cybill, Cybilla, Sabilla, Sabylla, Sib, Sibbell, Sibel, Sibell, Sibella, Sibelle, Sibilla, Sibyll, Sibylla, Sybel, Sybella, Sybelle, Sybill, Sybilla, Sybille

Sicily Place name: large island off the tip of Italy's "boot." Many Italian immigrants to the United States have roots in Sicily.
Sicilia, Sicillia, Sicilly

Sidney OE. "From Saint Denis." Famous English last name turned first name in the 18th century, very fashionable in the late 19th century, now little used for boys but beginning to be fashionable for girls in the Kelly/Ashley mold. O.J. Simpson's daughter is named Sydney.
Siddeny, Sideny, Sidneigh, Sidni, Sidnie, Sydney, Sydnie

Sidonie Lat. "From Sidonia." Sidon was an area in the Middle East. Not uncommon in France, but easily confused with Sidney in the U.S.
Sidaine, Sidonia, Sidony, Sydona, Sydonah, Sydonia, Syndonia

Sidra Lat. "Of the stars."

Siena Place name: town in Tuscany not far from Florence, home of many art treasures. The town gave its name to a reddish shade of brown.
Sienna

Sierra Place name. Sierra is Spanish for "saw," and was the name Spanish settlers gave to the sharp, irregular peaks of some of the Western mountains like the Sierra Nevada (literally, "snowy saw"). Now used from time to time as a proper name, along with other geographical features like Savannah and Mesa.
Ciera, Cierra, Siera

Sigfreda OG. "Peaceful victory."
Sigfreida, Sigfrida, Sigfrieda, Sigfryda

Sigismonda It. From OG. "Victorious shield."
Sigismunda, Sigmonda, Sigmunda

Signa Unknown Scandinavian meaning: "Victory" is a possibility. The name is very unusual.
Signe, Signild, Signilda, Signilde, Signy

Sigourney Origin unclear, and made familiar almost single-handedly by actress Sigourney Weaver, who was christened Susan.
Sigornee, Sigournie

Sigrid ONorse. "Fair victory." Little used outside of Scandinavian countries. Novelist Sigrid Undset.
Sigred

Silence Puritan virtue name. No longer considered a virtue.

Silken Modern name, adapted from the fabric. Rower Silken Laumann.
Silkie, Silkya

Silja Scand. dim. **Cecilia** (Lat. "Blind").
Silia, Silija, Siliya, Sillia, Sillija, Silliya, Silya

Silver Name of the precious metal. Could describe a baby's pale coloring, perhaps.
Silverey, Silverie

Silvia Var. **Sylvia** (Lat. "From the woods"). This was the original form of the name, eclipsed by the "-y" spelling in the 19th century.
Silva, Silvana, Silvanna, Silvie, Silvija, Sirvana, Sirvanna, Silvy, Silvya, Sylvia, Sylvie

Simcha Heb. "Joy."

Simla Place name: hill town in northern India where, in the days of the Raj, the British spent the hot summers.

Simone (Fem. **Simon**) Heb. "Listening intently." Used outside of France from the middle of the 20th century. Actress Simone Signoret; writer Simone de Beauvoir; gymnast Simona Amanar.

Shimona, Shimonah, Simeona, Simmina, Simona, Simonetta, Simonette, Simonia, Simonina, Simonna, Simonne, Symona, Symone

Sinead Ir. Var. **Janet** (Fem. **John**, Heb. "The Lord is gracious"). This name and Siobhan are a little more common than most Gaelic names, possibly influenced by actresses Sinead Cusack and Siobhan McKenna. Sheena is a short version of Sinead. Singer Sinead O'Connor.

Shinead, Seonaid, Sina, Sine

Siobhan Ir. Var. **Joan** (Fem. **John**, Heb. "the Lord is gracious"). Many of the phonetic forms of this name are probably intended as a combination of the "Sha-" prefix and Yvonne. Actress Siobhan McKenna.

Chavonne, Chevonne, Chivon, Chyvonne, Shavaun, Shavon, Shervan, Shevon, Shevonne, Shirvaun, Shivahn, Shivaun, Shovonne, Shyvonne, Sh'vonne, Sioban, Siobahn, Siobhian, Syvonne

Sintra Place name: town in Portugal. Because it sounds so much like Cynthia, Sintra has more plausibility as a first name than some place names.

Cintra

Sirena Gk. "Entangler." In Greek myth, sirens were creatures that were half-woman, half-bird, and sang so sweetly that men dropped everything to listen, and starved to death. Odysseus outwitted them in his travels. Easily confused with Serena, which has very different connotations.

Sireena, Sirene, Syrena

Siria Sp. from Per. "Sun-bright, glowing." Sirius, the Dog Star, is the brightest star in the heavens.

Seeria, Syria

Sissy Dim. **Cecilia** (Lat. "Blind"). Also a common nickname for a sister, since this is the way a younger sibling may say that word. Actress Sissy Spacek.

Cissee, Cissey, Cissi, Cissie, Cissy, Sissee, Sissey, Sissie

Sitka Place name: city in western Alaska. It is the second oldest city in Alaska, having been founded as a fur-trading post by Russians in 1799.

Sivney Ir. Gael. "Well-going." Rare Irish last name.
Sivneigh, Sivnie

Skye Scot. Place name: the name of a spectacular island off the west coast of Scotland. With the current trend toward nature and geography names, it may also refer to the big blue bowl overhead.
Skie, Sky

Skyler Dutch. "Giving shelter." Most probably an adaptation of the Dutch last name of Schuyler, which was brought to New York by 17th-century settlers. Used a bit for both boys and girls now, possibly prompted by the fashionable Kyle/Kyla.
Schyler, Schuyler, Skyla, Skylar, Skyllar

Sloane Ir. Gael. "Man of arms." An Irish last name that has become well entrenched in Britain and the U.S. Sometimes makes the leap to first-name status, perhaps as a maternal maiden name. Given extra prominence by the fact that Britain's preppy cousins are known as "Sloane Rangers," for the area in London where they congregate.
Sloan

Snowdrop Flower name. The snowdrop, a modest white flower, blooms very early in the spring.

Socorro Sp. "Aid, help." Currently popular in Spain. Most likely refers to the aid or help provided by the Almighty.
Secorra, Socaria, Socorra, Sucorra

Soki Possibly var. **Sukey**, dim. **Susan** (Heb. "Lily").
Sokey, Sukie

Solana Sp. "Sunlight."
Solenne, Solina, Soline, Souline, Soulle

Solange Fr. "With dignity."
Souline, Zeline

Soledad Sp. "Solitude."

Soleil Fr. "Sun."

Solveig Scand. "Woman of the house."
Solvag, Solvej

Soma Indo-Pakistani. "Moon."

Somers Probably short for an Old English place name having to do with summer, like "Somerset."
Sommer, Sommers

Sondra Var. **Sandra** (Dim. **Alexandra**, Gk. "Defender of mankind"). Actress Sondra Locke.
Saundra, Sohndra, Sonndra, Zohndra, Zondra

Sonia Var. **Sophia** (Gk. "Wisdom"). Used since early in the 20th century. The current Queen of Norway is named Sonja. Skater/actress Sonja Henie; painter Sonia Delaunay.
Sohnia, Sohnnja, Sondja, Sondya, Sonja, Sonje, Sonnja, Sonya

Sonoma Place name: an extremely picturesque county in Northern California.
Senoma, Sonohma

Sonora Place name: state in northwestern Mexico.

Sophia Gk. "Wisdom." Used in English-speaking countries since the 17th century, though the French form, Sophie, has given it much competition in Britain. The famous Istanbul mosque Hagia Sofia was once a Christian church, but it was dedicated not to Saint Sophia (an obscure and possibly nonexistent martyr), but to the Holy Wisdom, i.e., the Word of God. The name is not particularly common, and would seem ripe for revival with other "old-fashioned" names, but its unfamiliar sound (resembling neither the three-syllable "-a" ending names, nor the two-syllable "-ey" ending names) may hold it back. Actress Sophia Loren.
Saffi, Sofia, Sofie, Soficita, Sofka, Sofy, Sofya, Sonia, Sonja, Sonnie, Sonya, Sophey, Sophie, Sophy, Zofia, Zofi, Zofya, Zosia

Sophronia Gk. "Sensible, prudent."
Soffrona, Sofronia

Soraya Persian name of unknown meaning, brought to prominence by the last Empress of Iran.

Sorcha Ir. Gael. "Bright, shining." Used almost exclusively in Ireland. Actress Sorcha Cusack.

Sorrel Botanical name. Sorrel is a wild herb. Much less common than Laurel or Rosemary, but the herb itself is delicate and not widely found.
Sorel, Sorelle, Sorrell, Sorrelle

...rette Dramatic term: the traditional part of a coquet-
~~tish~~ ladies' maid in 18th and 19th century plays.

Spencer ME. Occupational name: "Provider." Used for
the person in a large household who dispensed food and
drink. Usually a last name, but occurs as a first name,
more commonly in Britain.
Spenser

Speranza It. "Hope."
Esperance, Esperanza, Speranca

Spring OE. "Springtime." Use as a given name dates from
(and is almost exclusive to) the 1970s.

Stacy Gk. "Resurrection." Dim. **Anastasia**. Most popular
since the 1970s, and has long since outstripped its source.
It was substantially popular for a while, but has dropped
out of the top 100 U.S. names.
**Stace, Stacee, Stacey, Staci, Stacia, Stacie, Stasa, Sta-
see, Stasey, Stasia, Stasie, Stasey, Stasha, Staska,
Stasy, Staycee, Staycey, Staysie, Staysy, Tacy, Taisie**

Star Word as name. Translations, such as Stella (Greek)
and Esther (Persian), are far more common.
Starla, Starlene, Starletta, Starlette, Starr

Starling Bird name. The starling is a fairly common bird
with drab plumage, so the name's appeal may reside in
its resemblance to the word "star."

Stella Lat. "Star." Use was mostly literary until the 19th
century, when the name became fashionable. For this generation of parents brought up on classic movies, it is hard
to dissociate from Marlon Brando bellowing "Stella!" in
A Streetcar Named Desire.
Estelle, Estella, Estrella, Stela, Stelle

Stephanie (Fem. **Stephen**) Gk. "Crowned." Cropped up
in the 1920s and current since then. In the last ten years
use has soared, and in 1994, Stephanie was in the top five
names given to girls in both San Francisco and New York
City. Tennis star Steffi Graff; actresses Stefanie Powers,
Stephanie Zimbalist; poet Stevie Smith.
**Fania, Fanya, Phanie, Phanya, Stefa, Stefania, Stefanie,
Stefenney, Stefcia, Steffa, Steffaney, Steffanie, Stef-
fenie, Steffie, Stefinney, Stefka, Stefya, Stepa, Stepania,
Stepanida, Stepanyda, Stepahnie, Stepfanie, Stepha,
Stephana, Stephania, Stephanina, Stephanine, Stephan-**

nie, Stephene, Stepheney, Stephine, Stephney, ney, Stesha, Steshka, Stevana, Stevena, Stevie, Stevonna, Stevonne

Stetson Probably Old English surname meaning "Stephen's son." Extremely unusual, and more likely to be used for boys, though it has a certain rakish air for girls, probably conveyed by the associations of the famous Stetson "ten-gallon" hat, worn by cowboys in the late 19th century.

Stetcyn, Stettson

Stina Dim. **Christina** (Gk. "Anointed, Christian").

Stine

Stockard Probably an Old English place name referring to a tree stump (the "stock-" particle). Used as a first name and brought to public attention by actress Stockard Channing, whose given first name, like Sigourney Weaver's, was Susan.

Storm OE. Use of the word as a name: may be a last name transferred. The adjective "stormy" is occasionally used to describe temperament.

Stormee, Stormie, Stormy

Sukey Dim. **Susan** (Heb. "Lily") Appeared in the 18th century and revived in the 20th, following the popularity of Susan itself.

Soki, Sokie, Sukee, Sukie, Suky

— **Summer** OE. Name of the season. Like Spring and Season, largely a phenomenon of the 1970s. Swimmer Summer Sanders.

Somer, Sommers, Summers

Sunny Eng. Word as name: most likely to be a nickname characterizing a child's temperament.

Sunnee, Sunnie, Sunshine

Surya Hindi. Name of the sun god. Figure skater Surya Bonaly.

Susan Heb. "Lily." After 18th-century use, neglected until a huge surge of popularity made it a top choice in the middle years of the 20th century. Parents who had three Susans in their first-grade class are likely to pass over the name for their own children. The huge range of variations attest to the popularity of this name throughout Europe and the United States. Suffragist Susan B. Anthony; authors Susan Cheever, Susan Isaacs; actresses Susan Hampshire, Susan Dey, Susan Sarandon.

Sanna, Shoshana, Shoshanah, Shoshanna, Shushana, Shu Shu, Sioux, Siouxsie, Siusan, Soosan, Soosanna, Sosanna, Suanny, Sue, Suesann, Suesonne, Suezanne, Sukee, Sukey, Sukie, Sonel, Sunel, Susana, Susanetta, Susanka, Susann, Susanna, Susannagh, Susannah, Susanne, Suse, Susee, Susette, Susi, Susie, Susy, Suzan, Suzana, Suzane, Suzanna, Suzanne, Suze, Suzee, Suzetta, Suzette, Suzie, Suzon, Suzy, Suzzanne, Zanna, Zanne, Zannie

Susannah Heb. "Lily." The original version of the name, and ripe for revival, combining as it does the nostalgic and the unusual (like Molly and Emma). Actress Susannah York.

Sanna, Sannah, Shoshanna, Shanna, Shu Shu, Suesanna, Susana, Susanna, Susannagh, Suzanna, Zanna, Zannie

Suzanne Fr.Var. **Susan**. It has more or less followed Susan into and out of fashion. Ballerina Suzanne Farrell; actresses Suzanne Pleshette, Suzanne Sommers.

Suesana, Susanna, Susanne, Suzane, Suzannah, Suzette, Suzzanne, Zanne, Zannie

Svetlana Rus. Meaning unclear, though some sources suggest "Star." The name is quite popular in Russia. Author Svetlana Stalin.

Svetlanna, Svjetlana, Swetlana

Swanhild Saxon. "Battle swan."

Swanild, Swanilda, Swanilde, Swanhilda, Swanhilde, Swannie, Swanny

Sybil Var. **Sibyl**. The most common spelling of the name, though it only became prevalent in the last century. Actress Cybill Shepherd.

Cybele, Cybill, Sibell, Sibilla, Sibyl, Sibylla, Sybel, Sybella, Sybelle, Sybill, Sybilla

Sydney OF. Place name: "Saint Denis." Originally Saint Denis would have been the name of a village, and the name Sydney would have indicated a resident there. The name used to be almost exclusively male, but was given prominence as a woman's name in the 1980s by madam/celebrity Sydney Biddle Barrows. With today's trend toward choosing unisex names, Sydney is looking more and more like a fresh alternative fo Courtney or Whitney.

Cydney, Cydnie, Sidnee, Sidney, Sidnie, Sydel, Sydelle, Sydnie

Sylvia Lat. ''From the forest.'' The Latin form, Silvia, predominated for centuries, but when the name was at its most popular (from the 19th century into the 1940s), Sylvia was the spelling of choice. Poet Sylvia Plath; actress Silvana Mangano.

Silva, Silvaine, Silvana, Silvania, Silvanna, Silvia, Silviana, Silvianne, Silvie, Sylva, Sylvana, Sylvanna, Sylvee, Sylvette, Sylviana, Sylvianne, Sylvie, Sylvine, Sylwia, Zilvia, Zylvia

---

HOW WOULD BILL GATES DO IT?

He's never been cool, that's clear. And all the money in the world isn't going to make him cool, either. But Bill Gates doesn't seem to mind. He just goes on his merry way, oblivious to social trends—and when he and bride Melinda French had a baby, they chose the name Jennifer, which has been so popular for so long that it approaches classic stature, like Michael or Matthew. And you know what? Jennifer Gates will never have to spell her name for anybody.

Tabina Arab. "Muhammad's follower."

Tabitha Aramaic. "Gazelle." New Testament name reintroduced in the 17th century passion for biblical names. Neglected in this century until a minor revival in the 1960s. Possibly too unfamiliar to gain much from the current old-name trend, but its Old New England aura may make it appealing to some parents. Journalist Tabitha Soren.

Tabatha, Tabbee, Tabbey, Tabbi, Tabbie, Tabbitha, Tabby, Tabatha, Tabetha, Tabita, Tabotha, Tabytha

Tacita Lat. "Silence." Never a standard, but somewhat more common in eras when a woman's role was to be quiet.

Tace, Tacey, Tacia, Tacie, Tacye

Taffy Welsh. "Loved one."

Tahira Arab. "Virginal, pure."

Tahnee Name of actress Tahnee Welch, Raquel Welch's daughter. The name may be a variant spelling of **Tawny**.

Taima NAm Ind. "Peal of thunder."

Taimah, Taoimah

Taisie Meaning and origin uncertain: possibly Maisie spelled with a "T," or a variation of Tacey. May even be a derivation of Stacey, with the initial "S" left off. Another possibility is a shortening of the Russian Taisiya, derived from the Greek Thais.

Tayzie

Taisiya Russian. Meaning uncertain: possibly "Bond," or an adaptation of Thais, which itself is an old name of uncertain meaning.

Taisia, Taisie, Tasia, Tasiya, Tasya, Taya

Talbot Meaning unknown. An aristocratic last name in England, used as a first name since the 19th century. The women's clothing concern The Talbots sells very conservative preppy apparel.

Talbert, Talbott, Tallbot, Tallbot

Talia Heb. "Heaven's dew." May also be a variant [of] lia, or a derivative of **Natalie**. A pretty name, b[ut infre]quently used. Actress Talia Shire.

Tal, Tali, Talie, Talija, Talley, Tallia, Tallie, Tally, Tallya, Talora, Talya

Talicia Modern name: Alicia with an initial "T" added. Ballet superstars Peter Martins and Darci Kistler used this name for their first child.

Taliesin Welsh. "Shining brow." Also the name of a Welsh bard of the 6th century, who is mentioned in Tennyson's *Idylls of the King*. More famous in the U.S. as the name of architect Frank Lloyd Wright's houses in Wisconsin and Arizona.

Taliessin, Talliesin

Talise NAm Ind. "Lovely water."

Talitha Aramaic. "Young girl." Actress Talitha Soto.

Taleetha, Taletha, Talicia, Talisha, Talita

Tallulah Choctaw Indian. "Leaping water." Not, as one might expect, an invented name, nor even one assumed by its most famous bearer, actress Tallulah Bankhead. It was a Bankhead family name, and is also a place name in Georgia. Could not now be used without reference to the actress, however.

Talley, Tallie, Tallula, Tally, Talula

Tally Diminutive of **Talia** (Heb. "Heaven's dew") or creative respelling of Sally.

Tallee, Talley, Tallie

Talma Heb. "Hillock, mound."

Talmah, Talmit

Tamara Heb. "Palm tree." Old Testament name with a hint of the picturesque. Tamar was the more common version until this century, when Tamara, the Russian form, overtook it. Quite fashionable in the 1970s. Skiing champion Tamara McKinney; author Tama Janowitz.

Tama, Tamar, Tamarah, Tamarra, Tamary, Tamera, Tamma, Tammara, Tammi, Tammy, Tamora, Tamra, Tamrah, Thamar, Thamara, Thamarra, Thamera

Tamika Modern U.S. name of unknown origin. Some sources suggest a Japanese root meaning "People," but this seems farfetched, since the name is not used in the

Japanese community. More likely to be a variant of the popular **Tanisha**.

Tameeka, Tamiecka, Tamieka, Tamike, Tamiko, Taminique, Tamiqua, Temeequa, Temika, Timeeka, Tomika, Tonica, Tonique, Tymmeeka, Tymmiecka

Tammy Dim. **Tamara** (or other "Tam-" names). A nickname that took on a life of its own in the 1950s and 1960s, and was probably used without much interest in its source or meaning. Now out of fashion. Actress Tammy Grimes; singer Tammy Wynette; evangelist Tammy Faye Bakker.

Tami, Tamie, Tammee, Tammey, Tammie

Tamsin Var. **Thomasina** (Heb. "Twin"). Very old name that was revived by British parents in the middle of the 20th century, but did not spread widely to the U.S.

Tamasin, Tamasine, Tamsine, Tamsinne, Tamsyn, Tamzen, Tamzin

Tandy Origin unclear: probably a modern name created by substituting "T" for the initial letter "S" or "M" of Sandy or Mandy. Parents seeking novelty often switch initial letters on an old favorite, and for some reason the initial "T" is especially popular as in Taryn (probably from **Karen**) and Tally (a variant of **Sally**). Actress Thandie Newton.

Tandee, Tandie, Thandee, Thandey, Thandie, Thandy

Tanga Modern name, possibly a combination of the informal Kanga and the sultry Latin dance the tango.

Tangela Modern name: Angela (Gk. "Angel") with an initial "T."

Tanjela, Tanjella, Tanngela

Tanisha Modern name of unclear meaning, though several sources propose an African origin. Its popularity may stem from a contemporary fondness for three-syllable names ending in "-a." And while the "Ta-" prefix doesn't approach the popularity of "La-" or "Sha-," the similarity of sound probably contributes to Tanisha's widespread use. This is probably a combination of "Ta-" and the much-favored Aisha.

Taneesha, Taniesha, Tanitia, Tannicia, Tanniece, Tannisha, Teinicia, Teneesha, Tinecia, Tiniesha, Tynisha

Tansy Gk. "Everlasting life." Also the name of a fairly unusual herb. Used mostly since the 1960s, by parents whose acquaintance with herbs goes beyond the supermarket shelf.

Tanazia, Tandie, Tandy, Tansee, Tansey, Tansia, Tanzey, Tanzia

Tanya Dim. **Tatiana**, an ancient Italian name. This diminutive has been more popular than the full name, especially in the 1970s. Notorious figure skater Tonya Harding has probably given the name bad connotations for years to come. Photographer Tana Hoban; singer Tanya Tucker.

Tana, Tanazia, Tahnee, Tahnya, Taneea, Tania, Tanita, Tanja, Tarnya, Tawnya, Tonnya, Tonya, Tonyah

Tara Ir. Gael. "Rocky hill." Though Irish legends mention a place called Tara, its real prominence came in the 1940s when most Americans knew that Scarlett O'Hara's plantation home was called Tara. This seems to have launched the use of the name, which is now quite steadily used.

Tarah, Tarra, Tarrah

Tarleton OE. "Thor's settlement." Margaret Mitchell fans will remember the Tarleton twins, admirers of Scarlett O'Hara, in the early pages of *Gone with the Wind*. This name is unusual even for boys.

Tarlton

Taryn Var. **Tara**, or respelling of a group of names that was popular in the 1950s and '60s, Karen, Sharon, and Darren.

Taran, Tarin, Tarina, Tarnia, Tarren, Tarryn, Taryna, Teryn

Tasha Dim. **Natasha** (Rus. "Christmas"). Author Tasha Tudor.

Tahsha, Tashey, Tashina, Tasia, Tasenka, Taska, Tasya

Tasmine Possibly a variant of **Tamsin**, or the highly popular Jasmine with a new initial consonant.

Tasmeen, Tasmeena, Tasmin, Tasmina, Tasmyne

Tate Middle English. "Happy, cheerful."

Tait, Taitt, Tayte

Tatiana Rus. Var. of an ancient Italian name. Has penetrated the U.S. somewhat in recent years. Opera star Tatiana Troyannos.

Tania, Tanya, Tati, Tatianna, Tatie, Tatijana, Tatiyana, Tatjana, Tatyana, Tatyanna, Tonya

Tatum Possibly ME. "Light-hearted." Made famous by actress Tatum O'Neal, but not generally used.

Tawny OE. "Golden brown." A descriptive name first used in the mid–20th century.

   Tahnee, Taney, Tauney, Tawnee, Tawney, Tawni, Tawnie

Taylor ME. Occupational name: "Tailor." Probably considered a girl's name based on the fame of novelist Taylor Caldwell, whose middle name it is. The "last name as first name" trend has brought Taylor into the top forty names for girls in the U.S., though it is still being strongly used for boys as well.

   Tahlor, Tailor, Tayler

Tea Var. **Thea,** Gk. "Goddess." Or possibly diminutive of **Dorotea** (Gk. "Gift of God"). Actress Tea Leoni.

Teague Ir. Gael. "Bard, poet."

   Teage, Teigue

Teal Bird name: a kind of duck noted for its dark greenish blue feathers. Also, by extension, a shade of blue.

   Teall, Tealle, Teil, Teill, Teille

Tecla Gk. "Fame of God." Traditionally, Saint Thecla, converted by Saint Paul, was the first female Christian martyr, but her legend seems to be largely fantastic. The name has been most popular in Greece.

   Teccla, Tekla, Tekli, Telca, Telka, Thecla, Thekla

Tehila Heb. "Praise song."

   Tehilla

Temira Heb. "Tall."

   Temora, Timora

Temperance Puritan virtue name. Temperance is moderate consumption of food and drink: the temperance movement of the late 19th and early 20th centuries went a step further and attempted to ban liquor entirely.

Tempest OF. "Storm." Rare usage is probably a matter of a family name transposed, since few parents wish for a child with a stormy temperament. Actress Tempestt Bledsoe.

   Tempesta, Tempeste, Tempestt

Terena (Fem. **Terence**) Roman clan name. Used mostly in the middle of the 20th century.

   Tareena, Tarena, Tarina, Tereena, Terenia, Terenne, Terriell, Terriella, Terina, Terrena, Terrene, Terrin, Terrina, Teryl, Teryll, Teryna, Therena

Teresa Popular alternate spelling of Theresa (Gk. "Harvest").

    Techa, Terasa, Terasina, Terasita, Terecena, Teresia, Teresina, Teresita, Tereska, Teresse, Tereza, Terezilya, Terezita, Terosina, Terrie, Terrosina, Terry, Tersa, Tersia, Terushka, Teruska, Tesa, Tesia, Teskia, Tess, Tessa, Tessie, Tessy

Terra May be used as a derivation of the female Terence names, or short for Teresa, or even as a reference to the earth, which is *terra* in Latin.

    Tera, Terah, Terrah, Tiera, Tierra

Terry Dim. Theresa (Gk. "Harvest"). This and other nicknames for Theresa were at their most popular in the middle of the 20th century. Actress Teri Garr.

    Terall, Terea, Teree, Tereigh, Terell, Terella, Terelynn, Terelynn, Teri, Terie, Terree, Terreigh, Terrey, Terri, Terrye

Teryl Modern name, either a variant of **Teresa** or combination of **Terry** and **Cheryl**.

    Terelyn, Terrall, Terrell, Terrena, Terrene, Terrill, Terryl

Tertia Lat. "Third." Unusual, as most of these number names (Prima, Secunda) are. Curiously, Octavia is the only one that has taken on a life of its own.

    Tercia, Tersia, Tersha

Tesla Name of a rock band, and before that, of a pioneer electrical engineer named Nikolai Tesla.

    Tessla

Tessa Dim. Theresa. Some sources also suggest Gk. "Fourth child." Pretty, simple, and uncommon.

    Tess, Tessie, Tessy, Teza

Texana Modern name, possibly respelling of Rexana or homage to the state of Texas.

    Texanna

Thaddea (Fem. **Thaddeus**) Gk., meaning unsure: "Brave" is one possibility.

    Tada, Tadda, Taddie, Thada, Thadda, Thadée, Thaddie

Thaïs Ancient Greek name, meaning unknown. There was a famous Athenian courtesan named Thaïs who traveled with Alexander the Great. Some stories add that she then went to Egypt and became the mistress of the reigning Ptolemy. Massenet based an 1894 opera on her story.

    Taïs, Taisa, Taisse, Thaisa

Thalassa Gk. "Sea, ocean."
> **Talassa**

Thalia Gk. "Blooming, in flower." In Greek legend Thalia is one of the Three Graces (along with Aglaia and Euphrosyne); she is also one of the Nine Muses, daughters of Zeus and Mnemosyne, each of whom represents an art or a science. Thalia represents Comedy.
> **Talia, Talie, Talley, Tally, Thaleia, Thalie, Thalya**

Thana Arab. "Thanksgiving."

Thea Gk. "Goddess." Also dim. **Dorothea** (Gk. "Gift of God"). Actress Tea Leoni.
> **Tea, Theia, Thia**

Theda Possibly diminutive of **Theodosia**, or derived from Old German "People." Reminiscent of exotic silent film star Theda Bara.
> **Theida, Thida, Theta**

Thelma Gk. "Will." Literary name coined in the late 19th century, at its peak in the first third of this century. It has the aura of a bygone era, but not so bygone that it is attractive to modern parents. Even the great success of the film *Thelma and Louise* hasn't done much to make it popular.
> **Telma, Thellma**

Themis Greek mythology name: Themis is the goddess of justice who is so often depicted with scales.
> **Temis, Temiss, Themiss**

Theodora Gk. "Gift of God." Much less common than its synonym, Dorothy. At its peak in the middle third of the 20th century, but never a standard. Actress/vamp Theda Bara.
> **Dora, Fedora, Feodora, Fyodora, Teddey, Teddie, Tedra, Teodora, Teodory, Theadora, Theda, Theo, Theodosia, Todora**

Theodosia Gk. "Gift of God." Little-used variant given some prominence by Anya Seton's 1941 historical novel *My Theodosia*, about Aaron Burr's daughter.
> **Docia, Dosia, Feodosia, Theda, Teodosia, Tossa, Tossia**

Theone Gk. "Name of God." Costume designer Theoni V. Aldredge.
> **Teone, Teoni, Theoni**

Theophania Gk. "God's appearance." Immensely popular

in its contracted modern form, Tiffany, but almost unheard of in this full version.

Theofania, Theophanie, Teofanie, Teophania, Teophanie

Theophila Gk. "God-loving." The masculine form, **Theophilus**, is slightly less rare.

Teofila, Teophile, Teophila, Theofila

Theresa Gk. "Harvest." May also stem from a Greek place name. The name owes its popularity to two important Catholic saints, the astringent, intellectual mystic Saint Teresa of Avila, and the humble young nun, Saint Thérèse of Lisieux. It seems to have spread from Catholic families to wider acceptance, and was especially common in the 1960s. Actress Teresa Russell; Mother Teresa; basketball player Theresa Edwards.

Resi, Rezi, Rezka, Taresa, Tera, Terasa, Teresa, Térèse, Teresia, Teresina, Teresita, Teressa, Tereza, Terezinha, Terezsa, Teri, Terrasa, Terresa, Terresia, Terri, Terrosina, Terry, Terrya, Tersa, Tersina, Tersita, Terza, Tess, Tessa, Tessey, Tessi, Tessie, Tessy, Thérèse, Theresina, Theresita, Theressa, Tracey, Tracie, Tracy, Treesa, Tresa, Tressa, Trescha, Treza, Zita

Therma Possibly a compound name, combining the first syllable of Theresa with the end of Irma. May also refer to warmth, since *therme* is the Greek word for heat.

Thermia

Thisbe Greek name from myth. Ovid's *Metamorphoses* tells the tragic tale of the lovers Pyramus and Thisbe, which is reprised in Shakespeare's *A Midsummer Night's Dream.*

Thomasina (Fem. **Thomas**) Heb. "Twin." Thomasin was the earliest form, replaced by Thomasina in the Victorian era, and Tamsin a hundred years later. Now quite scarce.

Tammi, Tammie, Thomasa, Thomasin, Thomasine, Thomazine, Toma, Tomasina, Tomasine, Tomina, Tommie, Tommy

Thora Scan. "Thor's struggle." Thor is the Norse god of thunder.

Thordia, Thordis, Thyra, Tyra

Thurayya Arab. "Star." Actually refers to the Pleiades.

Soraya, Surayya, Surayyah, Thuraia

Tia Sp. "Aunt." Probably used as a first name with little

reference to its actual meaning, but fondness for its sound.
Thia, Tiana, Tiara

Tiara Lat. "Coronet, jeweled headband." Pretty-sounding name for a very attractive object. A kind of small, potently scented gardenia known as "tiaré" grows in the Pacific islands.
Teara, Tiarra

Tiberia Lat. Place name: The River Tiber flows through Rome, and Tiberius was a Roman clan name.
Tibbie, Tibby, Tyberia

Tierney Ir. Gael. "Lord." Unusual as a last name, though Gene Tierney's fame has made it familiar. Has potential as a girl's first name, if the unisex trend continues.
Tiernan, Tierneigh, Tiernie

Tierra Sp. "Land." In keeping with the current trend toward geography names, and rhyming with the rather more popular "Sierra," this name is unusual but not outlandish.

Tifara Heb. "Splendor, brilliance, beauty."
Tiferet

Tiffany Gk. "God's appearance." Literally, Theophania. Traditionally used for babies born on Epiphany, the day when the Three Kings first saw the Christ Child. Now associated with Tiffany & Co., the New York City jeweler. The name has become shorthand for upper-class luxury, and was hugely popular in the 1980s. By 1990 it was sliding down the list of popularity, out of the top twenty, but Donald Trump still named his baby with Marla Maples "Tiffany." Likely to fade even further as the bulk of Tiffanys reach childbearing age themselves.
Theophanie, Tifara, Tifennie, Tiffaney, Tiffani, Tiffanie, Tiffeny, Tiffenie, Tiffie, Tiffney, Tiffy, Tiphanie, Tiphara, Tiphenie, Tipheny, Tyffany, Tyffenie

Tigris Ir. Gael. from Lat. "Tiger." According to legend, Saint Patrick had a sister named Tigris. It is also the name of a significant river that runs through Iraq.

Tikva Heb. "Hope."
Tikvah

Tilda Dim. **Matilda** (OG. "Battle-mighty"). Actress Tilda Swinton.
Thilda, Thilde, Tildie, Tildy, Tilley, Tillie, Tilly

Timothea (Fem. **Timothy**) Gk. "Honoring God." Uncommon feminization of a well-established boy's name.
Thea, Timaula, Timmey, Timmi, Timmie, Timotheya

Tina Dim. **Christina**, etc. Used in the 20th century, but especially popular in the 1960s. Rock star Tina Turner; actress Tina Louise.
Teena, Teenie, Teina, Tena, Tine, Tiny

Tirion Welsh. "Kindly, gentle."
Tirian, Tirien, Tirrian, Tirrien, Tiryan, Tiryon

Tirza Heb. "Pleasantness." Although many versions of the name exist, it is rarely used in modern times. It is one of the few Old Testament female names that was not used widely in the Puritan era.
Thersa, Thirsa, Thirza, Thirzah, Thursa, Thurza, Tierza, Tirzah, Tyrzah

Tisa Invented name: probably Lisa with an initial "T."

Tita Probably derived from Spanish diminutives like Martita; may be considered a feminization of **Titus** (or **Tito**).
Teeta, Tyta

Titania Gk. "Giant." The Titans in Greek myth were a race of giants. A more familiar use of the name, though, is the Queen of the Fairies in Shakespeare's *A Midsummer Night's Dream.* Easily confused with the more familiar Tatiana.
Tania, Tita, Titaniya, Titanya, Tiziana

Tivian Invented name: Vivian with a "T." Unusual.
Tivyan, Tyvyan

Toby Heb. "God is good." More commonly a boy's name, used from time to time for girls.
Taube, Taubey, Taubie, Thobey, Thobie, Thoby, Tobe, Tobee, Tobey, Tobi, Tova, Tovah, Tove

Toni Dim. **Antoinette** (Lat. "Beyond price, invaluable"). Unusual in this era of full-length first names. Author Toni Morrison; actress Toni Collete.
Toinette, Toinon, Tola, Tona, Tonee, Toney, Tonia, Tonie, Tonina, Tony, Tonya, Twanette

Topaz Lat. Jewel name. Less common than Ruby and Pearl, but a good candidate for a November baby (it is that month's birthstone) or for a baby with topaz (golden) coloring.

im. **Victoria** (Lat. "Victory"). Actress Tori Spell-

> **Torey, Tori, Toria, Torie, Torrey, Torrye**

Tosca It. "From Tuscany."

Tosha Slavic var. **Antoinette** (Lat. "Beyond price, invaluable").

> **Toshka, Tosia, Tosiya, Toskia**

Tossa Dim. **Theodosia**.

Tova Heb. "Good." Actress Tovah Feldshuh.

> **Tovah**

Toya Modern U.S. name, perhaps a diminutive of **Latoya**, one of the most popular "La-" names. It has no particular meaning.

> **Toia**

Tracy Dim. **Theresa** (Gk. "Harvest"). First used in numbers in the 1940s, probably in response to the film *The Philadelphia Story*. This touched off a long period of popularity that is now distinctly fading. Actress Tracey Ullman; tennis player Tracy Austin; singer Tracy Chapman; swimmer Tracy Caulkins.

> **Trace, Tracee, Tracey, Traci, Tracie, Trasey, Treacy, Treasa, Treasey, Treasa**

Tranquilina Sp. from Lat. "Calm, peaceful."

> **Tranquila, Tranquilinia**

Traviata It. "One who goes astray." As in the great Verdi opera *La Traviata*.

Trea Modern name possibly related to the Latin term for "third" (*tertia*). The name Trey is scantily used for boys.

> **Treia, Treya**

Treasure The word as name, of the same school of thought as Precious. What all doting parents feel their babies to be.

> **Tesora, Trésor**

Trelane Possibly an invented name, following the pattern of Delaney (Ir. Gael. "Offspring of the challenger.")

> **Tralaine, Trelaine, Trelaney**

Treva Fem. **Trevor** (Welsh. "Large homestead").

> **Trevia, Trevina**

Tricia Dim. **Patricia** (Lat. "Aristocratic"). Choreographer Trisha Brown.

> **Treasha, Trichia, Tris, Trisa, Trish, Trisha, Trisia, Trissina**

Trilby Literary name coined at the turn of the 20th century. Trilby, the central character of the eponymous novel and play, became a great singer. (The name may refer to vocal trills.) A trilby hat, worn by the character in the 1895 stage production, is a soft felt hat with a dented crown.

Trilbea, Trilbee, Trilbeigh, Trilbey, Trilbie, Trillby

Trina Dim. **Katrina** (Gk. "Pure").

Treena, Treina, Trine, Trinette, Trinnette

Trinity Lat. "Triad." Refers to the Holy Trinity, the three forms of God in the Christian faith. Used mostly among Spanish-speaking families. Actress Trini Alvarado.

Trini, Trinidad, Trinidade, Trinita, Trinitee, Trinitey

Trista Lat. "Sad." An inauspicious name for a baby, however pretty it sounds.

Tristana Fem. **Tristan** (Welsh. Meaning unknown). In the medieval legends Tristan is a knight, in love with Isolde, the wife of his uncle. The tale has been told in many forms, including an epic poem by Tennyson and an opera by Wagner.

Tristen, Tristenna

Trixie Dim. **Beatrice** (Lat. "Bringer of gladness").

Trix, Trixee, Trixy

Trudy Dim. **Gertrude** (OG. "Strength of a spear"). Cropped up in the middle of the 20th century, but little heard now.

Truda, Trude, Trudey, Trudi, Trudie, Trudye

Truth Concept as name. Akin to the Puritan virtue names but quite scantily used. Truly, a variant, turns up occasionally as a first or last name. Civil rights activist Sojourner Truth.

Truley, Truly

Tryphena Gk. "Delicacy." Mentioned in one of Paul's epistles to the Romans. Very scarce.

Trifena, Triphena, Tryphana, Tryphaena, Tryphenia

Tsifira Heb. "Crown, diadem."

Tsila Heb. "Shade."

Tzelya, Tsilah, Tzila, Tzilah, Tzili

Tuesday OE. Day of the week. Given exposure by actress Tuesday Weld, but not in general use.

Tuesdee

Tully Ir. Gael. "Powerful people."

Tulia Sp. from Lat. "Bound for glory."
Toolia, Toulia, Toolya, Toulya, Tula, Tulla, Tulya

Tundra Geography name: an arctic plain with permanently
frozen subsoil. Most likely to be used by well-traveled
parents who have actually seen the tundra—or by parents
who simply like the way the name sounds.
Tunndra

Turkessa Modern name, probably related to the color tur-
quoise. That word is French for "from Turkey," and the
color originally got its name from the opaque blue-green
stones originally mined in Turkestan and Persia.
Turquessa, Turkissa, Turkwessa, Turquissa

Twyla Modern name of uncertain meaning and derivation.
Some sources suggest it may related to twilight, others to
the French word for star, *étoile*, while others still suggest
a relationship to the manufacture of twill, a kind of fabric.
Choreographer Twyla Tharp.
Tuwyla, Twila, Twilla

Tyler Occupational name: "Maker of tiles." The name of
one of the country's less memorable presidents (John Tyler, 1841–1845). Very unusual as a girl's name, but could
become more popular with the current fashion for gender-
switching names.
Tyller

Tyra Var. **Thora** (Scand. "Thor's struggle"). Model Tyra
Banks.
Thyra, Tyria

Tzefira Var. **Zephyr** (Gk. "West wind").
Zefira

Tzipporah Var. **Zippora** (Heb. "Bird"). Zipporah was the
wife of Moses. Despite its Biblical prominence, the name
is not popular.
Tzipora, Tzippora, Zipporah

Tzigane Hung. "Gypsy."
Tsigana, Tsigane

Uberta It. var. **Huberta** (OG. "Bright or shining intellect").

    Uberrta, Ubertha, Yuberta

Udele OE. "Wealthy."

    Uda, Udella, Udelle, Yewdelle, Yudella, Yudelle

Ula Celt. "Gem of the sea."

    Eula, Ulla, Ulli, Yulla

Ulani Haw. "Cheerful."

Ulima Arab. "Astute, wise."

    Uleema, Ulima, Ullima

Ulla ONorse. "Will, determination." Also possibly short for Ulrica.

    Oula, Ula

Ulrica (Fem. Ulric) OG. "Power of the wolf" or "Power of the home." Very unusual outside of Germany.

    Rieka, Rica, Ricka, Uhlrike, Ulka, Ullrica, Ullricka, Ulrika, Ulrike, Uulrica

Ultima Lat. "End, farthest point." In English, hard to dissociate from "ultimate." There is a brand of cosmetics called Ultima.

    Ulltima, Ultimata

Ulva OG. "Wolf."

Uma Sanskrit. "Flax or turmeric." Uma is also the name of the Indian goddess Sakti, in her guise as light, and is a Hebrew name meaning "nation." For all the fame of actress Uma Thurman, the name may be too exotic for widespread use.

    Ooma

Umnia Arab. "Desire, longing."

    Umniah, Umniya, Umniyah

Una Lat. "One." The origin of the name may be Irish, though its Celtic meaning is lost. Very unusual. In Edmund Spenser's 16th-century epic poem *The Faerie*

Queen, the heroine of the first book is Una. She is the personification of truth and unity.

Euna, Oona, Oonagh, Unah

Undine Lat. "Little wave." In myth, Undine is the spirit of the waters. Edith Wharton created a character in *The Custom of the Country* who was named Undine for the haircurling (or "waving") tonic that had made her father rich.

Ondina, Ondine, Undeen, Undene, Undina

Unice Var. **Eunice** (Gk. "Victorious").

Uniss

Unique Adjective used as first name. Every child is, of course, unique, and perhaps no one feels that more intensely than parents of a newborn.

Uniqua

Unity ME. "Oneness." Used by the Puritans and extremely uncommon. Most people have heard of it only in connection with Unity Mitford, one of the famous English Mitford sisters.

Unita, Unite, Unitey

Urania Gk. "Heavenly." Urania was one of the Greek Muses, the nine daughters of Zeus and Mnemosyne identified with particular arts and sciences. Urania was in charge of astronomy. The seventh planet away from the sun, discovered in 1781, is called "Uranus" after the Greek sky god, however, not after the muse.

Ourania, Ouranie, Urainia, Uraniya, Uranya

Urbana Lat. "Of the city." The male form, **Urban**, is a bit more familiar, having been used by eight popes. In the U.S. the name is likely to be associated with the town where the University of Illinois is located.

Urbanna

Uriela Heb. "God's light." An appropriate name for girls born during Hannukah.

Uriella, Uriyella

Urit Heb. "Brightness."

Urena, Urina, Uriya, Urith

Ursula Lat. "Little female bear." Saint Ursula was a much-venerated virgin martyr, allegedly executed by Attila the Hun, though her story has little basis in fact. The name was most popular in the 17th century. Fans of Disney cartoons will be bound to associate it with the overweight octopus sea-witch in *The Little Mermaid.* Author K. Le Guin; actress Ursula Andress.

Orsa, Orsala, Orsola, Orsolla, Seula, Sula, Ulla, Ursa, Ursala, Urselina, Ursella, Ursie, Ursley, Ursola, Ursule, Ursulette, Ursulina, Ursuline, Ursy, Urszula, Urszuli

Uta Origin unclear: possibly dim. **Otthild** (OG. "Prospers in battle"). Actress Uta Hagen.

Ute, Utte, Yuta

Val Dim. **Valentina, Valerie.** Occasionally an independent name.

Vala OG. "Singled out."

Valla

Valda (Fem. **Waldemar**) OG. "Renowned ruler." Occurs in some northern European countries, and from time to time in Britain, but very scarce in the U.S.

Vallda, Velda

Valencia Place name: city on the Mediterranean coast of Spain, noted for its oranges.

Valentina Lat. "Strong." This name and Valerie come from the same Latin root. Valentia was the earliest form, but it entered the modern age as Valentina. Valentine is used for both boys and girls (the former more frequently in Britain), and the early Christian martyr for whom the holiday is named was male. Cosmonaut Valentina Tereshkova.

Teena, Teina, Tena, Tina, Val, Vale, Valeda, Valena, Valencia, Valenteen, Valenteena, Valentia, Valentijn, Valentine, Valenzia, Valera, Valida, Valina, Valja, Vallatina, Valli, Vallie, Vally, Velora

Valera Name of a famous Irish statesman, Eamon de Valera, who was born in New York of a Spanish father and an Irish mother. He was very active in the process that ultimately formed the Irish Republic.

Valerie Lat. "Strong." The French form of an early Christian name (Valeria) that was revived at the turn of the 20th century. It was very popular in the middle of the

20th century, but is less so now. Actresses Valerie Harper, Valerie Bertinelli, Valerie Perrine.

Val, Valaree, Valarey, Valaria, Valarie, Vale, Valeree, Valeria, Valeriana, Valery, Valerye, Valka, Vallarie, Valleree, Vallerie, Vallery, Vallie, Vallorey, Vallorie, Vallory, Valorie, Vallrie, Valry, Valka

Valeska (Fem. **Vladislav**) Old Slavic. "Splendid leader."

Valetta Place name: principal city on the Mediterranean island of Malta. Also, and more likely, a modern name made up of the popular "Val-" element with the feminine diminutive "-etta" ending.

Valeda, Valeta, Valletta

Valkyrie Scandinavian mythology figures: the attendants of Odin, who conduct the heroes slain in battle to the feasting hall in Valhalla. The Valkyrie fight with each other for pleasure, but their wounds magically heal each day.

Valkyria, Valkyrria, Vallkyrie

Valley Geography name: a low spot in a landscape. Well adapted to first name use because of the "-ey" ending, which is usually interpreted as feminine. Could also be construed as a diminute for Valerie.

Vallee, Vallia, Vallie

Vallombrosa It. "Shady valley." The name of a forest resort southeast of Florence in Italy, famous for the Benedictine monastery sited there. A name for Italophile parents.

Valombrosa

Valonia Lat. Place name: "Shallow valley."

Vallonia, Valonya

Valora Lat. "Courageous." From the same root that gives us "valor."

Vallora, Valoria, Valorie, Valory, Valorya, Valoura, Valouria

Vanda Var. **Wanda** (OG. Tribal name). Mostly used at the turn of the century.

Vahnda, Vannda, Vohnda, Vonda

Vanessa Literary name, invented by *Gulliver's Travels* author Jonathan Swift. Suddenly leapt into everyday use in the middle years of the 20th century, achieving some popularity in the 1970s, and quite considerable use recently.

It was in the top 100 U.S. names for girls in 1990, owing partly to strong popularity among Spanish-speaking parents. It is also the name of a genus of butterflies that includes the Red Admiral and the Painted Lady. Actress Vanessa Redgrave; celebrity Vanna White; singer Vanessa Williams.

Nessa, Nessie, Nessy, Van, Vanesa, Vanesse, Vanetta, Vannessa, Vannetta, Vania, Vanija, Vanna, Vannie, Vanya, Venesa, Venessa, Venetta, Vinessa, Vonessa, Vonesse, Vonnessa

Vanora Old Welsh. ''White wave.''

Vannora

Varda Heb. ''Rose.''

Vardia, Vardice, Vardina, Vardis, Vardit, Vardith

Varina Name of unknown origin, though it may be a respelling of Verena. It has strong emotional resonance for Southerners, and Virginians in particular. Varina was the name of one of the earliest Virginia plantations, and also of the wife of Jefferson Davis, hero of the Confederacy.

Verina

Varvara Var. **Barbara** (Gk. ''Stranger''). In Greek pronunciation the ''V'' and ''B'' sounds are quite close, hence the ties between these names.

Varenka, Varina, Varinka, Varka, Varya, Vava, Vavka

Vashti Per. ''Lovely.'' In the Old Testament, the wife of the proud King Ahasuerus of Persia. Passed over by the Puritans (perhaps because she became a divorcée), but revived very slightly in the 19th century.

Vashtee

Vasilia Fem. **Basil** (Gk. ''Royal, kingly''). In languages like Greek and Russian, the ''B'' and ''V'' sounds are very similar. This name with the initial ''B'' was quite common in the Middle Ages.

Vaseelia, Vasilija, Vasiliya, Vasillia, Vasilliya, Vazeelia, Vazeeliya, Vaseelia

Veda Sanskrit. ''Knowledge, wisdom.'' The Vedas are the four sacred books of the Hindus.

Vedis, Veeda, Veida, Veta, Vida

Vedette It. ''Sentry, scout.'' By extension, because a sentry or a scout is often singled out or separated from the group,

the French term *vedette* means something (like a headline)
that is singled out graphically. And by further extension,
in everyday usage, *vedette* is the French word for a movie
star.

Vedetta

Vega Arab. ''Falling.'' or Swed. from Lat. ''Star.'' Vega
is the name of one of the largest and brightest stars. It is
also the name of a car manufactured by Chevrolet, and
any parent who has ever driven one is unlikely to use that
name for a daughter.

Vaga, Vaiga, Vayga

Velda Var. Valda.

Vellda

Velika Old Slavic. ''Great, wondrous.''

Velma Origin disputed. Possibly dim. **Wilhelmina** (OG.
''Will-helmet''), possibly a late-19th-century invention.
In general use since the 1920s, but not fashionable.

Vehlma, Vellma

Velvet OF. ''Shaggy.'' The name of the fabric, which has
connotations of great luxury and sensuousness.

Vellva, Velva, Velvetta, Velvette, Velveina, Velvina

Venerada Sp. ''Venerated.''

Venetia Place name. Never reached the stature of that other
great Italian tourist mecca, Florence. Cropped up from the
17th century onward; use increased in the 19th century,
but the name would still be considered a bit fanciful. The
English form, Venice, is also used occasionally.

**Vanecia, Vanetia, Venecia, Venetta, Venezia, Venice,
Venise, Venita, Venize, Venitia, Vennice, Vinetia, Vonitia,
Vonizia**

Venus Name of the Roman goddess of love and beauty.
Used in Britain in the 16th century through the 19th, but
very scarce now. It creates a lot of expectations for a
female baby. Tennis player Venus Williams.

Venusa, Venusette, Venusina, Venusita

Vera Slavic. ''Faith'' or Lat. ''Truth.'' Use by two popular
novelists in the late 19th century promoted the name to
high fashion, but it is hardly found now. Actress Vera
Miles.

Veradis, Verasha, Veera, Veira, Vere, Verena, Verene,

Verina, Verine, Verinka, Verka, Verla, Verochka, Veroshka, Veruschka, Verushka

Verbena Lat. "Holy plants." Originally referred to olive, laurel, and myrtle, plants with spiritual significance to the Romans. In modern times, a class of plants with medicinal properties and, frequently, pleasant scents.

Verbeena, Verbeina, Verbina, Verbyna

Verdad Sp. "Truth."

Verde Sp. "Green." A descriptive name to commemorate spring, perhaps.

Verda

Verena Lat. "True." Derives from the same root as Vera. Primarily English use.

Varena, Varina, Vereena, Verina, Veruchka, Veruschka, Veryna

Verity Lat. "Truth." Puritan virtue name, much less common than Constance, Prudence, Hope, etc. Still occurs from time to time in Britain, however.

Veretie, Verety, Verita, Veritie

Verna Lat. "Springtime." Use spans the late years of the 19th century to the middle of the 20th, but the name has a dated air and is rare today. Actress Virna Lisi.

Verda, Verne, Verneta, Vernetta, Vernette, Vernice, Vernie, Vernis, Vernise, Vernisse, Vernita, Virna

Verona Dim. **Veronica**. Also the name of a northern Italian city well known to tourists, so it may be used by reminiscent parents.

Varona, Veron, Verone, Verowna

Veronica Lat. "True image" or Var. **Bernice** (Gk. "She who brings victory"). According to a legend that sprang up in the Middle Ages, a young girl wiped Jesus' sweating brow on his way to Calvary. The handkerchief she used later showed a perfect image of his face. (Three separate Italian churches now claim to own this holy relic.) The name first appeared in Britain in the 17th century, spread beyond Catholic families in the 19th century, and became popular in the 1950s. To baby boomers, reminiscent of the Archie and Veronica comic books. Also, in an age that avoids nicknames, four syllables is awfully long. Actress Veronica Lake.

Rana, Ranna, Roni, Ronica, Ronika, Ronna, Ronnee,

Ronni, Ronnica, Ronnie, Ronny, Veera, Veira, Vera, Veranica, Veranique, Verinique, Vernice, Vernicka, Vernika, Verohnica, Verohnicca, Veronice, Veronicka, Veronika, Veronike, Veroniqua, Veronique, Veronka, Veronqua, Vonnie

Vespera Lat. "Evening star." The source of the term "vespers" for an early evening church service.

Vesperina, Vespers

Vesta Lat. The Roman household goddess. Her altar was tended by six virgins (the "vestal virgins"), who were kept under severe discipline. They were buried alive if they lost their virginity. Most common late 19th to early 20th century, when these things still mattered a great deal.

Vevina Ir. Gael. "Sweet lady." This is an anglicization of the Gaelic word that produces the name Bevan or Bevin.

Vica Hung. from Heb. "Life."

Vicenza Place name: Italian city famous for several architectural features, notably buildings designed by the great Renaissance architect Palladio.

Vicensa, Vicenzia, Vichensa, Vichensia, Vichenza

Vicky Dim. **Victoria**. Author Vicki Baum; actress Vicki Lawrence.

Vicci, Vickee, Vickey, Vicki, Vicky, Vicqui, Vikkey, Vikki, Vikky, Viqui

Victoria (Fem. **Victor**) Lat. "Victory." Extremely common in Christian Rome, but curiously not fashionable during the reign (1837–1901) of the woman who gave her name to the Victorian age. Most recently popular in the 1950s and 1960s, but daughters in those days were probably called "Vicky." Parents who use it now are more likely to insist on the whole mouthful, or Tory in a pinch. In the top fifty names in 1990, just above the name of another English queen, Alexandra. Actress Victoria Principal.

Tori, Toria, Torie, Tory, Toya, Vic, Vicci, Vickee, Vickey, Vicki, Vickie, Vicky, Victoriana, Victorie, Victorina, Victorine, Victory, Vika, Vikkey, Vikki, Vikky, Viktoria, Viktorija, Viktorina, Viktorine, Viktorka, Viqui, Vitoria, Vittoria

Vida Dim. **Davita** (Heb. "Loved one") or Sp. "Life."

Veda, Veeda, Vidette, Vieda, Vita, Vitia

Vidonia Port. "Branch of a vine."
  Veedonia, Vidonya
Vienna Place name: the capital of Austria, a city known for
  its music and culture.
  Vienne, Viennia
Vigilia Lat. "Wakefulness."
Vigdis Nor. "War goddess."
  Vigdess
Vilhelmina Var. **Wilhelmina** (OG. "Will-helmet").
  Vilhelmine, Villhelmina, Wilhelmina
Villette Fr. "Small town." The name of one of Charlotte
  Brontë's lesser-known novels.
Vilma Rus. Dim. **Vilhelmina**.
  Wilma
Vina dim. **Davina, Lavinia**, etc. or Sp. "Vineyard." In ei-
  ther case, probably a name whose use was promoted by
  the feminine ending "-a." A name parents may choose
  simply because they like the way it sounds.
  **Veena, Vena, Veina, Vinetta, Vinette, Vinia, Vinica, Vin-
  ita, Vinya, Vyna, Vynetta, Vynette**
Vincentia (Fem. **Vincent**) Lat. "Conquering." An unusual
  feminization of a name that has not been very common
  in America.
  **Vicenta, Vicentia, Vincenta, Vincentena, Vincentina, Vin-
  centine, Vincenza, Vincenzia, Vincetta, Vinetta**
Vinia Dim. **Lavinia** (Lat. "Woman of Rome"). Used as an
  independent name.
  Veenia, Veenya, Venia, Vinya
Violante Gk./Lat. "Purple flower." This may be considered the root of Yolanda.
  Violanthe
Violet Lat. "Purple." A flower name in longer use than
  most. Occurred first in the 1830s and lasted nearly a hundred years, but always more popular in Britain (whose
  cool, damp climate is more hospitable to the spring flow-
  ers). Viola has been a less-used choice. Ballerina Violette
  Verdy.
  **Eolande, Iolande, Iolanthe, Jolanda, Jolande, Jolanta,
  Jolantha, Jolanthe, Vi, Viola, Violaine, Violanta, Violante, Violanthe, Viole, Violeine, Violetta, Violette, Viol-**

let, Violletta, Viollette, Vyolet, Vyoletta, Vyolette, Yolanda, Yolande, Yolane, Yolantha, Yolanthe

Virginia Lat. "Virgin." The name probably derives from a Roman clan name, but the current meaning has been assumed for hundreds of years. A great favorite in the U.S. from the mid–19th century to the mid–20th; the first child born in the U.S. was Virginia Dare, in 1597. The state of Virginia was named in compliment to the Virgin Queen, Elizabeth I. A good candidate for 21st-century revival, though it is currently quite scarce. Author Virginia Woolf; tennis player Virginia Wade.

Geena, Geenia, Geenya, Genia, Genya, Gigi, Gina, Ginella, Ginelle, Ginger, Gingia, Ginia, Ginnee, Ginni, Ginnie, Ginny, Ginya, Jenell, Jenella, Jenelle, Jinia, Jinjer, Jinnie, Jinny, Verginia, Verginya, Virge, Virgenya, Virgie, Virgine, Virginie, Virginnia, Virgy

Viridis Lat. "Green."

Virdis, Viridia, Viridian, Viridiana, Viridianna, Viridianne

Virtue Lat. "Strength." The original virtue name. In this case, virtue means strength to resist sin, though originally there was probably some connotation of manliness (the Latin *vir* means "man").

Visitacion Sp. from Lat. "Visitation." Refers to the visit the pregnant Mary paid to her cousin Elizabeth on July 2, according to the New Testament.

Vita Lat. "Life." Also occasionally a nickname for Victoria, as in the case of English writer Vita Sackville-West.

Veeta, Vitel, Vitella, Vitka

Viveca Scand. "Alive." Var. **Viva**. Actress Viveca Lindfors.

Vivecka, Viveka, Vivica, Vivika

Viva Lat. "Alive." Most familiar from the expression meaning "Long live ..." as in *"Viva l'España"* or *"Vive la France."* Actress Viva.

Veeva, Viveca, Vivva

Vivian Lat. "Full of life." Used for boys in Britain (although infrequently), generally for girls in the U.S. In spite of the early martyr Saint Vivian, the name has been current only since the 19th century, and has never been a real favorite. Actresses Vivien Leigh, Vivian Vance.

Bibi, Bibiana, Bibiane, Bibianna, Bibianne, Bibyana, Ve-

vay, Vi, Vibiana, Viv, Vivee, Vivi, Vivia, Viviana, Viviane, Vivianna, Vivianne, Vivie, Vivien, Vivienne, Vivyan, Vivyana, Vivyanne, Vyvyan, Vyvyana, Vyvyanne

Volusia Place name: county in Florida.

Walburga OG. "Strong protection." Saint's name very rarely trotted out in modern times. Saint Walburga was an 8th-century missionary in Germany whose feast day was May 1, the traditional pagan festival day. Walpurgisnacht has come down in legend as the night of the witches' sabbath.

Walberga, Wallburga, Walpurgis

Walda (Fem. **Waldo**) OG. "Ruler." Extremely unusual feminization of a name that is also unusual for boys.

Waldena, Waldette, Waldina, Wallda, Welda, Wellda

Walker OE. Occupational name: "Cloth-walker." The era that saw the rise of last names was also the great English era of the wool trade, giving us such cloth-manufacturing names as Fuller, Tailor, and Weaver. In that medieval era, workers trod on the wool to clean it. This name is very unusual for girls.

Wallker

Walkiria Var. **Valkyrie** (Ger. Myth name).

Wallis Var. **Wallace** (OE. "From Wales"). Famous as a feminine name because of Wallis Simpson, the woman who very badly wanted to be queen of England, but became Duchess of Windsor instead.

Walless, Wallie, Walliss, Wally, Wallys

Waltrina Fem. **Walter** (OG. "People of power").

Walteena, Walterine, Waltina

Wanda Probably a Slavic tribal name, though some sources suggest OG. "Wanderer." Use has been pretty well confined to the middle of the 20th century. Harpsichordist Wanda Landowska.

Vanda, Wahnda, Wandah, Wandie, Wandis, Wandy, Wannda, Wenda, Wendaline, Wendall, Wendeline, Wendy, Wohnda, Wonda, Wonnda

Wanetta OE. "Pale-skinned." From the same root that gives us "wan," which is not exactly a complimentary term. In the U.S. this name is more likely a phonetic spelling or variant of **Juanita**.
Waneta, Wanette, Wanita

Warda (Fem. **Ward**) OG. "Guardian."
Wardia, Wardine

Warna (Fem. **Warner**) OG. "Fighting defender."

Waverly OE. Place name: "Meadow of quivering aspens." Pretty sound, pretty meaning; good potential for a crossover boy/girl name.
Waverley

Wendell OG. "Wanderer." Probably acceptable as a girl's name because of its resemblance to the familiar Wendy.
Wendaline, Wendall, Wendelle

Wendy Literary name: coined by James Barrie for the human heroine of *Peter Pan*. The parents who used it in great numbers in the middle of the 20th century may have been inspired by either the musical play or the animated movie. Some, wishing to call a daughter Wendy, no doubt named her Gwendolyn, but the names aren't actually related. It is very rarely used today. Ballerina Wendy Whelan; playwright Wendy Wasserstein; actress Dame Wendy Hiller.
Wenda, Wendaline, Wendee, Wendeline, Wendey, Wendi, Wendie, Wendye, Windy

Weslia Fem. **Wesley** (OE. "Western meadow"). Usually used in honor of John and Charles Wesley, who founded the Methodist church in the 18th century.
Wesleya, Weslie

Whitley OE. Place name: "White meadow." Related to other "-ley" names like Ashley, as well as to Whitney. The name has been brought to public notice by a character on *A Different World*.
Whitelea, Whitlea, Whittley

Whitney OE. Place name: "White island." Boys' name that became hugely popular for girls in the early 1980s, possibly because of its connotations of old wealth. It was sliding out of the top fifty names by the early 1990s. Singer Whitney Houston.

Whitnea, Whitneigh, Whiteney, Whitnee, Whitni, Whitnie, Whitny, Whittaney, Whittany, Whittney, Whittnie

Wibeke Ger. var. **Viveca** (Scand. "Alive").
Wiebke, Wiweca

Wilda OE. "Willow"; OG. "Untamed."
Willda, Wylda

Wilfreda Fem. **Wilfred** (OE. "Purposeful peace"). Unusual feminization of a rarely used name.
Wilfridda, Wilfrieda

Wilhelmina OG. "Will-helmet." Despite the number of variants spawned by the name, it hasn't been very popular in any form. Probably used more often to honor a beloved relative named William rather than on its own merits. Actress Billie Burke; author Willa Cather.
Billa, Billee, Billey, Billie, Billy, Ellma, Elma, Guglielma, Guillelmina, Guillelmine, Guillema, Guillemette, Guillemine, Helma, Helmina, Helmine, Helminette, Min, Mina, Minna, Minnie, Minny, Valma, Velma, Vilhelmina, Villhelmina, Villhelmine, Vilma, Wileen, Wilene, Wilhelmine, Willa, Willabella, Willabelle, Willamina, Willamine, Willeen, Willene, Willemina, Willetta, Willette, Williamina, Willie, Williebelle, Wilmette, Willmina, Willmine, Willy, Willybella, Wilma, Wilmette, Wilmina, Wilna, Wylma

Willow Tree name. A phenomenon of the 1970s. Fashion model Willow Bay.

Wilma Dim. **Wilhelmina.** Less of a mouthful than its source, but reminiscent of the dizzy Stone Age housewife Wilma Flintstone in the TV cartoon show *The Flintstones*; track star Wilma Rudolph.
Valma, Vilma, Willma, Wilmina, Wylma

Wilmot OE. Last or diminutive name related to William, Wilhelmina, etc.
Wilmotina, Wilmott

Wilona OE. "Longed-for."
Wilone

Winifred Welsh. "Holy peacemaking." Also often explained as Old German "Friend of peace." Popular in Britain for fifty years around the turn of the 20th century, but little used otherwise.
Fred, Freddie, Freddy, Fredi, Fredy, Wina, Winafred, Winefred, Winefride, Winefried, Winfreda, Winfrieda, Wini-

fryd, **Winne, Winnie, Winnifred, Wynafred, Wynifred, Wynn, Wynne, Wynnifred**

Winola OG. "Charming friend."

Winona Sioux Indian. "Firstborn daughter." This is one of the very few Native American names that has achieved wide usage among European-American families, probably because it was popularized by poets such as Henry Wadsworth Longfellow. Actress Winona Ryder; country singer Wynonna Judd.

Wenona, Wenonah, Winnie, Winnona, Winoena, Winonah, Wynnona, Wynona, Wynnona

Winsome OE. "Agreeable, light-hearted."

Wynsome

Winter OE. Season name. Like Summer, used mostly in the 1970s.

Wintar

Wisdom English: virtue name. Exceedingly rare.

Wistar Ger. Last name of uncertain meaning. Used with pride as a first name among Philadelphia families: Caspar Wistar was a very prominent doctor in late–18th-century Philadelphia, and taught at what became the University of Pennsylvania. An earlier Caspar Wistar (in all likelihood the doctor's father) founded a thriving glass factory in southern New Jersey in the 1740s.

Wistarr, Wister

Wisteria Flower name: vine with cascading purple-blue blossoms. Named for the 18th-century Philadelphia physician Caspar Wistar.

Wistaria

Wren OE. Bird name: a wren is a small brown songbird.

Wyanet Native American. "Beautiful."

Wyanetta, Wyonet, Wyonetta

Wyetta Fem. **Wyatt** (OF. "Small fighter").

Wyette

Wynne Welsh. "Fair, pure." Uncommon, simple, but distinctive in a way that may appeal to today's parents.

Win, Winne, Winnie, Winny, Wyn, Wynn

Wynstelle Comb. form **Wynne** (Welsh. "Fair, pure") and Stella (Lat. "Star").

Winstella, Winstelle, Wynnestella, Wynnestelle

Wyome NAm Ind. "Wide plain." The name of the state

of Wyoming comes from this word. Track star Wyomia Tyus.

Wyomia, Wyomie

Wysandra Comb. form **Wynne** (Welsh, "Fair, pure") and **Sandra** (Gk. "Defender of mankind").

HARKING BACK TO THE OLD COUNTRY

If there's one sentiment that distinguishes today's parents from those of, say, fifty years ago, it's the willingness to choose un-Anglicized names for their children. See how this plays among some celebrity parents:

Rosanna Arquette and Paul Rossi: Enzo

Sinead O'Connor: Brigidine

Connie Sellecca and John Tesh: Prima

Frank (Sylvester's father) and Kathleen Stallone: Dante

Sylvester Stallone and Jennifer Flavin: Sophia

Quincy Jones and Nastassja Kinski: Kenya

Mikhail Baryshnikov and Jessica Lange: Alexandra (called Shura)

Mikhail Baryshnikov and Lisa Rinehart: Anna Katerina

Nicole Kidman and Tom Cruise: Connor

Frances McDormand and Joel Coen: Pedro

Xanthe Gk. "Yellow." A description of someone's coloring. Almost unknown.
Xantha, Xanthia, Zanthe
Xaviera (Fem. **Xavier**) Basque. "New house." Given some exposure by Xaviera Hollander, the author of a book that caused some stir in the early 1970s. It was called *The Happy Hooker*.
Exaviera, Exavyera, Xavienna, Xavyera, Zaveeyera, Zaviera
Xenia Gk. "Welcoming." Occasionally spelled with the "X"; occurs once in a while with a "Z." Or you might recognize the variation Xena, as in the Warrior Princess.
Xeenia, Xena, Xiomara, Zeena, Zena, Zenia, Zina, Zyna
Ximena Possibly a variant of **Xenia**, or an archaic Spanish form of **Simone**.
Xylia Gk. "Wood-dweller." Related to the far more common Sylvia.
Xylina, Xylona, Zylina

Yaffa Heb. "Lovely."
Jaffa, Yaffah
Yahaloma Heb. "Diamond."
Yaira Heb. "To illuminate."
Yeira
Yakira Heb. "Costly, precious."
Yekara
Yalena Rus. Var. **Helen** (Gk. "Light").
Yelena, Lenuschka, Lenushka, Lenya, Lenyushka
Yaminah Arab. "Suitable, proper."
Yamina, Yemina

Yancey Name of unclear origin: possibly a Native American word that, misunderstood by its hearers, resulted in the term "Yankee." Carries a whiff of the West about it, courtesy of Edna Ferber's novel *Cimarron*, whose hero was named Yancey. Rare for boys or girls, but oddly enough for a name that rhymes with Nancy, more often masculine.

Yancee, Yancie, Yancy

Yannick Fr. var. **John** (Heb. "The Lord is gracious"). This form originates in Brittany, and is used more for boys than for girls in France.

Yanick, Yann, Yannic

Yarina Rus. var. **Irene** (Gk. "Peace").

Yaryna, Yerina

Yarmilla Slavic. "Trader."

Yarona Heb. "She will rejoice."

Yasmin Arab. "Jasmine." A variation of a flower name that has been quite popular in the late eighties and early nineties. Princess Yasmin Aga Khan.

Yasamin, Yasiman, Yasmeen, Yasmeena, Yasmena, Yasmene, Yasmina, Yasminda, Yasmine

Yekaterina Rus. Var. **Katherine** (Gk. "Pure"). Figure skater Yekaterina Gordeeva.

Ekaterina

Yelisabeta Rus. Var. **Elizabeth** (Heb. "Pledged to God").

Yelisabetta, Yelizabet, Yelizavetha

Yerusha Var. **Jerusha** (Heb. "Married, belonging to someone").

Yeruscha

Yesenia Form of Jesenia, a popular name in the Hispanic community. Its origin is unclear but its popularity stems from that of a character in a Spanish-language soap opera.

Yasenia, Yazenia, Yesemia, Yessenia, Yessenya

Yessica Var. **Jessica** (Heb. "He sees"). In 1994 and 1995 figures, Jessica is one of the top five girls' names all over the country. This kind of popularity often prompts variations in spelling and pronunciation as parents seek a name that is fashionable but a little bit different.

Yesseca, Yessika

Yetta OE. Dim. **Henrietta** (OG. "Ruler of the house").

Used at the turn of the 20th century, but virtually unheard-of now.
Yette

Yeva Rus. Var. **Eve** (Heb. "Life").
Yevka

Ynez Sp.Var. **Agnes** (Gk. "Pure").
Inès, Inez, Ynes, Ynesita

Yoana Var. **Joanna**, fem. **John** (" The Lord is gracious").
Yana, Yanna, Yoanah, Yoanna, Yoannah

Yoconda Sp. var. **Gioconda** (It. "Delight").

Yoko Jap. "Good, positive." Would probably be unknown outside Japanese families without the fame of Beatle wife Yoko Ono.

Yolanda Gk. "Violet flower." The Spanish version of Violet. Used in English-speaking countries in the 20th century, particularly during the 1960s.
Eolande, Eolantha, Iola, Iolanda, Iolande, Iolantha, Iolanthe, Jolan, Jolanna, Jolanne, Jolanta, Jolantha, Jolanthe, Yalinda, Yalonda, Yola, Yolaiza, Yoland, Yolande, Yollande, Yolantha, Yolanthe, Yolette, Yolie, Yulanda

Yonina Heb. "Dove."
Jona, Jonati, Jonina, Yona, Yonah, Yonina, Yoninah, Yonit, Yonita

Yordan Var. **Jordan** (Heb. "Descend"). The substitution of "Y" for "J" at the beginning of a name is particularly comfortable for speakers of Spanish, in which the two letters are pronounced similarly.
Yordana, Yordanna

Yoslene Var. **Jocelyn**, derivation unclear. This is an unusual and inventive modern adaptation of a very old name.
Yosleen, Yoslina, Yosline

Yosepha (Fem. **Joseph**) Heb. "Jehovah increases." A possibility for parents who don't like Josephine.
Josefa, Josepha, Yosefa, Yuseffa

Ysabel Var. **Elizabeth** (Heb. "Pledged to God") via **Isabel**.
Yabell, Yabella, Yabelle, Ysabell, Ysabella, Ysabelle, Ysbel, Ysbella, Ysobel

Ysanne Modern name, combination of **Ysabel** and **Anne**. Found in Britain.
Ysande, Ysanna

Yudit Heb. "Praise."
  Yehudit, Yudelka, Yudif, Judit, Judith, Yudita, Yuta
Yuliya Rus. Var. **Julia** (Lat. "Youthful").
  Youliya, Yula, Yulenka, Yulinka, Yulka
Yuma Place name: desert and city in southwestern Arizona.
Yuridiana Probably an invented name, related to the Russian Yuri (cognate of George).
Yvette Dim. **Yvonne**. Actress Yvette Mimieux.
  Ivett, Ivetta, Ivette, Yevette, Yvedt, Yvetta
Yvonne (Fem. **Ivo**) Fr. from OG. "Yew wood." Since yew wood was used for bows, Ivo may have been an occupational name meaning "Archer." The most common male form is probably Yves, but Yvonne is more widespread in English-speaking countries. It was particularly popular in Britain in the 1970s. Tennis star Evonne Goolagong; actress Yvonne DeCarlo.
  Eevonne, Evonne, Ivonne, Yevette, Yvetta, Yvette

Zada Arab. "Fortunate, prosperous."
  Zaida, Zayeeda, Zayda
Zahavah Heb. "Gilded."
  Zachava, Zachavah, Zahava, Zechava, Zehavah, Zehavit
Zahira Arab. "Brilliant, shining."
  Zaheera, Zahirah
Zahra Arab. "White" or "Flower." Currently popular in Arabic-speaking countries.
  Zahrah
Zandra Var. **Sandra**, dim. **Alexandra** (Gk. "Defender of mankind"). Fashion designer Zandra Rhodes.
  Zahndra, Zandie, Zandy, Zanndra, Zohndra, Zondra
Zanna Dim. **Susanna** (Heb. "Lily").
  Zana, Zanne, Zannie
Zara Heb. "Eastern brightness, dawn." May also be a form of **Sarah** (Heb. "Princess"). Literary name used often over the centuries for exotic characters. Taken up in the

1960s in Britain (Princess Anne's daughter is named Zara), but unusual in the U.S.

Zaira, Zarah, Zaria, Zarina, Zarinda, Zayeera

Zarya Name from Slavic mythology: Zarya is a water priestess and protector of warriors.

Zaria

Zea Lat. "Grain."

Zefira Heb. "Morning."

Zifira

Zelda Dim. **Griselda** (OG. "Gray fighting maid"). The original name has long been eclipsed by this nickname, which was made famous by F. Scott Fitzgerald's neurotic wife.

Selda, Zelde, Zellda

Zelenia Var. **Selena** (Gk. "Moon goddess").

Zelaina, Zelenya

Zelia Origin unclear; perhaps Gk. "Zeal" or Fr. "Solemn," from a saint's name. Also possibly a variant of **Cecilia** (Lat. "Blind.") Rare.

Zalia, Zailie, Zaylia, Zele, Zelene, Zélie, Zelina, Zéline

Zelma Dim. **Anselma** (OG. "God-helmet"). A less common form than Selma.

Zellma

Zena Var. **Xenia** (Gk. "Welcoming"). This is the slightly more common form of the name. Tennis star Zina Garrison.

Zeena, Zeenia, Zeenya, Zenia, Zenya, Zina

Zénaïde Var. **Zenobia**.

Zenaida

Zenobia Gk. "Power of Zeus." A 3rd-century empress of Palmyra, whose name was revived in the 19th century but has a rather quaint sound today.

Cenobia, Cenobie, Zeba, Zeena, Zena, Zenaida, Zénaïde, Zenayda, Zenda, Zenina, Zénobie, Zenna

Zephyr Gk. "West wind."

Cefirina, Sefira, Sefarina, Sephira, Tzefira, Tzephira, Tzephyra, Tzifira, Zefeera, Zefir, Zefiryn, Zephira, Zephirine, Zephyra, Zephyrine

Zerlinda Heb./Sp. "Beautiful dawn."

Zerlina

Zetta Heb. "Olive."
Zeta, Zetana

Zia Lat. "Grain."
Zea

Zigana Hung. "Gypsy."
Tsigana, Tsigane, Tzigana, Tzigane, Ziganna

Zilla Heb. "Shadow." Old Testament name revived by the Puritans and again in the 19th century, when it was more popular than one might suppose, given its current obscurity.
Zila, Zillah, Zylla

Zilpha Heb. Meaning unclear. Old Testament name revived in the 18th century and gradually fading ever since. Children's author Zilpha Keatley Snyder.
Zilpah, Zillpha, Zylpha

Zinaida Rus. from Gk. "Belonging to Zeus."
Zena, Zenaida, Zénaïde, Zinaide

Zinnia Lat. Flower name. In this case the flower itself was named for its classifier, 18th-century German botanist Johann Zinn.
Zinia, Zinnya, Zinya

Zippora Heb. "Bird." Another Old Testament name; Zipporah was the wife of Moses. This biblical prominence has not translated into great popularity for the name, which sounds to some people like a way to do up a skirt.
Zipora, Ziporah, Zipporah

Zita Gk. "Seeker." Also dim. **Teresita, Rosita**, etc. The name of the last Hapsburg empress, who was given the name when it was at its most popular, at the turn of the century.
Zeeta, Zyta

Zitomira Slavonic. "Renowned life."

Ziva Heb. "Brilliance, brightness."
Zeeva, Ziv

Zivanka Slavonic. "Full of life."
Zivka

Zizi Hung. Dim. **Elizabeth** (Heb. "Pledged to God"). Analogous to the Hungarian diminutive for Susan, Zsa Zsa. French singer Zizi Jeanmaire.
ZsiZsi

Zlata Czech/Slavonic. "Golden."
Zlatina, Alatinka, Zlatka

Zoë Gk. "Life." Currently popular in Greece, and catching on strongly in English-speaking countries, especially in Britain. Increasingly used as the 1990s roll past. Actress Zoe Caldwell.
Zoee, Zoélie, Zoeline, Zoelle, Zoey, Zoie, Zoya

Zohara Heb. "Light, splendor."
Zahara, Zaharira

Zoila Sp. from Gk. "Full of vigor."
Soila, Soilina, Soilla, Soyla, Zoilina, Zolla, Zoyla

Zola It. "Lump of earth." Like Zona, probably used more for its sound than for its meaning. Runner Zola Budd.
Zoela

Zona Lat. "Belt, girdle." The name given to the constellation in Orion's belt. Generally U.S. use.
Zonia

Zora Slavic. "Dawn's light." Author Zora Neale Hurston.
Zorah, Zorana, Zorina, Zorine, Zorra, Zorrah, Zorya

Zoya Rus. Var. Zoë.
Zoia, Zoyenka, Zoyya

ZsaZsa Hung. Dim. **Susan** (Heb. "Lily"). Made famous by actress and celebrity Zsa Zsa Gabor.
Zsuzsa, Zsuzsanna

Zsofia Hung. Var. **Sofia** (Gk. "Wisdom").

Zuleika Arab. "Brilliant and lovely." Inseparable from Max Beerbohm's comic heroine *Zuleika Dobson*, for the sake of whose love all the undergraduates of Oxford University drown themselves. Not, perhaps, an inspiring example for parents.
Zulaica, Zuleica

Zulma Arab. "Healthy, full of life."
Zulema, Zuma

Zuñi Native American tribe: the Zuñi Indians live in New Mexico and are known for their beautiful pottery, weaving, and basketmaking.

Zureidy Sp. from Arab. "Well-spoken, articulate."
Zoraïda, Zuraide, Zureida

The Groundbreaking #1
New York Times Bestseller by
ADELE FABER & ELAINE MAZLISH

"Have I got a book for you!...Run, don't walk, to your
nearest bookstore."
Ann Landers

SIBLINGS WITHOUT RIVALRY
How to Help Your Children Live Together So
You Can Live Too
79900-6/$12.00 US/$16.00 Can

Don't miss their landmark book

HOW TO TALK SO KIDS WILL LISTEN
AND LISTEN SO KIDS WILL TALK
57000-9/$12.50 US/$16.50 Can

"Will get more cooperation from children than all the yelling
and pleading in the world." *Christian Science Monitor*

and also

LIBERATED PARENTS, LIBERATED CHILDREN
71134-6/$11.00 US/$15.00 Can